Renaissance Dictionaries

English-Latin *and* Latin-English

Promptuariū paruulorum clericor̄ quod apud nos Medullā grammatice appellatur Scolasticis q̄ maxime necessariū. Impressū Lōdonijs per wynādū de worde hac i vrbe in parochia sancte Brigide (in the flete strete) ad signū solis cōmorātē

Title page of the 1510 edition of the Promptorium *printed by Wynkyn de Worde, from a copy in the British Museum*

Renaissance Dictionaries

English-Latin *and* Latin-English

By DeWitt T. Starnes

Austin · University of Texas Press · *1954*

Library of Congress Catalogue Card No. 53–6001
Copyright 1954 by the University of Texas Press
Manufactured in the United States of America

Second Printing

Foreword

ALTHOUGH there are some more or less adequate accounts of individual lexicographers and of individual texts, there is until now no comprehensive and systematic history of English-Latin and Latin-English dictionaries. The reasons for this deficiency in the history of lexicography are not far to seek. No library in America or abroad has a complete collection of the early bilingual dictionaries with which this study is largely concerned. Progress has been made in recent years in collecting such texts, but these still are widely dispersed and few libraries have even a broadly representative collection. And there is no complete and exhaustive bibliography, though in this field we are better off. Arthur G. Kennedy's monumental *Bibliography of Writings on the English Language* (1927), indispensable in this study, is hardly final for the scholar who wishes to know the history of a given text which has gone through many editions, with intermittent revisions and augmentations.

The difficulty which still confronts the historian and the bibliographer of Renaissance dictionaries is exemplified in a study by the English classical scholar J. E. B. Mayor, who in 1855 and 1857 contributed to the *Journal of Classical and Sacred Philology* two articles on English-Latin and Latin-English dictionaries. In his discussion of the Elyot-Cooper dictionaries, for example, Mayor based his conclusions on a copy of the 1559 *Bibliotheca Eliotae* and a copy of the 1565 *Thesaurus* by Thomas Cooper. Elyot's dictionaries of 1538, 1542, and 1545 and the Elyot-Cooper of 1552 Mayor had not been able to consult; the *Bibliotheca* of

v

1548 he examined only after his articles were written. And Mayor had easy access to the great repositories of the British Museum, of Oxford, and of Cambridge.

Since Mayor's day more attention has been paid to the collecting of dictionaries, and the great libraries which he had access to are now much richer in their holdings. But neither in England nor in America are the various editions of a popular text easy to find in a single collection. The wide distribution of copies of a text presents many difficulties to the student who wishes to make a comparative study of different editions of the same dictionary, or a comparative study of dictionaries by different compilers.

The gathering of materials for this book, for example, has involved study, through a period of more than fifteen years, at the Huntington Library, the Newberry, the Folger Shakespeare, the Library of Congress, the British Museum, the Bodleian, and the University of Cambridge Library. In the course of years since this study was begun, our own Library at the University of Texas has acquired an excellent collection of original texts and microfilms of early dictionaries, which have been extremely useful in the latter stages of this work.

Although I employ the general title *Renaissance Dictionaries* for this book, and although the concentration is in the period from about 1500 to 1660, it has seemed desirable to indicate links with the past, that is, with the fifteenth century, and to trace the progress after 1660 to the consummation of a classical dictionary in the *Thesaurus* of Robert Ainsworth (1736, 1746). For the fifteenth century, or about 1440 to 1499, I attempt only an intensive survey as a background for the study of the subsequent centuries. An exhaustive study of fifteenth-century dictionaries, printed and in manuscript, would require a separate volume. With this modification, we may state that, chronologically, this study covers approximately the period of 1440 to 1740. And though the heart of the matter is found between the years 1500 and 1660, even within these bounds it would be rash to claim an exhaustive treatment of all phases of the lexicography. To a subject so extensive and so complex many more years could be devoted. But here are the essential features in the history of English-Latin and Latin-English lexicography down to the eighteenth century.

In general the aim in this study is to give a complete history of each text with respect to the principal sources, the link with antecedents and successors; the editions, with special attention to revision and augmentation; the technical aspects, including arrangement of entries, etymologies, pronunciation, grammatical information, definitions, and usage; the establishment of the authority of the dictionary; the progress towards a classical Latin-English dictionary; and the relation in content and technique to the English dictionary. Not all of these topics are involved in the discussion of each text; in some cases they are not applicable. But these subjects are kept steadily in mind throughout this account. As to the complicated problem of sources and interrelationships of the various lexicons in an age in which there was free borrowing back and forth, finality can scarcely be claimed. It is my hope, however, that the more essential interrelationships are here demonstrated.

The importance of this study needs little emphasis. To the student interested, for example, in tracing definitions or etymologies, English and Latin, through the sixteenth and seventeenth centuries, the value of knowing the chronology and interrelationships of the various dictionaries is at once apparent. Those interested in discovering the impact of foreign languages, especially Latin, French, and German, on the English vocabulary during the Renaissance will find it advantageous to note the foreign sources of certain texts and the translations or adaptations of foreign words, as, for example, in the Elyot-Cooper dictionaries. Finally, no history of English lexicography proper can be adequate without taking into account the close rela*' *nship of Latin-English and English-Latin dictionaries to the purely *.nglish dictionaries of the seventeenth and early eighteenth centuries, * illustrated, to mention a single example, by the relationship in cor.tent and technique of Robert Ainsworth's *Thesaurus* to the *Lingua Britannica reformata* (1749) of Benjamin Martin and to the Dictionary (1755) of Samuel Johnson.

Indebtedness to various scholars has been acknowledged, when known, at the apposite places in the notes. Special thanks are due, however, to Mr. A. F. Scholfield, librarian (1948) at Cambridge University Library, for generously putting at my disposal copies of the early editions of Thomas Thomas's Latin-English dictionary for comparison with later editions at the British Museum; to Professor James Sledd of the University of Chicago for the privilege of using matter in his unpublished dissertation (University of Texas, 1947) on John Baret's *Alvearie;* to Dr. Charles E. Noyes, University of Tennessee, for information derived from his unpublished manuscript on Adam Littleton and Robert Ainsworth; and to my colleague Professor Rudolph Willard for a critical and helpful reading of an early draft of the manuscript of this book.

For permission to use, in revised form, matter from one article printed earlier in *Studies in Philology* and three articles in the University of Texas *Studies in English,* I am indebted to the editors of these journals. To Miss Julia Harris, reference librarian of the University of Texas, I wish to express my thanks for assistance in compiling the list of Latin-English and English-Latin dictionaries in American libraries. For the making of the index, I am deeply grateful to my colleague on the English staff, Miss Lucetta Teagarden.

Finally, completion of this book would have been far more difficult without the generous aid of the Research Council of the University of Texas. To the Council, I am grateful for the award of funds for a research leave and for partial subsidy in the publication of this book.

DE WITT T. STARNES

Austin, Texas
January 2, 1953

Contents

Illustrations

PART I

The Fifteenth Century

CHAPTER I

Promptorium parvulorum (*ca.* 1440)

I HUMBLY with prayers entreat all pedagogues, teachers, and masters, that when they have examined this little work, they will approve what may by God's assistance have been rightly written, and will piously correct and emend what is written ill or erringly; since humble grammarians and boys may look on this short volume as on a mirror, and find freely and immediately the common words which belong to the Latin tongue." In these words and in this spirit wrote the modest author in his Preambulum to the *Promptorium parvulorum* (*ca.* 1440). The title of this our earliest English-Latin dictionary means "a storeroom for young scholars," or a repository of English and Latin words designed to assist schoolboys in learning the Latin language. This is the first of a whole progeny of dictionaries in England evoked by the need of young scholars and compiled by schoolmasters to promote learning. The history of the text is therefore of especial interest in this study.

Of the *Promptorium* there are six manuscripts, at least five early printed editions, dating from 1499 to 1528, and two modern editions based on manuscripts of the fifteenth century.[1] The earliest printed text of the *Promptorium* is a small folio of 115 leaves, from the press of Richard Pynson, 1499.[2] There is no title page. The first page is blank; the prologue on the reverse of the leaf begins thus:

Incipit prologus in libellum qui dicitur promptorius puerorum. Cernentibus solicite clericorum condiciones. . . .

and concludes:

. . . pro me peccatore misericorditer intercedant dominum nostrum ihesum christum. . . .
Explicit prologus.

3

The text proper begins on signature *aii:*

> Incipit liber qui dicitur Promptorium paruulorum siue clericorum.

The colophon, on signature *tiii,* reads as follows:

> Ad laudem et ad honorem omnipotentis dei et intemerate genitricis ejus. Finit excellentissimum opus exiguis magnisque scolasticis vtillissimum quod nuncupatur Medulla grammatice. Inpressum per egregium Richardum pynson, in expensis virtuosorum virorum Fredrici egmondt et Petri post pascha. anno domini .m.cccc. nonagesimo nono. Decima Vᵃ die mensis Maii.

This book is printed in double columns with running heads "Nomina *A,*" "Verba *A,*" etc., throughout the alphabet, distinguishing nouns and other parts of speech from the verbs.

Editions of the *Promptorium* issued by other presses in the early sixteenth century, though varying somewhat in content from Pynson's of 1499, tend to follow the general pattern. In no instance is there a claim of revision or augmentation. Variations in the printed editions might be explained by each printer's having used a different manuscript for his edition. But no printer refers to the manuscript which he used or to an effort to produce an edition based on the collation of manuscripts.

In point of time the next early printed edition is that by Julian Notary, in 1508. This is a small quarto of seventy-three leaves, preserved in a single copy in the Grenville Library of the British Museum (G. 7498).[3] The words on the title page are these: "Promptoriū paruūlorum clericorum quod apud nos Medulla grāmatice appellatur Scolasticis quam maxiē necessariū." On the reverse of the title page begins the prologue: "Incipit prologus in libellū qui dicitur promptoriū. Cernentibus solicite clericorum cōdiciōes nunc statuū graduum diversorum numerose videntur. . . ."

As in Pynson, the Notary text is printed in double columns, with the headings "Nomina" and "Verba," listing nouns and other parts of speech in groups distinct from verbs, and giving grammatical information.

Of the early printings, more editions from the press of Wynkyn de Worde have come down to us than from any other printer. Bibliographical works, as Way observes, have recorded Wynkyn de Worde editions of 1510, 1512, 1516, 1518, 1519(?), 1522, and 1528.[4] Examination of editions of 1510 (see frontispiece, copy of title page), 1516, and 1528 [5] reveals that, though these are independent editions, the variations in the texts are slight. There is, for example, a close correspondence in the number of entries, printers' signatures, etc. They are similar to each other also, and to the 1499 Pynson, in the method of recording entries, as in listing nouns and other parts of speech separately from the verbs, and in giving grammatical information.

Representative of the Wynkyn de Worde texts is that of 1510. The wording of the title page, with abbreviations spelled out, is thus:

Promptuarium ⁶ paruulorum clericorum quod apud nos Medulla grammatice appellatur Scolasticis quam maxime necessarium. Impressum Londonijs Per wynandum de worde hac in vrbe in parochia sancte Brigide (in the fletestrete) ad signum solis commorantem.

After the text proper, we find the following notice:

Ad Lectorem

And yf ye can not fynde a laten worde, or englysshe to your purpose, in thys present boke so shall ye take ortus vocabulorum, the whyche is more redyer to fynden a latyn worde after the ABC. and englysshe thereof folwynge for thys boke is thus ordened for to fynde a laten after ony maner of worde in englysshe for them that wyl lerne to wryte or speke latyn. and because that no man or chylde shall herafter have ony diffyculte more to serche for ony latyn or englysshe worde. therfore we have ordened this lybell in small volum for to bynde with Ortus vocabulorum moost necessary for chyldren.

This is followed by the colophon:

Ad laudem et honorem omnipotentis dei et intemerate genitricis eius finit excellentissimum opus scolasticis anglie quam maxime necessarium. quod merito medulla grammatices apud nos, vel paruulorum promptuarium nuncupatur. Impressum Londoniis per wynandum de worde in vico anglice (the flete strete) appellato sub solis intersignio commorantem. Anno incarnacionis Dominice. M.CCCCC.X die vero. xvij mensis Januarij.

The Ad Lectorem and the colophon, with necessary changes in date, reappear in subsequent editions of the *Promptorium* by Wynkyn de Worde. Reference to the *Ortus vocabulorum* (discussed in Chapter 4), a Latin-English dictionary printed in 1500, is of interest as expressing the need of a double dictionary, English-Latin and Latin-English. And the existence of a volume in the British Museum (G. 7497 [2]) in which a copy of the 1516 *Promptorium* is bound with an *Ortus* of 1520 may be evidence that the injunction of the printer was frequently carried out.

A significant detail of the 1510 colophon transcribed above is the reference to *Medulla grammatices* as a title by which the *Promptorium* was generally known. This title or subtitle was first used in the colophon of Richard Pynson's edition of the *Promptorium* (1499); it reappeared as *Medulla grammatice* on the title page of Julian Notary's edition of 1508, and on the title pages of the various editions printed by Wynkyn de Worde. It seems obvious then that *Medulla grammatice* was, at the turn of the century, the title generally applied to the English-Latin dictionary first printed as the *Promptorium parvulorum*. Reference in Thomas's *Dictionarium*, after 1600, to the *Promptorium* as "*Medull.*" or "*Medull. Gram.*" would indicate that the *Promptorium* was so called throughout the sixteenth century. The name *Medulla grammatice* is, however, confusing, since there are a considerable number of fifteenth-century manuscripts of a Latin-English dictionary of the same title (see the discussion of *Medulla grammatice* in Chapter 3). To avoid confusion, one has to remember that the term *Medulla grammatice* has, unfortunately, two distinct applications: (1) to fifteenth-century manuscript versions of a Latin-English dictionary, never printed, or, if so, with modifications and change of title; (2) as an alternate title to the printed editions of the first English-Latin dictionary, today better known as the *Promptorium parvulorum*.

In this survey no attempt is made to study manuscript versions of the *Promptorium*. These are described in some detail by Albert Way in his edition of the *Promptorium*.[7] Way's edition is based upon the Harleian MS 221, with additions from other manuscripts and from Pynson's printed edition of 1499. But Way's rearrangement of the grouping of entries, throwing all into one alphabetical order and omitting grammatical information concerning the Latin words, precludes consideration of his text as representative of the *Promptorium*.

More satisfactory, though not a critical text, is the edition prepared by A. L. Mayhew for the Early English Text Society. In this edition, the text of the Winchester manuscript, as the editor explains, is printed precisely as it stands. He observes the original arrangement, omitting nothing from the text. "It has been thought better," Mayhew writes, "to give the text in its entirety, and in its original order, in order that one may be able to see what the first English-Latin Dictionary was really like, and what help the 'parvuli,' or 'clerici' obtained from their *Promptorium* for the manufacture of the Latin prose of the period." [8] The text of Mayhew's edition begins with a Preambulum, which refers to the compiler as a preaching brother or friar of Lynn, gives the date of compilation as 1440, and lists some of the books from which the *Promptorium* derived. Then follow remarks on the need and the value of such a book, on the method of procedure in compiling it, and on the author himself as *rudis et inscius* and better fitted to learn than to teach, concluding with the hope that masters and teachers may approve what is done well and amend what is ill.[9] The word list which follows has rather more Latin equivalents for English entries and perhaps more grammatical information than are found in other texts. The transcribed entries following will show how Mayhew's text based on the Winchester manuscript compares with Pynson's (1499).

PYNSON
Nomina *A*

Abacke or bacward. *retro retrorsum. aduerbia.*

Abasshyd or aferd. *Territus ta tum. participia.*

Abasshment. *Terror. roris. Pauor. uoris. Ambo ma. ge. tercie de. Formido is. fe. ge. ter. de.*

Abatement or a withdrawyng of weyte or mesure. *Subtractio. nis. fe. ge. ter. decli.*

Abbey: *Abacia. e. fem. ge. prime decli.*

Abesse. *Abbatissa se. fem. ge. prime decli.*

Abydyng. *Expectatio. nis. fe. ge. ter. decli.*

Abyte. *Habitus tus. mascu. ge. quarte. declin.*

Abyl or abul. *Habiles le. omnis ge. tercie decli. Ydoneus a um. Aptus ta tum.*

Abochement. *Augmentum ti. Amplificamentum ti.* Catholicon *in augmentum ambo n. g. se. de.*

.   .   .   .   .

Verba incipiencia cum *A.*

Abatyn. *Subtraho traxi here di do ditur. tractum tu. tercie coniugacionis. acti.*

Abyden. *Expecto tas taui are di do dum. tatum, tatu prime coniugationis. acti. Prestolor aris atus sum are di atum pri. con. Deponens.*

.   .   .   .   .

Abownden or haue plente. *Habundo das aui re di datum. Prime coniugacionis. neutrum.*

MAYHEW
[Nomina *A*]

Abakke, or bakwarde: *Retro, retrorsum; aduerbia.*

Abashyd, or aferd: *Territus, -a, -um, uel perterritus, -a, -um; participia sunt.*

Abashment: *Terror, -ris; pauor, -ris; omnia masculi generis et tercie declinacionis: fformido, -is; feminini generis et 3 de* [*clinacionis*].

Abatement, or withdrawyng of mete or mesure, or oþer thyng: *Subtraccio, -is; defalcacio, -is; omnia feminini generis, tercie declinacionis.*

Abbey: *Abbathia, -e; Abbatia, secundum* 'catholicon'; *omnia feminini generis, prime declinacionis.*

Abesse: *Abbatissa, -e; feminini generis, prime de* [*clinacionis*].

Abydyng: *Expectacio, -is; feminini generis, 3° de* [*clinacionis*].

Abyte, Clothyng: *habitus; Masculi generis, 4 declinacionis.*

Able, or abul: *Abilis, -le; omnis generis, 3° decli* [*nacionis*].

Abochement, or abushment: *Augmentum, Amplificamentum, -ti;* 'catholicon' *in augmentum, -i, -o; omnia neutri generis, secunde declinacionis.*

.   .   .   .   .

Verba incipiencia cum *A.*

Abatyn: *Subtraho, -is, -traxi, -re;* 3 *con* [*iugacionis*], *actiuum.*

Abydyn: *Expecto, -as, -aui, -are; prime con* [*iugacionis*], *actiuum: Prestolor, -aris, -atus, -ari; prime con* [*iugacionis*], *depo* [*nens*].

.   .   .   .   .

Abundyn, or haue plente: *Abundo, -as.*

Although Mayhew has silently introduced modern punctuation into the transcript of the text, he has kept intact the original entries and the grammatical information. As his text is representative, and as it is more readily available than the printed editions of the fifteenth and sixteenth centuries, it is used largely as the basis of illustrations in this account of the *Promptorium*.

Probably the most trustworthy information we have concerning the compiler, the date, and the sources of the *Promptorium* is found in the *preambula* of the manuscripts edited by Way and by Mayhew. At the end of the Preambulum in Harleian MS 221, edited by Way (Part I, 3), appears the following:

> Isti sunt auctores ex quorum libris collecta sunt vocabula hujus libelli, per fratrem predicatorem reclusum Lenne Episcopi, Anno Domini millesimo cccc. xl°. Cujus anime propicietur Deus. Et intitulatur liber iste Promptorium parvulorum. Hoc modo scribuntur nomina auctorum infra in hoc libro.

Januensis in suo Catholicon	cath.
Uguitio in majori volumine	ug.
Uguitio versificatus	ug. v.
Brito	brit.
Mirivalensis in campo florum	c. f.
Johannes de Garlondia, in	
Diccionario scolastico	dicc.
Commentarius curialium	comm.
Libellus misteriorum qui dicitur	
Anglia que fulget	lib. mist.
Merarius	mer.
Distigius	dist.
Robertus Kylwarbi	kylw.
Alexander Neccham	necc.

> Cum aliis variis libris et libellis inspectis et intellectis, Deo adjuvante cum tota curia celesti.

A variation of this passage appears at the beginning of the Preambulum (col. 1) of Mayhew's edition of the Winchester manuscript, giving the same information as to date and compiler, and listing, in abbreviated form, the same authorities.

This evidence from the *preambula* of the manuscripts seems to establish the date of composition of the *Promptorium* as the year 1440. Commentators and editors generally have not been disposed to question this date.[10] Acceptable also is the information these documents afford concerning the compiler: he was a Dominican friar of Lynn Episcopi, Norfolk. Statements in the *preambula*, besides those already quoted or referred to, support this general identification. Such are the following:

> Vnde ego, dictus indigne frater predicatorum lenne, sub regula paupertatis. . . .

> Comitatus tamen norfolchie loquendi modum sum solum secutus, quem solum ab infancia didici, et solo tenus plenius perfec[t]iusque cognoui.

> Explicit preambulum in librum predictum, secundum vulgarem modum loquendi orientalium anglorum.[11]

These manuscripts afford no information as to the name of the Friar of Lynn Episcopi, but scholars have sought to christen him. In his edition of Peter Langtoft's *Chronicle,* Hearne, referring to Richard Pynson's edition of the *Promptorium,* writes:

The author was a preaching or black Fryer, and follow'd the dialect of the East parts of England, to which he had been used from his infancy, as he tells us in his Prologue. His name was Richard Frauncis, as I find by this note written in an old hand at the beginning of a copy of this book that was lent me by Mr. Ward of Longbridge, viz. Nomen Compilatoris istius libri est Frater Ricardus Fraunces, inter quatuor parietes pro Christo inclusus.[12]

Although Way rightly rejects Hearne's quoted statement as "at most the anonymous note or tradition of some previous possessor of the book," he quotes with approval a note from a copy of the same edition by Pynson in the public library at Cambridge: "Autor hujus operis fuit Galfredus Grammaticus dictus, frater Ordinis S. Dominici." [13] Way admits that this note is of "equal authority"—and therefore of no value without supporting evidence—with that quoted by Hearne. Yet Way accepts at its face value the note from the Pynson copy of the *Promptorium* in the Cambridge Public Library, the more perhaps because Bale, whom Way quotes, and after Bale, Pits and Tanner, attempt to identify the compiler of the *Promptorium* as Galfridus Grammaticus.[14] But Bale has no real evidence for his ascription to Galfridus—no more than he does for attributing to the same compiler the *Ortus vocabulorum* and the *Medulla grammatice.* The name Galfridus may have been suggested to Bale by editions of John of Garland's *Equivoca* and *Synonyma,* in which the name of "Magister Galfridus Anglicus" appears as expounder of the texts. Bale does indeed identify this Galfridus with "Galfridus Grammaticus," the alleged author of the *Promptorium.* Bale's conclusions are obviously acceptable to Way, who writes: "Whatever may have been his patronymic, I think that we may confidently ascribe to the Dominican recluse of Lynn, Galfridus, designated, from his special studies . . . 'Grammaticus,' the laborious achievement of the first English-Latin and Latin-English Dictionaries." Mayhew paraphrases this statement, changing the conclusion to read "the laborious achievement of the first English-Latin Dictionary." [15]

It must be said, however, that these editors and the commentators whom they follow present no conclusive evidence that the recluse of Lynn, the compiler of the *Promptorium,* bore the name Galfridus Grammaticus. In the present state of our knowledge we can only say that the real name of the compiler of the first English-Latin dictionary is not known.

Although we do not know the name of the compiler, we are on firmer ground when we consider the content, the method, and the sources of the *Promptorium.* A conservative estimate of the number of English entries is about twelve thousand.[16] This is, however, a bilingual dictionary, in which relatively more emphasis is placed upon the Latin than upon the English, and there are, on the average, two Latin equivalents for every English entry. The result is a dictionary of some thirty thousand terms. The value of such a compilation for the student of medieval and Tudor English and Medieval Latin needs no commentary.

As to the method, the compiler of the *Promptorium* arranges the English entries in alphabetical order, in two groups under each letter: "Nomina," the nouns and other parts of speech except verbs; and "Verba," the verbs. For the Latin words, the equivalents of the English terms to be defined, the author indicates the gender and declension of nouns, the nominative endings of adjectives, the principal parts and the conjugations of verbs, and adverbial forms. For the Latin words also he frequently cites his medieval authorities and thus furnishes a clue to a study of the sources of his Latinity. It is regrettable that he affords no such leads for the sources of the English entries.

Possible sources of the English, however, there are. These may be found in the numerous English-Latin and Latin-English vocabularies in existence in the fourteenth and fifteenth centuries. Some of these have been printed by Thomas Wright in *A Volume of Vocabularies* and, in a revised and enlarged edition, by Richard Paul Wülcker, under the title *Anglo-Saxon and Old English Vocabularies*.[17] Turning to a portion of a Latin-English vocabulary of the early fifteenth century (Wright, *op. cit.*, 199), we read these entries of words pertaining to the household:

Hoc pecten, A combe.	*Hic fusus*, A spyndylle.
Hoc colobium, A tabarde.	*Hec madula*, A jurdan.
Hec armilansa, A cloke.	*Hic jurdanus, idem est.*
Hoc capicium, A hode.	*Hoc tapetum*, A tapyt.
Hec tunica, A cote.	*Hoc coopertorium*, A coverlyde.
Hec manica, A sleve.	*Hoc carentrevillum*, A canwas.
Hec sista, A kyst.	*Hic lectus*, A bede.
Hic nodulus, A boton.	*Hoc stratum*, A bed-lytter.
Hoc monile, A broche.	

Here are seventeen entries from the first thirty in Wright's list, which have a fairly close correspondence to entries, in reverse order, in the *Promptorium*. The inference is not that the *Promptorium* drew from this particular vocabulary, but that such compilations in the period may well have contributed to the English word list. Support for this inference is strengthened by checking the Wright-Wülcker English Index (*op. cit.*, 411–85) with the vocabularies on which it is based and with the *Promptorium*. W. M. Lindsay's edition of the *Corpus Glossary* (Cambridge, 1921) and his study of the relationship of the Corpus to the Epinal and

Erfurt and Leyden glossaries constitute the best basis for a study of the ultimate sources of the *Promptorium*.

The principal immediate sources for the Latin words in the *Promptorium* can be determined beyond a reasonable doubt. These are listed in the Preambulum and are cited frequently in the entries of the text proper. Moreover, comparative study of the texts cited as authorities, so far as these are available, and the *Promptorium* substantiates the compiler's claims concerning the sources of his Latinity. His candor in acknowledgment and in recurrent citation of sources and authorities is in refreshing contrast to a tendency, later developed among lexicographers, of concealing the names of the major authors and works upon which they depended.

Pertinent comment on the authors and texts cited as sources in the Preambulum is presented by Way in the Preface to his edition of the *Promptorium* and repeated, with some revision, by Mayhew in the Introduction to his edition for the Early English Text Society.[18] It is not my aim to travel again entirely the ground thus covered. Yet a few of the authors, because of their special relation to the *Promptorium* and their importance to the subsequent history of lexicography, seem to require further discussion.

Foremost among these is Joannes Balbus Januensis, compiler of the *Catholicon*, or *Summa*.[19] According to Du Cange, the author, a native of Genoa in the thirteenth century, combined the works of Papias and Uguitio and reproduced a dictionary largely augmented *ex multis diversis doctorum texturis elaboratum atque contextum*, as stated in a colophon from which we learn that his labors were completed in the year 1286.[20] The *Catholicon* was first printed at Mayence in 1460 and frequently thereafter, in the original form and in abridgments, through the fifteenth century.[21] A representative copy of an edition printed at Strasbourg, *ca.* 1482,[22] may be briefly described. This is a thick folio in Gothic type, consisting of 392 leaves (784 pages), unnumbered, with two columns on each page. On the first page is the heading "Prima Pars," and, beneath, this line: "Incipit summa que vocatur catholicon edita a fratre iohanne de ianua ordinis fratrum predicatorum." There follow four sections (fols. 1–69) devoted to "Orthographia," "Ethimologia," "Diasintastica," and "Prosodia." Then comes the text proper (fols. 69–392). The word list begins with these entries: *alma, ab, abactus, abacuc, abacus, abalieno, abamita, abarim, abatis, abax, abba, abbas, abbatia*, etc., proper names of persons and places (*Baal, Babilonia, Bachanalia, Barabas, Belphegor, Belus*, and *Belzebub*) being distributed alphabetically throughout the text.

The *Catholicon* is an encyclopedic dictionary, a type which reappears frequently in the annals of lexicography, and a convenient source of information on many subjects. Small wonder it was in much demand by lexicographers and scholars generally. Its availability, owing to frequent printings, made it one of the most influential books of the fifteenth century. Modern critics who characterize the *Catholicon* as abounding in barbarisms and lacking the solid foundation of a classical vocabulary[23] are beside the point. The *Catholicon* is not a classical dictionary; it is medieval. And in this fact lies its value for this study.

In citing the *Catholicon* as a source for Latin words, the compiler of the *Promptorium* was following a well-established authority. That the Friar of Lynn had open before him the text of Balbus' work, nearly every column of the English-Latin dictionary affords evidence. Random openings of Mayhew's text of the *Promptorium* show the following results: columns 433–34, seven references to *Catholicon;* column 455, seven; columns 457–68, thirty-two; columns 500–510, twenty-eight. To express the relationship in another way, we may say that Latin words under the following English entries, to mention only a few, are supported by citation of the *Catholicon: bobet; boch; boystows; care, or lytyl cart; daff, or dastard; dagge of cloth; debate makere; dyner; dish berar; eyre; galegge or galoch; garywyndyl; gentyl; gloton; glovyng; gootys berde; gryse; growndyn; hale, or tente; hasard.* Following to their original source the Latin words cited, we find that the compiler was giving the meaning which he found in the *Catholicon.* The *Catholicon* is then a basic source for the *Promptorium,* as it seems to have been for most lexicons, Latin and bilingual, in the second half of the fifteenth century.

Another authority listed in the Preambulum of the *Promptorium* and cited with frequency in the text (EETS) as "Ugucio" and "Ugucio versificatus" is identified as Hugo of Pisa. Brief accounts of this compiler are given by Way and by Mayhew, deriving from Du Cange and other authorities.[24] The records indicate that Hugo was professor of ecclesiastical jurisprudence at Bologna about 1178 and Bishop of Ferrara from 1190 till his death in 1210. Of importance for this study is his dictionary, or "Huguitionis Pisani derivationes magnae sive dictionarium etymologicum." The purpose and scope of the *Magnae* are stated in the preface:

Opus divina favente gratia componere statuimus, in quo, prae aliis, vocabulorum significationes, significationum distinctiones, derivationum origines, etymologiarum assignationes, et interpretationum reperientur expositiones, quorum ignorantia Latinitas naturaliter indiga quadam doctorum pigritia non modicum coarctatur.[25]

First page of the dictionary proper of Joannes Balbus' Catholicon, or Summa, printed at Strasbourg, 1482, from a copy in the University of Texas Library (opposite)

Alma interpretatur

virgo abscondita vel abscosio vir-
ginitatis. sicut dr in interptatoibus.
Dieronim[9] vo dicit q aalma significat absconditas vignem et secre-
tam. De boc dicu in virgo
Aaron interptat mons fortis. vt
mons fortitudinis siue montan[9] vt dr interptatoibus
Lug. vo dicit Aaron interptat mons fortitudi. quia
tburibulu aureu accipies inter mortuos et viuos stetit.
et ruina mortis qsi qdam mons fortis exclusit.

· A · ante · B ·

Ab pposito omnib[9] in ppositoe pponit lris absq[3] c. vt
q. vel t. vt supra pleni[9] dixi in pma pte capi.de b. Unde
versus Ab si coponis elementa queq[3] sequuni. C. q. t. tã-
tum simul be tres excipiuntur
Abactus cta ctu.i.fugat[9] dispersus sepatul. et dr ab abs
Abacuc.luctator fortis vel lucta9 . i. ego abigis
tor rigidus seu pplerans eos aut suscepto cor[3] interpra-
tur. Sm aut biero. abacuc ppbeta. amplexans interptat

qi vel ex eo q amabilis domi fuit vocat amplexio. vl q2
un certamē cū domio deo agreditur.amplexatis.i.luctans
fortis vocabulū Nullus enim tam audax voce ausus est
deū ad disceptoēm iusticie puocare et dicere ei. Cur i re
bus bũanis et modi isti[9] popa tãta rex vlet iniqtas
Abacus ab abax cis qd interptat decē.denuat bic aba
cus ci.qsi decu plato q: i abaco sunt decē arc[9] sese decu
plantes In pmo est vnitas i secūdo denarii i tercō cēte
narius Est ena abac[9] vel abax.riga geometrie.vl tabu
la quã babet pbilosopbi vbi figuras ipuluere suposi-
to faciut.q alio nomie dr pinax vt Abax ena vl abac[9]
dr supio2 po capitellu.i.sariu quadrangulu qd sup colū-
nas ponit Et etias quelibet mēsa marmorea sic dr et est
mas.generis abacus et cor2.penulē. vide in abax
Abalieno as.pponit ex ab et alieno as.cta.pmo abalienati sunt retro2sum.i.alieni facti sunt.
Abamita te.fo.2o aut ex ab et amita coponit
Abarim mons in q obijt moyses vt babet deut.xxxii ·
Abans barus qd est qdam mēsura.pponit cū ab et
ablata dr bic et bec abantis ideclinabile po mēs casus.
id est q vel que cū bato diuidit auena vel aliud sim bug
vel abans.pponit ab assultes et batis dro plurali. vnde
dicit maister bene Pluralia cū singularib[9].pponunt.
vt a secretis. a calaculis a respõsis.abantis a comentarius
Dec eni.pponunt ab assultes et ab illis dris de nomia sue
officio2 tamē ideclinabilia vel possunt coponi ab a pre
positoe latina et pdicro2 ablatis vt a secretis ab boc ab
latiuo secretis.quonia ab ipso secretis que ei comunun-
tur dr aliqs a secretis. similiter abans.pponi pot ab a
et batis.qi ab ipsis batis siue mēsuris que ei comuniutur
vel qs exercet dr aliqs abans Et ide pot de alijs poicris
i similibus iudicari et cor2.penulema abans
Abax cis iterptat decē vide in abac[9] et cor2.a ante x.na
turaliter Unde dicit psan vl.li. vbi agit de terminatioib[9]
septuagintaocto tercie declinatois.q in a2 cor2.desunt
abax.cis.qd tamē dr bic abacus ci.frequéter iuenit.vt su
pra babes i tercia pte vbi agit de tercia declinatioe Et
sic patet q abax in gro cor2.penul.vt ostendi i secūda pr
te vbi egi de desinēdbus in x.
Abba sit nomē patr iterptat Ro.viii. et accetuat in fi.
Abbas ab abba pater dr bic abbas abbatis monadi
Abbatia ab abbas abbatis dr bec ab2   orum pat
batia.te.p ecclesia vbi est abbas Et aliqndo largi2 acci
pitur.p collectoe omniũ ecclesia2 et que sunt sub aliquo
abbate et p ista dignitate   bas abbans.
Abbatilla sle.monadba2 mater vel domia et dr ab abs
Abdenago ideclinabile interptatur seruies taceo Ide
a2 a2rias et accentuat in fine.
Abdias interptat buus domi.qi legatus missus ad gē
tes poicauit que ppbetali digna sunt ministerio et buis
tute.et inde seruus domini dicit.
Abdicatiu[9] ab abdico cap.dr abdicatiuus ua.uū.i.ne
gatiuus ua.uū qd pponit p upabdicatiu[9] id est supne
gatiuus.vnde supabdicatiua dr negatō que addit nega
toni.et nibil coopatur plus q3 poedces. vt i vulgari solet
dici ego nō babeo nibil qd nō plus valet q3 si diceretur
ego nibil babeo

This work, derived largely from Isidore's *Origines* and Papias' *Elementarium doctrinae rudimentum* (*ca.* 1060), had a wide vogue in the Middle Ages as evidenced by the large number of manuscripts still in existence.[26] It has never been printed, though much of it is incorporated in the *Catholicon* of Joannes Balbus, and a Modern Language Association rotograph (No. 30) of the Laud manuscript has made it readily available to American scholars. Paget Toynbee's suggestion of the indebtedness of Dante to the *Magnae* has served to direct the attention of scholars to a closer scrutiny of this Latin dictionary.[27]

Characteristic references to "Ugucio" in Mayhew's edition of the *Promptorium* appear in the following English entries: *boos of a boke, bookbyndere, cardyacle, catrypel, cercle, dawnyng, elf, eloquent, ganokyr, garbage, garyt, gate schodel, geldyng, gyrth, glofare, gryndyngston, gronyn, growyn, hangyng, hasard,* and *heyward.* In detail, some of these entries follow.

Boos of a boke, or othyr lyke: *Turgiolum, -i; neut.,* 2, vgucio in turgeo.
Bookbyndere, or mendere: *Socius, -ij; Masc.,* 2, vgucio in feros.
Cardyacle: Cardiaca, -ce; Vgucio in cardian.
Cercle, clepyd þe snayle, as of *serpentis* or oþer lyke: *Spira, -re; fem., prime,* vgucio, In spasium.
Elf, spyryt: *lamia, -e; fem., prime* . . . vgucio in lanio. . . .
Eloquent, or wel spok man or woman: *Eloquens, -tis; omnis gen.,* 3: *Dicosus, -a, -um;* vgucio in dico.
Geldyng, or gelt hors: *Canterius, -ij: Masc.,* 2, vgucio in cano. . . .
Gyrth, horsys gyrdyl . . . *singlum, -li est hominum* vgucio in cingo.
Gryndyngston, or mylle-stoon: *Molaris, -is; Masc.,* 3, vgucio in molo.

Among other documents referred to as sources by the compiler of the *Promptorium* are the *Dictionarius* of John of Garland, listed in the Preambulum, and the *Liber distigii,* or *Distigium,* cited in the text, and ascribed to Garland by Way. Born in England, probably in the second half of the twelfth century, John of Garland studied at Oxford and Paris and was professor at the University of Toulouse, 1229–31. Besides the *Dictionarius,* he was author of *Synonyma* and *Equivoca,* or *Multorum vocabulorum interpretatio,* books of interest to the grammarian and the lexicographer; of *Compendium alchymiae cum dictionario;* and of treatises on counterpoint, plain song, and other musical subjects.[28] It is not strange that Englishmen compiling dictionaries in the fifteenth century should turn to the work of this celebrated scholar of their own country.

The *Distigium,* preserved among the grammatical writings of Garland in the Library of Caius College, Cambridge, and printed by Thomas Wright (*A Volume of Vocabularies,* 175–82), is a metrical tract with an interlinear gloss in English and Latin. The first line, omitting the

gloss, reads thus: "Cespitat in phaleris yppus, blattaque suppinus."
Though not extensively employed in the *Promptorium* (for a typical
reference, see *s.v.* "Kervare before a lorde . . . *Cironomon, -tis;* 'liber dis-
tigij' ''), it is of interest for its arrangement and content and its possible
anticipation of later vocabularies.

The first 41 lines are a series of unrelated distichs, of sententious or
proverbial sayings, as shown by the following:

tavenere i. estus aeris

Fecula non acinum   caupo   canina   repellit,

vermes, Anglice myntys   *drastus*

et bibulus musti   bibiones   arcet   amurca.

i. sanctus   *i. vana gloria*

Non est hic   agnus   quem   sinodoxia   tangit,

i. gravat   malus mos   bonum opus orationis dicte

quemque   premit   cathesis   non potest   diasinaxis.

i. homines cubitales   qui obliquo videt

Inter   pigmeos   nanus   regnat,   strabo luscos. . . .

The remaining 120 lines of the *Distigium* are similar to these in arrangement. They form a vocabulary listing vocables associated with these
topics: the names of animals; a house and furnishings of a house; the
parts of the body; a mill and objects associated with it; a blacksmith's
shop; instruments of the household and farm, including distaff, spindle,
plow, and wagon; musical instruments; various artificers, such as cobbler,
tailor, dyer, tanner, mason, and carpenter; species of trees; dress materials; and various classes of people.

There is nothing novel in the author's choice of topics. Listing of the
names of parts of the body, houses and furniture, artificers, trees, birds,
animals, etc., was recurrent in the bilingual vocabularies from the tenth
to the fifteenth century. And such lists, generally more systematically arranged, continued to be employed in manuals for teaching Latin, French,
and Italian, as well as in the smaller English-Latin and Latin-English
dictionaries, through the sixteenth century.[29]

Better known and more extensively used than the *Distigium* was the
Dictionarius (*ca.* 1220) of John of Garland.[30] This book is not, as the title
might suggest, a list of words with definitions, in double columns of the
page. It is, in appearance, an informal prose tract with annotations and
interlinear glosses. Its purpose, as the author informs us, is to bring
together the more necessary words which the young scholar must hold
firmly in mind. It will begin with the members of the human body and,
from this beginning, evolve a *promptuarium*, or treasure house of words.
Proceeding with this topic, the author manages to introduce, in descriptive and expository discourse, words for all the parts of the human body

and to make clear the relationship of the parts. So he continues through other groups of words. After a paragraph, or even a sentence, the author interpolates from time to time explanations of certain words or phrases. At intervals also he uses interlinear English glosses of Latin terms.

bogelers   *bogyls*
Pluscularii sunt divites per plusculas suas, et lingulas, et mordacula, per limas, et
brydels
loralia equina.
Plusicularii dicuntur Gallice boucliers [buclers]. *Plusculas, Gallice* boucles. *Lingula, de lingua, dicitur Gallice* hardilon [hardeliun]. *Mordaculum, id est* mordaunt. *Loralia dicuntur Gallice* lorains, *id est* poitraus. [*Gallice* loreins, *Anglice* peytereles.]
                                                                    nedyls
Willelmus, vicinus noster, habet in foro ista vendenda ante se, acus, et
nedylcasys   *sope*   *myrrys*   *rasors wetstonys   vyrehyryns*
  acuaria, smigma sive saponem, et specula, et rasoria, cotes, et piricudia,
  spyndels
et   fusillos.
Acuaria dicuntur instrumenta illa ubi servantur acus. . . .[31]

In this manner the *Dictionarius* sets forth a wide range of words in common use. From terms applicable to parts of the human body, it continues with others pertaining to trades and manufactures, to the house of a citizen and its furniture, to the author's own wardrobe, to an ecclesiastical library, to the occupations and employments peculiar to women, to a fisherman and a list of fish, to a fowler and wild fowls, and to plants, herbs, and fruits. It supplies thus an informal but comprehensive list of common words together with an English gloss and commentaries on the more difficult terms.

In the *Promptorium* the *Dictionarius* is cited as an authority for Latin equivalents under the following English entries: *here boond, hoone, hoope, hopyr off a myl or a tramel, lace, losange, mader, malkyn, mydrym, myteyn, nowch, pane of a furrure, pendawnt, percyle.*

The *Dictionarius* was not printed until the nineteenth century, though, according to Wright (*op. cit.*, 120), manuscripts of it are not uncommon either in England or on the Continent, and it may have been well known in the fifteenth century. As to the vogue of the *Synonyma* and *Equivoca* there is no doubt. Numerous editions of these books were printed by Pynson and Wynkyn de Worde from 1496 to 1518.[32] These texts were probably used as schoolbooks; they are echoed also in the *Catholicon Anglicum* and the *Ortus vocabulorum.*

No less esteemed than John of Garland, in the fifteenth century, was Alexander Neckam (1157–1217). In the Preambulum of the *Promptorium* Neckam is cited, by his full name, among the authorities, and the name Neckam is repeated frequently under entries in the text. No work is mentioned, but the compiler seems to have been using the *De nominibus utensilium*. Alexander Neckam was a distinguished scholar, who, having gained renown as a professor in the University of Paris, returned to England in 1187 to direct the celebrated school at Dunstable. The *De nominibus* may have been composed while he was master at Dunstable. The number of manuscripts extant indicates that this was probably a popular schoolbook, as Wright suggests. It is printed in Wright's *Volume of Vocabularies* (pp. 96–119).

The *De nominibus* is a Latin vocabulary with an interlinear gloss, largely in Latin and French, though with a few terms glossed in English. In arrangement it is somewhat similar to the *Dictionarius* of Garland, but without the interspersed comments which appear in the latter text. Keeping the words together in their different classes (as those concerned with farm implements and agriculture), Neckam, like Garland, arranges them in a sort of continuous discourse. He begins with a description of the kitchen and its furniture and implements and the methods of preparing food. By a process of association of ideas, many other topics, with the appropriate terms and glosses, follow: the owner of a house, the chambermaid, and household employments; building, fortifying, and defending a feudal castle; occupations of the country; agriculture and farm implements; navigation and ships; the duties of a medieval scribe; the operations of a goldsmith; and ecclesiastical furniture.

In the *Promptorium* some of the references to Neckam are found in these entries: *garbage of fowlys, gonge hole, helme or roder, iowpe, lach, or snek, laththe for howsyng, perre,* and *staunch*.

Promptorium	*De nominibus utensilium*
Garbage of fowlys: *In plurali numero: Entera, -orum,* neckam. . . .	. . . et avium domesticarum entera.
Iowpe, garment: *Iupa, -pe; fem., prime,* neckam. . . .	Perhendinaturus jupam habeat penulatam.
Lach, or snek: *Pessulum, -i; neut.,* 2 . . . *vel pessula, -e;* neckam.	Ostium seram habeat, pensulam vel pensulum.
Perre, Drynke: *piretum, -ti; neut.,* 2, neckam. . . .	In promptuario . . . sint . . . medus, siue ydromellum, piretum. . . .

Of the other authorities mentioned in the Preambulum, three require brief comment: William Brito, *Campus florum*, and Robert Kilwardby.[33] William Brito (d. 1356) was a native of Wales and a monk of the Franciscan order. He compiled a *Summa, sive opusculum difficilium vocabulorum biblie,* sometimes entitled *Lexicon sive vocabularium biblie*. This is probably the work referred to by the compiler of the *Promptorium*. The *Campus florum*, ascribed to Thomas Walleys (fl. 1333), is more frequently cited as an authority for the Latin terms of the *Promptorium* than any other book excepting the *Catholicon*. Leland refers to the *Campus florum* as the *copiosus index juris Canonici*. Robert Kilwardby, a native of England, was educated at the University of Paris and probably Oxford, and rose to be Archbishop of Canterbury in 1272. He wrote commentaries on Priscian, Donatus, and Aristotle. Some of his grammatical treatises probably supplied materials to the compiler of the *Promptorium*.

These and other authorities cited, *passim*, in the text, such as Aristotle, Cato, Boethius, Donatus, Petrus Comestor, Henricus Suso, Gregory the Great, and the Decretum of Gratian, add up to a considerable body of source materials and show, as Way suggests, "how extensive a store of learning must have been treasured up in the library of the Austin Friars at Lynn" and in that of the neighboring convent of the Dominicans.[34]

CHAPTER II

Catholicon Anglicum (ca. 1483)

I N HIS EDITION of the *Promptorium,* Albert Way used for illustrative purposes a manuscript version of another English-Latin dictionary. He refers to this document in these words: "A highly valuable MS., dated 1483, consisting of an English and Latin Dictionary, wholly distinct from the Promptorium, and written apparently in the North-Eastern parts of England, is cited as the Catholicon Anglicum." [1] This manuscript was owned by Lord Monson [2] and was apparently christened *Catholicon Anglicum* by Way himself on the basis of these words in what he calls the colophon: "Explicit Catholicon in lingua materna. . . ." Almost forty years after Way had called attention to the Monson manuscript and had supplied a title for it, it was published by the Early English Text Society with an informative title page, reading:

Catholicon Anglicum, an English-Latin Wordbook, dated 1483. Edited, from the MS. No. 168 in the library of Lord Monson, collated with the Additional MS. 15,562, British Museum, with Introduction and Notes, by Sidney J. H. Herrtage . . . London . . . MDCCCLXXXI.

Herrtage assures us that he has sought to make this volume a companion to the *Promptorium* (i.e., to Way's edition), and to this end he has marked with a dagger all words which do not occur in the *Promptorium,* and marked with an asterisk those which are annotated by Way. [3]

The author of the *Catholicon Anglicum* is not known. The date of the Monson manuscript is 1483; that of Additional MS 15562, about 1475, according to Herrtage, [4] and the Additional manuscript was probably a copy from a still earlier manuscript. The date of the original we do not know. A conservative estimate of the number of English entries in the *Catholicon* is eight thousand as compared with twelve thousand in the *Promptorium*. But the number of Latin equivalents or synonyms in the *Catholicon Anglicum* is far greater than that in the *Promptorium*, and thus is of especial interest to students of fifteenth-century Latin. In the *Catholicon* the nouns, verbs, and other parts of speech are arranged in a single list, in alphabetical order. Grammatical information on the declension of nouns and adjectives and the conjugation of verbs, present in the manuscript, has been largely omitted from the printed text. "After the first few pages," writes Herrtage, "I have, in order to economise space, omitted the inflexional endings of the genitive cases of nouns, and the feminine and neuter genders of adjectives." [5]

Way points out, and Herrtage quotes him, that the principal authorities cited in the *Catholicon Anglicum* are Brito, the *Catholicon*, the *Doctrinale*, the gloss on the *Liber equivocorum* of John of Garland, Hugutio, Papias, Virgil, and Ysidore (i.e., Isidore of Seville); and of these only Hugutio and the *Liber equivocorum* occur at all frequently.[6] These editors note also that a large number of verses are quoted, probably from some work of John of Garland. If the names of the authorities listed above are cited in the manuscript, they have been silently omitted from Herrtage's printed edition. It seems quite likely that the compiler of the *Catholicon Anglicum* was familiar with Brito, Hugutio, the *Catholicon* of Joannes Balbus—authorities discussed by Way in his edition of the *Promptorium*—and made use of them. His more obvious indebtedness is, however, to John of Garland's *Synonyma*, a work not specifically mentioned by Way or Herrtage.

The *Synonyma*, composed probably at the beginning of the thirteenth century, had a renewed vogue after the invention of printing. In the British Museum there are copies of nine different editions, ranging in date from 1496 to 1518.[7] The plan of the book was to arrange in metrical form groups of words of similar meaning (synonyms), perhaps primarily as an aid to the memory, but also as a way of distinguishing differences in meaning among words in a closely related group. Editions of the *Synonyma*, from 1496, included an exposition by Master Geoffrey the Englishman (*cum expositione magistri Galfredi Anglici*), in which more grammatical information, as well as instruction on the use of each word of the group, is given. Characteristic passages in the *Synonyma* together with parallels from the *Catholicon Anglicum* [8] are presented herewith:

Synonyma

Catholicon Anglicum

an Helpe: Auxilium extraneis datur, presidium est a loco vtili positum, subsidium est quod superuenit, beneficium equalibus; versus:

Auxilium vel opem: suffragia dic et asilum,

    Auxilium vel opem, suffragia dic, & Asilum,

Presidium: vel subsidium: quibus adde iuuamen:

    Presidium vel subsidium, quibus Adde iuvamen;

His adiumentum: simul adiutoria iunge

    Hijs Adiumentum simul Adiutoria iungas,

His amminiculum: simul addas opitulamen

    Hijs Adminiculum simul Addas opitulamen,

Et de propitior fit propitiatio nomen.

    Et de propicior sit propiciacio nomen. . . .

Felle; Acer, Acerbus, asper, atrox, austerus . . . barbarus . . . crudus, crudelis, dirus, efferus, feralis, ferox, furus; . . . vnde versus:

Crudus/ crudelis/ austerus & improbus/ atrox,

    Crudus, crudelis, Austerus & improbus, Atrox,

Est ferus/ atque ferox violentus/ acerbus ac acer

    Est ferus, atque ferox, violentus, Acerbus & Acer:

Impius immitis/ seuusque/ molestus iniquus

    Impius, inmitis, seuusque, molestus, iniquus:

Asper inhumanusque/ tyrannus/ siue proteruus

    Asper, inhumanusque tirannus, siue proteruus.

Toruus/ & indomitus/ his iungaturque seuerus.

    Toruus & indomitus, hijs iungitur atque seuerus,

Predictis dirus/ sociabitur et truculentus.

    Predictis dirus sociabitur, & truculentus.

to Die; mori, obire, exalare, commori, & cetera; versus:

Interit/ expirat/ moritur/ defungitur atque

    Interit, expirat, moritur, defungitur atque

Occumbit vel obit: dissoluitur: examinatque

    Occumbit vel obit, dissoluitur, exanimatque.

Excidit/ exaltat/ discedit eis sociatur.

    Interit, occumbit, mortem signant violentam.

Interit/ occumbit/ mortem signant violentam

    Excidit, exalat . . . decedit, eis sociatur,

Ad naturalem concordant cetera mortem

    Ad naturalem concordant cetera mortem,

Et potes illum idem complexa dicere voce.

    Et potes illud idem complexa dicere voce:

Tollitur e medio: natura debita soluit

    Tollitur e medio, nature debita soluit;

Nature nostre: soluit generale tributum

    Nature nostre soluit generale tributum;

Synonyma	*Catholicon Anglicum*
Clausit presentem supremo funere vitam	Clausit suppremo presentem funere vitam;
Carcere corporeo/ resolutus spiritus exit	Carcere corporeo resolutus spiritus exit;
Mortuus est mundo: victurus postea Christo.	Mortuus est mundo victurus postea Christo.

to Dye.

vel prosaice sic:—presentis vite cursum feliciter consummauit; vel sic:—de corporeo spiritus sese re-laxauit argatustulo; vel sic:—anima resoluta est ab argastulo carnis: cum similibus; mori hominibus et ani-malibus commune est, sed obire conuenit tantum hominibus bonis; est enim obire quaci obuiam jre.

Many other passages in the two texts show close correspondences be-tween the *Synonyma* of Garland and the anonymous *Catholicon Angli-cum* [9] and suggest that the *Synonyma* is a major source, ultimate if not direct, of this English-Latin dictionary. There are of course other sources, but the Garland seems most important. Its importance lies not so much in the direct contribution of materials, i.e. the verses, as in the emphasis on certain linguistic principles, which seem to be exemplified by the com-piler of the *Catholicon Anglicum* even when he is not employing matter from his Latin source.

The first is the principle of synonymy, which, basic in John of Garland's Latin text, is extended in the borrowed materials and made widely ap-plicable throughout the *Catholicon*. In the second example above (*crudus; felle*), the compiler of the English-Latin text introduces thirty-two pos-sible synonyms (see the full text in Herrtage), extending the list in *Synonyma* by ten terms. In the materials not derived from the *Synonyma*, the principle is also in force, as in "to Blame; *accusare, culpare, culpitare, criminare, increpare, improperari, inhonorare, redarguere, reprehendere, probare, vituperare.*" *To begyle* has twenty-eight Latin equivalents or synonyms; *besy* has twenty-four; *to fille*, nineteen; and so on throughout. The principle of synonymy here exhibited is, in the sixteenth century, more consciously employed to gain copiousness and variety.[10] This is the earliest example of it in English-Latin lexicography.

A second principle in the *Catholicon* which seems to derive from John of Garland's treatise and to be elaborated in the English-Latin text is that of making distinctions in the meaning and usage of terms often re-garded as synonymous. In many of the metrical groupings of the *Syn-onyma* (as *morior*, etc., in the third example above) the author distinguishes different applications of the terms; and distinctions are made perhaps in most of the *versus* set down in the *Synonyma*. The author of the *Catholicon Anglicum* can be seen extending the principle in the prose entry *to dye*, a piece of exposition added to supplement the borrowing from Garland. But the principle also is exhibited independently, as in these terms: *alle, a bataile, to cry, resonabylle, synne*, and *a stewarde*. Under *to cry* the author lists sixty-odd verbs to indicate the cries of various animals and birds. Here is the procedure under *alle*:

Alle; universus, universalis, cunctus, singulus quibus quisque vnusquisque, totalis, pan grece, sesqui, Totus ad magnitudinem pertinet: ut totum corpus, tota terra; cuncti qui vbique sunt; vniuersi qui in loco, omnis qui in diuersis sunt locis; omnis ad multitudinem & numerum pertinet, ut omnis homo & omnes homines, omnis distribuit inter partes subiectiuas, ut omnis homo currit ergo iste & iste, & cetera.

For the logician or theologian the distinction of terms under *resonabylle* might have an appeal:

Resonabylle; racionabilis, racionalis. Sed differunt; Racionale est illud quod vtitur vel aptum natum est vti racione, vt homo, angelus. Sed racionabile est quod racione agitur vel ducitur & racionabiliter viuit: vnde multi homines sunt racionales. i. aptitudinem habent vtendi racione, sed non omnes sunt racionabiles quia non ducuntur racione & proprie homo dicitur racionalis, Angelus vero jntellectualis.

As the *Catholicon Anglicum* was never printed until 1881 and as there are few manuscripts of the text extant, it is difficult to assess its influence on subsequent lexicographers. The *Catholicon* does, however, exemplify the significant features of synonymy and of differentiation in meanings and usage of terms, which have their place in the history of lexicography.

A *page from the* Medulla grammatice, *Harleian MS 2257, folio 68ʳ, in the British Museum*

CHAPTER III

Medulla grammatice

W E HAVE NOTICED above that in the early printed editions
of the *Promptorium, Medulla grammatice* appeared as an alternate title, and that, throughout the sixteenth century, this
alternate title was generally employed instead of *Promptorium* to refer
to our first English-Latin dictionary. Later discovery of numerous
fifteenth-century manuscripts of a Latin-English dictionary entitled
Medulla grammatice [1] has led to some confusion respecting the lexicons
mentioned. Into the details of this ambiguity, it seems unnecessary to
proceed further. But since the *Medulla* has much in common with the
Promptorium [2] and the *Ortus vocabulorum,* and since it has been variously ascribed to one or the other of the compilers of these texts, it seems
desirable to place the *Medulla,* at the risk of transcending the limits of
my study of printed texts.

Medulla grammatice, as we here use the title, is a manuscript Latin-
English (not English-Latin) dictionary of the fifteenth century. That
this was a popular and probably influential lexicon, though never printed,
we may infer from the large number of manuscripts in existence. Way
(*op. cit.,* Part III, *l–liv*) describes briefly sixteen and refers to another,
which he had not been able to trace. Robert T. Meyer, in an unpublished
dissertation,[3] studies the sources of the Stonyhurst *Medulla,* a manuscript
apparently not known to Way. Among the more valuable manuscripts
of the *Medulla* described by Way are those numbered in his list 6, 7, and
10, respectively. These are Harleian MS 2257, Harleian MS 2270, and a
manuscript in the Library of St. John's College, Cambridge.

Meyer's study of the *Medulla* is based upon a facsimile copy of an original manuscript in the Jesuit College at Stonyhurst, Lancashire, England. This, Meyer regards as the most complete of all known manuscripts of the text. According to Robert Flower, Meyer states, the Stonyhurst *Medulla* antedates 1400. The earliest copy known to Way is conjecturally dated 1460. The author is unknown; and Meyer is probably right in thinking the text had not one author but many. "The authors . . . are a host of obscure persons, unknown teachers: monks, friars, and obscure clerks who expounded the classics and Scriptures in the cloister or in the schools" (p. 14). The glossary, arranged in ABC order, contains about twenty thousand words, chiefly Latin, which are defined in Latin or in English. Proper names of persons and places are distributed, alphabetically, throughout.

Following the method of W. M. Lindsay in his investigation of the English group of glossaries—the Corpus, Erfurt, Epinal, and Leyden—Meyer studies the sources of the Stonyhurst *Medulla*. In conclusion (pp. 132–36), he states that the search for the sources of the *Medulla* shows material to be found in three very distinct places: (1) The oldest strata, glosses from the classics and the Bible. To the *glossae collectae*, the original source of many glossaries, the *Medulla* has many correspondences, as the author demonstrates with respect to the Corpus, the Leyden, the Epinal, and the Erfurt collections. The inference is that the *Medulla* drew part of its material from the same source as did these earlier glosses. (2) The vocabulary (class glossary) or *nominale* was the basis for the greater part of the *Medulla*. (3) The medieval *summa* or encyclopedia of knowledge was a favorite book. Compilers of the late Middle Ages drew, for example, from such books as the *Magnae derivationes* of Hugo of Pisa, which was much indebted to Isidore's *Etymologia*.

Within the limits of his dissertation, Meyer was able to deal with only the first of the possible sources mentioned in his summary. This is, of course, basic in determining ultimate sources. But the investigation needs to be carried further, as the author himself realizes. What is the process of transmission of the materials of the *glossae collectae* through a period of five hundred years or more? It is here that further study of the vocabularies or class glossaries, such as those published in the Wright-Wülcker volumes, and of the *summae*, such as the *Catholicon* of Joannes Balbus, is highly desirable. If, for example, we check the *Catholicon* against Meyer's comparative study of the Stonyhurst *Medulla* and the Epinal-Erfurt glossaries (pp. 64 ff.), we shall find that the Latin of the *Medulla* corresponds fairly closely with that in the *Catholicon*, as under *abimelech, abra, absinthium, acephali, ador, agygraphia, allium, amphitrites, anastasis,* and *angiportus.* The *Catholicon* could have been a source for some of these entries and for many others not accounted for by the eighth- and ninth-century glossaries. The *Medulla*, as Meyer seems to imply, grew by accretions through a long period of time. My own investigation shows that at least partial support for this theory is found in the correspondence of the word list and the definitions of the *Medulla* (I refer especially to the word lists in the texts of the Harleian MSS 2257 and 2270) to those in *Vocabularius breviloquus,* an abridgment of the *Catholicon;* to those in the popular Latin-German lexicon *Vocabularius Latino-Teutonicus* and its successor, *Gemma gemmarum;* and, finally, to those in the *Ortus vocabulorum*. But the history of the *Ortus* and its relation to the *Medulla* and other predecessors will be presented in the section which follows.

CHAPTER IV

[*H*]*ortus vocabulorum* (1500)

WE LIKE to think that the titles given to some of the dictionaries at the end of the fifteenth century reflect something of the fascination that words and the study of words had for the authors and their public, and were not merely publishers' devices for calling attention to their wares. Among the attractive titles are "A Treasure House for Young Scholars" (*Promptorium* or *Promptuarium parvulorum*), "The Marrow of Grammar" (*Medulla grammatice*), "The Horn of Plenty" (*Cornucopia*), "Gems of Words," or "Gems of Gems" (*Gemma vocabulorum, Gemma gemmarum*), and "The Garden of Words" (*Ortus vocabulorum*). Although the Humanists of the sixteenth century scorned the medieval Latinity of the books so designated, still the titles seem prophetic of the passion for words, foreign and native, and the faith in the power of the spoken word, which persisted through the Renaissance.

It is with the last-named title, *Ortus vocabulorum*, that we are now chiefly concerned.[1] This book, a Latin-English dictionary, containing much Latin and less English, was first printed in small folio by Wynkyn de Worde in the year 1500. In a copy of this edition (Brit. Mus., G. 7620) the title appears, in black letter (fol. 1ʳ) as *Ortus vocabulorum*. The lower portion of this page is blank. On the reverse side, in black letter: "Prologus in librū qui ortus vocabulorum incipit. Ut etenim multos. . . ." The dictionary proper consists of 266 folios, printed in double columns, with running heads "*A ante B*," etc. In the colophon is the statement that the *Ortus* contains the meaning of all words which are found in *Catholicon, Breviloquus, Cornucopia,* or *Medulla grammatice*—a

28

statement to be recalled in discussing the sources. The colophon concludes with these words:

Per virum laudabilem ciuem prouidum magistrum Winandum de worde prope cele-berrimum monasterium quod Westmynstre appellatur. Anno incarnaciones dominice. M. CCCCC. impressum.

My estimate of the number of entries is approximately twenty-seven thousand, many of these with their Latin or English equivalents occupying not more than a single line in the column. The name of the compiler or compilers is nowhere mentioned and thus far is unknown.

Bale, assuming a certain Galfridus Grammaticus to be the author of the *Promptorium*, assigns to him also the *Medulla* and the *Ortus*.[2] Certainly "Geoffrey the Grammarian" is a most appropriate name for the compiler of any one of these texts, but Bale presents no real evidence for the identification of Geoffrey, or for his association with any one of the three books. Way, who was familiar with Bale's ascription and had spent more than a score of years studying the texts and manuscripts of fifteenth-century dictionaries, laments, "I have sought in vain to ascertain who may have been the compiler of this Latin-English dictionary" (i.e., *Ortus vocabulorum*).[3] Robert T. Meyer, though rejecting Bale's ascription of the *Medulla* to Galfridus Grammaticus, seems to accept his conclusion that the compiler of the *Promptorium* and the compiler of the *Ortus* are one and the same. Meyer writes, "But the compiler of the *Promptorium* did write a Latin-English dictionary, the *Hortus Vocabulorum*."[4] In support of this statement Meyer quotes Wynkyn de Worde's Ad Lectorem, in his 1516 edition of the *Promptorium*, to the effect that the printer had this English-Latin wordbook bound with the *Ortus*, Latin-English, for the benefit of young scholars.[5] It is true that the same printer was publishing both texts at this time and wished to sell as many copies as possible. But does it follow that because the texts were bound together they were compiled by the same person? Chronologically, the theory is difficult. The *Promptorium* was compiled as early as 1440; the *Ortus* was first published in 1500, and no manuscript of an earlier date is known. It is unlikely that the same compiler would have put together the two works sixty years apart. In general, the evidence of individual authorship of any one of the three books is too scanty to warrant definite conclusions.

Although the name of the compiler has not been ascertained, there is good evidence of the vogue of the *Ortus*. Kennedy and Way list twelve editions, ranging in date from 1500 to 1533; the *Short-Title Catalogue* records nine.[6] Of editions I have examined—those of 1500, 1511, 1514, and 1528 by Wynkyn de Worde, and one of 1520 by Jaques Cousin—only that of 1514 claims any augmentation. On the title page of this copy we read: *cum perpulcris additionibus Ascensii.*[7] It is difficult to ascertain where such additions are, or from what work of Ascensius they come. They must be scanty indeed, for, though there are corrections and slight changes after the first edition of the *Ortus,* the catchwords in the copies subsequent to 1500 remain the same; and the number of entries in "*A* ante *P*," for example, is the same—186. These later editions seem, in some instances, to have corrected errors of the press; but in other respects, the first edition is, as Way notes, more accurate and has also a large number of hexameter lines illustrating the meaning of Latin words, here introduced under the heading "Versus," but omitted in subsequent editions.[8] Otherwise, there are no material changes. The *editio princeps* is then the one from which our illustrations are drawn.

The entries in the text of the *Ortus,* including a number of classical and Biblical proper names of persons and places, are arranged in alphabetical order, with indication of the inflection and gender of nouns and adjectives and the conjugation of verbs. The following entries [9] in "*D* ante *E*" show the arrangement and the grammatical information offered:

Despondeo es i. promittere. sponsam facere vel viro coniugere to promysse maryage. a. s.
Desponsatio onis.   a weddynge.   f. t.
Desponsatus a um.   wedded.   o. s.
Desponso as to wedde.   tor trix icis.   a. p.
Despotes in plurali. i. dominatores.
Despumo as. me pro. i. valde vel deorsum spumare vel purgare.   to fome or clense. a. p.
Despuo is. i. expuere.   to spytte downe.   a. t.
Desputo as. i. deorsum spuere vel sputo profundere.   a. p.
Despumatorium rii. anglice spytte.   n. s.
Desterno nis straui.   to cast down behynde.   a. t.

Among the proper names are these:

Eschynes et demosthenes fuerunt duo oratores.
Esebon est proprium nomen civitatis.
Ezechias nomen proprium. inter fortis dominus vel fortitudo domini.   m. p.
Ganges gis. quidam fluuius qui exiens de paradiso pergit ad regiones indie.   m. t.
Gehenna ne. est locus ignis vel nomen proprium.   f. p.

As we have noticed above, the colophon of the 1500 *Ortus* refers to four books, some or all of which may be considered as possible sources. The list, with one addition, is repeated in the colophon of subsequent editions which I have examined, as well as in the title page. The full list, with other interesting matter, is presented on the title page of the 1509 edition by Pynson, and may be paraphrased as follows:

The Garden of Words, in alphabetical order, containing almost all things that are in the Catholicon, the Breviloquus, the Cornucopia, the Gemma vocabulorum, and the Medulla grammatice, together with an exposition in the vernacular English. Not unworthily called "the garden of words," for just as in gardens are found abundance of flowers, of herbs, and of fruits with which our bodies are strengthened and our spirits refreshed, so in this work are diverse words accommodated to beginners desirous of the pleasures of learning. With these words they may furnish the mind, adorn their speech, and finally, if the fates permit, grow into very learned men. . . . Here in alphabetical order they may easily find whatever words they desire. The inflection and gender of nouns and the conjugation of verbs they will learn by a letter subjoined to such word. A work useful and profitable to all desirous of a knowledge of arts and sciences; and on account of the exposition of English speech, especially necessary to the realm of England. Hurry, therefore, all Englishmen, and spare not your small coins. Buy this volume while you can get it good cheap.

To be sold in London on Fleet Street at the sign of St. George, by Richard Pynson, printer to His Majesty.[10]

This is the sort of lively advertising we might expect to see today on the jacket of a new book, and, like the skit on the jacket, the matter of this title page should be read with due caution. The claim that the *Ortus* contains all that may be found in the five books named is, of course, absurd. The *Catholicon* of Joannes Balbus, to choose only one from the list, is a large folio of almost eight hundred pages. There is little doubt, however, that the compiler had access to the books he listed and made use of them. But only in the limited sense that the *Ortus* contained much medieval matter common to all the others, excepting Perottus' *Cornucopia*, could his claim have the least validity.

One of the most likely immediate sources of the *Ortus* is the *Medulla grammatice*, which is referred to in every surviving copy of the *Ortus*. Any author compiling a Latin-English dictionary about the year 1500 surely would think first of the *Medulla*, the only Latin-English dictionary then available, existing in many manuscripts and having an extensive word list and, above all, many definitions in English. Moreover, no manuscript of this work had been published, though the title had been used as an alternate by the publishers of the *Promptorium*. Why should not such a compiler make the *Medulla* basic in putting together a new Latin-English dictionary? Revision and enlargement of a *Medulla* manuscript would not be an insuperable task, especially if such a manuscript were already in possession of one of the printers, say Wynkyn de Worde. Furthermore, publication of a Latin-English dictionary as a companion volume to the *Promptorium* would be a most useful, and perchance profitable, undertaking. These suggestions are given added weight by the circumstance that every single edition of the *Ortus* refers to the *Medulla* and thereby implies indebtedness. This reasoning lends support to Way's statement that the *Ortus* is apparently based upon the *Medulla grammatice*, but with considerable modifications and additions from other sources.[11] Plausible as this theory is, conclusive supporting evidence concerning the Latin element of the *Medulla* is, because of the large body of conventional materials, most difficult to find.

Some agreement, especially in the English equivalents for Latin terms, between the *Medulla* and the *Ortus* will suggest a close relationship.[12]

Medulla	*Ortus*
Imaginor aris. i. absentem rem praecipere vel imaginem rei absentis anglice to ymagine. *veluti Imaginatio/ nis.*	*Imaginor ari.* to ymagyn or thynke. *d. p.* *Imaginatio onis. vis anime qua quis comprehendit formas cum materia re absente. anglice* a thoghte/ or imaginacion. *f. t.*
Imago an ymage/*f. g. representatio alicuius rei.*	*Imago inis representatio alicuius rei. anglice* an ymage. *f. t.*
Imbecillis la lum. et hic et haec Imbecillis et hoc le/ex in et becill. i. sine baculo et sine sustamento virium. i. debilis et fragilis/et dicitur debilis. i. totus in baculo withoute staffe or febul. *nam becillus est baculus.*	*Imbecilis et hoc le idest sine baculo. idest sustentamento virium. i. debilis fragilis. anglice* febyll wayke/or withoute a stafe. *o. t.*
Imbecilitas. i. debilitas.	*Imbecillitas. i. debilitas f. t.*
Imbellis et hoc le omnis generis compositus ab in et bellum. i. eneruis debilis.	*Imbellis et hoc le. eneruis fragilis debilis.* febylle. *o. t.*
Imbellia. i. debilitas.	*Imbellia. lie. idest debillitas fragilitas. f. g. prime decli.*
Imbecillus la lum. i. imbecillis.	*Imbecillus a um. idest imbecillis. omnis gen. scde. decli.*
Imbellius a um freele.	*Imbellius a um, angl.* frele *o. s.*
Imbrex est vas aquaticum.	*Imbrex cis vas aquaticum f. t.*
Imbricium a gotre.	*Imbrices etiam dicuntur tegule quia capiunt imbres f. t.*
*Imber. m. g./*reyne or dewe/ *pluuiavis repentina ad nubes et pluuiam pertinens dicitur ab in et ebrio as quasi terram inebriat/et ad germinandum aptus.*	*Imber bris angl.* rayne or a dewe or a showre. *m. t.*
Imberculus dim.	*Imbriculus li. diminutiuus parvus imber. m. t.*
Imbercus ca cum reyny.	*Imbricus ca cum. pe. cor. i. pluuiosus. et dicitur ab imber o. s.*
Imbibo bis bi tum. i. valde vel intus bibere cor bi ubique.	*Imbibo bis bibi. i. valde vel intus bibere cor bi ubique n. t.*
Imburso sas .i. im bursam ponere.	*Imburso as .i. in bursam ponere a. p.*
Imbulus a tent/or a waye brede. *et/dicitur ab intus et/. ambulo.*	*Imbulus est dictus qui in/hijs gens ambulat intus.*

Medulla	Ortus
Imbuo is .i. perfundere vel iniciare docere vel bibere extra mensuram/ or to larde with boutre—or fatte.	*Imbuo is. perfundere iniciare docere informare vel extra mensuram bibere.*
Imeon haterelle.	*Imeon vel imon grece dicitur ceruix g. indeclinabile.*
Imitatorius a um folowe able.	*Imitatorius a um. dignus imitatione vel qui aliquem imitatur o. s.*
Imitor taris .i. sequi to folowe in maners.	*Imitor aris.* to folowe in maners *Tor trix et tio verbale o. p.*
Immanis et hoc ne dicitur ingens terribilis informis non bonus et crudelis o. g. Ab in et/manum quod est bonum. quasi sine bono efferus crudelis.	*Immanis et hoc ne. qui non est bonus ingens terribilis informis.* hooge. *o. t.*

These parallels suggest a close kinship between the *Medulla* and the *Ortus;* and in entries where the English equivalents are given (*imago, imbecillis*), as in a few others where only Latin appears (*imbrex, imburso*), the *Ortus* seems definitely to depend on its predecessor. But also there is suggestion of a more complex relationship, involving perhaps common sources for these two texts. Among other books referred to on the title page of the *Ortus* are the *Catholicon* and the *Breviloquus* (*Vocabularius breviloquus*),[13] both popular Latin dictionaries and both available in printed editions in the latter half of the fifteenth century. The *Breviloquus,* as an abridgment of the larger *Catholicon,* may here represent the two texts, and from it are taken a few entries for comparison with those above.

Vocabularius breviloquus

Imaginatio onis f. t. vis anime qua quis comprehendit formas cum materia re absente. Sed hoc recordationis. aut imitationis. aut confictionis. Recordationis cum rem imaginarmur quae prius fuit subiecta nostro sensui. Imitationis cum rem similem non eandem. Confictionis quando conformamus aliquid mente quod in rerum numero natura non patitur inueniri. vt chimeram ex capite leonis, pectore hominis. ventre asini. cauda serpentis. Prima imaginatio nobis cōis est cum beluis. secunda et tercia est propria hominis.

Imago inis. f. g. representatio alicuius rei: & dicitur ab imitor aris. quasi imitago. quasi qui imitatur rem cuius est in corporalibus liniamentis & dispositione partium. Item imaginarius a um quod pertinet ad imaginem. Vel quod percipitur vmbratiliter et quadam imaginatione.

Imbecillus la lum. & h & h imbecillis. & hoc le in eodem sensu. i. sine baculo. i. sustentamento virium. i. debilis. fragilis.

Imbellia lie. i. debilitas. fragilitas.

Imbellis. lis & hoc imbelle. i. inervis. fragilis. debilis.

Imberbris. m. t. pluuievis repentina. ad nubes vel pluuiam pertinens. sic dictus quod terram inebriet ad germinandum.

Imbriculus li. dimi. paruus imber.

Imbricus. cu. cum. pe. cor. et imbricosus a um idest pluuiosus. & dicitur ad imber.

Imeon vel imon grece dicitur ceruix.

Immanis nis. m. t. & hoc ne. qui non est bonus crudelis. terribilis efferus et dicitur ab in et manum. quod est bonum. quasi sine manu id est bono. secundum Papiam. Immanis dicitur ingens. informis. hispidus & horrendus.

If we compare these entries from the *Breviloquus* with similar ones from the *Medulla* and *Ortus* above, we find that in *imaginatio, imbellia, imbriculus, imbricus,* and *imeon* the *Ortus* is nearer to the *Breviloquus,* and may well have derived from this lexicon or its ancestor *Catholicon.* In the case of *imber* (*imberbris*) even the *Medulla* seems to follow the *Breviloquus.* These details suggest how complicated is the problem of sources. Similar results appear from other comparisons of the *Ortus* and the *Medulla,* as, for example, in the entries *mica* to *migale.* There are variations in the order of entries, and there is some matter in each text not found in the other, but correspondences in the English equivalents seem significant.

Medulla	*Ortus*
Mica ce est minutum fragmentum panis a crome. et est quod cadit a pane dum frangitur.	*Mica ce. reliquis panis vel quod cadit de pane dum frangitur et comeditur. Et dicitur a minutus a. um. quasi minutatim cadens. anglice a crome of brede. f. p.*
Michael elis nomen proprium.	*Michael elis nomen proprium angeli. m. t.*
Michanea wittenes.	*Micania nie is est ingeniositas machinatio. anglice a wytnes.*
Microcosmus mi mo m. g. i. minor mundus.	*Microcosmus .i. minor mundus f. homo qui dicitur minor mundus m. s. . . .*
Micrologium .i. breviloquum.	*Micrologium. id est breviloquium anglice schorte worde.*
Micrologus a short speker.	*Micrologus gi qui breuiter loquitur vel qui magnam rem annullare cupiens quasi paruam despiciendo narrat. angl. a schorte speker.*
Micros vel cron interpretatur breuis.	*Micron vel micros interpretatur breuis vel minor.*

The *Medulla* may well be a source for the English in the *Ortus,* and sometimes for the Latin, though there are obvious expansions of the Latin, depending possibly on the *Breviloquus* and the *Catholicon,* or other books mentioned on the title page of the *Ortus.*

Among these is the *Gemma vocabulorum* or *Gemma gemmarum,* a small Latin-German dictionary which was very popular during the first quarter of the sixteenth century.[14] This book is listed in every edition of the *Ortus* after 1500, and could have been very useful to the compiler of the *Ortus.* A copy of the *Gemma* (1514) refers in the Prologus to

Brito, Huguito, Papias, *Catholicon, Braxiloquus,* and *Breviloquus* as authorities employed in the compilation of this book. Brunet lists editions of a *Vocabularum gemmula* for 1483, 1487, and 1493. If this is the same lexicon as the *Gemma,* there were printed editions before the *Ortus* was compiled in 1500. However this may be, the real predecessor of the *Gemma* was another Latin-German dictionary in great vogue from the 1470's to the end of the fifteenth century. This originally bore the title *Vocabularius Latino-Teutonicus.*[15] The compiler of the *Vocabularius* cites as his authorities Huguito, *Catholicon, Breviloquus,* Papias, and others. Although they claim common Latin sources, a comparison with especial attention to the German element indicates that the *Gemma* derived from the earlier work.

Vocabularius Latino-Teutonicus (1480)	*Gemma gemmarum* (1505)
Ebdomodarius. ein wochner.	*Ebdomodarius:* ein wochener.
Ebes. i. obtusus vel tardus. thüme.	*Ebes. i. obtusus vel tardus:* dum oder doll.
Ebetare. i. obtusum facere. thummachen.	*Hebetare. i. obtusum facere:* dum oder unvernunfftig machen.
Ebilus est quaedam herba. attych.	*Ebulus est quedam herba:* attich.
Ebrius. a. um. i. extra mensuram bibens. truncken.	*Ebrius a. um. i. extra mensuram bibens:* druncken oder voll.
Ebrietas. trunckenheyt.	*Ebrietas:* drunckenheit. volheyt.

In many instances the *Gemma* expands the earlier text, relying for the Latin upon the standard larger texts. Since the *Ortus* was compiled in 1500 or before, it may have drawn from the *Vocabularius,* which came to be known as *Gemma vocabulorum* or *Gemma gemmarum.* There are many correspondences between the *Gemma* and the *Ortus,* as Way noticed. Compare this entry in the two books.

Ortus	*Gemma*
A est nomen prime littere latine. generis neutri. Secundo est prepositio latina et significat anglice. of or from. *Tertio est dictio greca et significat idem quod sine vt achoris id est sine gratia. Quarto est interiectio dolentis et tunc aspiratur: vt ach domine deus.*	*A est nomen prime littere latine. generis neutri. Secundo est prepositio latina significat:* von. *Tertio est dictio greca. idem quod sine: vt achoris. i. sine gratia. Quarto est interiectio dolentis. & tunc aspiratur: vt Ach domine deus.*
Abactus a um id est fugatus ablactus dispersus & separatus. angl. Renaway.	*Abactus a um id est fugatus ablatus:* geteylet. vertriben.
Abalieno as .i. alienum facere & componitur ex ab & alieno. Esa j. Abalienati sunt retrorsum. i. alieni facti sunt. to mak strange. *a. p.*	*Abalieno as are:* entfremden. *Componitur ex ab & alieno. Esa. j. Abalienati sunt retrorsum. i. alieni facti sunt.*
Abauus .i. pater aui my gransyris fayther *m. s.*	*Abauus est pater proaui:* myn alten vatters vatter, od vrene. *m. s.*

The *Gemma* from which the entries above are taken is dated 1505, but these entries, except the first, seem to derive from the *Vocabularius Latino-Teutonicus* (1480), which has the following:

Abactus. ta. tum. i. fugatus, seperatus. geteylt *m. s.*
Abalieno. nas. nare. componitur ex ab & alieno. Ysa. j. Abalienati sunt retrorsum. i. alieni facti.
Abauus est pater proaui. eyn vranherr.

The *Ortus* may owe something to an edition of the Latin-German dictionary falling between the dates 1480 and 1505. Here, as elsewhere in a complicated pattern of conventional materials, dogmatic conclusions are hazardous. But the probability of the *Ortus'* indebtedness is a reasonable assumption in view of the reference to the *Gemma* and of the supporting parallels.

The *Cornucopia*, listed among the possible authorities of the *Ortus*, is the work of Nicolas Perottus and bears the full title *Cornucopiae sive linguae Latinae commentarii* (1489). This is an elaborate commentary on the *Spectacles* and *Epigrams* of Martial, forming a sort of analytical lexicon. Rich in classical illustrations of language and mythology and fruitful as a source for lexicographers in the Renaissance, it was less well adapted to the requirements of the *Ortus*. The compiler of the last-named work tended to follow the medieval tradition, and his use, if any, of the *Cornucopia* is negligible.

A book not mentioned on the title page or in the colophon of the *Ortus* but used as a source for certain illustrations is the *Equivoca* of John of Garland.[16] Of the vogue of this work and the *Synonyma*, a companion piece by the same author, we have spoken above.[17] In the first edition of the *Ortus* (1500) the compiler quotes, under the caption "Versus," hexameter lines of Latin to illustrate the meaning or usage of certain words. We know that similar illustrations were used in the *Equivoca*. To this work the *Ortus* refers under *chorus:* "*Chorus ri.* a quere or a cramake in *equiuocis.*" And the *versus* of the *Ortus* and *Equivoca* correspond closely, as shown below.

Ortus (1500)	Equivoca (1499)
Cardo onis est herba . . . Versus.	
Cardo subest foribus si cardinis est genitiuus	Cardo subest foribus/si cardinis est genitiuus
Cardo onis. est herba nociua colonis.	Et si cardonis est herba nociua colonis.
Coclea . . . Versus.	
Dic cocleam scalam. turris testamquoque limacis . . .	Dic cocleam turris scalam/testam quoque piscis
Est cochlear proprie quo pultes ponis in ore.	Est coclear proprie quo pultis in ore.

Ortus (1500)	*Equivoca* (1499)
Liber . . . Versus.	
Liber idest bachus: vel vir siue compede natus	Liber id est bacchus/ vel vir siue compede natus.
Ac liber est codex: vel raptus ab arbore cortex.	Estque liber codex/ vel raptus ab arbore cortex.
Prima beri faciunt genitiuum brique secunda.	Prima beri faciunt/genitiuum brique secunda.

Although in some of the *versus* the compiler of the *Ortus* seems to be following another authority, probably the *Catholicon* of Balbus or the *Breviloquus,* the evidence indicates familiarity with the *Equivoca* of John of Garland.

To refer back to the title page of the 1509 edition of the *Ortus,* printed by Pynson, we may say that our survey, while not substantiating the claim there made that this Latin-English dictionary contains all, or nearly all, words found in the *Catholicon,* the *Breviloquus,* the *Gemma,* and the *Medulla,* affords evidence of the compiler's familiarity with these books and of his use of similar materials, much of which very probably came from them. Owing to the great body of conventional lexicographic materials in manuscripts and in printed books at the end of the fifteenth century, the problem of establishing exact relationships is extremely difficult, and conclusions regarding sources necessarily tentative. But the study of the *Ortus* may at least suggest what are some of the problems in the history of fifteenth-century lexicography and what rewarding work remains to be done. Popular as the *Ortus* was for the first quarter of the sixteenth century, there is little evidence of its influence on subsequent lexicography—a circumstance which might be explained by the desire of the Humanists to start afresh and to avoid the use of medieval sources.

¶ De domo lactarea.

to mylke   a payle   idem   a presse
Mulgeo / lactesco / multrale / multraq3 / prelum

a bowle   a stremer   a mele   a chese fat   a chese racke
Sinus / colarium / mutellio / formula / crates

whyte mete   mylke   creme   fome   butter
Lacticinia / lac lactis / flos / spuma / butyrum

the sour- nes   bestondynge   wrenche mylke   the chese lep   whey
Acor / colustrum / oxigalum / coagulum / serum

to sethe/or to strayne   to make/or to turne   to knede   to presse
Percolo / coagulo / subigo / premo / caseusq3

hordenes   idem   clenlynes   idem
Lanugo / situs / mundina / mundiciesq3

a dounghylle   a stabla/or a stondynge to ferme   idem
Est sterquilinium / stabulum / fimu / extraho / purgo

a racke/or a maunger   a racke   a stable   a hey hous
Presepium crates / presepe equile / fenile

prouander/or mynged corne   hors brede
Condita cibaria / farrago / panis equinus

a brydle or a byt   a brydle dle/or a byt   a styrop   a rayne
Ephipium / frenum / lupatum / scanlile / habena

idem   a petrall   a croper   a packe sadle/or a panell
Lorum / anteleua / cum posteleua / clitella

a gyrth   a bernacle   an hors har neys   the cloth that coue reth the hors   an hors combe
Cingula / pastomis / phalare / instratum / strigilisq3

a packe   a ferdell   a boget   a male/or a wallet/ bo pges
Sarcina / sarcinula / manticula / mantica / bulga

a hors shoo equina   the pastures   the brest plates   a hofe   a mane/a toppynge.
Solea / suffragines / tori / vngula / iuba / caprona

to syt   to lyght vp   to descend downe/to gall   to lyght on
Insideo / ascendo / descendo / exulcero / scando

to neyth   to curry   to walke/ to ryde   to wrynche agay ne/or kyke   to spur
Hinnio / stringo / agito / equito / recalcitro / pungo

Sinus abosum corripit penul.

Pinguis bonus chese.
Mollis (softe chese). Viridis. (grene chese)
Tener (rue che se). Arido (drye chese). Fistulo sus(full of yes)
Crudus(whey Vetustus reces albus
Fasciculus (a bottel)
Substrato (lpt tre) Lora scan sillaria (styrop lethers.

A page from the 1510 edition of John Stanbridge's Vocabula, *in the British Museum*

CHAPTER V

John Stanbridge's *Vocabula* (1496) and *Vulgaria* (1508)

NGLISH-LATIN and Latin-English lexicography in the fifteenth century is best exemplified in the *Promptorium*, the *Catholicon Anglicum*, the *Medulla*, and the *Ortus*. These works, some of which continued to be printed through the first quarter of the sixteenth century, we have taken account of, together with their probable sources in Medieval Latin dictionaries, encyclopedias, and other compilations. We have noticed also the persistence from the early Middle Ages of bilingual class glossaries, in interlinear and other arrangements, and their probable relations to the dictionaries discussed. The *glossae collectae* and vocabularies are the materials from which dictionaries are made. These are best represented in the Wright-Wülcker collection of vocabularies and glosses. The medieval tradition which these compilations exemplify is carried on at the end of the fifteenth century and through the sixteenth in certain schoolbooks by John Stanbridge. Since Stanbridge's work keeps alive the tradition at a transition period, and since this tradition, after a lapse of time, continues in language manuals and small dictionaries, it requires some notice here.

John Stanbridge, born in Heyford in 1463, was educated at Wykeham's school at Winchester and New College, Oxford.[1] He was *informator* at Magdalen School (1488–94), master of the Hospital of St. John at Banbury (1501), vicar of Winwick (1507), and prebend of St. Botolph's in the Cathedral of Lincoln (1509). He died about 1510. His books, designed for teaching Latin to boys, are the *Vocabula* and *Vulgaria*.

39

The *Vocabula* was first printed in 1496. In content and arrangement this work is thoroughly conventional, exhibiting characteristics of the vocabularies and dictionaries back even to the Anglo-Saxon period. Topics about which the Latin and the English words and phrases are grouped are the parts of the body, diseases, the table and things associated with it, the baker, the carpenter, the smith, the mason, the goldsmith, the silversmith, the cobbler, various other craftsmen and artisans, the farmer and things pertaining to cultivation of the land, wild beasts, tame beasts, birds, fishes, trees and their fruits, herbs, weapons, and musical instruments. Most of these items could be matched in the *Dictionarius* of John of Garland, in Alexander Neckam's *De nominibus,* or even in Abbot Aelfric's Latin–Anglo-Saxon *Vocabulary* of the tenth century.[2] The first part (five pages) of the *Vocabula* is presented in columns—an arrangement similar to that in the *nominales*[3] and word lists—as follows:

> *Sinciput & Vertex Caput Occiput et*
> *Coma Crinis*
>
> *Hoc sinciput* - *tis* the foremost part of the head
> *Hec Vertex* - *tis* the crowne of the head
> *Hoc Caput* - *tis* the head
> *Hoc Occiput* - *tis* the hinder part of the head
> *Hec Coma* - *e* the plaites of a womans heere
> *Hic Crinis* - *is* for a heere

Thereafter, the text assumes the form of a glossary, similar to an interlinear translation, but arranged under general topics, thus:

De Mensa et attinentibus

a table	*a trestle*	*a chayre*	*a quishin*	*a bord*	*cloth idem*
Mēsa	tripos	cathedra	pulvinus	mapula	mappa

a towel	*a napkin*	*a laver*	*a basin*
Mantile	mantilielum	gutturnium	labrum

water basin	*salte*	*a salt cellar*	*a spone*	*a dyshe*
Manilium	sal	salinum	coclearque	catinus

a dyshe	*u saucer*	*a dyshe*	*a charger*	*a trencher*	*a platter*
Discus	cetabulū	patina	lanx	quadra	perapsis

Under this heading are fifty-one additional entries with the interlinear gloss, as above. (See also the reproduction of the gloss "De domo lactarea.") On the reverse side of the title page in the 1510 edition of the *Vocabula,* Stanbridge cites among his authorities Pliny, Cato, Columella, and the *Cornucopia* of Perottus. On occasion the author may have consulted these authorities, but the selection of classes of words, the arrangement, and many of the Latin words are those of the medieval glossaries.

In organization and subject matter the *Vulgaria* (1508) closely resembles the *Vocabula*. On the first few pages are the columns of Latin words with their English equivalents applicable to parts of the human body; thereafter, the author uses a metrical arrangement of Latin words with the interlinear glosses in English. Once again appear the conventional topics of class glossaries—clothes, the wardrobe, the drawing room, the kitchen, the cook, foods, herbs, and fishes. It is a variant of the *Vocabula* with repetition of some parts of this work. At the end of the metrically arranged Latin vocabulary with its English glosses, the author of the *Vulgaria* exhorts "all lytell chyldren besely" to apply themselves to the mastery of all Latin words in this "treatyse."

> And yf ye do not/the rodde must not spare
> You for to lerne with his sharpe morall sence
> Take now good hede/and herken your vulgare.

Despite similarities in content, the two texts of Stanbridge had each an independent vogue. For the *Vulgaria*, the *Short-Title Catalogue* records seven editions from 1508 to 1529; for the *Vocabula*, seventeen editions, ranging from 1496 to 1631. Thus, though the *Vocabula* underwent revision in the course of the sixteenth century, it served to keep alive the tradition of the medieval vocabularies and *nominales* and possibly to prepare the way for the popularity of John Withals' *Dictionarie for Yonge Begynners*.

On the basis of our survey of fifteenth-century lexicography, a few observations seem to be in order. It is obvious that there was in this period tremendous activity in the compilation of English-Latin and Latin-English glossaries, vocabularies, and dictionaries. Some of these have been printed; others, containing a large body of material for the lexicographer and the philologist, remain in manuscript. To most compilers the teaching of Latin was the chief stimulus. Latin was still a living language. It was the language of the Church, of the Holy Scriptures, of canon law, of logic, of scholarly discourse, and of learning generally. This was not, of course, the Latin of Cicero and Terence, but the Latin of the Church and the State and learning. The inclusion of English in these documents lends added importance to them as a basis for the study of both languages.

Ultimate sources extend back for a period of five hundred years or more. By the end of the fifteenth century much of the early material, the *glossae collectae*, then thoroughly conventional, was included in printed texts, such as the *Catholicon* of Joannes Balbus, and the *Breviloquus*, and thus perhaps given the stamp of authority. Such texts were cited as authorities and, as we have seen, were often immediate sources for the English-Latin and Latin-English lexicographers.

But these bilingual compilers did not attempt to include all words which they found in their authorities. Their word lists—those of the *Promptorium*, the *Catholicon Anglicum*, the *Medulla*, and the *Ortus*— represent rather a selection. There are, for example, many words applicable to the affairs of everyday life, such words as might be found in the earlier glossaries and *nominales*. Others, applicable to the Church and churchmen and worship and the Scriptures, to the law, etc., would be more fully expounded in the large Latin dictionaries. There is no reflection, in the word lists, of the new learning; and there is no attempt to include all words.

These earlier compilers frequently claim, as in the *Ortus*, an alphabetical order of words. An AB or ABC order is more nearly descriptive, and few follow rigorously even this arrangement. As a rule, definitions are slight, consisting in listing a single equivalent, sometimes two, of the opposite language (Latin or English), though there are noteworthy exceptions in the *Catholicon Anglicum* and sometimes in the *Promptorium*, as under *preyste*, in which entry the compiler employs ten lines in the column to distinguish *sacerdos*, *presbiter*, and *capellanus*. Grammatical information on the Latin words is given for the student. In the *Catholicon Anglicum* is the exceptional experiment in synonymy, foreshadowing the principles of copiousness and of varying in the sixteenth century.

Here are the beginnings of a technique in the making of English-Latin and Latin-English dictionaries. At first scorned by the classicists of the sixteenth century, the content and method of these early dictionaries are later exhibited, as we shall see, in the dictionaries of the Renaissance. Some of the Latin words which Erasmus condemned as barbarous persist even in the Latin-English dictionaries, such as Cooper's *Thesaurus*, which were compiled under the classical impulse. Not until the work of Ainsworth in the eighteenth century was a Latin-English and English-Latin dictionary published which closely approximated classical Latinity.

PART II

The Sixteenth Century

CHAPTER VI

The Dictionary of Syr Thomas Eliot (1538)

A PREVIEW of Part II shows that the dictionaries, in order of development and importance, arrange themselves into two fairly distinct groups: Latin-English and English-Latin. The first group begins with the *Dictionary of Syr Thomas Eliot* (1538) and includes the various revisions and augmentations of this volume, under the title *Bibliotheca Eliotae*, by Elyot himself and by Thomas Cooper; Cooper's *Thesaurus*; G. Morelius' *Verborum Latinorum . . . commentarii*, with the English terms added by Richard Hutton; and Thomas Thomas's *Dictionarium*. These are all Latin-English excepting the Hutton-Morelius, which has Latin, Greek, and English; and they are unified in content through the dominant influence of the Elyot-Cooper series. They were all published in the period 1538 to 1587. But as the latter date marks the publication of the first edition of Thomas's *Dictionarium*, it is necessary to take account of subsequent editions of this book, extending into the seventeenth century.

The second group consists of English-Latin dictionaries, or those in which the English terms stand first and the Latin follows. In some cases also, as in Higgins's revision of Huloet, a third language is employed. The exception in this group is John Veron's dictionary, in which the Latin is placed first as the "lemma," or term to be defined. This group begins indeed with Veron's *Dictionariolum* (1552), and embraces Huloet's *Abcedarium*, Higgins's revision of Huloet, Withals' *Dictionarie*, Baret's *Alvearie*, and Rider's *Bibliotheca scholastica* (1589). In each of these dictionaries the Elyot-Cooper influence is important but by no

45

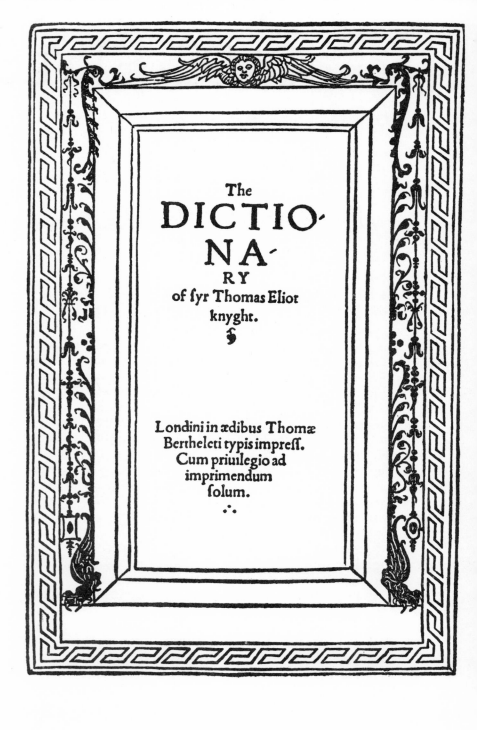

The
DICTIO-
NA-
RY
of ſyr Thomas Eliot
knyght.

Londini in ædibus Thomæ
Bertheleti typis impreſſ.
Cum priuilegio ad
imprimendum
ſolum.

means dominant. It is, however, a factor serving to relate this group to the first, or Latin-English, group. All of these were published within the period 1552 to 1589. Here again the study is projected into the seventeenth century in following the later editions of Withals' popular dictionary. We shall discuss first, in chronological order, the texts and authors within the Latin-English group and then proceed in a similar manner with the English-Latin, drawing together as far as possible, in the concluding chapter of Part II, the two lines of development.

In the study of the *Promptorium parvulorum,* the *Catholicon Anglicum,* the *Ortus vocabulorum,* and other wordbooks, we have been concerned with a native trend in dictionary-making and, essentially, with Medieval Latin and late medieval English, from about 1440 to 1530. Although we shall see later how this early work persists in the Tudor period, we have now to take account of new forces which served to establish another tradition in lexicography.

By the beginning of the sixteenth century the intellectual awakening, long current in Italy and France, was manifest in England. Among the factors inducing the intellectual ferment were the rediscovery and study of the classical Greek and Latin authors, the revival of a pagan philosophy of life, the expansion of the physical world through voyage and discovery, and the invention of the printing press and cheap paper. These and other forces altered the physical and intellectual world and powerfully stimulated man to utterance. But the expression of new ideas requires new symbols—words—and the meaning of new symbols must be made clear to those who would learn as well as to those who would teach. Convenient means of making available the revived language of Cicero and Terence and novel terms of English and other current living languages were enlarged wordbooks, lexicons, and dictionaries.

On the Continent, especially in Italy and France, response to the need of superior instruments for study of the ancient classical languages was made by such scholars as Laurentius Valla, Friar Calepine, Erasmus, Gulielmus Budaeus, Estienne Dolet, and the scholarly French family of Estiennes—Robert the Elder, Robert the Younger, Henri, and Charles.[1]

In England the first man to attempt the compilation of a dictionary commensurate with the demand created by changing conditions of life was Sir Thomas Elyot (1490?–1546).[2] Though not, so far as we know, a university man, Elyot received careful early training and became a voracious reader of ancient Greek and Latin literature. True Renaissance

Title page of the first edition of Sir Thomas Elyot's Dictionary, 1538, from the copy in the British Museum (opposite)

spirit that he was, he was athirst for knowledge. To realize his aim, he became author, translator, and compiler of books, in the vernacular, on the subjects of education, government, medicine, and language. In the early thirties he published *The Governour* (1531), *Of the Knowledge Whiche Maketh a Wise Man* (1533), *The Doctrinall of Princes* (1534), and the *Castel of Helth* (1534?). In *The Governour* and *The Castel*, Elyot exhibited his interest in the English language not only by writing in the vernacular but also by introducing many new words.[3]

This concern for the English vocabulary and the desire to promote learning and good citizenship were doubtless influences which turned Sir Thomas's thoughts to the compilation of a dictionary. From his own reading of the classics he had come to know the inadequacies of current dictionaries;[4] and he probably knew, also, the expressed desire of his fellow-Humanist, Luis Vives, for a better instrument in teaching the Latin language.[5] Under such a stimulus Elyot began the compilation of his Latin-English dictionary. This work was ready for publication in about two years, and, in 1538, was printed by Thomas Berthelet. The phrasing of the title page is: "The Dictionary of Syr Thomas Eliot, knyght. Londini in aedibus Thomae Bertheleti typis impress. Cum priuilegio ad imprimendum solum."

The volume is a small folio,[6] the leaves being numbered with Roman numerals from I to XXXVII, or to *"D ante O."* Thereafter the numbering is omitted. The printer's signatures are: Preface, A^{1-7}; text, A^6–Z^6, Aa^6–Ll^6. At signature *Ffij* begins "The Addicion of Syr Thomas Eliot knight vnto his Dictionarye." The "Addicion" continues through signature Ll^6, covering a total of thirty-six folios, or seventy-two pages, and includes new entries or augmentations under each letter of the alphabet—a procedure which will be explained below. The last three folios are devoted to a table of "poyses [weights], coines and measures," Roman, Greek, and Hebrew. Entries under the letters *A* to *L* are most augmented, *A* leading all others with an expansion of twenty-eight pages. The words thus added as a supplement in 1538 are in subsequent editions incorporated, with some exceptions, into the main body of the text. Throughout the text of this first edition are marginal references to Elyot's authorities. Plautus, Terence, and Erasmus (*Adagia*) are most frequently cited. Others are Pliny, Galen, Columella, Cicero, Salust, Livy, Servius, Budaeus, Virgil, Caesar, Quintilian, Ovid, Martial, Suetonius, Festus, Varro, and St. Jerome. In later editions the marginal references tend to disappear; in 1542 there are scanty references up to the letter *M;* in 1545, only to *D;* and in the revisions by Cooper they are omitted altogether.

The reason for the "Addicion" and the resultant patchy appearance of the 1538 edition is made clear in the author's revealing Preface. He explains that he had finished the compilation and, though ill satisfied with the result, had sent the manuscript to the press. It was then that Henry VIII heard of Elyot's efforts and his difficulties. He praised Elyot's work and even offered him a loan of books from the Royal Library to further his efforts. Referring to this event in the Preface, Elyot writes:

I receiued a newe spirite, as me semed: wherby I founde forthwith an augmentacion of my understandynge, in so moche, as I iuged all that whiche I had writen, not worthy to come in your gracis presence, *without an addicion* [italics mine]. Wherfore incontinent I caused the printer to cesse, and beginninge at the letter M, where I lefte, I passed forth to the last letter with a more diligent study. And that done I eftesones returned to the fyrst letter, and with a semblable diligence performed the remenant.

The King's encouragement and assistance, though it did not improve the organization of this first edition, undoubtedly made it more useful and stimulated the author to increased effort in subsequent editions.

A few entries from the text of the 1538 edition may throw some light on the arrangement and content.

Idea, a fygure conceyued in ymagynation, as it were a substance perpetuall: and lyke as of one seale procedeth manye pryntes, so of one Idea of a manne procedeth many thousandes of men, and semblably of other Ideas procedeth thynges innumerable. So that Ideae, be as it were external examples, wherby all other thynges be created: and this is Idea, wherof Plato speaketh.
Idiopathia, the propre passion of a disease.
Idem, the same thynge, or the same man.
Identidem, eftesones, in the same wyse.
Ideo, for that cause.
Idicus, ca, cum, of the mountayne of Ida.
Idiographum, a priuate wrytynge.
Idiographae literae, a priuate letter.
Idioma, matis, a propre forme of speche.
Idiota, Idiotes, a man or woman vnlerned.
Idolatra, a worshypper of idolles.
Idololatria, ydolatrie.
Idolium, a lyttell ydoll.
Idolothysia, offrynges to ydols.
Idolothytum, that which is offred to idols.
Idolum, an ydoll.
Idoneus, ea, eum, apte.
Idula, a shepe that was offred every Idus to Iupyter.
Idumea, a regyon in Syria ioynynge to Egypte, and bordereth upon Palestina.
Idus, Ides of monethes, whiche do diuide Nonas from Calendes.[7]

A few illustrative entries or definitions can, however, give but little information of the contents of the dictionary proper. On this topic and

Dvvmviratvs,us,dignitas duumuirorum Pli. li.4.Episto.ad Sempronium. Paul. lege honores.ff. de decur. Is qui non sit decurio, Duumuiratu,uel alijs honoribus ciuilibus fungi non potest.

Dvx,ducis,communis generis. Duca,quidã,α'γωγὸς, α'γωγὸς, qui, uel quæ ducit.Vir.1.Aen.Portantur auari Pygmalionis opes pelago:dux femina facti.Ci.i Ver.Relicti à duce,præfectóq; classis.

D ANTE Y

Dyn astes,huius dynastæ,qui in ciuitate plurimum pollet: à Græco δύναςαι,posse.Ci.ad Att.li.2.

Dyrrhachivm, δυῤῥάχιον, urbs est in parte Macedoniæ, quæ mari Adriatico incumbit,distans à Brundusio ccxx.M.pass.traiectu. Dictum uolunt Dyrrhachiü à nomine eius,qui urbi portum adiecit:nam antea Epidamnus uocabatur,teste Pli.li.3.c.23.

DE LITERA E

Et ex,ε'ᴋ,ᴋ, præpositiones sunt, quæ & separantur,& componuntur. Separatæ,modo temporales sunt : ut , Ex illo celebratus honos , hoc est,post illud tempus. Modo locales : ut , E cælo.Modo ponuntur pro à , uel ab . ut Audiui è patre meo.Modo significant pro,uel ad .(πρὸς, cum genitiuo)ut,Ex dignitate,Ex usu, Ex utilitate:hoc est,pro dignitate,uel ad dignitatem . E repub. pro repub.Modo secundum,ᴋαᴛὰ,ut,Ex Platonis sententia:id est,secundum Platonis sententiam. Modo in,Cicero:E renibus laborabat, id est morbum patiebatur in renibus . Compositæ quádoque priuationem indicant,ut Elinguis, Exanguis:quandoque uehementiam uel perfectionem,ut Eludo,Exoro. Quandoq; extra,ut Educo:Excludo. Componitur autem E, cum b,ut Ebibo:d,ut Educo:g,ut Egredior : i , ut Eiicio:l.ut Eludo : m , ut Emitto.n,ut Enitor : r , ut Erigo:u,ut Eueho.Et uero componitur cum a, ut Ex audio:c,ut Excurro.e,ut Exeo:f,ut Efficio:o , ut Exoleo : p, ut Expello:q,ut Exquiro:s,ut Exequor:t,ut Extendo : u,ut Exuro. Verum quando post ex sequitur f,mutatur x , in f,ut Effundo.Cú uero sequitur x,abijcitur s, ut Exequor, & Exicco:in alijs integra manet.

E ANTE A, ET B.

Eatenvs,p.c.Fin à tanto , ᴋαθ' ὅσον, ταύτο,significat usque,eo uel ad eum modum:cui respõdent quatenus,usq; quo, quod, ut, qua, ne quid. Causa in Instoria actione: Eatenus dabitur in eú actio, quatenus ex ea re locupletior factus est.Ci.1.de Leg. Hoc ciuile, quod uocant:eatenus exercuerunt, quoad populo præstare uolue runt. Idem de Opt.gene.or. Verba persequens eatenus ,ut ea non abhorreant a more nostro.Colu.li.12.c.9.Caules lactucæ ab imo depurgatos,eatenus,qua tenera folia uidebuntur.Suet.in Tib.Ea tenus interueniebat,ne quid perperam fieret.

Ebenvs,uel Ebenum.pe.c.Ebenus,ε'βενος,ᴋαι ε'βενο,Suid.lignum in tus nigrú,foris buxi aspectu,adeo solidum & ponderosum , ut in aqua non superfluitet. creditur tamé tenuis esse(ut Aetius tradit) substãtiæ,& abstergêdis uirtutis.unde oculorum caliginem discutere creditur.Hæc arbor nascitur in India,& cæsa durescit in lapidem,uriturq; odore iucundo.Vir.li.2.Georg. Sola India nigrum Fert ebenum.Vbi Seruius : Atqui & in Aegypto nascitur.sed Indiam,omnem plagam Aethiopiæ accipimus.Pli.li.12.c.4.

Ebibo,is,p.c.ε'ᴋᴘίνω,bibendo euacuo.Plaut.Amph.

Eblandior,diris,Togliere per lusinghe , est blanditijs aliquid extorquere.Liui.li.27. Neque omnia emebat,sed eblandiebatur.unde eblandita suffragia,quæ precibus & blanditijs impetrantur, apud Ci.pro Planc.

Eboratvs,a,um,quod extrinsecus ex ebore est, quod & Eburatum dicitur.Plau.in Persa:Lectos eburatos,auratos.

Ebvrnevs,uero , & eburnus, ab ebur : quòd est ex solido ebore. Quinct. libro.6.Cum in triumpho Cæsaris eborea oppida essent translata.

Ebriacvs,a,um,Ebriaco,meôduon,meôuciᴋòs.antiquis, teste Nonio in usu erat pro Ebrio,uel Inebriato.Plaut.in Adul. Homo ebriacus somno sanari solet.Ita enim legit Nonius. Alij tamé ibi Ebriatus legendum contendunt.ut sit a uerbo Ebrio,cuius compositum est Inebrio.

Ebrietas,μεῖθη , quam Cato dicebat nihil aliud esse , quàm insaniam uoluntariam.Pli. li.3.c.14.Ebrietatem arcet pecudum assus pulmo.

Ebriolvs,ab ebrius,Plaut.Curc.Tristes atque ebrioli incedunt.

Ebrivlo,as,p.c.μεθύσαι,ebrium facio.Laberius : Ebriulati mentem hilarem accipiunt.Nonius.

Ebriositas,propensio in ebrietaté.Ci.4.Tusc.Inter ebrietatem & ebriositatem interest , aliudq; est esse amatorem,aliud amantem.

Ebriosivs,Chestesso è ebriaco,oἰνωπλὴξ,qui sæpe sit ebrius. Cice.de Fato. Hunc scribunt ipsius familiares & ebriosum , & mulierosum fuisse.

Ebrivs,a,um, Ebrio,ebriaco,μεθύων,μεθυςθεὶς,μέθυσος , qui nimio potu alienatus est mente.Plau.Amph.Homo hic ebrius est.Cice.

Pæto lib.9.Habuisti in tua potestate,ex quo uel ex sobrio,uel certe ex ebrio scire posses.Vnde,Nõ sobrius,pro ebrio sumit. Mart. Et non sobria uerba subnotasti.Inter Ebrius & Ebriosus hoc interest,quòd Ebrius actum præsentem designat,Ebriosus habitum & consuetudinem.

Ebron,ε'βρὼν,mõs Palæstinorú,haud longe à Gaza Syriæ ciuitate.

Ebvdes,insulæ sunt quinque numero,in oceano Britannico,angusto freto diuisæ. a Plinio Hæbudes dicútur,a Stephano,α'ᴋᴋoῦσαι.

Ebvllio,is,Bollire,ε'ᴋᴘᵞᴏᵞᴊᴂᴌ. ὑπερζέω , inter bulliendum effundor.Per metaphoram pro iactabunde aliquid ostento.Ci.2.de Fi. Dixerit Epicurus,semper beatum esse sapiêtem, quod solet ebullire nonnunquam.

Ebvlvm,frutex ex sambuco folijs & baccis simillimus, in tantam ta men altitudinê non assurgens,neque arborescens. Vir.in Sileno : Sanguineis ebuli baccis. Col. Et rutilas ebuli creat uuida baccas.

Ebvr,eboris,Avoᴙᴎᴏᾓ'λᴂᴘᴂᴤ,dens elephanti,quasi è barro : sic enim elephantum uocabant ueteres,à barritu.Cic.4.Aca.Non est E laxo sculptus,aut ebore dolatus. Ebur pro uasis, aut alijs rebus ex ebore dolatis.Hora.lib.8.Carm.Ode 18.Non ebur neque aureum Mea renidet in domo lacunar. Antiquis in usu fuit nominatiuum Ebor: a quo remansit genitiuus Eboris, & adiectiuum Eboreum.

Ebvrneolvs,dimin. Ci.3.de Ora.Cum eburneola fistula.

Ebvrnevs,a,um,D'euorio,ε'λέφαντινος,ex ebore. Plin. lib.36.cap. 5.Iouem fecit eburneum in Metelli ædе . Aut quod instar eboris album est:ut Eburnea facies. Ouid. 3. Meta.Impubesq; genas,& eburnea colla.

Ebvrnvs,a,um,eburneus. Tibul. Plectro modulatus eburno.

Ebvrones,ε'βούρονοι, populi Galliæ Belgicæ.hodie Leodienses.

E ANTE C

Ecastor,aduerb.iurandi.Donatus,Ecastor, per Castorem & Pollucem.Plaut.in Amph . Ecastor te experior quanti facias uxorem tuam. Ter.in And. Perecastor scitus puer natus est Pamphilo.Sút qui per diphthongum malint scribere,ut Aecastor dictum sit,qua si per ædem Castoris.Hoc iuraméto(ut ait Macrob.)uiri non utebantur,nec mulieres per Herculem, Aedepol autem iuramentum erat tam mulieribus,quam uiris commune.

Ecbatana,num.plur.pen.corr.έᴋᴂᴛᴂᴠᴂ, metropolis est maioris Mediæ a Seleuco condita,teste Plin.lib 6.cap.14.Str. lib.11.Media in duas partes diuisa,quarum altera maiorem uocat,cuius metropolis fuit Ecbatana ciuitas,& Medici imperij caput, nunc etiã Parthi regia utuntur. Fuit & in ora Syriæ eiusdem nominis oppidú,in monte situm,postea Carmelum appellatum. Pli.lib.5.c.19.

Ecce,Ecco,ίδ'ᵞ,aduerbium demonstrandi apud Vir.aliquid repentinú,insperatumq; significat . ut,Ecce autê gemini a Tenedo tranquilla per alta.Scribit Asconius etiã hoc proprij esse Cicero nis,ut in rebus improuisis hac particula utatur, ut in oratione pro Clu.Ecce tibi eiusmodi sortitio,ut in primis Balbo esset iudicandum.Nonnunquã etiã in rebus lætis hac particula utimur. Oui.3. Am.Ecce Corinna uenit. Habet autê modo nominatiuum, modo accusatiuum.Cic.Att.lib.1.Ecce aliæ equitum.Idem 2.de Fin.Ecce miserum hominem,si dolor summum malum est.

Eccere,iusiurandum,ac si dicatur,per Cererem,ut Aecastor, Aedepol.Alij Eccere accipiunt per Cererem ac deae.Plaut. in Amph.Eccere,iam tu autem facis,ut tuis nulla apud te sit fides.

Ecclesia,Adunanzaε'ᴋᴋᴧᴇσία,Latine cœtus,concilium, cõcio. Io in de a Christianis Ecclesia dicitur,& Christus caput Ecclesiæ.

Eccvm,eccam,eccos,eccas,aduerbia sunt demonstrandi.Eccum, ecce hic,subintellige uirum,de quo agebamus.Eccã,ecce hic,subintellige feminã,de qua agebamus.Ellum,ecce illum , scilicet uirú, resoluendo per aduerbia,non per nomina. Ex his itaque non obscurum est,quid discriminis sit inter Eccum & Ellum, quòd scilicet Eccum demonstrat hominem, qui non procul abest a loco in quo sumus:ut Eccum Parmenonem, id est, Ecce hic Parmenonê:contra,Ellum,eum qui longius abest.

Ecdicvs,Latine uindex. Erant autem Ecdici , teste Budæo,in municipijs,qui Romæ tribuni plebis, qui,scilicet plebis caussam aduersus iniuriam optimatum tuebantur.Cic.ad Thermum. lib.13. epist.Fam. Dixerat mihi Enthymedus, se curaturum ut eedici Milesij Romam mitterentur.

Echeneis,ε'χενηὶς,genus pisciculi,quem Latini Remoram appellant.Pli.li.9.Est paruula admodum piscis assuetus petris, Echeneis appellatus,hoc carinis adhærente.naues tardius cire creduntur,unde nomine imposito Lura.lib.6.Non puppim retinens,Euro ten dête naidens,In medijs echeneis aquis.Qua re à Græcis ε'χένος, a nostris Remora à morádo remigio nominatur.uide Pl.l.32.c.1.

Echidna,ε'χιδνα,idem serpens esse creditur, qui à Latinis Vipera dicitur . A poetis accipitur pro quouis serpente, & præcipue pro hydra illa Lernæa,quæ ab Hercule interfecta est.Ouid.lib.3.Fasto.Sanguine Centauri Lernæa sanguis echidnæ Mistus.

Echinometra,ε'χινομήτρα,echinorum genus.Pli.li.9.c.31.

Echinvs,p.p.La coperta spinosa delle castagne,ε'χῖνος , tegmen spinosum , quo seruantur castaneæ.unde castaneæ echinatæ dicuntur. Plin. lib. 15.cap.23.Castaneis armatum echinato cortice uallum est. Ab

on Elyot's claims to have extended the bounds of lexicography in England, the Preface, once again, is revealing. It asserts that this volume contains, "besides the conference of phrases or fourmes of speakynge latin and englishe," the "propre termes belongynge to law and phisike, the name of diuers herbes knowen among us: also a good number of fishes founden as well in our ocean as in our riuers"; and "sondrie poysis [i.e., poises or weights], coynes, and measures, sometyme used among the auncient Romaynes, Grekes, and Hebrues." "Nor I haue omitted prouerbes, callyd Adagia, or other quicke sentences, whiche I thought necessarie to be had in remembraunce. . . . " As a result of such additions, the author concludes, this volume contains "a thousande mo latine wordes than were together in any one Dictionarie publyshed in this royalme." [8]

It is perhaps significant that the statement just quoted contains the only allusion ever made by Elyot to other dictionaries published in England. Neither in his Preface nor in his list of authors, referred to below, nor in marginal citations does he mention the *Promptorium,* the *Catholicon,* the *Ortus,* or any other text. He deliberately ignores these works, and the reason for his attitude is patent. Elyot was a Humanist; and the authors he read and admired were, with a few exceptions, the ancient Greeks and Romans. He expected, furthermore, that the ancient classical writers would be taught and studied in the schools.[9] It is quite natural, then, that in the compilation of his *Dictionary* Elyot should turn to those compilers who had been concerned largely with classical writers and with classical Latin. Among those he lists and comments upon are Festus, Varro, Nestor, Tortellius, Laurentius Valla, Perottus, Nebrissensis, Budaeus, and Friar Calepine.[10] Among these Continental compilers and lexicographers, and others not mentioned in the Preface, we must look for Elyot's sources and his model.

A number of Elyot's biographical sketches, for example, come from Diogenes Laertius' *Lives and Opinions of Eminent Philosophers,* probably a Latin version of the fifteenth century, and from Walter Burley's *De vita et moribus philosophorum.*[11] His "quicke sentences" and proverbs are from Erasmus' *Adagia* and *Apophthegmata.*

But the chief source of Elyot's *Dictionary* is the Latin *Dictionarium* of Ambrosius Calepinus, of Bergamo, Italy. The author of this book styles himself "Ambrosius Calepinus Eremitanus," and he dedicates his work to the senate and the people of Bergamo. The first edition (1502), in Latin only, was published at Reggio. Subsequent editions (1510, 1515, 1520, and 1531) were issued in various towns. According to Brunet, at

A page of Friar Calepine's Dictionarium, *Venice, 1564, in the University of Texas Library (opposite)*

least sixteen editions were printed by the Aldus press between 1542 and 1583.[12] The "Calepine," as it came to be called, was gradually augmented to include various languages: Hebrew, Greek, French, Italian, German, Spanish, and English. It continued to be printed throughout the sixteenth and seventeenth centuries. During the whole period of the Renaissance scarcely an important dictionary was published which did not reflect directly or indirectly the influence of Calepine. On the title page of the early editions Calepine declares that his *Dictionarium* has been gathered from the best authors (*optimis authoribus*), and he lists these as Nonius Marcellus, Pompeius Festus, M. Varro, Pedianus, Servius, Donatus, Perottus, Laurentius Valla, Tortellius, Suidas, *aliisque compluribus*.[13] Two points of interest about this list are that (1) it shows the compiler's predilection for classical or what he believed to be classical sources; and (2) it is a curious anticipation of the authorities mentioned by Elyot in the Preface of his 1538 dictionary, seven of the references in the two lists being identical. Elyot's comments indicate that he had examined the authors listed. It seems probable, however, that he was led to them through Calepine.

Calepine's *Dictionarium* of Elyot's day is in Latin throughout. In general, the entries are arranged etymologically, the derivatives being placed after their primitives, as, for example, in the entries *capio* and *facio*.[14] In the early editions of Calepine, the etymological arrangement is not, however, consistently followed. The gender and declension of nouns and the conjugation of verbs are indicated; the three forms of the adjective in the nominative are given; adverbs are identified as such; and quotations from standard Latin authors, generally with definite references to their source, are employed to illustrate meaning and usage. Proper names are distributed alphabetically among other entries throughout the text. These are names of countries, islands, cities, rivers, mountains, and persons mythical and real, with descriptions or biographical sketches as the terms may require. The Calepine was thus at once a dictionary abounding in grammatical and etymological information and an encyclopedia especially instructive about men and matters of antiquity. It is not strange that Sir Thomas Elyot, seeking for his own dictionary a more satisfactory model than his country had to offer, should turn to the *Dictionarium* of Friar Calepine.

What is the evidence to prove Elyot's dependence upon Calepine? In his Preface (1538) the English compiler comments, not very favorably, upon the Latin dictionary of the Italian hermit, but later admits that his own work has some faults, due in part to "to moche trust had in Calepine." Elyot's indirect admission of indebtedness is supported by evidence found in the marginal citations of the 1538 text. In many instances, authorities which Elyot cites in the margin, opposite terms to be defined, and quotes in the definitions proper to establish meaning or usage are the same as those employed in Calepine's definitions. Some of the entries under which this special type of borrowing appears are *abyssus, altus, ampulla, boa, caro, circumfero, claudo, colligo, commereo, commitigo, conficio,* and *conferro.*

More convincing evidence is to be seen, however, in Elyot's definitions which translate Calepine's Latin.[15]

Elyot's *Dictionary* (1538)	Calepine's *Dictionarium* (1520)
Diodorus, a philosopher of Socrates sect; and Diodorus Siculus, a story writer. and an other Diodorus, a stoike phylosopher, of whome Cicero writeth.	Diodorus . . . nomen philosophi Socratici . . . Fuit & Diodorus Siculus historicus: & Diodorus Stoicus philosophus Cęcus de quo Cice. in Bruto sic ait. . . .
Diogenes, a famous philosophers name.	Diogenes . . . nomen philosophi cynici famosissimi. . . .
Dione, a goddesse of the see, mother of Venus.	Dione . . . una ex nymphis oceani & Tethyos filia: vt quidam perhibent: a qua Venus ex Iove nata sit. . . .
Dioptra, a geometricall instrument, to discerne altitudes and distaunce. Victruuius vseth it for wayinge or pluckynge vppe of water.	Dioptra instrumentum geometricum ab explorando perspiciendoque . . . Vict. lib. viij. accipit pro regula ad librandas aquas cum ait. Libratur aqua dioptris.
Dioscoron, an yle in the borders of Italy.	Dioscoron insula est in finibus Italiae e regione Lacinij Promontorij. Cc.
Diospolis, a cytie of Aegypte. There be foure other of the same name in Aegypte, but very small cities in comparyson of this.	Diospolis aegypti ciuitas . . . Sunt & aliae locis alijs hoc nomine in aegypto quatuor praeter hanc pusillae ciuitates. . . .
Diotae, vessels of erth with handels, wherein wyne was kepte.	Diotae sunt vasa seu dolia fictilia duas ansas habentia & ad servāda vina accōmodata. . . .
Diphthera, a shepeherdes cote, made with shepe skynnes.	Diphthera . . . vestis pastoritia ex pellibus ouium: aut caprarum consutis.
Diphthongus, two vowels ioyned togither called a diphthonge, as *ae, oe, au, ei.*	Diphthongus est conglutinatio duarum vocalium vim suam seruantium . . . fere ubique *a* & *u* vel *e* & *u* diuiduntur.
Diplois, idis, any garment lyned, but it is taken for a doublette.	Diplois . . . genus palij: quasi duplex pallium. . . .
Dipondium, a weight of two pounde.	Dipondium & dipondius . . . a duobus ponderibus dicitur. . . .

In the list above are eleven successive definitions in which Elyot is freely translating Calepine. These are typical in their adherence to their source. There are of course breaks in the succession, and borrowings from many other sources, but almost any opening in Elyot's text will show to what extent the English compiler follows the Latin of Calepine.

In some instances the two authors borrow from a common source, but the content and phrasing of Elyot's text are more frequently determined by Calepine than by any other source. The matter thus adapted from the Italian lexicographer continues through the various editions of the *Bibliotheca Eliotae* (as the *Dictionary* was called after the first edition), including the augmentations by Thomas Cooper.

Elyot not only derives much of the content of his *Dictionary* from Calepine but also adapts his method of presentation. Elyot's edition of 1538 has the etymological arrangement (as *s.v. capto, expergo, exploro, expostulo,* and *expungo*),[16] the distribution of proper names throughout the text, the use of illustrative quotations with citation of authorities, the indication of the conjugation of verbs,[17] the nominative singular forms of adjectives, and, occasionally, the genitive singular of nouns. Elyot does not attempt, however, as Calepine had done, to indicate accentuation, pronunciation, gender, or derivation. But, in general, the Latin dictionary of the Italian friar is the pattern of the first Latin-English dictionary produced in England under the influence of the new learning. True, Elyot adapts his pattern to the needs of his public, selecting from Calepine, adding matter from various other authors, and giving especial attention to the English phrasing. Like the translators of the Tudor period, Elyot cast the content of his foreign model into the idiom of the day. So, in Elyot's *Dictionary*, that which is perhaps of most general interest is the English vocabulary and the English idiom into which Calepine and other sources are converted. Another point worthy of emphasis is that the pattern, and indeed much of the matter, of this first sizable Latin-English dictionary come from the Continent. This circumstance is a presage of what may be expected in the subsequent history of the classical tradition in dictionary-making in England.

Although the *Dictionary* of 1538 was well received, Elyot, not satisfied with his first effort, began at once to correct and enlarge this volume. About 1542, Thomas Berthelet printed another edition of Elyot's *Dictionary*, with the running title *Bibliotheca Eliotae: Eliotis Librarie*.[18] This title, intending probably to suggest a more comprehensive work than the first, was retained during the various augmentations. The Proheme, addressed to Henry VIII, is so interesting and so instructive in Elyot's method of correcting and amplifying that I venture to quote freely from it. After some preliminary remarks, Elyot writes:

I therefore moste feruently styred by your gracis comforte, in perusyng my sayd Dictionary, haue proceded to the correction and amplyfycation thereof, in suche fourme, as herafter foloweth. Fyrst sequestrynge my selfe from all other busynesse (that only except, wherein I was bounden to serue your hyghnesse) I assembled all such authors as I thought shuld be necessary, for the achieuynge of that which I toke in enterpryse, whose names do immedyately folowe this proheme: [19] and layinge them before me I not onely dyd seriousely and dilygently trye and examyne euery worde, which eyther in sygnification or fourme of speakynge, called a phrase, moughte make any doubt to them that shulde reade it, and by the same authors dyd as truly correct it as my lernynge wolde serue me: but also with a new spirite of hardynesse, receyued by the often remembrance of your gracious sayde comforte, I folowynge the example of Suidas the greke,[20] aduentured to make a generall collection by the order of letters of all notable countrays, cities, mountaynes, and ryuers, with theyr true descriptions, boundes, the names and natures of sundry beastes, foules, serpentes, and fysshes: the declaration of a great number of herbes, trees, fruites, gummes, precyouse stones and metalles, whiche before me were neuer of any man (that I can here of) declared and sette forthe in englyshe: The true definitions of all syckenesses and kyndes of maladyes, whyche commonly doe happen to men, with the cause wherof they procede: [21] Fynally the names of most notable personages, who from the fyrst man Adam untyll thre hundred yeres after the incarnation of Christe, dyd any thynge worthy a speciall remembrance, expedient and necessary to the moderation of our actes and procedynges, with the hystoryes of lyues of the sayd persones compendyousely gathered.

I haue not omytted fables and inuentions of paynymes, for the more easy understandyng of poetes. I also thought it necessary to enterlace the detestable heretykes, with theyr sundry heresyes, concernynge the substance of our catholyke faythe iustly condemned by the hole consent of all true chrysten men, to the intente that those heresyes beinge in this wyse diuulgate, may be the sooner espyed and abhorred in suche bokes, where they be craftily enterlaced with holsom doctrine. . . . As well in this parte as in the hystories and fables, I haue sette out the computation of tyme callid Chronography, wherin it appereth how longe the persons were eyther before the incarnation of Christe, or howe longe after. Also I haue declared the auncient coynes, weyghtes, and measures, conferryng them with those whiche be currant and usuall amonge us. I haue planted in prouerbes, callyd *Adagia*, such as be founden in latyn authours, with theyr expositions. Also the proper termes belongyng to phisyke and surgery, and other dyuers and sundry artes and scyences. More ouer I haue declared dyuers greke wordes, whyche be usurped of latyne authors. In this fourme haue I fynyshed this worke, to the glorye of almyghty god, and the no lyttell profyte (I truste) of all englyshemen, which are and shall be desyrous of doctrine. . . .

Remembering that this Proheme was addressed to Henry VIII, we may make some allowance for overstatement by the compiler. When due allowance is made, we still have an interesting reflection of the ideal, if not the actual, method of the Tudor lexicographer. To verify every word or phrase by reference to reputable authors would be, for a single compiler, an arduous and almost unending task. Elyot's statement of his procedure should not, however, be discredited, but rather interpreted. My interpretation is that he did actually verify, correct, and extend the number of illustrative phrases of his first edition. In the Calepine, his pattern, he would find many specific references to his authorities. Having the books open before him, he would need only to turn to the passages specified by the Calepine for verification. Incidentally, he would accumulate additional illustrations in the process. Such an explanation makes more credible Elyot's own description of his method. It may be added, also, that his labor was reduced by his borrowing much, as we shall see below, from another contemporary Continental lexicographer, besides Calepine.

The Proheme reveals, further, the way in which the subject matter of the book was expanded. More biographical, historical, and legendary matter concerning men and events was added. For this, as also for the descriptions of countries, cities, mountains, and rivers, the compiler had a precedent and much information in Calepine. Much more he doubtless found in Suidas' Greek *Lexicon,* as he suggests.[22] The increase in the number of proverbs, *adagia,* etc., probably indicates further drawing from Erasmus, Diogenes Laertius, and Walter Burley.[23]

Other matter added to the 1542 edition of the *Bibliotheca* appears in the "names and natures of sundry beastes, foules, serpentes, and fysshes . . . herbes, trees, fruites . . . precyouse stones and metalles, whiche before me were neuer of any man (that I can here of) declared and sette forth in englyshe." Elyot's assertion that such matter had not hitherto been "sette forth in englyshe" requires qualification. As a matter of fact, such class names, in Latin and English, had been compiled, at intervals, from the Anglo-Saxon period to Stanbridge's *Vocabula* (1496), and the *Vocabula* was still current in Elyot's day. Elyot, the classical scholar, seems, however, to have disregarded native glossaries and vocabularies and to have drawn from Suidas and other authorities.

Despite the impressive list of authors cited in the Proheme as those from whom the compiler had gathered phrases, it is reasonable to infer that the expansion of his book represented by the 1542 edition was not the result of a close firsthand reading and selection from so wide a range. For such procedure, Elyot would have had neither time nor energy in the space of time between 1538 and 1542. He depended rather upon a few of those in the list who were themselves compilers. His dependence in the earlier volume upon Calepine, we have noted. From Calepine, Elyot turned, as he admits, to Suidas' *Lexicon,* a source of Calepine and a storehouse of such information as Elyot sought.

In the list of 1542 are certain contemporaries to whom Elyot owed much. One of these is Gulielmus Budaeus, a French Humanist, probably the most learned man of his time.[24] He was a student of the ancient Greek and Latin languages rather than a compiler of dictionaries, yet his researches contributed very greatly to lexicography in the period of the Renaissance. The works which proved to be the greatest boon to lexicographers are the *Annotationes in quattuor et viginti Pandectarum libros* (1508), a critical and philosophical study of the digest and glosses of the Justinian Code of Roman laws; *De asse* (1514), a treatise on coins and weights; and the *Commentarium linguae Graecae* (1529). Of the *An-*

notationes Jean Plattard writes: "Peut-être est-ce la première oeuvre de philologue que nous ayons eue en France: elle est, à coup sur, un modèle de critique philologique." [25] With equal praise does Delaruelle speak of the *Annotationes:* "Pour parler sans métaphore, c'est un precieux recueil de matériaux lexicographiques, les plus important qu'on eût encore rassemble, et Robert Estienne a reconnu lui-même que les emprunts par lui faits à Budé constituaient le meilleur de son grand *Thesaurus latin.*" [26] Of Robert Stephanus' relation to Budaeus, we shall speak later. Meanwhile, it may be said that Elyot's debt to the studies of Budaeus is, for the most part, indirect, coming probably by way of Stephanus.

Elyot is quite specific in his acknowledgment of indebtedness to Stephanus and Doletus. He writes: "A recentioribus R. Stephano ac Steph. Doleto gallis aliquid traduxi in lingua nostra, neutrum tamen usque adeo imitatus, quin diversitatis utriusque linguae rationem habuerim."

Stephanus Doletus (1508–46) was a French Humanist par excellence.[27] He studied at Paris and at Padua and Venice, and early became an ardent Ciceronian. It was indeed his championship of the Ciceronians that led him to attack Erasmus.[28] Student of the classics, writer, printer, and friend of Budaeus, of Marot, and of Rabelais, Doletus early won distinction among a few literary men; but for alleged blasphemy, sedition, and offering prohibited books for sale, he was burned at the stake in his thirty-ninth year.

The work upon which Doletus' fame as a scholar rests is his *Commentariorum linguae Latinae,*[29] an important contribution to sixteenth-century Latin scholarship. His plan of procedure in the *Commentaries* is neither alphabetical nor etymological. Doletus makes a logical arrangement of words according to related or contrasted ideas expressed.

> Thus after *amare,* with which the *Commentaries* commence, follow in order *adamare, redamare, amator, amabilis, diligere, observare, colere, amplecti, complecti, amicitia, amor, charitas, pietas, benevolentia, animus, voluntas,* and so on, until the author has completely exhausted the words expressing or having relation to this idea. The words are thus classed, not according to their sound or orthography, but according to their signification.[30]

For each word Doletus gives the primary and the secondary meaning, distinguishes the different uses, and cites examples from Cicero to illustrate.[31] Prepared on this scale, the *Commentaries* fill two folio volumes of 3,421 pages—a vast storehouse for other lexicographers. The wealth of illustration may be inferred from the seventy-odd examples of meaning and usage under *conficere.* Although Elyot admits that he adapted matter from Doletus, his specific borrowings are hard to detect, for Elyot owes much to Robert Stephanus, who also was a debtor to his countryman and contemporary. The relation of Elyot to Stephanus is more nearly demonstrable.

Robert Stephanus (1503–59) belonged to a famous French family of classical scholars, editors, and printers. In philology and lexicography the labors of Robert, his brother Charles, and his son Henri were a powerful influence in western Europe for almost two centuries.[32] The publications of Robert Stephanus that are significant for this study are the *Dictionarium, seu Latinae linguae thesaurus* (1532, 1543, 1573) and the *Dictionarium Latino-Gallicum* (1538, 1546, 1552). The *Thesaurus*, a comprehensive Latin dictionary, owes much to the *Dictionarium* of Calepine and the *Annotationes* of Budaeus,[33] but it embodies also, especially in the second edition, much matter gathered from Stephanus' own reading and from that of his friends.

Stephanus' Latin-French dictionary of 1538 is based in large part upon his own *Thesaurus*.[34] The bilingual volume, however, omits many entries of the earlier lexicon, abbreviates illustrations, simplifies the arrangement of matter on the page, and gives the French equivalents of Latin definitions and illustrations. The Latin-French work is thus better adapted than the *Thesaurus* to become a source of other bilingual dictionaries.

For too close following of Calepine, Elyot believed, in the first edition of his *Dictionary* he had fallen into many errors. In the augmentation of his volume in 1542, he turned to other authorities. That one of these was Robert Stephanus we know from Elyot's acknowledgment. We infer, too, that the work he used was the Latin-French dictionary, since he speaks of having translated words from the French. This inference is supported by evidence derived from a comparative study of the two texts. Before presenting the evidence, however, it is necessary to anticipate what might appear to be a valid objection. The Stephanus text of 1538, like the earlier Elyot, owes some of its definitions and illustrations, via Stephanus' own *Thesaurus*, to Calepine; [35] similarities, then, between the Elyot of 1542 and the Stephanus of 1538 might be explained by the common source. The answer is that many of the illustrations common to these two texts are not in the Calepine; and, in case of entries common to the three texts, Elyot follows the arrangement of the 1538 Stephanus. In his first edition Elyot had arranged entries and illustrations after the model of Calepine: each entry, together with its illustrative quotations, in solid block form, one illustration following on the heels of another, without a line break or indentation. This similarity of arrangement, as well as of content, is exemplified by these excerpts:

Elyot's *Dictionary* (1538)	Calepine's *Dictionarium* (1520)
Conferre in pauca, To conclude shortly. Also *conferre,* to lay togither. *Sitque utrique, proximum horreum, quo conferatur rusticum instrumentum,* To bothe, next there must be a barne, wherin maye be layde up togyther instrumentes longyng to husbandry. Also *confero,* I gyue. *Multa contuli in Catonem,* I have gyuen or attribute moch to. Cato. . . . *Contuli me domum,* I went home. *Contuli me ad Catonem,* I went vnto Cato.	Conferre in pauca est concludere inquit Cice. lib. iij offic. Conferre verba in pauca est reducere. . . . . Sitque utrique proximum horreum quo conferatur rusticum instrumentum id est in vnum reducatur. Et conferre donare: vt Multa contuli in Catonem. i. multa donaui Catoni. Similiter conferre ire: vt Contuli me domum & Contuli me ad Catonem.

If we turn now to the revised and augmented dictionary, the *Bibliotheca Eliotae* of 1542 (and the 1545 edition is almost identical, as we shall see), we shall find that, though Elyot retains in the block form the matter paraphrased from Calepine, he adds a number of new illustrations so arranged that each begins a new line in the column. The added illustrations and their arrangement correspond closely to matter under *confero* in Robert Stephanus' *Dictionarium Latino-Gallicum* (1538), Elyot translating the French into English. Compare, for example, the following: [36]

Bibliotheca Eliotae (1542, 1545)	*Dictionarium* (1538)
Confero me in campum, vel ad campum, I go into the felde.	*Confero me in campum, vel ad campum* . . . *id est vado.*
Conferre animum alio, to set his mind els where.	*Animum alio conferre,* Oster son amour d'aucun, & en aymer ung autre.
Conferre capita, to assemble for counsel, to lay theyr heaes togyther.	*Capita conferre,* S'assembler ensemble, Quant deux ou plusieurs apportent leurs testes l'une aupres de l'autre pour parler de choses secrettes.
Confer gradum, come forthe.	*Gradum conferre,* Marcher aussi fort qu'ung autre, Aller quant & quant luy.
Conferre manus, to assayle eche other.	*Manum vel manus conferre,* S'entrebatre.
Conferre pedem, to come to the poynt. . . .	*Conferre pedem,* Venir au poinct.
Conferre studium, to employ his study.	*Conferre studium in rem aliquam,* Employer.
Conferre tempus in aleam, to spende the tyme in playenge at the dyce.	*Conferre tempus ad, vel in rem aliquam,* Employer & addoner son temps a faire quelque chose.
Conferre verba ad rem, to do as he sayth.	*Verba ad rem conferre,* Mettre en effect ce qu'on dict.
Confert, it is profitable.	*Confert* . . . Proufite, sert, ayde, est utile.

With three exceptions, all the illustrative phrases in the Elyot list above are in the 1538 Stephanus but not in Calepine. Here the case of the

English compiler's indebtedness to the Latin-French dictionary is clear. Elyot carries the arrangement a step further by placing the verb first in each phrase. The three exceptions are *confer gradum, conferre manus,* and *conferre verba ad rem.* These are among the phrases added by Elyot in 1542, and these three are found in both Calepine and Stephanus. In Calepine, however, each phrase is a part of a still longer phrase, as in "Et conferre gradum & procedere longius audet." From this, Stephanus had selected the phrase *gradum conferre,* which in the *Bibliotheca* becomes *confer gradum.* So in the other two examples, the short phrases of Elyot correspond to those selected by Stephanus from the longer phrases of his predecessor.

Of numerous other entries confirming the relationship of the English and the French lexicographer, let us consider a few examples from *conficio* and *persequor.*

Bibliotheca Eliotae	*Dictionarium*
Conficere pensum, to spyn out her threde. . . .	*Pensum conficere,* Acheuer sa fusee. . . .
Conficere prandium, to have dined. . . .	*Prandium conficere,* Acheuer de disner. . . .
Conficere solicitudines alicui, to bryng one into heuynes, or to make hym sorrowfull.	*Solicitudines alicui conficere,* Le mettre en soulcy.
Persequi ius suum, to defende his ryght.	*Persequi ius suum,* Deffendre & poursuiure son droict.
Persequi poenas alicuius, to reuenge ones deathe.	*Persequi poenas alicuius,* Venger la mort d'aucun.
Persequi promissa alicuius, to solicite one to kepe his promyse.	*Persequi promissa alterius,* soliciter qu'il tienne sa promesse.
Persequi uita disciplinam recte uiuendi, to lyue accordynge to the doctrine of lyuynge honestly.	*Persequi vita disciplinam recte uiuendi,* Viure selon la discipline de bien uiure.

Thus it appears from a comparative study that the chief source of augmentation in the 1542 *Bibliotheca* was Robert Stephanus' Latin-French dictionary of 1538. Having abandoned the Calepine after the first edition of his *Dictionary,* Elyot turned to the Stephanus, especially for illustrations of usage of Latin terms, and also modified his pattern in keeping with the new source. This modification is observable in the method of presenting illustrative phrases or sentences, so that the beginning of each illustration marks the beginning of a new line in the column. This order enhances the readability and clearness. It is to be noted, however, that Elyot did not follow the modified etymological arrangement of entries in his French source. The Latin-French dictionary groups Latin derivatives under the root word, thus violating an alphabetical order. The words so grouped appear, however, in their regular position in the alphabet with cross references to the root word under which they are defined. In 1538, Elyot, following Calepine, approximated the etymological order. And though the Stephanus, the new source of inspiration, employed a similar method, Elyot returned in the 1542 and 1545 *Bibliotheca* to an order more nearly alphabetical. For these two editions of his text, Elyot levied upon other authorities, such as Suidas, Budaeus, and Doletus, but upon no other so much as upon Stephanus.

In discussing the augmentation of Elyot's *Dictionary* during his lifetime and therefore, presumably, under the author's personal supervision, we have referred to the *Bibliotheca* of 1542, which incorporates the revisions and augmentations, and that of 1545 as the same in content. While this is true, it is necessary, because of the rarity of the edition here referred to as of 1542, to make clear that two distinct editions are involved. The title page of what is clearly the earlier edition is missing, but this edition is dated, with a query, in the British Museum *Catalogue*, as 1542. This date is partially supported by the later edition, which has the date 1545 on the title page but 1542 in the colophon. Furthermore, the copy without a title page has immediately preceding the text two pages of errata. In the 1545 copy there is no such list, but the errors specified have been corrected in the text proper. In the earlier text, also, the marginal references to authorities stop with the letter *M;* in 1545, with the letter *D.* It should be observed that in subsequent revisions by Cooper, to be discussed in the next chapter, the marginal references are omitted altogether. There are other differences, but none to indicate that the 1545 text is an appreciable augmentation of the earlier one. The printers' signatures are the same in the two editions: A^8–Z^8, Aa^8–Nn^5.

Some definite idea of the thoroughgoing augmentation of the 1538 *Dictionary* as represented in the *Bibliotheca* may be gained by comparison of the number of entries under various letters of the alphabet, as in the table below.

HEADING	NUMBER OF ENTRIES	
	1538 ed.	*1542* ed.
E ante *R*	72	89
E ante *S*	13	20
E ante *T*	16	22
E ante *V*	76	94

Such a representation could suggest merely part of the story. It does not, for example, take into account numerous new illustrations, the rejection of former entries, or the insertion of new ones. But it does support the conclusion that the 1542–1545 *Bibliotheca* shows a notable augmentation of Elyot's *Dictionary* of 1538.

Elyot died in 1546. Since subsequent issues of his *Dictionary* were edited by Thomas Cooper, it is desirable at this point to indicate what progress Elyot had made. He was the first English compiler to sense the need of a comprehensive Latin-English dictionary and to set to work to fulfill this need. He pointed the way to Continental lexicons as rich sources of information and as models for English lexicographers. The *Dictionarium* of Friar Calepine was the main source and the chief model of the 1538 edition of Elyot's *Dictionary*. In the issues of 1542 and 1545, Suidas' Greek *Lexicon* and Doletus' *Commentaries* served as subsidiary sources, and Robert Stephanus' Latin-French *Dictionarium* became a main source. This work of Stephanus was based upon his own *Thesaurus*, a compilation which, admittedly, owed much to Budaeus's *Annotationes* and somewhat less to Calepine. The relation of Elyot's *Dictionary* to its principal sources may be graphically represented thus:

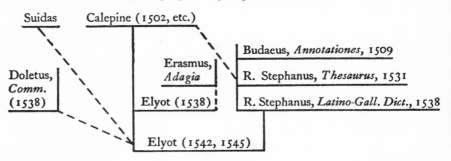

As the heavier lines indicate, the two important sources are Calepine and Robert Stephanus. These are especially to be kept in mind, for, as to form and content, they constitute the basis of Latin-English lexicography during the Renaissance.

Following his natural impulse to disseminate knowledge, inspired, too, perhaps by the examples of Suidas and Calepine and Erasmus, Elyot extended the scope of his *Dictionary* far beyond the bounds of any compilation in England before his time. A comparison of his 1538 volume with the *Ortus vocabulorum*, for example, will reveal at once how far he pushed out the boundaries of lexicography. One result of this extension is the incorporation of much matter, besides the definitions in the vernacular, that may well be termed literary features. These include biographical sketches, personal reminiscences, pseudo natural history and mythology, and proverbs and *adagia*. Elyot was the innovator of such features in English lexicography. One may question whether such items belong inside a dictionary, but one cannot doubt their interest to students of literary history.

Among the biographical sketches, supported by anecdotes and wise sayings, are those of Epimenides, the ancient Rip Van Winkle, from Diogenes Laertius; sketches of Philip of Macedon, Phocion, Pericles, and Paulus Aemilius, from a Latin version of Plutarch's *Lives;* and an incident in the life of Leaena. The sketch of Paulus Aemilius is filled with gorgeous pageantry and dramatic situations. At the end of this Elyot writes (1545):

This hystory haue I ben meued to wryte for the dyuerse pleasaunt and notable thynges, whyche be therin conteyned, with the unsuretie of prosperitie, wherin all menne are blynded, whiche do desyre to haue it.

Concluding the narrative under *Croesus,* we read:

Much more Herodotus the noble hystorian writeth herof in Clio, whiche I wold god were radde oftentymes of kynges and their counsaylours: for whose commoditie I haue written this Epitome or abbreuiation, to no man tedious, whiche hath a good nature.

An episode under *Leaena* has for readers of Shakespeare a literary association.

Leaena . . . the name of a common woman at Athenes who after that Harmodius and Aristogiton had slaine Hypparchum the tyrant, she being turmented in sundry facions, to the intent that she shuld dyscouer the confederates of that murder, she spake not one worde, but bytynge in sunder her tunge, she spyt it in the face of Hyppias the tyrant, who caused her to be tourmented.[37]

Sketches of ten Roman poets, Elyot seems to have translated from Petrus Crinitus. In the *Bibliotheca,* under *exconsules,* the lexicographer refers to Crinitus' *De honesta disciplina,* implying firsthand knowledge of this work. At Florence, in 1505, the *De honesta* and *De poetis Latinis* by Crinitus were published together in one volume. Possibly Elyot was familiar with some edition of this book. At any rate, biographical sketches under the following entries in the *Bibliotheca* correspond closely to essays from *De poetis Latinis: Accius, Livius Andronicus, Ennius, Horatius, Macer Aemilius, Ovidius, Pacuvius, Plautus, Propertius,* and *Terentius.* It is difficult to determine why the lexicographer did not also appropriate Crinitus' sketches of Juvenal, Martial, Seneca, Virgil, and others. Of the sketches that do appear in the dictionary, the most detailed are those of Horace, Plautus, and Ovid. To illustrate the nature of Elyot's borrowing, we herewith transcribe the sketches of Plautus from *De poetis* and *Bibliotheca,* respectively.

De poetis Latinis (1505)

.M. Plautus patria fuit ex umbria. quod ipse de se insinuat/ in fabula Mostellaria. & alii ueteres tradunt. Constat eum his temporibus Romae uixisse: atque in scaena praestitisse: quibus in ciuitate Pub. Scipio/ Fuluius nobilior: & M. Cato excellentes habiti sunt. . . . Cum erogasset omnem pecuniam scaenicis ornamentis ad summam paupertatem fuisse redactum. Eaque ratione in urbem rediisse: & operam pistori locasse ad uictum comparandum his molis circumagendis: quas trusatiles uocant. . . . Et cum aliquondam in pistrino uersaretur . . . tantumque scribendi elegantia & salibus uisus est praestitisse: ut Epius stolo affirmare non dubitauerit: Musas ipsas Plautino sermone fuisse locuturas: si latine loqui uoluissent. . . .

Bibliotheca Eliotae (1559)

Plautus, a comical poete, borne in Umbria: whan he had spent all his substaunce on players garmentes, and thereby was brought to extreme pouertee, he was fayne for his lyuyng to serue a baker in tournyng a querne, or handemill. Whan he was uacante from that labour, he wrote moste eloquente and pleasaunt comedies wherin he was reputed so excellent, that Epius Stolo saied of him, he doubted not, but that the muses woulde speake as Plautus did write if they shoulde speake latine. He was in the tyme of Cato Censorinus.

Reflections of personal observation or personal experience not infrequently appear. Under *glastum,* for example, Elyot commends Rowland Goodman [38] for his efforts to cultivate the plant *glastum,* which had once been used in England to make blue dye. Under *Britannia* he mentions his conference with Master Richard Pace about an ancient book unearthed at Ivy Church, near Salisbury. Under *Heliogabalus* he refers the reader to his *Image of Governaunce.* And under *gigas* Elyot relates that in company with his father, Sir Richard Elyot, he witnessed the exhumation of a thirteen-foot human skeleton at Ivy Church.

Many choice bits of pseudo natural history, deriving from Pliny and from medieval bestiaries, are inserted in these early editions of Elyot's *Dictionary* and *Bibliotheca.* Of the numerous examples, we here quote three:

Alce, a wylde beaste in the woodes of Germany, in fascion and skynne lyke to a gote, but greatter, which haue no ioyntes in theyr legges, and therfore they do neuer lye, but only do leane to trees, whan they do rest them, whiche the hunters knowynge, do sawe the trees that they leane to, halfe a sunder, wher by they fall downe, and be taken.

Alces, a beaste in Fraunce lyke a mule, but he hath his ouer lyp so longe, that whan he fedeth, he goeth backewarde, or elles he canne not byte of the grasse and herbes, which he shulde eate. The horsekynde of theym haue hornes on theyr ouer browes. Suche a beast was late brought in to Englande, and seene in the kynges parke at Westmister.

Belzahard, is a barbarous worde, but for the efficacy of the thing, it is necessary to knowe the signification therof. It is a specyal and soueraygne medicene agaynste poyson beinge drunke. Auenzoar wryteth that against poison, whyche is excedyngly hot, he made it in this fourme, thre graines of barley, with fiue ounces of the water of a gourde. But some men thynke, that the moste excellent Belzahard is this which foloweth: The propertie of the Harte is (as Plinius doth write) to be at contynuall debate with the serpente, in so much as he pursueth hym, and seketh for hym at the hoole, where he lyueth, and with the breath of his nosethrilles compelleth to come forthe. Now after that the hert hath fought with the serpent and eaten him, he be cometh thristie, and runneth unto some water, and leapeth into it, but he than doth not drynk. For if he shuld take neuer so lytel water, he shulde dye incontinent: than do yssue out of his eyes dropes, whiche by lyttell and lyttell do congeale, and waxe as greate as a chesten nutte. After that the heart is comme out of the water, men do awayt where those droppes do fall, and taketh them, and laieth them amonge treasure, as a thynge most precious, and agaynst all maner of poyson most certayne remedye. This haue I taken out of the boke of Ioan. Agricola *De recentioribus medicamentis.*

Proverbs or *adagia* in the *Dictionary* are fairly frequent. These derive, for the most part, from Erasmus' *Adagia* and continue to be a feature of the larger Latin-English dictionaries to the eighteenth century. The following examples will convey an idea of these:

Lac gallinaceus, the milke of an henne. A prouerbe applyed to theym, whiche lacke nothynge, or to thynges, whiche for the scarsitie of them be very pretious.

Noctuas Athenas, oules to Athenes, a prouerbe, where one sendeth to a man any thyng wherof he that receyueth it hath plenty.

Omne tulit punctum, he touched euery pointe. A prouerbe applyed to hym, whiche omytteth nothyng expedient or necesary, and is therfore of all men commended.

Ad pedem, a prouerbe whyche signyfieth agreable, as it were my shoe is meete for my foote. Accordynge to this prouerbe is the sentence of Paulus Aemilius, who herynge his wyfe Papyriam commended for her beaultie and dyuers other good qualities, he helde up his foote to them that praysed her, and asked howe they lyked his shoe. Than sayd Aemilius, ye se that it is a newe shoe, and a well made shoe, but yet none of you do know where he wryngeth me, but yet I do fele it.

Bos in lingua, a prouerbe touchyng them whiche dare not speake the truthe, or wyl not for bicause they have receiued money to hold theyr peace.

Caecus caeco dux, one blynde man leadeth an other. A prouerbe signifienge, one ignorant person to teache an other unlerned. One fole to gyue an other foole counsayle.

Caninum prandium, a dogges diner. A prouerb used where there is no wyne at dyner or supper, for dogges of theyr nature do abhor wine.

Clauum clauo pellere, to dryue out oone nayle with an other. A prouerbe, signifieng one yll to putte away an other, oone labour an other labour, oone griefe with an other griefe, one deceypte with an other deceypte, extreme pleasure with extreme peyne.[39]

Two other features of Elyot's dictionaries deserve special mention: *chronographia* and *copia.* In the Proheme of 1542 Elyot writes, "As well in this parte as in the histories [i.e., the brief biographies] and tables, I haue sette out the computation of tyme called Chronographie, wherein it appereth how longe the persons were either befor the incarnacion of Christe, or how long after." Although Elyot does not uniformly indicate chronology for his characters, there are many examples of this practice for pagan and Christian throughout his text. At the end of his sketch of Artaxerxes, for example, he writes, "He was before the incarnacion 485 yeres"; at the conclusion of Arthurus is the statement, "He flourished about the yere of our lorde .510"; Daniel "lyued before the incarnacion of Christ .619. yeres"; Jesus was "most cruelly nailed to the Crosse, the yere after the creacion of the worlde .3994."; Pythagoras "was before the incarnacion of Christe .522. yeeres." Elyot suggests his sources of information on chronology: under *lustrum*, he cites Glareanus' *Chronologia*, and under *Horatius* and *Origenes* he refers to Eusebius' *Ecclesiastica historica*. This latter work, or more convenient still, the same author's *Chronography*, is the most likely source. The custom of indicating chronology continues through the Elyot-Cooper dictionaries.

In the popular *Synonyma* of John of Garland and in the *Catholicon Anglicum* (Chapter 2 above) we noted the free and extensive use of synonyms as a means of supplying an abundance of words and affording the possibility of varying expression of thought in Latin. Although the idea goes back to antiquity, these compilers seemed to anticipate the revival of the principle in the sixteenth century. Vogue was early given to the idea by Erasmus' exposition in his *De copia verborum et rerum* (1512). *Copia* in Erasmus means the acquisition of an abundance of words and ideas, examples and illustrations, that will make possible the greatest variety in the expression of thought. *Copia* and the consequent possibilities of varying may be acquired, according to Erasmus, by the use of synonyms, figures of speech, historical examples, proverbs, and myth and fable. Abundant examples are supplied in the *De copia*, as well as in the *Adagia* and the *Apophthegmata*. The idea of *copia*, or "copie" in the Anglicized form, seems to have been an established principle from the time of Erasmus' treatise through the Renaissance.

With the *De copia* Sir Thomas Elyot was quite familiar. In *The Governour* (Book I, Chapter 11) Elyot recommends the study of rhetoric from Hermogenes or Quintilian or Cicero, and continues, "And in good faythe . . . for him that nedeth nat, or doth nat desire, to be an exquisite oratour, the litle boke made by the famous Erasmus . . . which he calleth Copiam Verborum et Rerum, that is to say, plentie of words and maters, shall be sufficient." In the Proheme of his *Bibliotheca* (1542), Elyot declares to Henry VIII that the first edition of his dictionary "neither in diligence, nor syncere exposicion, nor in copie of woordes, nor in abundance of mattier and sentence, is in any wise to be hereto compared." It is unusual and of some importance that Elyot should thus give especial emphasis to "copie" in his dictionary. Admiring Erasmus' *De copia* as he did, Elyot must have believed that the proverbs, the myths, the *sententiae,* the examples in the historical and biographical sketches, and, best of all, the groups of English equivalents placed compactly together after such Latin verbs as *expleo, explico,* and *expono,* together with illustrative phrases, exemplified the principle of *copia.* For this reason, Richard Sherry, in the dedicatory epistle to his *Treatise of Schemes and Tropes* (1550), gives special praise to Sir Thomas Elyot, who "in his dictionarye as it were generallye searchinge out the copye of our language in all kynde of wordes and phrases . . . hathe herebi declared the plentyfulness of our mother toūge." The principle is further exemplified, as we shall see, in Cooper's *Thesaurus,* and in other dictionaries in the sixteenth century.

Before discussing the revision and augmentation of the *Bibliotheca* under the editorship of Thomas Cooper, it seems desirable to make some further general observations on Elyot's contribution during his lifetime to the development of lexicography. His ideal, inspired by the new learning, was to compile a dictionary that would exemplify classical Latin and the English idiom of his own day. It should be obvious that his ideal of classical Latinity was but partially realized and that his lexicon, like many later ones, still contains a goodly amount of medieval matter. Nevertheless, under the influence of Continental predecessors, he laĭd the foundation for a system of lexicography in England, a foundation on which his successors continued to build during the sixteenth century. This system involves the alphabetical arrangement of terms to be defined; the giving of grammatical information; the use, on a limited scale, of quotations from standard Latin authors to establish meaning and usage; the occasional citation of authorities; and the insertion of much mythological, biographical, and historical matter. This system, with all its shortcomings, may be regarded as the beginning of modern Latin-English lexicography.[40]

CHAPTER VII

Bibliotheca Eliotae: Eliotis Librarie
(1548)

AFTER ELYOT'S death, in 1546, Berthelet, the publisher of the *Bibliotheca Eliotae*, persuaded Thomas Cooper (1517?–94) to assume editorship of the dictionary. For this task, Cooper's university training probably gave him better qualification than Elyot had had. Son of an Oxford tailor, Thomas Cooper received his B.A. and M.A. degrees from Magdalen College. He was master of Magdalen College School (1549–68), dean of Christ Church (1567), vice-chancellor of Oxford (1567–70), bishop of Lincoln (1570), and bishop of Winchester (1584–94).[1]

As revised and augmented by Thomas Cooper, the *Bibliotheca Eliotae* was published in 1548, reissued in 1552 as "the second tyme inriched," and again in 1559 as "the third tyme corrected and . . . enriched." That Cooper entered upon this labor with considerable misgiving, we learn from his remarkable Latin address to the reader.[2] In substance, Cooper writes that just as Elyot, once mistakes had been discovered in his book, had been lashed by the critics and an attempt made to discredit his whole work, so Cooper might expect similar criticism. There were indeed among the learned those whom almost no work, however well performed, ornate, or elegant, could please, except what they themselves did. The proposed task, Cooper further maintained, demanded more skill in languages and more knowledge in general than he himself possessed. There were surely others of greater talents and of better qualifications than he, by whom he hoped this work would be done.

Then the prospective reviser recounts Berthelet's reply to his objections—a reply worthy of recording. No one, Berthelet maintained, could be expected to know everything or to be absolutely faultless in his work, but such gifts as one had, deserved to be used for the benefit of others and for the welfare of the commonwealth. The work, to be sure, would be burdensome and would incite attacks by the envious and the malevolent. Nevertheless, the achieving of such a task was worthy of engaging all the power that one possesses. As for those endowed with extraordinary ability (*ingenia praestantissima*)—and there are many such in our day—some were intent on one thing, some on another, so that it could scarcely be hoped that they would undertake this task, especially since it offered a minimum of pleasure and very much labor and trouble. The carping of the learned who would not undertake the work themselves was no more to be feared than the contempt of the ignorant who did not understand intellectual labor. Such a bold challenge Cooper could not but heed. He engaged wholeheartedly in the labors of a lexicographer, seeking, despite hardships, to render a service to the youth of England and thereby contribute to the welfare of his country.

In the year 1548, Berthelet published Cooper's most important augmentation of Elyot's dictionary, with these words on the title page:

Bibliotheca Eliotae Eliotis Librarie. This Dictionarie now newly imprinted, Anno Domini M.D.XLVIII. is augmented and inriched with aboue xxxiii thousande wordes and phrases, very nedefull for the knowlage of the latine tonge: besyde the descriuyng of the true significacions of wordes, whiche were greatly amisse by ouer muche folowynge of Calepine. Cum priuilegio.[3]

To the work of revision, if we can judge by his words to the reader, Cooper brought a better understanding of the problems of a lexicographer than had his predecessor. Though he did not find a satisfactory solution to all the problems, Cooper produced in the revised *Bibliotheca* of 1548 a work which marks substantial progress in the development of lexicography in England. It is in the quality of the enrichment more than in the quantity that progress is shown.

But the quantity of augmentation must be noticed. According to the title page, the volume is "augmented and inriched with aboue xxxiii thousande wordes and phrases." The address to the reader is less explicit, stating merely that several thousand words (*aliquot millia*) have been added. If by "wordes" the author means terms to be defined and therefore new entries in the text, his estimates, vague though they are, are extravagant. But "wordes and phrases" is probably meant to include new terms for definition and phrases to illustrate meaning. Taken together they constitute considerable expansion—at least several thousand—as the increased size of the 1548 volume indicates. The counting of groups of entries throws light on the augmentation. From 1545 to 1548, for example, the entries under "*E* ante *R*" have increased from 89 to 154; under "*E* ante *S*," from 20 to 31; under "*E* ante *V*," from 94 to 219. But it is in the Latin phrases illustrating meaning and usage that the most notable augmentation appears. From 1545 to 1548 the number of illustrations under *evado* climbed from 1 to 20; under *evenio*, from 2 to 9; under *evoco*, from 1 to 13. A comparative study of *persequor, repeto,* and *repono* shows similar results. Many of these illustrations Cooper collected from his sources.

Some of the sources can be readily discovered. We noticed above that, in revising and enlarging the first and second editions of his dictionary, Elyot had drawn freely from the Latin-French dictionary of Robert Stephanus. Cooper also borrowed from Stephanus, and extended the debt. To the verbs *confero* and *conficio*, for example, Elyot had added a great number of illustrative phrases by free adaptation of Stephanus. In the edition of 1548, Cooper further increased the illustrations of meaning and usage by adding to *confero* thirty-seven and to *conficio* thirty-three more quotations, together with their English translations. All the added Latin phrases Cooper drew directly from Stephanus' Latin-French dictionary, the source which Elyot had used; and, like Elyot, Cooper translated the French equivalents into English. It would be superfluous to quote all the examples here, but confirmatory evidence is afforded by the parallels which follow.

Cooper's *Bibliotheca Eliotae* (1548)	Robert Stephanus' *Dictionarium Latino-Gallicum* (1538)
Conferre omnia sua studia in aliquem, to do all the pleasures that one can for a man.	*Conferre sua omnia studia in aliquem,* Luy faire tous plaisirs & seruices. . . .
Benignitatem in aliquem conferre, to shewe great liberalitie or gentilnesse to one, to dooe many pleasures for him.	*Conferre benignitatem in aliquem,* Accumuler beaucoup de plaisirs enuers aucun.
Castra castris conferre, to pitche or campe ouer ryght agaynst an other.	*Castra castris conferre,* Rapporter son camp au camp des ennemys; & mettre vis a vis.
Coram inter nos conferemus, we wyll deuyse and common of these matters, whan we meet together.	*Coram inter nos conferemus,* Nous parlerons & deuiserons ensemble.
Maledicta in aliquem conferre, to rayle or geue one shrewde wordes.	*Conferre maledicta in aliquem,* Dire beaucoup d'oultrages a aucun.
Ingenium ad rem aliquam, to geue ones minde to a thynge.	*Ingenium ad rem aliquam conferre,* Employer son esperit.

. . . .

Cooper's *Bibliotheca Eliotae* (1548)	Robert Stephanus' *Dictionarium Latino-Gallicum* (1538)
Conficere ambulationem, to walke.	*Conficere ambulationem, pomeridianam in aliquo loco,* S'y pourmener.
Absolutionem conficere, to dispache or quitte.	*Absolutionem conficere,* Expedier.
Propre centum annos confecit, He hath lyued well nere a hundred yeres.	*Propre centum confecit annos,* Il est uenu presque a bout de cent ans.
Conficere bellum, to atchiue or finish a warre; sometyme to fight.	*Conficere bellum,* Faire guerre, Batailler.
Pacem conficere, to pacifye or quyet a countrey.	*Pacem conficere,* Tranquiller & pacifier une contree.

It should be kept in mind that the above illustrations from the *Bibliotheca* of 1548 were not in the earlier editions of the text, but were all added by Cooper from the same source as Elyot had borrowed from—Stephanus' Latin-French dictionary. Although relatively few of the Latin verbs exhibit so great a range of meaning and usage as do *confero* and *conficio,* many other verbs, such as *confirmo,* for example, offer evidence of Cooper's borrowing and adapting matter from Stephanus' Latin-French dictionary. It may be said, too, that the instances of borrowing noted above, together with hundreds of others, are common to Cooper's three revisions: 1548, 1552, and 1559.

Another source for Cooper's augmentation of the *Bibliotheca* is Nicholas Udall's *Floures for Latine Speakyng selected and gathered out of Terence* (1533). In his *Shakespeare's Books,* H. R. D. Anders suggests that the Latin quotation *Redime te captum quam queas minimo* (*The Taming of the Shrew,* I, i, 167) derives from Terence via Lily's Latin grammar. Anders further observes that the same Latin sentence appears in Udall's *Floures* and that "Udall seems to have copied the sentence with the translation from the *Bibliotheca Eliotae.*" [4] Since, however, the same sentence with the translation had appeared in the 1533 edition of the *Floures,* five years before Elyot's *Dictionary* was published and fifteen years before Cooper's revision (1548), the relationship is actually the reverse: the *Bibliotheca* derived the sentence from the *Floures.* Whether Shakespeare borrowed from one of these sources or from some other need not concern us here. The point is that Anders' misleading note does serve to give the clue for further investigation.

Following the hint furnished by Anders, we turn again to the *Bibliotheca* of 1548. At the end of the address to the reader Cooper writes: "To the learned man Udall, by whose scholarly annotations our labors have been lightened in many places, give deserved praise and gratitude." [5] This is a clear-cut acknowledgment of Cooper's indebtedness. A comparative study of Udall's *Floures* (1533) and the *Bibliotheca* (1548) reveals that practically all of Udall's book, with some slight changes and with omission of specific references to Terence's plays, is incorporated in the *Bibliotheca,* either by Cooper himself or, as the acknowledgment may imply, by Udall working as Cooper's assistant.

The Latin phrases with the English translations, below, will serve to establish my conclusions.

Cooper's *Bibliotheca* (1548)	Udall's *Floures* (1533)
Excessit ex ephebis, he passed boyes age, he waxed a man.	*Excessit ex ephaebis,* He is paste childe-hode, Or, he wexeth a manne, or he groweth to mannes state. [fol. 1ʳ]
Expecto quid velis, I long, or I would fayne knowe, what your wyll, mynde, or pleasure is, or elles I desyre to knowe what you woulde.	*Expecto quid velis,* I wold fain know what your wyl or pleasure is, Or I longe or desyre to knowe your mynd, wyl or pleasure. [fol. 1ʳ]
Illices in fraudem, Thou bryngest them to displeasure and inconuenience: Thou doest entyce or allure theym to that thyng, whereby they shall haue hurte: Or thou tollest them into the snare or into daungier.	*In fraudem eos illicis,* Thou bryngeste them to displeasure and inconuenience: or thou entycest them to that thynge, whereby they shall haue hurte: or, thou tollest them into the snare, or in to daunger. . . . [fol. 31ʳ]
Manibus pedibusque, with all myght and maine, with hande and foote, with toothe and nayle, as much as in hym lieth, al that euere he may right busily.	*Manibus pedibusque obnixe omnia facit.* He doeth all thynges with hande and foote, or with tothe and nayle, as moche as in him lyeth, Or, he doeth all that euer he maye ryght busyly. [fol. 3ʳ]
Prudens, sciens, viuus, vidensque pereo, I die beyng ware or wittyng and knowyng thereof, beyng on lyue and seyng, Or I wilfully cast awaie my selfe.	*Prudens, sciens, uiuus, uidensque pereo:* I dye beinge ware or wyttynge and knowyng therof beinge aliue and seinge, or, I am wilfully caste awaye. [fol. 36ᵛ]
Redimas te captum quam queas minimo: to redeeme or raunsome thy selfe beynge taken prisoner, as good cheape as thou canst.⁶	*Redimas te captum quam queas minimo,* Redeme or raunsome thy selfe, beinge taken prisoner, as good chepe as thou mayste, or, if you be in any daunger come oute agayne as well as you may. [fol. 36ᵛ]

Although Cooper takes freely and literally from the *Floures,* he does not incorporate in the *Bibliotheca* Udall's detailed discussions of phrases and words, such as those under *investigare* and *fraus.* Udall's gatherings from Terence were, nevertheless, a most fruitful source for the *Bibliotheca* of 1548.

Another source of enrichment and augmentation Cooper found in proper-name dictionaries. He explains to his readers that proper names— the names of gods, men, countries, towns, and rivers—the knowledge of which is very necessary in the reading of poets, have been formerly for the most part neglected. Into this edition, however, he has transferred proper names from Stephanus and others who have written about them.[7]

Since Elyot, following the lead of Calepine and Suidas, had freely inserted such names in the earlier editions of his *Dictionary*, it is hardly clear what Cooper means by stating that they had been largely disregarded. It is true, however, that Cooper added a great many proper names, from "Stephanus and others," as he explains. The allusion is to Robert Stephanus. A new edition of the *Thesaurus linguae Latinae* had been printed in Paris in 1543 (2 vols., folio). As this work had proper names distributed through the alphabet, it could have been a source for Cooper. More likely, however, the allusion is to an earlier work devoted solely to proper names, a book compiled by Hermann Torrentinus, about 1490, and printed frequently through the first half of the sixteenth century, with slightly varying title, as *Elucidarius carminum . . . vel vocabularius poeticus* or *Elucidarius poeticus*.[8] This work, revised by Robert Stephanus and published as the *Elucidarius poeticus, siue dictionarium nominum propriorum* (Antwerp, 1545) in a single small volume, would have been most convenient for Cooper to consult. Correspondences between the *Bibliotheca* and the *Elucidarius* (1545) may be seen, for example, under *Canace, Candaules, Canobus, Capaneus, Capena, Carinea, Carmenta, Carneades, Cassandra, Cassiopea,* and *Catana*. Very similar matter, the English editor might have found elsewhere, as in Calepine, but his reference to Stephanus as a source lends probability to his use of the revised *Elucidarius*.

To survey our study of Cooper's augmentation of the *Bibliotheca* of 1548, we have discovered among his sources Robert Stephanus' *Dictionarium Latino-Gallicum* (1538), the same author's *Thesaurus* (1543), Stephanus' revision of the *Elucidarius poeticus* (1545), and Nicholas Udall's *Floures for Latine Speakyng* (1533). This list is not exhaustive. Of the sources named, however, Stephanus' Latin-French dictionary contributed the greatest amount of useful, classical material.

The two subsequent editions of 1552 and 1559 show less enrichment than the title pages imply. There are a number of corrections, especially with reference to plants and birds, involving sometimes the reduction of the length of descriptive items, sometimes expansion and the insertion of new entries. But the net result is no considerable augmentation of the texts.

The title page of the 1552 edition reads thus:

Bibliotheca Eliotae. Eliotis Dictionarie the second tyme inriched, and more perfectly corrected, by Thomas Cooper, schole maister of Maudlens in Oxforde.

This last edicion, beside the addicion and correction of verie manie thynges hath the proper names of most herbes that be agreed of among phisicians: the correction of weightes, measures and coynes, with the applyinge of the same to our tyme. Londini in aedibus. T. Bertheleti. Cum priuilegio.

The reviser's statement that this edition contains the "proper names of most herbes" requires explanation. It will be remembered that in the Preface of his 1538 *Dictionary* Elyot had urged that his book had the "names of diuers herbes knowen among us," and again in the Proheme of 1542 he wrote that he had added the "names of a great number of herbes," impliedly from Suidas. We know from consulting these earlier editions that Elyot did include the names of many herbs. He had, indeed, some special qualification on this subject. His *Castel of Helth*, for example, which according to some authorities [9] was first published in 1534, and of which there are extant copies of a 1539 edition and later ones, has descriptions of many herbs and an explanation of their medicinal and food values, based on Galen and numerous other authorities. Notwithstanding Elyot's special information on the subject and his inclusion of many plant names in his *Dictionary*, Cooper, by inference, ignores his predecessor. Such is the impression one gets from the title page of the 1552 edition.

Cooper's attitude is, however, intelligible in the light of his address to the reader in 1548. According to Cooper's explanation, Elyot, by too great haste or through errors of the printers or for some other reasons, had made many mistakes, not only in recording proper names but in other subjects as well, among them the names of plants and herbs. As Cooper himself knew little about this subject, his first thought was to omit all such nomenclature. Although certain physicians had scorned his requests for aid, others encouraged him and apparently approved Cooper's revised and selected list. Hence the words on the title page of the 1552 edition: "the proper names of most herbes that be agreed of among phisicians."

Cooper maintained further, in the same address, that the nomenclature of fruits and herbs lacked uniformity and consistency, and that some qualified person who had spent much of his life investigating the nature of plants should describe and name them. Such a man was William Turner, and Turner had promised such a study. Now William Turner did publish in 1548 *The Names of Herbes in Greke, Latin, English, Duch & Frenche*, but apparently too late for Cooper to use in his 1548 revision of the *Bibliotheca*. In 1551 Turner published *A Newe Herball*, which, though it utilized part of the matter of his earlier book, was a more elaborate treatise of the subject, accompanied by illustrations. Thus, when Cooper was revising the *Bibliotheca* for the 1552 edition, he could have secured information from either or both of Turner's books. Although in certain entries Cooper refers to Turner as his authority, he fails to mention the title of the book or books he is using. The parallels which follow indicate that the *Bibliotheca* (1552) is fairly close to *A Newe Herball* (1551).

Bibliotheca	*A Newe Herball*
Absynthium . . . is commonly called wormewood: how be it there be therof three kyndes: *Seriphium*, which seemeth to be our wormewood: *Santonicum*, wherof cometh wormseede, and may be called french wormwood: *Ponticum*, or *Romanum*, which hath a sweeter odour, it may be called wormwood gentle, our common wormwood is called in latin *Absinthium rusticum*.	*Absinthium* is named in . . . English wormwode . . . there are thre kyndes of wormwode, *ponticum*, *Marinum*, and *santonicum. Ponticum absinthium*, whych maye be named in english, wormwode gentle or wormwode Roman . . . But y^t hath both a lesse floure & lefe then the other Wormwodes have. The savvur of this . . . resembleth . . . a certain kynd of swete spice . . . As for this great cõmon wormwod it is called in latin *Absinthiũ rusticũ*. . . . *Absinthiũ marinũ* or *Seryphũ* . . . may be called in english sea wormwod . . . The thyrede kynde of Wormwood is called *Absinthium Santonicum*. . . . It maye be called well in Englysh, french wormwode. . . .
Anagallis . . . an herbe, called vulgarly *Morsus gallinae*, in englishe (as I suppose) Pimpernell: other take it for chikwede. This herbe hath both kyndes: the male beareth a red flower, the female a blue.	*Anagallis*. Pympernell is named both in Greke and in Latyne *Anagallis* . . . in french *Morgelyna*. Pympernell is of ij. kyndes: it that hath the blewe floure, is called the female, but it that hath ye cremesine is called ye male.
Antirrhino, an herbe, wherof be .ii. sortes, the one described of Plinie with leaues like flaxe, whiche groweth much in Germany, and may be called in Englishe calfe Snowte. the other of Diosco. with leaues like Pimpernell, whiche maister Turner saieth he hath it in his gardeyn, and calleth it broade calues snowte.	*Antirrhinum* . . . It is lyke unto gooshareth: called aparine with a very lytle roote, and almost none. It hath a fruit lyke unto a calfes snowt. . . . Plini giueth the leues of line or slaches unto antirrhinũ. . . . Y^e floures are purple . . . it hath a fruyte like unto a calfs snowt . . . groweth much in England in ye corne feldes. . . . This herbe maye be called in english calfes snowte.

Compare also with the *Newe Herball* matter in the *Bibliotheca* under *abrotonon, acanthus, adiantum,* and *anemone,* to list only a few. The use of Turner's books in the 1552 revision involved only slight augmentation, since most of the herbs had been described in earlier editions of the *Bibliotheca*. Cooper's task was to revise the entries in accord with his new authority.

Class names, including names of plants, herbs, trees, and birds, were traditional in English glossaries and vocabularies. Although Elyot and Cooper ostensibly disregarded the tradition, they nevertheless inserted many class names and descriptions in their dictionaries. Their prohemes and addresses to the reader remind us that such nomenclature is in the *Bibliotheca,* though they do not mention sources. In his 1548 address to the reader Cooper writes (to paraphrase): "Why should I waste time recounting the innumerable kinds of fishes, birds, insects, and precious stones, whose natures are to be examined and whose names learned by those who wish nothing to be missing in a vernacular dictionary?" Cooper inherited many descriptions of birds from Elyot. Some of these, in the revision of 1552, he modified or corrected; others he rejected; and he added many new entries, giving special attention to birds found in England. What was the source of his new information on birds?

Although Cooper refers to Pliny and Aristotle and other authorities, he does not reveal, either in his lines to the reader or in any of his entries on birds, the actual source of his corrections and augmentations in the edition of 1552. In 1544, William Turner published in Cologne a book entitled *Avium praecipuarum, quarum apud Plinium et Aristotelem mentio est, breuis & succincta historia.* In this little book, Turner has an alphabetical Latin list of birds, such as "De Ardea," followed by the names, added by Turner himself, in Greek, German, and English. He then gives a Latin excerpt from Pliny or Aristotle (Latin version), or both, on the appearance and characteristics of the bird in question. What is more important—and the best part of the book—is that Turner adds, in italics, his own commentary, modifying or correcting the descriptions of the classical authors and indicating the habits of the bird and its English name. He frequently supplied also names in the margin, Latin or English. This is the book that Cooper used in augmenting the *Bibliotheca* of 1552.[10] From Turner's book, he cites Pliny and Aristotle. Very frequently Cooper gets his special information, not from the classical authors, but from Turner's own comment. And though Cooper refers to Turner in association with herbal lore, he nowhere mentions the name in reference to birds. Yet the evidence indicates that Cooper practically took over Turner's book on birds. Compare the following parallels:[11]

Cooper's *Bibliotheca Eliotae* (1552)	Turner's *Historia avium* (1544)
Alcedo . . . a byrde of the sea. . . . This byrde is little more than a sparrowe, his fethers be purple of colour mixte with white, and hath a long necke and a small, his byll somwhat greene, long & sclender, and is sene very seldome,	*De Alcedone.* Ἀλκυών, alcedo, Anglice, the kynges fissher, *Germania* eyn leissvogel. (Plinius) *Ipsa auis pouli amplior pascere, colore cyanoe, ex/parte maiore, tantum purpureis & candidis admixtis pennis, collo gracili ac procero*

Cooper's *Bibliotheca Eliotae* (1552)

how be it this byrde is taken for that, which we call the kynges fysher. . . .

Attagen . . . a byrde, whiche is founde in Ionia, and is verie delicate, and hath fethers of sundry colours, and beyng at large, is alway syngyng and chatterynge, but beynge ones taken, he maketh no noyse, nor seemeth to haue any voyce. They are deceyued that take him for a woodcocke, it is most lyke a byrde called a monge us a godwitte.

Carduelis . . . a byrde called a lynnet, or some other little birde, that liueth by the seede of thistles, for I dare not affirm it to be a lynnet, which is named *Miliaria* . . . It, beynge (as Plinie sayth) of all birdes the least, is tought to do any thynge not only wyth the voyce, but also with the feete & byll in steede of handes.

Coeruleo . . . a birde, whiche appereth not in the winter, a clotbyrde, a smatche, an arlyng, a steincheke.

Diomedae aues, certayne birdes, whiche haue teethe, and eies of fierie colour, of the nature of theim reade Plinie.

Gracus . . . graculus . . . a byrde called of some a Iaye: but Erasmus in his adagies, so often as this worde Κολοιὸς, doeth come in use, doth still translate it *Graculus*, and Aristotle maketh .iii. kindes of those birdes . . . the description of the fyrste, agreeth in all poynctes unto the cornishe chough: the descripcion of the second unto our chough, properly called *monedula*, the thyrde I knowe not. . . .

Turner's *Historia avium* (1544)

. . . (Aristotle) . . . *rostrum subuiride, longum & tenue.* [Pp. 18, 19]

De Attagena. (Plinius de Attagene): *Attagen maxime Ionius celebratur, uocalis alias, captus uero obtumescit, quondam existimatus inter raras aues.* (Peter Gyllius) *Attagen, est . . . uersicoloribus picta plumis in dorso, & color ruffus est. . . . Falluntur igitur Britannici ludimagistri qui suum Wodcoccum attagenem faciunt. . . .*

De Carduelle. Carduelis . . . inter spiniuoras auiculas Aristoteles recenset. . . . Plinius scribit cardueles auium minimas imperata facere, nec uoce tantum, sed pedibus & ore pro manibus . . . Quin & hoc facit miliaria, quam linotam nostrates appellant.

Dictu mihi difficile uidetur, quamnam . . . Plinius carduelem fecerit, num thraupin aut acanthin, aut chrysomitrem. [from Turner's commentary, pp. 50–52]

De Coeruleone, Κυανός, *coeruleo, Anglice,* a clotburd, a smatche, an arlyng, a steinchek . . . *coeruleo . . . in hyeme non apparet.* [from Turner's identification and comment, p. 52]

De Diomedeis Avibus ex Plinio. Nec Diomedeas praeteribo aues. Iuba cataractas uocat, & eis esse dentes, oculosque igneo colore, caetera candidos tradens. . . . [p. 70]

De Graculis. Erasmus in eruditissimo adagiorum opere, quoties Κολοιὸς *occurrit . . . graculum reddit. Theodorum Gazam hac in re, licet alias libenter, minime secutus, qui* Κόλοιον *semper monedulam uertit.* (Aristoteles). *Monedularum tria sunt genera . . .* [Turner's comment] *Primum graculorum genus . . . est Anglis a* cornish choghe. . . . *Secundum genus . . . dictum. Latinis proprie monedula . . . Monedulam Anglie vocant,* a caddo, a chogh, or a Ka.

Additional illustrations of Cooper's debt to Turner in the field of ornithology may be found in the 1552 *Bibliotheca* under *Bosca, cinclus, iunco, lingulaca, lagopus, parus, picus martius, platalea, salus,* and *sitta.* There is, in fact, scarcely a page of Turner's book on birds which did not afford information to Cooper. It is mainly in the corrections and additions from William Turner's *Avium praecipuarum* (1544) and his *Newe Herball* (1551) that the *Bibliotheca* of 1552 reveals differences from that of 1548. Important though these changes are, they do not result in notable augmentation of the text.

Nor did the revision of 1559 show any appreciable increase in the number of entries, notwithstanding the claims made on the title page.

Bibliotheca Eliotae. Eliotis Dictionarie, by Thomas Cooper the third tyme corrected, and with a great number of phrases enriched, as to him that conferreth the other aeditions, it may easely appear. Londini in aedibus nuper Tho. Bertheleti. Anno Domini 1559. Cum priuilegio.

This claim to enrichment expresses an unfulfilled intention rather than an actual achievement. For after these four hundred years, we have "conferred the other aeditions," and the enrichment doth not "easely appear." We have seen, earlier in this chapter, that the numerous illustrative phrases added to the verbs *confero* and *conficio* in the 1548 revision continued without change in the editions of 1552 and 1559. Scrutiny of numerous other entries in the three editions of Cooper's revised *Bibliotheca* shows no essential changes after 1548. Definitions and illustrations of the following words, for example, are in the three editions practically identical: *ancilla, ciconia, curator, ecclesia, emblema, gratia, iustitia, leaena, oraculum, paganus, phantasia, pietas, prudentia, sapientia,* and *scientia.*

One reason why the *Bibliotheca* of 1559 did not receive the augmentation suggested on the title page is explained by Cooper himself in his "To the Reader" prefixed to the list of proper names.

I had purposed good reader, cleane taking out the proper names, to haue set them more perfectly corrected in a boke by them selfe, and to haue added in the Dictionarie in place of them, a great number of phrases, necessarie to declare the manyfold vse and construction of wordes in the Latine tongue. Which my purpose as I haue in some part perfourmed, addynge a number of profitable and necessarie phrases, ouer and besyde the correction of diuers thinges that before escaped: So yet by occasion of weakenes of body and sickelinesse, I was not hable to goe through with that I intended. Therefore that you may not be deceiued of any thinge that was in the former aedicion: I haue caused the Printer to adde here in the ende, all those proper names that he had left out before he vnderstode or had knowledge that I coulde not finishe that I had begonne and purposed. This I thought good, gentle reader, to aduertise thee, that thou shouldest not thinke eyther negligence in the Printer for omitting any thynge, or slouthfulnesse in me for not perfourminge that, which my health woulde not suffer me.

The author's illness, according to this account, forestalled his adding a "great number of phrases" and thus enhancing the usefulness of the *Bibliotheca* as he had planned to do. His illness also accounts for an odd feature of this 1559 edition. At the end of the general dictionary is a list of proper names pertaining to gods, men, places, together with the apposite information on each, extending, however, only part way through the letter *A*. The author's intention of taking out all proper names and arranging them in a separate section was thus only well begun. Being unable to finish this part of the book, and being unwilling to omit the words already taken from the text of the *Bibliotheca*, Cooper, probably under pressure by the printer for copy, submitted the unfinished list. Not until the publication of his *Thesaurus*, six years later, did Cooper finish and publish his "boke" of proper names. There it appears as the *Dictionarium historicum et poeticum propria locorum et personarum vocabula breviter complectens.*

References have been made frequently in this discussion to Cooper's Latin address to the reader in the *Bibliotheca* of 1548. This address was reprinted, without change, in the subsequent editions of 1552 and 1559. It is the compiler's own carefully thought-out statement of his conception of the work, of the purpose it should serve, of the difficulties encountered, and in general of his aims and methods. Some résumé of the contents of this document will be, therefore, a fitting commentary on Cooper's work thus far.

After explaining that he had been persuaded by the printer Berthelet to carry on the lexicographical work begun by Elyot, Cooper anticipates the criticism that he, and Elyot before him, had labored for but a single nation and chiefly for its young people. His reply is that they have so wrought; and that is their special glory. They have sought not fame abroad; rather they have preferred to serve youth at home. These Cooper has striven to please, and these would profit most; but his book should be valuable to all the studious, old and young.

Some there are, however, who object to the use of dictionaries or vocabularies on the ground that words should be learned from reading approved authors. With those who offer such objections Cooper disagrees. He has preferred to take his stand with Varro and Perottus, with Calepine and Nizolius,[12] with Doletus and Stephanus. He has imitated the industry of these learned men before him who devoted themselves to the study of language and the making of dictionaries. These men are held in high esteem in the learned world; and why should not Cooper himself receive due desert? Has he not converted into the vernacular for English youth what is most useful in the work of these honored scholars?

It will be urged, no doubt, that Cooper has simply adapted the work of others to the native idiom, and that that has been an easy task. True, he has been helped by the labor of his predecessors, just as their burdens were lightened by the sweat of others before them. Conversion into the vernacular has been, however, a far more difficult task than to have compiled a dictionary in Latin only. The attempt to define the six hundred rare Latin words which he has found in the writings of Columella, Cato, Varro, Pliny, and others shows some of the difficulties he has encountered. Of these words, no one hitherto has supplied adequate examples to show their usage, and the reader has thus been left to his own judgment. Cooper's task has required that he supply the correct meaning of the words and describe them concisely in the vernacular so that the force of each word may be understood by schoolboys.

And this is not all. It might be easy to convert into the vernacular common and familiar words, such as *ago, fero, duco,* and the like; but to find illustrations of the great variety of usages, and to set down in English apt and intelligible meanings so as to keep the grace and idiom of both languages—this has been labor. How great the labor involved in such a task, those would know who compared the infinite riches and elegancies of the Latin language with the leanness and penury of the English tongue. The work of converting and adapting the Latin into English is of great moment.[13] Others following his example have converted Latin works into English, to the great benefit of the English nation.

Another part of the address is of especial interest. It is concerned with the language of arts, crafts, trades, and sciences—a problem which every lexicographer since Cooper's day has had to face and for which he has had to seek a solution. How, Cooper inquires, is the lexicographer to know and to record with assurance the names of the tools and instruments with which builders, farmers, weavers, barbers, sailors, and others work? How is one to know the names of parts of single instruments? Think of the variety of terms relating to the building craft alone, for example, or to navigation and sailing. What of the special language or jargon of any one of these groups? These are searching questions for the lexicographer.

Cooper's answer to these and similar inquiries is that he who would make a lexicon that would contain the answers to the questions proposed, a lexicon in which there would be nothing lacking, would need to call into his counsel all craftsmen in order to learn from them the names of things in each craft. As for himself, he has frequently resorted to carpenters, gardeners, weavers, farmers, and people in the country generally, to find out the nomenclature of the instruments with which they worked.[14] How far Cooper actually consulted the craftsmen in their special fields, we do not know. But there can be little doubt that his scheme was a profitable one for lexicographers.

In conclusion, Cooper states explicitly what has been his program and therefore his plan of procedure in the *Bibliotheca*. He has arranged in alphabetical order all Latin words, and such foreign words as had been usurped by Latin authors.[15] Barbarisms and words not of approved usage among classical writers he has rejected. Many words and phrases, distributed without order in the former text, he has diligently restored to their proper places. He has noted the gender and inflection of nouns; given more correctly the preterites of verbs. He has added several thousand words and has indicated the numerous meanings of much-used verbs. To each Latin term he has supplied the fitting and idiomatic native words in one heap, as it were, and in so great variety that his labor would serve not more to expedite rapid learning of the Roman language than to bring grace and elegance to the English. From Cicero and other classical writers he has supplied phrases and forms of speech illustrating the apt uses of words.[16] Proper names of deities, men, towns, and cities he has added from Stephanus and others. Finally, he has made an incredible number of corrections in orthography and in other respects.

The address to the reader paraphrased above may be regarded as Cooper's considered statement of his aims and of what he believed he had accomplished in his revision of the *Bibliotheca*. There is, however, a slight discrepancy between his stated aims and his achievements, or between the ideal in his mind and the reality in the printed text. His effort to eliminate barbarisms, or words not of established classical usage, for example, is only partially successful; and it is hard to demonstrate that his quest for technical terms employed in the arts, crafts, and sciences went beyond what was available in printed sources. But even in these attempts he deserves credit for recognition of the problems.

In many respects he shows genuine progress in lexicography. He was careful in his choice of authorities, as in Udall for illustrations from Terence, Robert Stephanus' Latin-French text for illustrative phrases and the same author's *Thesaurus* or *Elucidarius* for proper names, and William Turner on herbs. He improved the arrangement of entries, approaching nearer than Elyot had done to an alphabetical order. He gave attention to the inflection and gender of nouns, a grammatical feature neglected by Elyot. In the 1559 edition Cooper proposed and partially executed the innovation of printing the proper names as an independent part of the text. More than Elyot, Cooper emphasized the necessity of classical Latin and the value of idiomatic English and, in practice, at least, the desirability of a copious and varied vocabulary. These ideas resulted in the extension of English definitions and a wealth of new illustrations from classical sources.

A few examples from the *Bibliotheca* of 1545, the last revision by Elyot, and from the revised text of 1548 will best confirm these conclusions.

Elyot's *Bibliotheca* (1545)	Cooper's revision of *Bibliotheca* (1548)
Expers, tis, withoute any parte, lackynge experyence.	*Expers, ertis, om. g.* without any parte, lackyng experience, rude, ignoraunt.
Expers doloris, without peyne.	*Expers doloris,* without paine.
Expers lucis, without lyght.	*Expers lucis,* without lyght.
Expers mortis, neuer dyinge.	*Expers mortis,* neuer diynge.
	Expers corporis, that hath no bodie.
	Ne quis expers tuae liberalitatis fieret, that euery man myght be partetaker of your liberalitee.
	Expers linguae graecae, that hath no knowlage in the greeke tongue.
	Expers amoris gnati, not knowyng that his sonne was in loue.
	Laboris expers, that dooeth labour and trauayle.
	Expers fama et fortunis, he that hath loste his credite and all his goodes.
Explano, aui, are, to make playne.	*Explano, aui, are,* to make plaine, to declare, to make manifeste, to expounde.
	Explanare verba, to pronounce distinctly and playnelye.
Expleo, eui, ere, to fyll, fulfyll. Also to saciate, to comforte.	*Expleo, eui, ere,* to fyll, to fulfyll, to fyll up. Also to saciate, to comforte, to make perfect, to accomplyshe, to content, sometime to make emptie or ιoyde.
Exple animum curis, put all care out of thy mynde.	*Exple animum curis,* put all care out of thy mynde.
	Explere aliquem scribendo, to satisfie and fyll one with writtynge letters to him.
	Explere animum alicui, to content ones mynd.
	Explere annos ducentos, to lyue fulle two hundred yeres.
	Supremum diem expleuit, he died, he ended his laste daye.
	Susceptum munus explere, to fulfil

Elyot's *Bibliotheca* (1545)

Cooper's revision of *Bibliotheca* (1548)
a charge that one hath taken upon him.

Numerum explere, to fyll up the numbre.

Famem explere, to satisfie or stynte ones hunger. . . .

Libidinem suam explere, to do and accomplish his pleasure.

Rimas explere, to stop and fyll up chynkes.

Quod summam talenti attici expleret, which was of the iust value of a talent.

Explico, aui, are, to extende. also to unfolde. to declare, to telle or shewe a thynge playnely.

Explicat ensem. He draweth out his sword.

Explicat & coenas unica mensa duas: He maketh twoo suppers at one table. Also to bryng to passe.

Explica aestem meum, put me out of this fantasy or doubte.

Explico, explicas . . . aui, are, to extende, to unfolde, to desplaie, to declare, to tell or shewe a thynge playnely, to delyuer, to rydde out of trouble, to bryng to passe, to dispatch or make an ende of.

Explicat ensem, he draweth out his sworde.

Explicat et coenas vnica mensa duas, he maketh two suppers at one table.

Explica aestum meum, putte me out of this fantasie or doubt.

Explicant acies, agmen, uel exercitum imperatores, whan they in an open fielde sette their souldiours in araye redy to battayle.

Explicare alas, to sprede & open the winges.

Explicare naues, to set shippes in an order redy to fyght.

Explicare epistolam, to open a letter.

Iter commode explicui, I haue prosperously atchieued and made an end of my iourney.

Explicatam tibi rem dabo, I wyll dispatch the matter for you.

Da operam, vt te explices, endeuour to ryd and dispatche your selfe out of businesse.

In the case of *expleo*, the 1548 edition has four derivatives not in the earlier text; in *explano*, four; in *explico*, six. These, not listed above, make a total of fourteen new entries in the 1548 text. The examples above are, of course, selected; there are many entries in the two texts that are practically identical. But the chosen examples are typical of the augmentation. They show Cooper expanding the definitions by adding synonyms and new meanings and supplying numerous illustrative phrases, taken largely from Stephanus. This procedure is a means of affording plenteousness, or copiousness, and the possibility of varying. The principle thus exemplified is continued, as we shall see, in the *Thesaurus* of 1565.

CHAPTER VIII

Thomas Cooper's *Thesaurus linguae Romanae & Britannicae* (1565)

FROM 1549 to 1568, Thomas Cooper was master of Magdalen College School. As this period corresponds fairly closely with his lexicographical and literary labors, we may infer that the duties of the master were not especially burdensome. It should be noted, however, that the first and most important augmentation of Elyot's *Bibliotheca* was completed in 1548, and may possibly have brought him into notice as a person qualified for the mastership. At any rate he found time in the midst of his duties as schoolmaster to publish a continuation of Lanquet's *Chronicle* (1549), known afterwards as *Cooper's Chronicle*, to write *An Answer* in defense of Jewel (1562), to continue his revisions of the *Bibliotheca* (1552, 1559), and to push forward the compilation of his *Thesaurus*.

Although his position afforded opportunity for extramural work, Cooper labored under certain handicaps. One of these was ill health, which, as we have seen, forestalled a part of the work he had planned for the revision of the *Bibliotheca* of 1559.[1] Another handicap to his labors, and undoubtedly a source of great annoyance, was the behavior of his wife. Her profligacy is reflected in contemporary doggerel verses,[2] in the Martin Marprelate tracts,[3] and, in the seventeenth century, in the notes of Aubrey. The comment of William Pierce, the editor of the Marprelate tracts, sums up concisely the reputation of Mrs. Cooper. "Mrs. Cooper," he writes, "appears to have been a woman of ungovernable temper, one who in an excess of rage would cast his manuscripts in the fire,[4] and, still worse, was of a profligate character. Martin . . . refers

85

to the scandal which associated her with Dr. Day, Canon of Christ Church
. . . who had to be bound in £100 not to come near her." Despite his
marital troubles, the reported destruction of his manuscript, and other
difficulties, Cooper managed to complete and to get published, in 1565,
his great dictionary.

The title page runs thus:

Thesaurus linguae Romanae & Britannicae, tam accurate congestus, vt nihil pene in
eo desyderari possit, quod vel Latine complectatur amplissimus Stephani Thesaurus,
vel Anglice, toties aucta Eliotae Bibliotheca: opera & industria Thomae Cooperi Mag-
dalenensis . . . Accessit Dictionarium Historicum & poeticum propria vocabula Virorum, Mulierum, Sectarum, Populorum, Vrbium, Montium & Caeterorum locorum
complectens, & in his incundissimas & omnium cognitione dignissimas historias . . .
Impressum Londini. 1565.

Subsequent editions of the *Thesaurus* appeared in 1573, 1578, 1584,
and 1587. As these differed in no material respect from that of 1565, we
may devote our attention to this volume. Before detailed discussion,
however, it should be noted that Cooper's elevation in the Church was,
after the publication of his dictionary, fairly rapid. He rose successively
to be dean of Christ Church (1567), dean of Gloucester (1569), bishop
of Lincoln (1570), and bishop of Winchester (1584). It seems probable
that his work as a lexicographer was a factor in his preferment in the
Church.[5]

What are the major sources of the *Thesaurus*, or what is the relation of
this dictionary to its predecessors? The statement on the title page that
Cooper's *Thesaurus* contained, in Latin, almost as much matter as the
great Latin *Thesaurus* of Robert Stephanus and, in English, as much
as the augmented *Bibliotheca Eliotae* is, if intended as an acknowledgment of indebtedness, somewhat equivocal. Ordinarily, free borrowing
without references to sources, in this period, would have passed un-
heeded. It was, in fact, a common practice. But by virtue of his high
position in the Church and his becoming a figure in the Marprelate controversy, Bishop Cooper became a target of adverse criticism; and
from the time of Martin Marprelate, in the 1580's, to the present day,
Cooper has been charged with plagiarism in the compilation of his
Thesaurus. It is a curious fact, however, that the critics are not in agreement as to what lexicographers or dictionaries Cooper pilfered, and not
one of the critics is entirely correct in his charges.

The first recorded accusation which we have found against Cooper
appeared in the Marprelate tracts in the late 1580's. In the tract entitled
"Oh Read Ouer Dr. John Bridges," the author writes: "To go forward.
His lordship of Winchester [Bishop Thomas Cooper] is a great clerk;
for he hath translated his Dictionary called Cooper's Dictionary verba-

tim out of Robert Stephanus' *Thesaurus;* and ill fauoured, too, they say. But what do I speak of our Bishops learning." [6] And, elsewhere: "He was corrector to the printer in Fleetstreet, that printed Eliot's Diction- ary: Cooper translated a piece of Robert Stephanus his Thesaurus, and joined to the same with a few phrases, and so bereued the famous knight of his labours." [7] One may well dismiss the Marprelate charge as the repetition of idle gossip by a hostile and ill-informed writer.

In 1606 a variation of this charge was made by Francis Holyoke. Holyoke himself had been charged with appropriating Thomas Thomas's *Dictionarium.* His defense, in the address to the reader, was that many lexicographers before him had so proceeded. Even Cooper had frankly avowed that he had plucked his *Thesaurus* from that of Stephanus and the *Bibliotheca* of Elyot. This was apparently Holyoke's interpretation of a statement on the title page of the *Thesaurus.* In 1633, when Holyoke was again under fire for appropriating "Thomasius," he made a similar defense, asserting, however, that Cooper translated his *Thesaurus* from the Latin-German dictionary of Johannes Frisius.[8]

In the Preface to his Latin dictionary, in 1664—a Preface surveying the history of Latin lexicography—Francis Gouldman seems to combine the two statements of Holyoke. Gouldman writes: "The Reverend and Learned Cooper, Bishop of Lincoln, reserving still as a foundation Eliots and his own former Labours upon him, and making great use of Stephens Thesaurus and Frisius his Dictionary (insomuch that F. Holyoke saith, he Translated Frisius his German into English) put forth his Thesaurus." Anthony à Wood (*ca.* 1690) has a variant of Gouldman's statement. Wood (*op. cit.,* II, 609) refers to Cooper's *Thesaurus,* "the foundation of which was taken from sir Tho. Eliot's dictionary, and the materials for the most part, from Rob. Stevens's Thesaurus and Joh. Frisius's Latin and German Dictionary."

In 1693, Kennett writes of Cooper's *Thesaurus:*

Yet this mighty work is very little more than a pure Transcript of the *Dictionarium Gallicum* by Charles Stephens at Paris, 1553. I have collated them in most parts, and find them literally the same in allmost all words, and the direct order of them, and in every classic phrase; with this only difference, that those phrases are rendered in French by Stephens, and in English by Cooper: whose disingenuity is much the greater, because in his preface and Dedication, he mentions the *Bibliotheca* of Sir Tho. Eliot, and the *Thesaurus* of Rob. Stephens; but speaks not a word of this other Dictionary of Charles Stephens which was the copy (I assure you) that he transcrib'd verbatim.[9]

In substantial agreement with Kennett is Mayor, except that he rightly ascribes the Latin-French dictionary to Robert Stephanus, not Charles, who only saw it through the press. Mayor writes: "A very cursory comparison will suffice to prove that Robert Stephens's *Dictionarium Latino-Gallicum* was employed by Cooper in the construction of his *Thesaurus;* indeed the resemblance is so great, extending even to the arrangement of examples and mode of printing, that there can be no doubt that Stephens's text was the copy from which Henry Wykes printed *in aedibus quondam Tho. Bertheleti.*"

How can we explain the diversity of opinion concerning the sources of Cooper's *Thesaurus,* for a period of three hundred years? Analysis of the expressed opinions reveals some of the reasons for the confusion. Cooper's own statements on the title page and in the dedication are misleading, whether he so intended them to be or not. His own oblique suggestion was repeated, with exaggeration and without verification, by Marprelate and by Francis Holyoke. We may add to the error of repetition without verification, that of writing with only partial information, as in the assertion of Holyoke, in 1633, that Cooper translated his book wholly from Frisius; and the opinions of Kennett and Mayor that Cooper based his *Thesaurus* wholly on the Latin-French dictionary of Stephanus. Apparently no one considered all the possibilities. The result is generalizations that do not reveal the truth about Cooper's sources and that reflect little credit on his critics.

Since there is confusion of long standing with respect to Cooper's procedure and to the sources of his dictionary, it is imperative that his case be reopened. We have referred above to the compiler's statement on the title page implying a close relationship of his *Thesaurus* to the volumes of Elyot and Stephanus. In the dedicatory epistle to the Earl of Leicester, Cooper is more explicit in his reference to Stephanus. He maintains that students will find in his *Thesaurus* not only a satisfactory interpretation of each Latin term in the vernacular but also numerous phrases and sentences collected from the very ample *Thesaurus* of Robert Stephanus, illustrating from approved authors the various uses of each term. Here is a specific acknowledgment of debt to Stephanus' *Thesaurus,* but to no other dictionary by the same author.

As to the relation of Cooper's *Thesaurus* to the *Bibliotheca Eliotae,* the only statement we have, until the 1587 edition of the *Thesaurus,* is that already referred to on the title page. Although this is an implied rather than a direct acknowledgment of indebtedness, Cooper doubtless thought, not without reason, that it was adequate. For a period of almost twenty years, he had served as editor and reviser of the *Bibliotheca,* and, as we have seen, had vastly augmented and improved Elyot's dictionary. He had, in fact, acquired a proprietary interest in the contents of his predecessor's work, just as Wykes, the successor of Berthelet, had acquired the right of printing the volume, with changed title if he desired.

Cooper's right to base his work on the *Bibliotheca* seems then justifiable. Finally, on the reverse of the title page of the 1587 *Thesaurus,* Cooper makes ample if somewhat belated acknowledgment of his debt to Elyot. Having recounted his work in three times revising the *Bibliotheca* and then in compiling the *Thesaurus,* Cooper states that, as everyone knows, he has been aided in the latter in no moderate degree (*non mediocriter*) by the labors of Elyot. It is fitting, Cooper thinks, that this fact should be noted lest, through change of title, the memory of the unusual industry of that noble man should perish, or Cooper himself be deservedly esteemed as ungrateful.[10]

That Cooper did use freely the materials of the revised *Bibliotheca* is evident on every page of the *Thesaurus.* Characteristic of the matter retained by Cooper are the Latin terms followed by a group of English words or phrases, copious equivalents of the Latin, as under *conduco, consecro, consector, consilium,* and *constituo.* Three of these, without the examples of usage, are as follows:

Conduco . . . To bring with: to hire: to bie: to take an house or lande. Also to gather or assemble in one place: to conuert: to take in hand to doe a worke or businesse for hyre or wages. And in the third person it is to profite.
Consecro . . . to dedicate or consecrate: to make holy: to make a thing remaine: to put in remembrance by writing. Also to attribute to.
Consilium . . . Counsaile, iudgement, or aduice: a purpose or intent: a pollicie: an appoyntment.

Except for slight differences in spelling and punctuation, this part of the entries is the same in both volumes. But the *Thesaurus* has for *conduco* 18 examples of usage, the *Bibliotheca* 10; for *consecro,* the *Thesaurus* 34, the *Bibliotheca* 6; for *consilium,* the *Thesaurus* 135, the *Bibliotheca* 19. These transcribed entries show not only the nature of Cooper's dependence on Elyot but also one method of expansion—that of supplying numerous additional examples of meaning and usage from a source other than the *Bibliotheca Eliotae.*

Although Cooper was greatly obligated to the *Bibliotheca,* the charges that he plagiarized Elyot are farfetched. With respect to his relation to Robert Stephanus the problem is much more complex. Between 1531 and 1552 Stephanus published five different dictionaries, all of which were popular,[11] but only two of which concern us here. The first, published in 1531, is the *Dictionarium seu Latinae linguae thesaurus,* with Latin terms commonly interpreted in French. A second and augmented edition of this work appeared in 1536, and a third in 1543. All French interpretations were omitted from the third edition, and thereafter Stephanus' *Thesaurus* was Latin throughout.

In the meantime Robert Stephanus published, in 1538, his *Dictio-*

narium Latino-Gallicum, or Latin-French dictionary, based in large part upon the *Thesaurus.* New impressions appeared in 1543 and in 1544–45; a second edition in 1546, and a third in 1552. This last edition was reissued with a different title in 1561. As the first two editions of Stephanus' *Thesaurus* had many French definitions for the Latin, it is not improbable that this work was sometimes confused with the Latin-French dictionary proper. Cooper's contemporaries, such as the writers of the Marprelate tracts, may have made this mistake. But, as we have seen, Cooper himself was thoroughly familiar with the Latin-French dictionary, and knew beyond the shadow of a doubt the difference between this text and Stephanus' *Thesaurus.* It is to the latter work, however, that Cooper acknowledges indebtedness, making no mention of the Latin-French dictionary of the same compiler, or of the Latin-German dictionary of Frisius; [12] and yet to either of these, Cooper's *Thesaurus* is nearer in content and arrangement of matter than to Stephanus' *Thesaurus.*

This statement is supported by the block of entries, under *conferre,* from corresponding sections of the four texts.

Stephanus' *Thesaurus* (1531)

Conferre, pro Mutare. Ovid. 4. Metamorphoses.
Vulgatos taceo, dixit, pastoris amores.
Daphnidis Idaei, quem Nymphe pellicis ira.
Contulit in saxum.
Aes conferre. Ovid. 4. Fast.
Falso conferre aliquid in aliquem. Cic. 5. Fam. 5.
Amorem conferre. Plaut. Curcul. 1. 1. 28
Ita tuum conferto amorem semper si sapis, ne id quod ames, populus si sciat, tibi sit
 probro.
Conferre se in fugam. Cic. pro Cecinna.
Amorem conferre alicui. Propert. lib. 2. eleg. 25.
Animum alio. Terent. Heaut. 2. 4.
Haec ubi immutata est, illi suum animum alio conferunt. Id est alios amant.
Animum ad fodiendos puteos. Hirtius de Bell. Alex. lib. 4.

Stephanus' *Dictionarium* (1538)

Conferre, pro Mutare. Ovid. Muer
Falso conferre aliquid in aliquem. Cic.
Amorem conferre alicui. Propert. Donner son amour a aucun, L'aimer.
Ita tuum conferto amorem semper si sapis, Ne id, &c. Plaut. Mets, ou iecte ton amour
 en tel lieu, &c.
Animum alio. Terent. Oster son amour d'aucun, & en aimer un autre.
Animum ad fodiendos puteos. Hirtius. Appliquer son esprit, Mettre son entente,
 S'addoner.

Frisius' *Dictionarium* (1556)

Conferre, pro Mutare. Ovid. Verwandeln/ Verenderen in ein andere gestalt.
Falso conferre aliquid in aliquem. Cic.
Amorem conferre alicui. Propert. Liebe an einen legen / oder einen lieb haben.

Ita tuum conferto amorem semper si sapis, Ne id, &c. Plaut. Wend dein liebe dahin/&c. oder/ Leg dein liebe also an.

Animum alio. Terent. Sein gemut anderschwo hin keeren oder wenden / und ein andere lieb haben.

Animum ad fodiendos puteos. Hirtius. Sein sinn und gedanck auff fod zegraben legen / Sich geben auff fod zegraben.

Cooper's Thesaurus (1565)

Conferre, pro Mutare. Ovid. To chaunge.

Falso conferre aliquid in aliquem. Cic. To attribute falsely to one.

Amorem conferre alicui. Propert. To loue: to cast his loue vpō.

Ita tuum conferto amorem semper si sapis, Ne id &c. Plaut. So bestow or employ thy loue, &c.

Animum alio. Terent. To turne his minde from one and cast it to another.

Animum ad fodiendos puteos. Hirtius. To set or bende hys minde: to minde to digge pittes.[13]

With these excerpts before us and with the chronology of the various texts in mind, we may state, without giving the basic details supplied by the excerpts themselves, some of the obvious conclusions: Stephanus' Latin *Thesaurus* is the source of his Latin-French dictionary, which in turn is the source of Frisius' Latin-German dictionary; and one or both of these bilingual dictionaries stand as the source of Cooper's *Thesaurus*. This conclusion eliminates Stephanus' *Thesaurus* as a direct source of Cooper in this and many other entries, and with it the charge that Cooper plagiarized Stephanus' *Thesaurus*. But what shall we say of Cooper's acknowledgment of indebtedness to this *Thesaurus?* For the answer to this question we must wait.

We have still to consider the relationships of Stephanus' Latin-French dictionary, Frisius' Latin-German dictionary, and Cooper's *Thesaurus*. The following excerpts, under *conficio*, will further our understanding.

Stephanus' *Dictionarium* (1538)	Frisius' *Dictionarium* (1556)	Cooper's *Thesaurus* (1565)
Conficio, conficis, pen. corr. confeci. pen. prod. confectum, conficere, Ex Con & Facio, idem significat quod facere vel perficere. Cic. Acheuer & parfaire.	*Conficio, conficis pen. corr. confeci, pen. prod. confectum, conficere, Ex Con & Facio, idem significat quod facere vel perficere.* Cic. Machen und aussmachen / Vollbringen.	*Conficio, conficis, p. cor. confeci. pen. pr. confectum, conficere, Ex Con & Facio, idem significat quod facere vel perficere.* Ci.
		To destroy or slea: to grieve, vex or torment: to perform: to finish or dispatch: to make an ende of: to bring to passe: to explicate or declare: to gather money: to breake: to consume or waste: to

Stephanus' *Dictionarium* (1538)	Frisius' *Dictionarium* (1556)	Cooper's *Thesaurus* (1565)
		make: to chawe meate: to digest.
Conficere exercitatione. Cic.	*Conficere exercitatione.* Cic.	*Conficere exercitatione.* Cic. By exercise to bring to passe.
Magna cura, multa opera, & labore conficere aliquid. Cic.	*Magna Cura, multa opera & labore conficere aliquid.* Cic.	*Magna cura, multa opera & labore conficere aliquid.* Cic.
Vi manuque conficere aliquid. Cic.	*Vi manuque conficere aliquid.* Cic.	*Vi manuque conficere aliquid.* Cic. To doe by force and strong hande.
Amanter diligenterque conficere aliquid. Cic.	*Amanter diligenterque conficere aliquid.* Cic.	*Amanter diligenterque conficere aliquid.* Ci. To dispatch.
Conficere nucem. Plin. Rompre, Casser, Mascher.	*Conficere nucem.* Plin. Ein nussz zerbrechen / oder zerknütschen / oder zerküwen.	*Conficere nucem.* Plin. To breake or knacke a nutte.
Conficere hominem. Cic. Meurdrir Assomer, Tuer.	*Conficere hominem.* Cic. Einen aussmachen / umbbringen / oder toden.	*Conficere hominem.* Cic. To murther or kill.
Duodecim propugnatores totidem sagittarum confecit ictibus. Il a tué.	*Duodecim propugnatores totidem sagittarum confecit ictibus.* Sueton. Hat er umbracht.	*Duodecim propugnatores totidem sagittarum confecit ictibus.* Sueton. He killed twelve at .XII. shootes.
Ignes conficiunt sylvas. Lucret. Bruslent & consument.	*Ignes conficiunt sylvas.* Lucret. Verbrennend od verzeerend.	*Ignes conficiunt sylvas.* Lucret. Burne and consume.
. . . .	. . . .	. . . .
Diem extremum morte conficere. Cic. Mourir.	*Diem extremum morte conficere.* Cic. Den letsten tag vollbringen oder enden / Starben.	*Diem extremum morte conficere.* Cic. To die.
Escas conficere dicuntur dentes intimi. Cic. Mascher & comminuer ou rompre bien menu.	*Escas conficere dicuntur dentes intimi.* Cic. Zerbeyssen / keüwen.	*Escas conficere dicuntur dentes intimi.* Cicero. To chawe or worke the meate.
Exercitum. Cic. Faire amas des gensdarms, Lever un armee, Dresser sus.	*Exercitum.* Cic. Ein kreigszeug versamlen / Knacht annemmen.	*Exercitum.* Cic. To levie or gather an armie.
Facinus. Cic. Commettre quelque cas meschant.	*Facinus.* Cic. Ein frafel oder schandtliche thaat begon.	*Facinus.* Cic.
Famam. Cic. Bailler bruit.	*Famam.* Cic. Ein geschrey machen oder aufbringen.	*Famam.* Cic. To procure a name or brute.

Stephanus' *Dictionarium* (1538)	Frisius' *Dictionarium* (1556)	Cooper's *Thesaurus* (1565)
Flagitium. Terent. Faire quelque meschancete.	*Flagitium.* Terent. Ein gross laster od ein grosse schand begon.	*Flagitium.* Cic. To commit some naughtie deede.
Funera iusta. Caes. Faire & parfaire les obseques d'un trespasse.	*Funera iusta.* Caesar. Eerlich und wol bestatten oder begrebnuss begon.	*Funera iusta.* Caesar. To make ones funerall.
Iter. Caesar. Parfaire son chemin.	*Iter.* Caesar. Sein reiss vollbringen.	*Iter.* Caesar. To dispatch or go a iourney.

Analysis of these entries leads to three generalizations: (1) The ample general definition under the first entry in Cooper's *Thesaurus* derives neither from Stephanus' *Dictionarium* nor from Frisius, but has been carried over by Cooper from his revised *Bibliotheca Eliotae*. (2) Cooper's *Thesaurus* shows a number of English equivalents of Latin phrases for which there is no corresponding source in Stephanus' *Dictionarium* or in Frisius. (3) In each entry in which the three texts show corresponding vernacular interpretations, Cooper's *Thesaurus* derives in most instances from Stephanus.[14] On the basis of these generalizations, for which there is much more supporting evidence than space permits us to cite, we may conclude that Stephanus' Latin-French dictionary is one main source of Cooper's *Thesaurus*. Cooper, in other words, when compiling his *Thesaurus*, continued to draw heavily from Robert Stephanus' *Dictionarium Latino-Gallicum*, early editions of which he and Elyot had used in the augmentation of the *Bibliotheca Eliotae*.

This conclusion does not, however, rule out Frisius as a subordinate source of Cooper's *Thesaurus*. To return to the illustrations above, we find that, in the interpretations of *conficere nucem* and *escas conficere*, Cooper is as near to Frisius as to Stephanus, if not nearer. Searching the texts more widely, we find a number of examples which, in my opinion, show Cooper drawing from Frisius rather than from Stephanus. In the examples below, the entire entry from Stephanus' *Dictionarium Latino-Gallicum* is given first, followed by only the German portion of Frisius' entry and the English portion of Cooper's. The Latin in all three texts is the same, except that Cooper and Frisius abbreviate *Ovidius*.

Stephanus' *Dictionarium*	Frisius' *Dictionarium*	Cooper's *Thesaurus*
Ore suo cibos conferre. Quintil. Comme font les oiseaulx qui baillent la besquee a leurs petits.	... Mit dem schnabel zeessen geben oder speysen wie die vogel jre jungen.	... To feede with the bill, as byrdes doe their yong.
In medium singulos denarios in singulos talos conferre.	... Alles in spil setzen oder in die schantz	... To holde or lay downe a penny for

Stephanus' *Dictionarium*	Frisius' *Dictionarium*	Cooper's *Thesaurus*
Sueton. Bailler, Coucher, Mettre sur le ieu.	schlahen Alle wurff ein pfennig schlahen.	everye bone or dye, in play.
Pedem. Plaut. S'approcher.	... Zuhinston oder Zuhintratten Nahen.	... To approach or come nie to.
Rationes conferre. Cic. Compter ensemble & uenir a compte.	... Miteinanderen rechnen zu einer rechnung kommen.	... To cast account, or reckon with one.
Rem in pauca. Plaut. Abbreger, Despescher.	... Kurtz machen oder mit kurtzen worten aufrichten.	... To make short, to conclude in few words.[15]
Voluntatem conferre in aliquem. Cic. Mettre son affection a aucun.	... Sein gunst an einen legen Zu eim einen guten willen haben.	... To set his good will upon one.
Conferre se totum ad amicitiam alicuius. Cic. S'addoner du tout a aimer aucun.	... Sich gantz und gar in eines freundtschafft geben.	... To applie himself wholly to ones friendship.
Conficere nucem. Plin. Rompre, Casser, Mascher.	... Ein nussz zerbrechen oder zerknütschen oder zerküwen.	... To breake or knacke a nutte.[16]
Conferre se ad umbram arboris. Ovidius. Se mettre a l'ombre d'un arbre.	... Ovid. Under einen baum ann schatten gon.	... Ovid. To go under the shadow of a tree.[17]
Conficere ambulationem pomeridianam in aliquo loco. Cic. Se y pourmener.	... Ein spatzier oder abentgang thun Sich nach mittag erspatzieren.	... To walke in the after noone, or to make his after noones walke in.[18]
Permagna pecunia ex ea re confici potest. Cic. Il y a bien a gaigner. Bud.[19]	... Es mag da ein gross galt zewagen bracht werden.	... A great substance may be made of that.
Tabulas. Cic. Faire registre de ce qu'on a faict & prins.	... Ein rodel oder register machen dess eynnemmens und aussgabens.	... To make a reckening booke of things received and layde out.
Pestem hominibus haec conferunt. Columel. Engendrent la peste, ou apportent.	... Dise ding machend oder bringend ein pestilentz.	... These things engender and bring pestilence among men.
Castris collatis. Silius. Mis uis a uis.	... Die lager gegen einanderen geschlagen.	... Their campes being pitched one over right agaynst the other.
Animum alio. Terent. Oster son amour d'aucun, & en aimer un autre.	... Sein gemut anderschwo hin keeren oder wenden und ein andere lieb haben.	... To turne his minde from one and cast it to another.[20]

In these illustrative entries the English phrasing of Cooper is, in my opinion, nearer to the German of Frisius than to the French of Stephanus; Cooper and Frisius write *Ovid.* where Stephanus has *Ovidius,* and both omit *Bud.*, which appears in Stephanus; finally Cooper changes certain English entries, which had appeared in his revisions of the *Bibliotheca*, apparently to conform to the corresponding German entries in Frisius.

It is evident, of course, that Stephanus' *Dictionarium Latino-Gallicum* as a common source of Frisius' Latin-German dictionary and Cooper's *Thesaurus* would account for a great many similarities in the latter two. But whenever Frisius and Cooper differ from Stephanus and agree with each other, then we need another explanation. And the obvious one, as Frisius' dictionary is earlier than Cooper's *Thesaurus* in date of compilation, is that Cooper is drawing from Frisius. In other words, the evidence shows beyond a reasonable doubt that Cooper used Frisius' Latin-German dictionary as one of his sources. Although he probably consulted the German's work constantly, the *Thesaurus* is by no means a mere translation of Frisius, as Holyoke asserted. The Frisius is a minor source, which sometimes determined Cooper's English phrasing.

The relationships of the Stephanus-Frisius-Cooper texts may now be restated. Stephanus' own *Thesaurus* is the source of his *Dictionarium Latino-Gallicum*, the latter text having omitted many Latin phrases of the original and abridged many others, and, for most of those used, having given the French equivalents. In this form the *Dictionarium Latino-Gallicum* becomes the direct source of Frisius' dictionary. The German compiler acknowledges his indebtedness, and comparison of the texts confirms the truth of his acknowledgment.[21] Stephanus' *Dictionarium* is also a major source of Cooper's *Thesaurus*, Cooper having adopted his pattern after the 1552 version of the *Dictionarium*, and having borrowed from this more examples of meaning and usage than from any other volume.[22] But here the relationships become much more complex because Cooper also derives some definitions and interpretations from Frisius.

To summarize: in the compilation of his *Thesaurus linguae Romanae et Britannicae* (1565), Thomas Cooper used as a model and a main source Robert Stephanus' *Dictionarium Latino-Gallicum* (1552), the Latin part of which is an abridgment of the same compiler's *Thesaurus linguae Latinae*. Into the framework of this pattern Cooper introduced considerable matter which he, as reviser, had thrice employed in augmentation of Elyot's *Bibliotheca*; he also drew a number of definitions and illustrations from the German of Johannes Frisius' *Dictionarium Latino-Germanicum* (1556). In addition to these sources, Cooper translated a large number of Latin phrases, which, though in the text of

A page of Robert Stephanus' Dictionarium Latino-Gallicum, 1552, from a copy in the British Museum; and a page in Thomas Cooper's Thesaurus, 1565, in the University of Texas Library; selected so comparisons can be made (two pages following)

Valde bona conditio si fuerit,fortaſſe non omittam. Cic. *Si le parti eſt fort bon.*

Controuerſiæ conditio. Quintil.

Pacis conditio cum aliquo.Cic.

Præſentis diſcriminis conditio. Quintil.

Petitionum conditio.Quintil.

Nulla conditione.Cic *Par nul moyen.*

℃Accedere ad conditionem & pactionem.Cic.

Accipere conditionem.Cic.Vide A C C I P I O.

Conditionibus accipere populos in ſocietatem.Liu. A *cer- tains pactes,ou charges cy conditions.*

Ad aliquam conditionem adducere aliquem. Balbus Ci- ceroni.

Aſtringere aliquem ſuis conditionibus.Cic.

Audire conditionem.Ouid.

Capere conditionem,& In conditionem.Vide C A P I O.

Dare alicuius rei conditionem alicui.Cic.

Ad conditionem deſcendere.Cælius Ciceroni.

Ferre conditionem.Plaut. *Faire une offre cy parti, Offrir un parti.*

Conditio noua & luculenta fertur per me interpretem. Terentius.

Ferre côditiones,eſt victoris & ſuperioris . Accipere con- ditiones,victi Cic.

Conditiones ferre,leges imponere Cic.*Faire les offres.*

Fugere à conditionibus. Cic. *Ne point tenir les pactions qu'on a accordé,Se partir de l'offre,cy ne le uouloir entretenir.*

Manere in conditione.Cic.   Manet conditio.Cic.

Mutare conditionem.Quintil.

Offerre conditionem pacis, apud Liuium. *Offrir les moyens de paix.*

Perducere aliquem ad ſuas conditiones.Cic.

Producere aliquem conditionibus.Cic.

Proponere conditionem ſupplicii alicui.Cic.

Iniquam conditionem recipere Quintil.

Repudiare æquiſſimam conditionem Cic. *Refuſer un parti treſequitable,cy qui n'eſt point plus auātageux à l'un qu'à l'autre.*

Reſpuere conditionem aliquam.Cic.

Stare conditionibus.Cic *Tenir les pactions qu'on a faictes.*

Statuere conditionem ſibi.Cic.

In eandem conditionem vocari.Cælius Ciceroni.

Vti conditione alicuius. Cic. *Ne refuſer point l'offre, Accepter ſon offre.*

Conditione tua non vtar.Caius.

℃Conditione pro Creatura ſæpe vſurpauit Tertullianus.

Conditionâlis,& hoc conditionâle pen prod.Adiectiuû vt Pars conditionalis Martianus. *Conditionelle.*

Contractus conditionalis.Vlpian. *Vn contract conditionel.*

Conditionâliter,pen.corr.Aduerbium.Paulus. *Conditionelle- ment,Soubs condition.*

Condus,condî,maſcul. gen. Plaut. *Celuy qui ha la charge de ſerrer cy garder les biens de ſon maiſtre,Deſpenſier.*

Condoceo,côndoces,pen.cor.condôcui,condôctû, con- docêre.Hirtius.*Enſeigner,Apprendre,Inſtruire.*

Condocefacio,condocefacis,penul.corr. condocefêci, pen. prod.condocefactum,condocefâcere,Idem.Cic.

Vtamur domitis & condocefact animalibus.Cic. *Qui ſont appriuoiſees.*

Condoleo,côndoles,pen.corr.côdolui,condolêre.Plaut. *Eſtre malade,ou fort malade.*

Caput condolet.Tibul.

Condoluit caput de vento.Plautus. *Le uent m'a faict mal en la teſte.*

Corpus condoluit tentatum frigore.Horat.

Si pes condoluit,ſi dens,ferre non poſſumus.Cic.

Condoleſco,condoleſcis,condolêſcere.Cic.Idem.

Condono,condônas,pen.prod.condonâre.Plaut. *Donner, Dare & condonare.*

℃Condono te.Plaut.

Condonare alicui munuſculum.Cic.

Condonare aliquem pecuniam, debitum, &c. Plaut. *Luy remettre ou quicter une debte.*

Condonare pecunias debitoribus.Cic.

℃Condonare peccatum Salluſt. *Pardonner.*

Remittere alicui & condonare animaduerſionem & ſup- plicium.Vatinius Ciceroni.

Condonâtus,pen.prod Participium à Condonor:vt Con- donatum iudicium alicui. Cic. *Le iugement par lequel le ne- abſoult ou condamne quelqu'un en faueur d'un autre, ſans regar- der au droict.*

℃Condonatus.Plin.iunior. *A qui on a pardonné.*

Condonâtio,Verbale Cic.*Donation, Largeſſe.*

Condormio, condormis, condormiui , condormitum, pen.prod.condormîre.Plaut.*Dormir auec d'autres.*

Condormiſco,condormiſcis,condormiſcere.Plaut. Idem.

Condryllon, ſiue Condrylle , Herba . Plin. *De la cicorée ſauuage.*

Conduco, condûcis pen. prod conduxi,côductum,con- dûcere Plaut. *Emmener, Mener auec ſoy.*

℃Conducere,Congregare.Cic. Virgines in vnum locum conduxerunt *ils aſſemblé en un lieu.*

Exercitus in vnum conducere.Tacit.

Partes conducere in vnum.Lucret.

℃Conducere.Plaut *Acheter.*

Nimium magno conducere.Cic.*Acheter trop cher.*

℃Côducere aliquem.Plaut. *Louer aucun a faire quelque choſe.*

Aliquem ad cædem faciendam conducere.Cic.

Hortum conducere.Cic.   Domum conducere.Cic.

Alicui locum in proximo conducere.Cic.

Nauigium conducere.Horat.

Conducere mercede Cic.

Conducere nauem.Plaut. *Louer,ou prendre a louage.*

℃Conducere, etiam dicitur is qui pretium pro re aliqua facienda Iulianus Iureconſultus. *Entreprendre quel- que beſongne a faire pour quelque pris.*

Ad pecuniam numeratam conducere. Caius *A l'argent.*

Redemptor qui columnam illam de Cotta & de Torqua- to conduxerat faciendam.Cic.Id eſt,à Cotta,&c.

Multitudo conducta.Cic.*Aſſemblee de mercenaires.*

℃Conducit,in tertiis perſonis, pro Vtile eſt. Plaut. Cic. *Vtile cy prouffitable,Il duit,il eſt duiſante.*

Ea maxime conducunt,quæ ſunt rectiſſima.Cic.

Neque homini infanti aut impotenti iniuſtè facta condu- cunt.Cic.

Conducit hoc tuæ laudi.Cic.

Propoſito conducere res dicitur . Horat . *Qui conuient ou propos.*

Rationibus noſtris conducit id fieri.Cic.

Conducit hoc Reip.rationibus.Cic.

Saluti tuæ conducunt.Cic.

Conducunt hæc ad ventris victum.Plaut.

In rem quod rectè conducat tuam.Plaut.

Conductus, Participium. Plaut. Nummo ſum conductus. *Ie ſuis loué.*

Conductus mercede diurna Horat. *Mercenaire.*

Conductus ſum coctum.Plaut.

Auxilia regum in vnum conducta.Tacit. *Aſſemblez.*

In vnum conducti.Tacit.

Bella côducta , dicuntur bella militû mercenarioru. Sil.

Conducta nauis.Terent.

Nummi conducti Horat *Argent prins a uſure,ou a intereſt.*

Conducta opera alicuius.Plaut.

Operæ conductæ.Cic.

Telæ côductæ.Tibul.   Sccere tellure conducta Virgil.

Teſtes conducti.Ouid.   Torus conductus.Ouid.

Conducta dicta ad fallaciam.Plaut.

Conductum,Subſtantiuum:vt Habere aliquid côducti.Cic. *Quelque petit louage.*

Conductor, Verbale. Cic. *Qui loue ou prend a louage aucun pour faire quelque beſongne. C'eſt auſſi celuy qui entreprend quelque be- ſongne a faire pour quelque pris.*

Conductio,Verbale.Cic.*Louage.*

Conducibilis,& hoc conducibile, penul.corr. Plaut. *Vtile cy prouffitable.*

Vtile & conducibile.Author ad Herennium.

Conductitius, Adiectiuum.Plaut.*Qui eſt loué.*

Temporum conditione aliquid mutari. Quintil. with the ſtate of time.

Victoriæ conditio. Cic.   Conditio vitæ. Cic.

Mortalis conditio vitæ. Cic.

Eaſdem vitæ conditiones non perferre. Cic.

Sequi aliquam vitæ conditione. Cic. To folow a maner of life.

Vuendi conditio. Horat.   Bona conditio. Horat.

Communis. Horat.   Dulcis. Horat.

Fœda. Horat.   Humana. Cic.

Infima conditio & fortuna ſeruorum. Cic.

Iniqua. Cic.   Inſidioſiſſima. Plin.   Triſtis. Claud.

¶ Aequa conditione cauſam dicere. Cic. when one hath equalitie with an aduerſarie in pleadyng.

Iniqua conditione cauſam dicere. Cic. when one hath moze aduauntage then the other.

Commodiore conditione eſſe dicuntur prædia. Cic. Fermes, not very chargeable.

Meliore conditione eſt ſenex quàm adoleſcens. Cic.

Longè alia conditione eſſe ac cæteri. Vatinius Ciceroni. To be in ſtate farre diuers from other men.

Conuellere conditionem amicitiæ. Cic.

Excutere conditionem alicuius. Ouid. To examine ones ſtate diligently.

Facere diſparem conditionem. Cic. Unlike ſtate.

Mortali conditione generari. Cic. To be bozne moztall.

Ea conditione nati ſumus, vt nihil quod homini accidere poſſie, recuſare debeamus. Cic. we be bozne in ſuch condition that.

Immortalium poſtulare. Cic.

Preuidere conditioni ciuium contra periculoſiſſimas hominum potentias. Cic.

¶ Conditio. Plautus. An offer oz condition in a couenant.

Luculenta conditio. Plaut. A great oz large offer.

Ea conditione dare aliquid. Cecinna Ciceroni. To giue under that condition.   Sub ea conditione. Cic.

Optima conditione prædia. Vide I V s. Cic. Fermes pziuileged, oz charged with nothyng.

Valde bona conditio ſi fuerit, fortaſſe non omittam. Cic. If the offer ſhall be very good.

Controuerſiæ conditio. Quintil.

Pacis conditio cum aliquo. Cic.

Præſentis diſcriminis conditio. Quintil.

Nulla conditione. Cic. In no meanes.

¶ Accedere ad conditionem & pactionem. Cic. To agree to.

Accipere conditionem. Cic. Vide A C C I P I O.

Conditionibus accipere populos in ſocietatem. Liu. Under certayne couenantes oz conditions.

Ad aliquam cōditionem adducere aliquem. Balbus Ciceroni. To perſuade to a certayne condition.

Aſtringere aliquem ſuis conditionibus. Cic. To wzappe in ſuche couenantes and conditions as he will himſelfe.

Capere conditionem, & In conditionem. Vide C A P I O.

Dare alicuius rei conditionem alicui. Cic. To offer the conditiō.

Ad conditionem deſcendere. Cælius Cicer. To condeſcende to.

Conditio noua & luculenta fertur per me interpretem. Terentius. Is offered.

Ferre conditiones, eſt victoris & ſuperioris: Accipere conditiones, victi. Cic. To apoynte the couenantes.

Conditiones ferre, leges imponere. Cicer. To apoynte the couenantes.

Fugere à conditionibus. Cic. Not to keepe couenantes.

Manere in conditione. Cic.   Manet conditio. Cic.

Mutare conditionem. Quintil.

Offerre conditionem pacis, apud Liuium. To offer meanes of peace.

Perducere aliquem ad ſuas conditiones. Cic. To bzyng to ſuche conditions as he will himſelfe.

Producere aliquem conditionibus. Cic. To delay with offers.

Proponere conditionem ſupplicij alicui. Cic.

Iniquam conditionem recipere. Quintil. Nothyng reaſonable.

Repudiare æquiſſimam conditionem. Cic. To refuſe a very indifferent offer.   Reſpuere conditionem aliquam. Cic.

Stare conditionibus. Cic. To ſtande to couenantes.

Statuere duriorem conditionē ſibi. Ci. To make an agreement ſmally to his owne aduantage.

In eandem conditionem vocari. Cælius Ciceroni.

Vt conditione alicuius. Cic. Not to refuſe his offer.

¶ Conditionem pro Creatura ſæpe vſurpauit Tertullian.

Conditionalis, & hoc conditionāle, pen. prod. Adiectiuum. Perteyning to condition oz offer. vt, Pars cōditionalis. Martianus. Contractus conditionalis. Vlpian. A conditionall bargayne.

Conditionaliter, penul. corr. Aduerbium. Paulus. Conditionally.

Condus, condi, m. gen. Plaut. A ſtewarde, oz he that kepeth the ſtoze of houſeholde.

Condoceo, cōndoces, pen. cor. condōcui, condoctum, condocēre. Hirtius. To teach.

Condocefacio, condocefacis, penuil. corr. condocefēci, pen. prod. condocefactū, condocefacere, Idem. Cic. To make to know. Vramur domitis & condocefactis animalibus. Cicer. Tamed and taught to doe thinges.

Condoleo, cōndoles, pen. corr. condōlui, condolēre. Plaut. To be very ſicke oz much payned.

Caput condolet. Tibul. His head aketh foze.

Condoluit caput de vento. Plautus. The winde made his heade ake.

Si pes condoluit, ſi dens, ferre non poſſumus. Cic.

Condoleſco, condoleſcis, condolēſcere. Cic. Idem.

Condono, cōndōnas, pen. prod. codonāre. Plaut. To giue: to fozgeuei to pardon.   Dare & condonare. Cic.

Condonare alicui munuſculum. Ci. To geue a pzeſent.

¶ Condono te. Plaut. I pardonne thee.

Condonare aliquem pecuniam, debitum, &c. Plaut. To fozgeue one money, &c.

Condonare pecuniam debitoribus. Cic.

¶ Condonare peccatum. Salluſt. To pardon an offence.

Remittere alicui & condonare animaduerſionem & ſupplicium. Vatinius Ciceroni. To remitte and pardon.

Condonātus, pen. prod. Participium à Condonor. Fozgeuē: pardoned. vt, Condonatum iudicium alicui. Cicer. A iudgement wherein without regarde of right, the iudge condemneth oz quiteth fez fauour of one.

Condonatio, onis, f. g. Verbale. Cic. A geuyng oz fozgeuyng.

Condormio, condormis, condormiui, cōdormītum, pen. prod. condormire. Plaut. To ſleape with other.

Condormiſco, condormiſcis, condormiſcere. Plaut. Idem.

Condryllon, ſiue Condrylle, Herba. Plin. Chondrilla melius ſcribitur. wilde fuckery.

Condris, dris, f. g. The hearbe called falſe Dittany.

Conduco, condūcis, penult. prod. conduxi, conductum, condūcere. Plaut. To bzyng with: to bye: to take an houſe oz lande. Alſo to gather oz aſſemble in one place: to conuerte: to take in hande to doe a wozthe oz buſſineſſe foz hyze oz wages. And in the thirde perſon it is to pzofite.

¶ Conducere, Cōgregare. Cic. Virgines in vnū cōduxerūt. Exercitus in vnum conducere. Tacit. To gather together.

Partes conducere in vnum. Lucret. To bzyng together.

¶ Conducere. Plaut. To pzocure oz bye.

Nimium magno conducere. Cic. To bye to deare.

¶ Conducere aliquem. Plaut. To hyze oz pzocure one.

Aliquem ad cædem faciendam conducere. Cicer. To hyze oz pzocure one.

Hortum conducere. Cic. To take: to hyze.

Domum conducere. Cicer.

Alicui locum in proximo conducere. Cic.

Conducere mercede. Cic. To hyze fez money.

Conducere nauem. Plaut. To hyze a ſhippe.

¶ Conducere, etiam dicitur is qui pretiū accipit pro re aliqua facienda. Iulianus Iureconſultus. To vndertake to doe thyng at a pzyſe.

Ad pecuniam numeratam cōducere. Caius. To vndertake to doe a wozthe fez ready money.

Redemptor qui columnā illam de Cotta & de Torquato conduxerat faciendā. Cic. Id eſt, à Cotta, &c. That was hyzed of Cotta, oz vndertohe at Cottaes hande to make, &c.

Multitudo conducta. Cic.

¶ Conducit, in tertijs perſonis, pro Vtile eſt. Plaut. Cicer. It is pzofitable.

Ea maxime conducunt, quæ ſunt rectiſſima. Cicer. Are moſt pzofitable.

Conducit hoc tuæ laudi. Cic. This maketh muche foz your pzayſe.

Stephanus' Latin-French dictionary, had there no vernacular translation.

Elyot's *Bibliotheca*, Robert Stephanus' Latin-French dictionary of 1552, and Johannes Frisius' Latin-German dictionary of 1556—these are the predecessors to whom Cooper's *Thesaurus* owes most. Other sources of information will be discussed below. Meantime, how do Cooper and his critics and commentators stand with respect to his leading sources? The answer has been already partially supplied. His critics come off rather badly. Some were content to repeat unverified statements; others, as Kennett, based dogmatic conclusions on inadequate information. No one extended his investigation far enough to exhaust all the alternatives.

What of Cooper himself? Judged by the standards of his day, little adverse criticism would seem to be warranted. But his contemporaries and successors were inclined to judge him by a higher standard than they applied to the average. Their charges that Cooper plagiarized Elyot's *Bibliotheca* and Stephanus' *Thesaurus* are, in the light of the compiler's own statements, without foundation. More pertinent would be criticism of his silence on the use of Stephanus' Latin-French and Frisius' Latin-German dictionary. Was Cooper in this disingenuous, as Kennett suggests? Or did he suppose—if indeed he thought at all about specifying sources—that blanket acknowledgment of his obligation to Stephanus' *Thesaurus*, the Latin basis of the other two dictionaries, was sufficient? Whatever our judgment concerning Cooper's relation to his predecessors, he had no reason to be ashamed of them. They were the best of the time. And a full and explicit statement of his obligation to them would have precluded adverse criticism and could hardly have injured his reputation.

Although the dictionaries of Elyot, Stephanus, and Frisius are, as we have seen, the more important sources of Cooper's *Thesaurus,* Cooper cites in his text other authorities, such as Erasmus, Budaeus, Celsus, and Nizolius, and he includes matter corresponding to what may be found in these authors. It is, however, often impossible to determine whether Cooper has consulted these authorities directly or derived his material by way of Elyot or Stephanus.

Cooper writes, for example, under *Cadmus* (*Cadmea victoria*), "Read herof in Chil. Erasmi"; and under *termerium* (*termeria mala*), "*Vide* Adag. Eras.*" But these entries, with the proverbs and the citations of Erasmus, are carried over from the *Bibliotheca* of 1559. These may, however, have been borrowed earlier from Erasmus, by Cooper. It will be recalled that Elyot, in his Preface to his *Dictionary* of 1538, and again in 1542, made a point of introducing proverbs, or *adagia*. In the text of 1538 he had only 57 proverbs, Latin and English; in 1542 (1545), 114.

In the revision of 1548, Cooper increased the number of proverbs to some 275. These continued through the editions of 1552 and 1559. As far as we can determine, these all derived from Erasmus' *Adagia*, some introduced by Elyot, many more added by Cooper. Of much interest is the fact that though these lexicographers took the Latin phrasing of the proverb from the *Adagia* and supplied in English a part of Erasmus' exposition, they frequently added to the *adagium*, from the common store, an English proverb of more or less similar meaning. But to return to the *Thesaurus*, Cooper here inserts proverbs in only the poetic dictionary or proper-name section; and the number is reduced from 275 in the *Bibliotheca* of 1559 to about 40 in the *Thesaurus*. Why the reduction, we are not told. But the source is still Erasmus' *Adagia*, and, with two or three exceptions, via the *Bibliotheca*.

To the *Annotationes Pandectarum*, the *De asse*, and the *Commentaries* of Budaeus, we have referred above. Elyot lists Budaeus among his authorities as early as 1538, and cites him frequently in the *Bibliotheca*. Robert Stephanus, a friend and admirer of Budaeus, acknowledges great indebtedness to his labors and quotes him more often than Elyot does. Citations to him are recurrent also in Cooper's *Thesaurus*. But most of these citations are from the *Bibliotheca*, as under *choenix, congius,* and *medimnus;* or from Stephanus' *Dictionarium Latino-Gallicum*, as under *chus, lancearius, lascivire, lumbus, schedion, symbolum,* and *ultra.*

Names and descriptions of diseases occupy a relatively large place in the Elyot-Cooper dictionaries. Having compiled the *Castel of Helth*, Elyot early became familiar with many medical writers and books, including Galen, Aëtius, Aegineta, Trallianus, Mesue, and Celsus, to mention a few. These he cites in the *Castel of Helth* and in his *Dictionary*. The *De medicina* of Celsus, Elyot knew well. Phrases from this book abound in Stephanus. Cooper, in the *Thesaurus*, draws from both sources. Sometimes he carries over what was in the *Bibliotheca*, as under *Attalus emplastrun, hyposarcha,* and *psylli;* sometimes he draws from Stephanus, as under *atrophia, cancer, cardia, cardiacus, lien,* and *tabes*. In many entries, Cooper, citing Celsus, has a composite of the two sources, as under *angina, lethargus, lethum,* and *febris*. There is no evidence that Cooper gathered illustrations directly from the *De medicina* of Celsus.

In his words to the candid reader (*candido lectori*), in the *Bibliotheca* (1548), Cooper states in substance that, despite the critics, he will follow the examples of Doletus, Robert Stephanus, Nizolius, and others who have won great praise for themselves in compiling dictionaries. The *Thesaurus Ciceronianus* of Nizolius was a treasure house for lexicographers, and we might infer from Cooper's reference that he used the

Ciceronianus in assembling his own *Thesaurus*. This inference is supported by comparison of the texts. In the *Thesaurus*, under *abalieno, aculeus, adhaeresco, ascendo, cervix, charitas, contumelia, custodia, diligo, exemplum, firmamentum, gradatim, huber* (*uber*), *impertio,* and *macula,* are seven to ten illustrations each from Cicero. These also appear in the Nizolius. Yet every example is in Stephanus' Latin-French dictionary, which Cooper was following. The debt to Nizolius is, as in the case of Budaeus and Celsus, through Stephanus, Cooper's primary source.

We have seen that in the *Bibliotheca* (1552, 1559) Cooper borrowed freely from Turner's *Herball* and his *Avium historia.* The *Thesaurus,* likewise, is much indebted to the same books. Apparently, the bird lore and herbal lore from Turner are carried over from the *Bibliotheca,* sometimes condensed or slightly rephrased. Turner's name is mentioned in the same entries, as under *aconitum, antirrhino,* and *chamaecyparissus,* in the *Thesaurus* and the *Bibliotheca.* It would be difficult to prove that in compiling the *Thesaurus* Cooper directly consulted Turner's books. He employed the lore gathered earlier for expansion of the *Bibliotheca.*

What has been said thus far concerning the sources of Cooper's *Thesaurus* is applicable to the dictionary proper, not to the section at the end, on proper names. Proper names did not appear in the Latin-French dictionary of Stephanus or the Latin-German of Frisius, Cooper's principal authorities. Even in the 1559 revision of the *Bibliotheca,* Cooper had intended to place proper names in a separate and independent alphabetical list, an intention which was not then fully carried out. In the *Thesaurus,* 1565, however, the compiler's aim is realized and the independent section is placed at the end of the volume, under the heading "Dictionarium Historicum & Poeticum propria locorum & Personarum vocabula breviter complectens."

Many of the proper-name entries Cooper had at hand. They had been originally collected by Elyot for his *Dictionary* and *Bibliotheca* and retained, though distributed through the text, in the various revisions. In fact, not a few of the sketches gathered by Elyot and printed in the *Bibliotheca,* Cooper had used in his continuation of Lanquet's *Chronicle.* These, perhaps as a matter of economy, he continued to employ even in the *Thesaurus.* Some of the sketches thus made by Elyot, used by Cooper in the *Chronicle* and later editions of the *Bibliotheca,* and retained in the *Thesaurus* are under *Ambrose, Aristides, Athanasius, Augustine, Basilides, Basilius, Cherinthus, Ebionites, Eunomius, Indae, Machabeus, Noe,* and *Origenes.* There are many others.

In addition to the proper names inherited from Elyot, Cooper added many, with descriptive sketches, gathered from other sources. In the address to the reader in his revision of the *Bibliotheca* (1548) Cooper explains that he has translated from Stephanus and others many of the proper-name items.

Robert Stephanus was a versatile and extremely industrious lexicographer. A new edition of his *Thesaurus* (2 vols.) had appeared in 1543, in which proper names were distributed through the alphabet, together with common nouns and other parts of speech. In 1545 he published a revised and augmented edition of the *Vocabularius poeticus*, a work originally compiled by Torrentinus at the end of the fifteenth century. This work, devoted solely to proper names, arranged alphabetically, was a most convenient source for Cooper and other lexicographers. The revised *Vocabularius* naturally had a great deal in common with Stephanus' *Thesaurus*. To both of these Cooper was indebted. There are numerous correspondences between the revised *Bibliotheca* and the two works by Stephanus. Furthermore, Charles Stephanus, brother of Robert, assumed editorship of the revised *Vocabularius* and, in 1553, published a much augmented edition, with the title changed to *Dictionarium historicum, geographicum, poeticum.* This book overlapped the two earlier publications of Robert Stephanus mentioned above. Although Cooper could have used Charles Stephanus' *Dictionarium* (1553) in his final revision of Elyot's *Bibliotheca* (1559), there is no conclusive evidence that he did so. Nevertheless, the revised *Bibliotheca* contained hundreds of entries which came from Robert Stephanus via his *Thesaurus* and his edition of the *Vocabularius.*

When Cooper came to prepare his "Dictionarium Historicum & Poeticum" as an appendix for his *Thesaurus* (1565), he had at hand a considerable body of matter in the revised *Bibliotheca*—some from Elyot, more from Robert Stephanus. All these entries he took over, sometimes with revision, often verbatim. The proper-name list and descriptive items from the *Bibliotheca* constitute the bulk of Cooper's matter for the *Thesaurus*. But the idea of an independent proper-name section and the title given to it seem to derive from Charles Stephanus' *Dictionarium*, as do many of the amplified sketches. The case of Cooper's indebtedness is fairly complex. But a close scrutiny of the 1543 *Thesaurus* of Robert Stephanus, the 1559 *Bibliotheca*, the 1553 *Dictionarium* of Charles Stephanus, and Cooper's *Thesaurus* reveals that though in many instances Cooper could have derived from either Robert or Charles Stephanus, he did, in fact, have matter from both.[23] In short, though Cooper has some entries not found in the Stephanus dictionaries, he derived most of his entries on proper names from Robert Stephanus' *Thesaurus*, generally by way of the revised *Bibliotheca*, and from Charles Stephanus' *Dictionarium*.

Having noticed the more important sources of Cooper's *Thesaurus*, we may now ask whether this volume exhibits any development or modification of technique in English lexicography. The compiler's aims and method of procedure in the revisions of the *Bibliotheca* have already been stated. In a similar manner, Cooper writes explicitly of the technical features or method in the *Thesaurus*, both in the Latin dedicatory epistle to Robert Dudley, Lord Leicester, and in the instructions (in English) to young scholars who would wish to make frequent use of this dictionary.

In the arrangement, the author tells us, he has observed diligently the alphabetical order, save in derivatives.[24] "For al the deriuatiues are set with their significations and phrases, in a contrarie Latine letter after their Primitiues. As for example after this Primitiue *Duco*, followeth *Ducens, Ductus, Ducatus, Dux, Ductor, Ductarius, Ductilis, Ductim*. Whereby with great profite they may learn, as it were, the whole progenie and offspring of anie worde." He has indicated, we learn further, for each word the part of speech, the accent and pronunciation; for nouns and substantives, the gender and declension; and for verbs, the conjugation. Various meanings, uses, and constructions of words he has signified, and also illustrated by quotations from approved Latin authors, whose names he has always specified.[25] "This diuersitie of significations I haue not onely noted togither confusely in the first exposition of the worde, but afterwards also distinctly eche by it selfe, with the phrases to the same belonging: which he [the student] may finde out by thys Paragraffe (¶) which is noted wheresoeuer the signification, or the use of the thing altereth." The author here cites examples, from the text, of words which have various meanings and constructions. "It is also to be noted what aduerbs authours doe vse wyth uerbes. . . . Moreouer, the phrases of elegancies, and specially such as haue any good grace of Metaphores. . . . It helpeth much also to the apt vse of the Latine tongue to obserue in Verbes, with what Nownes they be well vsed: and in Nownes what Verbes and Adiectiues they haue ioyned with them." Finally, the compiler declares, he has striven to reproduce in English idiom the real meaning of the Latin words and phrases.

The technical aspects of Cooper's *Thesaurus* as thus paraphrased from his own statement are exemplified in the text. To understand which of these are new and significant in English lexicography, we should remember that, in 1565, the dictionaries of Higgins (that is, the revised Huloet), Baret, Thomas, and Rider had not yet been published. Only the small volumes of Huloet, Veron, and Withals and the augmented *Bibliotheca* of Elyot were in vogue in England. No one of these exhibited in combination the various technical aspects of Cooper's *Thesaurus*. What then are the features in the latter work? These are (1) the modified etymological arrangement. Employed slightly by Elyot in his *Dictionary* of 1538, this system was thereafter abandoned in favor of the alphabetical order. In the *Thesaurus* Cooper returns to the earlier arrangement and thus emphasizes (2) derivatives as a convenience to the student. He indicates (3) accent and pronunciation of the terms to be defined; he gives (4) full grammatical information. He establishes (5) the meanings and usage of Latin terms by a wealth of illustrations from classical writers far beyond the precedent in the *Bibliotheca Eliotae*. Under *gratia*, for example, are a hundred new illustrations in the *Thesaurus;* under *oraculum*, twenty; under *prudentia*, sixteen; and under *scientia*, thirty.

To Cooper goes the credit for having introduced or re-emphasized these technical features in English lexicography. He cannot, however, be said to have invented them. He simply took over the technique of Robert Stephanus' Latin-French dictionary (Frisius' Latin-German dictionary, from which Cooper borrowed occasionally, used the same method), the source from which he derived innumerable Latin phrases and illustrations, and in which he found a French basis for much of his English. The adoption of the system of Stephanus' dictionary is so complete as to extend to the arrangement on the page of entries and illustrations and to the use of the paragraph symbol to indicate a new meaning or use of a word.

In other ways besides the technical innovations does Cooper exhibit in the *Thesaurus* the influence of his model. Barbarisms, for example, which had appeared in his revisions of the *Bibliotheca* are here expunged.[26] Examples of such words are *abditamentum, aberuncasso, aborsus, athophia, atimus, distito, gelotopaeus, ingitas, nequino, paspale, passarina,* and *passili.* These were omitted, one must infer, because they were not in Cooper's principal source. On the other hand, a number of Greek words were retained for the reason that they were in the Stephanus. Some of these are *abaphus, abaptistum, abbreviatura, catacrysis, cnipologus, cnopodion, codones, eucareia, galanga, gammoides, garyophillus, gelatina, novuncium,* and *sitocomia.*[27]

In the fabulous stories of men, beasts, countries, plants, accounts of diseases, etc., there are also reductions or omissions. The articles on *gazella, hyacinthus, lethargia, panthera,* and *lecanomantia* are, in 1565, reduced to about one-third of their original length. Condensed and changed, also, are the comments on *batrachion, effascino, garyophillus,* and *glastum.* Condensation of these items and the revision of many others seem to indicate good critical judgment of the relative value of entries.

To students of English language and literature, that which is of greatest interest in the *Thesaurus* is the English phrases and sentences— in short, the English idiom of the Elizabethan period. In converting foreign phrases, whether Latin, French, or German, into English, Cooper did his most original work. Although his foreign source may convey the sense of a phrase, it can rarely give the English idiom. Transforming foreign definitions into the vernacular was Cooper's special effort and his pride. His comment on this phase of his work, we noted earlier.[28] Vernacular interpretation he again emphasized in the preliminary matter of the *Thesaurus*. In the dedicatory letter, for example, he writes concerning young men who will use this work: "Here they will find a varied and copious interpretation of each entry in their mother tongue." Again, in the instructions (*annotationes*) to the reader Cooper writes that he has put into the vernacular not what at first glance seems to be the sense of the Latin but what represents the real thought of the Latin author he has cited. Of the phrase *Viui peruenimus illuc*, for example, readers may expect this literal interpretation: "We came thyther alyue." But the author's actual meaning is "We haue lyued to see that." So throughout, Cooper endeavors, often with the aid of his foreign interpreters, to determine the real drift of the Latin author and to make his thought live again in Elizabethan dress.

A glance through a few entries yields such examples as these: "*Foelicites tibi cedat*. Plin. God send you good of it"; "*Cedo coram ipso*. Ter. Say it to his face"; "*Citatis volare equis . . .* to fling out as fast as horses can gallop"; "*Equum ascendere stimulis*, to fetch up with the spur"; "*Nec latuere doli fratrem Junonis, & irae*. Virg. Iunoes brother knew full well . . . of his crafty fetch and stomacke agaynst them"; "*Superstitio . . .* Spiced conscience in vayne things"; "*Corde est mihi*. Cic. It lyketh or pleaseth me"; "*Bene emere*. Cic. To bie good cheape"; "*Male emere*. Cic. To bye deare"; "*Emere pretio spem*. Ter. I will not bie a birde in the bush"; "*It in auras*. Ovid. It vanisheth into ayre"; "*I in crucem*. Plaut. Go and be hanged: go with a mischiefe"; "*Ire in opus alienum*. Plaut. To meddle with another mans work"; "*Eunt praecipites mores*. Liv. Honest manners fall soon in decay"; "*Iram euomere in aliquem*. Terent. To vtter his stomacke and anger against one spitefully"; "*Iam nos fabulae sumus*. Ter. Nowe we be a talking stocke to euery man"; "*Mare acerrimum meretrix*. Plaut. An hoore is an horrible and daungerous sea"; "*Nulla mente animi habeo*. Plaut. I am cleane beside myself"; "*Stomacho suo viuere*. Pli. Iu. To liue after his owne fantasie and pleasure"; "*Diobolares meretrices quae duobus obolis conducuntur*. Plaut. Three halfe-pennie harlots"; "*Exegi monimentum aere perennius*. Horat. I haue finished a worke to the remembrance of my name of longer continuance than ymages of brasse"; "*. . . Te redimas captum quam queas Minimo*. Ter. Raunsome or delyuer thy selfe being taken in loue snares as good cheape as thou canst."

The English interpretations of the Latin phrases and sentences listed above serve to suggest the wealth of Elizabethan idiom in the Elyot-Cooper dictionaries. In these volumes are also many English words and expressions less well known than those cited. Of these, Mayor, using the 1559 *Bibliotheca*, makes a partial list.[29] These, Mayor maintains in 1857, "still wait for admittance into our English dictionaries." Although most words in his list have since been recorded in the *New English Dictionary*, the list is worth reproducing. The italicized English words in the following abridged entries are those noted by Mayor.

Indignor . . . to be stampyng and *staryng* wood.
Induco . . . to rase or strike out, to *defete*. . . .
Inarmis . . . unarmed, a man *yolden.*
Infricatus . . . *frotted* or rubbed.
Infurnibulum . . . a *piele*, wherwith breade is set into the ouen.
Inops ab amicis, dispurueied of friendes, without friendes.
Insitium, a *iegot* or other lyke meate stuffed with egges and fleshe chopped or mynced.
Inspico . . . to make a thynge smal or sharpe lyke to a wheate eare, whan it shooteth out of the *hose.*
Instar . . . a *platte*, a paterne.
Murmurillo . . . to *croole*, or rumble [cf. *Thesaurus* (1565); *Bibliotheca* (1559), s.v. murmuro: "*Intestina murmurant* . . . the bealye *crooleth*"].
Naphtha . . . a sort of *mawnde* or chaulkie clay.
Nauis vulnerata, a shyppe striken . . . or *bouged* with ordinaunce.
Nigrum papauer, gith.
Vas, or *Colum niuarium,* a colander or a bolle . . . to streygne lycour thorough, a *cieboll.*
Nodus . . . a knotte, a *knurle.*
Nouendiale sacrum, the *terrement* the nynth day after the buriyng.
Obductus . . . couered, *hylled.*
Obelus . . . a spitte, or *broche.* . . .
Obgannio . . . to *whyster* in ones eare.
Obstrepo . . . to *stere* and make a noyse or rustlyng with the feete or otherwyse agaynst one.

The italicized English words noticed by Mayor in the entries above must have been somewhat rare even in the sixteenth century. It is interesting to observe, as Mayor could not do in 1857, the information, or lack of information, on these words in the *New English Dictionary*. According to the *NED,* two of these words, *piele* and *hylled,* appear in Old English or Middle English; three, *crool, gith,* and *yolden,* are recorded as before 1600 but later than the *Bibliotheca* (1559); eight, *bouge, cieboll, defete, dispurueied, frotted, knurle, platte,* and *staryng,* as after 1600; and six, *broche, iegot, mawnde, stere, terrement,* and *whyster,* with the meaning indicated in the Elyot-Cooper dictionaries, are not recorded. In a sampling of better-known English words in the dictionaries, such as *academic, affectation,* and *confiscate,* Professor James Sledd has found fifty examples antedating instances cited in the *NED.*[30]

The discovery in the Elyot-Cooper dictionaries of English words used earlier than recorded instances in the *NED* does not, as the list above shows, imply a collection of strange, outlandish terms, but rather a very wide range of words, most of which were then current. These dictionaries have indeed such an abundance of words as to constitute a great treasury. They illustrate the Elizabethan idea of "copie." The beginnings of this principle in lexicography we have noted above, having observed the tendency in John of Garland, the *Catholicon Anglicum*, and Elyot's *Bibliotheca* (1542, 1545). As an indication of the vogue of the idea of copiousness in the 1540's, we have Rudolph Walter's translation (1542) of Julius Pollux's *Onomasticon*, with the statement on the title page, "Hoc est instructissimum Rerum et Synonymarum Dictionarium," suggesting the title of Erasmus' *De copia verborum et rerum* and exemplifying the principle of this work. Walter lists (p. 22) fifty-one epithets, words, or phrases one might use in praise of a king and, on the same page, some forty convenient terms for reviling a tyrant.

Cooper was in sympathy with the idea of copiousness. He enunciates the principle in his revisions of the *Bibliotheca* and re-emphasizes it in the *Thesaurus*. In the 1548 *Bibliotheca* Cooper writes that, for every Latin term, he has collected an abundance of native words, as it were in a single heap, and in so great variety that this our labor will help not only to the speedy knowledge of the Latin language but very much to the adornment and elegance of our own.[31] The following entries, from the *Bibliotheca* (1559), seem to exemplify the principle Cooper had in mind:

Statuo . . . to ordeyne, to determine, to appoynte, to defyne, to iudge or esteme, to thynke or iudge of a suretie, to set faste, to set up, to stable a thyng, to purpose surely, to geue iudgement or sentence against one, to dedicate, to beate one thynge agaynst an other . . . [twenty-four illustrative phrases in Latin and English follow].

Stadium . . . an ernest bendyng or settyng of the mind on a thyng, a great affection or desire that one hath to do a thyng good or ill, studie: sometyme exercyse, endeuoir, will or appetite, fantasie, desire, diligence, labour, fauour, loue, sometyme a thing that one fantasieth . . . [seventeen illustrations follow].

This custom of presenting immediately after the Latin term the whole group of English equivalents, a method not used by contemporary lexicographers, continues through the *Thesaurus*, probably as a studied device to give fullness.

On the subject of copiousness in the *Thesaurus* Cooper is very explicit and emphatic. Having pointed out to young scholars the uses of the book in learning accent and pronunciation, grammatical information, divers meanings and uses and constructions of Latin words, elegant phrases and metaphors, Cooper states: "Last of all a studious yong man, with small paines, by the helpe of thys booke may gather to himselfe good furniture both of wordes and approoued phrases and fashions of speaking for any thing, that he shall eyther write or speake of, and so make unto his use, as it were a common place booke for such a purpose." If, for example, one wishes to write on love or friendship, he might choose two or three words, *amicus, amo, amor,* and consider the words derived from them and phrases belonging to them; there is nothing "pertaynyng to that matter, but that he shall be able copiously to utter it." But to show at length the idea of "copie" would be longer than the place requires. "I will declare it by a matter of smaller use and copie." Then choosing the subject of shooting and the words *arcus* and *sagitta* and the phrases which go with them, Cooper demonstrates, with a passage of some 250 words, how young scholars "may procure this store and furniture." An examination of a few pages of the text of the *Thesaurus* gives ample proof of the variety and abundance which the lexicographer emphasizes.

Commendatory verses by Cooper's colleagues stress the same principle. The terms *copia, opes,* and *munus* are recurrent. One of these poems by James Calfhill will illustrate. A prose translation reads thus: "The Nymphs nursed Jove in the vale of Ida, and the reward of the nurses was a goat's horn. From this fecund horn flowed all copie, copie not lacking any benefit. If Jupiter is therefore so called from aiding the world, he who favors and aids all, he also cherishes Jupiter. Copie should not be lacking to anyone who nourishes those things which aid his country with richer enjoyment. Cooper, therefore, sucking the Muses, as it were, in his rich work has the exuberant horn of plenty. Here, youths with your studies draw out the rewards; here, nothing explicit that you desire is lacking. For the cornucopia of Cooper gives more richly than that of Amalthea, which was a goat's horn."

Although the *Thesaurus* was in high repute and the standard reference dictionary for a period of thirty years (there were editions in 1565, 1573, 1584, and 1587) not all of his contemporaries esteemed it as highly as his friends who penned the commendatory verses. William Turner, to whom Cooper was much indebted for bird lore and herbal lore, was sharply critical. In *A New Boke of the Nature of All Wines* (1568) Turner tells of his search in the *Thesaurus* for the right word to express the meaning of *acer.*

I found great plentie both of good Latin wordes and fine maners of speaking, gathered wyth great paines, and ordered with no small learning and iudgement, but in the English, as I found to muche plentie of light, and new inckhorne termes: so in some places I founde such scarcenesse, lacke, and want of proper and true Englishe names, that the author is faine to give one name to diverse Latin wordes, for when

I looked how he englished *Acer* he englished it thus: *Eger, sharpe, tart, soure,* or
fell [Turner omits *cruell, vehement; swift: valiant: diligent, circumspect: strong,
sore, fierce, earnest*]. Lo, here is great plentie of wordes, and yet we can not tell what
acer in taste doth properly signifie.[32]

Turner admits the "great plentie" of the *Thesaurus*. Cooper gives
ninety-seven illustrations from classical authors, which should have been
sufficient for students of language and literature. He has the descriptive
words for *acer* listed above by Turner, and these illustrations: *"Cibi
acres.* Plin. Eger and sharpe meates, byting"; *"Gustus acer.* Plin. Quicke
taste"; *"Gustu acri mordet.* It biteth with a sharp taste, as garlike . . ."
Turner was not easy to please; he seems to have expected in the *Thesaurus*
the sharp distinctions that only the scientist could make. Such distinctions
were hardly to be found for another hundred years or so. His reputed
discovery of "plentie of light, and new inckhorne termes" in the dictionary is not supported by the evidence. In the numerous illustrations
under *acer,* for example, there is not one English word that could be
termed "inkhorn." On this subject Professor Sledd writes:

Careful sampling of the English columns in the dictionaries of Elyot and Cooper
reveals no evidence that the lexicographers had an undue predilection for inkhorn
terms or a real aversion to them. Rather they seem to be in the main stream of Elizabethan English, and Turner's criticism of the *Thesaurus* seems a mere commonplace
of literary argument. . . . As they [Elyot and Cooper] said themselves, they undertook
"the conference of phrases or fourmes of speakynge latin and englishe," and provided
such a wealth of English synonyms that their works might increase the student's
mastery of both tongues.[33]

Cooper's reputation in later periods seems to have been fairly high,
if we except the criticisms for alleged plagiarism. For the lexicographers
of the seventeenth century, Adam Littleton, a learned theologian, lin-
guist, and philologist, may speak. Critical of former lexicographers for
transcribing corrupt or barbarous words, without distinction, he thinks
of Cooper as an exception, as one who set forth a distinguished work
most profitable in revealing the purity of the Latin language by examples
drawn from approved authors.

Mayor, in 1857, admits the shortcomings of Cooper, especially the
geographical and historical blunders, but insists that Cooper explains
some words that most Latin lexicons have been in error about. One of
these is *memoriter,* not satisfactorily explained by Faber, Gesner, Forcel-
lini, Scheller, Freund, Klotz, or Smith. Schaefer says that in the phrase
Sic memoriter citavit: ne quid reconditi hic latere putes it plainly means
"without book." Madvig had proved, however, that this word, the true
adverb of *memor,* denotes a ready and exact exercise of memory, and

never means merely "without book," "by rote," *auswendig*.[34] Compare the *Bibliotheca* (1552, 1559):

Memoriter, perfectly by herte, or with good remembrance, redyly.
Memoriter cognoscere, to knowe perfectely by herte.
Memoriter respondere, to answer promptly.

In the *Thesaurus* (1565) other examples are added:

Oratio quae est habita memoriter. Oration or talke uttered readily.
Memoriter colligere. To gather together readily without forgetting of any.
Memoriter memorat. Rehearseth readily, and by harte.
Memoriter exponere aliquid. Readily not forgettynge any parte.[35]

The final word of Mayor on Cooper's *Thesaurus*, not so apt as when written, still is worthy of repetition.

It may perhaps be Utopian to expect in modern purveyors of school books the Socratic curiosity which leads men to the farmyard or to the workshop to learn their own native language; but we have a right to grumble when we see the raciest of all our dictionaries compiled in the genial spring of our literature, neglected by the most successful of our lexicographers, who, with its aid might escape the debasing influences which make it daily more difficult to write plain English.

To this statement may be added the remark that Cooper's *Thesaurus* was the standard reference work during the formative period of Spenser, Marlowe, Shakespeare, and Ben Jonson, and must have been one of the books consulted in common by them and their contemporaries.[36]

In the Elyot-Cooper dictionaries there is a new trend in lexicography in England. Elyot's aim, in keeping with the times, was to compile a volume that would be serviceable in the study of classical authors, retaining, however, much that by present-day standards might be regarded as medieval or barbarous. Cooper, under the influence of Humanists on the Continent, especially Robert Stephanus, in the three revisions of the *Bibliotheca* and in the compilation of the *Thesaurus*, gradually modified or ruled out Latin terms regarded as medieval and barbarous and introduced more and more classical Latin, supported by abundant quotations from approved classical writers, such as Cicero, Terence, and Virgil. Although he retained many terms that in the course of 125 years were to be condemned as nonclassical Latin, his *Thesaurus* marks the consummation of the classical tradition in Latin-English lexicography in the Tudor period. Comparison of the thick folio of 1565 with the small, thin folio of Elyot's *Dictionary* of 1538 shows how great was the progress in quantity as well as in classical quality.

Of the copiousness as well as the classical character of the *Thesaurus*, Thomas Wykes writes in the commendatory verses. He reflects that the barbarous *Hortus* (*[H]ortus vocabulorum,* 1500) should in our times keep silent, and not even Calepine should vaunt his great riches, nor Nizolius longer speak from Cicero, nor Doletus have immoderate praise, nor Stephanus draw his *Thesaurus* above the stars: Cooper is easily first (*princeps*); he is to be sung before all others. This is an obvious exaggeration; Cooper would have profited, for example, in following more scrupulously Stephanus' *Thesaurus* and giving specific references to author, work, and page for his classical authorities. But Wykes probably does echo the sentiment of the times regarding the *Thesaurus,* especially the copious quality of it.

Copiousness as a feature of the Elyot-Cooper dictionaries we have noted above, and the principle was applicable to the English as well as the Latin of these dictionaries. In this emphasis they were of the period, as they were in the care for English idiom throughout. Cooper translates hundreds of Latin illustrative phrases and sentences which had no French or German equivalents in Stephanus or Frisius, authorities which he was following at the time. There being no English dictionaries, it is fairly certain that the Latin-English of Elyot and Cooper in a measure filled that lack, and were intended so to do. Judged from the point of view of the classical scholar, the *Thesaurus,* as the consummation of the Elyot-Cooper lexicography, stands above the *Hortus,* regarded by the Elizabethans as barbarous, but far below Ainsworth's *Thesaurus,* in which every suspect Latin word was challenged and only those admitted that could be supported by specific quotations from classical authors. Judged, however, from the point of view of its adaptation to the needs of the times and from its general usefulness, we must say that for many years the place of the *Thesaurus* was unique, and that its influence on lexicography in England was far reaching.

CHAPTER IX

Gulielmus Morelius' *Verborum Latinorum cum Graecis Anglicisque* (1583)

IT WAS ALMOST inevitable that the copious *Thesaurus* of Thomas Cooper should become a treasure house for subsequent lexicographers. In the *Thesaurus* was a great abundance—"a God's plenty," as Dryden might have said—of Latin from approved authors, together with English equivalents. And this dictionary had soon gained high repute. Among the earlier debtors to Cooper was Richard Hutton in his edition of Morelius' *Commentarii*.

Guillaume Morel, or Gulielmus Morelius (1505–64), as his name appears on the title page of his book, was a French Humanist, who published at Paris, in 1558, his *Verborum Latinorum cum Graecis Gallicisque conjunctorum commentarij, ex optimis quibusque auctoribus*. One of the interesting features of this book, according to the *Biographie universelle* (*s.v. G. Morel*), is that it contains a host of citations of Greek authors drawn from manuscripts, still unedited, of the Bibliothèque de Paris. Also according to the *Biographie*, the *Commentarii*, under the title *Thesaurus vocum omnium Latinorum ordine alphabetico digestorum*, was reprinted many times in the sixteenth and seventeenth centuries. Our concern is with a special version of the *Commentarii* published in England, in 1583. In this edition, English is substituted for French. The language of the title page follows:

Gulielmus Morelius, Verborum Latinorum cum Graecis Anglicisque Coniunctorum, locupletissimi Commentarij: Ad Elaboratum Vocum Passim Insertorum Accessione adaucti, vt stellulae, quae singulis lucent paginis, indicabunt. 1583. Londini, In aedibus Henrici Bynnemani, pr. assignationem Richardi Huttoni. Cum Priuilegio Regiae Maiestatis.

The dedication is to Robert Dudley, Count Leicester, Baron Denbygh, and so forth, by "Richardus Huttonus." Since the book was printed for Hutton, and since he writes the Dedication and discusses the method and content of the volume, it seems fairly certain that he was the editor of this edition and was therefore responsible for translating the French into English and for adding many English definitions. In the Dedication, Hutton refers to Dudley's patronage of Cooper and pays high tribute to the *Thesaurus*. It is significant that Cooper is the only English lexicographer mentioned. At any rate, the English portion of the Hutton-Morelius shows on every page close following of the *Thesaurus*. In the entries transcribed below for comparison, the Greek words of the Morelius are omitted.

Thesaurus (1565)	*Commentarii* (1583)
Conduco, condûcis, penul. prod. conduxi, conductum, conducere. Plaut. To bring with: to hire: to bie: to take an house or lande. Also to gather or assemble in one place: to conuert: to take in hande: to doe a worke or businesse for hyre or wages. And in the third person it is to profite.	*Condûco, dûcis, dúxi, dúctum, ducere, ex Cum & Duco,* Cic. . . . To bring with: to hire: to buy: to take an house or lande: also to gather or assemble togeather in one place: to conuert: to take in hande: to doe a worke or businesse for hire or wages: and in the third person it is to profite.
Condurdon. An herbe that in August beareth a redde flower, and hanged about the necke taketh away the disease called the kings euill.	*Condúrdon.* An hearb that in August beareth a redde flower, and taketh away the disease called the King's euill.
Condylus, cóndyli. pen. cor. Martial. The roundnesse or knots of the bones in the knee, ancle, elbow, knuckles, &c. Also a ring or thimble. Festus.	*Condylus, cóndyli, m. g. Graecum,* Martial . . . The roundnesse or knottes of the bones in the knee, ankle, elbowe, knuckles, &c. Also a ring or thimble.
Confarreo, confarreas, confarreâre. A quo *Confarreatus, & confarreatis.* Plin. To marrie with certaine solemnities before the bishop, when their children or infants were dedicated to priesthoode.	*Confarreo, confarreas, confarreâui, confarreâtum, ex Cum & Far, farris.* Tacitus . . . To marrie with certaine solemnities, before the Bishoppe, when their children or Infantes were dedicated to priesthood.

These are representative entries in the two texts. They show that in many of the English definitions Hutton followed Cooper verbatim, observing the order of words and even the punctuation. In other instances, Hutton borrowed the main entry from the *Thesaurus* and supplemented it by taking additional English meanings from the illustrations, as the following terms will show.

Thesaurus (1565)	*Commentarii* (1583)
Confingo, confingis, confinxi, confictum, confingere. To forme or make. *Hirundines . . . nidos confingunt.* Plin.	*Confingo, fingis, finxi, fictum, fingere, ex Cum & Fingo,* Plin. . . . To forme or make: to feigne to be true: to inuent

Thesaurus (1565)

Make or fashion their neastes. *Configere*. Colum. To feigne to be true: to inuent or ymagine: to comment.

Meta, metae, f. g. Plin. A butte or pricke to shoote at, properly made broade beneath & sharpe toward the toppe. A marke or goale in the fielde whereunto men or horses doo runne. . . .
Meta. Verg. The ende or bounde of any thyng: the limite.
Meta, quandoque accipitur pro inferiore parte molde . . . The lower stone of a mille.

Commentarii (1583)

or imagine: to comment: to giue shape or fashion.

Meta, metae, f. g. prima longa, Plin. . . . A butte or pricke to shoote at, properly made broad beneath, and sharpe toward the top: a marke or goale in the fielde whereunto men or horses do runne: the ende or bound of any thing: the limite: the lower stone of a mille.

Further confirmation of Hutton's debt to Cooper may be seen by comparisons of blocks of entries in the two texts: from *agabus* to *aggregare, Haliaeetus* to *haud,* and *praetexta* to *praevaricor.* Hutton's borrowing, as will be seen from the examples above, is of a very literal, not to say servile, kind. He absorbs many of the main definitions of Cooper, and if a main definition seems inadequate, he supplements it by drawing additional matter from the English in Cooper's illustrations. This method of procedure is of special interest because it anticipates, as we shall see, the method employed by subsequent debtors to Cooper.

Although Hutton's dependence upon Cooper is evident on every page and the debt to the *Thesaurus* very great, he also has much matter derived from other sources, part no doubt from his translation of the French. And the *Thesaurus* has a considerable body of matter not touched by Hutton. In method also the compilers differ: Hutton follows the alphabetical order of the original *Commentarii* rather than the etymological order of the *Thesaurus;* he includes also the Greek equivalents of the Latin terms, as Cooper does not. Hutton insists that he makes clear at a glance the accent, the quantity, the inflection, gender, case, conjugation, mood, and tense of each Latin word. He seems to have been the first English lexicographer to employ consistently the marks of accentuation: grave, acute, and circumflex.

Hutton's revision of Morelius apparently was not popular in England. Only the one edition of 1583 was published. The competition of such texts as Baret's *Alvearie* (1573, 1580), Cooper's *Thesaurus,* and Thomas Thomas's *Dictionarium* (1587) probably crowded out the Hutton-Morelius. Its importance lies in its close relation to Cooper's *Thesaurus,* its emphasis upon the alphabetical order of entries and upon accent, and its position as a transition text between Cooper and Thomas Thomas.

CHAPTER X

Thomas Thomas's *Dictionarium linguae Latinae et Anglicanae* (1587)

FROM ABOUT 1565 to 1595, Bishop Cooper's *Thesaurus* was the standard Latin-English dictionary. There was probably a copy of this thick folio in every reputable grammar school, and many people of the upper and upper middle classes possessed their own copies. But in the very year in which the fifth edition of Cooper's dictionary came from the press there was penned by Thomas Thomas (1553–88) an Epistola Dedicatoria to Lord Burleigh, commending another Latin-English dictionary, destined to supplant the Cooper and to become the standard popular reference work in England for the next twenty-five years.

Records of the compiler's life are scanty. From such as we have, we learn that Thomas Thomas was born in 1553, that he was educated at Eton and at King's College, Cambridge (Fellow, 1574; M.A., 1579), and that in 1582 he became the first printer for Cambridge University. In 1583 his press was seized by the Stationers' Company, on the grounds that, in printing the works of William Whitaker and other items, Thomas was infringing on their privileges. But his rights were upheld by Lord Burleigh, Chancellor. Thomas died on August 9, 1588,[1] less than a year after the first edition of his dictionary had come from the press. John Legate (Legatt) succeeded Thomas as University printer and as editor of the dictionary, which he continued to print under Thomas's name. The wording on the title page of the first edition of Thomas's dictionary is here transcribed.

Dictionarium Linguae Latinae et Anglicanae. In Hoc Qvid sit praestitum, & ad superiores λεξιχογράφος adiectum, docebit epistola ad Lectorem. Cantabrigiae, ex officina Thomae Thomasii, inclytae Academicae Typographi. Extant Londini apud Richardum Boyle ad insigne Rosae in Coemeterio D. Pauli.

Although the title page has no reference to the date of publication, the Epistola Dedicatoria addressed to William Cecil, Lord Burleigh, concludes with these words: "Ex officina nostra tertio Nonas Septemb. 1587." And at the end of the printer's address to the reader, are these words: "Cantabrigiae ex nostris aedibus, carptim inter operarum sussurros, Tertio Nonas Septembres, Anno salutis per Christum Dominum partae, 1587." According to these statements by the printer, the *Dictionarium* was brought out piecemeal, as it were, even during the hum of the press at other printing jobs, and finished on September 3, 1587.[2]

The *Dictionarium* thus launched seems to have won immediate popularity and, if we can judge by the number of printed editions which followed, to have maintained its vogue for many years. Editions appeared as follows: first, 1587; second, 1589; third, 1592; fourth, 1594; fifth, 1596; sixth, 1600; seventh, 1606; eighth, 1610; tenth, 1615; eleventh, 1619; twelfth, 1620; thirteenth, 1631; and fourteenth, 1644. No copy of the ninth edition has been located, though it obviously falls between 1610 and 1615. The more important revisions and augmentations were made in 1589, 1592, 1596, 1615, and 1631. The editions of 1600, 1610, and 1619 constitute a special and identical group, probably printed for use in schools. The details of the revisions and changes will emerge in our discussion of sources, a problem, in the Thomasius, closely related to that of the augmentations.

On the sources of the *Dictionarium*, we have an interesting comment by Francis Holyoke. From 1606 on for twenty-five years Holyoke, as editor of Rider's dictionary and his own *Dictionarium etymologicum*, published with the Rider, had been a competitor of the Thomasius and a free borrower therefrom. In the address to the reader in a 1633 edition of his dictionary Holyoke, feeling it necessary to justify himself for excessive borrowing from the Thomasius, maintains that he was following the practice of other lexicographers, including Thomas himself, and then states:

Thomas first compiled his dictionary from Calepine and Cooper, traces of whom are still discernible in the Thomasius. Afterward, he augmented his dictionary with matter from the *Nomenclator* of Junius and from certain glossaries and herbals. Finally, the reverend Philemon Holland, the learned physician and philologist, so wonderfully enriched the Thomasius from the works of reputable authors that no dictionary in that kind yet exists which, in the number of terms defined and in the illustration of meaning by selected phrases, is equal in merit to the Thomasius.[3]

What Holyoke writes about the relation of Thomas to Junius and Philemon Holland is true of the later editions of the *Dictionarium* What he says of the relation to Cooper is only partly true. Holyoke obviously did not know that Thomas used two dictionaries as primary sources: the Hutton-Morelius *Commentarii*, itself heavily indebted to Cooper's *Thesaurus*; and the *Thesaurus*. For the alphabetical arrangement of words, part of the word list, and possibly the suggestion for marking long and short syllables, Thomas followed Hutton-Morelius; for extending the word list and augmenting Morelius' definitions Thomas resorted to Cooper. Single entries frequently are composites from the two earlier dictionaries. In the revisions of 1592 and 1596, the same texts are used, as we shall see, as sources of the augmentations. A few illustrations will show the relationship of the 1587 Thomasius to the two major sources.

Cooper (1565)	Hutton (1583)	Thomas (1587)
	Mellifluus . . . Sweete as honie, that out of which honie floweth.	*Mellifluus.* Sweet as honie that out of which honie floweth.
Melligenus . . . Plin. That is of the same kinde that honie is.	*Melligenus* . . . Plin. . . . That is of the same kinde that honie is.	*Melligenus* . . . Plin. That is of the same kinde that honie is.
	Melliloquus . . . A sweete speaker.	*Melliloquus,* A sweete speaker.
Mellilus . . . Plaut. My honie one: my sweeting.	*Mellilus* . . . Plaut. My piggesnie: my sweeting: my dearling.	*Mellilus* . . . Plaut. My pigsnie, my sweeting, my darling, my honie one.
	Mellisones. They which practise dressing of honie.	*Mellisones,* They which practise dressing of honie.
Mellitus . . . Pli. Mixt with honie: condite in honie: sweete: pleasant: delectable.	*Mellitus* . . . Plin. . . . Homer. Mixt with honie: condite in honie: sweete: pleasaunt: delectable.	*Mellitus* . . . Mixt with hony, sweet, pleasant, delectable, as sweete as honie.
Mellium, lij, n. g. A dogs coller.	*Mellium, lij, n. g.* A dogs choller.	*Mellium, ii, n. g.* a dogges choller.
Melodes . . . Sidon. A sweete and cunning singer.	*Melodes* . . . A sweete singer.	*Melodes* . . . Sidon. A sweete and cunning singer.
Melodia . . . Melodie: sweete singing.	*Melodia* . . . A sweete song: melodie.	*Melodia* . . . Melodie, sweete singing.
Mesentericae venae. Unnumberable branches of the vaine called Porta, whiche restynge	*Mesentericae venae,* Braunches of the vaine called Porta, which conuey the iuyce of the	*Mesentericae venae, gr.* Branches of the vein called Porta, which conuey the iuyce of the meate

Cooper (1565)
on the skinnes that fasten the guttes doo conueigh the iuice of the meate concocted from the stomacke to the liuer.

Mesocraneum. The crowne of the head.

Mesolucos. An herbe like to Mercurie.

Mesonauta. A drudge in a shippe: a shippe page, which doth all druggerie.

Meta . . . Plin. A butte or pricke to shoote at, properly made broade beneath & sharpe toward the toppe. A marke or goale in the fielde whereunto men or horses do runne. . . .
Meta. Verg. The ende or bounde of any thyng: the limite.
Meta, quandoque accipitur pro inferiore parte molde . . . The lower stone of a mille.
Metator . . . Cic. He that planteth, disposeth, or setteth in order.
Metatores. Cic. They that measure and apoynte out a place to pitch a campe in.

Hutton (1583)
meate concocted, from the stomach to the liuer.

Mesocraneum . . . The crowne of the head: the middest of the skull.
Mesoleucus . . . A precious stone, blacke, hauing a white strake in the middest: also the herbe Mercurie.
Mesonauta . . . A drudge in a shippe: a gallie slaue.

Meta . . . Plin. . . . A butte or pricke to shoote at, properly made broad beneath, and sharpe toward the top: a marke or goale in the fielde whereunto men or horses do runne: the ende or bound of any thing: the limite: the lower stone of a mille.

Metator . . . Cic. . . . He that planteth, disposeth, or setteth in order: he that measureth and appointeth out the place to pitch a campe in.

Thomas (1587)
concocted from the stomache to the liuer.

Mesocraneum, gr. The crowne of the head, the midst of the skull.

Mesoleucus . . . Plin. A pretious stone, blacke, hauing a white strake in the middest: also the hearbe Mercurie.
Mesonauta . . . He that doth some worke and yet paieth something as a passenger: also a drudge in a ship, a gallie slaue, that doth all vile and abiect seruice in a ship.
Meta . . . A butte, or pricke to shoote at, properly made broade beneath, and sharpe toward the top: a marke or goale in the fielde whereunto men or horses doe runne . . . the end or bound of any thing, the limit, the lower or nether stone of a mil.

Metator . . . He that planteth, disposeth, or setteth in order: he that measureth and appointeth out the place to pitch a campe in: a land meater, a measurer of ground.

Analysis of the parallels above shows that Thomas employed both the earlier texts in compiling the *Dictionarium*. In some entries he follows Hutton only, as in *mellifluus, melliloquus,* and *mellisones,* terms not

in Cooper; in certain entries common to the three texts, Thomas prefer
Hutton, as in *mesentericae venae, mesoleucus,* and *mesocraneum;* in
others Thomas follows Cooper, as in *melodes* and *melodia;* in still others
Thomas has composite definitions, deriving matter from both earlier
texts, as in *mellilus, mesonauta,* and *metator.*

The shorter definitions, used for convenience in the examples above
do not suggest adequately the debt of Thomas to Cooper. The Cambridge printer frequently appropriated the English phrases in Cooper's
general definitions and supplemented them by others taken from the
examples of meaning and usage in the *Thesaurus.* The matter under
conficio in the two texts will illustrate.

Cooper (1565)	Thomas (1587)
Conficio . . . To destroy or slea: to grieue, vexe or torment: to performe: to finish or dispatche: to make an ende of: to bring to passe: to explicate or declare: to gather money: to breake: to consume or waste: to make: to chawe meate: to digest.	*Conficĭo, is, ēci, ctum, ĕre.* To finish o dispatch, to make an end of, t bring to passe, fulfill or accomplish to moue, to destroy or slea, to hur grieue, vex or torment: to explicate o declare: to gather, prouide, get, pro cure, or worke: to breake, to consum or wast: to make, to commit, to chew meate, to digest, to runne, to pass ouer, to conclude.

It will be observed that to Cooper's definitions Thomas has added *to
hurt, to moue, prouide, get, procure, worke, to commit, to runne, to pass
ouer,* and *to conclude.* The added matter is from Cooper's illustration
under *conficio.* Compare, for example:

Se conficere. Plancus. Cic. *To hurt* himseffe with traveile.
Aequor spatijs immensum conficere. Virg. *To passe ouer* the maine sea.
Conficere cibos. Liv. *To woorke* in the mouthe, &c.
Conficere de re aliqua cum aliquo. Cicer. *To conclude* of a matter with one.
Reditum alicui. Cic. *To procure* that one may returne.
Flagitium. Ter. *To commit* some naughtie deede.

The 1587 and 1589 Thomasius concentrated on the general definitions
using the method indicated of borrowing from Cooper, and offering no
examples of meaning and usage. In augmentations in the 1590's examples are supplied, and these too come largely from Cooper. The first
revision and augmentation of the Thomasius occurred in 1589. Here is
the wording of the title page:

Dictionarium Linguae Latjnae et Anglicanae Nunc Denuo Summa cura ac diligenti
recognitum, ac ultra priorem editionem verborum cumulo auctum. Huic etiam ac
cessit Dictionarium Historicum & Poeticum, ad prophanas historias, poetarumqu
fabulas intelligendas valde necessarium. Cantabrigiae Ex officina Iohannis Legat

celeberrimae Academiae Typographi. 1589. Extant Londini apud Abrahamum Kitson, ad insigne Solis in Camiterio D Pauli.

At the end of the text proper is the dictionary of proper names, with the heading "Dictionarium Propria Locorum et Personarum Vocabula breviter complectens." The title page claims a twofold augmentation: an increase by a heap (*cumulo*) of words (terms to be defined) and the addition of a dictionary of proper names. In the dictionary proper there are some additional entries and slight expansions of entries from the 1587 edition. But the increase is not impressive, as the following table may suggest.

	NO. OF TERMS DEFINED	
	1587 ed.	*1589* ed.
A ante B	280	283
A ante G	124	128
A ante H	10	12
A ante I	6	7

The table does not refer to occasional expansions of individual entries, but it does represent the relative increase of the text by addition of new terms. The important augmentation in the 1589 edition is in the proper-name dictionary. This part of the book occupies the last 76 leaves, or 152 pages, with two columns to a page, an estimated 6,500 entries. These are generally very brief, running to one or two lines, rarely more than four. They are little more than brief identifications of persons or places. Although the proper-name, or historical and poetical, dictionary continued as a feature of the Thomas dictionaries, it was never played up as important, and but slightly increased in the course of years. The 1631 edition, for example, has only about 7,500 entries.

In studying the sources of the proper-name section, we find a pattern similar to that used in the dictionary proper of the 1587 Thomasius. The editors use two major works as the basis for their information: Charles Stephanus' *Dictionarium historicum, geographicum, poeticum* (1553) and the proper-name section of Cooper's *Thesaurus*. The paralleled entries which follow will serve to show the close relationship of the proper-name division of the Thomasius to the basic sources.

C. Stephanus (1553)	Cooper (1565)	Thomas (1589)
Aba, Xenophanis filia, quae, Olbi Ciciliae urbis tyrannidē, quam pater procuratorio nomine administrarat cultu obsequiisque ab Antonio & Cleopatra sibi impertrauit. . . .	*Aba*, A towne in Arabie, and a Citie of Phocis. Also an hill of Armenia, out of which the riuer Euphrates springeth.	*Aba*, Daughter to Xenophanes, who obtained of Anthonie the gouernment of Olbia in Cilicia. Also a towne in Arabie, and a citie in Phocis. Also a hill

Caballīnus, a, um, p. b. Plin. *Of a horsse.*

Căballus, li, m. g. nunquam ferè sine derisione dicitur, Hor. *A horsse: a caple.*

Căballītío, siue Caballatio, onis, Fest. *The office of horsekeeping.*

Cabus, bi, m. g. *A measure containing two sextaries & a halse, or as other thinke, foure sextaries.*

Căcăbo, as, Ovid. *To call or sing like a partrich.*

Căcăbus, bi, m. g. Plin. *A Caudron, brasse potte, or skillet, wherin meat is sodde.*

Căcălĭa, æ, f. g. Plin. *An hearbe called wilde carowaies.*

Cacatura, æ, f. g. *Ordure, scumme, or silthe.*

Căcătŭrio, is, ivi, itum, Desiderat. Mart. *To lust to goe to the stoole.*

Căcătus, a, um, part. vel nom. è part. Catul. *Filed with ordure, that one hath used at the stoole.*

Căcētăphon, vel Cacophaton, græc. *An ill and unpleasant sound.*

Căchectus, & Cacheticus, i, m. g Pli. *A man of ill disposition or complexion of the bodie, whereby nothing prouueth with him, but that he pineth awaie.*

Căchexĭa, æ, f. g. *An euill disposition or state of the bodie, whereby it commeth to passe that all the nourishment is corrupt & this happeneth either when by reasō of long sickenes, the body is not refreshed, or by euill medecines, distempered, or by badde diet a long time receiued.*

Căchinnătĭo, onis, f. g. verb. à Cachinno. *A great or vnmeasurable laughter.*

Căchinno, as, & Cachinnor, aris. *To laugh a loude or vnmeasurable, so make a great sound.*

Căchinno, ōnis, Pers. *A great laughter, a scorner.*

Căchinnus, ni. *A scorne, a loud laughter in derision: a loud sound.*

Cachla, Plin. Idem quod Buphthalmus.

Cachryes, Plin. *Such a thing as groweth in hazells, hanging like Aglets before the leafe come forth, compact together as it were scales.*

Cachryi. *The seede of Rosemarie.*

Cacia, græc. *A fault in a thing, naughtines.*

Cacobasilea, æ, f. g. græc. *An ill kingdome.*

Căco, as, Mart. *To goe to the stoole.*

Cacoblepa. *A beaste in the bankes of Nilus, that killeth with the sight whome it beholdeth.*

Căcŏchyla, t. b. græc. *Things of euill iuice,*

Căcŏchĭmĭa, æ. f. g. gr. *Ill digestion.*

Căchŏdæmon, ōnis, f. g. Val. Max. gr. *An euill spirit or deuill.*

Căcŏëthe, n. g. Plin. *A bile or sore, ill to be cured.*

Căcŏëthes, n. g. Iuv. græc. *An euill or preposterous condition or custome, a venemous sore.*

Cacologia. *Ill speach.* Cacologus, græ. *An euill speaker.*

Căcŏstŏmăchos, græc. *That hath an euill and weake stomacke.*

Căcŏsyntheton, græc. Mala, seu desormis compositio.

Căcŏtechnĭa, Quint. græc. Ars mala & ad perniciem inuenta.

Căcŏzēlĭa, æ, f. g. Quint. græc. *An euill affection or imitation.*

Căcŏzēlus, Suct. græ. *One that doth not imitate well, one that is ill minded or affectioned.*

Cactos, Plin. *A kinde of thistle, after some an Artichoke.*

Cacubalum, Plin. Herba acinos ferens nigros, quæ etiam vocatur Sarichnos, & Strumus.

Căcŭla, æ, m. g. Plaut. *A souldiours slaue or boy page.*

Caculatum, ti, n. g. Servitinm, Fest.

Căcumen, ĭnis, n. g. Plin. *The toppe, height, or sharpe ende of a thing: the ridge of an house: also persectenes.*

Căcūmĭnātus, a, um, part. vel nom. è part. Plin *Sharpe topped, with sharpe toppes.*

Căcūmĭno, as, Ovid. *To make copped or sharpe at the toppes.*

Cădāver, ĕris, n. g. *A deade bodie, carrion. a carkasse, a corse: also ruine.*

Cădāvĕrōsus, a, um, Terent. *Full of carraine: like a dead corps or carcas, deadly, gastlie.*

H 3   Cădiscus,

C. Stephanus (1553)	Cooper (1565)	Thomas (1589)
Aba, oppidū in Arabia foelici . . . ciuitas Phocidis . . . & mons Armeniae, vnde oritur Euphrates. . . .		in Armenia. Also a king of Hungarie that spoiled Bauaria and Austria.
Aba, Vngarorum rex, Austriam & Bauariam depopulatus est.		
Abacaena, ciuitas Medorum & item Siciliae. Ptolem.	*Abacaena*, A citie of Mede, and also of Sicily.	*Abacaena*, A citie of Mede: an other of Sicilie.
Abacus, Ceuolae regionis apud Indos metropolis, quae Granata vulgo vocatur. . . .		*Abacus*, The chiefe citie of Cevola, in India, now called Grenata.
Abae, *Abarum*, oppidum Phocidis. . . .	*Abae, arum*, A towne of Phocis.	*Abae, arum*, A towne of Phocis, and a place in Lycia.
Abae, Lyciae locus. . . .		
Abala, oppidum in Africa, Trogloditarum, non procul a mari rubro.	*Abala*, A towne in Afrike.	*Abala*, A towne of the Troglodites by the redde sea: also a hauen by Messalia.
Abala, portus Messaliae proximus.		
Abarimon, Scythiae regio iuxta Imaum montem super Antropophagos, in qua syluestres homines degunt, auersis post crura plantis, maximam habentes velocitatem, passimque cum feris vagantes. . . .	*Abarimon*, A countrie in Tartary, where men haue feete turned backwarde, and be wonderfull swift and wild.	*Abarimon*, A countrey in Tartarie, the people hauing their feete turned backeward, notwithstanding are very swift.
Abalites, sinus maris Trogloditici. . . .	*Abalites*, A bosome or goulfe in the sea, called Trogoniticum.	*Abalites*, A gulfe in the sea Trogloditicum.
Babactes, & *Bactes*, Bacchi cognomen. . . .	*Babactes*, One of the names of Bacchus.	*Babactes*, One of the names of Bacchus.
Babyrsa, castellum munitissimum Atropatiae regionis in Asia, prope Artaxatam urbem. . . .	*Babyrsa*, A strong town of Asia, in the countrey Atropatia, neere to the citie Artaxata.	*Babyrsa*, A strong towne of Atropatia in Asia.
Bacchemon, Lactantio, Persei & Andromedae filius.	*Bacchaemon*, The sonne of Perseus and Andromede.	*Bacchaemon*, Sonne to Perseus and Andromada.
Bacchides, dux, Sinopem urbem Lucullo prodidit. Strabo. lib. 12.	*Bacchides*, A capitaine that betrayed the citie Sinopis to Lucullus.	*Bacchides*, A captaine that betrayed Synope to Lucullus.

It is not necessary to multiply illustrations. They all exemplify the conclusion that in compiling the "Dictionarium Propria Locorum et Personarum Vocabula" the editors of the Thomasius kept open before them

both the Stephanus and the Cooper. Sometimes they followed one
authority, sometimes the other, and frequently their entry is a composite of the two. The great source of information is, of course,
Stephanus. His text is devoted exclusively to proper names. To him,
not only Cooper and Thomas were indebted but also almost every other
lexicographer of the sixteenth and seventeenth centuries.

In 1592 appeared the third edition of the Thomasius, much augmented,
with these words on the title page:

Thomas Thomasii Dictionarivm Tertio Iam summa fide ac diligentia accuratissimè
emendatum, magnaque insuper rerum scitu dignarum, et vocabulorum accessione,
longè auctiùs locupletiùsque; redditum. Huic etiam (praeter Dictionarium Historicum & Poeticum, ad prophanas historias, poetarumque fabulas intelligendas valde
necessarium) novissime accessit utilissimus de Ponderum, Mensurarum, & Monetarum
veterum reductione ad ea quae sunt Anglis iam in usu Tractatus. Cantabrigiae . . .
1592.

The new feature in this edition of the Thomasius is the table of weights,
measures, and moneys of the ancients expressed in English equivalents
of the sixteenth century. For this, the editor (now John Legate) had a
precedent in the work of his antecedents. Elyot had given a place to
these topics in the first edition of his *Dictionary*, and Cooper had asserted
on the title page of the *Bibliotheca Eliotae* (1548) that the weights and
measures had been corrected. Legate did not, however, take his information from his English forebears. He states, at the beginning of tables,
that in giving English equivalents of weights, measures, and coins, he is
following closely the interpretation of Georgius Agricola,[4] though of
course he did not disdain the opinion of Budaeus [5] and others who had
written on the subject. Legate's treatise has the advantage over that in
Elyot or Cooper of being placed in an independent section of his dictionary and made easy of use.

Of more interest in this study, probably, is the way in which, as the
title page affirms, the editor increased and enriched the text proper. Investigation shows that the principal source of enrichment in this third
edition was again Bishop Cooper's *Thesaurus*. This work, as we have
seen, served as a basis for general definitions of many words in the earlier
editions of the Thomasius. But in these were no quoted Latin phrases to
illustrate meaning and usage. The editor now adds selected quotations
to supplement his general definitions. And these quotations derive, in
most cases, from Cooper's *Thesaurus*.

To the general definition of *confero*, for example, the Thomasius of
1592 adds the following illustrative phrases:

Conferre manum, vel manus, To fight together.
Conferre se Romam, In urbem, vel ad urbem, In campum, vel ad campum, To goe in or unto.
Conferre se in fugam; & conferre se in pedes. Plaut. To betake him to his heeles, to run away.
Conferre novissima primis, To compare the last with the first.
Dicimus autem Conferre se isti, & cum isto.
Tempus ad, vel in rem aliquem conferre, Plin. iun. To bestow or employ.

These Latin phrases, together with the citation of authors, come from the illustrations under *confero* in Cooper's *Thesaurus*.

The procedure is similar in Thomasius under *conficio*. Here are added these phrases, all from Cooper:

Vi manuque conficere aliquid, To doe by force and strong hand.
Conficere malum alicui, Terent. To doe one a mischiefe.
Pecuniam ex re aliqua conficere, To make money of a thing.

Many other entries in the 1592 Thomasius furnish evidence of a similar method of augmentation. For example, *abrogo* has four illustrative phrases, in both the Latin and its English equivalent; *absolvo* has three; *adverto*, five; *consisto*, three; *effero*, three; and *illido*, two—the illustrations all from the *Thesaurus*.

Holyoke's reference to Calepine and Junius as sources for Thomasius requires brief notice. The *Dictionarium* of Friar Calepine, or the Calepinus, as it was generally called, was of course known to all the Renaissance lexicographers. As we have seen, Elyot drew freely from this dictionary; Robert Stephanus at one time edited the Calepinus and took over materials from it for his own dictionaries. Cooper, indebted to both Elyot and Stephanus, owed, indirectly, much to the Italian's Latin *Dictionarium*. Thomas likewise was, through Cooper, an indirect debtor to Calepine. There is evidence, also, proving that Thomas went directly to the same source. After *vectatio* and *vomitoria spectaculis* the compiler writes *Calep.*, indicating Calepine as the source. As these terms are not in Cooper, we are safe in assuming that they come directly from the original Calepine. In many other words, such as *caprificatio, caprificus,* and *caprimulgi* the Thomasius is nearer to Calepine than to Cooper. Although Calepine is hardly a major source, the evidence supports Holyoke's statement that the Italian hermit's work was used by Thomas in 1592.

As early as 1567, Hadrian Junius published his *Nomenclator omnium rerum propria nomina,* a book of class names in the medieval vocabulary tradition. This popular work was translated into English and published as *The Nomenclator, or Remembrancer of Adrianus Junius, Physician,* "conteining proper names and apt termes for all things under their convenient titles . . . Written by the said Ad. Ju. in Latine, Greeke, French and other foreign Tongues: and now in English, by John Higgins, 1585." It was probably this edition to which Holyoke referred. The Junius was an obvious source of information for lexicographers from 1585, or earlier, to well into the seventeenth century. Although there is little evidence that Thomas used the *Nomenclator* in the 1587 edition of his *Dictionarium,* there are references to Junius in the 1589 and subsequent editions, as under *canicularis, caninus, canna, cannabaceus, capreolus, capsella, carbunculus, caseus,* and *cataplasmata,* which seem to indicate direct borrowing from this source.

With added illustrations from Cooper's *Thesaurus* and matter from Calepine and Junius, the 1592 Thomasius was considerably augmented. Since the various editions of the dictionary are without pagination, and since the pages differ in size and in the number of columns to the page, it is difficult to estimate accurately the extent of the increase. The text of 1589, for example, is a small quarto with two columns of words to the page, whereas the text of 1592 is a large quarto with three columns to the page. Thus the increase in the word list, and particularly in phrases illustrative of meaning and usage, must run to several thousand.

No augmentation is indicated for the 1594 edition of Thomasius.

The title page of the 1596 edition of the Thomas is identical in phrasing with that of 1592, excepting this added statement: "Qvinta Editio Superioribus cum Graecarum Dictionum, tum eorundem primitivorum adiectione multo auctior." Interpreted, this language refers to a twofold augmentation: (1) a separate list of Greek primitives, and (2) Greek equivalents inserted after the Latin terms to be defined. For primitives a special heading, after the dictionary proper, reads: "Primitiva Omnia Totius Graecae Linguae Vocabula." This section consists of fifteen pages, three columns to a page, of Greek primates with Latin equivalents. The source of the matter on these pages is the popular Greek-Latin lexicon (1589 and later editions) of John Scapula.[6] Comparison of the first fifty Greek words and the Latin interpretations in the Scapula with corresponding entries in the Thomasius shows a close relationship.

For the Greek equivalents of Latin entries, the editors of the Thomasius, in 1596, turned back to the Hutton-Morelius *Commentarii* of 1583, the volume used in compiling the 1587 edition. In the earlier editions of Thomasius, Greek equivalents were not inserted, but now the Morelius is the convenient source for the Greek. Parallels which follow will show the relationship.

Hutton-Morelius (1583)

Praéferox, ferôcis, adiectiuum, ex Prae &
Ferox, Liu. ὁ πάνυ χαλεπὸς . . . ἀπηνὴς
σφόδρα. Verie fierce and hastie: verie
rigorous, eger, and cruell.

Praeferrātus, ta, tum, Plin. . . . σιδερόδετος κατ' ἄκρον. Pointed or shod with
iron, as a speare is at the fore end.

Perféruidus, da, dum, ex Prae & Férui-
dus, Columel. . . . ὑπέρθερμος. Verie
hot, and burning: scalding or scortch-
ing hot.

Praefestinâtim, aduérbium, Sisenna, &
Praefestine, Plaut. . . . ἀνυπερθέτως
. . . Verie hastily: ouerhastily: in post
hast.

Praefestino, festínas, festinâre, ex Prae &
Festino, Columel. προεπείγω . . . To
make ouer much hast: to make post
hast: to hast before due time.

Praéficae, praeficorum, f. g. plural num.
Plautus. ἡ θρηνοῦσα. Women hired to
lament and mourne at ones buriall, and
to praise the life and deedes of the
dead parties.

Thomas (1596)

Praeferox, ōcis, adiect. Liv. Πάνυ
χαλεπὸς, ἀπηνὴς σφόδρα. Very fierce
& hastie, very rigorous, eger, and
cruell.

Praeferrātus, a, um, Plin. σιδερόδετος
κατ' ἄκρον. Pointed or shodde with
iron, as a speare is at the foreende: also
that is bound with yron, Plaut.

Praefervidus, a, um. Columel. ὑπέρθερμος.
Very hot, and burning: scalding or
scorching hotte.

Praefestinātim, Sisen. & Praefestine, ad-
verb. Plaut. ἀγυπερθέτως. Very hastily,
ouer hastily, in post hast.

Praefestino, as, Colum. προεπείγω . . . To
make ouer much hast, to make post hast
before due time.

Praefica, ae, f. g. Plaut. ἡ θρηνοῦσα. A
woman hired to lament & mourne ones
buriall going before the corpes.

Although the 1596 edition of the Thomasius claims on the title page
augmentation only in respect to the Greek primates and Greek equivalents of Latin entries, there is, in fact, a considerable number of new
entries. These are usually short, occupying one or two lines in a column,
and many of them are followed by the marks *Gl.* or *Gloss.*, indicating a
glossary or glossaries as their source. What glossaries are used or who
gathered these words, we do not know. These are the kind of words
supplied later by Philemon Holland, but there is no evidence to prove
that, in 1596, Holland was in any way associated with the editors of the
Thomasius. The table which follows shows the number of entries between
key words and suggests to what extent the 1596 edition is augmented.[7]

| | NO. OF TERMS DEFINED | | |
	1592 ed.	*1596* ed.	*1600* ed.
Confero to *confugella*	100	207	176
Mollugo to *montifringilla*	100	118	112
Spargo to *sphaeromachia*	100	114	104

Analysis of the added words in each block reveals that about 50 per
cent of them are indicated as coming from glossaries. The third group,

Condoctor,oris, m.g. Gloss. *A fellow teacher.*

Condóléo, es, & Condolesco, is,ui,ére, & elcére. συνάγχια. *To be verie sicke or much pained: to ake, to be sorowfull.* Condoluit caput de vento, Plaut. *The wind made his head ake.*

Condolo,as, Apull. *To make smooth.*

Condolentia,æ,fœ.g.Gloss. *A sympathy of greefe.*

Condolentèr, adverb. Firmic. *With griefe.*

Condominari,Livius. *To beare rule.*

Condomo,as,ui,Gloss. *To tame togither.*

Condominatus,m.g.Gloss. *A bearing rule togither.*

Condónatio,ónis,fœ.g.verbal. χάρισμα. *A giving or forgiving.*

Condónatus,a,um, part. συγχωρηθείς. *Forgiuen,pardoned.*

Condóno,as, δωρέομαι. *To give willingly and freely:to remit,forgive, and pardon.* συγχωρέω. Condonare alicui munusculum, *To give a present.* ¶Condono tc,Plaut.*I pardon thee.*¶Condonare aliquem pecuniam,debitum,&c. Plaut.& Condonare pecuniam debitoribus.*To forgiue one the mony which he ought.* ¶Condonare peccatum, Saluft. *To pardon an offence.*

Condormio, is, ivi, itum, ire, & Condormisco,Plaut. συγκαθεύδω. *To sleepe with other,to take a noppe.*

Condormitator,oris,m.g.Glo. *That sleepeth with one.*

Condormitio,f.g. Firm. *A sleeping togither.*

Condormito,as,Gloss.*To sleep togither.*

Condotalis,le,Cod. *Having his dowrie togither.*

Condotari, Cod. *To have a dowrie with another.*

Condotatus,a,um,Digest.*Having a dowrie with other.*

Condrille,es, & Condrilla, æ, fœ.g. vel Condrillum,li,n.g. Plin. gr. vide Chondrilla.

Condris,siue potiùs Chondris, fœ. g. Plin. *The bearbe called false ditanie.*

Condubitalis, le, Gloss. *That doubteth or is in doubt.*

Condubitatim, adverb. Gloss. *Doubtingly.*

Condubitantèr,Glo. *Doubting togither.*

Condubitatus, a, um, Firmic. *Doubted of by many.*

Condubito,as,Marc. *To doubt of.*

Condubius,a,um,Gloss. *Which doubteth.*

Conduçibilis. le. ad Heren. λυσιτελής,ὠφέλιμος. *Profitable, compendious. good that might bired.*

Condúcit,συμφέρει. *It is profitable,expedient,good,or availeable: it maketh much for.*

Conduco,is,xi,ctum,ére, συνάγω. *To bring with: to hire or procure: to buy: to take an house or land :* μίσθωμα, *also to gather or assemble togither in one place :to convert: to take in hand, to undertake to doe a thing at a price , to doe a worke or businesse for hire or wages.* μισθόω. Exercitus in unum conducere, Tacit. *To gather togither.* ¶ Aliquem ad cædem faciendam conducere, *To hire or procure one to,&c.* ¶ Qui columnam illam de Cotta conduxerat. *Who undertooke at Cottas hands to make, &c.* ¶Conducit hoc tuæ laudi, *This makeih much for your praise.*¶Conducunt hæc ad ventris victum, Plaut. *Are good to fill the bellie.* ¶In rem quod rectè conducat tuam, Plaut. *Makeih well for thy profite.*

Conductarius,a,um,Glo.*That guideth togither.*

Conducor, eris. Firmic. *To be brought togither.*

Conductilis,le,Firm. *Easie to be hired.*

Conductim,adverb. Cap. *Bringing togither.*

Conductio,ónis,f.g.verb. μίσθωσις. *An hiring,an undertaking to doe a' a price,hire: a gathering togither.*

Conductitius, a, um, Plaut μισθωτός. *That may be or is hired or taken.*

Conducto,as, Gloss. *To bring togither.*

Conductor,aris,Gloss.*To be led togither.*

Conductor,oris,m.g.verb.μισθωτής. *He that taketh or hireth: bee that is hired to doe : that undertaketh.*

Conductum,di,n.g.* *A thing hired.*

Conductus,a,um,part. à Conducor, μεμισθωμένος. *Hired, procured, brought togither.*

Condulus, Fest. vide Condalum.

condum,di,n.g. Gloss. *A cup or pot.*

Condúplicatio,ónis. f g. verb. Plaut. διπλασιασμός. *A doubling: also a figure when one worde is twise repeated,Ad Heren.*

Condúplico,as, διπλόω. *To double.*

Conduplor, atis, Gloss. *To be doubled.*

Conduplicatò, adverb. Gloss. *Doubling.*

Conduplicatus, a, um, Gloss. *Deubled.*

Conduplicor,atis, Digest. *To be doubled.*

Condurdon,Plin. *An hearbe that in August beareth a red floure, and bealeth the disease called the Kings evill.*

Condus, di, & Conduspromus, mi,m.g.Plaut. ταμίας,ταμιείον.*A butler,a yenman of the larder.*

Condylóma,átis,n.g. s.b. Plin. græ *A swelling of the fundament, proceeding of an inflammation.*

Condylus,li,m g. s b. Mart. gr. *The roun inesse or knots of the bones in the knee, ankle, elbowe ,knuckles, &c A lso a ring or thimble.*

Confabrè,adverb.Firm. *Fitly, handsomely.*

Confabrefacio, is, Digest. *To make fitte or fine.*

Confabrefactus, a, um, Gloss. *Male handsome.*

Confabricator,Glo. *That doth devise*

A page from the 1596 edition of Thomas Thomas's Dictionarium, in the University of Texas Library

spargo to *sphaeromachia,* for example, has the following new entries with sources indicated in the parentheses:

Sparicellus (Gloss.)	*Sparulus* (Gloss.)	*Speculabilis* (Lucret.)
Spargana (Gloss.)	*Spatiabundus* (Capell.)	*Speror* (August.)
Spargor (Virg.)	*Spatiatio* (Gloss.)	*Sperum* (Gloss.)
Sparsor (August.)	*Spector* (Ouid.)	*Sphaeroides* (Boet.)
Spartarius (Gloss.)		

These words, typical of the various additions, seem to show that at least one editor had a preference for words from medieval glossaries and the Church Fathers over those of classical origin. Thus the Thomasius appears to move a step away from the idea of a classical dictionary which was in the minds of Elyot and Cooper.

Since the editions of 1592 and 1596 are both fairly large quartos with three columns to a page, it is possible to estimate the extent of the augmentation. Although the texts are without pagination, the printers' signatures indicate that the later edition was augmented by about 10,000 words. While there were changes, additions, and also omissions, in subsequent editions, probably no edition contained a larger word list than that of 1596.

The edition of 1600 differs from all preceding editions of the Thomasius. Earlier editions had been printed in quarto, those of 1592 and 1596 being fairly large quartos; the edition of 1600 is a small octavo. The quarto of 1596 had introduced Greek primates and Greek equivalents for most Latin terms; the 1600 octavo omits all matter pertaining to Greek, and also reduces somewhat the Latin word list of 1596. Referring to the table above, we find that the octavo of 1600 has in the first group (*confero,* etc.) 176 entries as compared with 207 for the 1596 quarto and 100 for the 1592; in the second group (*mollugo,* etc.) 112 as against 118 and 100; and in the third group (*spargo,* etc.) 104 as against 114 and 100, respectively. Thus in number of words listed the 1600 octavo falls between the quartos of 1592 and 1596. The octavo bases its word list on the 1596 quarto, omitting some of the words, especially those derived from glossaries.

Examination of the editions of 1610 and 1619, both octavo, shows that they correspond with that of 1600 as to word lists, omission of Greek primates, equivalents for Latin terms, and printers' signatures. They appear to be, in fact, reprints of the 1600 octavo. These small volumes, similar in format, size, and content, and printed at Cambridge and London, may have been intended for schoolboys. Color is given to this theory by the fact that a copy of the 1600 Thomasius in the Cambridge University Library is bound (contemporary binding) with a copy of Lyly's Latin grammar (1606), once owned by Mrs. Elizabeth Colles.

In 1606 the editors of the Thomasius return to the quarto-size volume, instead of octavo. The title page of this edition is the same in phrasing as that of 1596, except for the substitution of *Septima Editio* for *Quinta Editio*. In the word list there is a slight reduction. The 1606 quarto has slightly more entries in the dictionary proper than has the 1600 octavo, but fewer than the 1596 quarto. The Greek primates and Greek equivalents are restored. Probably the basic list for the 1606 edition was in the 1600 volume, though some additions seem to have been made from the 1596 quarto. Changes though there were in the 1600 octavo and its reprints and in the 1606 volume, these represent no augmentations, but rather slight reductions, in the main word list.

A notable augmentation occurs in the Thomasius of 1615. This edition is in quarto, with three columns to a page, similar to the 1606 and earlier quartos, and with a title page corresponding to the earlier ones, except for the specification of this as the *Decima Editio,* and the following important addition: "Cui demum adiectum est Supplementum, Authore Ph. Hollando Med. Doctore, nova aliquot Dictionum millia complectens: Vnà cum nouo Anglolatino Dictionario." It should be said at the outset that the word list in the dictionary proper corresponds rather closely with that of the quarto of 1606. The augmentation for the 1615 edition is found in the innovations specified by the Latin sentence just quoted from the title page: the supplement added by Philemon Holland, and the small English-Latin dictionary.

The *Supplementum* by Holland is printed at the end of the volume, with a separate title page, the wording of which follows: "Lexici Latino-Anglici Paralipomena/Londini, Excudebat Joannes Legatus, Typographus Celeberrimae Academiae Cantabrigiensis. 1615." Following the title page is Holland's address, dated "Coventriae 17 Calendas Februarii 1615," and directed to the reader studious of Latin grammar. Holland writes, in substance, that for almost fifteen years, as often as he could find an idle moment in his medical work, he was drawn by some power (*nescio quo ingenij siue ductu siue impetu*) to the pleasant gardens of grammar and to the reading of historians and poets. When, in the reading of various approved classical authors, he had collected many words and phrases, not, so far as he knew, observed by lexicographers, it seemed to him worth while to arrange these in alphabetical order and to make a supplement to a dictionary. These observations, he thought, should be made available to posterity. He then comments on the useful work of Thomas Linacre, Sir Thomas Elyot, Cooper, and Junius; he also pays tribute to Thomas Thomasius and to John Legate, who had continued Thomas's work. Holland then states that he has permitted his collection to be used by Legate as a supplement to the Thomasius.

The *Supplementum*, or *Paralipomena*, according to the independent title page, contains 80 leaves, or 160 pages, with three columns to a page. An estimate of the entries, or Latin terms defined, is about 6,600. A study of the word list of Holland's *Paralipomena* indicates some overlapping with the Thomasius proper, but Holland has many terms not in the larger text, and others, though common to the two texts, with different shades of meaning. Holland cites his authorities, not mentioning specific texts except in the case of Pliny, where he seems to be alluding to the *Natural History*. The most frequent citations appear to be to Pliny and to Ammianus Marcellinus. References to Plautus are numerous; others cited are Apuleius, Arnobius, Macrobius, *Medulla grammatice*, and Suetonius. We might expect frequent citations of classical physicians. There are in this edition a few to Celsus and fewer to others. The first 26 entries, transcribed below, will give some specific idea of the content of the *Paralipomena*.

Abdicativus, a, um. Abdicativa propositio, in Logicke, a negatiue proposition, Apul.

Abigeus, i. m. gen. A theefe that stealeth, and driueth away cattell. Vlpian.

Abominor, aris. To wish in cursing manner, *Crurum eius fragium abominata*, Wishing his legges had beene broken. Apul.

Aborior, eris, vel Aboriris. To end, or to die. *Cui opponitur Orior.* Varro.

Abortivi senatores. Suet. Sor. Orcivi.

Abrodiaetus. A delicate or dainty person. Plin. 35.

Abrupta discrimina vel pericula. Extreme, imminent and present dangers. Am. Marcel.

Abrupta mulier, a curst, shrewd, wilfull and froward woman, Am. Marcel.

In Abrupto necessitatis, at the pointe of necessitie. Am. Marcel.

Abruptà, adverb. Without order, *vt, Abrupti damnari*, To bee condemned downe right, without all order, Am. Marc.

Abruptè, Wilfull. Am. Marcel.

Abscedor, is, di, ère. To lose the sight of a place, Virgil. *Aerias Phaecum abscondimus arces.*

Absocer, èri. My wiues great grandfather, Iul. Capitol. in Gordianis.

Absolvo, is, ère. To cleere one or resolue one. *Hoc primum te absolvo.* I resolue you first of this point. Or, I would cleere this point unto you first. Plaut. Menech.

Absoluta lingua, Loose at libertie, not tied. Plin.

Absolutoria tabula, or *tabella*, A bill or verdict giuen up by the Iury noted with this letter, *A.* to acquit a prisoner, Sueton. August.

Absque, Praep. Except, or sauing. *Absque Mesopotamia.* Am. Marcel. Besides, *Absque mortuis. Id.* Ouer and aboue. *Absque fructuosis petitionibus multis.* Ouer and besides many good and gainfull suites, Am. Marcel.

Abstinor passivè, To bee pent or kept from. *Si inclusus abstineatur die ac nocte.* If he be pend up and kept from meat, *&c.* Plin. 15.

Abstinens, Part. forbearing extortion, or taking other mens goods. *Ita sunt abstinentes.* Am. Marcel.

Absumēdo, inis, a waste, or consumption, Plaut.

Absumor, eris, To be worried, or deuoured, Plin. 9.46.

Aberusus, part. Idem quod Abstrusus, Am. Marcel.

Abusus, a, um, Spent or worne with using.

Abutor, ěris, To vse, or make vse of. *Cuius abutimini fontibus?* Whose springs be they that ye vse, and drinke of? *Sic* Am. Marcel. *Temporis spatio abusus.*

Abusivus, a, um. Adi. Disused, *Abusivus aries,* a Ramme (i. an engin) laid by and disused. Am. Marcel.

Acacia, a kinde of thorne tree the gum wherof is Gum Arabicke. Dodon.

As we noticed above, the title page of the 1615 Thomasius mentioned not only the *Supplementum* by Dr. Holland but *Vna cum nouo Anglo-latino Dictionario.* In the text the English-Latin dictionary has the running title "Vocabularium Anglolatinum ex Dictionario." It consists of 70 leaves (signatures *Aaaa*⁸–*Kkkk*⁸), or 140 pages. These abbreviated English entries, words or phrases, run to more than 16,000; and each English entry has a number of Latin equivalents, or synonyms. Although these increase the physical size of the general *Dictionarium,* they do not essentially increase the Latin word list, for, as the running title suggests, they are all from the Latin-English dictionary. They represent a selection and setting down in abbreviated form and in reverse, the English before the Latin, of what could be found in the Latin-English dictionary of the 1615 Thomasius. The reason for this belated section is to be found in the competition at this time offered by the Rider-Holyoke dictionaries, which had both the Latin-English and English-Latin *in extenso.*

Addressing "All Young Learners of the Latin Tongue," in 1615, Legate the printer states that he is now carrying out his long-intended purpose of supplying, in the *Vocabularium,* the English before the Latin. He continues:

This though it bee not in that copious and ample manner performed, as by others heretofore haue beene, who intending their owne priuate ends, haue heaped whatso-euer they could rake together out of other mens labours: yet my trust is that I haue heerein effected so much, as shall bee for your vse, who are young grammarians. For to what end are obsolete words to be stuffed into this worke, when better are as ready to be had, vnlesse it be to make vp a number of some thousands, that the volume may seeme the greater, though not the worthier.

In a Latin address to the reader, the printer explains that the *Vocabularium* has been completed by a very learned man, but he supplies no name. The *Vocabularium* comes from Thomas's *Dictionarium,* but not directly as the heading and the running title suggest. As early as 1589, John Rider had performed the feat, in his *Bibliotheca scholastica,* of making an English-Latin dictionary by reversing and abridging Thomas's Latin-English. Of the trouble resulting from Rider's procedure, we shall hear later. The point of interest relative to the 1615 Thomasius is that the editors, with absolute justification, selected their English-Latin *Vocabularium* from an early edition of Rider. The only wonder is that they had not done so earlier.

The quarto of 1620, excepting the important dedication to Lord Bacon, to be referred to later, corresponds in all respects to that of 1615, and is probably a reprint of the latter. The 1620 edition need not, therefore, detain us here.

Before proceeding to a consideration of the final revision and augmentation of the Thomasius, a point of biographical and bibliographical interest must be touched upon here. We learned earlier that upon the death of Thomas Thomas, in 1588, John Legate succeeded him and continued to print and, at intervals, to revise and augment Thomas's *Dictionarium*. In 1619, John Legate the Younger, also a printer, succeeded his father in the right to print Thomas's dictionary. No explanation has been given of the reason why the Legates came, apparently, so easily by this right, and this is perhaps not the place to discuss the subject in detail. It is sufficient to state here that, from John Legate the Younger's dedication in the 1619 edition of Thomasius (reprinted in the 1620 edition), we learn that the younger Legate was the grandson of Thomas Thomas and that therefore the elder Legate must at one time have been the son-in-law of Thomas. These facts, not observed by bibliographers, are probably of considerable importance respecting the literary and property rights of the Legates in the *Dictionarium* of Thomas Thomas.[8]

In the 1631 edition, to which Holland contributed, we have the last augmentation of the book and the final form. The title page of this edition reads the same as that of 1592, quoted above, with the following addition:

> Decima Tertia Editio Superioribus cum Graecarum Dictionum, tum earundem primitivorum adiectione multo auctior. Cui demum illud intextum est Supplementum, quod priori editioni adjecerat Ph. Hollandus Med. Doctor, una cum Auctario novo, aliquot Dictionum millia complectens—Novum insuper Dictionarium Anglo-latinum. . . . Londini, Ex officina Iohannis Legati . . . MDCXXXI.

In an address to the reader Holland explains that his *Paralipomena,* which appeared as a supplement to earlier editions (1615, 1620), has now with his consent been woven into the dictionary proper, each word in its place in the general alphabet. Not only so, but more than 600 additional words which Holland has later collected have likewise been placed in the text. Apparently, the phrase *aliquot Dictionum millia complectens* ("comprising several thousand words") of the title page is intended to include the new collection of 600 words, the 6,600 in the

Paralipomena, and an unspecified number of entries and illustrations from medieval sources, as Holland informs the reader. All these are now inserted in the Thomasius proper. Of the words from the Middle Ages and the late fifteenth century, Holland himself mentions two specific sources and suggests others that are probably of the same general period.

Hijs [that is, to these 600 words] etiam accedunt . . . Versiculi aliquot, ex Ioannis de Ianua Fratris, viri ut illa secula ferebant eruditi & de re Literaria optime meriti, Catholico: ex Medulla item Grammaticae, alijsque illius Notae authoribus: quotquot videlicet Lumen aliquod Literaturae adferre, & nitorem seu elegantiam conciliare videbantur.

The *Catholicon,* referred to by Holland, was compiled by the Dominican Joannes Balbus in 1286. This encyclopedic Latin dictionary, first printed in 1460, and frequently thereafter, was one of the principal sources for lexicographers of the fifteenth century. It may be significant that Philemon Holland, the classical scholar and "translator general," at the turn of the sixteenth century, deemed it worth while to collect words from the *Catholicon.* The *versicùli* from this lexicon are easily found in the 1631 Thomasius. Entries also from the *Medulla grammatice* (probably the same here as the *Promptorium parvulorum*) are readily observable, since they are designated *Medull. Gram.* All told, Holland's contribution to the Thomasius probably amounted to 8,000 or 9,000 entries. These words are wide in range, coming from Holland's extensive reading and translating of classical literature and his study of medieval glossaries and lexicons. Through Holland's enrichment, the *Dictionarium,* already a copious dictionary, becomes the great repository of Latin and English words in the Renaissance.

As there was no further augmentation of the Thomasius in the final edition of 1644, we may now briefly summarize the important revisions and changes made in the course of the history of the text. (1) The second edition, 1589, shows a slight increase in the word list and the addition of a concise dictionary of proper names, from Cooper and Charles Stephanus, extending to about 6,600 entries, a list which was ultimately extended to 7,500. (2) In 1592, the word list was further augmented, additions being made from Calepine and Junius, and phrases and sentences to illustrate meaning and usage were supplied largely from Cooper's *Thesaurus.* (3) In 1596, a considerable number of new entires were inserted from early glosses; Greek equivalents for most Latin entries were drawn from the Hutton-Morelius *Commentaries;* and a table of Greek primates with Latin equivalents was added from Scapula. (4) The editions of 1600, 1610, and 1619, all in small octavo, slightly reduced the word list, omitting all Greek terms and Greek primates. These editions were probably prepared for use in schools. (5) The *Paralipomena* of Philemon Holland and a concise English-Latin dictionary were added at the end of the text in 1615. (6) In 1631 the entries of the *Paralipomena* and several hundred additional terms and definitions assembled by Holland were woven into the text proper of the Thomasius.

The divisions and content of the text thus developed through a period of more than forty years may be briefly indicated by a tabulation of the headings of the 1631 (and the 1644) edition.

"Dictionarium Linguae Latinae et Anglicanae" (the Latin-English dictionary of 730 pages, quarto, three columns to the page, containing about 45,000 words).

"Dictionarium Propria Locorum et Personarum Vocabula breviter complectens" (the proper-name dictionary of 82 pages, three columns to the page, with approximately 7,500 entries).

"Ponderum, Mensurarum, et Monetarum Veterum reductio ad ea, quae sunt Anglis jam in vsu" (an index of Latin and Greek terms pertaining to ancient weights, measures, and moneys, followed by an exposition of the terms, together with their equivalents in English; 12 pages).

"Primitiva Omnia Totius Graecae Linguae Vocabula" (a list of Greek primates with Latin equivalents, drawn from Scapula; 14 pages).

"Vocabularium Anglo-Latinum ex Dictionario" (an elementary English-Latin vocabulary of 140 pages, drawn from the Latin-English section via Rider's *Bibliotheca scholastica*).

The technical features of the Thomasius were probably determined in large part by the basic sources. In employing the alphabetical order, for example, as in adding Greek equivalents for many entries, Thomas was following the Hutton-Morelius *Commentarii*. In the intermittent indications of etymology, the Cambridge printer had a precedent in both Hutton and Cooper. The practice of marking long and short syllables of Latin terms with the symbols of the macron and the breve, as in *dīvĭdo* or *dīversōrium* or *dŭbĭtātio*, was a departure from the major sources. Cooper had indicated the stress by the abbreviations *pen. cor.* and *pen. prod.*, and Hutton had used the accentual symbols. For the giving of grammatical information—indicating the part of speech, the gender and declension of nouns, the principal parts of verbs, etc.—Thomas had ample precedent, though he seems to be nearest to Hutton and Cooper. Either of these authorities he could have followed in the matter of inserting phrases and sentences from classical writers to illustrate meaning and usage. In this practice, however, Cooper among English lexicographers offered the great precedent and abundance of illustrations, many of which Thomas borrowed. In selecting a few choice illustrations from the many, the edi-

tors of the Thomasius worked economically and made possible the presentation of a greater number of terms in smaller compass than in the
Cooper. The various editions of the Thomasius served to establish the
alphabetical order of arrangement, and in this as in most other technical
aspects Thomas was the model for lexicographers of the seventeenth
century.

Closely related to the technical aspects of lexicography—if not actually
a part of them—is the exemplification of the principle of copiousness. We
have seen earlier how this principle, through the use of synonymy, was
illustrated in the *Catholicon Anglicum*, in Elyot's *Bibliotheca*, and most
elaborately and consciously in Cooper's *Thesaurus*. Although Thomas and
the subsequent editors of his text do not employ the word *copie* or its
derivatives in their comments on the dictionary, they show by their actual
practice that the precedent of Cooper was not lost on them. They elaborate
the practice of the Elyot-Cooper dictionaries in placing immediately after
the term to be defined a larger number of English synonyms than generally appeared in Cooper. This is seen in the main entries of *confero* and
conficio (pp. 118 and 122 above) and in various others. Three additional
words illustrate the principle of copiousness:

Incurro . . . To run in or against, to incurre, to iustle, to meete with one by chance,
to take or befall, to extend or lie in length one with another: to light, run, or
happen upon, to inueigh against, to make incursions or inuasions, to assaile, to encounter, to run togither, or each at other.

Iners . . . Without Science or any Craft: idle, slouthfull, negligent, lither, not
occupied, nothing liuely, foolish or dull, without courage or spirit: not able to
helpe it selfe, unprofitable, barren, fruitlesse, unsauorie, without good taste or
smacke: rude, negligently made, unapt, unfit.

Inuidia . . . Enuie, hatred, ill will, spite, grudging, ill opinion that the people
haue of one, malice, procuring of ones displeasure by word or deed, great displeasure against one. . . .

Copiousness in the Thomasius definitely anticipates the work of John
Florio in his *Worlde of Wordes*, an Italian-English dictionary, published in 1598. Florio follows the system of Thomas, borrows freely
from his dictionary, and employs the running title "A Copious and exact
Dictionarie."

Our conception of the final editions of the Thomasius, in all its copiousness, would hardly be complete without noting further the diversity of
materials, much of which was drawn into the text after compilation of
the earlier editions. There are, for example, a great many entries concerned with the identification and description of birds. Some of these
are borrowed from Cooper, who, as we have seen, derived a considerable
amount from Turner's *Avium historia* (1544), inserted it in the *Bibli-*

otheca of 1552, and carried it over to the *Thesaurus,* without ever mentioning the name of Turner. For the borrowings from Cooper, compare the *Thesaurus* and the *Dictionarium* under *alcedo, ardea, attagena, atricapilla, bosca, carduello, certhia, cinclo, collurio, crex, parus, platea, salus,* and *sitta.* The editors of the Thomasius also went directly to Turner. Under *aesola, iunco,* and *lutea,* they quote Turner, whose name is not mentioned by Cooper; and *tetrao,* common to Turner and Thomas, is not in Cooper. A similar process is observable with respect to the herbal lore in the Thomasius. The play is from Turner to Cooper to Thomas. But again the compilers insert additional entries on herbs directly from Turner's *Herball.* See in the respective texts the words *abrotonum, absinthium, acanthion, acanthus, aconitum, adiantum, alsine, amaranthus, amomum, anagallis,* and *anemone.*

Festus also is much cited in the later Thomas dictionaries. In some instances, the citation and the accompanying definition, as in *alicariae* and *ambrices,* are from Cooper. But in many other cases, as in *ambaxioqui, ambegni, ampedices, amtermini, anas & aditas, anculo,* and *ancumulentae,* the revisers of the Thomasius seem to have gone directly to the *De significatione verborum* of Festus.

With the supplements of Philemon Holland in 1615, and again in 1631, there appear more quotations from, and a greater number of references to, Nonius, Varro, Ammianus Marcellinus, and Petronius Arbiter.[9] As Holland himself was a learned physician, it was but natural that he should supply medical terms from earlier writers of the same profession. Hence the increased number, in the 1631 edition, of references to Dioscorides, Celsus, and Paracelsus.[10] To judge from the number of citations of Paracelsus and the numerous Latin quotations from him, one would infer that he was greatly admired by Holland. Under the following entries Paracelsus is quoted: *scacurculla, scaiolae, scirona, sebel, sedativa medicamenta, spagyrus, spara, sparallium, truphat, turbith, trigonum, vegetabilia, viltrum, ulissipena, unquasi, vomitivum, xenechtum, xeniphidei,* and many others.

Although Holland undoubtedly had a predilection for classical literature and language, he did not neglect the native and the vernacular. He states explicitly that he has taken matter from the *Catholicon,* the *Medulla grammatice,* and other such works. Among the *versiculi* which Holland admittedly drew from the *Catholicon* of Joannes Balbus and which were inserted in the Thomasius are these:

> Est cevere virum, sed crissari mulierum,   Cathol.
> Sternitur aequivoce, mare, Iectulus, hostis, asellus,   Cathol.
> Subque iugo positus, bos dicitur ibi subiunx,   Cathol.
> Glebas saepe vomis, ideo nomen tibi vomis,   Cathol.

There are also in the Thomasius some definitions similar to those found in the fifteenth-century *Catholicon Anglicum*. As this work was never printed until modern times, it is possible that Holland or some other contributor had access to a manuscript of the *Catholicon Anglicum*, though the similarities might be accounted for by a common source, such as the *Catholicon* of Joannes Balbus. Below are a few definitions for comparison.

Thomas	Catholicon Anglicum
Vespertilio . . . a reremouse.	a Bakke, *blata, vespertilio.*
Maialis . . . a barrow hogge, a libd or gelded hogge.	a Bare . . . *aper* . . . *maialis.*
Iugum . . . the beame whereon weavers doe turn their webbe. . . .	a Beme of a webster: *iugum, liciatorium.*
Liciatorium . . . a weavers shuttle, or a silk womans tounell or tavell, whereon silke or thread is cast or shot through the loom or webbe; the yarne beame.	
Singultio . . . to yexe, to sobbe, to cloake.	to Zyske . . . *singultire, singultare.*
Singultus . . . a yexing or hicke, a sobbing, a clocking of hennes with chickens.	a Ziskynge: *singultus.*

In the first chapter of this study, we referred to the circumstance that the printed editions of the *Promptorium parvulorum* in the early sixteenth century carried on the title page and in the colophon the alternative title of *Medulla grammatice* and that there was a tendency to refer to this English-Latin work by the latter title. The evidence shows that this practice prevailed at the end of the sixteenth century. Holland, in the note to the reader before the Thomasius of 1631, states that he has gathered definitions from the *Medulla grammatice*, among other books, for his collections. A comparison of the words and definitions in the Thomasius which are ascribed to the "*Medul. Grammat.*" with corresponding entries in the *Promptorium* shows them to be identical. As there was no printed edition of the *Medulla*, it seems highly probable that all those entries marked *Medul. Grammat.* are in reality from the *Promptorium.*

Thomas	Promptorium
Antemurale . . . A Barbican before a Castle: the Outworkes, Medull. Grammat.	Barbican be-forne a castel: *antemurale.*
Candidarius, ii. A Bleichster, or Whitester. Medull. Gram.	Bleyster, or quytstare: *candidarius, ij.* Whytestare, or pleykstare: *candidarius, ij.*
Canthus . . . The yron wherewith the round ring of the cartwheele is bound, the strake of a cart . . . the fellow of a wheele, Medull. Gram.	ffelwe off a wheele: *cantus.*

Thomas	Promptorium
Carnisprivium vel carnibrevium . . . car-nivale or Shrovetide, Medul. Gram.	ffastgong: *carniprevium.*
Cervix . . . The Haitrell. Medul. Gram.	Nape of a hed: . . . *ceruex.* Naterel [Haterel?], *idem quod* nappe, *supra.*
Cheruchus . . . A Fane. Medull. Gram.	ffane of stypil or odyr lyk: *Ventilogium* . . . *Cherucus.*
Ventilogium . . . A fane or weathercocke. Medul. Gram.	Weder-koke: *Ventilogium* . . . *idem quod* fan, *supra.*
Granomellum . . . Grout, Medulla Gram.	Growte for ale: *Granomellum.*
Semidolium . . . A vessel containing halfe a tunne: a pipe.	Pype, vessel or half tunne: *Semidolium.*
Submeridianum . . . An vndermeale. Medul. Gram.	Underne: *submeridianum.* Undermele: *postmeridies.*

The definitions quoted above seem to support the theory that those in the Thomasius ascribed to the *Medulla* came actually from the *Promptorium*. But one cannot be positive. There is the possibility that Holland may have had access to a manuscript of the *Medulla*.[11] Whatever Holland's source was, the significant fact is that his contribution to the Thomasius prolonged the life of, or revived permanently, many words that had been current in the fifteenth and early sixteenth century. Incidentally, he thus enhanced the value of Thomas's dictionary as a compendium of the English language of the Renaissance.

It is interesting to observe that the Thomasius has many definitions not listed as from a medieval source, but parallel to definitions in the *Promptorium*. Compare, for example, the following:

Thomas	Promptorium
Saginarium . . . A place wherein beasts or birds are fatted or crammed: a coupe, a franke, a pen, an Oxe stall.	Cowle to closyn ffowlys: *saginarium.* frank, kepyng off fowlys to make fette: *saginarium.*
Saginatus . . . fatted, crammed, franked.	ffrankyd: *saginatus.*
Sagino . . . to franke, to make fat, to cram.	ffrankyng: *saginacio.*
Fascino . . . To transforme or disfigure by enchantment, to bewitche, to forspeake, to forelooke.	fforspekyn or charmyn: *ffascino.*
Fascinous . . . One that bewitcheth or forspeaketh.	
Solea . . . a sole of a shooe, a shooe called a galoge or paten. . . .	Galegge, or galoch under solyng off mannis ffete: *crepitum.*
Intestina . . . The entrals, the guts and garbage.	Garbage of fowlys: *Entera.*
Intestinum . . . An entrall, an inward part either of man or any living thing, a bowell, gut, or garbage.	

The *Dictionarium*, or Latin-English dictionary of Thomas Thomas, is perhaps the most representative Renaissance lexicon. This typical quality is evident in the range and character of its sources. Based originally on Cooper and Morelius, through these it derived matter indirectly from the Latin-French dictionaries and the *Thesaurus* of Robert Stephanus. To Calepine also Thomas was a debtor, direct and indirect. He borrowed from Junius' *Nomenclator*, from John Scapula's Greek-Latin lexicon, from Charles Stephanus' Latin dictionary of proper names, from William Turner's books on birds and herbs, and from medieval glossaries. Through Philemon Holland, the Thomasius was further enriched by gleanings from the *Promptorium*, from Joannes Balbus' *Catholicon*, from Pliny, from Marcellinus, from Festus, from Celsus, and from Paracelsus. The Thomasius thus brings together in a compact but copious volume Latin terms from the ancient and the medieval world, interpreted largely in the English idiom of the Elyot-Cooper dictionaries.

Briefly to anticipate later discussion, the richness and range of Thomas were almost immediately recognized by other lexicographers. Within two years after the first edition, John Rider converted a large proportion of the Thomas into his *Bibliotheca scholastica* (1589), an English-Latin dictionary with a Latin index. In 1606, Francis Holyoke transformed Rider's Latin index into a Latin-English dictionary, deriving his English definitions for the most part from Thomas. And the Rider-Holyoke dictionaries, thus sprung from Thomas, were in constant vogue until the middle of the seventeenth century. In 1664, Francis Gouldman based his *Copious Dictionary in Three Parts* on Thomas and on the Rider-Holyoke. Adam Littleton and Robert Ainsworth, deriving from Gouldman and his antecedents, continue to reflect the impact of the Elyot-Cooper-Thomas dictionaries to the eighteenth century.[12]

CHAPTER XI

John Veron's *Dictionariolum puerorum,*
tribus linguis (1552)

IN THE PRECEDING chapters on lexicography in the sixteenth century we discussed the Elyot-Cooper group of Latin-English dictionaries and their immediate successors. These constitute a closely related group, extending over a period of approximately one hundred years. We now return to the middle of the sixteenth century to consider another group, all with the English before the Latin, with one exception, and each text to some extent dependent upon the Elyot-Cooper dictionaries. The exception is a small dictionary compiled in Latin, English, and French, in 1552, by John Veron.

Veron was a native of France, who was born near Sens, and studied at Orleans in 1534. In 1536 he went to England and spent some time studying at Cambridge University. He was rector of St. Alphage, Cripplegate, London, 1552–54. After a term of imprisonment for seditious preaching (1553–58), Veron served as prebendary of St. Paul's and rector of St. Martin's, Ludgate. He published protestant and controversial tracts and translations (1548–62). He died in 1563.[1] The dictionary printed under Veron's name bore the title *Dictionariolum puerorum, tribus linguis, Latina, Anglica, et Gallica conscriptum.* The provenience of this book is set forth by Rudolph Waddington in his address to the reader (quoted below), prefacing a new and much altered edition (1575) of Veron's text. Waddington explains that Veron had added English to a short dictionary compiled by Robert Stephanus in Latin and French.

The Latin-French work which Waddington refers to as the basis of Veron's dictionary is the *Dictionariolum puerorum Latino-Gallicum* of

Robert Stephanus. This book was first published at Paris, in quarto, in 1542 and reissued in 1544 and 1547. There was a second edition in 1550 (reprinted in 1552), and a third edition in 1557.[2] A comparison of Veron's text with the *Dictionariolum* of Stephanus confirms Waddington's statement.[3]

R. Stephanus (1544)	Veron (1552)
Condémno, condémnas, condemnáui, condemnátum, condemnâre, Condamner. Faire condamner.	*Condémno, condémnas, condemnáui, condemnátum, condemnâre,* to condemne, to make to condemne, Condamner, Faire condamner.
Condénso . . . Espessir. Serrer.	*Condénso* . . . to thyck, to harde. Espessir, Serrer.
Condîco . . . Quand deux ou plusieurs se denoncent l'ung a l'autre quelque chose, & côuiennent en icelle. Conuenir de quelque chose. Promettre. Intenter action personelle contre quelqu'ung.	*Condîco* . . . when two or mo do denounce or declare one to an other some thyng, and agree upon the same, to agre upon some thyng, to promyse to laye action personall agaynst some body. Quand deux ou plusieurs se denoncent l'ung a l'autre quelque chose, & conuiennent en icelle. Conuenir de quelque chose. Promettre. Intenter action personelle contre quelqu'ung.
Confectus . . . *Participiũ à conficior,* Gasté & perdu, Mis au bas. Parfaict & acheué. Mis a fin. Faict.	*Confectus* . . . *Participiũ à conficior,* destroyed and lost, brought lowe, undoone, perfecte, atcheued, fynished, brought to an ende, done. Gasté & perdu, Mis au bas. Parfaict & acheué. Mis a fin. Faict.
Conféssus . . . Qui a dict ce qu'on luy auoit demandé. Recongneu & côfessé. Cler & manifeste. Dequoy en n'ha point de doubte.	*Conféssus* . . . whych sayeth that, which he was asked, recognised, and confessed plain and manifest, wherupon there i no doubt. Qui a dict ce qu'on luy auoi demandé, Recongneu & côfessé, Cler & manifeste, Dequoy en n'ha point de doubte.

The parallels are representative of the two texts throughout. Veron takes over the Latin and French of Stephanus, inserting between these his rather literal English translation of Stephanus' French. Apparently the Veron text of 1552 was not a very successful venture. No new edition was published for a period of twenty-three years.

In 1575, however, this dictionary was considerably altered and enlarged, by Rudolph Waddington, and published with the following title page:

A Dictionary in Latine and English, heretofore set foorth by Master Iohn Veron and now newly corrected and enlarged For the vtilitie and profit of all young student in the Latine tongue, as by further search therin they shall finde. By R W. Imprinted at London, by Henry Middleton, for Iohn Harison, dwelling in Paules Churchyarde, at the signe of the white Greyhounde. Anno Domini. 1575.

Waddington's "To the Reader" is so nearly typical of the Elizabethan lexicographer's attitude toward dictionary-making that it is here quoted in its entirety.

To the Reader

How profitable the skill of any forreine tongue is in these daies to such as seeke knowledge and desire conference with strange nations, needs no enforcing: whilst the enioyers thereof have so double advātage ouer the base and skillesse sort, as among them they are both worthily praysed and of the higher and skilfull daily aduanced and preferred: But aboue all how necessary the knowledge of the Latine tongue is to any of us, that eyther desire to be entred into other bordering tongues or to serch the depth of any Science, or the assurance of our saluation through the true understanding of holy scripture, is so cōmonly knowne, and so generally agreed on, that happie seemes he that may attaine therto, or procure and leaue it to his child as a sufficient heritage. Than how much beholden are cōmon weales to such, as neglecting their priuate calling, haue been contented herein to impart the fruites of their labours to many? But among other our cōmon weale to those, that being for skill worthily aduanced, or for birth sufficiently prouided for, haue notwithstanding voutchsaued . . . to bestow the benefite of their trauailes upon us their countrey men? Herein that learned Knight Syr Thomas Eliot trode the first path, louingly leauing his labour to posteritie as a seale of well wishing to furtherance in learning. This labour since that time with no lesse loue and three double paine that Reuerend father D Thomas Cooper, now Bishoppe of Lincolne, hath so amply enlarged and so painefully polished, as both Maister Eliot's wish is sufficiently performed, and the diligent students therein to their contentment (as I take it) satisfied.

But because so ritche a tongue in wordes, adorned with so many apt phrases, cannot be comprised in any smal volume fitte in price or bulke, for young students, therefore that worthy French Printer Robert Steuens, thought good to draw a short Dictionary into Latine and French for the use of his countrey schollers, wherunto Maister Iohn Veron Senouois, likewise a French man, and a painefull preacher of Gods Gospell here amongst us, desiring to profite our youth in the Latine tongue, wherein he was very skilfull, added the English. These Bookes being all sold, and the meaner learned youth of this land wholly unprouided, I was intreated by one desirous to further learning, to ouer looke and augment the same: and weighing the greate giftes of those that had trauayled therein before with my smal habilitie and also leasure to satisfie his request, could gladly haue denied my freend, if his earnest perswasions to the imitation of so excellent men, and my great desire to further youth in learning, according to my calling had not wholy ouercome me. Therefore with humble submission to the better learned at my freendes earnest request, and for discharge of duty to my countrey, I tooke this woorke in hand, and of purpose thought good to leaue out the french, both by cause I saw it not so necessary for english students in latine, as for that Maister Barret,[4] hath few yeares since set forth an Alueary sufficient to enstruct those which are desirous to travel in the understanding of the French tongue, and also because I coueted to haue the more roome to adde such woords, as I thought meete for the further instruction of the younger sort of schollers: how many they are or how long they were in gathering I may not say, for I dare not complaine of my small paines, while so excellent men haue so cheerfully gone through with so great labours.

Only this I will say, if anything be found in this book woorthy of my trauaile, I wholy Dedicate it to the toward youth of my Cuntrey, to whom I wish such further-ance in learning as they may therby not only attaine both praise and aduancement in the true understanding of Gods truth, whereby they may the more faithfully serue our Queene and common weale heere, but also assure themselues of euerlasting praise, and euerlasting aduancement in Christ Jesu Amen.

Rodolphus Waddingtonus Ludimagister Hospiti Christi scholae, in renouatam Veroni Bibliothecam: Ad studiosam Anglorum Iuuentutem.

From this address and also from the title page we learn that Wadding-ton has omitted the French from the text and thus left more space for the Latin and English. Although he retained the Latin word list and the English definitions of 1552, he corrected and much extended the list. The extent of increase in the word list may be inferred from the table which follows, showing the number of entries between the terminal words (the Stephanus of 1544 had the same number of entries shown for the Veron of 1552).

	NO. OF TERMS DEFINED	
	1552 ed.	*1575* ed.
Bacca to *bellulus*	100	177
Condemno to *convenientia*	188	269
Frons to *furox*	100	143
Occasio to *offula*	100	173
Secludo to *supervivum*	100	190

Although this table cannot show the augmentation of individual entries taken over from the 1552 edition or substitution for omissions from the earlier text, it suggests an increase of almost 60 per cent over Veron's text of 1552.

What were the sources of Waddington's augmentation? His expressed admiration for Elyot and Cooper, in "To the Reader," gives the clue for investigation. One source, a comparative study reveals, was Elyot's *Bib-liotheca* of 1548. Entries common to the *Bibliotheca* of 1548 and the Waddington-Veron of 1575 and lacking in the Stephanus of 1544, and therefore in the Veron of 1552, suggest the *Bibliotheca* as the source.

Elyot-Cooper (1548)	Stephanus (1544)	Veron (1575)
Abcedarium, the order of the letters or the crosse-rowe.		... the order or the letters or the cross rowe.
Abcedarius, he that set-teth any thyng in or-der by letter, or he that teacheth children theyr crosserowe, or he that learneth his crosse-rowe.		... he that setteth any thing in order by letter. He that teacheth children their crosserowe, or he that learneth his crosse rowe.

Elyot-Cooper (1548)	Stephanus (1544)	Veron (1575)
Comitia . . . a congregacion or assemble of the people, for election of officers, or for the promulgacion of lawes, lyke to our parliament.	. . . assemblees de tout le peuple, or d'une partie pour consulter de quelques affaires.	. . . the congregation or assemble of the whole people or of part therof to consult upon certaine affaires, as for election of officers, for promulgation of laws like to our parliament.
Conferrumino, as, to soulder.		. . . to soulder.
Conferveo . . . to be hote together.		. . . to be hot together.
Confidentia . . . *f. ge.* confidence, assurance, boldnesse, trust, hope, unshamefastnesse.	. . . confiace, & asseurance. Hardiesse.	. . . *f.g.* Confidence, assurance, boldenesse, trust, hope and unshamefastnesse.

In the parallels above, corresponding entries in the Veron of 1552 and Cooper's *Thesaurus* of 1565, though not specified, were considered. The results show that the augmented Veron of 1575 was indebted to the *Bibliotheca* of 1548. A wider investigation seems to show that though Waddington follows the 1548 *Bibliotheca* generally, he occasionally consults the *Thesaurus*. Compare these entries:

Elyot	(1548)	*Confertim*	. . . in a busshement together.
Veron	(1552)		. . . in heapes, together.
Cooper	(1565)		. . . In a heape togither.
Veron	(1575)		. . . in heapes, together, or in a bushment together.
Elyot	(1548)	*Confibula*	. . . a claspe or tache. Also a wooden pynne, or thinge made to clenche two peeces together.
Veron	(1552)		. . . a wodden pin. . . .
Cooper	(1565)		. . . A claspe or tache: also a wooden pinne, or thinge made to clenche two peeces together.
Veron	(1575)		. . . a wodden pinne, a claspe, or tache.
Elyot	(1548)	*Confisco*	. . . to seyse a thynge for a forfayture to the common weale, or to the prince.
Veron	(1552)		. . . to seyse a thyng, to confiscate. . . .
Cooper	(1565)		. . . To seyse a forfeyte to the prince.
Veron	(1575)		. . . to seise a thing, to confiscate, or forfayt.
Elyot	(1548)	*Confisio*	. . . an hopyng or trustynge.
Veron	(1552)		. . . confidence, affiaunce. . . .
Cooper	(1565)		. . . A hoping or trusting.
Veron	(1575)		. . . confidence, affiaunce, hoping or trusting.
Elyot	(1548)	*Confixus*	. . . thrust through, sticked. . . . a sticking or thrustyng in.
Veron	(1552)		
Cooper	(1565)		
Veron	(1575)		. . . a sticking, or thrusting in. . . . pricked, thrust through.

Elyot	(1548)	*Conflagito* . . . to desyre importunately.
Veron	(1552)	
Cooper	(1565)	. . . To request importunately.
Veron	(1575)	. . . to request importunately.

Elyot	(1548)	*Conflagro* . . . to be on fyre, to be inflamed to bourne.
Veron	(1552)	. . . to burne.
Cooper	(1565)	. . . To burne: to be on fire: to be inflamed.
Veron	(1575)	. . . to burne, or to be on fire.

In the *confertim* and *confixus* entries the Veron of 1575 borrows from Elyot's *Bibliotheca* of 1548; in the *conflagito* and *conflagro*, probably from Cooper; and in the *confibula, confisco,* and *confisio,* possibly from either Elyot or Cooper.[5]

It should be recalled that the English in Veron's *Dictionariolum* of 1552, being a translation of Stephanus' French, owes nothing to the English lexicographers. Only with the second edition, of 1575, did extensive borrowing of the English definitions begin through Waddington's levy upon the Elyot-Cooper dictionaries. And though the particular illustrations hardly indicate the relative proportion of borrowing, Waddington owed more to the *Bibliotheca* than he did to the *Thesaurus.*

The third and last edition of Veron's dictionary appeared in 1584, with the language of the title page identical with that of 1575, down to the initials "R. W." Thereafter are the words: "Imprinted at London by Rafe Newberie and Henrie Denham. Cum Priuilegio Regiae Maiestatis. 1584." The preliminary matter before the title page is missing, in the Cambridge University copy consulted, but the address to the reader is the same as that of 1575. There is on the title page no claim of augmentation or correction. At the end of the text appears this line: "Finis propositi, laus Christo nescia finis." This is followed by the statement that what gives excellence in this new edition of the dictionary is the correction by Abraham Fleming.[6] The author then enumerates various ways in which he has sought to improve the dictionary: by restoring or correcting the Latin-Greek words to a pure reading, by correcting genders, by substituting idiomatic English for semi-Gallic expressions, and by adding some hundreds (*centurias aliquot*) of select phrases (that is, to illustrate meaning and usage). He adds that he would have proceeded further but for the imminent appearance of the *Nomenclator* of Hadrian Junius.[7] Various tests show few new entries, but, as the reviser maintained, numerous illustrative phrases. Compare the following entries from the 1575 and 1584 editions.

(1575)

Digitus, ti, m. g. Verbale: a finger.

(1584)

Digitus, ti, m. ge. Verbale, a finger or toe. *Digito se colum attingere putat,* he thinketh himself the onelie man of the world. *Digiti in pedibus liuescunt,* his toes wax wan, or looke blacke and blew.

Ebibo, ebibis, ebibi, ebibitum, ebibere. to drinke all out without leauing any thing.

... to drinke all out without leauing anie thing. *imperum heri sui Ebibere,* with bibbing to forget his maisters bidding.

Hyemo, mas, maui, matum, mare, To make winter, and cold weather, to winter, to make winter weather, to passe the winter in some place.

... to make winter and cold wether, to winter, to make winter weather, to passe the winter in some place. *dies Hyemant,* the daies wax cold and winterlie.

Librarius, ria, rium, that pertaineth, or serueth for bookes, that weigheth a poūd.

Librarius, a, um, that pertaineth or serueth for bookes, that weigheth a pound. *Libraria taberna,* a bookebinders shop. *Librarium atramentum,* printers inke or writing inke.

Ludo, ludis, lusi, lusum, ludere, to play, to mocke, to deceiue, to laugh to scorn, and to write verses.

... to play, to mocke, to deceiue, to laugh to scorne, and to write verses. *Ludere operam,* to loose his labour. *Ludere otium,* to passe the time away. *Ludere sanguine hominis in conuiuio,* to make a pastime or sport to kill one at the table.

Pasco, pascis, paui, pastum, pascere, To feede, to eate, to keepe beastes in the fieldes, or at pasture.

... to feed, to eat, to keepe beasts in the fields or at pasture. *ouis pauit Pastum,* the sheepe did eat grasse. *canem seuo pingui Pascere,* to feed a dogge with tallow or greasie fat.

The additional illustrative phrases in the 1584 edition are taken from Cooper's *Thesaurus*.

For the Latin words, the Veron dictionaries give grammatical and etymological information. They tag adverbs, adjectives, verbals, and participles; they indicate the gender and declension of nouns, the principal parts and the conjugation of verbs, and frequently the word or words from which a term is derived. As a rule, this information is found in the sources—the Stephanus or the Elyot-Cooper. A few entries from the 1552 edition of the Veron, omitting the English and French, show the system of giving grammatical information.

> Conformátio, mationis, foem. gen. Verbàle. . . .
> Confóueo, confoues, foui, tum, uère. . . .
> Confragôsus, sa, sum, à Confringo. . . .
> Cónfrico, cas, cui, fríctum, fricâre. . . .

Confusus, confûsa, confusum, Participium à Confúndor. . . .
Confúse, Aduerbium.

Although the modest Stephanus-Veron dictionaries contribute nothing new to the technique of dictionary-making in England, they effect a fusion of the Latin-French of the Stephanus and the Latin-English of the Elyot-Cooper. Since both Elyot and Cooper had borrowed freely from Robert Stephanus' larger Latin-French dictionary, and since Waddington and after him Fleming took matter from the Elyot-Cooper dictionaries, the pattern of sources of the Veron texts has become complex. In Baret's *Alvearie* the complication is even more pronounced.

CHAPTER XII

Richard Huloet's *Abcedarium* *Anglico Latinum* (1552)

THE HISTORY of John Veron's *Dictionariolum* is paralleled by that of Richard Huloet's *Abcedarium*. Both books were designed to be useful to schoolboys, both were first published in 1552, and each was revised and augmented only after a period of twenty years. The *Dictionariolum*, first printed as a Latin-French-English text, was reduced, in the revision of 1575, to Latin and English. The *Abcedarium*, an English-Latin dictionary, appeared in the revised edition of 1572 as English-Latin-French. These are two of many small bilingual or trilingual dictionaries published in England or on the Continent from about 1540 to 1560.[1] Although Huloet claims that his book is a new pattern in the field of lexicography, it is not without antecedents.

Of Richard Huloet (or Howlet) very little is known. According to W. A. J. Archbold, in the *DNB*, he was born at Wisbech, Cambridgeshire. His book is dedicated to Thomas Goodrich, bishop of Ely, with whom Huloet was, presumably, on good terms. An entry under *prepare to speak* refers to "Lillius" as a former teacher, indicating that Huloet had probably studied Latin with William Lilly, the Humanist teacher of Latin-grammar fame. In "A Peroration to the English reader" Huloet declares that in compiling his book he has "emploied my industrye, laboure, and dilygence almoste these tenne yeres passed." If we accept this statement at its face value, we might infer that the *Abcedarium* was begun as early as 1542. A study of the sources seems to indicate that the bulk of the work was accomplished in the late forties, since at this period were published the books to which Huloet is most indebted. In the

E · R

ABCE=
DARIVM ANGLI-
CO LATINVM, PRO
Tyrunculis Richardo
Hulœto Exscri=
ptore.

LONDINI.

Ex officina Gulielmi
Riddel.

ANNO. M.D.LII.

Cum priuilegio ad imprimendum
solum.

ARISE FOR   IT IS DAY.

Peroration the author asserts also that his book "may be resembled to a paterne, or prothotipe newly inuented, and deuised by some simple craftis man."

The wording on the title page of Huloet's book is as follows:

Abcedarivm Anglico Latinvm, pro Tyrunculis Richardo Huloeto Exscriptore. Londini. Ex officina Gulielmi Riddel. Anno. M.D.LII. Cum priuilegio ad imprimendum solum.

In his Ad Lectorem Huloet makes mention of an important feature of his text—the introduction of numerous synonyms. Distinction in meanings among these, he explains, he will not attempt to make; he would not deprive the student of the pleasant task of finding out for himself the differences. Synonymy in the *Abcedarium* and its relation to copiousness we shall treat below.

According to contemporary dictionaries, including Huloet, the term *abcedarium* may be defined as a book from which a child learns his ABC's, or crossrow. For his purpose, Huloet extends the meaning of the word to signify an English-Latin dictionary for children, arranged alphabetically, each English entry being followed by its Latin equivalent.

Huloet himself offers, in the preliminary matter to his text, a clue to his model and his sources. He lists the names of authors, ancient, medieval, and contemporary, from whom he allegedly drew information and examples of usage for his own book. In his alphabetical list of writers are 214 names, but as more than half of these appear in a similar list by Sir Thomas Elyot in his *Bibliotheca* of 1545, it would seem that the roster of authorities is largely conventional. In this blanket acknowledgment we do find, however, the names of certain authors whom Huloet consulted and who can be shown to have furnished him the form and substance of his *Abcedarium*. Among these are Friar Calepine, Thomas Cooper, Sir Thomas Elyot, Erasmus, Robert Stephanus, and Polydore Vergil; and there are a few other creditors not included in the formidable Nomina Authorum.

Of the authorities listed by Huloet, Robert Stephanus may be first considered. In 1549, Stephanus published the second edition of his *Dictionnaire francois-latin*.[2] To this text, the *Abcedarium* is quite similar in the arrangement and presentation of materials, as the following entries show:

Dictionnaire (1549)	*Abcedarium* (1552)
Cruel, *Crudelis, Immanis, Ferus, Importunus, Improbus, Atrox, Saeuus, Tur-*	Cruell *atrox. cis, crudelis. le, cruentus. a. um, dirus, durus, Foedus, ferox. cis,*

Title page of the Abcedarium, *1552, from a copy in the Folger Shakespeare Library* (*opposite*)

Dictionnaire (1549)

pis, *Trux, Austerus homo, Teter in
aliquem, Praeditus crudelitate.*
Mort d'une cruelle mort, *Indigna morte
preemptus.*
Chose cruelle & come enuoyee de l'ire
de dieu, *Dira res.*
Le plus cruel qui fut iamais, *Saeuissimus
quam qui vnquam.*
Venir a estre cruel, *Deduci de animi leni-
tate.*
Cesser d'estre cruel, *Exacuire.*

Abcedarium (1552)

*ferus. a. um, Inclemens, Inhumanus.
a. um, Immanis. ne, Immitis. e, Malig-
nus. a. um, Proteruus, rigidus, San-
guinarius. a. um. sanguineus, sanguino-
lentus, seuerus, saeuus, Teter. ra. rum,
Toruus, Truculentus, Trux, cis, Tur-
pis, Violentus. a. um.*
Cruell or vnmarcifull gouernaunce. *Man-
liana imperia.*
Cruell swerde. *crudus ensis.*
Cruell in gouernaunce. *Imperiosus. a. um.*
Cruell rebelles or greate babblers. *Amor-
rhei.* . . .

For the main entry in each text a series of Latin synonyms, roughly
equivalent to the vernacular word, is given; then follow subordinate
entries, each using the key word in an illustrative phrase and giving its
Latin equivalent. There are of course, in each text, simple entries of the
vernacular word and its Latin counterpart, occupying not more than one
or two lines in a column. But for the vernacular words of extensive and
varied usage, the method employed is that illustrated by the entry *cruel*
(*cruell*) presented above. The exceptions are in Huloet's entry of proper
names, which have no place in the French-Latin dictionary. In other respects, the *Dictionnaire* is the obvious model for the *Abcedarium*.

We might expect also that the English compiler would borrow freely
from the copious text of his French predecessor. Although there are inevitable correspondences in the groups of Latin synonyms in the two
texts, Huloet takes few, if any, of these from the *Dictionnaire*, and apparently never derives his English from translating the French phrases.
His indebtedness to Stephanus consists primarily in adapting the method
of the French-Latin text to the English-Latin. Other possible sources for
the numerous Latin synonyms in the *Abcedarium* are John of Garland's
Synonyma,[3] a popular text in the early sixteenth century, and the anonymous *Catholicon Anglicum* (*ca.* 1480), then in manuscript. The *Catholicon* borrows much, especially synonyms, from Garland's work. But neither
of these is a source of Huloet's synonymy. We must then search further
for the real sources which supplied Huloet matter to fit into the framework of the *Abcedarium*.

The standard Latin-English dictionary at the time when Huloet began
his work in lexicography was Sir Thomas Elyot's *Bibliotheca Eliotae*
(1545), a text which was revised and much enlarged by Thomas Cooper,
in 1548. The names of both Cooper and Elyot appear in Huloet's list
of authorities. The mere presence of their names is of course not evidence

that Huloet consulted their books. A comparative study of the *Bibliotheca* and the *Abcedarium* does, however, reveal what at first appears to be occasional borrowings.

Bibliotheca (1545)	Abcedarium (1552)
Iuditia legittima, iudgementes gyuen according to the determined lawe writen, or by ancient custom approved.	Iudgement accordynge to law wrytten. *iuditia legitima.*
Iuditium capitis, iugement in causes criminall.	Iudgement in causes criminal, or capitall. *iudicium capitis.*
Obelus, a spytte or brooche. Also a long stryke in writynge for a note or diuersitye.	Stryke in writyng made in length like a spyt for a note or diuersitye . . . *Obelus.*
Praetexta, a longe garment myxte with purple silke, whiche was the vesture of noble mens sonnes, untyll they came into xvii yeeres of age.	Garment, or vesture mixte with purple sylke for noble mens chyldren to weare, untyl they come to seuentene yeres of age. *Praetexta.*

The parallels cited indicate that Huloet borrowed a certain amount of matter from the Elyot-Cooper *Bibliotheca,* and the indebtedness is further confirmed by Huloet's taking over intact from the Elyot-Cooper such proper-name entries as those under *Anabaptistes, Anacharsis, Anaxarchus, Anaximander, Anchises, Ania, Anna,* and *Anticyra.* Even so, the debt of the *Abcedarium,* estimated to contain 26,000 words,[4] seems thus far to be relatively small.

The Latin synonyms following a simple English entry in Huloet's text are, almost without exception, Latin words defined in the *Bibliotheca,* distributed, of course, according to their place in the alphabet. In each case the definition, given in English, has in it the key entry word or one closely approximating it. The first entry for *abide,* omitting conjugational endings, runs thus in the *Abcedarium:* "Abyde. *Contor . . . Cunctor . . . Maneo, . . . Moror . . . Operior . . . Residio . . . Resisto . . . Resto . . . Sedeo . . . Sisto.*" For eight of these synonyms, which are main entries in the *Bibliotheca, abyde* is given as one meaning. A similar procedure is observable throughout, as, for example, in the choice of synonyms after *abash, abate, abhor, delay,* and *continue,* indicating the *Bibliotheca* as Huloet's source. Likewise, in the subentries, which are English phrases containing the key word with Latin equivalents of the phrases, the Elyot-Cooper text is generally the source. The following entry, under *continue,* with corresponding matter from the *Bibliotheca,* will suggest Huloet's method of borrowing.

Abcedarium (1552)	Bibliotheca (1548)
Continue. *Continuo. as, Duro, as, Perenno, as, Pergo. is, Maneo. es, Perpetuo. as, Teneo. es.*	*Continuo* [5] *. . .* to continue; *Duro . . .* to endure or continue; *Perenno . . .* to dure or continue foreuer; *Pergo . . .*

Abcedarium (1552)	*Bibliotheca* (1548)
Continue for one yere. *Peranno. as.*	to continue as one hath begunne;
Continue in hope. *Bene sperare, Spem alere.*	*Maneo . . .* to remayne, to continue;
Continue long or euer. *Perenno. as.*	*Perpetuo . . .* to continue on a thing without ceassyng; *Teneo . . .* to holde
Continue with a stedfast mynde, constantly, or perseuerantly. *Perseuero. as.*	*. . .* to hold or keepe in.
	Peranno. . . . to lyue a yere to an ende.
	Bene de aliquo sperare [*s.v. spero*], to haue a good hope of one.
	Spem alere [*s.v. spes*], to make one hope and look still for a thing.
	Perenno . . . to dure or continue for euer.
	Perseuerantes, constantly.
	Perseuero . . . to continue with a stedfast mynde.

It will be observed that six out of seven definitions which the *Bibliotheca* gives of the *Abcedarium* synonyms for the English term *continue* contain this key word. The results suggest that Huloet not only collected the groups of synonymous Latin words from the Elyot-Cooper text but did so according to a preconceived method. The English phrases with their corresponding Latin, which follow the main entry *continue*, need little comment. These derive obviously from the *Bibliotheca* and tend to confirm the theory that the Latin synonyms are from the same source.

What Huloet's method was in thus collecting and arranging the synonyms and phrases we cannot be certain. A plausible conjecture is that the English lexicographer first made his English word list, in ABC order, leaving considerable space between entries. He then read through the Latin-English *Bibliotheca* to assemble his materials, placing the collected matter in two groups under each English entry: (1) synonymous Latin words, the definition of each of which in the *Bibliotheca* contained the English term to be defined, or, in some instances, a close approximation; and (2) English phrases, containing or suggesting the key English word (always put first), with their Latin equivalents. He reverses thus the Latin-English of the *Bibliotheca,* and makes further rearrangement, if necessary, to get the key word first. This readjustment constitutes a partial disguise for Huloet's very extensive indebtedness to a single source— the Elyot-Cooper *Bibliotheca.* Although the method thus described is conjectural, it is a possible explanation of the way the author compiled his text. The extent of Huloet's borrowing is demonstrable beyond any doubt.[6] Taking the major portion of his subject matter from the *Bibliotheca,* Huloet arranged it in a pattern—except for the insertion of proper names and a few other items to be noted—exactly similar to that of the French-Latin dictionary of Robert Stephanus. The *Abcedarium* exhibits the hand of Stephanus but the voice of Elyot-Cooper.

Although the *Bibliotheca* is the major source of Latin synonyms, definitions, and illustrative phrases, and the *Dictionnaire* of Robert Stephanus the model for the arrangement of materials, Huloet fills out his pattern with occasional borrowing from other books. "Calepinus" (Friar Ambrose Calepine) is listed among the authorities, and from the *Dictionarium* Huloet takes several passages, usually not translating Calepine's Latin. The following entry, excepting the English phrasing at the beginning, is almost verbatim from Calepine.

Prudens. Phronesis, prudentia, ae. one of the vertues or graces whom August. *de libero Arb.* thus diffineth *Prudentia est appetendarum, et Vitandarum rerum scientia.* Macrob. *prudentiae est ad rationis normam que agit Vniuersa dirigere, et nihil preter rectum, et laudabile facere. prudentiae insunt Ratio, intellectus, circumspectio, prouidentia, Docilitas, cautio. Et apud Socratem omnes uirtutes censebantur prudentias.* Aristot. *inquit impossibile quempiam esse prudentem, nisi sit bonus.* Plaut. *in leg. prudentia uirtutum dux, Idem in Tru. Quae hic habet phronesium, omnem ex pectore meo mouit phronesim.*

In his sketch of England, under "England . . . *Anglia*," Huloet has two columns in Latin. For the first nineteen lines, he seems to be paraphrasing Calepine, under *Anglia*.[7] Many more things about England, he then explains, he will transcribe from more recent writers. He then follows, still in Latin, Polydore Vergil's *Chronicle of England*. This description of the Island reappears in Higgins's edition of Huloet, in 1572, where Higgins cites Polydore Vergil as the source.

To the entry "consanguinitye . . . *consanguinitas*," Huloet devotes the better part of two pages. The exposition of the various degrees of consanguinity is in Latin, accompanied by a diagram or table of consanguinity. In the first part of the entry Huloet again depends upon Calepine, under *parens, parentalia*. For the diagram or tree of consanguinity and the numerous Latin terms of kinship associated therewith, the English compiler is indebted to a sixteenth-century edition of Isidore's *Etymologiae* (lib. ix. c. v.),[8] which, to accompany the chapter "De affinitatibus et gradibus," has a full-page, small-folio illustration of the *arbor consanguinitatis* with its numerous branches. This appears to be the direct inspiration of Huloet's graphic representation of the subject. It is not practical to transcribe here Huloet and his Latin sources and the drawings of the tree on the subject of consanguinity. Brought together, however, the treatments show Huloet combining, in this entry, subject matter from Calepine and Isidore.

Erasmus, listed among Huloet's authorities, is quoted under *laugh & laughing*. Huloet was doubtless familiar with the *Adagia*, but the reference here to *sardonius risus* may come by way of Calepine, who cites the *Chiliades* as his source. Other entries in the *Abcedarium*, generally brief, suggest that Huloet may have consulted the fifteenth-century *Promptorium parvulorum* and the *Catholicon Anglicum*, though again the indebtedness, if any, may well be indirect.[9] Compare the entries which follow.

Promptorium	*Abcedarium*
Brerre or brymmyl. *Tribulus . . . Vepris.*	Brymble or bryar. *Alba spina . . . tribulus, vepres.*
Chaumbyrleyn: *Camerarius . . . Cubicularius.*	Chamberlyn: *Camerarius . . . Cubicularius.*
Crany, or cranyys: *Rima . . . Rimula . . . Riscus.*	Chinck, clyft, crany or creves of earth . . . *Rima, ae. & Rimula. . . .*
Ffrank, kepyng off fowls to make fette: *saginarium.*	Ffrancke, cowle, or place wherein any thing is fedde to be fatte. *Saginarium, Utuarium.*
Ffrankyd: *saginatus.*	Ffrancked to be made fat, *attilis saginatus.*
Leep, or baskete: *Sporta, calathus, corbis, canistrum.*	Leape or basket. *Sporta. sportula . . .* Basket. *Calothus corbis . . . sporta.*
Leep, or fysch kepyng or takyng: *Nassa.*	Leape to take fyshe, called a iunckor. *Nassa.*
Rascayle, or simple peple . . . *popellus . . . Infimas. . . .*	Rascall people. *Popillus.*
Rere soper . . . *Obsonium.*	Rere suppar. *Obsonium.*

The parallel entries below suggest a possible indebtedness of Huloet's *Abcedarium* to the *Catholicon Anglicum* (ca. 1483).

Catholicon Anglicum	*Abcedarium*
a Bakke; *blata, vespertilio.*	Backe or Reremouse which sitteth in the darke, *Nicteris . . . Vespertilio, onis.*
a Balke of howse; *trabs, trabes, trabis & trabus, trabicula.*	Balke, or chiefe beame or piller in a house. *Têplum, Trabes, Trabs, Trabalis. . . .*
a Balke betwyx twa furris, *crebro, porca.*	Balke in a plowed lande . . . *Porca, ae, Scamnū. . . .*
to Belche (Belke or Bolke): *ructare, ructuare, ructari.*	Belke, or bolke, or breake wynde upward. *Eructo . . . Ructo . . . Rugo, Ruto . . . Rutor.*
Blabyrlyppd; *broccus, labrosus.*	Blabber lipped . . . *Labeo, onis.*
a Lawnder; *candidaria, lotrix.*	Launder, or woman washer. *Lotrix, cis.*

The sources of the *Abcedarium* so far discovered are the *Bibliotheca Eliotae*, probably the edition of 1548; and the *Dictionnaire francois-latin* of Robert Stephanus, 1549, as a model of arrangement; these are supplemented by matter from Calepine, Polydore Vergil, Isidore, and Erasmus, and possibly from the *Promptorium* and the *Catholicon Anglicum*.

Another feature of the *Abcedarium*, for the first time employed by an English lexicographer, is the short essays on the letters of the alphabet. For these, Huloet had a precedent in Calepine; and in the treatment of the letter *B*, here transcribed, Calepine is the source.

A letter amonge the mutes, boroweth hys soūde of the letter E. The Grecians do call B. *Vita.* the whyche hath his nature meanelye betwene P. and Ph. And that whyche they wryte with P and Ph. is traduced in the Latine in B. And agayne contrariwise, what in the Greke is written with Ph. in the latine is conuerted in B. and thys is done *Ob literarum affinitatem.* In composicions B. is transuerted into these letters C. F. G. P. V. And thus *Differentiae uel Euphoniae causa.*

This custom, begun by Huloet, is continued in more elaborate form by Higgins in the edition of 1572, by Baret in his *Alvearie* (1573, 1580), and is revived in 1678 by Adam Littleton.

Huloet's precedent for the extensive use of synonyms is found in John of Garland's *Synonyma* and *Equivoca*, very popular at the end of the fifteenth century, and in the *Catholicon Anglicum*, and is emphasized by Erasmus in his *De copia*, in which synonymy is an important device for gaining copiousness and variety. Huloet is thus in the tradition of the Elizabethan period. Notwithstanding its interesting features, the *Abcedarium* did not gain a wide vogue; twenty years passed before a second edition was printed. This was published, in 1572, under the title of *Huloets Dictionarie*, corrected and enlarged by John Higgins.

Higgins, whose literary efforts extended from about 1570 to the end of the century, was a poet (or versifier) and compiler. Besides his revision of Huloet, Higgins published *Flowers, or Eloquent Phrases of the Latin Speach* (1575)—an augmentation of Nicholas Udall's *Floures for Latine Speakyng selected and gathered out of Terence* (1533)—and wrote supplements to the *Mirror for Magistrates* (1575), and other works.[10] In revising Huloet, Higgins's principal innovation was the addition of French terms, equivalents of the Latin and English. Otherwise, he followed the pattern of Huloet, greatly expanding the original work by matter drawn from a variety of new sources. The title page which follows and Higgins's address to the reader are informative concerning the scope of the revised book and its sources.

Huloets Dictionarie, newely corrected, amended, set in Order and Enlarged with many names of Men, Townes, Beastes, Foules, Fishes, Trees, Shrubbes, Herbes, Fruites, Places, Instruments, etc. And in eche place fit Phrases, gathered out of the best Latin Authors. Also the Frenche thereunto annexed, by which you may finde the Latin or Frenche of anye English woorde you will. By IOhn Higgins late student in Oxeforde . . . Londini, In aedibus Thomae Marshij. Anno. 1572.

Higgins's address to the reader affords specific information on the sources of his augmentation.

And for yᵉ better attayning to the knowledge of words, I went not to cōmon Diction-aries only, but also to the Authors themselues, and vsed therein conference with them which wrote particularly of suche things, as yᵉ place requyred. As in herbes I followed the iudgemēt of Master Turner, Dodoneus, Pineus, Fuchsius, and sometime Plinius: In beastes, fishes and foules, Conradus Gesnerus: In instrumentes of warre Vegetius: In buildinge Vitruuius: generallye Hadrianus Iunius: In names of places Ptōlomeus: In the nature of wordes Valla & others: In Phrases Thierre out of which I confesse I haue taken a great part of this Booke, notinge the phrases wyth S. after the Frenche, for that Stephanus was the first Author thereof: and finallye I wrote not in the whole Booke one quyre, without perusinge and conference of many Authors. Therefore wher you finde in the Booke any of yᵉ first letters of the names aboue, or the like: that same standeth for a note of the Authors name, where I founde such Phrase, Frenche, name, or words as is there placed. And if any shall doubt hereof, let him but conferre Huloet and this together and peraduenture in one letters lookinge ouer he shal finde so muche added, as shall seeme more painful to him in accompte, then I demed the laboure in doinge it.

Higgins's boast that he has considerably expanded Huloet's *Abceda-rium* is amply supported by comparison of the two editions of the text. The expansion consists in augmentation of entries in the 1552 edition—that is, in generally increasing the number of Latin synonyms in the main entries and adding locutions or illustrative phrases. Higgins also adds many new entries from a variety of sources, and, for almost all entries and illustrations, he supplies French equivalents not found in the earlier text. The sources he lists in his address to the reader are demonstrably real sources, though some of these he drew upon but slightly. Those to whom he is most indebted are Thierry's edition of Robert Stephanus' *Dictionnaire francois-latin* (1564), William Turner's *Herball* (1568), and Hadrian Junius' *Nomenclator*, to which Higgins himself was to supply the English terms, in 1585. And there are other sources of which Higgins makes no mention.

Of these, the major source of new matter is the Stephanus-Thierry, as Higgins implies. The parallel entries which follow are typical; these show the nature and suggest the extent of the English compiler's debt to his French source.

Huloet-Higgins (1572)	Stephanus-Thierry (1564)
Assemble, to gather together. *Aggregare, Copulare, Coadunare, Cogere, Com-mittere, Concire, Cōgerere, Contra-here, Coagmentare.* Assembler.	Assēbler, *Aggregare, Copulare, Coadu-nare, Cogere, Comittere, Concire, Congerere, Contrahere, Coagmentare.*
Hide. *Abscondo, is, di. Abstrudo, is. Celo, as, Condo, is. Occulo, is. Occulto, as.*	Cacher, *Abdere, Abscondere, Abstrudere, Celare, Condere, Ab oculis remouere,*

Huloet-Higgins (1572)	Stephanus-Thierry (1564)
Operio, is, Pallio, as. Recondo, is. Remouere ab oculis. Tego, is. Abdo, dis. Supprimo, is. Velo, Obscuro, as. Cacher. S.	*Occulere, Occultare, Recondere, Tegere, Supprimere, Velare.*
Combate and to fighte. *Batuere, Confligere, Conflictare, Depugnare, Dimicare, Praelium edere, Preliari, Pugnam capessere, Certamen consere, Contrahere certamen, Belli fortunam tentare vel experiri.* Combatre & battailer. S.	Combattre c'est battailler. *Batuere, Confligere, Pugnare, Dimicare, Praeliari, Certamen conserere, Cōtrahere certamen.*
Comely. *Decenter, Decore, Apte, Congruenter, Conuenienter. Accommodate.* Conuenablement. S.	Conuenablement, *Apte, Congruenter, Conuenienter, Decenter, Accommodate.*
Compte. *Computare, Imputare, Reputare, Numerare, Numerum referre, Rationem subducere, Rationem & calculum ponere.* Compter. S.	Compter, *Computare, Imputare, Reputare, Numerare, Numerum referre, Rationem subducere, Rationem & calculum ponere.*

These parallels exemplify especially Higgins's borrowing of Latin synonyms for the vernacular entry and their French equivalents from Stephanus-Thierry. For this use of synonymous Latin terms, Higgins was of course following the precedent of Huloet in the *Abcedarium,* just as Huloet himself had as a model for this practice an earlier edition of the *Dictionnaire* (1549). Higgins indeed generally retained the Latin synonyms of the earlier Huloet, supplementing them with additional words from his French-Latin source. The entry *hide* above is a case in point: the synonyms are from Huloet, excepting *abdo, supprimo,* and *velo,* which are added from Stephanus-Thierry. The same procedure is observable in the entries *cruell, cruelly, cruelty,* and *dye.* The Latin synonyms for these words are from the *Abcedarium* plus the *Dictionnaire.* For synonyms of entries not found in the earlier Huloet, such as *compte* above, Higgins depends upon his French source.

His acknowledgment is comprehensive: "In Phrases Thierre out of which I confesse I haue taken a great part of this Booke, notinge the phrases wyth S. after the Frenche, for that Stephanus was the first author thereof." By "phrases" Higgins obviously means the illustrative phrases or locutions, in the vernacular and Latin, which follow a main entry and show the use of the term in various combinations, as under *pardon:* "Pardon, or forgeue me this faulte. *Vnam hanc noxiam mitte.* Pardonne moy ceste faulte. S." Another example is under *approche:* "I wil approche to (or nere) him. *Ad hominem accedam.* I'iray vers luy." Higgins implies by his acknowledgment that the Latin and the corresponding French phrases in these entries, and others, derive from the French-Latin of Thierry. Many do, of course, but by no means all.[11] It will be noted that the order of entries in the Huloet-Higgins *Dictionarie* is English, Latin, French. In augmenting the illustrative phrases, Higgins's chief concern was with the Latin and its French equivalents; the English would be easy. For the Latin and French, in this order, a Latin-French dictionary, especially one with numerous illustrations, would be the more convenient text for Higgins to use. Such a text was at hand in the *Dictionarium Latino-Gallicum* (1561) of Robert Stephanus. This Latin-French dictionary was first published in 1538, considerably enlarged in 1546, slightly augmented in 1552, and reissued in 1561.[12] The augmented text contained literally scores, in some cases hundreds, of illustrative phrases—Latin and French. To this, Higgins turned as a dictionary far more copious in illustrations than the Thierry and, for his purpose, economical of time.

The problem of Higgins's indebtedness to Stephanus' *Dictionarium Latino-Gallicum* is somewhat complicated by the close interrelationships of the Stephanus dictionaries. The *Dictionnaire francois-latin* (1539) drew much from the Latin-French of 1538.[13] The later Thierry, likewise, has much in common with the 1561 *Latino-Gallicum*. Higgins seems to have used both, turning to Latin-French as an ampler source of illustration and as a convenience in selecting. Another complicating factor is that Thomas Cooper's *Thesaurus*, Latin-English, derives a major portion of its illustrations from Stephanus' Latin-French. And Higgins was familiar with Cooper, using a number of the items on proper names and apparently consulting Cooper from time to time for his English phrasing. The following entries from the three texts—Stephanus' *Dictionarium Latino-Gallicum* (1561), Cooper's *Thesaurus* (1565), and the Huloet-Higgins *Dictionarie* (1572)—seem to indicate that both Cooper and Higgins borrowed from Stephanus.

Stephanus (1561)	Cooper (1565)	Huloet-Higgins (1572)
Redigo . . . redigere . . . Mener a force.	*Redigo . . . redigere.* To bring by force or cunning: to gather or heape togither: to restore.	Brynge in by force, or otherwyse. *Redigo . . . redigere.* Mener a force. S.
Eo redigis me, vt quid egerim, egomet nesciam. Terēt. Tu me mets en tel estat que, &c.	*Eo redigis me, vt quid egerim, egomet nesciam.* Terent. Thou bringest me in that case, that I my selfe can not tel what I haue done.	Thou bringest me in suche a doubte, I know not what to doe. *Eo redigis me, vt quid egerim, egomet nesciam.* Tu me mets en tel estat que, &c. S.
In concordiam redigere.	*In concordiam redigere.*	Bryng into concorde, or

Stephanus (1561)	Cooper (1565)	Huloet-Higgins (1572)
Plaut. Mettre d'accord.	Plaut. To set at one: to bring to concorde.	make them frendes. *In concordiam redigere.* Mettre d'accord.
In deditionem imperii Romani redigere. Cic. Contraindre de se rendre a l'empire Romain, Mettre en l'obeissance des Romains.	*In deditionem imperij Romani redigere.* Cic. To constraine them to yeelde and become subiect to the Romaine empire.	Bryng into th'obeysaunce of the Romane Empire. *In deditionem emperij Romani redigere.* Contraindre de se rendre a l'empire Romain, Mettre en l'obeissance des Romains.
In ditionem suam redigere. Cic. Mettre soubs sa seigneurie.	*In ditionem suam redigere.* Cic. To bring vnder his subiection.	Bryng him into his own iurisdiction, or vnder his subiection. *In ditionem suam redigere.* Mettre soubs sa seigneurie.
In gratiam redigere aliquos. Terent. Accorder aucuns, Faire leur appoinctement, Les appoincter.	*In gratiam redigere aliquos.* Ter. To set at one: to make agreed: to make friends agayne.	Bringe vnto favour, or to make them friendes againe. *In gratiam redigere aliquos.* Accorder aucuns, faire leur appoinctement, les appoincter.
Sub imperium Romanum redigere. Rediger, Reduire.	*Sub imperium Romanum redigere.* Caes. To bring vnder subiection of the Romaine empire.	Bringe some vnder the obeisaunce of the Romaine Empire. *Sub Emperium Romanum redigere.* Rediger, Reduire.

In the three groups of entries transcribed above, the lexicographers employ the same illustrative Latin phrases. As Stephanus is earlier, he seems to be the source for the Latin of Cooper, and in some instances, as in the fourth entry, the French is the basis of Cooper's English. The Stephanus is also basic for the Latin and French of Huloet-Higgins, as well as the English, though Higgins may have seen the English of Cooper, as in the first and sixth entries. The entry *causa* ("cause") in the three texts has a similar array of illustrations.

Two additional examples, involving only the Stephanus *Latino-Gallicum* and the Huloet-Higgins are pertinent here.

Stephanus (1561)	Huloet-Higgins (1572)
Precarius, Adiectiuum. Vlpian. Toute chose empruntee a la charge de la rendre quand il plaira au presteur.	Borowed at the wyll of the lender vntill it be required againe, or so long as the lender liste. *Precarius, a. um.* Toute chose empruntee a la charge de la rendre quand il plaira presteur.

Stephanus (1561)

[*s.v. versura.*] *Versuram facere.* Cic. Emprunter argent a gros interest pour payer vne debte qu'on doibt a moindre interest, Prendre a perte de finance, Descouurir sainct Pierre pour couurir sainct Pol.

Huloet-Higgins (1572)

Borowe of Peter to paye Paule, whiche is a vulgar speache, properly wheras a man doth borowe of one to paye an other. *Nomen transferre, Versuram facere, Soluere, uel uertere.* Discouurir saint Pierre pour couurir saint Pol, emprunter argent a gros interest pour payer vne debte qu'on doibt a moindre interest, prendre a perte de finance.

The evidence seems to indicate that in enlarging Huloet's *Abcedarium*, Higgins drew abundant matter from both the Stephanus-Thierry *Dictionnaire*, French-Latin, and the Stephanus *Dictionarium Latino-Gallicum*. Was Higgins, then, disingenuous in emphasizing his indebtedness to Thierry and failing to mention the Latin-French text? [14]

Higgins's entries of proper names of persons and places, with the accompanying sketches, have a variety of sources. Some he inherited from Huloet; others came from Calepine and the Elyot-Cooper dictionaries. From Cooper's *Thesaurus* he derived the sketches under the following entries: *Apulia, Aristotle, Asia, Atalanta, Athanasius, Athenodorus, Atlas, Augustinus, Augustus,* and *Attalus,* to mention a few.

"In herbes," writes Higgins to the reader, "I followed the iudgemēt of Master Turner." And in one entry in the *Dictionarie* we read: "Crowfoot herbe. *Ranunculus Secundum.* Turn. And there are seuē diuers kindes hereof, reade Turner in the seconde volume of his Herbale, fol. 114." Turning to the volume and folio cited, we find seven cuts illustrating the seven different kinds of *ranunculus.* In various entries Higgins borrows from Turner, as he admits.

Huloet-Higgins (1572)

Amomum, is a small bushe, about the quantitie of a mans hande, lyke a cluster of grapes soulden into him selfe like stickes of wode one within an other, after the maner of a nette, & it hath a swete sauour. . . .

Asparagus, an herbe called Sperage, of this herbe are two sortes, the first is called *Aspa altilis, Asparagus* alone, and this is the cōmon Sperage, the other kynde is called in latine *corruda,* or *Asparagus syluestris* . . . In Englishe Pricky sperage, in Frenche it is named Esperage.

Turner (1568)

Amomum is a smal bushe/ about the quantitie of a mannes hāde/ like unto a cluster of grapes solden into him selfe/ litle stickes of wood/ goynge one beside and ouer an other/ & partely it resembleth a net . . . yᵗ hath a good sauoure. . . .

Sperage is called in Latin *Asparagus*/ . . . in Frenche Esperage/ . . . *Asparagus* is of two sortes/ the one is called *Aspa altilis*/ *Asparagus* alone/ and this is the cōmon Sperage . . ./ The other kind is called in Latin *corruda,* or *Asparagus syluestris.* This kinde may be called in Englishe Pricky Sperage.

Huloet-Higgins (1572)	Turner (1568)
Aspe is a tree otherwyse called a Popler, of whiche there be three kyndes, that is to wytte, the whyte, the blacke, and that of Lybia, *Populus alba, populus nigra, Populus Lybica.*	There ar thre kyndes of Populus/ the whyte/ the blak/ and it that is called lybica . . . The Populus is called with us by two names/ som call it a poppler/ and other an Asp or an esp tre.

In 1585, Higgins himself supplied an English translation of Hadrian Junius' *Nomenclator*. But in 1572, Higgins obviously used a Latin (or multilingual) edition of Junius. He admits drawing matter from Junius and explains that he indicates the borrowings with the letter *H* at the end of the entry.[15] The following entries (in which I use the 1585 edition of Junius) confirm Higgins's statement.

Junius (1585)	Huloet-Higgins (1572)
Physiognomon, cic. *physiognomus, qui e totius corporis filo atque habitu, de ingenio cuiusque pronuntiat* . . . Aristot. [498*a*]	Physiognomer. *Phisiognomon, onis, m. g. Physiognomus . . . Qui a totius corporis filo atque habitu, de ingenio cuiusque pronunciat.* H.
Dielcystinda, quo duplices puerorum turmae, porrectis hinc inde manibus, alteros ad se pertrahere conantur, dum pars altera superior existat . . . Polluci. A kinde of play wherin two companies of boyes holding hands all in a rowe, doe pull with hard holde one another, till one side be ouercome; it is called sunne and moone. [299*a*]	Sonne and Moone, a playe that children & bigge boyes use to playe, wherein twoo companies drawe, th'one one waye and th'other an other till one part giue the other the foyle. *Dielcystinda.* H.
Ascoliasmus, empusae ludus . . . a kinde of playe wherein boyes lift up one leg, and hop on the other: it is called fox in thy hole. [298*a*]	Playe called hunte the foxe. *Ascoliasmus, Empusae ludis.*

In the *Abcedarium* Huloet, following the precedent of Calepine, devotes brief discussions to most letters of the alphabet, in order of appearance. This feature of the earlier edition Higgins retains, frequently expanding or changing the original expositions. A few examples will indicate the nature of the short essays on the letters as well as the changes made by Higgins.

1552 Edition	1572 Edition
D is a letter called in Greke *delta*, Δ or δ there signifiyng the numbre of foure, whyche in Latine or Englishe letters signifieth fyue thus wrytten. M.D.L.I. which is 1551. Also at Memphis the ryuer Nilus hath wyth hys course made a place after the fourme of thys Greke letter Δ and to thys daye is called *delta*.	D is a letter called in Greke *Delta*, there signifying the numbre foure, which in Latine or Englishe letters signifieth fiue, thus written. M.D. lxxi. whiche is 1571. Also at Memphis the ryuer Nilus hath with his course made a place after the fourme of this Greeke letter Δ and to this daye it is called *Delta.*

1552 Edition	1572 Edition
G. Letter coūted among the mutes is often in tences chaūged in ct. S. & X. for the whyche G, the Grecians do wryte K. *cappa*.	G. A letter in the number of the mutes, which often in the preterfect tēce of verbes is chaūged into ct, as *Legor, lectur, Agar, actus:* sometime into S, as *Spargo, sparsi, Mergo, mersi:* Not seldome into X, vt *Rego, rexi, Pingo, pinxi:* And certaine Greeke woordes written in that tongue with UK, when they are chaunged into latine are written with G, vt Κύκνος, latine *Cygnus.* In the notes of antiquitie G signified *Gaudium, Gens, Genius, Gellius, Gaius, & Gratia.* Also *Ga, Grauis,* &c.[16]
L. Letter is both a semiuowell and a liquid, and beynge a word, standeth in oure wrytynge figuratiuely for the numbre of fiftye.	L. A letter counted among the halfe vowelles, and also a liquid, the Grekes cal it *Lamda,* In latin following a mute in yᵉ same woorde, it maketh the syllable going before, if it be shorte, commune: in oure tongue it is used so dyuersly that it nedeth a lōger discourse, then is here necessary. For in dyuers woordes wee wryte the double and pronounce yᵉ single, as in *All, Wall,* &c. But time wyll take these away, as she dayly reacheth at the reste. L. in nombre is wrytten for .50.

Under the entry *gods,* Huloet had introduced a table with the title "Pantheon of the Gods." [17] This is a list of the pagan gods, indicating their place and function—a sort of theogony in miniature. This pantheon, a literary rather than a linguistic feature of the dictionary, Higgins takes over for his revised edition. Other literary features, which occupy considerable space in the new edition, Higgins inserted on his own initiative.

In illustrations of Latin terms, for example, Higgins quotes from Latin authors, giving his English versification of the quotations. Among the poets thus represented are Catullus, Horace, Juvenal, Lucretius, Mantuan, Martial, Ovid, Persius, Terence, and Virgil. From Virgil's *Eclogues* there are twenty-five excerpts—more than from any other Latin author.[18] Two examples will show how Higgins employs these verses in his *Dictionarie.*

A.A.A. lalare . . . But Pers. Satyr. 3 hath *Lallare,* to sucke.

> Et similis regum pueris pappare minutum
> Poscis, & iratus mammae lallare recusas.

> And like the princely infantes thou
>   desirest little pappe,
> And angry leauste to lall hir dugge
>   that lulles thee in hir lappe.

Attalus. To one Attalus Martial, the Poete wrate this Epigramme.

> Declamas belle, causas agis Attale belle.
> Historias bellas, carmina bella facis.
> Componis belle mimos, epigrammata belle
> Bellus Grammaticus, bellus es astrologus,
> Et belle cantas, & saltas Attale belle.
> Bellus es arte lyrae, bellus es arte pilae.
> Nil bene cum facias, facis attamen omnia belle
> Vis dicam qui sis? magnus es Ardelio.

> Frende Attalus thou declamste well,
> Thou pleadest causes well.
> The histories do passe thou makste,
> Thy verses do excell.
> Thou makest mery poemes, and
> Thy Epigrammes are fine:
> In Grammer, and the course of starres,
> Thy knowledge is deuine.
> Both well thou singest Attalus,
> And dauncest light withall:
> Thy arte doth passe to playe on harpe,
> Or tosse the tennisse balle.
> When nought thou doste is well, yet all
> Thou dost thou thinkest ryght.
> Wilt thou I tell what one thou arte?
> Ardelio, Thraso lyke.

This practice of inserting verses to illustrate words in the dictionary had been used in the *Catholicon Anglicum* (*ca.* 1483) and was to appear again, in elaborate form, in William Clerk's augmentation of Withals' *Dictionary*, in 1584.

We have noticed above that Huloet, following his French model, and perhaps remembering the example of John of Garland and Julius Pollux and the precepts of Erasmus, introduced into the *Abcedarium* numerous Latin synonyms.[19] These, as we have seen, Higgins retained and, under the influence of the Stephanus-Thierry dictionary as well as the Elizabethan desire for copiousness and variety of expression, greatly augmented. Higgins, more than Huloet, consciously emphasized the principle of synonymy and copiousness. Examples of his practice, in addition to these cited, are under such entries as *aide, advise,* and *detract,* as follows:

Aide, or to helpe out. *Iuuare, Adiuuare, Adiutare, Opitulari, Adiumento esse, Adiumentum dare, Adiumentum affere, Adiumenta importare, Auxilium afferre, Operam alicui dare, Operam praebere, Opera referre, Suppetias ferre, Ire opitulatum, Soluti esse alicui, Comministrare, Commodare alicui in re aliqua, Alicui auxilio venire, Auxiliari alicui.* Aider. . . .

Aduise or thinke of a thinge. *Animaduertere, Aspicere, Considerare, Deliberare, Consultare, Apud se reputare, Aduertere, Circumspectare, Despicere.* Aduiser.

Detract, or to speake ill of one. *Allatrare aliquem, Defama alicuius detrahere, De-*

trahere alicui, Insectari aliquem maledictis, Lacerare optimum virum incesto ore, Maledicere alicui, Male loqui alicui, Obloqui, Obtrectare laudibus alicuius, Premere aliquem, Sinistris sermonibus carpere aliquem, Vellicare. Mesdire & detracter de quelqu'vn. S.

It is true that many of the Latin equivalents supplied by Higgins derived, as he admits, from Stephanus by way of Thierry. Yet Higgins chose entries in which there were many synonyms, and not infrequently augmented the number.

That Higgins had in mind the principle of varying and copiousness is evidenced by another practice which had no precedent in Huloet or Stephanus: that of writing a sentence in English and then expressing the idea in Latin, in a great variety of ways, employing from twelve to sixty or more Latin phrases. It is as if Higgins had studied carefully Erasmus' *De copia* (especially Chapter 33, Book I), and here supplied additional examples to illustrate the principle. Similar matter Higgins could have found at the end of the *Colloquy,* "The Profane Feast," under the heading "A short rule concerning this Copia; it teaches how to vary a sentence pleasantly, copiously, easily, frequently, and elegantly. . . ." Then Erasmus lists with brief explanation eight ways of attaining *copia,* which may be paraphrased thus: (1) use apt and chosen words for the idea to be expressed; (2) use variety of words if they are to be found; (3) if proper words are wanting, use borrowed words; (4) secure variation by substituting the passive voice for what has been said in the active; (5) employ verbal nouns and participles; (6) change adverbs into nouns, and nouns sometimes into one part of speech, sometimes into another; (7) change affirmative sentences into negative, or the contrary; (8) use questions, or speak interrogatively what has been spoken indicatively. Erasmus then shows, step by step, how the instructions may be applied to the sentence "Your letters have delighted me very much" (an illustration also employed in the *De copia,* Chapter 33).

There can be no doubt that Higgins had learned his lesson well; practically all the methods of varying explained by Erasmus are exemplified by sentences which Higgins supplies in his augmentation of *Huloets Dictionarie* (1572). Such sentences with the variant Latin equivalents appear under *elegant, eloquent, experience, faire, faulte, finishe, foe, folowe, force, free, frende, gayne, gentlenesse, geometrie, giantes, giue, hope, infamie, ire,* and *loue.* Some of the English sentences for which Higgins supplies the Latin variants are these:

There is nothing can geue me consolation.
He wryteth elegantly.
He is eloquent.
Experience is the maistres of all thinges, or experience teacheth us many thinges.

There is no man more fortunate than you.
It is a faire or very beautifull virgin.
I am not in faulte.
I hope to finishe or ende this matter according to my mynde.
Thou hast sette my mynde free from all feare.

Typical of Higgins's method of varying is the passage which follows, transcribed from his edition of *Huloets Dictionarie* (1572).

Experience is the maistres of all things, or experience teacheth us many thinges. *Multa discuntur, percipiuntur ab experientia. Multarum rerum scientia, cognitio, intelligentia, doctrina capitur, sumitur, hauritur ab experientia & vsu. Multa cognoscuntur experientia duce. Multarum rerum magister est vsus, multa docet, ostendit, patefacit, viam aperit vsus ad multarum rerum scientiam. Erudimur valde, instituimur, expolimur. Ex ignorantiae tenebris educimur, ad scientiam multarum rerum experientia duce peruenimus. Multarum rerum scientiam consequimur, experientiam secuti, experientia docti, experientia magistra.*

In this passage and others, too long to quote here, are exemplified nearly all the methods suggested by Erasmus to attain copiousness and elegance and skill in varying the expression of thought.

The Huloet-Higgins dictionaries are in the English-Latin tradition of lexicography, stemming from the *Promptorium parvulorum* and the *Catholicon Anglicum* of the fifteenth century. In content they are, like their contemporaries, composite, deriving matter from many sources, but owing most to Calepine's Latin dictionary, the Elyot-Cooper Latin-English dictionaries, and the French-Latin and Latin-French lexicons of Robert Stephanus. The relationship of the Huloet-Higgins texts to these antecedents is perhaps even more complex than the foregoing discussion has indicated. In their technical features there is little that is novel; they give grammatical information concerning Latin words, such as case endings of nouns, principal parts of verbs, and identification of adverbs and adjectives, which is the practice in other lexicons. There is no attempt at etymology; definitions are slight, the real meaning being often determined by the Latin synonyms and by the illustrative phrases. In the extensive use of synonyms and in the elaborate exemplification of the Erasmian principle of copiousness, especially in the edition of 1572, the Huloet-Higgins dictionaries go beyond their antecedents. These latter features are taken over by an immediate successor, Baret's *Alvearie* (1573).

That *Huloets Dictionarie,* as revised and augmented by Higgins, did not reach another edition after 1572 was due first of all to the competition of the *Alvearie,* a more pretentious text in English, Latin, and French, with useful indexes to the Latin and French words. Other competitors were Withals' English-Latin *Dictionarie,* already well established; Veron's Latin-English text, revised by Waddington (1575); and, above all, Thomas Cooper's *Thesaurus,* Latin-English, then regarded as the authoritative classical dictionary and published at regular intervals from 1565 to 1587. Although the Huloet-Higgins of 1572 did not survive the powerful competition, it is, in range of matter and in its reflection of contemporary linguistic and literary principles, of no little importance in the history of lexicography.

CHAPTER XIII

John Withals' *Shorte Dictionarie*
for Yonge Begynners (1553)

IN THE 1550's there appears to have been a demand for small inexpensive dictionaries, possibly because they would be useful for
schoolboys. Yet neither Veron's *Dictionariolum* nor Huloet's *Abcedarium*, both published in 1552, seems to have had wide vogue, neither
being printed a second time until after the lapse of many years. As early
as 1553, John Withals published his little dictionary in English and
Latin, which, though slow in getting under way, was destined to become
the most widely used text in the second half of the century. The history
of Withals' book is an illuminating chapter in sixteenth-century lexicography.

Concerning the life of Withals, almost nothing is known; information
on the date of his birth, his education, or the time of his death is wanting.
As his text was obviously planned for schoolboys, it is a plausible conjecture that he was an obscure schoolmaster. His book, as printed in 1556,[1]
has on the title page: "A Shorte Dictionarie for Yonge Begynners.
Gathered of Good Authours, specially of Columell, Grapald, and Plini.
Anno. M.D.LVI." The running title is "A littell Dictionarie for children."

In the dedication to Sir Thomas Chaloner the author writes:

I am at this present bolde, hauing no acquaintance with your maistership, to dedicate this my rude collections vnto you, praiyng you to accepte it as a thinge written
by me to induce children to the latine tõgue, not moued thereto with the desire of
vaine glory but with a feruente affection and loue I beare vnto my countrey.

I haue resorted to the most famous and ancient Authours, out of the whiche, as
out of cleare fountaines, I haue drawen as diligently as I could the proper names of

167

thinges conteyned under one kynde, and disposed them in such ordre, that a very childe beyng able to reade, may with little labour profitely imprinte them in memory; whiche shal! not be onely profitable for them nowe in their tendre age, but hereafter when they shalbe of more judgement and yeres, it shalbe unto them a singular treasure: for the lack whereof they shalbe compelled, as I haue herde many profounde clerkes both in disputacion as also in familiar communication to use in steede of the proper and naturall woorde, a paraphrase or circumlocucion.

This "littell Dictionarie" designed "to induce children to the latine tongue" was, if we may judge from its vogue, a most successful venture. It was reprinted, occasionally with revisions and augmentations, in every decade, sometimes oftener, between 1556 and 1634. At least thirteen editions appeared during the seventy-odd years of its existence.[2] Of the important revisions, we shall speak below.

The Withals is an English-Latin dictionary, with series of words and phrases related by association rather than by origin and grouped under general topics. In each entry the English word or phrase is placed first and is followed by the Latin equivalent, as "The earth, *terra, ae*"; and the declension of the Latin nouns and the conjugation of the verbs are indicated. The range of topics for the groupings is fairly inclusive, going from the broad, general subjects to the specific but less well known. Beginning with the topic "aether, or air," the author proceeds to list English and Latin terms applicable to the seven planets; the twelve signs of the zodiac; the four elements of fire, air, earth, and water; the sea and all that belongs to it, as fishes and ships; the earth and what is therein, as beasts, birds, trees, plants, and man and the parts of his body, his buildings and institutions; also crafts and skills, as the baker, the carpenter, the miller, and so on, through a great part of man's activities.

Each related group of words and locutions has its appropriate caption or heading in both English and Latin,[3] and under the general heading one may find the specific related word or phrase. If one wished, for example, to find the Latin for *axe* or *saw*, he would look under the topic "Carpenter, with his instruments, and such as worke in tymbre"; and there he would find such entries as *a carpenter, the master carpenter, a builder, buildyng, an axe to hewe or cutte with, sharpe of edge, dull of edge, the helve or handle of the axe or other instrument, a chip axe, a sawe, a wymble,* together with the Latin equivalents of these terms.[4]

Such a grouping of entries scarcely lends itself to an alphabetical or etymological arrangement; it is topical. In range of subject and in disposition of matter, Withals' *Dictionarie* has many antecedents. It belongs to the bilingual vocabulary tradition, which, in England, may be traced back to the eighth century or earlier.[5] But vocabularies, Latin–Anglo-Saxon or Latin–Middle English, were not printed until the nineteenth century. Although Withals may have known some of these in manuscript, the evidence seems to indicate that his dictionary was compiled from printed texts. To "Grapald" (Grapaldus), the author of one of these texts, Withals acknowledges indebtedness, on the title page. Franciscus Grapaldus of Parma, Italy, first published, in 1494, his *Lexicon de partibus aedium.*[6] It is this book to which Withals refers. The *Lexicon* proved to be a popular book and was frequently reprinted on the Continent.

The title of Grapaldus' little book hardly suggests the comprehensive character of its contents. Although almost every chapter contains, at the outset, terms applicable to a building, the topics and the word list are extended to include what is in the building or in any way associated with it. Chapter 3 (Book I) with the heading, "Apotheca" ("wine shop"), begins with mention of a wine cellar and includes the terms signifying the various types of vessels used to contain wine, the kinds of wines, the colors and flavors, grapes and other fruits and plants from which wine is made, testing of wine (*vini probatio*) for dilution, the wholesome and pleasurable uses of wine, and so forth. Treated in a similar manner is "Gynaecium" (Book II, Chapter 5), the part of the house designed for women. This term suggests at once looking glass (*speculum*). Then follow rouge (*purpurissum*) for the lips and cheeks; ceruse, or white lead, for the neck and breast; medicines (*tetanothra*) to smooth wrinkles in the face; ointment (*psillothram*) to remove superfluous hair; an instrument (*volsella*) to pluck hairs from the body or face; instruments for trimming and for curling the hair; soap, perfume, and jewelry; also cradles (*incunabula*), and the feeding and training of children.

Under such topical headings a great many terms associated with the general subjects are brought together and their meaning and application made clear in a sort of connected discourse. The principal words thus defined are listed in the margin near their definitions as well as in their context on the page. As the summaries above may suggest, the twenty-four chapters of the Grapaldus contain a considerable list of Latin terms closely related to daily activities.

For the English-Latin *Dictionarie* of Withals, the compact Latin *Lexicon* of Grapaldus seems to have been the model. There is frequent correspondence in topical headings as well as in definitions. "The Partes of Housyng, with that belongeth: *Partes aedium cum appendicibus*," is a heading in the *Dictionarie* which echoes the title *De partibus aedium* of Grapaldus. In the topics pertaining to the stable, the bathhouse, the armory, diseases of the eye, and diseases of the head, to mention a few, Withals follows the lead of Grapaldus, sometimes translating the Latin, sometimes quoting it verbatim. The examples which follow serve to show the relationship.

Withals (1556)	Grapaldus (1535)
A stable, *stabulum, li, vel, equible. sed stabulum dicitur non tantum equorum, sed & hominum.*	Stabulum, ubi greges & armenta clauduntur, locū generaliter appellamus: nā equi tenentur, specialiter Equile ... Dicuntur & stabula hominum & diuersoria & hospitia. [p. 120]
The bitte of a brydle, *orea, reaem vel lupatum, ti.*	Oreas quibus ora frenantur. Est & inter frena Lupus, quem Lupatum nonnulli. [p. 132]
The reyne of a bridle, *retinaculum, li, vel lorum, ri.*	Habenae, quae & retinacula, frenis annexa sunt lora, manuque tenentur. [p. 133]
The manakle for the horse nose, *pastomis.*	Ast Pastomis ad cohibendam naribus imponitur.
But for the horse eares, *aureae dicuntur.*	Sicut aureas quae ad aures religantur. [p. 132]
Dorsualia dicuntur operimenta, quibus equorum dorsa teguntur, as with a panell or such other.	Operimanta ueró quibus mulorum, boumque, & equorum dorsa conteguntur, Dorsualia vocant. [p. 136]
[Lorica] *Dicitur sepimentum, quo vrbem cingunt obsessores.*	Nam lorica sepementum est apud historicas quo urbem cingunt obsessores. [p. 172]
The harneys of mayle about the necke, *Torques, quis a gorgette.*	Addito Torque ex anulis ferreis uel laminis ad iuguli imprimis tutamentum. [p. 324]
About the handes, *manicae.* About the armes, *brachialia.* *Sic humeralia & femoralia.*	Manicae a manibus dicuntur, quibus milites e ferro in praelijs pugnantes utantur ad earum defensionem: ueluti a brachia Brachialia, ab humeris Humeralia, & a femore Femoralia. [p. 324]
Balista, tae, dicitur instrumentum, quo maiora saxa, & grauiora mittuntur.	Balistae tormenta sunt, quibus saxa maiora & grauiora mittuntur. [p. 338]

These parallels, chosen after a comparative study of other possible sources, show Withals' dependence upon Grapaldus' *Lexicon* and confirm his acknowledgment of indebtedness, as expressed on the title page of the *Dictionarie*. In the *Lexicon*, Withals found the model for his own text, many of his major topics, part of his word list and definitions, and a great many Latin phrases and sentences, which he took over without translating. But Grapaldus was by no means a sole source. From a wordbook compiled thirteen hundred years earlier than the *Lexicon*, Withals supplemented the matter borrowed from Grapaldus. The allusion is to the work of Julius Pollux.

Pollux was a Greek Sophist and grammarian, who, about A.D. 177, compiled an extensive Greek vocabulary, called *Onomasticon*.[7] This was first printed by Aldus, at Venice, in 1502. In 1542 a Latin edition of this text was prepared by Rudolphus Gualtherus and printed at Basel. It was this Latin version of the *Onomasticon* that was known to Withals. In this book the arrangement of topics and the method of definition are quite similar to those in the *Lexicon* of Grapaldus, though the *Onomasticon* has a wider range of subjects. It lists also an abundance of synonyms and antonyms, a feature having no counterpart in the *Lexicon*.

Having modeled his *Dictionarie* upon Grapaldus, Withals found the copious Latin text of the *Onomasticon*, with a topical arrangement like that in his own compilation, a convenient supplementary source. From the vocabulary under the headings "De Nauibus, et Nauticis nominibus" (p. 32), "De partibus Nauis" (pp. 33–34), and "De Nauigantibus" (p. 35), Withals augmented his word list for his topic "A shyp with all Water vessels: *Nauis cum pertinencijs.*" From the "De Aegroto, et Sano" (p. 154) of the *Onomasticon*, Withals supplemented his "De Morbis & aegritudinibus"; and from Gualtherus' annotations on "Auium Voces" (p. 239), the English compiler added many terms to his vocabulary pertaining to birds. These terms appear in a poem, "De Philomela," supplied by Gualtherus among the annotations and ascribed to Ovid. The verses put in metrical form the Latin words used to signify the cries of birds and other animals. From these verses Withals takes numerous phrases or sentences to supplement his own entries. Among his borrowings are these:

Clangunt Aquilae	Pulpat vultur
Bubulat bubo	Modulatur pica
Vlulant vlulae	Frigulat graculus
Cucubat noctua	Gruit grus
Pipit passer	Regulus, merops, &
Pupulat pauus	progne zinzillant

These Latin sentences, derived from the verses inserted by Gualtherus, together with evidence of borrowing from other topics in the *Onomasticon*, seem to indicate that Withals consulted the Latin text of 1542.

In the *Lexicon de partibus aedium* of Grapaldus and Gualtherus' Latin edition of the *Onomasticon* of Pollux, Withals found, then, the pattern for his own *Dictionarie*, and a basic word list. He was not content, however, to depend wholly on these two authors. Into this pattern he wove words and phrases from various other sources. One of these was the *Dictionarium* of Friar Ambrosius Calepine. First published in 1502, this book went through many editions in the period, being gradually developed into a polyglot before the end of the century.[8] In the edition of 1542, which Withals may have used, the Calepine was still primarily a Latin dictionary, having added Greek equivalents for the Latin terms to be defined. The text has an etymological, or modified alphabetical, arrangement of entries, the derivatives being placed immediately after the root words. Having his basic word list, Withals could further enlarge it by reference to the systematically arranged and more extensive vocabulary in the Calepine. And the Calepine he drew from freely.

The problem of determining Withals' indebtedness is complicated, however, by the circumstance that Calepine had transferred into his own lexicon considerable portions of Grapaldus and had also drawn upon some of the same sources as Grapaldus, such as Pliny and Columella. It has been necessary, then, to examine the various texts involved in order to reach valid conclusions. Fortunately for the investigator, Withals frequently borrowed the Latin of his original without translation and thus renders comparison easy. Some of the examples that emerge from the comparative study and that show Withals' debt to Calepine are here presented.

Withals (1556)	Calepine (1542)
Sed forum quatuor modis intelligitur. Primo, negotiationis locus: Secundo, quo iudicia fieri solent: Tertio, quum is, qui prouinciae praeest, forum agere dicitur, quum ciuitates vocat, & de controuersijs earum cognoscit, ac sententiam fert: Quarto, quum id forum ueteres appellabant, quod nunc vestibulum sepulchri dici solet.	Forum . . . Et quatuor modis dicitur. Primo, negociationis locus, quo uenalia feruntur . . . Altero, in quo iudicia fieri, cum populo agi, & conciones haberi solent . . . Tertio, cum is qui prouinciae praeest, forum agere dicitur, cum ciuitates uocat, & de controuersijs cognoscit, ac sententiam fert. Quarto autem id forum ueteres appellabant, quod nunc vestibulum sepulchri dici solet.
The spoiles or porcions of goodes to be diuided among the souldiours after the battaile or conflicte is paste, *Manubiae, biarum, spolium, lij, & Spolia in plu.*	Manubiae . . . Ascon. scribit manubias praeda imperatorum pro portione de hostibus capta. Spolia quoque quaesita de hoste nobile per deditionem manubiae ueteres dicebant.
A foote man of warre, *pedes, ditis: sicut eques, equites, qui ex equo militat.*	Pes, peditis . . . miles, qui pedibus militiam exercet: sicut eques, qui equo militiam exercet.
Squint eied or gogle eied, *strabus, bi, vel strabo, nis, is dicitur, qui oculos habet distortos.*	Strabo, onis, qui oculos habet distortos.

From these Latin dictionaries—Grapaldus, Pollux-Gualtherus, and Calepine—Withals derived the essentials of his text. But since he was compiling an English-Latin dictionary, it was natural that he should avail himself, as far as possible, of bilingual lexicons, especially English-Latin and Latin-English. He appears to have done so. One such text was that of John Stanbridge, whose Latin-English *Vocabula*, for schoolboys, was first published in 1496 and frequently thereafter in the first half of the sixteenth century.[9] In this book Stanbridge employs the conventional topical groupings of man, the parts of his body, his diseases, his crafts and professions; animals, birds, fishes, etc. In the first pages of the text, he has the usual order of arrangement, in parallel columns. Although the disposition thereafter approximates that of an interlinear gloss, the author retains the headings of the traditional vocabularies. This book is one link between Withals and the older native vocabularies. To it he is indebted for certain entries, as the examples here transcribed will show.

Withals (1556)	Stanbridge (1496)
A head, *caput tis.*	*Hoc caput tis,* the head.
The crowne of the head, *vertex ticis.*	*Hec vertex cis,* the crowne of the head.
The brayne panne, *calva.*	*Hec calva, e,* for a braine panne.
The brayne, *cerebrum, bri.*	*Hoc cerebrum, bri,* the braine.
The seame of the head, *sutura re.*	*Hec sutura re,* the seame of the head.
The white of the eie, *albugo, ginis.*	*Hec albugo, ginis,* the white of the eie.
The eie lidde, *gena, ne.*	*Hec gena e,* the eie lidde.
The corner of the eie, *hirquus, qui.*	*Hic angulus, oculi,* the corner of the eie.
The space betweene the browes, *intercilium, lij.*	*Hoc intercilium, lii,* the space betweene the browes.

Withals' borrowing consists largely in reversing the order of entries and in omitting the qualifying adjectives which are found in Stanbridge. His debt to the *Vocabula* is relatively small.

To the Latin-English *Dictionary* of Sir Thomas Elyot, as revised by Thomas Cooper under the title *Bibliotheca Eliotae* (1548), Withals' obligation is much more extensive.[10] Although he makes no acknowledgment of indebtedness, Withals pays high tribute to Elyot and implies, in his Prologue, that he has received aid from the *Bibliotheca*. The implication is confirmed by a study of the texts. The problem of assessing the debt is by no means simple. Elyot had derived much matter from Calepine and some directly from Grapaldus. But Calepine also was indebted to Grapaldus; and Withals, to both Grapaldus and Calepine. Thus the debt to Elyot is fairly complex. The parallels which follow, based on a study of all the apposite texts, offer proof that Withals was a direct borrower from the *Bibliotheca*.

Withals (1556)	Elyot-Cooper (1548)
A Markettemanne, or he that useth Markettes or Faires, *agoreus.*	*Agoreus,* . . . a market man, an haunter of markets or faires.
A Loupe to looke out of a house, or wall, *Conspicilium.*	*Conspicilium,* . . . a loupe to looke out of an house or walle. . . .
The Chapiter of a piller, a little pilour, set upon a greater, *Epistylium.*	*Epistylium, lii,* . . . the chapiter of a pyllour, or a littell pillour sette upon a greatter.

Withals (1556)	Elyot-Cooper (1548)
A peele to sette in the breade, and take it out with, *infurnibulum*.	*Infurnibulum, li.* a piele wherewith breade is sette into the ouen.
Maceria, riae, and *Maceries, ei.* is a wal of stone, made without loome or mortar.	*Maceria, ae,* & *Maceries, ei* . . . a wall of stone withoute mortar.
Municeps, a citizen or bourgesse inioyinge the liberties of the town.	*Municeps* . . . a citizen or burgesse enioieyng the libertees of the towne.
Acetabulum, a littel vessell, as a measure of wyne, conteynyng two ounces and an halfe.	*Acetabulum, tabuli* . . . a measure conteinyng in it of wine .ii. ounces and an halfe. it is also a little vessell, as a saucer, or other like.
Batris, a vesselle with a longe handle.	*Batris,* a vessell with a long handell, after Calepin.
A gredyron, *cratis, tis, vel craticula, lae.*	*Craticula, lae* . . . a gredeyron, whereon meate is broyled.
Coronamentum, Roses, uillettes, & other flowers, wher of Garlandes be made.	*Coronamentum* . . . roses, violettes, and other floures, wherof garlandes be made.

In the dictionaries and vocabularies that he used, Withals had access to abundant matter on birds and plants. Some of this he obviously appropriated. But he was eclectic: he found in books current in his day, other than dictionaries, information on these subjects, which he must have regarded as more trustworthy. These, in preference to the conventional sources, he levied upon. Most worthy of notice are two books by the versatile Englishman William Turner: [11] *Avium historia, or History of Birds* (1544),[12] and *The Names of Herbes in Greke, Latin, English, Duch & Frenche* (1548). In both fields of study, Turner had read widely and critically, and had supplemented his reading with firsthand observation. His work has a definite place in the history of science. Withals was one of the first, but by no means the last, of English lexicographers to incorporate the results of Turner's investigations in his dictionary. From the *Historia* as well as the *Names,* Withals drew freely. Traces of Turner's work are everywhere evident in the parts of the *Dictionarie* devoted to birds and to herbs, as examples below will testify.

Withals (1556)	Turner's *Historia* (1544)
A martlet, whiche is of the quantitie of a swalowe hauyng no feete to goe, but onely stumpes, *cypsellus, li, apus vel apos, podis, graece.*	[*Apodes.*] *Plurimum uolant, que apodes vocantur, quia carent usu pedum. Ab alijs Cypselli appellantur, hirundinum specie.* [p. 100]
A sea cobbe, *gauia alba.*	. . . *gauia,* a se cob or a seegell. *Gauiarum duo genera* Aristot. *facit: alterum album, quod apud mare, alterum cinerium.* [p. 78]
A gull, *gauia cinericia.*	
A redshanke, *hematopodus.*	*Est apud Anglos* . . . *auis quaedam longis*

Withals (1556)	Turner's *Historia* (1544)
	& rubris cruribus, nostra lingua red-shanca *dicta, cui an descriptio haemotopodis.* [p. 102]
A stockdooue, *liuia, ae,* for stockdooues be not the great dooues that haue the whyte rynge about their neckes, but *palumbes* be they.	... *quae liuia Latine dicitur, est syluestris illa columba quam Angli* a stocdoue ... *nominant. Latine palumbes* ... *dicta ab Anglis* a coushot a ringged doue ... *appellatur.* [p. 60]
A kyte, gleade, or puttok, *Miluus, ui, miluius, uii.*	[*De Miluo siue miluio*] ... *miluus, Anglice,* a glede, a puttok, a kyte. [p. 116]
A hedge sparow, *curruca, cae, & passer sepiarius.*	[*De Passeribus.*] *Vocatur apud Anglos* an hedge sparrouu, *hoc est passer sepiarius.* [p. 157]
A wrenne, *regulus, li, trochilus, graece.*	... *trochilus, senator, regulus, Anglice* a uuren. [p. 152]

We have presented above a few of many items which Withals derived from Turner's *Avium historia*. Evidence of the lexicographer's indebtedness to *The Names of Herbes* is just as conclusive, as the following parallels will show—parallels deduced after all other possibilities had been tested.

Withals (1556)	Turner's *Names* (1548)
Shepherdes purse, *bursa pastoris.*	*Bursa pastoris* is also called in englishe ... Shepherdes bag or shepherdes purse. [p. 83]
Two penie grasse, *centimorbia.*	*Centimorbia* ... may be called in englishe Herbe .ii. pence or two peni-grasse. [p. 84]
Petypanicke or grescorne, *phalaris.*	*Phalaris* ... may be called in englishe petie panicke, or ... grasse corne. [p. 61]
Cinke foile, or fiue fingered grasse, *quinquefolium.*	*Quinquefolium* is called ... in english Cynkfoly or fyue fyngered grasse. [p. 66]
Stone Rue, or Wall Rue, *Ruta muralis.*	*Saluia vita* or *Ruta muralis* ... may be called in english Stone Rue, or wal Rue. [p. 86]
Unsauerie margerum, *symphytum.*	*Symphytum* ... may be called in english Vnsauery Margerum. [p. 77] [13]

Our investigation thus far indicates that in the compilation of his *Dictionarie*, Withals selected and adapted materials from at least seven different books: Grapaldus' *Lexicon de partibus aedium*, a Latin edition of Pollux' *Onomasticon*, Calepine's *Dictionarium*, Stanbridge's *Vocabula*, the Elyot-Cooper *Bibliotheca*, and Turner's *Historia* and *Names of*

Herbes. The list may not be exhaustive,[14] but it is enough to suggest a heroic effort "to induce children to the latine tongue."

Such are the provenance and the sources of Withals' *Dictionarie* in its earliest form. But in the course of its subsequent history it underwent a sea change. Although it retained the original plan of organization, it was several times revised and augmented to keep abreast of the times and to hold its own with competitors. The text thereby incurred indebtedness to other sources, indebtedness which will be noted at the apposite places in this account. It may be stated here, however, that the edition of 1568 represents no change from that of 1556. The revisions of 1574 and 1581, the second and third respectively, by Lewis Evans, show the addition of some words and locutions under various topics, a few corrections, and, at the end of the 1581 copy, a three-page list of adjectives. These revisions seem to be of no great consequence.

The more important revisions and augmentations of Withals' *Dictionarie* occurred in the editions of 1584, 1602, and 1616. The phrasing of the title page of the 1584 edition is thus:

A Shorte Dictionarie in Latine and English, verie profitable for yong beginners. Compiled at the first by Iohn Withals: afterwards reuised and increased with Phrases and necessary additions by Lewis Evans. And nowe lastlie augmented with more than six hundred rythmicall verses, wherof many be prouerbial, some heretofore found in olde authors, and other some neuer before this time seene or read in the Latine tongue, as hauing their originall grace in English, by Abraham Fleming. . . . Printed at London by Thomas Purfoote, and are to be sold at his shop without Newgate, ouer against Saint Sepulchers Church. 1584.

The additions by Fleming are indicated by symbols and are of course obvious in the text. Examination of the revised text confirms the assertion on the title page of the considerable augmentation by Fleming. Among the "rythmicall verses" added are these:

Vita haec est fabula quaedam Scena autem mundus versatilis histrio & actor quilibet est hominum.

> This lyfe is a certaine Enterlude or Playe,
> The world is a stage full of change euerie way,
> Euerie man is a player, and therein a dealer.

Causidicis, erebo, fisco, fas viuere rapto.

> It's lawful for lawyers, th'exchequer, and Hell,
> By polling and pilling to liue verye well.

Qui satur est pleno, laudat ieiunia, ventre.

> The man whose belly filled is,
> Commendeth fasting much, iwis.

Diues macrescit, quanto plus copia crescit.

> The riche man waxeth leane and lanke,
> The greater growes his money banke.

Foemina pro dote nummorum dicit amo te.

> A woman for dowrie of money doth saye,
> I loue thee, *quis negat,* Who is saith nay?

Sero rubens coelum mane indicat esse serenum.

> The euening red, the morning gray,
> Foreshewes a clear and summers day.

Post sumptum vinum, loquitur mea lingua Latinum.

> After wine well taken,
> My tongue speakes good Latine.

Ni castigetur petulans mox clunis habetur.

> Except the buttockes beaten be,
> The boye prooues wanton as we see.

There are some six hundred of these "rythmicall verses," Fleming asserts, and it would be tedious and ungenerous to refute his statement. The point is that such verses do constitute much enlargement, and as most of these remained in subsequent editions, they must have proved acceptable to the "yong beginners" and to the schoolmasters. Other entries in the 1584 edition, some of which had come earlier into the *Dictionarie* and are, with one exception, not in verse, may here be quoted as of interest to students of Elizabethan literature.

Sea . . . It is too late to spare when all is spent: An old said-saw: when all is gone and nothing left, what helps the dagger with the dogeon heft? This is drawn from the bottom of the sea, thus: *Sera est in Fundo parsimonia.*

Tree . . . An Iuie tree, *Haedera . . . Vino vendibili non opus est suspensa haedera.* Good and saleable Wine needeth no Iuie bush hanged up to commend it.

Gudgeon . . . Gape Gogeon: An olde English Prouerb, spoken of him that is hongrie of treasure, *Gazis inhisto, Gaza, ae,* is treasure, and *inhio . . .* is to gape Gogeon-like, which is as wide as the chops will let him.

A truffe or packe, *Sarcina, nae.* It is a double poake, bagged at both the ends, and hangeth behind and before on his shoulders that doth weare it, and therof is our prouerb, *Non videmus manticae quod in tergo est,* We see not that wallet that hangeth behinde. It is spoken of reprehension in other mens faults by such as can not see their owne, who be supposed to put other mens faults in the wallet before them, and their owne in that behind them.

The principal sources of Fleming's augmentation of Withals seem to be the *Adagia* and the *Encomium moriae* of Erasmus and the *Proverbs* of John Heywood.[15]

Editions of Withals in 1586, 1594, and 1599, under the editorship of Fleming, and printed by Purfoot, remain almost identical in content to that of 1584. But in 1602, William Clerk, the new editor, greatly enlarged the *Dictionarie.*[16] The wording of the title page suggests the fresh matter of the text:

A Dictionarie in English and Latine for Children, and yong beginners: Compiled at the first by Iohn Withals (with the phrases, and Rythmicall, and prouerbial verses, &c. which haue bin added to the same, by Lewis Evans, and Abr. Fleming, succesively.) And (newlie) now augmented, with great plentie of latine words, sentences, and phrases: with many proper Epigrams: Descriptions: Inscriptions: Histories: Poeticall fictions besides. Framed (all) to their yong vnderstandings which be learners in the Latin tongue, to leade them on to riper knowledge, with delight. By William Clerk . . . Printed at London by Thomas Purfoot. Anno. Dom. 1602.

In the Preface, Clerk defends the method of Withals' *Dictionarie* in these words:

And though it leadeth not, as do the rest, by way of *Alphabet*, yet hath it *order*, and *method* both, and the fittest *order*, and the fittest *method* for yong beginners: for Example, he that would find the *Sunne*, the *Moone*, the *Starres*, or any such other excellent creatures aboue, he may looke for the *Skie*: that is more readie here, for his capacitie, and that is their place, and there they be readie for him in English, and Latine both. . . . Againe, *it is night, it is day, it is light, it is dark, it is cleare, it is clowdie,* &c. these do pertaine to the *Skie*, and there is the English and Latin of them.

As William Clerk was a schoolmaster and a lover of literature, his work as a reviser of Withals afforded him opportunity for self-expression. He increased the text by more than one hundred pages, his added materials being under the heading "Adiectives belonging some to the bodie, some to the minde." Retaining the adjectives from the earlier editions, Clerk illustrated their meaning and usage by selected passages from Latin literature. In this section of the text, for example, the author quotes and translates for illustration twenty-eight epigrams from Martial.[17] These phrase-by-phrase translations may well have been exercises which the author had used in the classroom. In addition to the epigrams, Clerk introduced illustrative passages from Locher's Latin version of the *Ship of Fools*, together with his own prose translations and Barclay's version in English. Clerk's method is best exemplified under the entry *obsequious* (pp. 415–17), where he has matter for illustration from Martial and Locher and Barclay. The example follows.

Such was the *obsequie, plyantnesse, service* . . . of Rufus to Naevia, wherof Martiall in his xcvij Epigram:

> Quicquid agit Rufus,
>   nihil est, nisi Naevia Rufo.
> Si gaudet, si flet,
>   si tacet, hanc loquitur,
> Coenat, propinat, poscit,
>   negat, innuit, una est
> Naevia: si non sit
>   Naevia, mutus erit.

Quicquid agit Rufus, Whatever Rufus doth, taketh in hand *Nihil est,* is nothing, *nisi Naevia Rufo,* if Naevia be not with him. Al things are nothing to Rufus but

Naevia, who with Rufus but Naevia? *Si gaudet*, if he be merrie, *si flet*, if he be sorrie, *si tacet*, if he be silent, *hanc loquitur*, Naevia is privie to it, he speaketh to Naevia, he consulteth with Naevia: *coenat*, hee cheereth, *propinat*, he saluteth with the Cap, *poscit*, he requireth, *negat*, he denyeth, *innuit*, hee noddeth with his head, he maketh signes, this or that token, he giveth of his mind, *una est Naevia*, Naevia maketh one: no cheering, no saluting, no demaunding, no denying, not a nod, but at Naevia: *si non sit Naevia*, if Naevia be not there, be missing, bee away, *mutus erit*, he is mute, dumme, all is mar'd.

> But this is not all:
> Scriberet hesterna patri
> cum luce salutem,
> Naevia Lux, inquit:
> Naevia lumen ave.

Cum scriberet (*Hesterna luce*) *salutem patri*, Yesterday when Rufus should have wrote to his Father, have greeted, have saluted (with his Letters) his Father. *Naevia Lux, inquit:* Thus he wrote in the Letter to his Father. *Naevia Lux*, Naevia my Life, *Naevia lumen*, Naevia my light, *Ave*, hayle to thee, health to thee, &c.

Rufum deridet, Naevia ita amore furentem, ut nihil aliquid, vel loqueretur, vel cogitaret. Martiall mocketh, he laugheth at Rufus, that was inflamed so, that was so madde with, so madde of the love of Naevia, that hee could not speake, nor thinke of any thing else but Naevia, Naevia. And the rather for the reason which the Poet yieldeth.

> Viz.
> *Naevia non una est:*

Shee is not thine alone: not proper, not peculiar unto thee, but common to all, a whore, a harlot, &c.

> *Quid vir inepte fueris?*

Foolish man that thou art, why art thou so madde: why doatest thou so on her? This folly is thus reprooved plainely, in the *Ship of Fooles*, Viz. *Is fatuus miseros casus, & fata subibit.*

> This is the description, viz.
> Qui tua blanda Venus
> sequitur fera iussa dolosque,
> Et properat diros
> tentare Cupidinis arcus,
> Is fatuus miseros casus, &c.

Blanda Venus, Thou flattering Goddesse Venus, thou deceivable lust, *qui ita sequitur fera iussa dolosque*, who so ensueth, followeth thy wicked hests, cruell commande-ments, and thy wiles, thy guiles, *Et properat*, and hieth him, maketh speede, maketh bost, *diros tentare Cupidinis arcus*, to trie to assay Cupid his damnable bowes, his damned desires, *is fatuus*, this Foole, such as this, *miseros casus, & fata subibit*, shall incurre hazard, lie open to all wretched states and conditions.

> Alex Barclay thus:
> Viz.
> O cruell Venus:
> who so doth ensue,
> Thy flattering evils
> and proud commandement,

> And hasteth not
>   the darts to eschew
> Of blind Cupido,
>   but followeth his intent,
> Suche fooles endure
>   much sorow and torment,
> Wasting their goods
>   dishonouring their name,
> As past feare of God,
>   and seeking after shame.

Besides the illustrations from Martial, Locher, and Barclay under the alphabetical entries of "Adjectives," Clerk derives matter from at least one other source, not acknowledged. At the end of the entries under each letter of the alphabet the author has a subheading: "Histories and Poeticall Fictions," that is, myths, legends, and biographical sketches. Under *A*, for example, are *Aaron, Aba, Abdala, Abydeni, Acanthus, Acca Laurentia, Aecius Naevius, Acco, Acestes, Achelous, Achemon, Acheron,* and *Achilles.* The source of these sketches is Thomas Thomas's *Dictionarium* (1587) in the section entitled "Dictionarium Propria Locorum et Personarum."

The 1608 issue of Withals is a reprint of the 1602. In 1616 occurred the final augmentation of the Withals *Dictionarie.* Here is the phrasing of the title page.

A Dictionarie in English and Latine; devised for the capacity of Children, and yong Beginners. At first set foorth by M. Withals, with Phrases both Rythmical and Prouerbial: Recognised by Dr. Evans; after by Abr. Fleming: and then by William Clerk. And now this last Impression enlarged with an encrease of Words, Sentences, Phrases, Epigrams, Histories, Poeticall fictions, and Alphabeticall Prouerbs; with a compendious Nomenclator newly added at the end. All composed for the ease, profit, and delight of those that desire Instruction, and the better perfection of the Latine tongue. Initio facillima, & optima sunt discenda. B. R. Printed at London by Thomas Purfoot. 1616.

The most obvious enlargement in this issue is the Nomenclator, of thirty-eight pages (pp. 585–623).[18] This section has the heading "Breuis succincta Verborum Nomenclatura." It is in the bilingual-vocabulary tradition, being arranged under such topics as "Nomina Dearum," "Nomina Deorum," and "De membris humanis," with the simple English word or phrase on the left and the corresponding Latin word opposite, on the right. This is a sort of ready reference supplementing the text proper. It may well have been inspired by John Higgins's translation of Junius' *Nomenclator* (1585).

Another new feature of the 1616 edition is the thirty-two-page (pp. 552–84) section of *adagia,* listed on the title page as "Alphabeticall

Prouerbs." As early as 1584, Fleming had introduced proverbs into Withals' *Dictionarie,* distributing them alphabetically throughout the text. For this practice, Fleming had ample precedent in earlier lexicons. In 1538, Elyot included adages or proverbs in his *Dictionary.* The number was increased by Cooper, in his revisions of Elyot, until the *Bibliotheca Eliotae* of 1559 contained about 275 proverbs. In the second edition of Baret's *Alvearie,* Fleming himself as reviser recorded some 260 *adagia* from Erasmus together with Fleming's own English translations. In these books the proverbs are inserted intermittently throughout to illustrate meaning and usage of words. Thus the reviser of Withals, in 1616, had precedent for including proverbs in the *Dictionarie,* but no lexicographer before him had presented them in a special section, independent of the text proper. This the 1616 reviser does, and he includes in his alphabetical list approximately 500 proverbs.

This part of his text, for which there is no corresponding section in the earlier editions, has the heading "Adagia Nonnulla, Latino-Anglica, non sine sale & facetijs nostratibus, condita & enucleata" ("Proverbs, Latin and English, expounded with our merry conceits and tempered with wisdom.") These adages are arranged in alphabetical order, according to the Latin, as *A fronte praecipitum, Absque scopo iacularis,* etc., with the English, in black type, following each Latin adage. The Latin phrases and sentences, with few exceptions, derive from Erasmus' *Adagia;* the English is the reviser's own paraphrase, or his selection of a native proverb approximating the meaning of the Latin. Here follow transcriptions of typical adages in his list.

Ad pristina praesepia. Home is home be it neuer so homely.

Aethiopem dealbas. You take great paine, but all is vaine.

Aesopicum denudas graculum. Hee that robs a scoller, robs twenty men.

Actum est. All is marde. All the fatt is in the fier.

Bis pueri senes. No foole to the old foole.

Corui luscinijs honoratiores. Doctor Dodipoll is more honored than a good Diuine.

Cretizandum cum Cretensi. Hee must haue a long spoone that will eate with the deuill.

Currus bouem trahit. The cart before the horse.

Dij tibi dent tuam mentem. God send you more wit, and me more money.

Dimidum facti, qui bene coepit, habet. Well begun is halfe done.

Elephantem ex musca facis. You make a mountaine of a molehill.

Ex tua officina venit. A pig of your owne sow.

Endymionis somnum dormis. You take but a nap of night long.

Exitus acta probat. All is well that ends well.

Faciem perfricuit. Hee blusheth like a blacke dogge, hee hath a brazen face.

Facies tua computat annos. A man need not looke in your mouth, to know how old you are.

Fac interim aliquid ipse deinde Deum inuoca. First lay your bones to worke, then call on God.

Flere ad nouercae tumulum. To weepe with an Onyon.
Gallus in suo sterquilino plurimum potest. A Cocke fights well on his owne dunghill.
Grata breuitas. Short and sweete.
Gallinae filius albae. A darling.
In vino veritas. When men are well whifled, their toungs run at randome.
In memorato habere. I haue it at my fingers ends.
In mari aquam quaeris. You cannot see wood for trees: The butcher looked for his
     knife, and that was in his mouth.
In sinus gaudere. To laugh in his sleeue.
Ineuitabile fatum. Wedding and hanging are both destiny.
Lingua amicus. A friend from the teeth outward.
Lingua quo vadis? Wit whither wilt thou?
Lucri bonus odore ex re qualibet. Somewhat hath some fauours, so we get the chincke,
     we will beare with the stinke.
Musco lapis volutus haud obducitur. The rowling stone, gathereth no moss.
Multum muli scabunt. Scratch my breech, and I will claw your elbow.
Mons cum monte miscetur. Friends may meete, but hils and mountaines neuer.
Neque natare, neque literas nouit. Hee knoweth not a B from a battle doore.

In giving prominence to proverbs, the reviser (his name is not known,
though the initials "B. R." on the title page may be his) had a precedent
in the Elyot-Cooper dictionaries and in the *Alvearie* of 1580. In the
collection of *sententiae*—here distinguished from proverbs—he had the
immediate example of William Clerk in the 1602 Withals; and also of
Elyot, who, however, did not devote a separate section to the wise
sayings. In the revision of 1602, Clerk inserted a series of Latin sentences
without the English (pp. 461–66) under the heading "Illustres quaedam
Sententiae ex optimis autoribus selectae." In 1616 the English paraphrases were added. A few examples of the *sententiae* follow.

Bene viuere, bis viuere est. Liue well, and liue alway.
Probitas laudatur, & alget. Honesty is praised, and little regarded.
Sola virtus expers sepulchri. Onely vertue shall neuer die.
Praeterita reprehendi possunt, corrigi non possunt. Things passed may be reproued,
     but not corrected.
Omne solum forti patria est. A valiant man accounteth euery place his owne Country.
Qui suis contentus, is vere ditissimus est. A contented mind is a kingdome.
Solus temporis honesta auaritia est. Auarice of time is only honest.
Varium & mutabile semper foemina. A womans mind is alwaies mutable.

The last edition of Withals' *Dictionarie* (1634) has no further augmentation or essential changes.

By 1600, or earlier, the term *dictionary* had come, generally, to be
applied to a collection of words with definitions arranged alphabetically
or etymologically. The etymological arrangement tended to be alphabetical, except in the grouping of derivatives under their root words; and
the derivatives were inserted in their places in the alphabet, with cross-
references to their primates, as in Cooper's *Thesaurus*. In the sense in

which the word was employed by the middle of Elizabeth's reign, *dictionary* was not strictly applicable to the text compiled by Withals. It should be observed, however, that Withals had a precedent in John of Garland's *Dictionarius,* a title given to his interlinear gloss or vocabulary at the end of the twelfth century.[19] Withals' *Dictionarie* is, in fact, a super-vocabulary, with topical groupings of words related by frequent association and current in the daily affairs of life. As the direct method of teaching Latin was in vogue in the Elizabethan school, the word list and even the order of arrangement proved most useful to schoolmasters and to "yong beginners" in the study of Latin. This method, tested by several centuries of use, was destined to prevail long after Withals' day.

Our study indicates that the *Shorte Dictionarie* of John Withals, though in the tradition of the medieval bilingual vocabulary, drew into its pages matter from at least a dozen different sources, including other dictionaries and scientific and literary treatises current in the sixteenth century. Its eclecticism was perhaps typical of the age in which it was compiled and was a means of adapting itself to the needs of the time. The character of the augmentations, from decade to decade, implies on the part of the editors or revisers a consciousness of the public interest in literature and in apt writing and speaking; hence the introduction of myths, legends, sketches, proverbs, and wise sayings from such sources as Martial, Erasmus, Locher, and Barclay,[20] and the "Poeticall Fictions" from Thomas Thomas. The principal enlargements were of a literary rather than a linguistic character.[21] This feature of the Withals, together with the traditional type of organization and its use as a school text, probably explains its continuous popularity through a period of more than seventy years. And it may be noted that in the *Nomenclator* of Junius, the *Janua linguarum* (1631) and the *Orbis pictus* (1657) of Comenius, the *Nomenclator classicus* (1675) of John Ray, and the *London Vocabulary* (*ca.* 1700) of James Greenwood, the tradition, of which the Withals is a part, persisted to the nineteenth century.[22]

CHAPTER XIV

John Baret's *Alvearie* (1573)

THE *Shorte Dictionarie* of John Withals, consisting of some six thousand words, was, in fact, little more than a glorified English-Latin vocabulary adapted for use as a school text. About the time the fourth edition of the Withals appeared, another dictionary, compiled largely by a schoolmaster and his pupils, was published in London. This was the *Alvearie* of John Baret (d. 1578?).[1] Though much more comprehensive than the Withals, Baret's book in its inception was obviously intended for use in schools.

John Baret, or Barrett, was Fellow of Trinity College, Cambridge, where he received the B.A. degree in 1544–45, and the M.A. in 1558. In a dedicatory letter (1573) to Lord Burleigh, Baret relates that about eighteen years earlier, or in 1555, he had had pupils at Cambridge "studious of the Latin Tongue." In later years he is said to have taught in London and to have traveled abroad. He received an M.D. degree from Peterhouse, Cambridge, in 1577, though there is no evidence that he ever practiced medicine. His will was proved in 1578.[2]

The mere factual record reveals little concerning the character of the man. More intimate glimpses appear in occasional entries of the *Alvearie* and in the author's "Address to the Reader," explaining the genesis of his book. Characteristic of the Elizabethan schoolmaster with his predilection for punning is Baret's account, under *interest*, of what happens to the man who falls into the hands of loan sharks:

Me thinke it is prettily sayd in Grammar that *Interest* will be ioyned with *Mea*, *Tua*, *Sua*, *Nostra*, *vestra*, & *Cuia*, onely in the ablatiue case, because they are pronounes possessiues. For how great so euer his possessions, goodes or lands be that haunteth the company of this impersonall, if now perchaunce he be able to kepe three persons, at length he shall not be able to keepe one: yea, he himselfe shall shortly become such an impersonall, that he shall be counted as no body, without any countenaūce, credit, person, or estimation amonges men. And when he has thus filched, & fleeced his *Possessiue* so long till he hath made him as rich as a new shorn shepe, then he will turne him to commons in to Ludgate: where for his ablatiue case, he shall haue a datiue cage crauing and crying at the grate, your woorships charitie for the Lordes sake. Therefore *tuo te pede* & *modulo metire*, & then shalt thou neuer need vsury. Cut thy coat according to thy cloth, spend according to thy ability.[3]

We like to think that this discourse and others, such as those under *feathers*, *felon*, and *gaill*, are expressions of Baret's personal opinion. Some of them doubtless are. But when we remember that these may be simply conventional Elizabethan attitudes, the insertions of a collaborator, or even adaptations of an earlier lexicographer, we are hardly warranted in regarding them as authentic biographical details.

The "Address to the Reader" is an alluring account of the way the *Alvearie* came into existence. It reads:

About eyghteene yeares agone, hauing pupils at Cambridge studious of the Latin tongue, I vsed them often to write epistles and themes togither, and daily to translate some peece of English into Latin, for the more speedy, and easie attaining of the same. And after we had a little begunne, perceyuing what great trouble it was to come running to mee for euery word they missed, (knowing then of no other Dictionarie to helpe vs, but Sir Thomas Eliots Librarie, which was come out a little before) I appoynted them certaine leaues of the same booke euery day to write the English before ye Latin, and likewise to gather a number of fine phrases out of Cicero, Terence, Caesar, Liuia, &c. and to set them vnder seuerall Tytles, for the more ready finding them againe at their neede. Thus within a yeare or two they had gathered togither a great volume, which (for the apt similitude betweene the good scholars and diligent Bees in gathering their wax and hony into their Hiue) I called then their Aluearie, both for a memoriall by whom it was made, and also by this name to incourage other to the like diligence, for that they should not see their worthy prayse for the same, vnworthily drowned in obliuion.

Not long after, diuers of our friendes borrowing this our worke which we had thus contriued and wrought onely for our owne priuate vse, often and many wayes mooued mee to put it in print for the common profit of others, and the publike propagation of the Latin tongue: or else to suffer them to get it printed at their proper costes and charges. But I both vnwilling, and halfe ashamed to haue our rude notes come abrode vnder the viewe of so many learned eyes, and especially finding no leasure from my prefixed studies for the polishing of the same, vtterly denied their request, vntill at length comming to London, the right worshipfull Maister Powle, & Maister Garth,[4] with other, &c. singuler fauourers of all good learning, and my very especiall friendes, with their importunate & earnest exhortations had cleane ouercome my contrary minde. Then immediately laying aside all other studies, I was fayne to seeke for writers and workemen about the same, to make it readie for the presse. Therefore I went to diuers of mine olde pupils then being at the Innes of court, deliuering each of them some part of their olde discontinued worke to see it written faire againe, & for other peeces which I thought vnperfect, I gat certayne of ye best scolers of two or three schooles in London to write after my prescription: but in the Frenche and Tables, although I had before traueyled in diuers countries beyonde the seas, both for language and learning: yet not trusting to mine owne skill, I vsed the helpe of M. Chaloner, and M. Claudius.[5]

Uppon this occasion I being much conuersant about the Innes of Court, and also sometime occupied among scolers in the schooles, there came vnto mee a Printer shewing mee Huloets Dictionarie (which before I neuer sawe) & told me he intended to print it out of hand, augmented with our notes also if I woulde. But this bargaine went not forward with him for diuers causes which here it were to long to rehearse. And surely had not the right honorable Sir Thomas Smith knight, principall secretarye to the Queenes Maiestie, that noble *Theseus* of learning and comfortable patron to all students, and the right worshipfull Maister Nowell Deane of Pawles, many wayes incouraged mee in this weary worke, (the charges were so great, and the losse of my time so much grieued mee) I had neuer bene able alone to haue wrastled against so many troubles, but long ere this had cleane broken of our worke begunne, and cast it by for euer.

This "Address" has the ring of an authentic personal document, yet analysis of it and comparison with the text of the *Alvearie* raise a number of puzzling questions. According to the author's account, this was, in its inception at any rate, a co-operative work, each busy little student contributing his lexicographical honey. Although there are inequalities and inconsistencies in the text, it is difficult to see the work of many hands therein. In Baret's statement that he "appoynted" his students "to gather a number of fine phrases out of Cicero, Terence, Caesar, Liuia, &c." is the implication that these were gathered directly from the classical Latin writers. True, Cicero, Terence, and the others, are recurrent in the list of classical authorities cited in the text, but in almost every instance, the cited authority, together with other matter, derives from Baret's immediate source—Calepine, Robert Stephanus, or Cooper.

Who were some of Baret's "old pupils," then at the "Innes of court"? How responsive would they have been in resuming the project after years of separation from their master?

Another implication in the "Address" is that Baret and his pupils began their compilation with the use of *Bibliotheca Eliotae, Eliotis Librarie*. This would have been the logical procedure if, as Baret states, the work was begun eighteen years before 1573. Comparative study of texts shows, however, that the phrasing of English entries—derived from the Elyot-Cooper dictionaries—is almost always that of Cooper's *Thesaurus*, not the *Bibliotheca*. If we accept Baret's statement concerning the *Bibliotheca*, then we must assume later revision of the manuscript of the *Alvearie* to make it conform to the phrasing in the *Thesaurus*.

Baret's insistence that he was at length induced to publish the *Alvearie* by the "importunate and earnest exhortations" of friends is the age-old excuse for publications of various kinds. Only three years before, Peter Levins had poked fun at similar excuses, stating that he himself had, from the beginning, intended to publish his *Manipulus vocabulorum*.

It is evident from these observations that the "Address" is not to be accepted at its face value. Yet the general drift of the address, namely, that the compilation was begun on the basis of the *Bibliotheca* and much later, probably a short time before publication, reworked, is probably true. Such a procedure is, as we shall see, in harmony with the content of the published text.

The *Alvearie*, thus described by Baret, was printed by Henry Denham, in 1573, with the title page worded as follows:

An Aluearie or Triple Dictionarie, in Englishe, Latin, and French: Very profitable for all such as be desirous of any of those three Languages. Also by the two Tables in the ende of this booke, they may contrariwise, finde the most necessary Latin or French wordes, placed after the order of an Alphabet, whatsoeuer are to be founde in any other Dictionarie: And so to turne them backwardes againe into Englishe when they reade any Latin or French Aucthors, & doubt of any harde worde therein.

After the title page, there follow the introductory matter of the dedication, the "Address to the Reader," and the commendatory verses; then come the preambles and the text proper, and the Latin and French indexes.

Baret begins the text proper with a preamble to the letter *A*, in which, as Professor Sledd notes, the author opens the discussion of English spelling reform. This he continues through twenty-two letters of the alphabet, not distinguishing *J* from *I* or *V* from *U*, and not discussing *X* and *Z*. More on this topic later.

The order of languages in the entries is English, Latin, Greek (only occasional in the 1573 edition), and French. Entries are arranged alphabetically according to the key word in the English, though there are variations from a strictly alphabetical order, resulting from variant spellings of the key word, from the repetition of entries under different headings, and from the tendency to etymological groupings. For the Latin words, Baret indicates the part of speech, the genitives of nouns to show the declension, and the principal parts of verbs to designate conjugation. By means of the abbreviations *pen. corr.* and *pen. prod.* the author reveals the accent and the pronunciation of Latin words.[6]

At the end of the text are the "tables" or indexes of Latin and French words referred to on the title page. These are designed to assist students readily to find the English equivalent of any "harde worde," Latin or French, they may meet in their reading. To facilitate the search, each word in the indexes is marked with a letter and a number. To discover the English equivalent, one turns to the specified letter of the alphabet and locates the number in the margin. If a reader wished to know, for example, the meaning of *abiuro,* he would find this word entered in the Latin index, as *"Abiuro.* f. 934." Turning to the marginal number 934 under the letter *F,* he would read: "To Forswere, to deny with an oth. *Abiuro, ras.* . . ."

A few entries from the text will best illustrate the system of the *Alvearie:* [7]

a Bagpipe. *Vtriculus, li: vel vtricularis tibia, vel Ascaula, lae, f.g.* Cornemuse.

* A baggepiper. *Vtricularis, rij. m.g.* Sueton. Vn cornemuseur.

a Baye tree. *Laurus, ri. vel rus, rui, f.g.* Plin. δαφνὴ. Vng laurier.

* Of baye. *Laureus, rea, um.* δάφνινος. *vt: Laurea corona.* Liu. De laurier.

Oyle of baye. *Oleum laurinum.* Plin. Ouile de laurier.

A browne bay. *Equus fuscus.* Ouid.

Bay windowes. *Cauae fenestrae.* Virgil. Fenestres ouuertes.

Of bay colour, bayarde. *Badius color, id est phoeniceus siue spadiceus, inde equus Badius.*

a Bayle, promesse or bonde of appearance before a iudge at a day appointed. *Vadimonium, nij, n.g.* Promesse ou obligation de comparoir deuant le iuge, an iour assigne.

a Bayly: gouernour: an ouerseer. *Dioecetes, tae, pen. prod.* Cic. *Procurator, vel qui procurationem alicuius rei suscipit. Nomarcha, ae.* Bud. Qui ha la charge de quelque chose.

Although the range of source material for the *Alvearie* of 1573 is fairly wide, the bulk of the matter derives from earlier lexicographers, English and French. Of these, the Elyot-Cooper dictionaries contributed most, as far as the English is concerned. If we may trust Baret's statement, his students began the compilation of the *Alvearie,* about 1555, by converting certain leaves daily of the Latin-English *Bibliotheca Eliotae, Eliotis Librarie* into English-Latin. From such procedure, we should expect to find a great many close correspondences between the *Alvearie* and the *Bibliotheca.* There are some agreements, but in almost every instance these can be better explained by the compilers' use of Cooper's *Thesaurus,* where they would have found grammatical information, indication of accent and pronunciation, and mention of Latin sources—generally present in the *Alvearie* but wanting in the *Bibliotheca.* Furthermore, the *Alvearie* follows, probably in the majority of entries, the phrasing and the punctuation of the *Thesaurus.* If, as seems likely, the earlier manuscript of the *Alvearie* depended much upon the *Bibliotheca,* then it must have been revised, after 1565, and made to conform to the more concise phrasing of Cooper's *Thesaurus.*

Title page of the 1573 edition of John Baret's Alvearie, *from a copy in the Folger Shakespeare Library (opposite)*

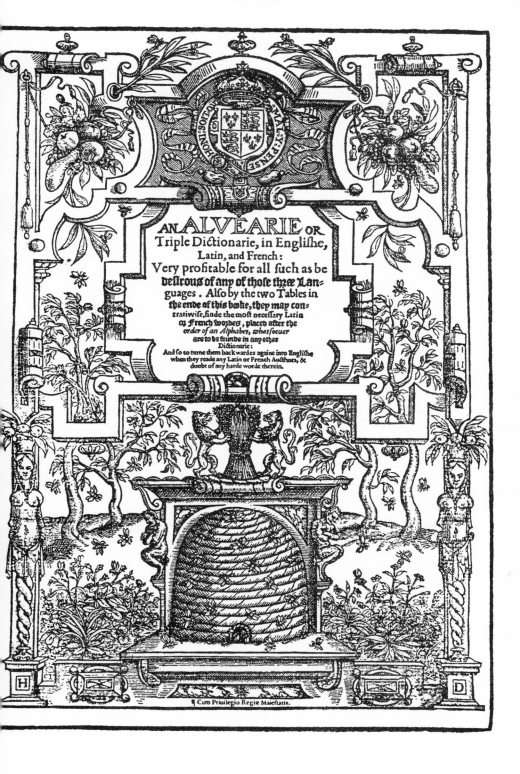

AN **ALVEARIE** OR
Triple Dictionarie, in Englishe,
Latin, and French:
Very profitable for all such as be
desirous of any of those three Lan=
guages. Also by the two Tables in
the ende of this booke, they may con=
tratiwise, finde the most necessary Latin
or French wordes, placed after the
order of an Alphabet, whatsoeuer
are to be founde in any other
Dictionarie:
And so to turne them back wardes againe into Englishe
when they reade any Latin or French Authors, &
doubt of any harde worde therein.

¶ Cum Priuilegio Regiæ Maiestatis.

For such a revision, there is possibly a suggestion in the latter part of Baret's "Address to the Reader." Obviously some years had elapsed since the compilation had begun. Resolved at last to prepare his work for the press, Baret explains that he farmed out to his "olde pupils then being at the Innes of court," "their olde discontinued worke to see it written faire againe." There may be a question whether the "olde pupils" undertook the task; but apparently somebody at this time, possibly a year or so before the *Alvearie* went to press, made a thoroughgoing revision of the manuscript. By virtue of the revision, Cooper's *Thesaurus* became the most important source in the phrasing of the English definitions. This theory would explain the discrepancy between Baret's suggestion that the *Bibliotheca* was a major source and the fact that the *Thesaurus* actually is.

Granted revision,[8] the entries below show what changes Baret and his assistants made to bring the *Alvearie* into conformity with Cooper's *Thesaurus*.

Bibliotheca (1548)	*Thesaurus* (1565)	*Alvearie* (1573)
Plango, xi, plangere, to weepe or bewayle, to strike or hit, to thumpe, to knocke.	*Plango, plangis, planxi, planctum, plangere.* Ouid. To weepe: to bewayle: to stryke: to hitte: to thumpe or knocke.	to Bewaile: to weepe: to hitte: to thumpe, or knocke. *Plango, gis, planxi, planctū, gere,* Ouid.
Redimiculum, li. n. g., the attyre, ornamentes or apparayle of a womans head, as it were a veluet bonet, a frenche hood, or such like.	*Redimiculum, redimiculi, pen. corr.* Iuuenal. The attyre or ornamentes of a womans heade or necke, as a bonet, a french hoodde, a paste, or such like.	Billementes: the attire or ornamentes of a womans head, or necke, as a bonet, a frenche hoode, a paste, or such like. *Redimiculum, li, pen. corr. n. g.* Iuuen.
Remordeo, mordi, dere, to byte hym agayne, of whome he was bitte, to vexe or trouble hym, of whom he was vexed, to tourmente the mynde, to make one heauy, to greeue.	*Remordeo, remordes, remordi, remorsum, remordere.* To bite him againe of whome he was bitten: to vexe or grieue him, of whome he was vexed.	To bite him againe, of whome he was bitten, to vexe or grieue him againe of whome he was vexed. *Remordeo, des, di, morsum, dere.*
Supplico, aui, are, to beseche humbly, to make request.	*Súpplico, súpplicas, pe. cor. supplicáui, supplicâtum, supplicare.* cicer. To beseeche humbly: to make request: humbly to intreate.	to Beseech humbly, to request, humbly to intreate. *Supplico, cas, pen. corr.* cicer. . . .

Bibliotheca (1548)	Thesaurus (1565)	Alvearie (1573)
Scopae, arum, f. ge. plu., a browme or besome to sweepe houses.	Scopae, scoparum, f. g. pluralis numeri. Plaut. A broome or beesome to sweepe houses.	Besomes, or broomes to sweepe houses. Scopae, parū, f. g. Plur. Plaut....[9]

These examples show that, in the various entries in which the *Alvearie* is in the Elyot-Cooper tradition, the final form of Baret's definition is determined by Cooper's *Thesaurus* of 1565. In instances in which the English of the *Bibliotheca* and the *Thesaurus* is so nearly identical that Baret and his helpers might have used one or the other, the grammatical information and the ascription of sources in the *Alvearie*—matter not in the *Bibliotheca*—show that the source was the *Thesaurus*, which does have this information. Compare, for example, the parallels above, under *plango, scopae,* and *remordeo*. Similar results are reached by tracing through the three texts the following entries: *ales, clauus, clibanus, follis, interpunctus, irrepo, minerual, mutulus, palimpsestus, prodo, recito, sistere ruinas, tortus,* and *veterator*. To test results in another way, we may study the entries in the *Alvearie* (1573) from *C, 501* to *C, 535*. In thirty-five successive entries, the *Thesaurus* determines the English phrasing in all except four, which derive from some source other than the Elyot-Cooper dictionaries.

If we broaden the scope of the investigation and consider entries in which the main definitions change but slightly in the Elyot-Cooper dictionaries from 1538 to 1565, we reach a similar conclusion. In the following list of entries thus traced, the English definitions with grammatical forms and citations of sources in the *Alvearie* are finally determined by the *Thesaurus: agoranomus, castratio arborum, contiguo, decursio, expressio, grallatores, perflo, presso, prospectus, saltus, subrogo, suppilo, talio,* and *titubanter*.[10]

The assembled evidence points to the conclusion that the *Alvearie* is in the tradition, as far as the English and Latin are concerned, of the Elyot-Cooper dictionaries; that in its formative stage it may have drawn freely from the *Bibliotheca Eliotae*, but that in the published form of 1573, Cooper's *Thesaurus* is the major English influence. The *Thesaurus*, together with Robert Stephanus' *Dictionarium Latino-Gallicum* (1552, 1561), probably furnished the major portion of the content; but this topic must be developed later.

Although the *Alvearie* owed much to Cooper, it also incurred smaller debts to various other English lexicographers in the sixteenth century. Among the earlier texts was Richard Huloet's *Abcedarium*, first published in 1552 and revised by John Higgins, in 1572, as *Huloets Dictionarie*.

According to Baret's preface, a printer showed Baret the revised Huloet and asked him to augment it with notes. Baret declined the invitation, and his attitude implies that he would have nothing to do with a book that was now become his competitor—in fact, had slightly anticipated his own. Nevertheless, the compilers of the *Alvearie* of 1573 seem to have made use of the Huloet-Higgins dictionaries. The debt is not easy to assess, for as both Baret and the Huloet-Higgins had borrowed from the Elyot-Cooper and Robert Stephanus, some of the parallels could be explained by common sources. Only those parallels which correspond in Latin and English (and are not therefore accounted for by borrowing from the French-Latin or Latin-French of Stephanus) and which have no corresponding passages in the Elyot-Cooper may be regarded as valid. The entries which follow meet these requirements.

Huloet (1552)	Huloet-Higgins (1572)	Alvearie (1573)
Gilthed or goldney fishe which cheweth like a beast. *Aurata marina, scarus . . . Orata.*	Gilthead, or goldney fishe whiche cheweth lyke a beaste. *Aurata marina, Scarus, . . . Orata. Brame de mer.* . . .	a Gilthed, or goldney fishe which cheweth like a beast. *Aurata vel Orata marina, Scarus . . . Brame de mer.* [G, 205]
Actiuitie or exercise in all martial feates. *Pāncratium . . . Strenuitas. . . .*	Actiuitie or exercise in all martial feates. *Pancratiū . . . Strenuitas. . . .*	Actiuity, or exercise in all martial feates. *Pancratium . . . Strenuitas. . . .* [A, 126]
Gymmow or ringe to hange at ones eare as the Egyptians haue. *Staloginum, Inauris.* . . .	Gemoll or gemmow. *Stalagnium . . .* It is suche as the Egiptians vse to hange at their eares.	a Gemowe such as Egiptians vse to hang at their eares. *Stalagnium. . . .* [G, 128]
Cupbord cloth or carpet. *Tapes . . . Tapete. Tapetum.*	Cupbord cloth or carpet. *Tapes . . . Tapete, Tapetum. Tapis. . . .*	A cupbord cloth, or carpet. *Tapes . . . Tapetum . . . Tapete . . . Vng tapis.* [C, 1646]

Another parallel under *gayne*, represents a borrowing by Baret of a longer passage in the Huloet-Higgins, inserted, as we have seen, to illustrate the principle of "copie" and varying.

Huloet-Higgins (1572)	Alvearie (1573)
Many come into the courte for gayne and lucre sake. In forum multi veniunt, vt lucri plurimum faciant: vt lucrētur plurimū, vt quaestus maximos faciat, lucri cupiditate adducti, lucri dulcedine illecti, lucrum spectantes, lucrū secuti, lucro vel lucri spe cōmoti. Mul-	*Many come to the courte for gaine & lucre sake.* In forum multi veniunt vt lucri plurimum faciant: vt lucrentur plurimum, vt quaestus maximos faciant, lucri cupiditate adducti, lucri dulcedine illecti, lucrum spectantes, lucrum sequuti, lucro vel lucri spe com-

Huloet-Higgins (1572)

tos in forū lucri cupiditas adducit, ad agendas causas impellit, facit augēdae rei cupiditas, ditandi spes, congerendarū opum, comparandarū diuitiarū, pecuniae colligende, vt in forum se conferant, vocem in quaestum conferant, vt agendis causis se dent, vt industriam suam in agendis causis exerceant.

Alvearie (1573)

moti. Multos in forum lucri cupiditas adducit, ad agendas causas impellit, facit augendae rei cupiditas, ditandi spes, congerendarum opum, cōparandarum diuitatum, pecuniae colligendae, vt in forum se conferant, vocem in quaestum conferant, vt agendis & actitandis causis se dent, vt industriam in agendis causis exerceant. [*G*, 19] [11]

Fleming, editor of the 1580 *Alvearie*, obviously thought well of such passages and took over many others from the Huloet, as we shall see in the discussion of the 1580 text.

A few of the shorter entries in Baret derive from the *Manipulus vocabulorum* (1570) of Peter Levins. The following parallels are illustrative.[12]

Levins (1570)

An Egge caudel, *ouaceum, i.* [56, 35]

Chamblet, cloth, *sericum undulatum.* [86, 37]

Cockish, *salox, acis.* [145, 2]

A Dag, *tormentiolum, i.* [10, 6]

A Dodkin, *hilum, i.* [133, 27]

To Dowke, *Vrinare.* [218, 2]

Baret (1573)

a Caudel of egges. *Ouaceum, cei.* . . . [*B*, 232]

Chamblet . . . *sericum undulatum.* [*C*, 247]

Cockishe, or lecherous, lustie. *Salox, acis.* [*C*, 695]

a Dag. *Tormentiolum, li.* . . . [*D*, 2]

a Dodkin: of small value: a thing of naught. *Hilum, li.* [*D*, 891]

To diue or ducke under the water. *Vrino.* [*D*, 864]

From the popular English-Latin dictionary of John Withals, we might expect that Baret would have drawn freely. There is evidence of some borrowing, but the topical arrangement of items in the Withals rendered it less convenient for the compilers of the *Alvearie* to use. In the parallels listed below Baret appears to be nearer to Withals than he is to the Elyot-Cooper or the Huloet-Higgins, and the examples are not in Veron's dictionary.

Withals (1556)

Stiffe colde, *rigor.* . . .

A daie and a halfe, *sesquidies.*

the east parte of the worlde, *Oriens.* . . .

The noyse of winde amonge trees, *fragor.* . . .

Baret (1573)

Stiffe colde. *Rigor.* . . . [*C*, 745]

A day & an a [*sic*] halfe. *Sesquidies.* . . . [*D*, 9]

the East parte of the world. *Oriens.* . . . [*E*, 45]

The noize of wind among trees. *Fragor.* . . . [*N*, 156]

These and four additional examples are cited by Sledd to establish the debt of Baret to Withals.[13]

Nearly all the dictionaries of the sixteenth century are probably indebted, directly or indirectly, to Friar Calepine's *Dictionarium*. We have earlier noted extensive borrowing from this source by the Elyot-Cooper dictionaries. To Calepine, Baret also has many obligations. Even in the 1573 *Alvearie* there are a number of Greek words or phrases, equivalents of Latin terms used, and these are drawn largely from Calepine. In addition Calepine supplies Baret with some of his etymologies and with rather lengthy expositions in Latin. For parallel Greek entries in Baret and Calepine, the following list affords examples. The references are grouped in pairs, the letter and number, as *B*, 412, being to the 1573 *Alvearie*, the Latin word, as *allucinor*, to the Aldine 1542 Calepine: *B*, 412–*allucinor; B*, 419–*decallo; B*, 404–*origo; B*, 420–*retro* & *retrorsus; B*, 427–*contemplor; B*, 444–*ructo; B*, 448–*tintinnabulum; B*, 450–*venter; B*, 451–*ventriosus vel ventrosus; B*, 453–*charus; B*, 456–*mugio; B*, 465–*scannum; B*, 468–*intendo*. Although Calepine does not account for all Greek words and phrases in the 1573 *Alvearie*, he is a principal source. The parallel entries which follow give evidence of the more extensive debt of Baret:

Baret (1573)	Calepine (1542)
To aske or inquire diligently. *Percontor* . . . ἀνέρομαι. *Diligenter inquiro, à cōto, quo nautae vtuntur ad inquirenda loca nauibus opportuna. Nam aquae altitudinem conto pertentant. Percontor itaque est quasi conto inuestigare, & inquirere.* [A, 515]	Percontor, ἀνέρομαι . . . à conto dicitur, quo nautae utuntur ad loca nauibus opportuna. Nam aquae altitudinem conto pertentant . . . Significat autem idem quod percunctor: id est, diligenter interrogo.
a Chaine. *Catena* . . . σειρά *Vinculum est ferreum quo vel seruos vel captiuos, vel animalia irretimus ne effugiant.* [C, 280]	Catena, σειρά . . . Vinculum est ferreum, quo vel seruos, vel captiuos vel animalia irretimus ne effugiāt. . . .
The common or mean people. *Vulgus* . . . τὸ πλῆθος. *Pars populi ignobilior, a voluendo nomen habens, quod inconstanter huc illuc voluatur.* . . . [P, 228]	*Vulgus* . . . τὸ πλῆθος . . . Significat multitudinem ignobiliorem . . . Et à uolendo quidam dici putant, quod stulte huc, atque illuc uoluatur.

Baret has a long passage, too long to be inserted here, under *age*. The discourse which follows the English entry is in Latin and is almost a verbatim copy of Calepine's Latin under *aetas*.

Another source for the *Alvearie* of 1573 is John Veron's *Dictionariolum puerorum, tribus linguis, Latina, Anglica, et Gallica* (1552). This text is based upon Robert Stephanus' *Dictionariolum*, Veron having added the English, a rather literal translation of Stephanus' French. As the Stephanus-Veron text is then important as a source of both French and English, it will be discussed below along with the French sources of the *Alvearie*.

We have seen earlier that William Turner was well known to the lexicographers. His *Libellus de re herbaria, The Names of Herbes, The Newe Herball*, and *Avium historia* all furnished matter to the Elyot-Cooper and the Huloet-Higgins dictionaries. Baret, too, was familiar with Turner and seems to have drawn firsthand from the 1562 *Herball*. In a number of entries he refers to Turner by name: *E*, 99, "Eiebright ... *Euphrasia*. Turn. 30"; *E*, 187, "Endyue ... *Intubus*. Turn. folio 21"; and *L*, 114, "Lauander ... *Lauendula* ... Turn. 39." Confirmation of Baret's familiarity with Turner's work is found in the close parallels of the *Alvearie* and the *Herball*.

Baret (1573)	Turner (1562)

The tender and freshe leaues of elder with perched barley, are good for burninges and bitinges of dogges. . . . [*E*, 119]

The tendre and freshe leaues swage inflammaciones layd to emplasterwise with perched barley and they are good for burning and the bitinges of dogges. . . . [125*a*]

The roote of elecampana seasoned and laied vp in maluasie is good for the stomake. *Helenij radix stomacho Vtilis est in passo cōdita*. Dios. li. 1. cu. 27. The sucket or sawce makers drie the roote of elecampana a little first, & then seeth it, & afterwarde steepe it in cold water, & laie it vp in sodden wine for diuers uses. . . . The roote of Elecampana broken and drunken is very good against the spitting of bloud . . . Dios. *ibi*. [*E*, 121]

Elecampane seasoned and layde vp in maluasey is good for the stomake. The succot makers and saucemakers take the roote and drye it a lytle first and then seth it and afterward stepe it in colde water and laye it vp in sodden wine for diuerse vses. The roote broken and dronken is very good against the spitting of blode. [22*a*]

There is a iuyce pressed out of strawberries, which by cōtinuāce of time encreaseth in strēgth, and that is a present remedie, against the sores and wheales of the face, and against the bloudshotten eies . . . Fuchsius, 807.

There is a inice [*sic*] pressed out of strawberries whiche by cōtinuance of tyme encreaseth in strēgh [*sic*] and that is a present remedy against the sores and wheales of the face & against the blood-shotten eyes. [6*a*]

If the roote of Lillies be bruysed with honie, it healeth scurfinesse, scabbes, and lepers, & scoureth away the running sores in the head, it scoureth the face and taketh away wrinkles . . . Diosc. lib. 3. cap. 99. [*l*, 2]

The roote . . . broken and brused w^t hony . . . healeth scurfyness scales scabbes and Lepres & it scoureth away the rynning sores in the heade. It scoureth ye face and taketh away the wrynkles. [38*b*] [14]

For the Latin and the English of the 1573 *Alvearie,* Baret owed most to the Elyot-Cooper dictionaries, particularly to Cooper's *Thesaurus.* Smaller debts he contracted to Calepine, Huloet-Higgins, Levins, Withals, and Turner's *Herball.* The problem of Baret's French source is more complex. In the "Address to the Reader" Baret writes that "in the Frenche and Tables," "not trusting to mine own skill, I vsed the helpe of M. Chaloner and M. Claudius." Neither of these suggested collaborators has been identified beyond a reasonable doubt. For "M. Chaloner," Sir Thomas Chaloner the Elder has been suggested. Sir Thomas was doubtless qualified to do this work, and, conjecturally, he was of St. John's College, Cambridge, Baret's old school. But the real difficulty is, as Professor Sledd suggests, in dates.[15] Baret matriculated sizar in 1551; Chaloner had already attained knighthood in 1547 and was in the service of the State, as envoy to France (1553) and to Scotland (1556), by the time Baret began the compilation of his dictionary. Baret began with the English and the Latin, as he explains to the reader, and the French was added many years later, probably after 1565. Even if the French were added before 1565, what is the likelihood of Sir Thomas's assistance? He was envoy to Emperor Ferdinand in 1559, to the Spanish Netherlands, 1559–60, and to Spain, 1561–64. There was little time in his busy career for lexicographical work. Sir Thomas died in 1565. If, as we believe, the French was added after this date, Sir Thomas was not a collaborator.

As to the "M. Claudius" whom Baret refers to, Miss Lucy E. Farrer was the first to raise the question whether this Claudius might possibly be identified with Claudius Holyband, a popular teacher of French in London from about 1565 to 1580.[16] On the title page of his *French Schoolemaister* (1573), he refers to himself as "professor of the Latin, Frenche, and English tongues." He compiled five textbooks for Englishmen studious of French: *The French Schoolemaister* (1565?; second edition, 1573?); *The French Littleton* (1566?); *The Treasurie of the French Tong* (1580); *Campo di Fior* (1583), including English, Latin, French, and Italian; and a *Dictionarie French and English* (1593).[17] Thus Holyband, often referred to as "Maistre Claude," would seem to be qualified as a collaborator of Baret in the French, and so a logical candidate for the "M. Claudius" mentioned by Baret. But Miss Farrer is herself wary of making the identification. She writes: "Who is this M. Claudius? Is he an ancestor of the Claude family, which is distinguished among the Protestants of the seventeenth century? He might be the David Claudius who translated into Latin and published in 1604 the sermons of John Calvin. But I have not been able to do the necessary research to establish his identity." [18]

Although Miss Farrer nowhere identifies M. Claudius as Holyband, she observes that Baret's *Alvearie* and Holyband's *Dictionarie French and English* (1593) have several traits in common, and cites some fifteen parallels in evidence.[19] These, if valid, would prove at most that Holyband borrowed from Baret. But most of the parallels can be better accounted for by a common source, or sources. Consider, for example, a single entry, for which Miss Farrer cites, with abridgment, only Baret and Holyband.

Robert Stephanus' *Dictionarium* (1561)

Speculator, pen. prod. Verbale. Caes. Vn espion, Espie & guette, Guetteur, Eschauguetteur.

Cooper's *Thesaurus* (1565)

Speculator, pen. prod. Verbale. Caes. An espiall in warres: a scoutewatch: a beholder: a viewer.

Baret's *Alvearie* (1580)

An espyall in warre: a scoutewatche: a beholder: a viewer. *Speculator, ris . . . pen. prod. Verbal.* Caesari . . . Vn espion: Espie & guette, Guetreur, Eschauguetteur. [*B*, 469]

Holyband, *Dictionarie* (1593)

Eschauguetteur. a viewer, a beholder whilest they fight in battell, a spie, an espiall in warres, a scoute-watch.

An analysis of this entry, as it appears in the four lexicons, shows that Cooper drew from Stephanus, making his own English translation; and that Baret used both Cooper and Stephanus. What of Holyband? He could have drawn from Cooper and Stephanus or from Baret. Since so many of the suggested parallels of Baret and Holyband may be accounted for by common sources, it is farfetched to speculate, as does one scholar to be noticed presently, that Holyband is using in his *Dictionarie* materials which he had furnished to Baret.

Miss Kathleen Lambley gives brief notice to the *Alvearie* and remarks: "By 'M. Claudius' Baret possibly meant Holyband, who was often called 'Maistre Claude.' M. Chaloner may have been the author of the French dictionary published by Harrison in 1571." [20] These statements contribute nothing to the problem. Nor does Professor Warren B. Austin, who writes with an assurance that, in the light of the facts, is difficult to understand. He states:

Although it has not been previously noticed, Hollyband was a substantial collaborator in John Baret's 'Alvearie' or Triple Dictionarie in English, Latin, and French. . . . Baret's M. Claudius was of course no other than Claudius Hollyband. . . . Together with Chaloner, then Hollyband compiled the French definitions for the 'Alvearie' and the elaborate "Tables" appended to the work.[21]

Austin's inferences are based upon the large number of parallels which he finds between the *Alvearie* and the *Dictionarie French and English* (1593). His parallels cannot be examined since he quotes not one. Granted that these exist, as Miss Farrer shows, we have seen the danger of basing conclusions on these alone. Miss Farrer refrained from doing so. To assert, as Austin does, on the basis of these, that M. Claudius is Holyband and that in his *Dictionarie* of 1593, Holyband is transferring from the *Alvearie* "some of his early work" [22] is to go quite beyond the known facts.

The French Schoolemaister and *The French Littleton,* the two works of Holyband published before the *Alvearie,* offer no striking resemblances. Parallels between the *Alvearie* and either *The Treasurie* (1580) or the *Dictionarie* (1593), when not explainable by common sources, prove only that Holyband knew Baret's work. That M. Claudius and Claudius Holyband are identical is, to be sure, an eminent possibility, but the identification remains to be proved. Correct is Professor Sledd's conclusion: "The most careful weighing of the evidence leaves the issue still in doubt." [23]

Whoever the collaborators of Baret, so far as the French element in the *Alvearie* is concerned, they need not have been noted scholars in the French language. Probably any of Baret's former pupils could have inserted the French as well as Sir Thomas Chaloner and Maister Claudius Holyband or his counterpart; and the former pupils are more likely to have done so. They would have needed only to be able to read the dictionaries of Robert Stephanus and Bishop Cooper and to insert the English and the French at the proper places in the text of the *Alvearie.* As to the French, there is little that is original: it depends largely upon the dictionaries of Robert Stephanus.

Owing to the staggering industry of Stephanus as a lexicographer, it is difficult to determine with finality which of his dictionaries the collaborators of Baret used in compiling the *Alvearie.* Stephanus compiled, as we have seen, five different dictionaries, all of which were popular. In 1531 he first published his *Dictionarium, seu Latinae linguae thesaurus;* a second edition, in two folio volumes, appeared in 1536, and a third in 1543. With this third edition, the French terms, which had appeared sparingly in the earlier editions of the *Thesaurus,* were ruled out, and the text was a purely Latin dictionary. In this form it was printed again in 1570. Meanwhile, Stephanus had published in 1538 his *Dictionarium Latino-Gallicum,* abridged with respect to the Latin, from the *Thesaurus,* with French equivalents given for all Latin entries. A second edition, much amplified, appeared in 1546, a third in 1552, and a reprint of this in

1561. The *Dictionnaire francois-latin* was first published at Paris in 1539; a second edition in 1549; and a third, corrected and augmented by Jehan Thierry, in 1564. In addition to these larger works, Stephanus published two small dictionaries: *Dictionariolum puerorum* (1544, 1552, 1557) and *Les mots français* (1544, 1557).[24] The problem of Baret's relation to the Stephanus dictionaries is rendered no easier by the fact that the Elyot-Cooper dictionaries drew freely from the *Dictionarium Latino-Gallicum*, Veron from the *Dictionariolum*, and Higgins, in his revision of Huloet, from the Stephanus-Thierry of 1564.

It is possible, however, to indicate some of the Stephanus dictionaries which the collaborators of Baret did use as sources. The *Thesaurus*, which after 1536 contained only Latin, is least likely to have been a source. At the time when the French was added to the *Alvearie*, the *Thesaurus*, which contained some of the French equivalents, was at least thirty-five years old, and Stephanus, meanwhile, had published his *Dictionnaire francois-latin*, his *Dictionariolum puerorum*, and his *Dictionarium Latino-Gallicum*, any one of these a more likely source for the English-Latin-French *Alvearie*. It is true that there are some parallels between the *Alvearie* and Stephanus' *Thesaurus*, but in every instance the *Dictionarium Latino-Gallicum* better accounts for Baret's French and Latin, including grammatical information and stress, than does the *Thesaurus*. And, as we shall see below, the *Latino-Gallicum* was extensively used elsewhere in the *Alvearie*.

From Stephanus' *Dictionnaire francois-latin*, the *Alvearie* derived a large number of its etymologies, as shown in the entries *aduenture, alarme, almanach, approche, attayne,* and others to be considered in the discussion of etymology in the latter part of this chapter. Certain other entries, not concerned with etymology, also derive partly or wholly from the *Dictionnaire*, as the following:

Dictionnaire (1549)	*Alvearie* (1573)
S'accorder à aucun, *Côformare sed ad alicuius voluntatê, Annuere, Cedere alicui, Concedere in sententiam alicuius, Alicui accedere, Assentire, Astipulari, Consentire, Fauere sententiae alicuius.*	To agree to one, or be of his opinion. *Conformare se ad alicuius voluntatem. Annuere. Cedere alicui. Concedere in sententiam alicuius. Alicui accedere. Assentiri. Astipulari. Consentire. Fauere sententiae alicuius.* S'accorder à aucun. [*A,* 199]
Abondance. *Abundantia, Affluentia, Feracitas, Fertilitas, Hubertas, Profluentia.* Abondance de quelque chose que ce soit, *Copia.*	Abundance or plenty. *Abundantia. Affluentia, Feracitas, Redundantia, Fertilitas, Vbertas, Profluentia, Copia.* Abondance, foyson. [*A,* 57]
Fort aagé, ou qui est de grand aage.	Very old, or aged. *Grauis aetate, vel an-*

Dictionnaire (1549)	Alvearie (1573)
Grauis aetate, vel annis, Magno natu, Obsitus aeuo, Plenus annis, Grādaeuus, Prouecta aetate homo, Grandis natu. Non pas fort aagé, *Non admodum grandis natu.*	*nis. Magno natu. Obsitus aeuo. Plenus annis. Grandaeuus. Prouecta aetate. Homo admodum grandis natu. Annosus* . . . Fort aagé, ou qu'est de grande aagé. [A, 183]

These are among the correspondences in the *Dictionnaire* and the *Alvearie* which are not explainable by common sources, such as Stephanus' *Dictionarium Latino-Gallicum* or Cooper's *Thesaurus*. We shall see below (pp. 211–12) examples of near-parallels between the two texts, in which, however, the *Alvearie* has been modified or supplemented by use of other sources.

We have referred to the debt of the *Alvearie* to the Stephanus-Veron *Dictionariolum puerorum tribus linguis Latina, Anglica, et Gallica* (1552). The following parallels, tested by comparison with other possible sources, offer evidence of the *Alvearie*'s debt to the *Dictionariolum:*

Dictionariolum (1552)	Alvearie (1573)
Congius, congii, m. g. a measure of liquides contayning syx sextarios, which is of our measure a pottell & one pynte. Vne mesure de choses liquides, cotenant six sextiers.	A measure of liquides contayning sixe sextarios which is of our measure a pottell and one pinte. *Congius, gij, m. g.* Vne mesure de choses liquides, contenant six sextiers. [M, 213]
Conicio, conijcis, conieci, coniectum, conijcere, to caste togyther, to hurle, to put, to haue some opinion by coniectures onely, without hauynge necessary arguments and tokens, to coniect, to diuine. Iecter ensemble. Iecter. Mettre. Auoir quelque opinion par seules coniectures, sans ce qu'on ait argumens necessaires, Coniecturer, Deuiner.	To cast togither: to hurle: to put: to haue some opinion by coniectures onely, without hauing necessarie argumentes and tokens: coniect: to deuine. *Conijcio, cis, ieci, iectum, conijcere.* Iecter ensemble, Iecter metre, auoir quelque opinion . . . necessaires, coniecturer, deuiner. [C, 179]
Conniueo, conniues . . . to wynk with the eyen, to make as though we did not see and perceaue some thyng, to beare paciently, to let it passe as though we knewe nothyng. Cliner les yeulx, Faire semblant de ne uoir on apparceuoir quelque chose, Porter patienment. La laisser passer comme qui n'en scauroyt rien.	To wincke with the eyen, to make as though we did not see and perceiue some thing: to beare paciently, to let it passe as though we knew nothing. *Conniueo, conniues* . . . Cliner les yeulx, &c. [W, 251]

Of all the Stephanus lexicons, the *Dictionarium Latino-Gallicum* (1552, 1561) contributed most to the French terms and, indirectly, to the English in the *Alvearie*. To understand why this is true, it is necessary to recall briefly the history of the text and its use by the Elyot-Cooper dictionaries. First published in 1538, the *Dictionarium* became an important source, as we have seen, for the augmentation of Elyot's *Bibliotheca* in 1542 and in subsequent editions. By 1552 the *Dictionarium* had been considerably augmented, so that it contained much of the Latin of Stephanus' *Thesaurus* together with the French equivalents. In this form it became a major source and model for Cooper's *Thesaurus* (1565).

Baret and his assistants, having begun their compilation by converting Latin-English entries into English-Latin, were familiar with the process. Wishing to improve the English definitions and to revise and supplement the French equivalents of the Latin and English, they must have acquired, in or after 1565, two of the most comprehensive and scholarly texts: Stephanus' *Dictionarium Latino-Gallicum*, with the Latin before the French, and Cooper's *Thesaurus*, with an almost identical Latin word list and with the Latin before the English. To enrich the *Alvearie*—a triple dictionary in English, Latin, and French—Baret and his collaborators needed only to keep the Cooper and the Stephanus open before them and to transcribe the desired matter. This they apparently did.

Entries made in the *Alvearie* before 1565, on the basis of the Elyot-Cooper *Bibliotheca*, the Stephanus *Dictionnaire* (1549), or the Stephanus-Veron *Dictionariolum* (1552) were often rephrased to conform to Cooper's English and to the French equivalents in Stephanus' *Dictionarium*. In both Stephanus and Cooper the compilers would have found identical information on grammar, stress, and Latin authorities. Such information, with identical abbreviations—information which was very slight or entirely wanting in the *Bibliotheca* and the *Dictionnaire*—reappears in most of the main entries in the *Alvearie*. Very frequently Baret's main entry has the English of Cooper's *Thesaurus*, the French of Stephanus' *Dictionarium*, and the grammatical information common to both. Sometimes Baret depends upon the *Dictionarium* only, correcting with its aid the French; sometimes he draws only from Cooper, omitting the French; and in a number of instances Baret reveals the use of at least two of the French sources and Cooper's *Thesaurus*. These composite entries are probably evidence of late reworking of entries in preparation of the *Alvearie* for the press.

In the illustrations which follow we shall see how the collaborators in the *Alvearie* modified or corrected, by the use of Cooper's *Thesaurus* and Stephanus' *Dictionarium*, borrowings from (1) Stephanus' *Dictionnaire* and (2) the Stephanus-Veron *Dictionariolum*, and how they depended for many entries upon the joint use of (3) the *Thesaurus* and the *Dictionarium*. The entries below illustrate the borrowing in the first category, from the *Dictionnaire*.

Dictionnaire: Abolir, *Abolere, Abrogare, Antiquare, Conuellere, Exterminare, In-*
(1549) *ducere, Interuertere, Obliterare, Resignare.*

Dictionarium: *Aboleo, aboles, pen. cor. aboleui & abolui, abolitum, pen. cor. abolere.*
(1561) Cic. Abolir, Mettre a neant, Anicheler.

Thesaurus: *Aboleo, aboles, pen. corr. aboleui, & abolui, abolitum, pen. corr.* Cic.
(1565) To abolishe: to undoe: to put out: to rase: to disanull.

Bibliotheca: *Aboleo, aboles, eui, ere, act.* to put out, to rase out, to anull, to undoe
(1559) foreuer.

Alvearie: to Abolishe: to vndooe: to repeale: reuerse or disanull: to put out.
(1573) *Aboles, boles. penult. cor. aboleui & abolui, abolitum, lere.* Cic. *Abrogare, Antiquare, Conuellere, Exterminare, Inducere, Obliterare, Resignare, Delere.* Abolir, Mettre a neant, Anichiler. [*A*, 45]

Analysis of the transcribed entries above shows that the *Alvearie* as printed in 1573 owes something to the *Dictionnaire*, the *Dictionarium*, and the *Thesaurus*. In all probability the earlier manuscript of the *Alvearie* had an entry that corresponded in its English to the *Bibliotheca* (1559), and in the French and Latin, to the *Dictionnaire* (1549). The form finally printed may have been the result of revision of the entry on the basis of the *Dictionarium* and the *Thesaurus*. The entry *atrocitas* exemplifies a similar procedure.

Dictionnaire: Cruaulte, *Crudelitas, Diritas, Atrocitas, Saeuitia, Immanitas, Impetu-
ositas, Indignitas.*

Dictionarium: *Atrocitas, penult, corr. atrocitatis, f. g. Denominatiuum.* Cic. Oultrage,
Cruaulté, Felonnie.

Thesaurus: *Atrocitas, pen. cor. atrocitatis, f. g. Denominatiuum.* Ci. Crueltie,
fiercenesse: outragiousnesse: grieuousnesse.

Bibliotheca: *Atrocitas, tatis, f. g.* crueltee, fiersnesse, outragiousnesse.

Alvearie: Crueltie, fiercenesse, outragiousnesse. *Atrocitas, penult. corr. tatis.
foemin. gene.* Cicer. . . . *Saeuitia, Immanitas, Crudelitas,* Cruaulte,
felonie, outrage. [*C*, 1574]

Congrerro and *coniunx* represent borrowings in the second category, from the *Dictionariolum* (1552). These entries, like certain ones from the *Dictionnaire*, seem to have undergone revision in the course of the compilation of the *Alvearie*.

Dictionariolum: *Congerro, congerronis, mas. gen.* a companyon to talke and comon
meryly. Compaignon a caqueter & plaisanter.

Dictionarium: *Congerro, huius congerronis, masc. g.* Plaut. Compaignon a quaqueter
& plaisanter.

Thesaurus: *Congerro, huius congerronis, mas. g.* Plautus. A merry companion:
that keepeth companie in merrye conceytes and pleasant deuises.

Bibliotheca: *Congerro, onis, ma. ge.* a mery companyon, he that keepeth company
only in pastime and merie deuysyng.

Alvearie: A companion to talke, and common merily. *Congerro, ronis, mas. gene.* Plaut. Compaignon a caqueter, & plaisanter. [*C*, 914]

Dictionariolum: *Coniunx, ugis: vel Coniux, ugis, co. gen.* the husband or wyfe of one. Le marri ou la femme de quelqu'ung.

Dictionarium: *Coniux, coniugis, pen. cor. com. gen. a Coniugo, coniugas, vt ait* Phocas. Le marie ou la mariee, Le mari ou la femme de quelqu'vn.

Thesaurus: *Coniux, coniugis, pen. cor. com. g. a Coniugo, coniugas, vt ait* Phocas. A mate: a husband or wyfe.

Bibliotheca: *Coniux, ugis,* or *Coniunx, ugis co. g.* a mate, a husbande or wyfe.

Alvearie: The husband or wife of one. *Coniux, vel Coniunx. coniugis, com. g. A Coniugo, coniugas, vt ait* Phocas. Le mari ou la femme de quelqu'vng. [*W*, 204]

Many of Baret's entries are accounted for by the joint use of Stephanus' *Dictionarium* and Cooper's *Thesaurus,* as are these below.

Stephanus (1561)	Cooper (1565)	Baret (1573)
Follis, huius follis, masc. gen. Toute chose faicts de cuir pour y mettre quelque chose dedens, comme vn bource, sac & semblables. *Follis.* Plaut. Vn soufflet a souffler le feu. *Follis.* Martial. Vne bale ou grosse pelotte a ioueur, laquelle est pleine de vent.	*Follis, huius follis, mas. gene.* A purse, bagge, or any thing of leather made to be fylled: a bellow to blow fire: a ball filled with winde . . . *Follis.* Martial. A great ball stuffed onely with winde.	a Bellowes to blowe the fire with, any maner of thing that is made of leather for to put something in, as a purse, a sacke, and such like, a ball to playe with, a great ball puffed vp with winde. *Follis, huius follis, m. g.* Plaut. Vn soufflet a souffler le feu. Toute chose faicte de cuir pour y mettre quelque chose dedens, comme vne bourse, vn sac & semblables. Vne bale a iouer, ou grosse pelote enflee de vent. [*B*, 461]
Mutulus, mutuli, pen. corr. Varro. Columel. Vn appuy sortant la murialle pour soustenir vne poultre, lequel on appele Corbeau, ou Modillon.	*Mutulus, mutuli, pen. cor.* Varro. Colu. A stay cut out of stone or timber in buylding to beare up the summer or other part: In masonrie they call it a corbell: In tymber worke a bragget, shouldering, or such like.	a Bragget or staie cut out of stone or timber in building to beare vp the sommer or other part: in masonrie they call it a corbell, in timber woorke a shouldring or such like. *Mutulu, tuli, m. g.* Col. Vng appuy sortant de la murialle pour soustenir vne poultre lequel on appelle Corteau. [*B*, 1004]
Ales, huius álitis, pen. corr. Absoluté positum. Auis dicta alarum mag-	*Ales, huius alitis, pen. cor. Absolute positum. Auis dicta ab alarum*	a Birde: all great birdes, as hen, goose, rauen, crane, and such like. *Ales, tis.*

Stephanus (1561)	Cooper (1565)	Baret (1573)
nitudïne. Alites. Proprement ce sont toutes sortes de grands oiseaux. comme Gelines, Oyes, Corneilles, Corbeauls, Grues, & semblables.	*magnitudine. Alites.* Properly all great foule. . . .	*Substant. m. g. vel f. g.* . . . *Auis.* Oiseau, tout oiseaux grãd, comme geline, oye, corbeau, grue, & semblables. [*B*, 640]
Tortus, Participiũ: vt Vino tortus & ira. Horat. Geine de vin & de courroux, Contrainct par vin & par ire de dire tout ce qu'on scait . . . *Baculus tortus.* Ouid. Tortu, Gauché.	*Tortus, Particip.* Crooked: bowed: wrested: wrong: tormented: grieued. *vt Vino tortus & ira.* Hor. Constrayned with dronkennesse and anger to vtter.	Crooked, bowed, wrested, wrong, tormented, grieued. *Tortus. Partic.* Cicer. *vt vino tortus & ira.* Ci. Tortu, Courbé, Geine de vin & de corroux, contrainct par vin & par ire de dire tout ce qu'on scait. [*C*, 1519]
Veterâtor, pen. prod. veteratoris. Terent. Vn vieil routier qui de long temps est vsité a quelque chose que ce soit, & principalement à finesse. Vn ruzé & affette, Qui scait ses deffaictes, Vn vieulx singe.	*Veterâtor, pen. prod. veteratoris, m. g.* Ter. A crafty beguiler: a false deceiuour: a subtile knaue, that hath long practised falshoode: an olde crafty foxe.	A craftie beguiler: a false deceiuer: a subtile knaue, that hath long practised falshood, an old craftie fox. *Veterator, pen. prod. toris, m. g.* Ter. . . . Vn routier, qui de longe temps vsité a finesse, vn Ruzé & affette, vn vieulx renart. [*C*, 1442]

On the basis of various parallels presented and on Baret's "Address to the Reader," not to be taken too literally, it is possible to reconstruct the process of compilation which terminated in the *Alvearie*. In the earlier stage, much of the English-Latin was derived by the simple method of inverting the Latin-English of the Elyot-Cooper *Bibliotheca* (1548 or 1552 edition) and probably by supplementing the results with small borrowings from Withals and Calepine. For the French, the *Dictionnaire* (1549) of Robert Stephanus and the Stephanus-Veron *Dictionariolum* were drawn upon, the latter furnishing also English entries corresponding to the French. Much later, certainly after 1565 and possibly in 1572, after the publication of the Huloet-Higgins, the manuscript of the *Alvearie*, containing the earlier materials specified above, was corrected and augmented by the use, probably simultaneously, of Cooper's *Thesaurus* for the English and Latin and Stephanus' *Dictionarium Latino-Gallicum* for the French. At this later period also may have occurred the borrowings from Levins and the Huloet-Higgins. Although this reconstruction is necessarily conjectural, it is in harmony with Baret's own explanation in the address, and more particularly with the comparative study and analysis of numerous entries in the text.

Thus reworked, corrected, and supplemented, and also prefaced with commendatory verses by Baret's friends, the *Alvearie* was published in 1573. The verses, laudatory of Baret and censorious of the Huloet-Higgins, were contributed by men well known in their day. Among the contributors were John Cooke, headmaster of St. Paul's School from 1559 to 1573; Richard Mulcaster, then headmaster of the Merchant Taylors' School; John Depup, master of Nottingham Grammar School in 1578; Edward Grant, poet and lexicographer in his own name and headmaster of Westminster School for twenty years; and Arthur Golding, translator of Ovid.[25] Notwithstanding the prominence of the versifiers, Baret is praised for virtues not his own, and the Huloet-Higgins uncritically condemned. These efforts in behalf of Baret seem to have been successful. The *Alvearie* of 1573 took precedence over the much-feared competitor, the Huloet-Higgins of 1572. No other edition of the latter work appeared. The *Alvearie* was in the process of revision in 1578, when Baret died; and, under the direction of Abraham Fleming, a new edition was published in 1580.

Abraham Fleming (1552?-1607), B.A., Peterhouse, Cambridge, 1582, chaplain to the Countess of Nottingham and rector of St. Pancras, London, was an antiquary, poet, and lexicographer of tremendous industry, though of little originality. To him are ascribed in the *DNB* fifty-nine items, including *A Panoplie of Epistles* (1576), translations of Virgil's *Bukolikes* (1575), John Caius' *Of English Dogges* (1576), and various other works. In the field of lexicography, Fleming seems, generally, to have had a subordinate role. Besides revising the *Alvearie* (1580), he revised and augmented the Veron-Waddington dictionary (1584), supplied a "dictional" index to the Junius-Higgins *Nomenclator* (1585), and augmented with more than "sixe hundred rhythmicall verses" Withals' *Shorte Dictionarie* (1586). In Cooper's *Athenae Cantabrigienses*, Fleming appears to be credited with supplying the English to the 1583 edition of G. Morelius' *Verborum Latinorum cum Graecis Anglicisque*. For this there seems to be no authority.[26]

In his augmentation of the *Alvearie* in 1580, Fleming extended the range of sources. To the Huloet-Higgins *Dictionarie* of 1572, from which we noted instances of borrowing in the *Alvearie* of 1573, Fleming now returns for larger drafts of material. Despite the prefatory verses in both editions of the *Alvearie* severely attacking Huloet, Fleming unblushingly took what he required from the Huloet-Higgins *Dictionarie*. And his requirements seem to have been fairly great. A partial explanation is found in the nature of much of the matter he appropriated from his competitor.

As we have explained earlier (Chapter 12), Higgins, in revising the Huloet, sought to emphasize the principle of copiousness by means of synonymy and variety. The Latin synonyms Higgins drew largely from the Stephanus-Thierry *Dictionnaire francois-latin* (1564); the sentences with phrases for varying the expression of the idea seem to have been Higgins's own, though the *De copia* of Erasmus was the obvious model. This feature of copiousness, almost absent from the *Alvearie* of 1573, Fleming must have thought desirable. At any rate, he silently took over many of the Huloet-Higgins entries illustrating the principle. The excerpts below, from the Stephanus-Thierry, the Huloet-Higgins, and the Baret-Fleming (i.e., the *Alvearie* of 1580), show that Fleming followed the Huloet-Higgins rather than the Stephanus.

Stephanus-Thierry (1564)	Huloet-Higgins (1572)	Baret-Fleming (1580)
Se taire, *Tacere, Conticere, Conticescere, Obticere, Facere finem sermoni, Silere, Silentium facere, Silentium dare, In silentium descendere, Immutescere, Obmutescere, Vocem premere, Consilere, Comprimere vocem.*	Kepe silence, or to holde his peace. *Muffo, as. Fauere linguis. Ne mi sonare, Sileo, es. Reticeo, es. Supprimo, is. Taceo, es. Verba premere, vel vocem. Conticeo, ces. Conticesco, cis. Obticeo, ces. Facere finem sermoni, Silentium facere, Silentium dare, In silentium descendere, Immutesco, cis. Consileo, les. Comprimere vocem.* Se taire. S.	To keepe silence. *Muffo, as, Fauere linguis, Sileo. Reticeo. Supprimo. Taceo. Verba vel vocem premere. Conticeo. Conticesco. Obticeo. Finem facere sermonis, silentium facere, silentium dare, in silentium descendere, Immutesco, Obmutesco, Consileo, Comprimere vocem. [K, 27]*
Aller au deuant de quelqu'un. *Exire obuiam alicui, Ire alicui obuiam, Obsistere alicui obuiam, Obuiam accedere, Obuiare, Occurrere, Proficisci obuiam, Progredi obuiam, Sese obuiam alicui ferre, Prouisere, Venire alicui aduersum, Aduersum ire, Adire contra.*	Meete, or to goe to meete one. *Obeo, is. Obuiam ire, Obuius esse, Obuiam fio, Obuiam dare, Obuenio, is. Exire obuiam alicui, Ire alicui obuiam, Obsistere alicui obuiam, Obuiam accedere, Obuiare, Occurrere, Proficisci obuiam, Progredi obuiam, Sese obuiam alicui ferre, Prouisere, Venire alicui aduersum, Aduersum ire, Adire contra.* Aller au de quelqu'un. S.	To go to meete one. *Obeo, obuiam ire, obuius esse, obuiam fio, obuiam dare, obuenio. Exire obuiam alicui, ire alicui obuiam, obsistere alicui obuiam, obuiam accedere, obuiare, occurrere. Proficisci obuiam, progredi obuiam, sese obuiam alicui ferre, prouisere, venire alicui aduersum, aduersum ire, adire contra. [G, 367]*

Other entries in the 1580 *Alvearie*, illustrating synonymy and variety and deriving from Stephanus through Huloet-Higgins, are *to die* (*D*, 632); *to beare, or suffer patiently* (*P*, 5); *to paine, or to punish* (*P*, 29); and *to do one a pleasure, or good turne* (*P*, 481). The lengthy entry under *partrich* (*P*, 139) comes directly from Huloet-Higgins and has no ultimate source in Stephanus.

Perhaps even more obvious is Fleming's incorporation in the *Alvearie* of Higgins's own lengthy entries to illustrate the principle of varying. Characteristic are the following:

Huloet-Higgins *Dictionarie* (1572)	*Alvearie* (1580)
Only iustice contayneth all vertues, or al other vertues are cōprehēdēd in iustice. *Omnes insūt in vna iustitia virtutes. iustitia cōtinētur, comprehenduntur, continet iustitia, comprehendit, complectitur omnes virtutes, omnes ad vnam iustitiam virtutes referuntur, ab vna iustitia pendent, in vna iustitia includūtur. qui iustitiam tenet, non est vt virtutem vllam praeterea desideret, requirat, expetat. nulla virtute iustus caret. nulla virtus abest à iusto. coniunctae sunt, colligatae, connexae cum iustitia virtutes omnes.*	Only Iustice containeth all vertues, or all other vertues are comprehended vnder Iustice. *Omnes insunt in vna Iustitia virtutes. Iustitia continentur, comprehenduntur; continet Iustitia, comprehendit, complectitur omnes virtutes. Omnes ad vnam Iustitiam virtutes referentur, ab vna Iustitia pendent, in vna Iustitia includuntur. Qui Iustitiam tenet, non est vt virtutem vllam praeterea desideret, requirat, expetat; nulla virtute Iustus caret. Nulla virtus abest a Iusto. Coniunctae sunt, colligatae, connexae cum Iustitia virtutes omnes.* [*I*, 349]
Thou shouldest leade a more ioyfull, quiet, and pleasaunt lyfe, if thou couldest forgette thy misfortunes: *Laetior tibi vita esset, iucundior, tranquillior, tranquillius ageres: si tuos casus obliuiscereris, ex animo tuo, mēte, memoria deleres, euelleres: si memoriam tuorum temporum omitteres, deponeres, abijceres, ex animo deleres: si tua pristina mala, tuos casus, tuorum temporum varietatem obliuione voluntaria contereres, apud te deleret obliuio.*	Thou shouldest lead a more ioyfull, quiet, and pleasant life, if thou couldest forget thy misfortunes. *Laetior tibi vita esset, iucundior, tranquillior, tranquillius ageres, si tuos casus obliuisci posses, ex animo tuo, mente, memoria deleres, euelleres: si memoriam tuorum temporum omitteres, deponeres, abijceres, ex animo deleres: si tua pristina mala, tuos casus tuorum temporum varietatem, obliuione voluntaria contereres, apud te deleret obliuio.* [*F*, 908]

A dozen other similar entries Fleming takes from the Huloet-Higgins and places in the *Alvearie* of 1580. The sentences, omitting Latin variations, are these:

> He wryteth elegantly. [*E*, 147]
> Experience is the maistres of all thinges. . . . [*E*, 475]
> It is a faire or very beautifull virgin. [*F*, 48]

I am not in faulte. [*F*, 226]
I hope to finishe, or ende this matter. . . . [*F*, 564]
There is no man more fortunate than you. [*F*, 985]
If you intende to folowe your ancestours. . . . [*F*, 825]
In prosperitie thou shalt haue frendes enough. . . . [*F*, 1101]
Many come into the courte for gayne and lucre sake. [*G*, 21]
I see not why thou shouldest hope. [*H*, 626]
Thou indeuoureste to bring me to infamie. [*I*, 140]
I loue thee chiefly. . . . [*L*, 709]

There are other borrowings, of more normal kind, from the Huloet-Higgins, but those cited are sufficient to indicate the heavy debt of Fleming to this source.

In 1578 appeared Henry Lyte's English translation of Dodoens, a translation based upon De l'Esclusse's French version of Dodoens' *Cruydeboeck*. Lyte's work was printed in London by Gerard Dewes with the title the *Niewe Herball*.[27] From Lyte's text Fleming supplemented the herbal lore of the *Alvearie*, hitherto dependent largely upon Turner, as we have seen. A few illustrations will show the rather literal quality of Fleming's borrowings.

Niewe Herball (1578)

There be foure kindes of *Ranunculus*, or Crowfoote, as Dioscorides and Galen do affirme. . . . Crowfoote is called in Greke βατράχιον: in Latin *Ranunculus*, of Apuleius *Herba scelerata* . . . in French *Bassinet*. . . . The first of the first kinde is called of some in Greeke σέλινον ἄγιον, καὶ σέλινον ὑδατίον: in Latine *Apium palustre*, *Ranunculus palustris*: in French *Grenoillette aquatique*, or *Bassinet d'eaue*. [pp. 415 ff.]

The great Daysie, and the small wilde Daysie, do grow in medowes, and moyste pastures. The fayre dooble garden Daysie is planted and set in gardens. . . . These floures are called of Plinie in Latine *Bellis* and *Bellius*, and now they are called in Latine *consolida minor*, and *Herba margarita*, of some *Primula veris* . . . in English Daysies: in French *Marguerites* or *Pasquettes*. [p. 170]

Mandrage groweth willingly in darke and shadowie places. . . . Mandrage is

Alvearie (1580)

Crowfoote, wherof be many kindes, as Dioscorides and Galen do affirme, which certaine of them are not vsuall in this countrie. *Ranunculus*, *herba scelerata*, *Apium palustre*, *Ranunculus palustris*. βατράχιον, σέλινον ἄγιον, καὶ σέλινον ὑδατίον. Bassinet, Grenoillette aquatique, or bassinet d'eaue. [*C*, 1687]

Daisies, a certaine flowre most common with vs both in gardens and pastures, they are of nature cold and moist. Plinie calleth them *Bellis, vel Bellius*. *Consolida minor*. *Herba margarita*. *Primula veris*. Marguerites & pasquettes. [*D*, 23]

Mandrage, this groweth willingly in shadowie places, the roote and barke

Niewe Herball (1578)	*Alvearie* (1580)
called in Greeke μανδραγόρας in Latine *Mandragoras*, of some *Circaea*, and *Antimalium*, and of Pythagoras also *Anthropomorphus*. . . . The roote of Mandrake, and especially the barke, is colde and drie euen harde to the fourth degree. . . . [p. 437]	is cold and drie to the fourth degree. *Mandragoras, Circaea, Antimalium, Anthropomorphus.* [M, 79]

We have observed in preceding chapters the general interest in proverbs in the sixteenth century and the tendency of lexicographers to include them in their dictionaries, notably in the Elyot-Cooper texts and in the later issues of Withals' dictionary. The *Alvearie* of 1573 included no proverbs; Fleming seems to have thought this a shortcoming of the earlier text if we may judge by his action. In his revision he introduced 264 proverbs, together with a Latin index to render them useful. The major source, as usual, was Erasmus' *Adagia*. In the *Bibliotheca Eliotae* Fleming could have found, already converted into English, some 275 proverbs, mostly from Erasmus. A half-dozen of these Fleming seems to have used, as *Adrastia nemesis, Delius natator, Hydram secare, Lerna malorum, Ilias malorum*, and *Thassus bonorum*.[28] But Fleming preferred for the most part to go directly to Erasmus, to include the Latin and Greek of the *Adagia*, and to make his own translation, usually only of the words which indicate the application of the proverbs. The parallels which follow, the Greek terms being omitted, show the quality of Fleming's adaptation of the *Adagia*.[29]

Adagia (1703)	*Alvearie* (1580)
A fronte atque a tergo. Proverbii vice receptum, pro eo, quod est diligenter inspicere, & praeterita cum praesentibus ac futuris conferre. . . . [p. 729c]	*A fronte atque a tergo* . . . A Prouerbe, which causeth diligent circumspection, comparing things past, with things present. [A, 206]
Janus alter. Quadrabit vel in providum ac circumspectum, vel in ancipitem & perfidum. Persius: O Jane, a tergo cui nulla ciconia pinsit. Sunitum a Jano bifronte, cujus notior est fabula, quam sit hoc loco percensenda. [p. 1007a]	*Alter Ianus* . . . A Prouerbe to be applyed to those, which are very circumspect and warie in their affayres. [A, 324]
Altera manu fert aquam, altera ignem. In eum torqueas licebit, qui cum coram sit blandus, occulte noceat. Aut in bilinguem, & nunc laudantem, nunc vituperantem, aut in diversa sentientem. [p. 1041e]	*Altera manu fert aquam, altera ignem* . . . A Prouerbe to be applyed to those, which befor a mans face can vse glosing termes, & behinde his backe, rayse contumelies against him. [A, 327]
Amico amicus . . . Quadrabit in eos qui	*Amicus amico* . . . A Prouerbe to be ap-

Adagia (1703)	*Alvearie* (1580)
nullum officium refugiunt, modo gratum faciant amicis. . . . [p. 119*e*]	plyed to those which eschewe no perill or daunger, so that they may gratifie or pleasure theire friende. [*A*, 360]

What with the insertion of more than 260 proverbs, the extension of Greek terms and herbal lore, and countless minor alterations, Fleming did not leave the *Alvearie* "almost unchanged." References in the *NED* to the *Alvearie* of 1573 and 1580, numbering Baret's entries according to the 1580 edition, are not adequate, for references in the two editions rarely coincide.[30] Confirmation of this fact can be readily made by a comparative study of successive entries under any letter in the two texts. In the 1580 *Alvearie* are

countless quiet additions, corrections, and omissions within the text, which show that someone, presumably Fleming, had gone through the *Alvearie* page by page and had either seen it written fair again or had annotated it heavily. Though in 1580 the English renderings are in general much the same, and though whole series of entries can be discovered which are quite unaltered, the fact remains and must be emphasized that the two editions are not interchangeable. . . .

Although Fleming himself introduced some errors, there are, as Sledd has remarked, "numerous instances in which Fleming corrected mistakes involving misspellings, false punctuations, the omission of words, wrong repetitions, the mistaking of one word for another similar to it in sound or appearance, and even the creation of ghost words."[31]

Fleming's tendency to eliminate archaisms, uncommon words and usages, and what he regarded as vulgar forms does not enhance for the philologist the value of the *Alvearie*. It should be added, however, that he rearranged and sometimes elaborated English definitions and supplied more cross references, more French, more Latin synonyms (from the Stephanus-Thierry and the Huloet-Higgins), more herbal lore, and some etymologies.

Having considered the sources of the two editions of the *Alvearie* and the differences in the texts, it remains to treat briefly two special features, common to the two texts but slightly dealt with by other English lexicographers of the sixteenth century. I refer to etymology and the elaborate discussion of the letters of the alphabet, involving the reform of English spelling. It is not my purpose to go into the intricacies of these complex subjects. I can only record their presence and give some idea of Baret's treatment of them and the sources of his information.

For his treatment of etymology, Baret had but slight precedent in the Elyot-Cooper dictionaries or in any other predecessors among English lexicographers. The subject was, however, not new. It can be traced back to antiquity. Baret and his assistants occasionally drew from the ancients in their etymologizing, but as a rule they drew from lexicographers of a more recent period, especially Stephanus and Calepine, in whose texts they found references to the ancients. The number of entries in the two editions of the *Alvearie* in which there are obvious attempts at etymology are somewhat fewer than one hundred. Professor Sledd lists and quotes seventy-two examples,[32] and this number can be extended. The examples quoted below are fairly typical of those appearing throughout the *Alvearie*.

Abbay is a french woorde, & signifieth barking against somme thing. *Latratus vel oblatratus* . . . For when the dere is vtterly wearied & out of breath, then is he faine (setting him self to some hedge, tree, &c.) to stande at defiance against all ye houdes barking rounde about him, & to defende him selfe with his hornes as it were at the swoorde pointe, as long as he is able. Herevpon we say commonly of men at variance. He will hold or keepe him at abbay. . . .

Aduenture is deriued of the Latin woord *Aduenio,* for *Euenio.* To chaunge, happen, or fortune. *Casus, Fors, Fortuna, Euentus.*

Alarme, is borrowed of the Frenche, as who say to the armour, or to prepare and make the souldiars ready with their harnessee and weapons to fight in battaile. *Ad arma.* A'larme.

Appease is a woorde borowed of the french Appaiser, *Quasi ad pacem adducere.*

Bagage, is borowed of the french, & signifieth al such stuffe as may hinder or trouble vs in warre or traueyling, being not woorth cariage. . . .

Braue seemeth to come of this greeke woorde βραβεύω. i. *Prior sum.* As to looke aloft and go gailie desiring to haue preheminence.

a Felon, i. malefactour, is borowed of the french, Felon, ou felon & despit, Cruell, outragious, vnmercifull, *Atrox, Importunus, Immisericors.* And the vice is called Felonie which signifieth outragious disorder & cruelty. For those hell houndes, which will lay violent handes vpon other mens bodyes or their gooddes & liue of the spoyll, are lyke byles or botches in the body of the common weale: & must be cured either by incysion and letting bloud in the necke veyn, or by searing with a hoate yron, or else with a cawdle of hempsede chopt halter wise, & so at lest to vomit thē out, & cut thē of from the quiet society of citizens or honest christiãs. . . .

Spouts in buildings like anticks or leopards faces called Gargelles bicause ye water floweth out by their mouthes, &c. as they which gargyle or washe their mouthes and throtes. . . . [1573, *S*, 658; 1580, *S*, 756]

Vertue tooke hir name first of Vir, that is a worthie man. *a viro virtus nomē est* (*sortita*) *mutuata.* [1573, *T*, 25; 1580, *T*, 29]

In the examples transcribed from the *Alvearie* the number ascribed to French influence is relatively larger than in the text as a whole. There, approximately 50 per cent of the words etymologized are said to be of French origin; the remainder from Latin, or Greek, or occasionally another language. But the total proportion of etymologies relative to the entire word list is comparatively small. Here follow a few entries to illustrate the French influence.

Dictionnaire (1549)

Admiral. Semble qu'on doibue escrire Almyral, *ab ἁλμυρὶς id est a salsugine, vel re maritima* . . . Emir en lāgue Moresque signifîe ce que nous disons Admiral: & peult estre que nous deburions escrire Amira, a cause de Emir.

Almanach. *Videtur Arabica dictio aut Chaldea. Al est articulus, Le. & Mana, Hebraicè siue Chaldaicè est numerare. In Calendrio enim numerantur menses & dies.*

Approcher. De Appropinquare syncopez la syllabe moyenne, restera Approquare. Il est notoire que cuault qu, & se muent fort souuent l'ung en l'autre. . . .

Enuiron, *quasi in gyro, g in v.*

Pantoufle, *quasi παντόφελλος. πᾶν, id est omne: φελλος dicitur Latine Suber,* Liege. *Sunt igitur crepidae, quarum solum subere constat* . . . B[ude].

Alvearie

the Admirall . . . Admiral. Semble qu'on doibue escrire Almyral. *Ab ἁλμυρὶς, id est, à salsugine, vel re maritima.* [*A,* 161]

Almanach (which also we call a prognosticatiō) seemeth to be either an Arabic or a chaldie woorde. Al, is an article in their language, as Le, is in french, and The in English. And Mana in Hebrue or Chaldie tongue signifieth to numbre, for in the Calendare moneths and daies are compted and numbred. *Fasti . . . vel Fastilibri.* [*A,* 316]

Approche is borowed of the french, Approcher, which also is deriued of the latin woorde Appropinquare, by the figure syncope, taking away the middle syllable and there remayneth Approquare, for C. is vsed often in french in steede of Qu. in latin. [*A,* 503]

Enuiron, is a french woorde made of the latine. *Quasi in gyro. G, verso in V.* [*E,* 288]

A shooe called a pantoufle or a slipper. *Crépida . . . Sandálium . . .* Pantoufle. *Quasi παντόφελλος. πᾶν i. omne: φελλος. i. suber.* Liege. *Sunt igitur crepidae, quarum solum subere constat.* Bud. [1573, *S,* 326; 1580, *S,* 366]

Of Calepine's *Dictionarium* as a source for Greek terms and for entries in the *Alvearie,* we have treated above, noting especially Baret's etymology of "common or mean people," after Calepine, from *volvendo* because the vulgar roll hither and thither. For various other etymologies, Baret is indebted to Calepine. Consider the following:

Dictionarium (1542)

Mvlier, γυνή. à mollicie (vt inquit Varro) dicta est & immutata detracta litera, quasi mollier. Vlpian. Mulier dicitur quae virgo non est.

Nihilum, οὐδ' ὁ, τί οὖν, ex non, & hilum

Alvearie

a Woman. *Mulier, lieris.* γυνή. Femme *à mollitie dicta est, immutata & detracta litera quasi mollier, & proprie Mulier dicitur quae virgo non est.* [*W,* 315]

Nothing or a thing of naught. *Nihilum,*

Dictionarium (1542)	*Alvearie*
componitur, quod significat ullum . . . Sunt qui putent Hilum significare illud quod grano fabae adhaeret . . . ex quo nihilum, & Nihil per apocopen, quod significat quantitatem . . . Nil, ὀυδὲν, syncopatum est à nihil. . . .	*li.* ὀυδεν, μῆδεν, *ex non & hilum conponitur quod* (authore Festo) *significat illud quod grano fabae adhaeret. Inde fit Nihil per Apocopen quae significat quantitatis priuationem & Nil per syncopen factum est.* [*N*, 182]
Lacunar, δοκὸς, pen. prod. diminutiuum à lacus, & accipiter pro trabe . . . Hoc etiam Laquear & Laquearium per antistichon. Verg. . . . Dicitur & Lacunarium: potius tamen Lacunar dicitur interstitium tignorum, a similitudine lacuum.	The roofe of a chamber embowed or fretted: also a playne beame in a roofe. *Laquear, laquearis, pen. prod. Diminut. a lacus.* Plin. σανίδωμα. *Haec etiam lacunaria appellantur, propterea quod tignorum interualla, quondam lacuum speciem praebere videantur.* . . . [*B*, 268]

It is hardly within the scope of this study to account for every etymology in the *Alvearie*, even if it were possible to do so. Although Stephanus and Calepine are the basis of a great many, probably most, of the etymologies, they do not explain all. Some are probably original with Baret; others from sources not found in this survey. Derivations suggested for words of foreign origin are generally traditional, drawn from other lexicographers. For native English words, the compiler offers few etymologies. He shows, in fact, no detailed knowledge of the earlier stages of his native tongue. "The measure of his failure," as Professor Sledd aptly writes, "is that he chose the old familiar paths when new roads were opening before him." [33]

We have referred earlier to the preambles, or essays at the beginning of the letters of the alphabet, in the *Alvearie*. In Calepine and Huloet-Higgins were precedents for such discussions. Their essays were, however, relatively brief; Baret goes quite beyond these, drawing from a wide range of sources and developing his preambles into essays on the reform of English spelling. Perhaps these were read with interest by Baret's contemporaries, but they do not seem to have established a precedent among lexicographers for detailed treatment of the letters. In England, at any rate, it was almost exactly a hundred years later when the practice was resumed. Adam Littleton, in his *Latine Dictionary, in Four Parts* (1678), had erudite discussions of the letters. His essays were appropriated by the editors of the Cambridge *Novum luculentum* (1693), and paraphrased by Robert Ainsworth in his *Thesaurus* (1736). Thereafter, such essays seem to have disappeared from the dictionaries.

Our interest is, however, not in the history of the practice, but in the use Baret made of the preambles and the sources of the ideas therein ex-

Is one of the dumme consonants, and hath no power of it self to speake or vtter any voice before it heare the sound of some vowell, as paper. This letter p seemeth both by his name and forme to be of kind to b, and as it were b turned vpside downe: And therefore the latin writers in translating gréeke bookes haue turned many gréeke wordes beginning with ϖ into the romane b, as πύξος is made buxus. ἄμφω is made ambo, Where ph is chaunged for b. Hereupon I thinke it came that so many diuers and doubtfull opinions are risen among the latin grammarians about the power and pronuntiation of Φ. for the grand capitaine Priscian (as Quintilian affirmeth) thought it was not vsed among the old grecians altogither as we doo ph, but rather in sound somewhat inclining to b as many doe corruptly pronounce it. And that ph can not truely aunswere in the voyce and sound of f, I haue partly shewed my selfe before, and also the propre nature of p and h, doe plainly confirme the same. But sith that in writing of English we haue no great néede of the helpe of ph (being already sufficiently furnished with f) me thinke we may write such degenerate gréeke wordes (which long vse and continuall prescription of time hath made ours) with f, as the Italians doe Filosofie, Filippus, Fantasie.

P. ANTE. A.

Pace in going, a steppe. Gradus, dus, Passus, sus, m. g. Virgil. *Vn pas, marchement, le marcher, Marcheure.*

A swift pace. Citatus gradus. Sen.

To go a stalking or stealing pace, softly. Suspenso gradu ire. Ter. *Tout bellement sans bruit, En fac de larron.*

¶ **Pacient:** quiet: calme: still. Placidus, da, dū. Ter. Patiens, Clemens, tis, om. g.

✳ **Pacience:** sufferance. Patientia, Clementia, Tolerantia, tæ, f. g. Gell. *Pacience: Souffrance.*

✳ **Paciently: quietly.** Pacienter, Sedáte, Clementer, Plácidé. Tolleranter, tius, tissimé. Aduerb. Plin. *Passablement, Tolerablement.*

✳ **Pacience,** when a man taketh a thing well, without troubling or vexing him self. Aequanimitas, tatis, foem. gener. Animi æquitas Cicer. *Quand ou prend bien vne chose, sans se contrister ou esmouoir.*

To suffer or take paciently. Lenté, placaté, leuiter, moderaté ferre. Cic. Aequo animo aliquid accipere. Toleranter dolorem pati. Cic.

To heare one paciently without disturbing him. Audire cum bona venia. Cic.

¶ **Pacience** hearbe. Vide **Docke.**

¶ to **Pacifie:** to appease: to quiet. Placo, as, are. Ter. Sedo Paco, Pacifico. Plin. *Appaiser: Seder: Accoiser.* Vide **Appeaze.**

To pacifie a man toward one. Placare aliquem alicui. Cic.

✳ **Pleased: appeased: pacified: quiet.** Placatus, ta, tum. Plin.

✳ **I pacifying: an asswaging: a pleasing: a peace making.** Pacificátio, onis, f.g. Verbale. Cic. *Appaisement*

✳ **To pacifie god with satisfaction or prayers:** to purge by sacrifice. Expio, as. Plin.

✳ **That cannot be pleased, pacified, appeased, or reconsilied.** Implacábilis, le. Plin. *Qu'on ne peult appaiser. vt,* Implacabilem sese inexpiabilemque præbere alicui. Cic.

He will easily pacifie his father and make him condescende to doe what he will. Facillimé patris pacem in leges conficiet suas. Ter.

May be pacified. Numina leniri possunt. Ouid.

✳ **Not pacified: not appeased.** Impacatus, penult. prod. Adiect. Virg.

✳ **He that pacifieth, asswageth or tameth: he that quieteth.** Pacátor, & Pacificator, toris, ma. gener. Seneca.

✳ **To pacifie or asswage againe.** Remulceo, ces, cere. Virgil.

Be not so angry, pacifie your selfe. Reprime iracundiam. Ter.

I will pacifie and comforte all my great longyng for you with &c. Omne desiderium literis mittendis accipiendisque leniam.

¶ a **Packe** or fardell that a man doth beare with him in the way, truffe, or cariage. Sárcina, cinæ, f.g. Plaut. *Vng pacquet & fardeau qu'on porte auec soy sur le chemin, Bagage.* And Sarcínula, æ. Iuuen. a litle packe or fardell.

Packe horses or mules. Sarcinaria iumenta. Cæs. Dossualia iumenta. Varro. Clitellarij equi.

✳ **A packe saddle, or sumpter saddle: a packe:** an

pressed. What Baret writes on the letter *K* suggests his interest in orthography and spelling reform which runs through the various preambles. He writes:

Some sluggish head perchaũce (which would haue all men sleap with him quietly in slouth and security, because he would not haue his idlenesse espied) will say I am to curious about orthographie: and what nede I beat my braine about so fruteles & trifeling a matter? Other some y*t* wallowe in welth, and being in some fat office of writing haue filled their barnes and bagges with old Cacographie, say all is well ynough, and that it is impossible to amend it, & but folly to go about to make it any better. Indede I graunt measure is a merie meane. But as our forefathers in olde time haue by their diligent and daily serch, traced out the truth in letters, syllables and single woordes, and at lenghe [*sic*] by their vigilant and painfull industry haue framed and builded vp the art of Grammar, and left it all ready polished to our handes to their great commendation and immortall fame: So methinke to be ouer careless, not looking to amend faults betimes, but suffer it to fall in decay, as not being able to kepe it now in reparation, we shall be all worthy of perpetuall shame. And although theis heauy heads are loth to learne, & theis cunning clerks thinke scorn to be taught: yet the poore young infant which learneth to spell I know suerly should finde much ease and readinesse by this meanes, and much sooner come to a perfect ripenesse, both in reading and writing. For I meane not here to set them to scholl again which haue allready learned, but I wuold fayne help and further young beginners which would be learned.

The laudable aim of being helpful to "young beginners" by improving English orthography, Baret was not to realize. He was led, as examination of his preambles shows, into a maze of classical and Renaissance discussions of Greek and Latin pronunciation and orthography as well as of English, and he emerged with no clear-cut system for young beginners to follow. Among the documents he must have consulted, and therefore among the sources of his essays, are Erasmus' *De recta Latini Graecique sermonis pronunciatione* (1528), Sir Thomas Smith's *De recta et emendata linguae Anglicae scriptione* (1568), John Hart's *Orthographie* (1569), the Calepine, the Huloet-Higgins, and the letters of Cheke and Gardiner. The preamble of the letter *H*, involving some knowledge of Erasmus, Smith, Hart, Huloet-Higgins, and possibly Quintilian and Donatus, is fairly representative.

H Which corruptly wee name Ache is commonly called *aspirationis nota*, and among our grekishe Grammarians is vtterly denied to be a letter, because the Grekes vse it onely before vowels, and most commonly in the beginning of woordes. But whether it be a letter in Grece, or onely a breath as they say: yet surely they must needes graunt that we in England haue great neede of it, and vse it both before & also after our english vowels, as Sih, Tauht, Siht, &c. And me thinke such woordes cannot well be written, or plainly sounded without an h actually placed among them. Many

A page of the 1573 edition of John Baret's Alvearie, *in the University of Texas Library* (*opposite*)

therefore now a daies to be sure they will want nothing haue h foysted in, also an idle g, (Sigh, Taught, Sight) which to our eare soundeth nothing at all. For euery vowell compacted in dipthongs, and consonants in compounding woordes, ought to be seene seuerally to the eye, and also distinctly to be heard to the eare. And that is the true Orthography and right vse of all letters, as I haue before shewed out of *Aristotle* and *Quintilian*. And whereas H is seuerally ioyned in one syllable with C, S, D, & T. as they corruptly write Chese, She, The te, and The i. *rem facere* to thriue: Sir Thomas Smith very properly sheweth by a pretie similitude of Musicke that it should not be so, but rather some fit characters to be devized for them, where h should nomore be seene, then it is heard. For Musicke is therefore called *Symphonia*, because both the base, triple, and meane are so equally tempered together in iust proportion of time, breathe, and tune, that no parte drowneth an other, but euery one may sensibly be heard in like measure of sounde to the eare: So in Grammar euery letter that is written, must likewise audibly be pronounced with the rest, or els to be left cleane out. But as for ph, ch, &c. because we seeme to borowe them of the Greeke, I for my part will passe them ouer in silence, leauing that language with Latin also and Hebrue, to be reuiued and repolished of the learned vniuersities, and then I trust we also shal be better able to write true Ortographie in compiling our english Dictionaries.

In concluding our survey of Baret's treatment of the letters of the alphabet and his interest in spelling reform, we quote from Professor Sledd, whose study of the *Alvearie* is the most searching and informative work in the field. Sledd writes:

The proposals for spelling reform in the *Alvearie* are highly representative and only slightly original; the specific suggestions may most of them be traced to earlier improvers of English spelling, and the background of ideas on which these suggestions are superimposed may be traced in large part to the restorers of Greek pronunciation. . . . Combining the ideas of the English orthographers with those of the Grecians, he [Baret] affords an insight into the contemporary state of linguistic thought among educated men, and he might very well have been less valuable, as an index, if he had been more original.[34]

The foregoing detailed discussion of Baret and his *Alvearie* requires a summarizing statement. Perhaps the first noteworthy feature of the *Alvearie* is that it is a collaborative work. Whether or not Baret accurately describes the procedure in the compilation of the 1573 edition, it seems evident that, in both editions, several hands were engaged. This circumstance of assembling the materials may account for the wide range of sources, mostly secondary. In the *Alvearie* of 1573, for example, Baret and his assistants borrow from the Elyot-Cooper dictionaries—the *Bibliotheca* (1548) and the *Thesaurus* (1565)—the Huloet-Higgins dictionaries (1552, 1572); Levins' *Manipulus vocabulorum* (1570); Withals' *Dictionarie* (1553); the Stephanus-Veron *Dictionariolum* (1552); Calepine's *Dictionarium* (1564); and William Turner's *Newe Herball* (1552). For the *Alvearie* of 1580, Fleming and his co-workers extend the debt to the Huloet-Higgins of 1572; borrow freely from the Stephanus-Thierry *Dictionnaire francois-latin* (1564); and take what they need from Robert Stephanus' *Dictionarium Latino-Gallicum* (1552), Henry Lyte's *Niewe Herball* (1578), and Erasmus' *Adagia*, which yields 275 Latin proverbs.

For etymologies, the compilers owe much to Calepine and to Stephanus' French-Latin text of 1549. In the discussion of spelling reform, in the preambles, Baret shows familiarity with Erasmus' *De recta Latini Graecique sermonis pronunciatione*, Sir Thomas Smith's *De recta et emendata linguae Anglicae scriptione* (1568), and John Hart's *Orthographie* (1569).

The *Alvearie* shows perhaps more than other dictionaries of the sixteenth century the impact of French lexicography on English, and, indirectly, on the English language. Baret is, for example, the only English lexicographer in this period to give noteworthy attention to etymology of the vernacular. In this he is following the precedent of Robert Stephanus and borrowing freely from the French author. In his emphasis upon copiousness, Baret follows the lead of the Huloet-Higgins dictionaries. For the discussion of letters of the alphabet, he has a precedent in the same compilers as well as in Calepine; but in directing these expositions towards spelling reform, he reflects the learned contemporary discussions of Latin and Greek and the current need of his contemporaries in writing the English language.

CHAPTER XV

John Rider's *Bibliotheca scholastica* (1589)

NINE YEARS after the appearance of the second edition of the *Alvearie*, there was published at Oxford a comprehensive English-Latin dictionary. The compiler, John Rider, or Ryder, was born at Carrington, Cheshire, in 1562. He was educated at Jesus College, Oxford, from which institution he received the B.A. degree (1581) and the M.A. (1583). He took holy orders, and held the rectory at Waterstock (1580) and at South Ockendon (1581–83). In 1597 he was appointed dean of St. Patrick's Cathedral, Dublin, and spent his life thereafter chiefly in Ireland. He rose, in 1612, to be bishop of Killaloe. His early life was devoted mainly to study or tutorial work at Oxford. It may well have been his experience as tutor that first aroused his interest in making a dictionary.[1]

In 1589, Joseph Barnes published for Rider at the University of Oxford Press his *Bibliotheca scholastica. A Double Dictionarie.* The wording of the title page follows.

Bibliotheca Scholastica. A Dovble Dictionarie, Penned for all those that would haue within short space the vse of the Latin tongue, either to speake, or write. Verie profitable and necessarie for Scholers, Courtiers, Lawyers and their Clarkes, Apprentices of London, Traveliers, Factors for Marchants, and briefly for all Discontinuers within her Maiesties Realmes of England and Ireland. Compiled by Iohn Rider, Master of Artes, and preacher of Gods word. First reade [me] With others conferre [me] Then censure me. Read the Preface, Learne the vse. Printed by Ioseph Barnes, Printer to the Vniversitie of Oxford, and are to be sold at the Tygers head in Paules Church-yarde. 1589. Cum privilegio Regiae Majestatis.

218

This volume, described as "A Double Dictionarie," is a small quarto, with three columns to the page, consisting all told of eighteen hundred columns. It is primarily an English-Latin dictionary, with a Latin Index after the model of that in Baret's *Alvearie*. The wording of this title, together with the manner of the *Bibliotheca*'s publication in the seventeenth century, has given rise to an error about the nature of this book which has persisted from the early seventeenth century to Sidney Lee's sketch of Rider in the *DNB*.[2] Lee perpetuates the error by referring to Rider's work as "an elaborate English-Latin and Latin-English dictionary." On the basis of this error, long current before Sidney Lee's day, other mistaken inferences have been made about Rider and his book. These mistakes will be cleared up in the discussion of the Bishop of Killaloe and his immediate successor, Francis Holyoke. Meanwhile, let it be understood that the *Bibliotheca scholastica* of 1589, notwithstanding the language of the subtitle, is primarily an English-Latin dictionary. The Latin index with its numbered references is something far different from a Latin-English dictionary.

After the title page there follow the Latin dedication to Francis Walsingham and a body of preliminary matter, much of which is pertinent to our consideration of Rider's text. As copies of Rider's *Bibliotheca* (1589) are scarce in America, it seems desirable to include here Rider's address to the reader and other matter.

To the Reader

Courteous Reader, I may seeme to some ouer-bold in setting forth a new treasure of wordes unto the world, when the workes of so honorable and learned men, who haue laboured in this kinde, are so learnedly penned, and highly esteemed. In truth I must, and doe most willingly confesse, that neither in age, witte, learning, or experience, I am to be compared with the least of them, nay, unfit to carie the bookes, where some of the honorable learned would read the lecture; whose learned labors haue yielded these manie years to England great profite. Yet notwithstanding, considering the great vtilitie of a Dictionarie, whose matter is manifold, and vse generall, and also that no one Dictionarie, as yet extant, hath the English before the Latine, with a ful Index of al such Latine words as are in any one common Dictionarie amongst vs: and also because the poore estate of most students is not able to furnish themselues with al such Dictionaries, their seuerall prices amounting to so much; and also weighing the great want that poore scholers haue in not hauing most, or all of the common Dictionaries: I haue thought it good therfore, for thy benefite, courteous Reader, to epitomize and contract the learned workes of all the learnedst and best Dictionaries in England, with vs now extant, into a lesser roome, reducing al those learned Volumes into a portable Enchiridion, & into so great treasures to cast, for thy vse, some smal mites of mine owne, which amount to 4000 wordes more then any one Dictionarie now extant affoords.

Which I haue done not without great paines and charges: which heauie burden of charge, if it had not bene supported by the Right honorable, my very good Lorde, the Earle of Sussex, and the Right worshipfull Master William Waade. Esquier,[3] one of the Clarkes of her Maiesties most honourable privie Counsel, with other of my good loving Parishioners of Barmonsey neere London, & good friends in and neare Banburie, it might haue bene said of me, as it was of the foolish builder, This man began to builde, but was not able to make an ende. But at last, though long, by Gods prouidence, it is come to this issue, that I must present it (howsoeuer it be finished) to thy courteous viewe & friendly censure: requesting thee to reproue with judgement charitable, what I haue ouerpast, in haste: In recompence whereof, I wil be no lesse willing to reforme, then thy courtesie to admonish. Thus assuring my selfe, that thou, learned reader, wilt my faultes escaped, either with thy pen correct, or in courtesie conceale: Remembring that the first shadowes of young painters maie haue some blemishes & first editions of young writers, (yea & best works) some faultes. I commit thee, gentle Reader, to his tuition that must present both thee and me faultles, in his owne righteousnesse, before the great Iudge at the coming of our Lord Iesus Christ. From Oxon. this xxx. of September

> Thin to his power.
> JoH. RIDER.

The author's remark that "no one Dictionarie, as yet extant, hath the English before the Latine, with a ful Index of al such Latine words as are in any one common Dictionarie amongst vs" is hardly in keeping with the facts. Baret's *Alvearie* of 1573 (and 1580) had the English before the Latin and an index of Latin words (probably the model for Rider's text); *The Nomenclator* (1585) of Junius had a similar index; and the Huloet-Higgins of 1572, the Huloet of 1552, and the Withals of 1556 (and at fairly regular intervals until 1634) had the English before the Latin, though none except Baret and Junius had the Latin index. Rider's stated aim—"to epitomize and contract the learned workes of all the learnedst and best Dictionaries in England"—is partially realized, though this implied acknowledgment does scant justice to the one dictionary to which he owed the greatest debt.

Besides his "To the Reader," Rider has "Directions for the Reader," to be included below, and a series of laudatory poems and tracts. First, Rider himself has two Latin poems to his patron or Maecenas; [4] then follow a commendatory prose paragraph by John Case [5] to youths studious of the Latin language, and complimentary poems on Rider and his book "by Io. Vnderhill, Doctor of Theology; Tho. Holland, Regius Professor of S. Theology; Rob. Ralli, Dr. of Theology; by Iohannes Purefey, Robertus Cranus, Tho. Dochen, R. H., socius Novi Collegij, Io. Williams, Iohn Pelleno, Richard Hartley, Iohn Dove, Thomas Basterd, John Hoskins, Laurence Mychelborn, T. W.; E. M.; P. M." Thus Rider's book was launched with a chorus of praise very similar to that employed by Baret in publishing his *Alvearie* in 1573.

Rider's words to the reader, supported by the commendations of his colleagues, carefully set forth his reasons for compiling his *Bibliotheca* and its value for students of the Latin language. Eager to make clear its system, the compiler gives explicit instructions to the prospective users. As these "directions" are informative for all, they are here inserted in Rider's own language.

Directions for the Reader

In the English of every word I observe vsually this order. First I put the verbe (if it haue any) then the participle, after the Nownes substantiues, and adjectiues, and lastly the Adverbs.

In the Latine vnder the English I generally obserue this order. First I place the proper Latine word vnder the figure of 1: then the figuratiue or translate vnder the figure of 2; and lastly those that be obsolete, or words out of vse, vnder the figure of 3. These words that be old and out of vse, I put them downe, not that in writing any Latine exercise, having other choice, thou shouldst vse them: for to prevent that I brand them in the forehead with the figure of 3. But when thou readest them in several authors, thou shouldest be eased of a farther toile, in knowing their significations.

The author here explains the symbols (such as *ad.* for *adjective, m* for *masculine,* etc.) to indicate the parts of speech, inflection, and gender, and observes that, after the English-Latin dictionary, he has, in alphabetical order, certain general heads—"Birdes, Colours, Dogges, Fishes, Herbes, Stones, Trees, Weights," etc.—matter similar to that which had been recurrent in the vocabularies from the Middle Ages on. A few transcribed entries show how the "directions" apply to the text.

To Blossome, bloome, or beare flowers. 1 *Floreo.*
To blossome before dew time. 1 *Praefloreo, praegermino.*
A blossome, or bloome. 1 *Flos, m.* 3 *Botrio, quintina, quinticia f.*
To Blot out, wipe awaie, or deface. 1 *Deleo, deluo, delino, oblitero,* 2 *Deformo,* 3 *Lituro.*
Blotted out. 1 *Deletus, obliteratus, maculatus.* 2 *Interlitus, complanatus, p.*
He that blotteth out. 1 *Deletor, m.*
A blotting out. 1 *Obliteratio, deletio, complanatio, f.*
A blot, or blurre. 1 *Litura, macula, f. erratum, n. vide* bleamish.
To imbrewe with Bloude, or to make blouddie. 1 *Cruento, sangvino.*
To let bloude. 1 *phlebotomo, as.*
Bloudshotten, or raied with bloud. 1 *Cruentatus, p.*
Bloude. 1 *Sanguis, m. anima, f.*
The bloud of a wound. 1 *Cruor, m.*
A little bloud, or bloud whereof puddings be made. 3 *sanguiculus, m.*
Blackebloud. 1 *Tabum, m.*
Corrupt or attainted bloude. 1 *Sanies, f.*
An inflammation of bloude. 1 *Plegmone, es.*
Bloudeshed. 1 *Sanguis, m. sanguinis emissio.*
The letting of bloude out of a vein. 1 *phlebotomia, phlebotomatio, f.*
A letter of bloude. 1 *Phlebotomator, m.*
Spitting of bloude. 1 *Haemoptysis, sanguinis, expuitio.*[6]

These entries indicate that, in general, Rider is in the tradition of the English-Latin lexicographers from the *Promptorium parvulorum* to the Huloet-Higgins and Baret, being in method near his immediate predecessors and in content, as additional examples would show, somewhat more comprehensive than any of his antecedents. In his use of the numbers 1, 2, 3, to indicate the status of Latin words as "proper," "figurative," or "obsolete," Rider goes a step beyond his predecessors. Unlike the Huloet-Higgins of 1572 or the Baret of 1573, Rider does not introduce the French equivalents of his Latin and English terms.

In Baret's *Alvearie*, Rider had a precedent for his Latin Index, but into his Index, Rider introduces much more grammatical and rhetorical information than appears in that of his predecessor.[7] Rider explains, in his "Directions for the Second Dictionarie," or Index, the method of using it and the information to be found on the Latin words. "First you have the word declined at large as far as it is needful, thē the Quātities of Syllables accēted. . . . You have also the *Derivations, Etymologies, Affinities*, and *Differences* of many hundred words, gathered from *Martial, Isidor, Tardivus*, and other good authors." For most verbs, he asserts, you will find what cases they govern: accusative, dative, ablative, etc. "Also when you would know the Signification of any latine woorde that is in the Index, or secōd Dictionarie, marke what figures be vnder that woord, for the first Figures show the Colume, & the next the Line of the saide Colume where you shall see that woorde you seeke for Englished. . . ."

Rider's statement about the information—derivation, quantity of syllables, and inflection—to be found in his Latin Index is correct, as is his suggestion that the Latin words were gathered from a wide range of classical sources. But for the word list and the grammatical information, Rider was simply selecting and transcribing words, accents, and symbols of inflection from his basic source for the Index. A discussion of his sources is therefore immediately pertinent.

The major source of Rider's *Bibliotheca scholastica* (1589) is Thomas Thomas's *Dictionarium linguae Latinae et Anglicanae* (1587). Evidence of Rider's indebtedness is at once apparent through comparison of his "Index Alphabeticum omnium verborū quae in hoc opere exponuntur," to give the full title, with corresponding entries in Thomas's *Dictionarium*.

Rider's Index (1589)	Thomas's *Dictionarium* (1587)
A & Ab, Praepositiones sunt ejusdem significationis: Ablat. casum regunt. 526. 17. 622, 24. 1012. 56.	A et Ab praepositiones sunt eiusdem significationis. . . .
A, vel ab, junctum cum certis nominibus, ministros significat: vt a consilijo, a cubiculo . . . Sic: Misi a pedibus, &c.	A, vel ab, iunctum cum certis nominibus, ministros significat. ut A poculis . . . A pedibus. . . .

Rider's Index (1589)	Thomas's *Dictionarium* (1587)
Abacēs, Iabol. vasa quaedam viliora, in quibus pretiosiora reponuntur.	Abăcēs. Iabol. vasa quaedam viliora, in quibus pretiosiora reponuntur.
Abacion, cij. n. g. dim: ab abax idē quod abaculus: Ammonius.	Abăcĭon, ij, n. g. dim. ab. Abax: idem quod Abaculus. Ammonius.
Abacti, orum. m. g. 1016, 29.	
Abăctor, oris, masc. g. ab abigo, Apul. 1407, 14.	Abăctor, oris, m. g. verb. ab Abigo, Apul. . . .
Abăctus, a, um. part. ab abigor, 216, 54. 479, 56.	Abāctus, us, m. g. Plin. . . .
Abăctus, tus, m. g. ipse abigendi actus, & violenta expulsio, Plin.	Abāctus, a, um, part. ab Abigor. . . .
Abăcus, ci, masc. g. 9, 49.	Abăcus. ci. m. g. . . .
Abăcŭlus, li, masc. dim: a nomine abax.	Abăcŭlus, li, m. g. dim. a nomine Abax, Plin. . . .
Abăcŭli, orum, mas. sunt calculi, quibus in dispunctione, & supputatione numerorum vtebantur antiqui.	Abăcŭli. . . .
Abăgĭo, onis, f. Var: vox obsoleta, significans adagium.	Abăgĭo, onis, f. g. Varr. . . .
Abălĭēnătĭo, onis, f. 1666, 53.	Abălĭēnătĭo, onis, f. g. verb. . . .
Abălĭēnātus, a, um, part. 30, 20. . . .	Abălĭēnātus, a, um. Part.
Abălĭēno, as, atum, are, ex ab & alieno, Accus. addito, Ablat. cū Praep. vt abalienare animum ab aliquo. 30, 13. . . .	Abălĭēno, as, are. . . .
Abălĭēnor, aris, atus, sum Plau. 30, 18. . . .	Abălĭēnor, aris, are, atus sum, Plaut. . . .
Abambŭlo, as, avi, atum, are, Fest. i. ab aliquo loco, vel persona ambulare.	Abambŭlo, as, avi, atum, are. Fest. . . .
Abămita, tae, f. g. Iustin. 8, 11.	Abămĭta, itae, f. g. Iustinian. . . .
Abanec, dictio peregrina, 654, 55.	Abanec, dictio peregrina. . . .

For the sake of clearness in the comparison, the English definitions in the entries above from Thomas are omitted, only the entries with the markings of long and short syllables and with grammatical and etymological information being given. Following the numbers in the excerpt from Rider's Index, as in "*Abacus* . . . 9, 49," we find in reverse order (the English before the Latin) Thomas's English definition. So with the other entries in the two texts. The two following excerpts offer supporting evidence of the relation of Rider's Index to Thomas's *Dictionarium*.

Rider's Index (1589)	Thomas's *Dictionarium* (1587)
Faba, bae, f.	*Faba, ae, f. g. p. b.* A beane.
Faba Iovis, faba suilla, porcina vel lupina, i. hyosciamus, Iun.	*Faba fresa,* Plin. A beane bruised or broken.
Faba fresa, ae, f. Plin.	*Fabae tunica, concha, valvulus vel operculamentum,* Iun. A beane shale,
Fabacĭus, a, um, ad. Plin.	huske, or peele. *Fabae scapus, fabalis*
Fabācĭa, ae, f. Plin.	

Rider's Index (1589)

Fabae tunica, vel concha, valvulus, vel operculamentum, Iun.
Fábāgĭnus, a, um. ad. vt fabaginum acus, idem quod fabaricus, Cato.
Fábāle, lis, n. Plin.
Fábālĭa, orum, neut. Iun.
Fábāgo, ginis, f. vel fabagium, gij.
Fábālis, le. ad. Ovid.
Fábārĭus, a, um, ad. Catul.
Fábātĭum, ij. n. id est, stipula fabalis.
Fābella, ae, f. dim. a fabula, Cic.
Făber, bri, m. C.
Faber, aerarius, vel aeris, Horat.
Faber automarius, Iuni.
Faber aurarius. C.
Faber cuparius.
Faber ferrarius, Plin.
Faber lignarius, Cicer.
Faber ocularius, Iun.
Faberculus, li, m. dim. a Faber.
Faberrime.

Thomas's *Dictionarium* (1587)

stipula, Iun. Beanhelme, or beane strawe. *Fabae hilum,* Iun. The black of the beane being like an eie. *Faba Iovis, faba suilla, faba lupina.* Iun. Henbane. *Faba Graeca, vel Syriaca, Vid. Lotos. Faba porcina, Vid. Hyosciamus.*
Faba inversa. Some think it to be called the hearb *Lunaria,* or *Fabricia, ae, f. g.* a beane cake. *satanum somnificu. n.*
Făbācia, ae, f. g. Plin. A beane cake.
Făbāgĭnus, a, um. Cato. Of beanes.
Făbāle, is, n. g. Plin. Beane straw or stalke.
Fabālia, fabāgo, fabaginum acus, Iun. Beanchaff, or the clensing of beanes.
Făbālis, le, Ovid. Of a beane.
Făbārĭus, a, um, Catull. Pertaining to beanes.
Făbella, ae, f. g. dim. a *Fabula.* A short tale or fable, a little enterlude.
Făber, bri, m. g. A workman that maketh any thing of hard matter or stuff . . . *Faber aerarius, vel aeris,* Horat. A coppersmith, a brasier, a tinker. *Automarius,* Iun. A maker of devises and motions, that goe and turne of themselues, as clockes, jackes to turne spits, &c. *Aurarius,* A goldsmith. *Ferrarius,* Pli. A forge man or iron smith. *Lignarius,* A carpenter. *Ocularius,* Iun. A spectacle maker. . . .
Faberrĭmus, a, um. Apull. Verie cunningly wrought.

From the information supplied above, it is evident that Rider's Index depends upon the *Dictionarium* for its Latin word list, for its grammatical information, and for the authorities from whom the Latin words and phrases are derived. Comparison of the texts proper—the English-Latin of Rider and the Latin-English of Thomas—shows that Rider was not content to borrow his Latin word list from Thomas; he also took over hundreds of Thomas's English definitions.

Rider's *Bibliotheca* (1589)

To graffe Ly cutting a round hole in the barke of a tree, and with claie to set in the budde of another tree. 1 *Inoculo.*

Thomas's *Dictionarium* (1587)

Inoculo, as Plin. To graffe by cutting a round hole in the barke of a tree, and with clay to set in the budde of another tree.

Rider's *Bibliotheca* (1589)	Thomas's *Dictionarium* (1587)
A graffe of a foote long, cutte from a tree, & set in the ground: or a graft cut on both sides to be set in the earth or a stock set in the ground to graft on. 1 *Talea*.	*Talea, f. g.* Plin. A stocke set in the ground to graffe on, or a graffe of a foote long cut from a tree, & set in the ground: a graffe cut on both sides to be set in the earth.
A graffing, when a budde of one tree is cut off rounde with part of the barcke, and set on an other: or when an hole is bored in a tree, & a kernell put in with a little lome. 1 *Inoculatio*.	*Inoculatio . . .* Graffing, when a budde of one tree is cut off round with a part of the barke, & set on an other: or when a hole is bored in a tree, and a kernell put in with a little lome.
Ten noble men appointed amongest the Romans, in steed of Consuls, to gouerne the common wealth. 1 *Decemuiri*.	*Decemuiri . . .* Tenne noble men appointed among the Romanes, in stead of the Consuls, to gouerne their common wealth. . . .
The gouernance which the people haue amongest themselues, without any other superiours, or gouernours, except such as they themselues make, or by themselues are established. 1 *Democratia, f.*	*Democratia, ae, f. g.* The gouernance or ruledom that a people haue upon themselues and their commonweale, without hauing other superiours or gouernours, except those officers that they themselues haue made, or by them are established.
Māna, delicate bread that god caused to fall from heauen in manner of a dewe, white, and like coriander seede, in eating very pleasaunt. 1 *manna, f.* Manna or aire dewe congealed vpon trees and plantes, which the physitions vse gentlie to purge choler. 1 *Manna, f. Mel aērium . . . Syriacus.*	*Manna, ae, f. g.* Plin. In the Scripture it is a delicate thing that God caused to fall from heauen in great abboundance in manner of a dewe, white, and like a coriander seede, in eating very pleasant: in phisicke it is a manner of dewe congealed on trees and plants . . . and reserued as a gentle purger of choller. Galen calleth it *Mel aerium*, Ayer or dewe Manna. . . .
A maide that maketh readie her Mistress. 1 *Ornatrix, f.*	*Ornatrix . . .* also a waiting maid that trimmeth & maketh readie her mistresse.
A maide bearing a basket on her head, wherein were images, or iewels of the Gods. 1 *Canephora, f.*	*Canephora, ae.* A maide bearing on her heade a basket, wherein were Images or Iewels of the goddes.
A young maide whose breastes are ready to be imbossed, or set out to the shewe. 1 *Sororians Virgo.*	*Sororians Virgo*, Plaut. A young maid whose breasts begin to be embossed and round: or be set out to shew.

Examples of Rider's borrowings from Thomas could be multiplied almost indefinitely. Not all are as literal as those indicated above. Some definitions are abridged, some rearranged or changed slightly in wording; but matter from Thomas is evident throughout. Even in the groups of Latin synonyms following many English entries and in the English-Latin lists of birds, dogs, and fishes, under "Certaine Generall Headings" at the end of the text proper—groups and lists borrowed freely from other sources—Rider constantly consulted Thomas.

For his synonymy as an adjunct of "copie" and variety, Rider had ample precedent in the French-Latin dictionaries of Robert Stephanus, the *Abcedarium* (1552) of Huloet, Higgins's revision of Huloet (1572),[8] the *Alvearie* (1573, 1580) of Baret; and the *Synonymorum sylva* of Pelegromius, translated by "H. F." and current from about 1580.[9] To all of these Rider is, directly or indirectly, indebted, though it may have been the popular appeal of the *Sylva* which caused Rider to emphasize synonymy. At any rate, Rider shows familiarity with the *Sylva*. Compare the following:

Synonymorum silva (1609)	Rider's *Bibliotheca* (1589)
a Complaint, a Lamentation, or mone. *Querula, Querimonia. Questus, Eiulatus. Fletus, Gemitus. Lamentatio, Questio. Conquestio. . . .*	A complaint or moane making. 1 *Querela, querimònia, questus, conquestus, gemitus.*
to Consent, to agree. *Conuenire . . . Concordare, Cohaere . . . Congruere, Suffragari. Consentire, Assentire. Quadrare, Consonare. . . .*	To consent or agree together. 1 *Consentio, conspiro, congruo, conuenio, concordo.* 2 *Quadro, cohaereo.*

Other examples of Rider's indebtedness may be found by comparison of the following English entries in the two texts: *deadly, excellent, cold, luxurious, lecherous, poverty or poorenesse,* and *slanderer.*[10] Although Rider has in his English headings and Latin synonyms many general correspondences to the *Sylva*, his actual borrowings are relatively scanty. The *Sylva* may well have served as a guide to Rider in his selection and arrangement of matter from Thomas and other sources.

One of these additional sources is the Huloet-Higgins *Dictionarie* (1572). Higgins, like Huloet before him, emphasized synonymy and, in his revision, greatly augmented the number of Latin synonyms collected by his predecessor. From the Latin synonyms and from the English definitions and phrases of the Huloet-Higgins, Rider drew generously. Compare the following entries:

Huloet-Higgins (1572)	Rider (1589)
Deceyue. *Caluo, Circumuenio, Contechnor, Circumscribo . . . Decipio, Decollo, Deludo, Defraudo, Eludo, Fallo, Fraudo, Frustro, Frustror, Illudo, Implano, Impono, Inesco, Ludo . . . Offundere errorem alicui, Seduco, Subduco, Subsendo.*	To deceve, or beguile. 1 *Impono, fallo, decipio, caluo, caluor, implano.* 2 *contechnor, circumduco, seduco, circumuenio, circumuento, interuerto, circumscribo, inesco, insidior, capto, ducto, lacto, sustendo, cretizo, excaeco, exbalisto.*

Huloet-Higgins (1572)	Rider (1589)
Deceaued. *Circumspectus, Circumuentus, Deceptus, Illusus, Proditus, Defraudatus, Inductus, Ludificatus, Captus, Fraudatus.*	Deceiued. *Circumspectus, falsus, deceptus, seductus, elusus, fraudatus, illusus, defraudatus, captus, circumuentus.*
Deceauour. *Circumscriptor, Fraudator, Deceptor, Pellax, Pellicator, Ludificator, Lusor, Frustrator, Impostor, Dolosus, Fallax.*	A deceiuer or beguiler. *Fraudator, defraudator, deceptor, circumuentor, insidiator, seductor, ludificator, planus, circumscriptor, impostor.*
Deceitfull. *Dolosus, Fallax, Fraudulentus, Pellax, Fraudulosus, Subdolus, Versutus, Vulpinus.*	Deceitful. *Fraudulentus, dolosus, subdolus, versutus, vafer, veteratorius, perfidiosus, fallax, bilinguis, vulpinus, captatorius.*
Deceitfully. *Dolose, Fallaciter, Fraudulenter, Fraudulose, Subdole, Versute.*[11]	Deceitfully. *Dolose, subdole, fraudulenter, fallaciter, astute, versuto, vafre, insidiose.*

In the examples given the Huloet-Higgins accounts for more of the Latin synonyms employed by Rider than does any other dictionary of the period. Rider supplemented his list, however, by drawing from other sources. As he had worked through the Thomas thoroughly, he found in this text ready reinforcement. Under *deceitful,* for example, Rider supplies *bilinguis, captatorius, perfidiosus, vafer,* and *veteratorius,* for each of which one meaning given by Thomas is "deceitful." Likewise, under *deceitfully,* Rider adds from the same source *astute, insidiose,* and *vafre.* A similar procedure is exemplified by Rider in the entries *decay, declare, defile, destroy,* and many others. The debt to the Huloet-Higgins is even more obvious in entries not involving synonyms, as in these:

Huloet-Higgins (1572)	Rider (1589)
Declare in presence. *Repraesento.* . . .	To declare in presence. *Repraesento.*
Declare a message. *Annuntio.*	To declare a message. *Annuncio.*
Declaration or a plea in lawe of any accion. *Libellus.*	A declaration in the law of any Action. *Libellus.*

Beginning with *an apple* and continuing with the various kinds of apples and related terms, such as *apple monger,* Rider has fifty entries. Of these, thirty-seven derive from Huloet-Higgins and thirteen from Thomas. Typical of entries on this topic are the following:

Huloet-Higgins (1572)	Rider (1589)
Apples named winter gouldinges. *Mala scandiana.* . . .	Winter goldings. *Scandiana.*
Apples which we call sommer gouldinges, or queene apples. *Mala sanguinea vel rubelliana, vel rubella & purpurea.* . . .	Summer goldings. 1 *Mala sanguinea, purpurea, rubella, rubelliana.*

Huloet-Higgins (1572)	Rider (1589)
Apples of the herbe called Mandragge. *Mala canina.*	Apples of the herb called Mandrag. 1 *Mala canina.*
Apples of no worthe, whiche we call wyldinges . . . *Gregalia.*	Wildings. *Gregalia poma.* . . .

In the Huloet-Higgins, Rider found a copious word list, abundance of Latin synonyms and illustrative phrases, all arranged under key entry words and so spaced as to be most convenient to follow. The result is that, next to Thomas, the Huloet-Higgins is Rider's most fertile source.

Rider's Index in the *Bibliotheca* may well have been suggested by that in Baret's *Alvearie*.[12] The index in the *Alvearie* has after each Latin word a letter and a number, the letter referring to the alphabetical position of the English equivalent, the number, to the entry. Consider, for example, "*Abiuratio* . . . f. 967." Turning to the letter *F* in the text and looking down the margin, we find the number 967. Immediately opposite is this entry: "A forswearing. *Abiuratio, onis. foem. gen.*" The Index in the *Bibliotheca scholastica* is similar, except that instead of a letter and a number after each Latin word, there are two numbers, the first referring to the column of the text and the second to the number of the entry, as "*Acanthis* . . . 1745, 46." In column 1745 and at entry 46 we find "Grounsell . . . *acanthis.*"

A comparative study of the two texts along with other contemporary dictionaries indicates that Rider owed to Baret more than the suggestion for his Index. Rider borrowed from the *Alvearie* certain of his definitions, as the following parallels suggest:

Baret (1580)	Rider (1589)
A beadle, or crier of the court, etc. which calleth for men by their names. *Nomenclator, toris, pen. prod. m. g.*	A Beadle or crier in the Courte, which calleth foorth men by their names. *Nomenclator, m.*
A beadle, such as cryeth congregations in the vniuersities, or to disputations, going before the graduates there to the schooles. *Cerys, ryces, m. g.* . . .	A Beadle in vniuersities, which crieth conuocations, or to disputations, going before them to the scholes. *Preco, accensus, caerix. m.*
A Beadle of brydewell. *Lictor pistrinalis.*	A Beadle of beggars, or bridewell. *Fustiarius, flagellarius, lictor pistrinalis, castifer.*
A Beadle to arrest or do execution upon malefactours. *Lictor, toris, m. g.*	A Beadle to arrest, or doe execution upon malefactours. *Lictor, m.*

In these entries under *beadle*, as in two or more under *parchment*, Rider borrows from Baret matter not found in the Huloet-Higgins. Even when he is, in the main, following the latter source, as in *decay, deceive,* and *declare,* Rider supplements his text with illustrations from Baret.

Baret (1580)	Rider (1589)
To fall downe and decaie by little and little. *Sublabor.*	To decay by little and little. 1 *Sublabor.*
That will die, decaie, or perish. *Periturus.*	That will decay. *Casurus . . . periturus.*
To mocke: to deceiue. *Ludifico . . . Ludificor . . . Deludo.*	To deceiue or mock. *Ludo . . . deludo . . . ludifico, ludificor, deludificor.*
Adde to: and put to any thing. *Addere, Adjicere, Subiungere, Adiungere, Subtexere, Adtexere, Annumerare, Aponere, Subnectere, Inserere.*	To add. 1 *Addo, appono, adjicio, adjungo, subdo, referro, injicio, subjungo.* 2 *Attexo, annexo, subtexo, ascribo, affero.*[13]

The evidence indicates that Rider was quite familiar with Baret's *Alvearie* and that from this book he got the idea for the Latin Index in the *Bibliotheca scholastica,* some entries not found in other sources, and supplementary illustrations.

Under "Certaine Generall Headings" at the end of the dictionary proper Rider inserts, in English and Latin, lists of birds, colors, dogs, fishes, herbs, trees, and stones. Such lists, or class names, are traditional in bilingual glossaries and vocabularies from the early Middle Ages to the eighteenth century. Although some of Rider's entries in the specific lists are simply names, English and Latin, in the manner of earlier vocabularies, or *nominales,* the compiler adds some information pertinent to a dictionary proper. His immediate model and, in part, his source of information is *The Nomenclator, or Remembrancer* of Hadrian Junius,[14] supplemented with the English terms by John Higgins, in 1585. In every group of class names, Rider borrows, rather literally, considerable matter directly from Junius. Characteristic are the following:

Junius (1585)	Rider (1589)
Arborem in orbem caedere . . . to cut a tree round.	To cut a tree round. *Arborem in orbem caedere.*
Arborem in pulpam caedere. To cut a tree in long wise, as it were in plankes.	To cut a tree in longwise, as it were in planckes. *Arborem in pulpam caedere.*
Arbores in quincuncem digerere vel dirigere . . . To plant trees in checker wise.	To plant trees in checker wise. *Arbores in quincūcem digerere vel dirigere.*
Arbuscula topiaria . . . Trees wrethed over head archewise . . . an arbour.	An arbour, trees wreathed over head archwise. *Arbuscula topiaria.*

But many entries under "Trees" have no antecedents in Junius. Such, for example, is *sycamorus.* This and other terms derive from Thomas. Under "Fishes . . . *Pisces,*" Rider takes the first seventeen items straight from Junius. Then follow thirty-seven entries not in Junius. These are all found, verbatim as to English and Latin, in Thomas. In the lists of birds, colors, herbs, and stones, Rider's procedure is similar: he has a composite of Junius and Thomas. In the names of dogs, there are a number of entries common to Junius, Thomas, and Rider, Ovid being an ultimate source.[15] But, in this topic also, Rider takes from Thomas items not discoverable in common sources.

For the "Certaine Generall Headings" and for a proportion of the items introduced under each heading, Rider follows Junius' *Nomenclator*. But his lists are considerably augmented by borrowings from Thomas, as the following parallels indicate. Rider's first series is under "Birdes."

Rider (1589)	Thomas (1587)
A sea-bird great and rauenous. *Charadrius, m.*	*Charadrius* . . . A seabird great and rauenous. . . .
A shoueler, or shofler. *Platalea.*	*Platalea* . . . it is called a Shoueller.
A Siskin. *Ligurinus, luteola.*	*Ligurinus* . . . A bird called a Siskin, vide *luteola.*
A wilde swanne braying like an asse. *Onocrotalus, m.*	*Onocrotalus* . . . A birde like to a swanne, braying like an Asse.
Certaine rauenous birds like to swannes hauing beneath their mouth a little gorge into which they swallow their meat greedily. *Oenocratali.*	*Oenocratali* . . . Certaine rauenous birdes like to swannes but they haue beneath their mouth a little gorge, into which they swallow their meete greedilie. . . .
The great Titmouse. *Frigillago, vel fringillago.*	*Frigillago, vel fringillago* . . . The bird called the great Titmouse.
A Wagtaile, or washer. *Motacilla, motacula.* . . .	*Motacilla,* or *motacula* . . . A wagtaile.
A witwall, or woodwall. *Vireo.* . . .	*Vireo,* A greene birde called of some a witwall, of others a green finch, or canarie bird.
A sea woodcock, because it hath a long bill not unlike a woodcock. *Trochilos, vel trochilus.*	*Trochilos, vel trochilus* . . . a sea woodcocke, because it hath a long bill not vnlike a woodcocke.[16]

Borrowings from Thomas are discoverable also under "Hearbes":

Rider (1589)	Thomas (1587)
An hearbe called also *Volubilis. combretum, n.*	*Combretum, ti, n. g.* An hearbe called *Volubilis.*
An hearb that in August beareth red flowres, and taketh away a Disease called the Kings Evill. *condurdon.*	*Condurdon,* Plin. An hearbe that in August beareth a redde flower, and healeth the disease called the Kings evill.
An hearb like Hemlock. Comon, latine *cicuta.*	*Cicuta, ae, f. g.* An herbe much like to our hemlocke. . . .
An hearb called also *cunilago. conyza, f.*	*Conyza* . . . An hearb called also *cunilago.* . . .
An hearb called *Polygonion,* it groweth much in stones and wals, and is alwayes greene. *Osteocollon.*	*Osteocollon, gr.* An hearb called also *Polygonion:* it groweth much in stones, and walls, and is alwaies greene.
An hearb called also *Cynocephalia,* because it is like a Dogges head. *Osirites.*	*Osirites* . . . An hearb called also *cynocephalia,* because it is like a dogs head.

Rider (1589)	Thomas (1587)
A certain hearb with a stalke like Fennell, and leaues like Madir. *Myagros*.	*Myagros* . . . A certaine hearb with a stalke like fenell and leaues like madder. . . .
An hearb called *Nyctegretum*, because it shineth farre in the night time. *Nyctilops*.	*Nyctilops* . . . An hearb called also *nyctegretum*, because that it shineth a farre of in the night time. . . .
An hearbe which Theodore doth translate sometimes *Cicram*, sometimes *Eruiliam*. *Ochras*. *Ocharon*.	*Ochres*, or *Ocharon*. An herb which Theodore doth translate sometimes *Cicram*, sometimes *Eruiliam*.

As the descriptive and expository items thus introduced are widely distributed in Thomas, it would be interesting to know Rider's procedure in collecting them. A fair conjecture is that, having made his headings and a partial list of items under each, on the basis of Junius' *Nomenclator*, Rider supplemented these as he found apposite matter reading through Thomas.

Rider's lists of class names are of interest not only as additional evidence of dependence on Thomas but also for what these lists reveal, incidentally, concerning Thomas's *Dictionarium*. On birds and herbs, for example, Rider gives, in abridged form, much of the lore on these subjects which appears in Thomas, and which Thomas derives largely from the Elyot-Cooper dictionaries and from Turner directly. But Elyot and Cooper had made free use of Turner's book on birds and the various treatises on herbs—the *Libellus* (1538), *The Names of Herbes* (1548), and the *Herball* (1551). Rider thus, through Thomas and the Elyot-Cooper dictionaries, reflects part of the debt of Renaissance lexicographers to Turner.

In column 1706 of the *Bibliotheca* Rider lists, in Latin only, words indicating the cries of birds and of quadrupeds, according, as he states, to Sidonius, Ovid, and Julius Pollux. The reference is to Rudolphus Gualtherus' Latin edition (1542) of Pollux' *Onomasticon*. Gualtherus had inserted in the annotations of his edition a poem entitled "De Philomela," which he ascribed to Ovid. The poem is too long to quote, but from it Rider apparently compiled the matter transcribed below.

Voces Inarticulatae Volatilium Quorundam

Philomela modulatur. Aquila clangit: Accipiter pipit: Corvus crocitat, crocit, corniculat: Perdix cacabat: Anser gratitat, glacitat: Cygnus drensat: Turtur atque Columba gemunt: Palumbes plausitat: Ciconia gloterat: Gallus cururrit: gallina gracillat, glocit, glocitat: Pavo pupillat: Grus gruit: Vultur pulpat: graculus frigulat: Milvius lipit, lugit: Anas tetrinit: hirundo trinsat: Passer pipit: Cicada fritinit: Sturnus pisitat: Turdus trutilat: Acredula mittat: Coturnix grylissat: Galgulus glocitat. Merula stridet: Pica picatur, vel modulatur: Upupa papissat: Meleagris cacissat: Vespertilio stridet:

cuculus cuculat: Bubo bubulat: Noctua cucubat: Ulula ululat: Butio bubit: Regulus, meros zinzilutat: apes bombilat: Parus tinninat.

Voces etiam quadrupedum animalium

Leo rugit: Tigris raucat: Panther caurit: Pardus felit: Lupus ululat: Aper frendet: Barrus barrit: Cervus, onager glocitat: Taurus mugit: Equus hinnit: Verres quiritat: Asellus uncat: Aries blacterat: Ovis balat: Sus grunnit: Caper, hircus mutit: Canis latrat: Vulpecula gannit: Catulus glaucitat: Lepus vagit: Mus mintrat: Mustela dintrit: Grillus grillat: Sorex disticat: Serpens, & anguis sibilant: Rana coaxat.

The *Onomasticon* may also have been suggestive to Rider in his accumulation of synonyms, though there is no conclusive evidence that he borrowed matter other than the terms applicable to the cries of birds and animals.

The major source, then, of Rider's *Bibliotheca scholastica*, an English-Latin dictionary with a Latin Index, was the Latin-English dictionary of Thomas Thomas. On Thomas, Rider depended largely for his Latin word list, for the marking of long and short vowels and the grammatical information supplied in the Index, and for the greater part of his English definitions. If we remember that Thomas was based on Cooper and Morelius, and Cooper on Elyot and Robert Stephanus and Frisius, and also that Rider supplemented the matter from Thomas by Pelegromius' *Synonymorum sylva*, Gualtherus' Latin edition of Julius Pollux' *Onomasticon*, the Huloet-Higgins, Baret, and Junius, we may agree that Rider's dictionary is an epitome of the "learned workes of all the learnedst and best Dictionaries in England." Rider's own contribution was somewhat more than that of a mere compiler: he distinguished levels of usage as respects the Latin vocabulary, made a superior collection of Latin synonyms, and, by his collection of class names, incidentally revealed the riches of Thomas's *Dictionarium*. The compilation thus made was destined to continue, with little change, in the Rider-Holyoke dictionaries through the seventeenth century. But the account of these dictionaries and the clash of Francis Holyoke with the heirs of Thomas must be recorded in a subsequent chapter.

Before beginning the account of seventeenth-century dictionaries, it may be profitable here to recall the more important facts in the history of Latin-English and English-Latin lexicography in the sixteenth century. The *Dictionary of Syr Thomas Eliot* (1538) was the first attempt in the century to compile a Latin-English dictionary commensurate with the needs incident to the new learning. Elyot's model and main source seems to have been the *Dictionarium* (1502) of Friar Calepine of Bergamo.

This was supplemented, however, by matter from Suidas, Perottus, Erasmus, the herbals, and other sources. In subsequent editions (1542, 1545) Elyot extended his word list, and especially his illustrations of meaning and usage, by free borrowing from Robert Stephanus' Latin-French dictionary of 1538, William Turner's *Libellus de re herbaria* (1538), and Erasmus' *Adagia*. Under the title *Bibliotheca Eliotae*, Elyot's *Dictionary* was much augmented by Thomas Cooper, in 1548, 1552, and 1559. The sources of Cooper's augmentation were, once again, Robert Stephanus' Latin-French dictionary and Erasmus' *Adagia*. He used also Nicholas Udall's *Floures for Latine Speakyng selected and gathered out of Terence;* some edition of Torrentinus' *Vocabularius poeticus*, edited by Robert Stephanus; probably Stephanus' *Thesaurus;* and, beginning with the 1552 *Bibliotheca Eliotae*, matter from William Turner's *Avium historia* (1544), *The Names of Herbes* (1548), and the *Newe Herball* (1551).

Cooper's *Thesaurus* (1565), utilizing much of the matter of the 1559 *Bibliotheca*, vastly extended the word list and illustrations by drawing heavily upon Robert Stephanus' augmented Latin-French dictionary of 1552, supplementing this by some matter from Johannes Frisius' Latin-German dictionary of 1556. Cooper's "Dictionarium Poeticum," a dictionary of proper names supplementing the *Thesaurus*, used, besides the proper-name entries in the *Bibliotheca*, much matter from Robert Stephanus' *Thesaurus* and Charles Stephanus' *Dictionarium historicum, geographicum, poeticum* (1553).

In 1583, Richard Hutton edited, supplying English definitions, the *Verborum Latinorum . . . commentarii* of G. Morelius. For his English definitions he drew heavily from Cooper's *Thesaurus*. Thomas Thomas in his *Dictionarium* (1587) copied from both Cooper and the Morelius-Hutton, supplementing his compilation, in subsequent editions, with matter from Junius and Calepine.

These Latin-English dictionaries constitute a closely unified group, in which the Elyot-Cooper dictionaries are dominant. Their influence continues, as we shall see, through the seventeenth century.

In the smaller dictionaries, intended generally for schools, there is an analogous situation as to sources and interrelationships. John Veron's dictionary in three languages, Latin, French, and English (1552) was based upon Robert Stephanus' *Dictionariolum . . . Latino-Gallicum*. The Veron, augmented by Rudolph Waddington (1575) and Abraham Fleming (1584), drew freely from the Elyot-Cooper dictionaries. Huloet's *Abcedarium* (1552) was indebted for its plan to Stephanus' *Dictionnaire francois-latin* (1549); it drew also from the *Bibliotheca Eliotae*, from the *Promptorium parvulorum,* and from Calepine, Isidore, and Polydore Vergil. Higgins's revision of Huloet (1572) borrows heavily from the French-Latin dictionary of Stephanus, augmented by Jehan Thierry (1564), from Stephanus' *Dictionarium Latino-Gallicum,* from Cooper's *Thesaurus,* and from Turner, Gesner, Junius, *et alii.* The short dictionary of John Withals, perhaps better than any other in the period, illustrates the native tradition of the bilingual vocabulary. In the course of its history, however, it collects materials from many sources—from Grapaldus' *Lexicon,* Gualtherus' edition of Pollux' *Onomasticon,* Calepine, Stanbridge's *Vocabula,* the Elyot-Cooper *Bibliotheca,* Turner's *Avium historia* and *Names of Herbes,* Erasmus' *Adagia,* Barclay's and Locher's versions of *The Ship of Fools,* Martial's *Epigrams,* and Thomas Thomas's *Dictionarium.*

Baret's *Alvearie,* in its two editions of 1573 and 1580, shows a similar tendency to utilize materials from a wide range of sources. Although its heaviest debt is probably to the Elyot-Cooper dictionaries, the *Alvearie* drew also from the Huloet-Higgins, Peter Levins' *Manipulus vocabulorum,* the Stephanus-Veron, Withals, Calepine, and various dictionaries of Robert Stephanus. For special information, Baret consulted Turner's *Herball,* Lyte's translation of Dodoens' *Herball,* Erasmus' *Adagia* and his *De recta Latini Graecique sermonis pronunciatione* (1528), Sir Thomas Smith's *De recta et emendata linguae Anglicae scriptione* (1568), John Hart's *Orthographie* (1569), and possibly Clenardus, Priscian, and Quintilian. For diversity of source materials, Baret's *Alvearie* is scarcely surpassed.

With the mention again of Rider's *Bibliotheca scholastica,* whose dependence upon Thomas Thomas and whose borrowings from Pelegromius, Julius Pollux, Huloet-Higgins, Baret, and Junius are noted above, we conclude the résumé for the sixteenth century of titles and sources. Worthy of emphasis in the survey are not only the interdependence and interrelationships of dictionaries compiled in England but also their debt, in content and method, to Continental lexicographers, especially Calepine and Robert Stephanus.

This survey would hardly be complete without some notice of the technical aspects of the dictionaries of the period. In the Elyot-Cooper dictionaries, perhaps most nearly representative of the century, there appears to be definite progress toward a dictionary exemplifying classical principles. Nearest to this ideal is Cooper's *Thesaurus,* which rules out many Latin terms regarded as barbarous or medieval and aims, according to the compiler, to supply examples of meaning and usage chosen from standard classical authors. There remain, however, many terms later to be challenged. The times were hardly ripe for a purely classical dictionary.

As to organization or arrangement of materials in the dictionary, there were two competing systems (if we except the very popular Withals, which carried on the medieval-vocabulary tradition of arrangement by class names): the etymological and the alphabetical. Elyot seems to have wavered between the two systems, finally settling upon the alphabetical, a system which continued in Cooper's revisions of the *Bibliotheca*. Other lexicographers, though generally favoring an alphabetical arrangement, only approximated it. When Cooper published his *Thesaurus* (1565), he employed a modified etymological system, grouping families of words together, with cross references in alphabetical order—the result of the influence of Robert Stephanus' Latin-French dictionary, Cooper's model. Thomas Thomas chose, however, to follow the alphabetical arangement of G. Morelius rather than Cooper. And the proved usefulness and vogue of Thomas seem to have established the alphabetical arrangement.

In the second half of the sixteenth century some attention was given to pronunciation of Latin words. Cooper, following Calepine, used the symbols *pen. cor.* and *pen. prod.* to indicate where the stress would fall on a given word. Baret used these symbols also. Thomas, following Morelius, employed the breve and the macron to indicate short and long vowels; and Rider, in his Latin Index, followed Thomas. It can hardly be said, however, that any definite system was established, owing, possibly, to the controversy in the century on the question of Latin pronunciation.

In etymology there was growth in quantity, if not in quality. The principle was not new. Joannes Balbus in the *Catholicon* offered a precedent in the fifteenth century, and Calepine in the sixteenth. In general, etymologies in Cooper, Thomas, and Rider are simple statements of the make-up of compound words. Thomas, influenced by Morelius, has far the greatest number of etymologies. These were taken over by Rider. John Baret, following Stephanus and Calepine, devoted more attention than any of his English contemporaries to etymology.

In the choice, and gradual increase, of classical examples to illustrate usage, there was a notable development. This practice derived from the Continental lexicographers Calepine and Robert Stephanus, especially Stephanus. Elyot, in 1538, used such illustrations sparingly, citing his authorities in marginal notes. In subsequent editions of his *Dictionary*, by himself and later by Cooper, the citation of the authors' names tended to drop out, though the illustrations increased in number. In his *Thesaurus* of 1565, Cooper, following Stephanus, mightily increased the number of classical illustrations and cited his classical authors, though not the work and section from which the quoted matter derived. Thomas and others followed Cooper, but tended to select rather than include all the wealth of matter in the *Thesaurus*.

It may be sufficient simply to mention other features of sixteenth-century dictionaries, already discussed: the exemplification of synonymy and *copia*, the extensive use of proverbs, and the introduction of proper names, together with the historical and legendary matter associated with them.

PART III

The Seventeenth Century

CHAPTER XVI

The Rider-Holyoke Dictionaries (1589–1659)

I N THE LAST chapter we discussed John Rider's *Bibliotheca scholastica*, published at Oxford, in 1589. Although this book came to be known as *Riders Dictionarie*, Rider himself seems to have had no further active interest in it after the publication of the first edition. Apparently he devoted his time thereafter to ecclesiastical affairs. From 1597, when he was appointed dean of St. Patrick's Cathedral, Dublin, he lived for the rest of his life chiefly in Ireland.[1] When a London syndicate, about 1604, wished to have the Rider revised and expanded, they turned not to the original compiler but to Francis Holyoke, another Oxford man, for assistance.[2] For the revised edition of 1606, and for all subsequent editions of the *Dictionarie*, except one by Nicholas Gray, in 1626, Holyoke alone is responsible. In not one of these seventeenth-century editions is Rider mentioned as a collaborator. Augmentations claimed for the dictionary bearing Rider's name are by Francis Holyoke. The title *Riders Dictionarie* is a sort of publisher's trade-mark.

Francis Holyoke (1567–1653) studied as a commoner at Queen's College, Oxford, about 1582, but left without a degree. Afterwards he taught school, first at Oxford and then in Warwickshire, where in February, 1604, he became rector of Southam.[3] It was probably about this time that he began reworking the *Bibliotheca scholastica* and preparing it for publication under the title *Riders Dictionarie*. The changes wrought by Holyoke in this work and the way in which, under his editorship, the Rider was published from time to time for a period of fifty years have resulted in confusion regarding the relationship of Holyoke, Rider, and

239

Thomas Thomas, and in the bibliography of the Rider-Holyoke dictionaries. It is now time to examine some of the conjectures concerning the Rider-Holyoke-Thomas relationship and to determine whether they have any basis in fact.

One of the first of these, and probably the source of subsequent confusion, is that made by Thomas Fuller [4] in 1662, about seventy-three years after the publication of Rider's *Bibliotheca,* and fifty-six years after Francis Holyoke had first assumed responsibility for editing the Rider. Fuller's comment, the source of later statements, runs thus:

> Francis Holyoake (Latining himself *de sacra Quercu*), and minister of Southam, born at Whitacre in this county. He set forth that stable book which school-boys called "Rider's Dictionarie." This Rider did borrow (to say no worse) both his saddle and his bridle from Thomas Thomatius, who, being bred fellow of King's College in Cambridge, set forth that dictionary known by his name; than which men have not a better and truer; children no plainer and briefer. But Rider, after Thomas's death, set forth his dictionary, the same in effect, under his own name, the property therof being but little disguised with any additions.
>
> Such plagiaryship ill becometh authors or printers; and the dove being the crest of the Stationers' arms, should mind them, not (like rooks) to filch copies one from another. The excutors [*sic*] of Thomas Thomatius entering an action against Rider, occasioned him, in his own defence, to make those numerous additions to his dictionary, that it seems to differ rather in kind than degree from his first edition.
>
> I am forced to place this child, rather with his guardian than father: I mean to mention this dictionary rather under the name of Master Holyoake than Rider, both because the residence of the latter is wholly unknown to me, and because Mr. Holyoake added many (and his learned son hath since more) wonders therunto. Master Holyoake died Oct. 2, anno Domini, 1661.

Fuller's comment requires examination. That Rider in 1589 did depend largely upon Thomas's Latin-English dictionary is, as we have seen in the foregoing chapter, undeniable. That the heirs of Thomas brought action against Rider and that Rider himself as a result had "to make those numerous additions to his dictionary" is a misrepresentation. Although Legate and other heirs of Thomas probably realized Rider's extensive debt to Thomas, they made no complaint. Editions of Thomasius appeared in 1592, 1594, 1596, and 1600; and in not one of these is there a reference to Rider's *Bibliotheca.* Why should there be? As an English-Latin dictionary, Rider's was hardly a competitor of the Latin-English by Thomas. Furthermore, the lexicon compiled by Rider was evidently a drug on the market, no second edition being required for a period of seventeen years. Rider had nothing to do with the second and subsequent editions of the dictionary. He did not make "numerous additions" to the English-Latin dictionary originally compiled by him; nor did Holyoke, though he claimed augmentation by himself. Every extant contemporary criticism is directed against Francis Holyoke, not Rider, after Holyoke had begun converting the Rider Latin index into a Latin-English dictionary which would then be a competitor of the Thomasius. Fuller's report condemning Rider for borrowing "both his saddle and his bridle from Thomas Thomatius," and commending Holyoke, is based on insufficient knowledge of the facts and is misleading.

Fuller's error is followed in the *DNB,* where, under *Rider,* we read, "Fuller says that Rider borrowed 'both his saddle and bridle' from Thomas"; and under *Thomas* we read further that John Rider, in editions of his dictionary subsequent to 1589, was obliged to make numerous additions and alterations in consequence of an action brought against him by Thomas's executors. In the sketch of Francis Holyoke (*DNB*) the writer is a little nearer to the truth, though he does not correct the earlier statements. He writes: "In 1617 Francis Holyoke recast and edited Rider's dictionary, and was charged by Thomas's executors with extensive plagiarism. In subsequent issues of Rider's book in 1626, 1633, and 1640 Holyoke's contributions were modified and amplified by Holyoke himself, by Nicholas Gray. . . ." The sketch takes no cognizance of the editions of 1606, 1612, and 1627 in which Holyoke is still unregenerate.

Fuller's account is confused and misleading, as is that of the critics who follow him. One source of this confusion is that neither Fuller nor subsequent commentators had examined critically the early editions of Rider, especially that of 1589, and the first edition revised by Francis Holyoke, in 1606. Fuller, reporting gossip almost thirty years after Rider's death, obviously did not have correct information, and those who accepted his account were likewise in error. Fuller's story is, however, not entirely a fabrication; it is rather an inadvertent distortion of the facts.

In order to discover the basis of his story, we need to survey briefly the early history of the text. Although Rider's *Bibliotheca scholastica* (1589) undoubtedly had merit, it was not a profitable venture for the printer and publisher. Already current were Huloet's *Dictionarie,* revised by Higgins (1572), and Baret's *Alvearie* (1573, 1580), both containing the English, Latin, and French, in the order named. Then there was the less expensive and more popular small English-Latin dictionary of John Withals, published at regular intervals during the eighties and nineties. Rider's text seems to have fallen between the larger works of Baret and Huloet and the smaller one of Withals, and to have taken the place of neither. Scholars desiring an inexpensive English-Latin dictionary would doubtless prefer the Withals; those wishing a more elaborate and authoritative lexicon would consult the Huloet or the Baret, since these contained not only the English and Latin but the French as well. The place of the Rider seems to have been anomalous. This condition was probably one factor accounting for the seventeen-year interval between the publication of the first and the second edition.

Entries in the *Stationers' Register* seem to support this inference.[5]

7 June 1602
> John Barnes. Entred for his copies these bookes . . . Riders Dictionary 4[to]. . . .

6 December 1602
> John Barnes. Entred for his copie master Riders Dictionary upon condicion that yt shalbe printed onely in London and not elswhere.

27 January 1603
> Master Burby. Assigned over unto hym from John Barnes a booke called Ryders Dictionary which was entred for the said John Barnes copie as appeareth 6 decembris ultimo 1602 & 7 June *eodem anno.*

26 November 1604

Master man Master Master Norton Master Leake Wardens M. Edward Whyte M. Waterson M. Addames M. Burbie M. Banckworth	Entred for their Copies by consent of Master Burbye A Booke (formerlie assigned unto him) called Ryders dixionarie.

It is not entirely clear what these entries mean.[6] Although the Rider was entered as early as 1602, it was not printed, as far as I can learn, until 1606, and then in much expanded form. Why the transfers, as the records indicate, from Barnes to Burby and from Burby to others, and the postponing of printing from year to year? The explanation is probably that no publisher was willing to risk the losses that might be involved in publishing an expensive text which had not been greatly in demand during the first twelve years of its existence. Revision and expansion might, however, put the Rider back in the game.

Perhaps with such thought in mind certain London booksellers (*bibliopolae*), according to Francis Holyoke in the address to the reader of the 1606 edition, when they had bought from the Oxford publisher the right to print Rider's dictionary, employed Holyoke to make revisions and corrections before the book should go to press. And the changes were to be thoroughgoing. One of the problems, Holyoke explains, was to convert the Latin Index of the original Rider into a Latin-English dictionary. This procedure would of course greatly enhance the value of the book and increase the demand for it. But this task would require time and would involve further delay. We do not know when Holyoke began making over the Rider, but he explains that he was delayed considerably on account of the ravages of the plague in London, and for various other reasons. It seems very probable that the failure of publishers to see an adequate financial return in reissuing a not-very-popular Rider, and the obstacles which prolonged the work of Holyoke, once revision was decided upon, would account for the long interval between the original edition (1589) and the revised and expanded text (1606).

It is noteworthy that no mention is made of Rider as reviser of the text, or of his having any further interest in the publication. Moreover, I find no record before 1606 protesting against Rider's borrowing from Thomas Thomas. There is, however, a hitherto unnoticed item, bearing directly on Francis Holyoke's use of Thomas's text in the transformation of Rider's Latin Index into a Latin-English dictionary—a piece of work which constituted the second half of the Rider in 1606. Though hindered by the plague and other obstacles, Holyoke insists, in his remarks to the reader, that the booksellers were nevertheless pressing him to finish the revision. Under such pressure, Holyoke continues, he distributed part of the work among twelve assistants to hasten the preparation of copy. These helpers, it seemed, borrowed a great many definitions from the Latin dictionary of Thomas Thomas; and besides they incorporated into "our Rider" [7] many strange and rare words which Thomas had gathered from various glossaries.

As a grudging acknowledgment of his heavy borrowing from Thomas and a statement of alleged reasons for doing so, this explanation is important. The subsequent part of Holyoke's words to the reader are no less significant, though they require some explanation. Having acknowledged the borrowing, for which he makes his assistants responsible, Holyoke continues: "Hence these tears, these beginnings of litigation, as if we had caused the great damage to the heirs of Thomas." He confesses the aforesaid borrowing, but denies any damage or harm. If this procedure is to commit an injury, then Thomas himself did the same kind of wrong to Cooper and Calepine, from whose dictionaries Thomas compiled his own, excepting the addition of a few foreign phrases. Furthermore, even Bishop Cooper, Holyoke continues, excerpted his text from Stephanus' *Thesaurus* and Elyot's *Bibliotheca*. It can escape no one's attention, he urges, that Stephanus, Scapula, and other lexicographers proceeded in the same way. So runs his defense, concluding that, after all, there is a greater difference between his *Dictionarium etymologicum* and the Thomasius than there is between Cooper and Elyot.

The pertinent part of Holyoke's Latin address follows.

De tertia huius laboris parte, videlicet de Rideriani Indicis interpretatione, quam ex ipsius Rideri Dictionario Anglico-latino descripsisse, & cuius libet verbi significationem in proprium redigisse locum destinaveram, paucula mihi adhuc dicenda sunt. Cum propter pestem iam tum undique grassantem, aliaque pene infinita impedimenta, ab hoc studio abductus fui, & Bibliopolae interim opus inchoatum a me absolvendum efflagitabant. Ego vero quoniam aliter promissis stare non potui, hanc huius negotij partem, maxima exparte, alijs duodecim studiosis partitim perficiendam commisi: Qui plurimas verborum interpretationes ex Thomasii Dictionario mutuati sunt: Multa etiam Glossemata, quae Thomasius ex quibusdam Glossographis descripsisset, in nostrum Riderum retulerunt. Hinc scilicet lachrymae: Haec harum litium initia: Quasi Thomasii haeredibus summam iniuriam intulissemus. Ad quam accusationem ut breviter, & sicut res est, respondeamus, actionem supradictam confitemur, iniuriam actionem denegamus. Nam si hoc sit iniuriam inferre, eandem ipse Thomasius iniuriam Coupero & Calepino antea intulit, ex quorum Thesauris, missis quibusdam phrasibus, & additis quibusdam vocabulis peregrinis suum Dictionarium composuit. Couperus etiam & ipse ex Stephani Thesauro & Eliotae Bibliotheca, Thesaurum suum decerpsisse ingenue profitetur. Idem etiam Stephanum, Caelium Secundum, Scapulam, aliosque Lexicographos factitasse neminem latere potest. Qui omnes sua Dictionaria ex aliis, vel ex se invicem, addendo, diminuendo, vel alio quovis modo mutuando composuerunt. Adeo ut id verum esse probat proverbium, quod Comicus Poeta simili de causa ad suam defensionem attulit. Nullum iam dictum verbum, quod non dictum prius. Et cum be verbis solummodo agitur, ut in Dictionariis, multo rectius ad nostram defensionem possit accommodari, Sed ut uno verbo dicam, maior est differentia inter Etymologicum Dictionarium, & Thomasium, quam inter Couperum & Eliotam, & de hac re satis.

Thus, according to his own account, protest was directed against Holyoke for his borrowing; and as complaint was obviously made before the printing of the 1606 edition, the first with which Holyoke was associated, we naturally are curious to know how the publisher of the Thomas had discovered Holyoke's plagiarism even before the text was published. So far, no document has come to notice—though there may be one—which reveals the details of the discovery or the nature of the action preferred.

Here are the circumstances, however, which may throw light on the manner of the early discovery of Holyoke's plagiarism. At the time Holyoke began his revision of Rider, John Legate the Elder, son-in-law of Thomas Thomas, was printing in London and had the exclusive right to print Thomas's dictionary. It is quite possible that through a journeyman printer, or a spy, or some one of the twelve assistants of Holyoke, Legate learned of the heavy borrowing from Thomas. He may even have acquired parts of the manuscript of Holyoke's revision as evidence of its relation to the Thomasius. As a result, Legate made vigorous protest, or, as Holyoke's explanation to the reader suggests, may even have brought legal action in an effort to forestall the publication of Holyoke's *Dictionarium etymologicum*, which was to be the Latin-English section of the revised Rider. However Legate acquired information, and whatever the precise nature of his action, he seems not to have accomplished his purpose; for Holyoke and his publisher proceeded, apparently without making any alterations.

The importance of Holyoke's explanation to the reader is that it contains his own acknowledgment of indebtedness to Thomas and refers to the action brought against him by Thomas's heirs. That action was taken against Holyoke for his plundering Thomas's dictionary to compile his own *Dictionarium etymologicum*, or Latin-English dictionary. There is no intimation that Rider, personally, was in any way involved. After all, Legate, representing Thomas's heirs, would hardly now he prosecuting Rider for alleged violation of literary property rights in 1589. Possibly Fuller's comment was a vaguely remembered report of the case in 1606, though it could have concerned a later action. For Holyoke seems not to have been daunted. He continued to gather Thomas's harvest for years, as we shall see in the subsequent account of the Rider-Holyoke dictionaries. But now more particular attention must be devoted to revisions by Holyoke.

The title page of Holyoke's first revised edition of Rider runs thus:

Riders Dictionarie Corrected and Augmented Wherein Riders Index is transformed into a Dictionarie Etymologicall; deriving every word from his native Fountaine, with reasons of the derivations: none yet extant in that kind before. Here also the Barbarous words are ranged into a Dictionarie by themselves, and many words added, never yet in any: With a brief Index of proper names, Collected out of Stephane, Gesner, and others. By Francis Holyoke. London, Printed by Adam Islip. 1606.

The "Riders Dictionarie" in the first line of this title page has reference, of course, to the *Bibliotheca*, or English-Latin dictionary of 1589.[8] Notwithstanding the claim of the editor, the augmentation of this section is slight. In seventy-eight entries, from *to blossome* to *blustring winde*, for example, only two in the 1606 edition are new. This proportion seems to obtain for the rest of the text.

Had the next statement on the title page been noted by students of Rider and Holyoke (even if they had not read the address to the reader), they would have escaped the error of assuming that the original Rider was an English-Latin *and* Latin-English dictionary. The words I refer to are "wherein Riders Index is transformed into a Dictionarie Etymologicall." This is clear English, showing that the Latin-English section was not published until 1606; and for this section and the rest of the claim on the title page, Francis Holyoke alone is responsible. Thereby hangs a tale. What is the source of Holyoke's transformation of Rider's Latin Index? The answer, in part anticipated by the foregoing discussion, is confirmed by the parallels below showing Holyoke's dependence, in the *Dictionarium etymologicum* upon Thomas's *Dictionarium*. As Thomas had borrowed freely from Cooper's *Thesaurus*, it is necessary for this test to present matter from the three compilers.[9]

Cooper (1565)

Confero . . . To beare, cary, put, bring or lay togither: to profite: to set forth: to prepare: to deuise: to talke togither: to giue: to compare or conferre: to employ or bestow: to go: to deferre: to lay or ioyne.

Confertior, confertissimus. Liu. In the thickest prease.

Confessio, Verbale. Cic. A confessing or acknowledging.

Confessus, Participium. That confesseth: also cleare: manifest: without doubt.

Confibula, pen. cor. Cato. A claspe or tache: also a wooden pinne: or thing made to clenche two peeces togither.

Conficio . . . To destroy or slea: to grieue, vexe or torment: to performe: to finish or dispatch: to make an ende of: to bring to passe: to explicate or declare:

Thomas (1596)

Confero . . . To beare, carrie, put, bring, set or lay together: to profit or serue . . . To set forth: to prepare: to deuise, commune or talk together: to giue or contribute: to compare: to conferre . . . To contend: to employ or bestow, to doe: to goe or come to: to lay, impute, or transferre: to attribute or cast vpon, to deferre, or to put off: to lay or ioyne: to turne, to set, bend or apply, to put and commit himselfe: to helpe. . . .

Confertior, issimus, Liv. & *Confertus, a, um* . . . Full, stuffed, replinished, heaped and gathered together, thicke and close together: Also in a flocke or multitude together.

Confessio, onis, f. g. a *Confiteor* . . . A confessing or acknowledging.

Confessus, a, um, part. Active & Passive. That confesseth, acknowledgeth, sheweth or declareth: manifest, certaine, without doubt, not to be denied, that which euery man graunteth. . . .

Confibula, ae, f. g. Cato . . . A claspe or tatche: a wooden pinne or thing made to clench or claspe two pieces together.

Conficio . . . To finish or dispatch, to make an end of . . . To bring to pass, fulfill or accomplish: to mooue: to destroy, murther, or slay, to hurt, grieue, vexe or torment:

Holyoke (1606)

Confero . . . to bear, carry, put, bring, set, to profit, to set forth, to prepare, to talke together, to give, to bestow, to come to, to impute, to deferre, to compare, to turn, to applie, to helpe, to ioyne.

Confertior, issimus, Liv. & *Confertus* . . . full, stuffed, heaped together, thick and close together, also in a flocke or multitude together.

Confessio, onis, fem. gen. a *Confiteor,* a confessing or acknowledging.

Confessus, a, um . . . that confesseth, acknowledgeth, manifest, certaine, without doubt, that which every man graunteth.

Confabula [sic], *ae. f. g.* Cato. a claspe or tache, a wooden pinne or other thing to clench or claspe two things together.

Conficio . . . to finish, to dispatch, to fulfill, to destroy, to slay, to kill, to grieve, to declare, to procure, to provide, to breake, to consume, to chew meate, to digest,

Cooper (1565)	Thomas (1596)	Holyoke (1606)
to gather money: to breake: to consume or waste: to make: to chawe meate: to digest.	to explicate or declare: to gather, prouide, get, procure, or worke: to breake, knacke, or cracke: to consume or waste: to make: to commit: to chew meate: to digest: to runne: to pass ouer: to conclude. . . .	to run, to passe over, to conclude.
Conficiens . . . That keepeth a diligent regester or booke of all that he doeth.	*Conficiens* . . . He which finisheth, dispatcheth, bringeth forth, procureth or worketh.	*Conficiens* . . . he which finisheth or dispatcheth, bringeth forth, procureth, worketh.
Confictio, confictionis, Verbale. A feigning or new inuenting.	*Confictio, onis, f. g. Verb. a confingo* . . . A faining or new inuenting.	*Confictio, onis, f. g. verb a confingo* . . . A faining.
Confictus . . . Deuised: feigned: counterfeyted: imagined. . . .	*Confictus* . . . Ter. Deuised, fained, counterfeited, inuented.	*Confictus* . . . Ter. Devised, counterfeited, invented.
Confido . . . To trust: to haue sure confidence: to bee sure: to dare.	*Confido* . . . To trust or put his trust in, to haue sure confidence: to be sure: to dare: to beleeue and esteeme, to haue a good hope, to depend upon. . . .	*Confido* . . . to trust, to dare, to believe or esteeme, to have a good hope, to depend upon, to be bold.

The entries above show that Holyoke derived quite literally from Thomas in compiling his Latin-English dictionary or *Dictionarium etymologicum,* printed with Rider's dictionary in the 1606 edition. Holyoke did not use every entry in the Thomas, nor did he borrow the phrases and sentences to illustrate meaning and usage. He has also a small proportion of terms not found in Thomas. But comparison of Holyoke with Thomas, Cooper, and others shows that Holyoke preferred Thomas and that this is the source of a large percentage of his word list, together with the English phrasing.

In the index of proper names (in subsequent editions, the "Dictionarium Propriorum Nominum Etymologicum") Holyoke also follows Thomas's precedent and borrows some of his sketches. Compare the following:

Thomas (1596)	Holyoke (1606)
Aaron, Was sonne to Amram, and brother to Moses . . . Also a King of the Persians. . . .	*Aaron* . . . the sonne of Amram, brother to Moses, also a king of the Persians: also a captaine of the Saracens.
Aba, Daughter to Xenophanes . . . Also a towne in Arabie, and a citie in Phocis. Also a hill in Armenia. Also a king of Hungarie. . . .	*Aba,* Daughter to Xenophanes: also a towne in Arabia, and a citty in Phocis, also a hill in Armenia: also a king of Hungarie.

Thomas (1596)	Holyoke (1606)
Abacus. The chiefe citie of Cevola in India, now called Granata.	*Abacus,* the chiefe cittie of Cevola in India, nowe called Granata.
Abadir, A stone which Saturne deuoured in steade of Iupiter.	*Abadir,* a stone which Saturne devoured in steed of Iupiter.
Abas . . . Sonne to Lynceus and to Hypermnestra . . . Also a Troiane companion to Aeneas.	*Abas* . . . sonne to Lynceus and Hypermēstra: also a companion of AEneas, also the name of a Poet, also a king of the Thuscians, also a Centaure.
Abas . . . A poet that built the towne Abae: also the name of a Tuscan king, and of a Centaure.	

As a concluding remark, we may say that in the Rider-Holyoke of 1606 we find *Riders Dictionarie,* the major portion of which Rider, in 1589, had adopted from Thomas Thomas; the *Dictionarium etymologicum,* Latin-English, which Holyoke had drawn largely from Thomas; and the index of proper names, which uses part of the matter from a similar section of Thomas. Is it any wonder that the heirs of Thomas made objection? They experienced the bitter irony of seeing the matter of their own dictionary virtually appropriated by Holyoke and turned into their most formidable competitor.

In 1612 a new edition of the Rider-Holyoke was printed at Oxford by Joseph Barnes.[10] The general title page asserts that this is *Riders Dictionarie,* corrected and enriched with above five hundred words, and that there is annexed a "Dictionarie Etymologicall." A second title page, in Latin, precedes the *Dictionarium etymologicum,* claiming for this part augmentation of more than four thousand words. For the Rider there is the running title "Bibliotheca Rideri Scholastica"; for the *Dictionarium,* there are two running titles: "Dictionarii Etymologici Pars Prima," containing approved Latin terms, and "Dictionarii Etymologici Pars Secunda," with the barbarous and obsolete words; finally, for the proper names, "Dictionarium Propriorum Nominum Etymologicum."

Holyoke's claim of augmentation of Rider, that is, the English-Latin, is recurrent throughout the series of Rider-Holyoke dictionaries. In 1606, we read "Corrected and Augmented"; in 1612, "Corrected and with the Addition of above Five Hundred Words Enriched"—a phrase repeated in the editions of 1617 and 1626, though in his address to the reader Nicholas Gray makes no such claim for the 1626 edition. In the edition of 1627, Holyoke asserts augmentation with the addition of many hundreds of words not extant in any former edition; and in 1633 he extends this boast by adding "both out of the Law, and out of the Latine, French, and other Languages." The last statement is repeated in the issues of 1640 and 1648. Various tests for amplification of Rider fail to substantiate Holyoke's claims. The 78 entries, for example, between *to blossome* and *blustering winde,* in the 1589 Rider, are increased by 2 in 1606 and 1612. Consider the entries between *exact* and *executioner:* 100 in 1589; 105 in 1606 and 1612; 106 in 1617 and 1626; and 108 in 1633, 1640, and 1648. In *"E ante V"* the number of entries varies from 58 in 1589 to 64 in 1648; in *"O ante V,"* from 153 to 157; in *"V ante E,"* from 79 to 83. Although there are some entries added and some corrections, the samplings indicate, despite Holyoke's claims, relatively little augmentation of Rider's English-Latin from 1589 to 1659.

As to augmentation of the *Dictionarium etymologicum,* or Latin-English, in the 1612 edition, Holyoke has a better case. Although there are not 4,000 added entries, as the compiler affirms, there is substantial increase. Evidence of amplification appears in the number of added entries between *confero* and *confido* and in other blocks in the "Prima Pars," or approved words, and especially in the "Pars Secunda," or barbarous and obsolete terms. Of the first 47 entries in "Pars Secunda," 40 are from Thomas, and of the 67 entries from *ablegmina* to *abstentus,* 57 are from Thomas. Thomas's dictionary seems, in fact, to be the principal source of augmentation for the Latin-English of 1612. Although Legate probably was aware of the continued augmentation of Holyoke's *Dictionarium etymologicum* at the expense of the Thomasius, we find no record of protest between 1606 and 1617. This silence may be due to the circumstance that the edition of 1612 was printed at Oxford. But the situation was changed when, in 1617, a new edition of the Rider-Holyoke was printed in London.[11]

The 1617 edition is very similar in the wording of title pages, in its running titles, and in arrangement and content to the Oxford edition of 1612. There is the innovation of introducing a certain number of Greek equivalents with the Latin entries, a practice in vogue in the Thomas dictionaries from 1596. For the Greek terms, somewhat increased in subsequent editions of the Rider-Holyoke, Thomas is one source, though Calepine and others are drawn upon in the course of the several editions. For the Latin-English of 1617, Thomas remains the primary source, as a comparative study of the following entries in Cooper, Thomas, and Holyoke reveals: *ancillor, ancus, anhelo, arbustum, astrum, astruo, augur, basis, bitumen, bucculae, calamitas, censor, clepsydra, digero, diuersorium, dolon, dorsum,* and *emeritum.* In these as in hundreds of other entries, Holyoke's following of Thomas's English phrasing is of a very literal, not to say servile, kind. More disturbing possibly to Legate and other heirs of Thomas than the continuous raids on their lexicon is the circumstance that the 1617 edition of the Rider-Holyoke appeared in three issues: printed by Adam Islip for Thomas Man, William Leake, and Thomas Adams.[12] It must have seemed to Legate and his sponsors that

Holyoke and his publishers were set on driving the Thomasius off the market. Complaint was probably made immediately, and by 1619 this was a matter of public record.

Meantime, John Legate the Younger succeeded his father as printer of the Thomasius. In the 1619 edition of Thomas's dictionary, the first to appear since the Rider-Holyoke of 1617, young Legate makes vigorous protest against Holyoke. This is found in the dedication to Baron Verulam, Lord Bacon. Legate charges that there are those who, without permission, have transcribed the Thomasius and dare sell it under the name of Rider. He will demand judgment. His accusation is not of Rider, but obviously of Holyoke and his publishers, though Legate does not here mention these names.

Idem adultus, longeque quàm à patre acceperam, auctior, cum iam iterum prodeat, vestrum (Honoratissime Domine) audet implorare patrocinium. Hoc si audacter nimis, nec fas sit aram tam sublimem, ac sacram vulgari attrectatione, temerari, benignitatem vestram adprecor, ne nutricij temerarij culpam luat alumnus innocens, ac nescius, ne, quod ego peccarim patronum quaerens, se pati queratur liber insons. Quo quidem patrocinio haud indigere vix poterit, cum in trahaci ac rapaci hoc saeculo, qui messem alienam inuadant nunquam sint defuturi. Persensimus sanè antehac artes quorundam dolosas, ac delusorias, qui hunc *Thomasii* mei filium genuinum, adoptiuum meum, ausi sunt inuitum in alienam familiam transcribere, ac ridenda audacia *Rideri* nomine venditare. Ita scilicet huiusce nostri frontem tantum immutarunt, qui prius perfricuerunt suam. Idem vero iam confidentius, si licuerit sub tanti Ducis vexillo praeliari, de vendicijs postulabit, ac, si denuo huiusmodi fucum, imò furtum fecerint, plagij reos aget; tua modo aequis faueat inceptis tutela ac clementia, dignissime, ac sub supremo *Iacobo* maximè iuris humani diribitior: quem Ecclesiae, Reipublicae, Academiisque, iustitiae, aequitati, foelicitati seruet incolumem, ac florentem Deus Opt. Max. Ita, cum omnibus bonis, comprecor

Honoris Vestri Obseruantissimus,
IOANNES LEGAT.

Here is not only the accusation of plagiarism but also an indication that Legate had for long observed the indiscriminate borrowing from the Thomasius. Legate's exposure of Holyoke seems not to have fazed the lexicographer, though the warning was heeded by Adam Islip, the printer and publisher. Before Islip published the next edition of the Rider-Holyoke, in 1626, he had it revised and modified considerably, not by Holyoke, but by Nicholas Gray. Gray had the M.A. degree from Christ Church, Oxford, June 10, 1613, had served as headmaster of Charterhouse School, and was, at the time of the revision of the dictionary, headmaster of Merchant Taylors' School.

The general title page of the new edition,[13] placed before *Riders Dictionarie*, is similar in phrasing to that of 1617, adding, however, "many vsefull alterations, emendations," etc. The title page for the Latin-

English part is much changed; it drops the old phrasing "Dictionarium Etymologicum," supplies "Rideri Dictionarium Seueriore Trutina Castigatum," and explains that the former divisions into pure, or approved, Latin words, obsolete and rare, and proper names are now placed together in a single alphabetical order. For the English-Latin of the original Rider, Gray claims, in the address to the reader, only corrections and emendations, despite the assertion on the title page of more than five hundred words enrichment. For the Latin-English part there are many changes, including omissions, alterations, and additions. Of course much of what Holyoke had borrowed from Thomas was retained, but there was a definite effort to get away from the *Dictionarium etymologicum,* and apparently no further borrowing from Thomas. New matter derived from Calepine and Becmanus. Gray's is a competent piece of work, in which the Rider-Holyoke is greatly improved. In the preparation of this edition Holyoke seems to have had no part. He was, in fact, busily engaged in preparing another edition, after the pattern of the 1617 one, for a printer away from London.

Disregarding the earlier exposure and warning by Legate, Holyoke continued to levy on Thomas; and in 1627 he had printed at Oxford by William Turner another edition of his dictionary. The general title page,[14] beginning "Dictionarivm Etymologicvm Latinvm," is literally filled with the compiler's exposition of the ways in which he has augmented and improved the various parts of the text: the Latin-English, the proper names, and the English-Latin. A second title page, prefacing the Rider, declares that this has been augmented by many hundreds of words not extant in any former edition. In this edition of 1627 the etymological, or Latin-English, dictionary is, for the first time, placed at the beginning of the volume. The twofold division of this part is abandoned and the pure and improper words placed in one alphabet, possibly in imitation of Gray's edition in the preceding year. The Greek equivalents, we are told, are here "in more exactnesse then ever were in Calepine, Morelius, or any other." The principal source for the slight augmentation of the Latin-English is still Thomas. The claim of augmentation of the English-Latin by many hundreds of words is not supported by the facts. Indeed both title pages constitute an exaggerated bit of advertising.

If the rearrangement of matter and the exaggerations of the title page were intended to deceive, they were not successful. After the appearance of the 1627 edition, John Legate repeated the accusation, indicating that he would now go to court. His statement, echoing in part the earlier one, is found in the dedication to Thomas Coventry, Baron of Alesbury, in the 1631 edition of the Thomasius.

Huiusce Author Dictionarij primarius, Thomasius erat, Avus meus maternus: cuius famae, me nepotem eius pijssimè parentatum iudicabunt omnes, vbi Posthumo suo Thomae, Sponsorem Te (nobilissime Domine) accersere conatus fuerim. Boni igitur (vt soles) humilitèr oro, istocce Dictionarium vt accipias; quod Decima iam tertia vice (ultrà numerum laborum Herculis, labore sanè plusquàm Herculeo) publici iuris fecerim: Digneris (obsecro) Tu qui Res gubernas publicas, & verba tutari publica. Tanto quidem patrocinio indigere vix poterit; cum in trahaci ac rapaci hoc saeculo, qui messem alienam invadant, nunquam sint defuturi. Persenserit etenim liber iste, persenserit (inquam) antehac artes quorundam dolosas ac delusorias, qui hunc Thomasij mei filium genuinum, adoptivum meum, ausi sunt invitum in alienam familiam transcribere, ac ridendâ audaciâ Rideri nomine venditare: ita (scilicet) huiusce nostri frontem tantùm immutaverunt, qui priùs perfricuerunt suam. Liceat igitur (Honoratissime Domine) mea mihi vendicare, & coràm Tanti Judicis tribunale, in tam iusto aequitatis foro, eos de vindicijs sic postulare, vt si denuò huiusmodi fucum imò furtum fecerint, Plagij reos agere. Deus Opt. Max. Te aequissimum Justitiae Diribitorem, Regis, Regni, & Ecclesiae bono, diù servet incolumem, florentem diù. Ita cum bonis omnibus comprecor,

Honoris vestri
observantissimus,
IOANNES LEGAT.

It is probable that Legate now took action against Holyoke. Confirmation of this inference is found in the 1633 edition of the Rider-Holyoke, printed in London by Adam Islip and Felix Kyngston. This volume shows considerable, if not fundamental, changes, as we shall see below. In the Ad Lectorem, Holyoke is on the defence.[15] He maintains that there are those who are bringing action to injure him. In borrowing from Thomas, he was following a common practice of lexicographers. Cooper, he insists, translated his *Thesaurus* from Frisius; Thomas himself borrowed from Cooper and Calepine and later from Junius. As this address is so revealing and so generally overlooked, I insert all the relevant portion:

Sed nunc tempus est ut eorum criminationibus respondeam, qui mihi iniuriam actionem intendunt, quasi ex alienis Dictionariis praecipue Thomasianis expoliatis, nostrum etymologicum construxerimus, grave crimen si modo verum & bonis viris indignum. Sed si nihil in his sit factum quod alii omnes Lexicographi ante me non factitarunt, spero bonos & aequos aestimatores eandem libertatem mihi indulturos, quam in alijs tantopere collaudarunt. Cooperus Tirisij [i.e., Frisii?] Tigurini Dictionarium Latino Germanicum, ni fallor, transtulit. Suum autem Thomasius ex Calepino & Coopero primum compilavit, quod vestigia adhuc recentia ostendunt. Postea ex Iunij nomenclatura & quibusdam glossarijs & herbarijs auxit & ampliavit: tandem reverendus vir D. Philemon Hollandus doctissimus medicus iuxta ac philologus, ipsum Thomasium ex bonis auctoribus adeo mirifice ditavit, ut nullum in eo genere Dictionarium adhuc exstet, quod pro vocabulorum numero, perfecta vocum interpretatione & phrasibus selectis huic Thomasiano adaequari merito possit: sibi habeat & per me licet, quod tanta cura & impendio comparavit. In prima huius Etymologici editione, quorundam verborum interpretamenta ex Thomasio decerpta, &

in nostrum translata eorum negligentia factum, quibus id oneris demandatum erat, ut eadem vocabula interpretata ex Ridero & Coopero excerperent, non nego: at vero in proximis editionibus ullam me voculam [*sic*], quod sciam attigisse, quam alibi non invenerim, nisi apposito Thomas. nomine aut T nominis signo, id vero pernego. Quos si idem in suo Anglicolatino [Latino-anglico?] Dictionario observasset, *literam caninam* ad nauseam usque recitasset.

What Holyoke writes in the Latin address quoted above is only part truth, apparently intended to confuse the issue. For example, he reluctantly admits that he borrowed freely from the Thomasius in the first, or 1606, edition of his *Etymologicum;* even so, he was following the example of Cooper and even Thomas himself. In subsequent editions, Holyoke maintains, he indicated by the name Thomas or by the letter *T* the terms that could be found only in the Thomasius. The alleged symbols to indicate borrowings from Thomas do not, however, appear in the Rider-Holyoke texts. On the other hand, Holyoke increased his debt to Thomas in the editions of 1612 and 1617 and made no further acknowledgment. It is true that many of the definitions which Holyoke took from Thomas had appeared in Cooper and Elyot, forebears of Thomas. But a comparative study of the various texts shows that in the earlier editions Holyoke's debt was almost wholly to Thomas. Holyoke's statement confuses the uncritical reader.

The plan of the 1633 edition,[16] with the Latin-English first, is similar to that of 1627. The title pages also are similar in content (and prolixity) but not identical. The heading of the *Dictionarium etymologicum* emphasizes the fact that Holyoke alone is responsible for the correction and amplification of this edition. And on the title page of the Latin-English, we read: "Now for the fourth time newly corrected and greatly augmented by the great industrie and paines of Francis Holyoke." Claims of increase in the Rider English-Latin are, as usual, much exaggerated. In the Latin-English there is definite expansion, not so much in the addition of new entries as in the extension of those already in the text. Into these Holyoke inserted Latin passages, often including synonyms, from a seventeenth-century edition of Calepine, or etymological information from Fungerus or Becmanus. The English phrasing, drawn from Thomas, is retained. There are, to be sure, some new entries, usually very short. But the general process of augmentation in the 1633 edition is as described. Such overelaboration of entries does not enhance their value. But this, apparently, was Holyoke's forced response to action brought against him by the heirs of Thomas Thomas.

A threefold comparison of texts—Thomas's *Dictionarium* (1596), Holyoke's *Etymologicum* (1627), and the revised *Etymologicum* (1633)— from the entries *expedio* to *exploro,* or almost any other series of entries, in the three texts offers ample evidence of Holyoke's procedure. Below are a few of the entries referred to.

Thomas (1596)	Holyoke (1627)	Holyoke (1633)
Expedio . . . To dispatch, quitte, discharge, or rid, to bring one out of trouble: to deliuer, to unloose, to undoe: to prepare, to set in a readiness: to bring to passe: to speeke: to declare, tell, utter, or show briefly: to determine: to come to passe, or take effect: to find means to get: to finish, or end: to conclude. . . .	. . . *Quasi pedum ligamenta dissolvo ab antiquo pedio a pes* . . . To dispatch, to discharge, to deliver, to unloose, to prepare, to bring to passe, to utter briefly, to conclude.	. . . *Quasi pedum ligamenta dissolvo, ab antiquo pedio, a pes* . . . *extrico, Libero; parcere, accingere, extollere: est etiam eventum habere.* To dispatch, to discharge, to deliver, to unloose, to prepare, to bring to passe, to utter briefly, to take effect, to conclude.
Expeditio . . . A setting forth towardes warre, an expedition, a voyage.	. . . A setting forward to the warre, a voyage.	. . . *exercitus, apparatus belli, bellum.* A setting forward to the war, a voyage.
Expeditus . . . Readie, in a readinesse: not letted or troubled: soon prouided and gotten: quick, nimble, light, prompt, easie to dispatch: deliuered, dispatched, ridde out of. *Expeditus miles.* Salust . . . A light harnessed soldier.	. . . Ready, soon prouided, quicke, light, dispatched, rid out, also light harnessed.	. . . *promptus, facilis, nullis impedimentis oneratus. Expediti milites armaturae & sine impedimentis. Expeditior comp., facilior.* Ready, soon provided, quick, light, dispatched, rid out: also light harnessed.
Expendo . . . To weigh, to ponder, consider, or examine straightly or diligently . . . to spend money . . . to lay out: to pay: to abide or sustain.	. . . To weigh, consider, to spend money . . . to lay out, to pay, to sustaine.	. . . *pondero, aliq. exacte examino, considero, quandoque lucere & exoluere.* To weigh, consider, to spend money . . . to lay out, to pay, to sustaine.
Expenso . . . to seale up and deliuer money by waight. Also to recompence. Macrob.	. . . To seale up and deliver money by weight, also to recompence, to lay forth.	. . . *expensare apud Juriconsultos est expensam pecuniam consignare, ac tradere: interdum est compensare.* To seale up and deliver money by weight, also to recompence, to lay forth.
Expergiscor . . . To	. . . Bec. *expergo, pergis-*	. . . Bec. *expergo, pergiscor*

Thomas (1596)	Holyoke (1627)	Holyoke (1633)
awake, to be stirred up.	*cor* . . . To awake, to be stirred up.	. . . *expergiscor habet passivam significationem, aut neutralem absolutam,* Cicero. *expergiscimini aliquando atque exurgite, ab expergiscor fit experrectus, expergitus autem ab expergor* . . . To awake, to be stirred up.
Expeto . . . To desire much, to couet: to happen, to indeauour to get, to aske, to inquire. *Expetere preces a Deo pro precari Deum.* Plaut.	. . . to desire much, to endeavour to get, to aske.	. . . *avide cupio, opto, desidero, expetere preces a Deo pro precari Deum,* Plaut. *expetere poenas ab aliquo, supplicium expetere, al. pro evenire.* To desire much, to endeavour, to get, to ask.
Expio . . . To pacifie God with satisfaction or praier, to recompence, to make satisfaction or amends for, to purge or clense by sacrifice, to hallow.	. . . To pacifie God with sacrifice or prayer, to make satisfaction, to purge by sacrifice, to hallow.	. . . *purgo, mundum ac purum facio, placo, expiare scelera est punire.* To pacific God with sacrifice or prayer, to make satisfaction, to purge by sacrifice, to hallow.[17]

The parallel entries above show one way in which Holyoke augmented his edition of 1633: he inserted, before the English phrases, Latin synonyms or explanatory phrases drawn from Calepine and others. This procedure of course made his text appear very different, in the particular definitions, from the Thomas. It should be observed, however, that Holyoke tenaciously held to the English phrases derived from Thomas. In many cases, such as in *expedit, expello, expes, expiabilis, expiatio, expilatio, expilator,* and other words not listed among the parallels, there are no changes from Thomas through the Holyoke of 1633. There are, however, occasional new entries, as in *expenno* and *expignoro.* In short, Holyoke made no radical or fundamental changes in the edition of 1633. The changes in general consist, not in the modification or omission of matter taken from Thomasius, but in insertions of passages from Calepine and others concerned mostly with etymology. The entries transcribed below are from the Calepine of 1609. Compared with the same words in the parallels given above, they show Calepine as a major source of augmentation.

Expedio . . . Extrico, libero, & quasi pedum ligamenta dissolvo. . . .
Expeditio . . . Exercitus apparatus belli, bellum. . . .

Riders

DICTIONARIE,

CORRECTED AND AUG-MENTED WITH THE ADDITION OF

many hundred Words both out of the Law, and out of the
Latine, French, and other languages, such as were and are
with us in common use, but never printed till now,
to the perfecting of the worke.

THE BARBAROVS WORDS WHICH WERE

many hundreds are expunged, to the helpe of young
Scholars, which before they used in stead of good Words.

In the end of the Dictionarie you shall finde certaine gene-
rall heads of Birds, Colours, Dogs, Fishes, Hawkes, Hearbs,
Numbers, Stones, Trees, Weights.

Lastly, the names of the chiefe places and Townes in England,
Scotland, and Ireland, &c. which were never in R I D E R S *before.*

Also hereunto is annexed certaine Tables of Weights and Measures, the va-
luation of auncient and moderne Coines; as also a table of the Hebrew, Greek,
and Latine Measures, reduced to our English Standard and Assise: and
the weights used in Physick, none of which were ever in
R I D E R S *worke.*

Whereunto is joyned a Dictionarie Etymolo-
gicall, deriving each word from his proper fountaine, the first that ever
was extant in this kind, with many worthy Castigations and Additions, in
this last Edition, as will appeare in the Title and
Epistle before it.

Now newly corrected and much augmented by
F R A N C I S H O L Y-O K E.

LONDON,
Imprinted by *Felix Kingston.* 1649.

Expeditus . . . Promptus, paratus, nullis impedimentis oneratus . . . Expediti milites, dicuntur leuioris armaturae & sine impedimentis . . . Expeditior labor, facilior. . . .

Expendo . . . Pondero . . . Quandoque significat exactè exanimo, considere . . . Quandoque luere, exoluere. . . .

Expensare; apud Iuriconsultos, est expensam pecuniam consignare ac tradere . . . Interdum expensare est compensare. . . .

Expergisco . . . Expergiscor autem passiuam habet significationem . . . aut certe neutralem absolutam. Cic. Expergiscimini aliquando, atque exurgite. Ab expergiscor fit Experrectus . . . expergitus autem ab expergor. . . .

By the process described, Holyoke expands considerably the bulk of the 1633 Latin-English dictionary. Although some new words are added and the total word list now exceeds considerably that in the editions, for example, of 1612 and 1617, we get the impression of considerable padding in this latest volume.

As early as 1617, Holyoke introduced into the *Dictionarium etymologicum,* or Latin-English, a certain number of Greek terms, equivalents of the Latin entries. Many of the Greek words are directly from Thomas, some from Calepine. These are supplemented by further borrowings of Greek from Joannes Fungerus' *Etymologicum Latinum opus* (1605), under *aborigines, abyssus,* and *acapnus;* and from Christianus Becmanus' *Manductio ad Latinam linguam: nec non de originibus Latinae linguae* (1619), under *grabatus, gracilis, grus, guberno,* and *gymnasium.* From the last two lexicographers Holyoke may have borrowed the Hebrew terms which appear in the 1633 and subsequent editions. The Greek and Hebrew constitute a source of augmentation for this volume.

In this edition also the proper-name dictionary is somewhat amplified. Matter from Thomas is retained and amplifications made from Gray's edition of 1626, from Becmanus, and possibly others.

The Rider-Holyoke of 1640,[18] "now the fifth time newly corrected and very much augmented" by Francis Holyoke, is, in content and sources, little different from that of 1633. Noteworthy, however, is the elimination of barbarous and obsolete words, and the reverting to the arrangement—the English-Latin of Rider first and the Latin-English of Holyoke last—of the editions of 1617 and earlier. The three issues, and a possible fourth, of this edition constitute a bibliographical problem.[19] This problem need not detain us here, since in content the issues seem to be identical. As a simple test of the persistence in this edition of the Latin word list and the English definitions from Thomas, compare the entries from *nasute* to *nates.* In the 1640 Holyoke there are twenty-seven entries in this block, twenty-five of which have English definitions. Of these, nine-

Title page of the 1649 edition of John Rider's dictionary as revised by Francis Holyoke, from a copy in the University of Texas Library (opposite)

teen correspond closely to the English in the 1631 Thomasius. In other series of consecutive definitions the percentage might vary somewhat, but the illustration is representative of the relationship of the two dictionaries in 1640.

To the years 1648–49 belongs the next issue of the dictionaries published under the editorship of Francis Holyoke. This volume was printed by Felix Kingston as "now the sixth time newly corrected." [20] In this edition the *Dictionarium etymologicum* is placed first, as in 1633, and dated 1648; at the end is *Riders Dictionarie*, English-Latin, with the date 1649 on its special title page. How much time elapsed between the printing of the two is not known; if they were printed, as apparently they were, to be bound in the same volume, the time could not have been long. It seems likely that the Latin-English part was printed late in 1648, and the Rider at the beginning of 1649. At any rate, the dates have been confusing; sometimes the earlier, sometimes the later, is stated as the time of publication. As the issues I have examined have the two parts in one volume always with the two dates, we record the double dating of 1648–49. This issue used the old title pages of the 1640 edition, simply shifting them in accordance with the rearrangement of the contents. And the contents are the same, including printer's signatures and catchwords, as in the 1640 edition. All that has been said of subject matter and sources of the 1640 edition is therefore applicable to the 1648–49.

The last edition of the Rider-Holyoke was printed in London "by J. T. for Andrew Crook," in 1659. Although this is an independent edition, the arrangement of materials within the text proper and the wording of the title page, except for slight differences in spelling and alignment, correspond to those of the 1640 edition. There is no augmentation.

On etymology in the Rider-Holyoke dictionaries, we have touched but lightly. It has seemed better to reserve this topic for a special word here. As we have seen, Holyoke termed his Latin-English lexicon an "Etymological Latin Dictionary," in 1606; and in the course of its history for more than forty years he emphasized on title pages, in addresses to the reader, and especially in the accumulation of etymologies in his text, this aspect of his work as lexicographer. For this work he had ample precedent, not in Elyot, Cooper, or Thomas, but in Varro, Festus, Isidore, Calepine, Robert Stephanus, Baret, and, in the seventeenth century, Fungerus and Becmanus and Minsheu. All of these, excepting Stephanus, Baret, and Minsheu, Holyoke cites at one time or another in his text. Probably his debt to Calepine is greatest, but in his assembling of etymologies for Latin terms, not English, Holyoke was eclectic. He seems to have gathered and selected from a wide range of sources. In this work he doubtless took considerable pride. This too was a kind of compensation for his excessive borrowing from Thomas. The etymologies in his text enabled Holyoke to reply to his accusers that there was a greater difference between his dictionary and Thomasius than there was between Cooper and Elyot.

Of course there is little, if anything, new in the assembled etymologies of Holyoke, interesting as some of them are. Perhaps the most that can be said is that Holyoke gave prominence to the subject through the first half of the seventeenth century and thus prepared the way for the more important etymological dictionaries of Skinner and Junius and others in the late seventeenth and early eighteenth centuries. Examples of Holyoke's more extensive etymologizing appear under *consilium*, where the compiler cites Varro, Festus, and Fungerus; and under *examen*, *etymologia*, and *fastii*. In support of the etymology of *fastii*, Holyoke cites Festus, Isidore, Fungerus, and Joseph Scaliger. Entertaining are the etymologies, recorded by Holyoke but developed much earlier, of *contemplate*, which derives from *temple*, a place which may be viewed from every side; of *congruo* ("to agree"), from *gruibus* ("cranes"), because they don't live apart from each other; of *conniveo* ("to wink"), from *con* and *nix*, *nivis* ("snow"), because snow dazzles the sight and causes one to open and close the eyes, to wink; and of *conjugium* ("marriage"), from *jugum* ("yoke"), by which a husband is yoked to his wife. Below is given a representative list of Holyoke's etymologies.

Congruo . . . *dict. à gruibus, quià non se segregant,* (*al. leg. quia non fere segregantur, sive cum volant, sive cum pascuntur.* Fest.) . . . To agree, to serve to the purpose, to bee of one minde.

Conjugium . . . *à coniugo, vel jugo, plurimi à jugo communi quo maritus jungitur uxori,* Isidor. *Conjugium dict. quasi sint conjuncti* . . . Marriage, wedlocke. . . .

Conniveo . . . *ex con & niveo, unde nicto, oculorum palpebras moveo, modo claudo, modo aperio, & ponitur pro dissimulo* . . . *alii ex con & nix, nivis, quia nix aciem oculorum perstringit, et al. a con & nitor, al. ex con & nuo* . . . To winke or twinkle with the eyes. . . .

Contemplor . . . *contemplari dictum est à templo, id est, loco qui omni parte aspici, vel ex quo omnis pars videri potest, quem antiqui templum nominabant.* Fest. To behold diligently, to muse upon, to consider, to take view of. . . .

Exercitus . . . *quod exercitatio, vel exercendo sit melior,* Varr. Ulp. *ab exercitatione itidem ducit, al. exercitus, ab ex & arceo, dict. quia expellit & hostes profligat* . . . An army. . . .

Equus . . . *quidam ab equus quod equipares solent quadriges jungi,* Isid. *equi dicti eo quod quando quadrigis jungebatur.* Scal. . . . An horse. . . .

Februarius . . . (*dict. quod tum in extremo mense anni populus februaretur, id est, lustraretur & purgaretur, vel à Junone februata, quam alii februalem vel febrilem, quod ipsi eo mense sacra fiebant.* V. Festus *cum* Scal. & Isid. & Var.) . . . The month of February.

Fortis . . . *quidam à ferendo adversa, vel à fors, nam fors adjuvat audaces, al. à ferro quod sit durus, nec molliatur* . . . Strong, valiant, mighty, constant, courageous. . . .

Frivolus . . . Plin. . . . *quasi fere valens obolum, MS.* Fest. *frivola sunt proprie vasa fictilia, quassa, unde dicta verba frivola . . . frivolum alii à frio as quod est inane, leve, nulliusque momenti.* Frivolous, of no account. . . .

Graculus . . . à garrulitate, graculi, à sono oris vocati, sive à gerendo dicti, quod jacta segetum semina plurimum gerant, vel quod ex olivetis cubitum se recipientis duas pedibus buccas tertiam ore ferant. haec Festus . . . The Cornish Chough. . . .

Importunus . . . quod caret portu vel quiete, ubi nullus portus est, ut opportunus ex ob & portus. Perot. Festus. *importunum est in quo nullum est auxilium, velut esse solet portus navigantibus . . .* Out of season, inconvenient, urgent, cruell. . . .

Aside from the etymologies, in which Holyoke apparently follows no one lexicographer consistently, a few words should be said concerning his method. Notwithstanding the title of his Latin-English dictionary, Holyoke lists his words in alphabetical order. He marks long and short vowels to show the pronunciation, indicates with abbreviations the part of speech, the declension of nouns and adjectives, the conjugation of verbs, and, often, the classical authority for the term. In all this, he follows closely Thomas. For his etymologies, except in compound verbs, there is in the Thomasius no precedent. The illustrative phrases and sentences from classical authorities to indicate meaning and usage—a laudable practice of Thomas and his forebears—Holyoke omits.

Such is the rather complex history of the Rider-Holyoke dictionaries. The role of Holyoke as reviser and editor is not praiseworthy. For the exaggerated claims of almost constant augmentation, the publishers may have been at least partly responsible. For the virtual appropriation of the Thomas dictionary, Holyoke alone is accountable. Even in an age when borrowing and imitation were widespread, there is no more flagrant disregard of literary property rights than in Holyoke's action.

The Thomas-Rider-Holyoke relationship seems now fairly clear. It is desirable, however, to restate succinctly the results of this investigation. The foundation for a misconception was laid in 1589, when John Rider gave to his *Bibliotheca scholastica* (an English-Latin dictionary) the subtitle of *A Double Dictionarie*—which it was not. Holyoke, as a reviser of Rider, actually made this a "double dictionarie" in 1606, being himself the compiler of the Latin-English part, which he called a "Dictionarie Etymologicall." This he extracted largely from Thomas's Latin-English dictionary, without permission. In subsequent editions (1612, 1617, and 1627) Holyoke continued his raids, not, however, without the protest of John Legate the Younger, heir of Thomas and printer of the dictionary. Legate accused Holyoke, not Rider, who had no hand after 1589 in the dictionary published under his name. Finally, Legate brought action, as Holyoke inadvertently admits in the Ad Lectorem to the *Etymologicum* of 1633, and forced Francis Holyoke to make changes, however unsatisfactory. Undoubtedly, Thomas Fuller had heard something of all this, though he did not have his facts straight. And Fuller's gossipy note has been a source of error from 1662 to the present day.

There is no adequate bibliography of the Rider-Holyoke dictionaries. The reasons for this deficiency are not far to seek. Periodically, for almost sixty years, the texts were printed; and for the first thirty-eight years they were issued alternately at Oxford and London. From 1612 on there were two title pages in each edition: one for *Riders Dictionarie*, English-Latin, and one for Holyoke's *Dictionarium etymologicum*, Latin-English. There were also running titles, or headings, for other sections, such as the dictionary of proper names, which need not be considered here. But the order of arrangement in the 1612 edition—Rider's English-Latin first and Holyoke's Latin-English later—does not hold for all subsequent issues. In the edition of 1627, for example, the order is reversed. First is the general title page, applicable to the whole volume, and indicating the arrangement of the parts as (1) *Dictionarium etymologicum*, (2) "Dictionarium Proprium Nominum," and (3) *Riders Dictionarie*. For the Rider, however, there is a second title page, which, though applicable to the English-Latin of Rider, adds, "Hereunto is joyned a dictionary Etymologicall." But as we have seen, Holyoke's etymological dictionary stands first in this volume; and the quoted statement is without discernible meaning. Though the arrangement of the 1627 edition holds for that of 1633, it reverts once more in 1640 to that of 1612.

To the confusion produced by alternating arrangements of materials and by overlapping title pages, we may add the complications resulting from multiple issues of a given edition, as, for example, three in 1617, and three, possibly four, in 1640; and also occasional erratic dating, as 1639 for 1640. If we recall, further, that some biographers and bibliographers, without examining original texts, copy mistakes made by predecessors in the field, it is possible to understand why there is no satisfactory bibliography for the Rider-Holyoke dictionaries.

Information concerning these dictionaries in *Athenae Oxonienses*, Watt, Allibone, Lowndes, *DNB*, and the *Cambridge Bibliography* is scanty and unreliable. Bateson, in the *Cambridge Bibliography*, for example, has one reference each to John Rider and Francis Holyoke. Under *Rider* is the entry "Bibliotheca Scholastica. Oxford, 1589. [Latin-English, and English-Latin]." Although Rider's title is misleading, it is hardly an excuse for terming the *Bibliotheca* a Latin-English and English-Latin dictionary. The 1589 edition is an English-Latin lexicon with a Latin index. Under *Francis Holyoke* the editor records, "Dictionarium Etymologicum Latinum. 1633," and remarks, "In the final form, 1677-6, there are three parts, English-Latin, Latin-English, and a Dictionary of Names." Apparently, the editor did not know of the various editions of the text, and that there are three parts of the Rider-Holyoke from 1606 on. Another entry, not in the *Cambridge Bibliography*, but in Watt, Allibone, and others, is the ascription to Rider of "Dictionarium, Latine et Anglice. Oxoniae. 1589." There is no such title, and the phrase does not apply to the *Bibliotheca*, as may have been intended. The *DNB* makes no mention of the Rider-Holyoke editions of 1606, 1612, and 1627; the abbreviated titles of the *Short-Title Catalogue* up to 1640 are not very helpful for the bibliography of these dictionaries; Kennedy (Nos. 2761, 2768, 2772, etc.) has a fairly comprehensive list, though he does not record the Oxford edition of 1627 and he apparently follows Watt in assigning to Rider "Dictionarium, Latine et Anglice." Falconer Madan (*op. cit.*, II, 28–29) has most nearly a correct list of the Rider-Holyoke dictionaries. His association of Holyoke with the *Bibliotheca* of 1589 seems to have no basis in fact; and he takes no account of the multiple issues of the editions of 1617 and 1640. Madan's account, compact and informative, is herewith transcribed.

This book [*Bibliotheca scholastica*] by bp. Rider (d. 1632) was taken up by F. Holyoke and modified for his issue of the dictionary in 1606, &c. . . . The successive editions seem to be Oxf. 1589 (Ri., Hol.), Lond. 1606 (Ri., Hol.), Oxf. 1612 (3rd ed., Ri., Hol.), Lond. 1617 (Ri., Hol.), Lond. 1626 (Rid., Hol., Gray), Oxf. 1627 (Ri., Hol.), Lond. 1633 (4th ed., Ri., Hol.), Lond. 1640 (Ri., Hol.), Lond. 1648 (6th ed., Ri., Hol.), Lond. 1676–7 (F. Hol., T. Hol.), publd. by C. Holyoke. The changes between 1589 and 1627, the first and last Oxford editions, can be given with some clearness owing to the discovery of a perfect copy of the 1612 Oxford edition, hitherto unrecorded. The English-Latin part is by Rider, and was always called, after the first edition, 'Bibliotheca Rideri Scholastica' or 'Rider's Dictionary': it is common to all editions, but of course was augmented and corrected by Holyoke from 1606 on. But the second part (Latin-English) was in Rider's first edition only an index, and accordingly when Holyoke made it into a much larger Dictionarium Etymologicum (in two sections of 'Pura . . .' and 'Barbara Vocabula,' which from 1626 on were amalgamated), he claimed it as his own, from the first enlargement. Rider's little additional list of Birds, other animals, herbs, weights, &c., occurs in all editions, except that the Roman Calendar is not found in 1606, 1612, or 1626. An Index of Proper names appears first in 1606, a geographical dictionary (Engl.-Lat.) first in 1611, 'Radices Graece Linguae' a short Greek-Latin dictionary by T[homas?] W[illis] in 1627, with an appendix of coins by W. T. P. . . .

Madan's reference to the Holyoke dictionary of 1676–77 requires comment. In 1664, Francis Gouldman published *A Copious Dictionary in Three Parts*, which was reissued in 1669, 1684, and later editions. Gouldman had incorporated much of the Rider-Holyoke of 1648, but he had also drawn freely from the later editions of Thomas Thomas and from other sources. Thomas Holyoke, seeing the debt of Gouldman to his father's book, set about compiling a new Holyoke dictionary, which he called *A Large Dictionary in Three Parts* (1677). Although this text contains much matter which had originally appeared in the Rider-Holyoke text, it includes also practically all that Gouldman had added from Thomas and others. Informative as Madan's entry is, it leaves much of the story of the Rider-Holyoke dictionaries to be told.

Even though the bibliographical problems of the Rider-Holyoke dictionaries may not be finally solved until we know more about the printing and distribution of books in the sixteenth and seventeenth centuries, it is possible to present a more accurate and informative account of the texts and their relation to each other than has been hitherto available. The description which follows, though based upon the study and comparison of texts, makes no claim of being scientific bibliography. It attempts rather to state in nontechnical language the contents of each edition, with necessary annotations, and incidentally to suggest the sources.

Bibliographical Summary

1589. John Rider.

Bibliotheca Scholastica. A Dovble Dictionarie, Penned for all those that would haue within short space the vse of the Latin tongue, either to speake, or write. Verie profitable and necessarie for Scholers, Courtiers, Lawyers and their Clarkes, Apprentices of London, Traveliers, Factors for Marchants, and briefly for all Discontinuers within her Maiesties Realmes of England and Ireland. Compiled by Iohn Rider, Master of Artes, and preacher of Gods word. [printer's device] First reade [me] With others conferre [me] Then censure me. Read the Preface, Learne the vse. Printed by Ioseph Barnes, Printer to the Vniversitie of Oxford, and are to be sold at the Tygers head in Paules Church-yarde. 1589. Cum privilegio Regiae Majestatis.

Contents, arrangement, sources: (1) English-Latin dictionary (cols. 1–1696). Based largely on Thomas's Latin-English dictionary, with some borrowings from Huloet-Higgins, Baret, and others (see the preceding chapter on Rider's *Bibliotheca*). (2) Certain general heads, as "Birds," "Colours," "Dogs," "Fishes," "Hawks," "Herbs," "Stones," "Trees," "Weights," and a Roman calendar. (3) "Index Alphabeticus omnium verborū quae in hoc opere exponuntur." This Latin word list, together with the information on grammar and classical authorities, derives from Thomas.

1606. Francis Holyoke.

Riders Dictionarie Corrected and Augmented. Wherein Riders Index is transformed into a Dictionarie Etymologicall; deriving every word from his native Fountaine, with reasons of the derivations: none yet extant in that kind before. Here also the Barbarous words are ranged into a Dictionarie by themselves, and many words added, never yet in any: With a briefe Index of proper names, Collected out of Stephane, Gesner, and others. By Francis Holyoke. [printer's device] London, Printed by Adam Islip. 1606.

Contents, arrangement, sources: Sig. *Aiii:* Dedication to Henry, Prince of Wales. Sig. *Aiiii:* "Lectori aequo. S.," Holyoke's informative Latin address to the reader, defending himself against charges of plagiarizing Thomas. (1) "Bibliotheca Rideri Scholastica." This is the running title for the original English-Latin dictionary, which despite Holyoke's claim shows almost no augmentation. (2) "Dictionarii Etymologici pars prima, in qua pura & probatis autoribus usitata vocabula, simul & seorsim explicantur." This is Holyoke's heading for the first and main division of what has now become the Latin-English part of the dictionary. The entries correspond closely to those found in Thomas's *Dictionarium*, except the attempts at etymology, in which the compiler leans heavily on Calepine. (3) "Dictionarii Etymologici pars secunda, in qua Barbara obsoleta & raro usitata vocabula explicantur." The heading is Holyoke's; the entries and definitions are largely from Thomas, in whose lexicon, though not separated from the main word list, they are marked obsolete or rare. (4) "Index Propriorum, sive Dictionariolum Poeticum & Historicum." This division, now first introduced into the Rider-Holyoke dictionaries, has antecedents in Charles Stephanus' *Dictionarium, historicum, geographicum, poeticum,* Cooper's *Thesaurus,* and Thomas's *Dictionarium.* Holyoke borrows from Thomas, Stephanus, and others.

1612. Francis Holyoke.

Riders Dictionarie Corrected, And With the Addition of Above Five Hundred Words Enriched. Hereunto is Annexed A Dictionarie Etymologicall deriving every word from his natiue fountaine, with reasons of the derivations, and many Romane antiquities, never any extant in that kinde before. By Francis Holyoke. The Third Edition. [arms of University] At Oxford. Printed by Ioseph Barnes. 1612.

This edition has a special title page for the Latin-English, as follows:

Dictionarium Etymologicum in Duas Divisvm Partes, quorum prior, pura, & a bonis autoribus Latinis, probata; altera, obsoleta & parum usitata vocabula, simul & seorsim explicat. [The compiler here claims augmentation of the *Dictionarium* by above four thousand words.] Omnia Svmmo Studio et Industria elaborata per Franciscum de Sacra Qvercu. Oxoniae, Excudebat Iosephus Barnesius. 1612.

Contents, arrangement, sources: Notwithstanding the general title page and the special one for the etymological or Latin-English part, the running titles are the same, except for one addition, as those in the 1606 edition: (1) "Bibliotheca Rideri Scholastica," (2) "Dictionarii Etymologici Pars Prima," (3) "Dictionarii Etymologici pars secunda," (4) "Dictionarium Propriorum nominum Etymologicum," and, added, (5) "Posthuma Quaedam Verba e Petronio, Lubino . . ." (11 pp. of 3 cols. each).

In general the sources, in the various divisions thus indicated, remain much the same, except in the fifth, which is self-explanatory. To Thomas Thomas is the great debt, and that debt is increased in the augmentation of Holyoke's *Dictionarium etymologicum* (see the discussion above). Holyoke's claim, on the title page, to have added five hundred words, or entries, to the English-Latin of Rider is exaggerated; the increase is almost negligible from 1606 to 1648. For the first time Holyoke supplies in this edition a certain number of Greek equivalents for Latin entries. In this he is following Thomas, whose dictionary had Greek equivalents from 1596 on. Holyoke borrows his Greek from Thomas and Calepine. In the preliminary matter to this volume is a Latin address by "Ro. Bvrton ex Aede Christi" (Robert Burton) making tantalizing allusion to litigation directed against Holyoke and defending the etymological dictionary against its critics. Burton mentions no names.

1617. Francis Holyoke.

"Riders Dictionarie Corrected. . . ." The general title page of this issue corresponds almost verbatim to that of 1612, down to and including "By Francis Holyoke"; the phrase "The Third Edition" is omitted, and the title page concludes, "London, Printed by Adam Islip for Thomas Man. 1617." The special title page for the *Dictionarium etymologicum* corresponds also to that of 1612, except the conclusion: "Londini, Excudebat Adam Islip. 1617."

Another issue of the 1617 edition (copies at the University of Illinois and the Library of Congress) concludes the general title page with "London, Printed by Adam Islip for William Leake. 1617." The title page of the *Dictionarium* in this issue is identical with that cited immediately above. With the exceptions noted, these two issues, in content and arrangement of matter, seem to be the same. They have the same divisions and running titles as the edition of 1612, and apparently represent no augmentation.

According to *STC*, there is still another issue of the 1617 edition: "London, Printed by Adam Islip for Thomas Adams. 1617." This issue I have not examined, but it is a fairly safe conjecture that it does not differ in content from the other two.

The fact that no other edition of the Rider-Holyoke appeared until

1626, and this one much changed under the direction of Nicholas Gray, may be the result of the vigorous protest of John Legate the Younger against the continued pilfering of the Thomas *Dictionarium*, of which Legate was the printer.

1626. Francis Holyoke and Nicholas Gray.

Riders Dictionarie. As It Was Heretofore Corrected, And with the Addition of Above Five Hundred Words Enriched. Hereunto is annexed a Dictionarie Etymologicall, deriuing euery word from his natiue fountaine, with reasons of the deriuations; and many Roman antiquities, neuer any extant in this kinde before. By Francis Holyoke. To which are ioyned (as may appeare more largely in the title and Epistle before the Latine Dictionary) many vsefull alterations, emendations, and additions of Etymologies, Differences, Antiquities, Histories, and their morals. By Nicholas Gray. [Greek motto.] London, Printed by Adam Islip. 1626.

The special title page for the Latin-English is phrased:

Rideri Dictionarium Severiore Trutina Casigatum. In quo (praeter ea quae olim elaboravit Franciscus de Sacra Quercu) Etyma Innumera Supplentur, Syntaxis Singularum Vocum Adiicitur, Voces cognatae significationis discriminantur, Complura Authorum loca, quae lectorem morari poterant, enodantur: Phrases, Adagia, Formulae, Historiae, Fabulae, cum earum Mythologijs, Plurima Venerandae antiquitatis monumenta (pro operis male) attexuntur: & vocabula Pura, vna cum Obsoletis & proprijs, sed suo quaeque charactere distincta, in vnum iam ordinem rediguntur . . . Operis & horis succiuis. N. Gray. Londini. Excudebat Adam Islip. 1626.

The first part of the general title page simply follows those of 1612 and 1617; in an address to the reader Gray states that he has made corrections in the English-Latin section but claims no augmentation.

Contents, arrangement, sources: (1) "Bibliotheca Rideri Scholastica." This is the running title for the English-Latin, not essentially changed from that of earlier editions. (2) "Rideri Dictionarium severiore iam trutina castigatum. . . ." This division, the Latin-English, corresponding in general to the *Dictionarium etymologicum,* places all words, including proper names, into one alphabetical order. Gray marks obsolete and barbarous words with a cross, proper names with a double cross, and indicates new matter with an asterisk. He greatly changes and improves the Latin-English of Holyoke. Gray appears to have done a careful and honest revision, modifying borrowings made earlier by Holyoke and refraining from further indebtedness to Thomas. It is fairly obvious from Gray's address to the reader that Holyoke had nothing to do with this revision. This seems to be confirmed also by the circumstances that in the following year, 1627, Holyoke published at Oxford another edition of the dictionary which, disregarding the improvements by Gray, reverts largely to the Holyoke-Rider of 1617 and to further borrowings from Thomas.

1627. Francis Holyoke.

Dictionarivm Etymologicvm Latinvm, Antiqvissimum & novissimum nunc demum infinitis penè laboribus & continuis vigilijs compositum & absolutum à Francisco de Sacra Quercu. That is, A Dictionarie declaring the originall and derivations of all words vsed in any Latine Authors, with the reason of their derivations and appellations; neuer any in this kinde extant before: the quantities of syllables, as also the differences of those words, whose affinitie in signification or otherwise, might cause a promiscuous and improper vse: the pure and improper words gathered into one Dictionarie, and distinguished by this marke: †. Wherevnto besides the hard and most vsefull words in Divinitie, Philosophie, Physicke, and Logicke, are added many thousand other words out of approved authors old and new, with their Greeke in more exactnesse then ever was in Calepine, Morelius, or any other: and also the coines, measures, weights, and Greeke Rootes, none of which are extant in any Edition formerly published. Herevnto is also annexed the proper names adorned with their Etymologies, illustrated, and explained, with Histories, Proverbes, Mythologies, &c. together with the Chronologie of the persons, and the beginning of noted Citties, and plantation of sundry Countries, the Geography, and the names both ancient and new of the most remarkable places, lastly Riders Dictionarie I the English before the Latine compiled by Rider, is augmented with many hundreds of words, both out of the Law, and out of the Latine, French, and other languages, such as were and are with vs in common vse, but never printed vntill now to the perfecting of that worke. Also the Romane Calender. By the great industrie and paines of Francis Holyoke. Oxford. Printed by William Turner, Printer to the famous Vniversity. Ann. Dom. 1627.

Here follows the special title page within this volume:

Riders Dictionarie Corrected and Augmented with the Addition of many hundred words not extant in any former edition. Herevnto are annexed Riders Calender, and certaine Tables explaining the names, weights, and valuations of auncient and modern coynes, as also a table of the Hebrew, Greeke & Latine measures reduced to our English standard and assise. Wherevnto is joyned A dictionary Etymologicall, deriving each word from his proper fountaine, the first that ever was extant in that kind . . . by Francis Holioke.

Contents, arrangement, sources: (1) *Dictionarium etymologicum.* For the first time Holyoke places first the Latin-English lexicon and throws into one alphabet all words formerly included in "Prima Pars" and "Secunda Pars." The principal source continues to be the Latin-English dictionary of Thomas Thomas, though there are some additions from Joannes Fungerus' *Etymologicum Latinum opus* (Frankfurt, 1605) and Christianus Becmanus' *Manductio ad Latinam linguam* (Hanover, 1619). (2) "Dictionarium etymologicum propriorum nominum." The section on proper names, from Thomas and various sources. (3) "Radices Graecae linguae." (4) "Bibliotheca Rideri Scholastica." This English-Latin lexicon retains all borrowings which Rider originally made from Thomas. (5) The list of birds, colors, etc., from Rider; and a short English-Latin geographical dictionary.

Despite the warning of Legate and the other heirs of Thomas, and the good example set by Gray in his revision of 1626, Holyoke continued, in the edition of 1627, to base his work mainly on Thomas. His shift in the arrangement of matter in the text and the exaggerated claims of the title page have little meaning. Some time after the appearance of this edition, action was taken against Holyoke (see his address to the reader in the 1633 edition, and the discussion above).

1633. Francis Holyoke.

Dictionarivm etymologicvm Latinvm Antiqvissimum & novissimum nunc demum infinitis pene laboribus & continuis vigilijs compositum & absolutum à Francisco de Sacra Quercu. Or, A Dictionarie Declaring The Originall and Deriuations of all Words vsed in any Latine Authors, with the reason of their Deriuations and Appellations; neuer any in this kind extant before. Whereunto besides the hard and most vsefull words in Diuinitie, Philosophie, Physicke, and Logicke, are added many thousand other Words out of the Ciuill and Canon Lawes, Glossaries, Criticks, and other approued Authors, old and new; with their Greeke in more exactnesse than euer was in Calepine, Morelius, or any other: and also the Coines, Measures, Weights, and Greeke Rootes; and many other vsefull Additions, as will appeare in the Epistle to the Reader, and better in the Work itselfe. Hereunto is also annexed the Proper Names, adorned with their Etymologies; illustrated and explained with Histories, Prouerbes, Mythologies, &c. Together with the Chronologie of the Persons, and the beginning of noted Cities, and plantation of sundry Countries; the Geographie, and the Names both antient and new, of the most remarkable Places. Lastly Riders Dictionarie (I) the English before the Latine, compiled by Rider, is augmented with many hundreds of Words, both out of the Law, and out of the Latine, French, and other Languages, such as were and are with vs in common vse, but neuer printed vntill now, to the perfecting of the Worke. Now the fourth time newly corrected, and very much augmented, by the great industrie and paines of Francis Holy-Oke. London, Printed by Adam Islip and Felix Kyngston, Anno. Dom. 1633.

Here is the title page of the Rider within the volume:

Riders Dictionarie, Corrected and Augmented with the Addition of many hundred words, both out of the Law, and out of Latine, French, and other Languages . . . Hereunto are anexed certaine Tables explaining the names, weights, and valuations of antient and moderne coynes, as also a Table of the Hebrew, Greeke, and Latine measures, reduced to our English Standard and Assise. Whereunto is ioyned a Dictionarie Etymologicall, deriuing each word from his proper fountaine; the first that euer was extant in this kinde: with many worthy castigations and Additions, as will appeare in the Title and Epistle before it. Now newly corrected and greatly augmented by Francis Holy-Oke. London, Printed by Adam Islip and Felix Kyngston. 1633.

These title pages are of course very similar, though not identical, to those in the 1627 issue, the 1633 volume being printed at London as "Now the fourth time newly corrected, and very much augmented."

Contents, arrangement, sources: (1) "Dictionarium Etymologicum Latinum . . . Nvnc DenVo Svmma Cvra et Diligenter ab Ipso Avthore Avctum et Recognitvm." Holyoke's heading here emphasizes the fact that he himself was responsible for the amplification and correction and, by inference, had made the changes required by legal action. And this Latin-English section shows considerable expansion, not by way of new entries, but generally in extension of those already in the text. The source of much of the new matter is a late edition, probably 1609, of Calepine (see discussion above) with some additional matter from Fungerus, Becmanus, and Martinius. Notwithstanding the augmentation, Holyoke apparently retains all the appropriated material hitherto made from the Thomasius. (2) "Dictionarium Etymologicum Propriorum Nominum." (3) "Bibliotheca Rideri Scholastica." This is the usual running title for the Rider dictionary, English-Latin, followed by the list of birds, etc., and by the brief geographical dictionary and the Roman calendar. Holyoke's claim of great augmentation of this section is untrue.

1640. Francis Holyoke.

Riders Dictionarie, Corrected and Augmented with the addition of many hundred Words both out of the Law, and out of the Latine, French, and other Languages, such as were and are with vs in common vse, but never printed till now, to the perfecting of the worke. The Barbarous Words Which were many hundreds are expunged to the help of young Scholars, which before they used instead of good Words. In the end of the Dictionarie you shall finde certaine generall heads of Birds, Colours, Dogs, Fishes, Hawkes, Hearbes, Numbers, Stones, Trees, Weights. Lastly, the names of the chief places and Townes in England, Scotland, and Ireland, &c. which were never in Riders before. Also hereunto is annexed certaine tables of Weights and Measures, the valuation of auncient and moderne Coines; as also a table of the Hebrew Standard and Assise; and the weights used in Physicke, none of which were ever in Riders worke. Whereunto is joyned a Dictionarie Etymologicall, deriving each word from his proper fountaine, the first that ever was extant in this kind, with many worthy Castigations and Additions, in this last Edition, as will appeare in the Title and Epistle before it. Now newly corrected and much augmented by Francis Holy-Oke. London. Imprinted by Felix Kingston for Andrew Crooke. 1640.

The Rider-Holyoke dictionary of 1640 offers bibliographical difficulties. Although the arrangement reverts to that of the earlier editions, with the English-Latin of Rider standing first in the volume, this edition is in content little different from that of 1633. But there are at least three different issues of 1640, possibly four. The phrasing transcribed above is from the title page of an unrecorded issue in the Folger Library.

Other issues having exactly the same title pages down to the imprint are here indicated: "London. Imprinted by Felix Kingston for John Waterson. 1640"; "London, Imprinted by Felix Kyngston for Richard Whitaker. 1640." Another possible issue of this edition is suggested by a volume (Rare Books Collection, University of Texas) which contains only the *Dictionarium etymologicum* and is dated 1639 on the title page.

But this title page corresponds word for word and also in arrangement on the page to the title page preceding the *Dictionarium etymologicum* in the 1640 issue for Andrew Crooke, down to the imprint. Compare the following:

Now the fifth time newly corrected, and very much augmented by the great industrie and paines of Francis Holy-Oke. London. Imprinted by Felix Kingston. 1639. Cvm Privilegio.
Now the fifth time newly corrected, and very much augmented by the great industrie and paines of Francis Holy-Oke. London. Imprinted by Felix Kingston for Andrew Crooke. 1640. Cvm Privilegio.

The phrase "Now the fifth time newly corrected" in the volume dated 1639 may indicate that the date should be 1640. If this is correct, the Texas volume indicates another issue of 1640.

Contents, arrangement, sources: (1) "Bibliotheca Rideri Scholastica," (2) "Dictionarium Etymologicum Latinum," (3) "Dictionarium Etymologicum Propriorum Nominum." These are the running titles, in the order listed. There are the usual materials from Rider, but no augmentation; and the matter in the Latin-English section corresponds fairly closely to that in the 1633 edition. Perhaps the significant changes are to be found in the exclusion of the obsolete and barbarous words. Greek and Hebrew equivalents for the Latin are made more prominent. The sources remain, of course, largely the same.

1648–49. Francis Holyoke.

In content the Rider-Holyoke dictionary of this date marks no change. The general title page, beginning "Dictionarium Etymologicum Latinum," is the same as the second title page in the 1640, except that it is brought up to date in these statements: "Now the sixth time newly corrected, and very much augmented by the great industry and paines of Francis Holyoke. London. Imprinted by Felix Kingston. 1648."

The Rider, or English-Latin lexicon, stands last in this volume. Its title page seems to be a reprint of that used in the 1640 edition, when the Rider stood first, except the imprint: "London. Imprinted by Felix Kingston. 1649."

In the three copies I have examined, the Holyoke Latin-English part bears the date 1648; the Rider, 1649. No wonder there is confusion. Madan (*op. cit.*, II, 109) first refers to this edition as of 1649, but later changes the date to 1648, asserting without explanation that the former date was a mistake. This edition belonging to the years 1648–49 is hardly more than a reprint of the 1640 edition, with rearrangement of major divisions.

1659. Francis Holyoke.

Madan (*op. cit.*) records no edition of the Rider-Holyoke for 1659. There is, however, a copy of this edition in the University of Illinois Library. The wording on the title page, including the phrase "Now newly corrected and much augmented," corresponds in general to that of 1640, down to the imprint, which reads: "London: Printed by J. F. for Andrew Crook, at the Green Dragon in St. Paul's Church-Yard, 1659." The arrangement of the parts of the text, with the English-Latin standing first, is similar to that of 1640, but the catchwords and the printer's signatures are different from those of the 1640 edition. There is apparently no augmentation, and none is claimed. The 1659 edition appears to be a slightly revised version of the 1640 text.

1677. Thomas Holyoke.

A Large Dictionary in Three Parts. This work by the son of Francis Holyoke is an attempt almost a generation later to rejuvenate the old Rider-Holyoke by large philological transfusions from Gouldman, Thomas, and others. The effort was not successful, but it is worth noting that Thomas Holyoke retained much of the matter which his father and Rider had taken from Thomas at the beginning of the seventeenth century.

CHAPTER XVII

Christopher Wase's *Dictionarium minus* (1662)

URING THE PERIOD of the Commonwealth, or from 1648 to 1661, there seems to have been little publishing in Latin-English lexicography. With the Restoration, at least half a dozen new dictionaries appeared within a few years. The first of these was compiled by Christopher Wase (1625?–90). Wase was a schoolmaster who had been educated at Eton and at King's College, Cambridge. From 1648 to 1668, he served as headmaster of Eton, of Dedham Royal Free School, and of Tonbridge School, respectively. Probably his experiences as a schoolmaster led him to compile his Latin-English and English-Latin dictionary, which was finished about the time he began his work at Tonbridge.

Since the title pages, one for each part of the dictionary, give explicit information on the plan and content of his work, I here transcribe them.

Dictionarium Minus: A Compendious Dictionary, English-Latin & Latin-English. Wherein the Classical Words of both Languages are aptly Rendred. And for the more sufficient Direction of Students In

    I. Construing: the divers Significations are distinguished, according to different Phrases, and the Tropical or Figurative sense is set after the Proper and Natural.

    II. Pearsing [Parsing?]: The various Constructions are specified.

    III. Making Latines: The Termination of the Genitive is added to the Noun, the Infinitive to the Verb, and the English Neuter is differenced from the Active.

Also The Received Names of Herbs, Plants, &c., are largely inserted; divers Proverbs

explain'd; and many Antiquities illustrated. By Christopher Wase, M.A. Master of the Free-School in Tunbridge, London . . .
Printed by Da: Maxwell, 1662.

The second half has a separate title page, thus:

Compendium Calepine. Being a Latine-English Dictionary, and an Abridgement of the last Calepine, augmented by Passeratius. Containing A List of the Classical Words of the Latine Tongue, an Explication of particular and proper Phrases, and a Recital of divers Proverbs. Abstracted by Christopher Wase, M.A. London: Printed by D. Maxwell. 1661.

As the title page of the latter half, or Latin-English part, has the earlier date, we may consider this part first. A comparison with Passeratius' Calepine of 1647 shows that Wase's claim is correct. All that he has in his Latin-English text may be found in expanded form in the Calepine. But Wase's small quarto is an abridgment, intended for the use of school-boys. It represents therefore a rigid selection, a selection designed to include only classical words. The emphasis on the classical quality of the word list is important as anticipating the development of a classical Latin dictionary at the end of the century. Like Calepine, Wase employs the etymological order of arrangement, placing derivations after the root words at the sacrifice of a strictly alphabetical order. The necessary grammatical information is given, as the title page states; and a few well-chosen Latin phrases are inserted after most entries to illustrate meaning and usage. Wase seems to be the first lexicographer in the century to express the definite aim of setting "the Tropical or Figurative sense" after "the Proper and Natural."

Proper names, which English lexicographers from Cooper on had placed in a separate section of the text and which Calepine had distributed throughout the word list, Wase omits. In his "Advertisements to the Judicious and Courteous Peruser," Wase comments:

Some might have expected the Proper Names of Men, or Countreys, to have been either distributed into the Work, or set after it: Not a few of the Pagan Gods are inserted; Remarkable places may to much more advantage be taken out of the Globe, Map, or Chart: As for the Proper Names of Heroes or Eminent Personages, these are indeed delightful and have their use; but being for substance the same in both (and indeed all) Languages, conduce not much (if at all) to the Artificial part of a Grammarian; the Advancement of which is throughout this whole Work immediately intended.

Wase's decision to rule out proper names was in keeping with his aim to put into small compass the essentials for teaching and learning the Latin language.

The fact that his dictionary was compiled primarily for beginners is emphasized in the Latin address to the reader. In this address also Wase briefly reviews the history of the English language, noting the Teutonic basis of English and the close relation of English to the Scandinavian languages. Wase proposes in his book to employ English current in his own day. Among his predecessors in lexicography, he names Thomas and Rider, but not Holyoke.

Placed first in the volume is the English-Latin section with the heading "Promptuarium Anglicanae & Latinae Linguae." This, like the Latin-English division, has three columns to the page. Each English entry is followed by a single Latin equivalent, only rarely by more. This is in accord with the compiler's belief that one Latin term in good standing is better than more words, among which the beginner would have to choose. There is not a close correspondence between the English-Latin and Latin-English parts of the volume; that is, the first section is not merely an inversion of the second, or Latin-English. In the English phrasing, as in the arrangement of entries, Wase doubtless took suggestions from Rider's English-Latin dictionary, a work he mentions favorably. Compare the following entries:

Wase (1662)	Rider (1589)
To abandon. *Derelinquo ere.*	To Abandon, put away or forsake. 1 *Amando, amoneo, abjicio, relinquo, defero, destituo.* 2 *Extermino.*
	To abandon or divorce, *vide* divorce.
Abandoned. *Derelictus.*	Abandoned and forsaken. 1 *Amandatus, relictus, desertus, destitutus.* 2 *Exterminatus.*
	An abandoner or forsaker. 1 *Amandator, relictor, desertor. destitutor.* 2 *Exterminator. m.*
An abandoning. *Derelictio nis.*	An abandoning or forsaking. 1 *Amandatio, relictio, desertio, destitutio.* 2 *Exterminatio.*
To abase. *Humilio are.*	To Abase or bring lowe. 1 *Humilio.* 2 *Dejicio, demitto. . . .*
Abased. *Humiliatus.*	Abased or brought lowe. 1 *Humiliatus.* 2 *Dejectus, demissus, depressus. p.*
An abasement, or abasing. *Depressio nis.*	An abasement or bringing lowe. 1 *Humiliatio.* 2 *Dejectio, demissio, depressio, f.*
To abash. *Pudefacio, confundo ere.*	To Abash or make ashamed. 1 *Pudefacio, pudore percello.* 2 *Consterno, vide* to astonish. . . .
Abashed. *Pudefactus, confusus.*	
To be abashed. *Pudefio ere, confundor.*	To be abashed. 1 *Pudefio.* 2 *Consternor, obmutesco, conticesco.*
	Abashed. 1 *Pudefactus, pudore perculsus.* 2 *Consternatus, p.*

Wase (1662)	Rider (1589)
An abashment. *Confusio nis.*	An abashment. 2 *Consternatio, demissio, f. Infructio animi. vid* astonishment.
To abate (act.) *Subduco ere.* To abate (neut.) *Decresco ere.*	To Abate or Diminish. 1 *Demo, minuo, imminuo, comminuo, Attenuo.* 2 *Destruo, remitto.*
Abated. *Subductus.* An abatement. *Diminutio nis.*	Abated or diminished. 1 *Demptus, comminutus, attenuatus.* 2 *Demissus, p.*
	An Abating or Diminishing. 1 *Diminutio, attenuatio. f.*
	To Abate in accomptes. 1 *Subduco, subtraho, deduco.*
	Abated in accompts. 1 *Subductus, subtractus, deductus. p.*
	An abating in accomptes. 1 *Subductio, subtractio, deductio. f.*
	To Abate ones courage. 1 *Percello, frangere, animum.*
	To abate or diminish ones credit, *vide* To Discredit.

A comparison of these entries shows the likenesses and the differences. In the choice of English words and phrases, beginning with the infinitive verb form and proceeding through verbals and other forms to the noun, Wase seems to be following his model. He exercises independent judgment, however, in the choice of Latin terms; and in selecting a single Latin word instead of three or more, as in Rider, Wase simplifies his text and makes it more useful and convenient for schoolboys. Apparently, Wase was little interested in the principle of copiousness, which was basic in Rider's compilation. The names of herbs, plants, etc., in Rider, were always placed together in their own alphabetical list. In Wase, notwithstanding the suggestion of the title pages, such names are distributed alphabetically throughout the text.

A second edition of Wase's dictionary appeared in 1675 with a single title page worded thus:

Dictionarium Minus: A compendious Dictionary, English-Latin & Latin-English. Wherein the Classical Words of both Languages are Aptly Rendred Also, The Received Names of Herbs, Plants, &c. Largely Inserted; divers Proverbs Explain'd; and many Antiquities Illustrated. The Second Edition. By Christopher Wase, Superiour Beadle of the Civil Law in Oxford. London. Printed by Thomas Newcomb for James Good Bookseller in *Oxford.* 1675.

The compiler modestly refrains from claiming augmentation or even corrections in this edition. There are indications, however, that he has made corrections and changes. In this edition he drops many of the past participles, as *abased* and *abbreviated,* whose infinitive and noun forms are given; and he adds entries, as *to abridge,* inadvertently omitted from the first edition. He thus improves the utility of his book without increasing the size or cost of it.

An innovation for English-Latin dictionaries is Wase's method of distinguishing the different meanings of certain English words by the use of explanatory words or phrases, as in the following entries:

To abide (or dwell) *commoror ari,* (or tarry) *Praestolor ari . . .* (or suffer) *Tolero ari.*
An able man (in skill) *Solers,* (in wealth) *opulentus,* (in strength) *validus.*
Nearness (in place) *Propinquitas, Vicina ae.* (of disposition) *Parsimonia ae.*
Sharp (in action) *Acer.* (in taste) *Acidus.* (of wit) *Acutus.*
To Twinkle (as the eye) *Nicto are.* (as a star) *Scintillo, mico are.*
Undone *Infectus.* (or slackened) *Remissus.* (ruined) *Perditus.* (untied) *Resolutus.*

As early as 1668, Bishop William Lloyd had employed a similar method in his English vocabulary at the end of Bishop Wilkins' "Essay Towards a Philosophical Language," and this may have been the precedent for Wase. This device for distinguishing meanings was to be adopted later, as we shall see, by Elisha Coles and Robert Ainsworth.

To some who had been critical of abridgments, Wase repeats that his book was chiefly intended for the learner, not "Masters or Criticks in the Latine Tongue." He concludes:

Other Tongues have their Manuals, as well as larger Treasuries; This, I hope, will neither over-lighten the Fathers Purse, nor over-load the Childs Sachel: Nor will it displease the Industrious and Learned Goldman, or the Judicious and Accurate Littleton, that some place be allow'd amongst the studious and less accomplish'd persons for these poor endeavors of

Thine and Their
Humble Servant,
CHRISTOPHER WASE.

Of Gouldman and Littleton here referred to, we shall learn more in the chapters which follow. It is sufficient to state that each esteemed Wase's little volume and each made use of it in his more pretentious dictionary. Constructed on sound principles, designed to be useful to students, and published without fanfare or boast, Wase's modest volume is in pleasing contrast to the pompous and pedantic lexicon edited by Francis Holyoke.

Facing the title page in the first edition of the *Dictionarium minus* is the "Royal Privilegium" insuring Wase protection in the printing and distribution of his book. This seems of sufficient interest to be reproduced here as an addendum to this chapter.

Charles R.

Charles the Second, by the Grace of God, King of *England, Scotland, France,* and *Ireland,* Defender of the Faith, &c. To all Our Loving Subjects, Greeting. Whereas *Christopher Wase,* Master of Arts, hath with great labour and diligence made a Compendious Dictionarie under the Title *Dictionarium minus*, &c. for the use of young Scholars, which hath been testified unto Us to be a Work of much use and benefit for their progress in Learning, and the said *Christopher Wase* hath been at great Expence in causing same to be Imprinted; of which Costs, and the Fruit of so laborious a Work, he may be defrauded, if any other shall Re-print the same thus fitted and prepared: Know Ye therefore, That it is Our Royal Pleasure, and We do by these Presents Grant unto the said *Christopher Wase*, his Heirs, Executors, Administrators and Assigns, upon his humble request unto Us made, such Privileges, Protection and Defence, as in Right and Equity may be allowed for an Undertaking so painful and advantagious. And We do hereby strictly prohibit all Our Subjects from the Re-printing the said Work, or any of those Collections from Foreign Writers accomodated to the use and benefit of our Nation, or any other Inventions by the Author inserted into this Book as parts and parcels of the Work, for the space of Fourteen years next coming, Except with the license and by the appointment of the said *Christopher Wase*, his Executors and Assigns. Or in case the said Book, or any part thereof be Re-printed in any Foreign parts, We do likewise forbid the importing, vending, or putting to sale the same in any of Our Dominions, upon pain of Our highest Displeasure, and Confiscation of all such Books so imprinted and imported, the one moiety of the Sum arising from the Sale of them to be paid into Our Exchequer, the other to the said *Christopher Wase*, his Heirs, Executors, Administrators or Assigns, and such Penalties as by the Law may be inflicted.

Given at Our Court at Whitehal, this third day of March, *in the Fourteenth Year of Our Reign.* 1661.

By His Majesties Command,
WILL. MORICE

CHAPTER XVIII

Francis Gouldman's *Copious Dictionary in Three Parts* (1664)

TWO YEARS AFTER Christopher Wase had printed the first edition of his *Dictionarium minus,* Francis Gouldman brought out a thick octavo English-Latin and Latin-English dictionary. Gouldman, M.A. (1630), Christ's College, Cambridge, was for many years rector at South Ockendon, Essex. Not until 1664 did he publish the first edition of his *Copious Dictionary.* A second edition appeared in 1669; a third in 1674, with additions by W. Robertson; and a fourth and final in 1678, enlarged by Anthony Scattergood. Each issue had three title pages: one for the text as a whole, one for the Latin-English, and one for the proper names. Here are the title pages for 1664.

A Copious Dictionary in Three Parts:
  I. The English before the Latin, Enriched with about Ten Thousand Words more than any former Dictionary contains.
 II. The Latin before the English, With correct and plentiful etymological Derivations, Philological Observations, and Phraseological Explications.
III. The Proper Names of Persons, Places, And other things necessary to the understanding of Historians and Poets. To which are adjoined A Table of Authors Names at large, which in this Book are made use of, or mentioned; and also some lesser Tractates. The whole being a Comprisal of Thomasius and Rider's Foundations; Holland's and Holyoke's Superstructure and Improvements: Together with Amendments and Enlargements very considerable for number and nature, promoted and carried on by a diligent search into, and perusal of several other Dictionaries, and many Authors ancient and modern: Rendring this Work the most complete and useful of any in this kind yet extant; As the Preface doth particularly declare, and the Book it self will more fully evidence.
By the care and industry of Francis Gouldman, M.A.
London, Printed by John Field, M. DC. LXIV.

The title page of the Latin-English part of the dictionary reads as follows:

Dictionarium Etymologicum, Philologicum, Phraseologicumque, omnium quae extant locupletissimum. In quo prioribus Lexicographis Consultis & perpensis, Aliorum Omissa non pauca inseruntur, Admissa non levia repurgantur, Omnia ex ipsis Fontibus, summa (qua fieri potuit) cura ac diligentia, repetita sunt & restituta. Cui annectuntur A fronte, Catalogus Auctorum nomina recensens; A calce, Dictionarium Propria Nomina complectens. Caetera Praeloquium jam indicavit. Londini, Excudebat Joannes Field, Anno M. DC. LXIV.

The title page of the proper-name dictionary:

Dictionarium Historico-Geographico-Poeticum: In quo debita serie tractantur Propria Nomina Deorum gentilium, hominum, regionum, urbium, marium, fluviorum, &c. Cum eorum Etymologia, Historia, Mythologia, Geographia, Chronologia, &c. multo magis, quam unquam ante hac, aucta & emaculata. Ex quibus Fax accenditur Historicis, Poetis, & aliis Auctoribus: adeoque Theologiae ethnica, & plurimarum rerum scitu dignissimarum penetralia referantur. Una cum minutiorum Tractatum Appendicibus non contemnendis. Londini, Excudebat Joannes Field, Anno M. DC. LXIV.

Identical in phrasing with the title pages transcribed above are those of the second edition in 1669, down to the imprint. Then we have for the first or general title page these words: "The Second Edition: Wherein the Quantities of Syllables not onely in Apellatives, but also Proper Names are more accurately noted then heretofore. Cambridge, Printed by John Field, and are to be sold by George Sawbridge. M. DC. LXIX." Title pages of the English-Latin and proper-name parts of the 1669 text correspond to those of 1664, except the imprint common to the two parts, which has this phrasing: "In hac Editione Syllabarum Quantitates, multo quam antehac accuratius, assiguntur. Cantabrigiae, Excudebat Joannes Field, Anno M. DC. LXIX." It may be stated summarily that the Gouldman dictionary published at Cambridge in 1669 is, excepting the more careful marking of quantities and the specified changes on the title pages, not different from that of 1664. The two texts correspond throughout as to printers' signatures and catchwords.

The third edition, 1673–74, seems to have been printed partly in Cambridge and partly in London, judging by the title pages. The wording of the general title page is the same as that of 1664, excepting slight differences in arrangement on the page, and the matter which follows, including the imprint.

And in this Third Edition (besides many other Additions) the most Textual, usual and proper Hebrew Roots and Derivatives, added to the Simple Theams and Compounds of the Latin, throughout the Whole Work, are Inserted By W. Robertson, A.M. Cambridge, Printed by John Hayes, to be sold by G. Sawbridge, J. Place, W. Place, T. Bassett, T. Dring and J. Leigh, Booksellers in London, 1674.

To **Dive** under water. Urino, inuriro, urinor.

One that diveth under water. Urinator, m. & trix, f.

A diving under the water. Urinatio, f.

To make **divers**. Vario, as.

Diversity, Diversitas, varietas, disparilitas, variatio, variantia, inconstantia, f.

A propriety of speech divers from the rest of the same language. Dialectus f.

Divers, sundry, or unlike. Varius, diversus, ad. dissimilis, absimilis, alienus, dissonus, adj. varians, distans, p.

Divers, or manifold. Multiplex, varius, anceps, multifarius, multimodus, omnigenus, multijugus, multijugis, omnifarius, adj.

Of divers kinds. Multigenus, multigeneris.

Of divers, or mixt colours. Versicolor, multicolor, adj.

Diversly. Varie, diverse, multiplicitèr, multifariam, distinctè, adv.

A diverticle. Diverticulum, To **divert**. Diverto.

To divide. V. Devide.

To **Divine** or prophesie. Divino, prædivino, hariolor, auguror, præfagio, auspico, ominor, vaticinor, conjecto, conjecturo.

A diviner, soothsayer, or wizard. Divinator, hariolus, augur, fatidicus, mantes, fatiloquus, vates, vaticinator, præsagus.

A diviner by looking in Beasts bowels. Aruspex, haruspex.

She that so divineth. Haruspica.

Divination, or divining. Auguratio, mantia, præsagitio, præsagium, auspicium, vaticinium, divinatio, augurium, conjectura, aruspicium.

The art of divination, or foretelling of things to come. Mantice, haruspicina, f.

Divination by the air. Aëromantia, f.

A divination by water. Hydromantia, lecanomantia.

He that useth that divination. Lecanomantes, Hydromantius.

Divination by looking into fire. Pyromantia, ignispicium.

A divination by lots. Sortilegium, n.

Divination by looking into a glass. Catoptromantia.

A divination by birds. Oscinum, n.

The dignity or state of diviners. Auguratus, us, m.

The ornaments of diviners. Augurale, lis, adj.

Established by divination. Auguratus, adj.

A towre or castle where men divined of matters. Auguraculum, n.

In divining a Bird that crieth from the top of any thing. Supervaganea avis.

Pertaining to divination. Auguralis, aruspicalis, haruspicinus, vaticinus adj.

By divination. Auguratò, adv.

A **Divine**, or professour of divinity. Theologus, gi 3 m.

A diviner or writer of holy Scripture. Hagiographus.

Divinity. Theologia, divinitas, f.

Divine or heavenly. Cœlestis, divinus, æthereus, divus, dius.

Divine or immortal. Nectareus, adj.

Very divine. Prædivinus, adj.

Belonging to divinity. Theologicus, adj.

Divinely. Divinè, adv.

To **divorce**. Abdico, repudio, repello, dimitto.

To be divourced. Diffideo.

Divourced. Repudiatus, dimissus.

A divorcer. Repudiator.

A divorcement. Repudium, divortium, repandium, dissidium, n.

A divorcing or vise. Repudiatio, f.

Diurnal. Diurnus.

To **divulgate**. Famigero, as.

To be divulgated. Permanesco, permano.

Dizzy. V. Giddy.

Dizziness. Vertigo.

D ante O.

Docile. Docilis.

Docility. Docilitas.

A **dock** where a ship is made and repaired. Navale, n. navigiorum textrina, f. textrinum.

A docked, or short introduction of a matter. Documentum.

A docket. Breve vel summa contentorum in scriptis.

Docked. Amputatus.

A **Doctor.** Doctor.

A Doctor of divinity. Doctor theologicus.

A doctor of Physick. Archiater, archiatrus.

A doctor of Law. Legisdoctor, m.

Doctrine. Doctrina. eruditio, præceptio, didascalia, institutio, disciplina.

Doctrinal. Protrepticus.

A document. Documentum, præceptio, syntagma.

Dock, i. the upper part of the horse tail.

To **dodge.** Vitiligo.

A dodger. Vitilitigator, prævaricator.

A **dodkin.** Hilum, n. teruncius, m.

A **Doe.** V. Buck.

To **Do.** Ago, facio, patro, efficio, perpetro.

To do a thing again. Itero, redintegro.

To do a thing slily, or to pick

---

a purse. Manticulor.

To do often. Actito, factito.

Togo about to do. Facesso.

To do or accomplish. Exequor, perago, conficio.

To do a thing diligently. Recuro, satago.

To do amiss. Erro, oberro, prolabor.

To do after the country fashion. Ruro.

To do a good turn. Gratificor, promereor.

To do and undo. Retexo.

To do all things at others commandment. Obsecundo.

To do any thing by measure or number. Modulor.

To do by turn. Alterno.

To do a thing in vain. Frustro, frustror.

To do a thing hastily. Maturo, propero.

To do a thing negligently. Varico, varicor.

To do like for like. Retalio.

To do a thing unadvisedly. Præcipito.

To do a thing before another. Præverto, anteverto.

To do well. Benefacio.

To be done. Fio, consio, effio. I will do. Faxo, pro faciam, def.

Done. Actus, factus, gestus, patratus, perpetratus, perfectus, transactus, p.

Done before. Anteactus.

Suddenly done. Approperatus.

That must be done. Obeundus.

Done and dispatched. Perfectus, transactus, p.

Done by stealth. Surreptitius.

Done curiously. Accuratus.

A doer. Factor, actor, effector, patrator.

He that doth any thing often. Factitator, m.

A thing done. V. Deed.

A doing. Executio, actio, factio, persunctio, factura, effectio, f.

The virtue or power to do. Efficientia, f.

Rightly doing. Catorthosis, f.

Enforcement to do. Nixus, ùs.

Late done. Nuperus.

A **DOG** or bitch. Canis.

A dog. Canis masculus.

A bitch or bratch. Canis fœmina.

A little dog, or whelp. Catulus, & catellus.

A young dog not yet well trained. Tyruncula canis.

A little bitch. Canicula, f.

A fierce dog. Canis acer.

A swift dog. Citus, vel celer canis.

That hath a shrill mouth. Argutus.

That hath a coller on his neck. Armillatus.

An old dog past the best. Ca-

---

nis emeritus.

A mad dog. Canis rabidus vel rabiosus.

A spaniel, hound, or other dog that hunteth by scent. Canis generosus, sagax, odorus, odorisequus.

A spaniel. Hispaniolus.

A water-spaniel. Hispaniolus aquaticus, villosus.

A land-spaniel. Hispaniolus agrarius. campestris.

A hound. Venaticus, adj.

A drawing-hound, or bloodhound. Investigarius, plaudus, canis Scoticus.

A Gase-hound. Agasæus.

A Grey-hound. Leporarius, Gallicus.

A Terriare. Terrarius, m.

A Tumbler. Vertagus, m.

A Mastiff, or band-dog. Molossus.

A Cur. Canis gregarius, degener,

A shepherds-dog, or herdmans dog. Canis pecuarius, pastoralis, aggregarius, pœmenis, pernox.

A Farmers cur to keep the house. Canis villaticus.

A little pretty dog which women use to play with : a Fisting hound. Melitæus canis.

A Mongrel. Hybris, hybrida.

A Mongrel engendred of a wolf and a dog. Lycisca, lyciscus, cracuta, Of a fox and a dog. Alopecida, alopecydes.

To bark like a dog. Latro.

To howl. Ululo, exululo, baubor.

To yaulp, or yelp like a dog, Gannio.

To go a saut as bitches do. Cutulio.

To set dogs on. Immittere canes.

To hunt. Venor, sector, indago.

To draw or follow by the foot. Investigo.

To quest, or open as Spaniels or Hounds do, when they have the scent or sight of their game. Nicto, is.

To chear the hounds. Hortari.

To cry like a young whelp. Glaucito.

Nomina Canum.

B

Blab, or Bark. Canache.
Black-foot. Melampus.
Blanch, or White coat. Leucon.
Bright. Vide Swift.

C

Catch, or Snatch. Harpagus.
Chaunter or wingwood. Hylactor, hylax.
Churl. Vide Wolf.
Close-biter. Læthargus.
Cole, or Cole-black. Asbolus, melaneus.
Crow. Corax.

h   Fawn-

A slight variant of this imprint appears in a copy in the University of Texas Library, concluding: "Printed by John Hayes, Printer to the University, 1674." This may possibly indicate another issue of the 1674 edition.

The two other title pages in this edition indicate that these parts were printed in London, not Cambridge. In phrasing they are identical with those of 1664, transcribed above, to the imprint and the sentence preceding. For the Latin-English of 1673–74, the end of the title page reads: "In hac Editione Syllabarum Quantitates, multo quam antehac accuratius, assiguntur. Londini, Excudebat Gulielmus Rawlins. Anno M. DC. LXXIII." The same imprint concludes the title page for the proper names.

As the 1674 edition represents the only real revision and augmentation (not extensive) of the Gouldman, it requires brief comment. The insertion of Hebrew roots and derivatives by W. Robertson is one element of amplification. For this innovation there was precedent in the later Rider-Holyoke dictionaries, though these were not the source of Robertson's Hebrew terms. The Hebrew roots and derivatives, roughly equivalent to the Latin entries, are fairly consistently inserted throughout the 1674 Gouldman; in the Rider-Holyoke they are few and far between. Perhaps it should be added here that from the first edition Gouldman had added Greek equivalents, largely from Thomas and Holyoke.

Possibly of more importance is a fair amount of augmentation in the English-Latin and Latin-English parts. A few illustrations of expansion in the English-Latin may be found under the signatures specified herewith.

Sig. *a*1ʳ   *s.v. abolish,* 5 more Latin synonyms are added, *s.v. abomination,* 2 short independent entries.

Sig. *b*7ʳ   no changes, except that *V* becomes *Vide.*

Sig. *d*7ʳ   14 short new entries are added; as the total number of entries on this page is 161, the new matter is less than 10 per cent.

Sig. *q*3ʳ   15 short new entries added. These, like other new entries, are marked with an asterisk.[1]

These are typical of the English-Latin; they indicate augmentation, though not in any considerable degree. Amplification in the Latin-English is relatively less.

The edition of 1678 seems to have been printed in all parts by the University Press at Cambridge. The title page of this edition is identical with that of 1674, except the imprint: "And in this Fourth Edition there

A page of the 1669 edition of Francis Gouldman's Copious Dictionary in Three Parts, from a copy in the University of Texas Library (opposite)

are many thousand Words more added, by the Skill and Pains of Dr. Scattergood. Cambridge, Printed by John Hayes, Printer to the University. M. DC. LXXVIII." For the Latin-English the title page reads: "Cantabrigiae, Ex officina Joan. Hayes, Celeberrimae Academiae Typographi. Anno M. DC. LXXVIII." For the proper-name, or historical-geographical dictionary, no printer's name or place of publication is given. Only this date: "Anno Dom. M. DC. LXXVII."

Despite the claim of the addition of "many thousand Words," by Dr. Scattergood, the augmentation of the 1678 Gouldman is negligible. Through the English-Latin and the proper-name sections, the printer's signatures and the catchwords are the same as those in 1674. In the Latin-English parts of the two volumes there is close correspondence in signatures, though there are slight variations in the catchwords. Dr. Scattergood's thousands of additions are so well distributed that we are left wondering where they are. The various texts indicate that the statement about the additions is another bit of exaggerated advertising.

It has seemed desirable to clear up the problem of editions, including changes and augmentations, before discussing the relation to antecedents, the sources, and other features of the Gouldman dictionary. As the edition of 1674 represents the only substantial augmentation, we shall draw illustrations from this, referring to other editions when occasion requires.

An interesting feature of the general title page is the compiler's candor—uncommon among lexicographers of the time—in stating, in effect, that his is not an original work: that the foundations were laid by Thomas and Rider, and the superstructure and improvements were made by Holyoke. Furthermore, near the end of the Preface to his dictionary, Gouldman again acknowledges the principal sources of his work. He writes, "In sum: Nothing considerable, nothing profitable in Thomasius,[2] Rider, or Holyoak . . . can be said to be wanting." In the Preface, Gouldman refers to Wase's dictionary as "a book of good use." To the compilers thus mentioned Gouldman is indebted for most, if not all, the matter in the English-Latin part of his dictionary. Compare the following entries:

Rider-Holyoke (1640)	Wase (1662)	Gouldman (1674)
Abacted. v. Driven away.		Abacted. v. Driven away.
To Abandon, put away, or forsake. 1 *Amando, amoneo, abjicio, relinquo, desero, destituo.*	To abandon. *Derelinquo ere.*	To abandon, put away, or forsake. *Amando, amoneo abjicio, relinquo, derelinquo, desero, destituo.*
To abandon or divorce, v. Divorce.		To abandon or divorce. *Vide* Divorce.

Rider-Holyoke (1640)	Wase (1662)	Gouldman (1674)

Rider-Holyoke (1640)

Abandoned or forsaken. 1 *Amandatus, relictus, desertus, destitutus.*

An abandoning, or forsaking. 1 *Amandatio, relictio, desertio.*

To abase, or bring low. 1 *Humilio.* 2 *Dejicio, demitto, deprimo. vide* Debase and humble.

. . . .

To abate or diminish. 1 *Demo, minuo, imminuo, comminuo, attenuo, decoquo.*

. . . .

An Abecedary or alphabet an a, b, c. 1 *Alphabetum, abcedarius. n.*

An abecedary, or pettie, or teacher of petties . . . 1 *Alphabetarius, abecedarius, m.*

To bee able. 1 *Possum, valeo, queo.*

To be very able, or more able than others. 1 *Praepossum, praepello, praevaleo, praevalesco.*

Able, strong or mighty. 1 *Potens, valens, p. validus, potis, efficax, ad.*

Able to rule himselfe. 1 *Compos fui.*

Very able, or more able than others. 1 *Praepotens, praepollens, p. praevalidus. ad.*

Abilitie, ablenesse, strength, or power. 1 *Facultas, potentia, efficacia, efficacitas, robur, n.*

Wase (1662)

Abandoned. *Derelictus.*

An abandoning. *Derelictio.*

To abase. *Humilio are.*

. . . .

To abate (act.) *Subduco ere.*
To abate (neut.) *Decresco ere.*

An A.B.C. *Alphabetum.*
An A.B.C. boy. *Elementarius puer.*

To be able. *Possum posse.*

Able, *Potens, idoneus, valens.*
An able man (in skill,) *Solers,* (in wealth,) *opulentus,* (in strength,) *validus.*
Ability or ableness. *Potentia.*

Gouldman (1674)

Abandoned or forsaken. *Amandatus, relictus, derelictus, desertus, destitutus.*

An abandoning, or forsaking. *Amandatio, relictio, derelictio, desertio, destitutio.*

To abase, or bring low. *Humilio, dejicio, abjicio, demitto, deprimo. Vide* Debase and humble.

. . . .

To abate or diminish, (act.) *Demo, minuo, detraho, imminuo, comminuo, attenuo, decoquo, subduco.*
To abate (neut.) *Decresco.*

An abecedary or alphabet, an A.b.c. *Alphabetum, abecedarium. n.*

An abecedary or petty, or teacher of petties . . . *Alphebetarius, abecedarius, m. elementarius puer.*

To be able. *Possum, valeo, queo.*

To be very able, or more able then others. *Praepossum, praepolleo, praevaleo, praevalesco.*

Able, strong or mighty. *Potens, valens, p. validus, potis, efficax, idoneus, adj.*
*An able man for skill, *Solers;* For wealth, *Opulentus;* For strength, *Validus.*

Able to rule himself. *Compos fui.*

Very able or more able then others: *Praepotens, praepollens, p. praevalidus, adj.*

Ability, ableness, strength or power. *Facultas, potentia, opis, efficacia, f. robur, n.*

The examples show Gouldman's procedure. For him, the Rider-Holyoke list was basic. This he supplemented from Wase. Gouldman's assertion on the title page that the English-Latin contains ten thousand more words than any other dictionary is sheer exaggeration. And his declaration in the Preface that he was helped by the use of a folio manuscript, "which seemeth to be of good Antiquity and precedent to Rider," we may query. Such manuscripts there might have been; [3] but the Rider and Wase account for so much of Gouldman's English that it is difficult to see what use he might have made of the alleged manuscript.

It will be observed that the title page of Gouldman's Latin-English division echoes that of Holyoke in his *Dictionarium etymologicum*. From this source and from the Thomasius, as Gouldman suggests on his general title page, he derives most of his Latin-English. The Latin terms and English definitions and illustrations, which, in the three texts, fall between *expedibo* and *exploro* reveal the character of Gouldman's indebtedness. Here are a few of the entries to illustrate the relationship: [4]

Thomas (1631)	Rider-Holyoke (1648)	Gouldman (1674)
Expedibo, pro expediam, Nonn.	*Expedibo pro expediam:* Nonnius.	*Expedibo, pro Expediam,* Non.
	Expedimentum, ii, n. B. Furtherance.	*Expedimentum, ti, n.* B. Furtherance.
Expello, is, puli, pulsum, ere . . . To expell: to put, thrust, drive, or chase out or away: also to reiect. *Expellere aliquem regno,* Caesar. *Ex urbe.* To expell or drive out of. *Expellere aliquem in opus,* Plin. To drive out to worke. *Per vulnera animam expellere,* Ovid. To kill. Also to thrust forth as the land doth. A cape or promontorie . . . *Criumetopon. Expellit.* Plin.	*Expello, is, puli, ulsum, ere* . . . To put or chase out or away, also to reject, to thrust forth, to expell.	*Expello, is, puli, pulsum, ere* . . . To expell: to put, thrust, drive or chase out or away: also to reject. *Expellere aliquem regno:* Caes. *Ex urbe;* To expel or drive out. *Expellere aliquem in opus,* Plin. To drive out to work. *Per vulnera animam expellere,* Ovid. To kill, also to thrust forth as the land doth a cape or promontory. *Criumetopon* . . . *expellit,* Plin.
	Expenno, as, Hadr. *i. depenno.* To pluck away feathers.	*Expenno, as;* Hadr. *i. depenno.* To pluck away feathers.
Expenso, as, Scaev. To seale up and deliver money by weight: also	*Expenso, as* Scaev. *expensare apud Juriconsultos est expensam pecuniam*	*Expenso, as;* Scaev. *Expensare, apud J.C. est Expensam pecuniam consig-*

Thomas (1631)	Rider-Holyoke (1648)	Gouldman (1674)
to recompense, Macrob. To use to lay forth, frequent. *Cui opponitur, Accepto,* Plaut.	*consignare, ac tradere: interdum est compensare.* To seale up and deliver money by weight, also to recompense, to lay forth.	*nare ac tradere: interdum est Compensare.* To seal up and deliver money by weight: also to recompense, Macrob. To use to lay forth, *saepe expendo: cui apponitur Accepto.* Plaut.
	Expensilatio, Gel. 14.2. *vel divisim expensi latio.*	*Expensilatio,* Gell. 14.2. *vel divisim Expensi latio.*
Expergefacio, is, eci, actum, ere . . . To waken out of sleepe, to stirre up that before was quiet: to take courage or a good heart.	*Expergefacio, is, eci, actum, ere* . . . to awake, to stirre up, to take courage.	*Expergefacio, is, eci, actum, ere;* . . . To waken out of sleep, to stir up that before was quiet: to take courage or a good heart.
Expergefactus, a, um, Lucret. Wakened out of sleep.	*Expergefactus, a, um;* Luc. Wakened.	*Expergefactus, a, um;* Luc. Wakened out of sleep.
Expergificus, a, um, That doth awaken. *Carmen expergificum gallorum,* The Cocke crow, Apull.	*Expergificus, a, um.* That doth awake.	*Expergificus, a, um.* That doth awaken. *Carmen expergificum gallorum.* The Cockcrow, Apul.
Experrectus, a, um, ab expergiscor . . . Quickened, stirred up, wakened: waking, or that awaketh or stirreth up himself.	*Experrectus, a, um* . . . *a porrigendo sc. vocatus quod fere facimus recentes, a somno experrectus est qui per se vigilare coepit.* Fest. Wakened, wakening, stirred up.	*Experrectus, a, um;* . . . *a porrigendo sc. vocatus, quod fero facimus recentes, a somno. Experrectus est qui per se vigilare coepit,* Fest. Wakened, wakening, stirred up.

Study of the definitions above will show that Gouldman had the texts of Thomas and Holyoke open before him and drew freely from both. In some cases he follows Thomas, in others Holyoke, and in still others he derives from both. This seems to be the principle of compilation throughout. Very rarely does Gouldman have a definition derived from any text other than these. In fifty consecutive entries, beginning with *expedibo,* Gouldman has not a single entry independent of the other two texts. There are at least fourteen entries which he derives from Thomas only, ten which he borrows from Holyoke only, twelve which derive from both, and many others which may have come from either. Almost nothing in either or in both of his predecessors is wanting in Gouldman. Quotations and phrases from standard authors to illustrate meanings and uses of terms, omitted in the Rider-Holyoke, Gouldman restores by drawing from Thomas.

The same sources are basic for Gouldman's geographic and poetic dictionary, or dictionary of proper names. In this section Gouldman draws more from a late Rider-Holyoke than from Thomasius, though he uses both. Compare the following:

Thomas (1596)	Rider-Holyoke (1640)	Gouldman (1674)
Aba, Daughter to Xenophanes, who obtained of Anthonie the government of Olbia in Silicia. Also a town in Arabie, and a citie in Phocis. Also a hill in Armenia. Also a King of Hungarie that spoiled Bavaria and Austria.	*Aba*, Daughter to Xenophanes: also a towne in Arabia, and a citie in Phocis: also a hill in Armenia: also a King of Hungarie.	*Aba*, Daughter to Xenophanes, who obtained of Anthony the government of Olbia in Silicia; also a town in Phocis: also a hill in Armenia; also a King of Hungary that spoiled Bavaria and Austria.
Abacaenum, A citie of sicile not farre from Messana. *Abacaeni incolae.*	*Abacaenum, urbs Siciliae, unde Abacaeni incolae.*	*Abacaenum, urbs Siciliae, unde Abacaeni incolae.*
Abaton, A place at Rhodes, made to defende the Image of Artemisia.	*Abaton, graece, ἄβατον ab a & βαίνω i. invium.* A place at Rhodes made to defend the Image of Artemysia.	*Abaton, graece, ἄβατον ab a & βαίνω i. invium.* A place at Rhodes, made to defend the Trophy of Artemisia.
Abel, Adams second sonne. Also a place in Palaestina, where Iephte fought with the Ammonites.	*Abel, i. luctus*, a place in Palestina: הבל, *i. vanitas, sive anhelitus*, the sonne of Adam.	*Abel, i. luctus* הבל *i. vanitas, sive anhelitas*, The son of Adam; also a place in Palestine where Jephte fought with the Ammonites.
Abi, A river in England called Humber. Abia, The daughter of Hercules. Also a citie, the same that Ira.	*Abi*, a river in England called Humber: also *Abi, i. pater meus* or *Abia*, אביה, *i. pater Domini, aut voluntas Domini.* The mother of King Ezechias: also the daughter of Hercules: also a Citie, the same that Ira: also the sonne of Samuel the Prophet.	*Abi*, a river in England called Humber; also *Abi, i. pater meus*, or *Abi*, אביה, *i. pater Domini, ut voluntas Domini.* The mother of King Ezechias. *Abia*, The daughter of Hercules. A city, the same with Ira; also a son of Samuel.

Following the practice of Thomas and of the later editions of Rider-Holyoke, Gouldman places under one alphabet the pure and the barbarous words. This, he explains, is the right procedure, since it is difficult often to distinguish between purity and barbarism, and since also the Latin-English section is used in reading, not in writing. The marking of vowels and the indication of grammatical information and classical authority are as in Thomas and Holyoke. In the use of phrases to illustrate meaning and usage Gouldman follows Thomasius, borrowing his illustrations. In his very brief discussions of letters of the alphabet, he is reviving a practice last used by Baret, but soon to be employed very learnedly by Littleton and Ainsworth.

Gouldman writes that he has etymologies in plenty, and thus repairs a defect in Thomas. His hint in the Preface is that the etymologies may have come from that "Excellent posthumous Work of the admirably Learned Gerardus Joannes Vossius, his Etymologicon linguae Latinae." His debt to Vossius is hard to establish. Under *contemplari, continuus, convexum,* and *fructus* in Gouldman and Vossius, there are definite correspondences; but since the same matter with references to Festus, Varro, and Calepine is also in the Rider-Holyoke, it is possible that Gouldman was drawing from the latter source. Etymologies cited earlier, under *congruo, conjugium, conniveo, exercitus, equus, fortis,* and *graculus,* as typical of Francis Holyoke, all appear in Gouldman. Most of his etymologies are from the same source.

The *minuter tractates* following the dictionary of proper names consist of (1) "Ponderum, Mensurarum Et Monetarum veterum reductio ad ea, quae sunt Anglis jam in usu," (2) "De Sestertio," (3) "Primitiva omnia Totius Graecae Linguae Vocabula," (4) "De Nominibus Mensium Graecorum," (5) a table of modern coins, with their weights and the relative value of foreign and English coins, and (6) Latin equivalents of English place names ("ex Cl. Camdeno"). The first four of these come directly from Thomas Thomas; the fifth and sixth from Rider-Holyoke.

As a survey, not without errors, of the history of Latin-English lexicography and an exposition of his own work, Gouldman's Preface is of unusual interest. It is here transcribed, with slight changes in paragraphing, as a conclusion to this chapter.

The Preface

It is not the Intendment of this Introductory Discourse, to perswade the World of the Usefulness, or rather the Necessity of such Gates of Language and Learning: The rational and convincing Prefaces of many learned men, the heavy progress of former times much wanting them, with the general acceptance of, and great improvement by these helps in later times, render such Labours useless. But the present Design is, to give a plain and brief account of Other Undertakings of this nature, especially by learned men of our own; and of what hath been endeavoured in this Present Work; and in both to give the Reader that Satisfaction he certainly will and justly may expect as to this Book offered to view.

To Languages as well as Dominions (with all other things under the Sun) there is an appointed time: they have had their Infancy, Foundations and Beginning; their Growth and Increase in purity and perfection, as also in spreading and propagation; their state of consistency; and their old age, declinings and decays. That thus it pleased the Divine Providence to deal with Rome in her Power and Tongue is abundantly manifest: For after that she that had been the Mistress and Glory of the World, grew ripe for the recompence of her Pride, Tyranny, Persecutions and all Abominations, the Barbarians (for Language and Manners) overran her and her Territories, and seven times in much less then an hundred years trampled upon her Glory. From these times, and peculiarly the Goths establishment, towards the end of the Fifth Century, the genuine purity of the Latin Tongue was sensibly imbased, and indeed as to a general acceptation, all real Learning (and Religion very much) ran low and dreggy. Onely, as God reserved in successive Ages of degeneracy and darkness some Witnesses to his Truth; so were there some worthy men now and then appearing for the Vindication of Learning, and those Tongues that did most befriend her.

One of the first most direct and considerable attempts of this kind (as to the Latin Tongue) was made by Papias a Lombard, whose Work, though wanting the best Method for use, viz. Alphabetical Order, and not wanting some Oversights and Impertinencies, yet was a good Essay for those times towards the Derivation and Explication of Latine Words: this was towards the end of the Twelfth Century, when as for a considerable time before and after, the Latine Tongue had scarce any Writers worthy notice, onely some few (and those but ordinary) Historians, and some schoolmen (with their Niceties wrapped up in Improper Language) appeared in the World, and indeed not many Learned men among the Grecians, onely in the Hebrew and Arabian Tongues Learning flourished. A considerable time after this Vocabulist (for so is he named) Nestor Dionysius of Novara in Dutchy of Millan succeeded, and what Papias his Vocabulary, and some other Works of like nature (some having, some wanting the Names of their Authors) had heaped up, and in some things had mistaken, or were themselves by their too ignorant Successours mistaken, he with considerable Amendments and Improvements reduced into Order by an Alphabetical handling: and this not without the Envy and Exclamations of his Contemporaries, who so far were strangers to good Latine, so little were sensible of its Depravations among them, and so much loved their barbarisms, that they hated, derided and opposed whatever offered at the redeeming of Learning from its present slavery.

After him many industrious and able restorers of Learning followed apace, and about the year 1494, Ambrosius Calepinus treading in his steps and method: But that work of his at its first Birth bare no proportion to its present stature, to which it hath gradually encreased at many Editions in several Places, by the Labours of Montanus, Passeratius and other excellent Builders upon his Foundation. Not to enlarge too far, take but two more: Robert Stephens, that Learned Printer, about the year 1536 put forth his Thesaurus, a book of great Industry and worth: of which Cooper saith, "The greatness is the onely inconvenience of that Golden Work." And not long after, Joannes Frisius published his Latine and German Dictionary.

To come to our own Writers of Dictionaries: About the same time Sir Th. Eliot, an able Lawyer, and every way a famous Scholar in those days first brake the Ice as to our English Tongue, with great pains Compiling a Latine and English Dictionary, called his Bibliotheca, in the Reign of King Henry the Eighth, to whome it is Dedicated. This work Thomas Cooper, in the beginning of the Reign of Edward the Sixth, Augmented and Enriched with Three and thirty thousand Words and Phrases, besides a fuller account of the true Signification of Words; farther declaring, That there was a complaint of innumerable Faults in Eliot, by too strict following Calepine, the mistakes of Impressions, or his own hast and oversight. Afterward the Reverend and Learned Cooper, Bishop of Lincoln, reserving still as a Foundation Eliot's and his own former Labours upon him, and making great use of Stephen's Thesaurus and Frisius his Dictionary (insomuch that F. Holyoak saith, he translated Frisius his German into English) put forth his Thesaurus linguae Romanae & Britannicae, about the year 1565. About these times Baret's Alvearium, being an English and Latine Dictionary, was prepared, and Printed 1573. In the year 1583, Richard Hutton makes the French-part of Guil. Morelius (that Learned Printer to the French King) his Comentarii, to speak English.

To come nearer our Present Work: In the year 1588, Tho. Thomasius, the Printer to the University of Cambridge, puts forth his Dictionary in Octavo which was so acceptable a Work, that in eight years it had Five Impressions with the Authors Corrections and Enlargements, in the carrying on of which Work he died. John Legate undertaketh, with his Place, the Printing of his Work 1596; in which Fifth Edition many words were added out of Physicians, Lawyers, Mathematicians, etc. Also Examples and Instances out of best Authours, and a Dictionary of Names of Places and Persons added thereto. Since this time it hath risen to Fourteen Editions, not without signall Improvement, especially by Doctour Philemon Holland, of which Fr. Holyoak freely and ingenuously acknowledgeth, That by that Learned person in Physick and Philology it was so wonderfully Inriched, that there was no Dictionary of that kind Extant, that for Number of Words, perfect Interpretation, and choice Phrases may be compared with it. John Rider, Minister of Saint M. Magdalen Bermondsey in Southwark, and afterward Bishop of Killaloo in Ireland, (not long after Tho. Thomasius) published his work, as an Epitomizer of all the Learnedst and best Dictionaries then in English, superadding much of his own to what was then Extant: That Part whereof which hath the Latine before the English was swallowed up by Francis Holyoak's greater attempt and performance: which Work of Holyoak's, however designed (as he Prefaceth) before Becmannus, Fungerus and Martinius came out, yet is not a little beholding to them, especially the last, as may appear to any one that shall Compare them in some few words. Very lately an ingenuous person, Christopher Wase, hath published a more contracted Dictionary, a compend of Calepine, a Book of good use.

Having thus led the Reader with the series of time through the most considerable Works of this Nature, now let him take this account of the Book before him. As to the adding this Dictionary after others that have been well reputed and are useful, let it be considered, That they were written one after another, and that was no hindrance to their Authours pains or others acceptance: yea others of late in other Countries have been and are still adding new to old: and who can fix the time when such Works are at the height of all desirable or possible Perfection, where Hercules's Pillars may be placed with a Ne plus ultra? Nay, it will appear by what followeth, that even the latter Dictionaries have been defective: Moreover they, as hath been represented, had their Amendments and Increase by successive Endeavours and Editions, raising them to that pitch wherein they stand. As to what hath been endeavoured, and (we doubt not) in good measure performed in this Edition, we will speak to the several parts of the Book distinctly.

As to that Part which hath the English before the Latin;

The English it self is very much restored where faulty and mis-spelled in former Dictionaries: And in the Latin of them many faults corrected.

The leading words are put generally into their natural Order and due place, whereas before they were much transposed.

Many Heads of English with their Latin supplied: And very many Additional Latin Words Inserted in their places under the former English; both, by a modest computation, amounting to at least Ten Thousand. And this not without furtherance by a Folio Manuscript, which seemeth to be of good Antiquity and Precedent to Rider. So that there is a considerable Accession, as may appear to the Peruser.

As to that part which hath the Latin before the English:

Multitudes of Faults amended in the Words, both Latin, Greek, Hebrew and English.

The Sense which was sometimes unintelligible, and sometimes lame and defective, is now made Entire and Plain, so far as brevity would permit.

The joyning with good Coherence of several Designs in other Dictionaries, in one Volume in This, is considerable. Formerly the Pure and Proper Latin Words were in one Alphabet; the Obsolete, Antique and Antiquated Words in an other, to the trouble of Him that searched for a Word. And if it be inquired, why those Words that are of a baser Allay are not by some Mark distinguished from the more currant and usual Words: Let it be considered; First, that it is hard to set the just Boundaries and Landmarks of the more approvable Latin, and that which by Degrees crept in with the Declinings of the Empire, decay of Learning and mixture of Barbarous Nations. Secondly, That this part of a Dictionary is little consulted, but for the understanding of a Word found in an Authour, and doth not considerably belong to the making of Latin. Besides, that the Nature of the Authours quoted generally intimateth when a Word is suspicious for purity, and when not. Moreover, formerly the Etymologies and Notations of the Word were chiefly minded by some; the Instances of Use, and Phrases in Authours most attended by others: This hath the former (and supplies that defect in Thomas) for the understanding of the whole Frame of the Latin Tongue, and its Derivations. This hath also the Later (therein supplying that great Defect in Rider and Holyoak;) Phrases being a Clavis to Authours, letting us in to their Sense and Meaning.

Chapter XIX

Thomas Holyoke's *Large Dictionary in Three Parts* (1677)

FRANCIS HOLYOKE, the first reviser of *Riders Dictionary* and the compiler of the *Dictionarium etymologicum,* died in 1653. His lexicographic work was continued, after a lapse of some years, by his son, Thomas Holyoke. Thomas was educated at Queen's College, Oxford, where at one time he was captain of the undergraduate Royalists. He took the degree of master of arts in 1639 and became chaplain of Queen's College. He was prebendary of Wolverhampton and a practicing physician until the Restoration. Sometime in the 1660's, apparently, he began the compilation of a dictionary based in part upon the work of his father. Two years after Wase had printed the second edition of his dictionary (1675), and one year before Gouldman had put out his fourth edition (1678), Thomas Holyoke published, in thick folio, his *Large Dictionary.* The general title page is phrased thus:

A Large Dictionary in Three Parts:
   I. The English before the Latin, containing above Ten Thousand more words than any Dictionary yet extant.
  II. The Latin before the English, with correct and plentiful Etymological Derivations, Philological Observations, and Phraseological Explications: To which there is added above Six Thousand words more than in any other Book of this Nature: as also the Phrases, difference of words of the same signification, the Greek and Roman Antiquities, viz. Their Magistrates, Habits, Customs, and Ceremonies, used at Sacrifices, Meals, etc. As also their Formulae, and likewise the most textual usual proper Hebrew Roots and Derivatives added to the simple Themes, and Compounds of the Latin are inserted.
 III. The Proper Names of Persons, Places, and other things necessary to the understanding of Historians and Poets. In the whole comprehending whatever is Ma-

terial in any Author upon this Subject. Together with very considerable and ample Additions, carried on by a diligent search into and perusal of very many Authors both Ancient and Modern. Whereby this Work is rendred the most Compleat and Useful of any that was ever yet extant in this kind.

Performed by the great Pains and many years Study of Thomas Holyoke, D. D. London, Printed by W. Rawlins, for G. Sawbridge, W. Place, T. Bassett, T. Dring, and J. Place. M. DC. LXXVII.

The title page for the Latin-English is, in part, as follows:

Lexicon Philologicum, Dictionarium Etymologicum. In quo Voces Latinae tum Purae tum Barbarae. Et quam multa Vocabula Anglicanae ex Originibus declarantur: Dictiones Hebraeae, Graecae, Syntaxisque singularum Vocum adjiciuntur . . . Propria Nomina, Et Fabulae cum suis Mythologiis . . . Summa Studio & Labore Thomae de Sacra-Quercu. Londini: Excudebat Guliel. Rawlins. MDCLXXVII.

For the title page of the proper-name section, this phrasing:

Dictionarium Historico-Geographico-Poeticum: In quo debita serie Tractantur Propria Nominum Deorum gentilium, Hominum, Regionum, Urbium, Marium, Fluviorum, &c. . . . Ex quibus fax accenditur Historicis, Poetis, Et Aliis Auctoribus . . . Londini, Excudebat Gulielmus Rawlins, Anno M. DC. LXXVI.

Immediately preceding the "Dictionarium Historico" is a brief section with the heading "Index Vocabulorum," containing tracts on the weights, measures, and moneys of the ancients, with their English equivalents; and also a catalogue of place names of ancient Britain. These all derive from Thomas and Rider-Holyoke by way of Gouldman.

At the beginning of the book, Thomas Holyoke has a lengthy "Epistola Lectori Benevolo," in which he refers to the more important lexicographers of the past, but nowhere mentions Thomas, Gouldman, or Wase, the three to whose work he is most indebted.[1] His attitude may be contrasted with that of Gouldman, who a mere compiler, like Holyoke, frankly lists the sources of his book.

To refer to the first or general title page of *A Large Dictionary*, we are struck by the similarity in phrasing to that of Gouldman's dictionary. Compare, for example, the following:

Gouldman	Holyoke
A Copious Dictionary in Three Parts:	A Large Dictionary in Three Parts:
I. The English before the Latin, Enriched with about Ten thousand Words more than any former Dictionary contains.	I. The English before the Latin, containing above Ten Thousand words more than any Dictionary yet extant.
II. The Latin before the English, with correct and plentiful Etymological Derivations, Philological Observations and Phraseological Explications.	II. The Latin before the English, with correct and plentiful Etymological Derivations, Philological Observations and Phraseological Explications. . . .

Gouldman	Holyoke
III. The Proper Names of Persons, Places, and other things necessary to the understanding of Historians and Poets. . . .	III. The Proper Names of Persons, Places, and other things necessary to the understanding of Historians and Poets. . . .

So far as we can determine, Thomas Holyoke nowhere refers to the dictionary of Gouldman. There can be little doubt, however, that he deliberately imitated the title page and borrowed freely from the text of Gouldman. To find the explanation of this procedure, we need to recall the discussion of Gouldman's compilation. We remember that his work practically absorbed that of Francis Holyoke (which we have referred to as the Rider-Holyoke), supplementing it with illustrations from Thomas Thomas's *Dictionarium*. Thomas Holyoke may have reasoned that, in incorporating in his own text the lexicon of Gouldman, he was but reclaiming the family heritage. Whatever may be the explanation of Holyoke's procedure, the evidence shows that he based his compilation upon the Gouldman and the Rider-Holyoke, with generous borrowings from Wase and possibly others.

For clearness and convenience we may discuss more specifically the sources of *A Large Dictionary* in the order of the major divisions listed on the title page: first, "The English before the Latin." For Restoration lexicographers, the principal model for English-Latin dictionaries was the compilation by John Rider, repeatedly printed, up to 1659, in the Rider-Holyoke dictionaries. A second book of this kind, after 1662, was that assembled by Christopher Wase. Though owing something to Rider, Wase exhibited considerable independence in his unpretentious English-Latin dictionary. Gouldman based his English-Latin on Rider, supplementing it occasionally with additions from Wase. The work of Thomas Holyoke is analogous. Apparently he used Gouldman as his major source, taking over all that Gouldman had collected from his twofold source. A comparison of texts—Rider, Gouldman, and Thomas Holyoke—will show that many of Holyoke's definitions, including spelling and punctuation, are determined by Gouldman.

Rider (1648)	Gouldman (1674)	T. Holyoke (1677)
A Dabbe 1 *alpha, f. vide* Blow.	A Dab. *Alpha, f. vide* Blow.	A Dab. *Alapa, foem. vide* Blow.
To dabble in the dirt. 1 *In luto versari.*	To dabble in the dirt. *In luto versari.*	To dabble in the dirt. *In luto versari.*
		Dabled. *Inquinatus.*
		A dabling. *Inquinatio.*
To call dadde, or daddie. 3 *Pappo.*	To call Dad or Daddy. *Pappo.*	To call Dad or Daddy. *Pappo.*
A Dad, or daddie, as	A Dad or Daddy as young	A dad or daddy, as young

Rider (1648)	Gouldman (1674)	T. Holyoke (1677)
young infants, do call them, when they begin to speake. 3 *Pappa, tata.*	infants do call them when they begin to speak. *Pappas, tata.*	infants do call them, when they begin to speak. *Pappas, tata.*
To dagge sheepe. i. to cut away the skirts of the fleece.	To dag sheep, i. to cut away the skirts of the fleece.	To dag sheep, i. to cut away the skirts of the fleece.
A dagge. 1 *Tormentiolum.*	A dag. *Tormentiolum, n.*	A dag. *Tormentiolum, n.*
A dagger. 1 *Pugio, m. cestrum, n.*	A dagger. *Pugio, m. ficu, f. cestrum, n.*	A dagger. *Pugio, m. ficu, f. cestrum, neut.*
A pocket dagger. 1 *Sicula, f.*	A pocket-dagger. *Sicula, f.*	A pocket-dagger. *Sicula, f.*
A hanging dagger. 1 *Parazonium, f.*	An hanging dagger. *Parazonium, n.*	An hanging dagger. *Parazonium, n.*
A little dagger. 1 *Pugiunculus, m.*	A little dagger. *Pugiunculus, masc.*	A little dagger. *Pugiunculus, m.*
To dagle or dag. 2 *Collutulo.*	To daggle or dag. *Collutulo.*	To daggle or dag. *Collutulo, irrorare vestem.*

It is not difficult to see, in these examples under "*D* ante *A,*" that Thomas Holyoke has followed Gouldman in capitalization and spelling, in the omission of the numbers (from the old Rider to indicate the status of a Latin word), and in the supplying of extra terms, as *ficu* (*s.v. a dagger*). Additions independent of Gouldman—"A dabbling. *Inquinatio*" and *irrorare vestem* (*s.v. to daggle*)—are from Wase. The following parallels will show more particularly Holyoke's borrowing from both Gouldman and Wase.

Wase (1675)	Gouldman (1674)	T. Holyoke (1677)
To gabble. *Praecipitantèr loqui.*	Gabbing. *V.* Lying.	Gabbing. *V.* Lying.
A Gabbler. *Praeceps in loquendo.*		
A Gabberdine. *Laena, ue.*		
The gable end of a house. *Fastigium, i.*	A Gabel. *Vectigalis genus.*	A gabel. *Vectigalis genus.*
A building having a gable end. *Fastigiatus, pyramidalis.*	Gable. *V.* Cable.	Gable. *V.* Cable.
A Gad of Steel. *Massa feri, Chalybis.*		
To gad up and down *Vagor, ari.*	To gad up and down. *Vagor, circumcurso, volito, ito, perigrinor.*	To gad up and down. *Vagor, circumcurso, volito, ito, peregrinor.*
A Gad-bee, or Gadflie. *Tabanus, Asilus i.*	A gadder abroad. *Vagus, adj. ambulo, m.*	A gadder abroad. *Vagabundus, adj. ambulo, m.*

Wase (1675)	Gouldman (1674)	T. Holyoke (1677)
A gadder. *Erro nis.*	A gadding gossip. *Ambulatrix f.*	A gadding gossip. *Ambulatrix, f.*
Gadding. *Errabundus.*	A gadding abroad. *Peregrinatio, f.*	A gadding abroad. *Peregrinatio, f.*
Always gadding up and down. *Vagabundus.*	Gaddingly. *Peregre, adv.*	Gaddingly. *Peregre, adv.*
	A gad of steel. *Massa chalybis.*	A gad of steel. *Massa chalybis.*

The Gaffle of a Cross-bow. *Chalybs flexor Ballistae.*

The gaffle of a Cross-bow. *Chalybs flexor balistae.*

A gage, or give a gage. *Oppignero are.* — A gage, *V.* pledge. — A gage. *V.* Pledge.

Gaged. *Pignori datus.*

A gaging. *Oppigneratio.*

To gage vessels or casks. *Capacitatem doliorum metiri.*

A Gage to measure Casks with. *Virga chorometrica.*

Gaged or measured. *Virga chorometrica probatus.*

A Gager. *Doliorum mensor.*

The gaging of cask. *Chorometria ae.*

To gage vessels, as casks. *Capacitatem doliorum metiri.*

A gage to measure casks with. *Virga chorometrica.*

Gaged or measured. *Virga chorometrica probatus.*

A gager. *Doliorum mensor.*

The gaging of casks. *Chorometria.*

The Rider-Holyoke (1648–49) is omitted from the parallels above. Adapting the material of the Rider, Gouldman makes several small changes; and Thomas Holyoke follows Gouldman. The interesting matter here is the six new entries introduced by Holyoke, beginning with *The gaffle of a Cross-bow.* These are all from Wase. Not every group of entries would offer relatively as much from Wase. But Thomas Holyoke's principle throughout is to employ Gouldman's text as a basis and to supplement with matter from Wase.

It may be recalled that the second part (Latin-English) of *A Large Dictionary* is described on the title page with phrases employed earlier by Gouldman as applicable to his own dictionary. As a heading for this Latin-English part of his work, Thomas Holyoke uses "Lexicon Philologicon et Dictionarium Etymologicum," recalling the earlier etymological dictionary by Francis Holyoke. Unlike the earlier Holyoke dictionaries, Thomas Holyoke's adds, for most words, phrases illustrating meaning and usage. This element alone would indicate considerable expansion above the Rider-Holyoke, in which such phrases were lacking.

Although the Latin-English division of Thomas Holyoke's *Large Dic-*

tionary occupies probably two-thirds of the folio text, the word list is not larger than that of any other dictionary of the kind. The word list corresponds fairly closely indeed to that of the Gouldman of 1674. There are entries not contained in Gouldman; and the Holyoke, printed in larger type, with more generous spacing on folio pages, gives the impression of a much greater vocabulary than that in smaller type on the quarto pages of Gouldman. But the differences are not so great as they appear to be. Thomas Holyoke seems indeed to have taken over Gouldman's word list, his Greek and Hebrew terms, and his illustrative phrases. The illustrations of usage he supplements by additions from Wase. Although there are borrowings from other sources, Gouldman and Wase are basic for the Latin-English, just as they are for the English-Latin, as shown above.[2] This is not to say that Holyoke neglected his father's text. There are whole blocks of entries, such as the twenty-eight from *exter* to *extersus*, in which the sole source seems to be the earlier *Dictionarium etymologicum*. Certain new entries, and especially the expansion of old ones by examples of usage, better show the matter derived from Gouldman and Wase. The parallels below are designed to show the relation of Thomas Holyoke's *Large Dictionary* to Francis Holyoke and Gouldman.

F. Holyoke (1648–49)	Gouldman (1674)	T. Holyoke (1677)
Expenso, as, Scaev. *expensare apud Juriconsultos est expensam pecuniam consignare, ac tradere: interdum est compensare.* To seale up and deliver money by weight, also to recompense, to lay forth.	*Expenso, as;* Scaev. *Expensare, apud J.C. est Expensam pecuniam consignare ac tradere: interdum est Compensare.* To seal up and deliver money by weight: also to recompense, Macrob. To use to lay forth, *saepe expendo: Cui apponitur Accepto,* Plaut.	*Expenso, as, act. acc.* Scaev. *Expensare apud J.C.tos est Expensam pecuniam consignare, ac tradere: Interdum est compensare.* To seal up and deliver money by weight: also to recompense, to lay forth, to pay one their expenses.
Expensus, a, um . . . Weighed, considered, laid out, reckoned.	*Expensus, a, um: part.* Weighed, pondered, considered, laid out, reckoned. *Expenso gradu.* Propert. With a slow pace. *Mihi feras expensum,* Write or set this on my head in your book: or Write that you have lent or delivered it to me.	*Expensus, a, um* . . . weighed, considered, laid out, reckoned. *Expenso gradu,* Propert. With a slow pace. *Mihi feras expensum.* Write or set this on my head in your books: or, write that you have lent, or delivered it to me.
Expertus, a, um, ad. ab experior: multum pe-	*Expertus, a, um: adj. ab Experior: multum pe-*	*Expertus, a, um, ior, issimus, part. ab Experior: mul-*

F. Holyoke (1648–49)	Gouldman (1674)	T. Holyoke (1677)
ritus ex n. hic pro valde ponitur . . . Isid. Taught by experience, skilfull.	*ritus. ex enim hic pro valde ponitur.* Isid . . . Attempted . . . taught by experience, that hath proved and tried, expert, skilfull, cunning, of good experience. *In rebus suis & alterius expertus,* cunning in his own and other mens affairs. *Expertus belli, & expertus bello.* Virg. Skilfull & expert in war. *Pericula mille expertus,* Lucan. That hath been in a thousand dangers. *Puella virum experta,* Hor. That hath had company with a man. *Expertus loquor,* I speak from certain experience.	*tum peritus, Ex. n. hic pro valde ponitur* . . . Isid. Taught by experience, skilful. *In rebus suis, & alterius, expertus,* Cic. Expert, and cunning in his own and other mens affairs. *Loquor expertus.* I speak from certain experience. *Expertus belli, & expertus bello,* Virg. Skillful in war. *Pericula mille expertus,* Lucan. That hath been in many dangers. *Puella virum experta,* Hor. That hath lost her maidenhead. *Expertae industriae homo,* Suet. A man of approved industry, and diligent.

In the examples above, the Thomas Holyoke entries are largely, if not entirely, determined by the Gouldman. There are many other instances of this procedure, just as there are of Thomas Holyoke's sole dependence, especially in shorter entries, upon his father's work. But for many of the longer entries, particularly of verbs with a variety of uses, we have in *A Large Dictionary* composite entries, deriving definitions and some of the illustrative phrases from Francis Holyoke and Gouldman, and supplying additional illustrations from Wase. In the entry *confero,* for example, the younger Holyoke takes his English definition mainly from Gouldman. His illustrations of usage—Latin phrases with English translations—he draws from at least three sources: eight from Francis Holyoke; five from Gouldman; and fifteen from Wase. Under *conficio,* he derives the English definition jointly from Francis Holyoke and Gouldman, eight illustrations from Gouldman and five from Wase. Although Gouldman's thick quarto had much more to offer than the small quarto of Wase, it is surprising how frequently Thomas Holyoke selects illustrations from the latter. It is probably a tribute to the competency of Wase's work.

That the texts discussed above constitute the sole sources of Thomas Holyoke's Latin-English dictionary cannot be maintained. They do serve to determine his method and to account for a considerable portion of the content. But in his somewhat pompous Preface, Holyoke mentions a number of lexicographers, native and foreign, including Thomas Cooper and Robert Stephanus and Dr. Henry Spelman. With all of these he was probably familiar, as he was with the Passeratius Calepine; and there is some indication that he consulted these authorities.

Spelman's *Glossarium* (1626, 1664) becomes, in fact, a major source for Latin passages in Holyoke's *Dictionary*. One test of this close relationship of the two texts is to compare the first thirty successive entries in Spelman (beginning *abba, abbas, abbatia, abbatis*) with the corresponding items in Holyoke. The latter, it will be found, has taken a part of every entry. So throughout, Holyoke draws constantly from Spelman, not using every entry, but, obviously, keeping the Spelman open before him. The *Glossarium* is a major source for the unconventional, often non-classical matter of Holyoke.

Another source for the longer passages, generally in Latin, is a seventeenth-century Calepine. From Calepine, Holyoke likewise draws freely. Examples of his borrowing may be seen under *asinus* and *canis*, long entries, in Latin, in which the various proverbs associated with each term are set down. Other borrowings from Calepine may be seen under *abanec, aedes, bulla, legem*, and *lex*. For what we might regard as encyclopedic matter or padding in the Holyoke, Spelman and Calepine are important sources.

The third part of *A Large Dictionary* has the special title "Dictionarium Historico-Geographico-Poeticum," borrowed from the corresponding part of Gouldman's *Copious Dictionary*. The title is a variant of Charles Stephanus' *Dictionarium, historicum, geographicum, poeticum*, a Latin text devoted solely to proper names and of great vogue from 1553 to the end of the seventeenth century. The custom of including in the large Latin-English lexicons a section on proper names was begun by Thomas Cooper, as we have observed earlier, and continued by Thomas, the Rider-Holyoke dictionaries, and Gouldman, though omitted in the small volume by Wase. The problem of Thomas Holyoke's source for this part of his *Large Dictionary* is comparatively simple: he follows, with few exceptions, Gouldman. The latter had used the Rider-Holyoke proper-name section, making expansions of certain entries and supplying additional sketches. This body of material Thomas Holyoke takes over *in toto*. In the first fifty-nine entries—"*A* to Abatas"—Holyoke follows Gouldman closely, excepting occasional rearrangement and the addition of a single entry (*abascui*). Holyoke's entries in "*C* ante *E*" and "*P* ante *A*" exemplify a similar procedure. Only occasionally does Holyoke add an entry. Here he owes nothing to Wase, for Wase had omitted proper names.

As for other features of Thomas Holyoke's text—the grammatical information, the Greek and Hebrew terms, the etymologies, the tables of measures and weights and coins, and English place names—he was following his immediate predecessors, Gouldman and Francis Holyoke.

Owing to the competition offered by the dictionaries of Elisha Coles and of Adam Littleton, published in the late seventies, Thomas Holyoke's *Large Dictionary* did not go into a second edition. We can hardly say that Holyoke made any innovation in lexicography. He seems to have been a competent compiler; his *Dictionary* is a composite bringing together much of what had appeared in Rider-Holyoke, Gouldman, and Wase, with additions from a seventeenth-century Calepine, Spelman's *Glossarium*, and possibly other sources. Containing the essential matter of these predecessors and printed in folio, in larger and more legible type, *A Large Dictionary* is for consultation preferable to any one of these.

CHAPTER XX

Elisha Coles's *Dictionary, English-Latin, and Latin-English* (1677)

O N FEBRUARY 27, 1677, Charles II granted to Elisha Coles a royal license for printing *A Dictionary, English-Latin, and Latin-English*. In the same year, Coles's *Dictionary* was published. Being a small, inexpensive quarto, the lexicon of Coles was obviously prepared for an audience different from that of Thomas Holyoke's large folio, which was also printed in 1677. Elisha Coles was a son of John Coles, schoolmaster of Wolverhampton, and a nephew of Elisha Coles, Calvinist. He attended Magdalen College, Oxford (1659), but left without taking a degree. In 1663 he went to London, where for several years he taught Latin to youths and English to foreigners. For a brief period (1677–78), he was second undermaster of Merchant Taylors' School, a post which he resigned to become master of Galway School. Here he remained until his death, in 1680. Coles wrote books on shorthand and schoolbooks, such as the *Compleat English Schoolmaster*, and compiled two dictionaries. *An English Dictionary* appeared in 1676,[1] and *A Dictionary, English-Latin, and Latin-English* in 1677. The title page of the bilingual dictionary runs thus:

A Dictionary, English-Latin, and Latin-English; Containing All things Necessary for the Translating of either Language into the other. To which end Many things that were Erroneous are rectified, many superfluities retrenched, and very many Defects supplied. And All suited to the meanest Capacities, in a plainer Method than heretofore: being (for ease) reduced into an Alphabetical Order, and Explained in the Mother Tongue. And Towards the completing of the English Part (which hath been long desired) here are added Thousands of Words, Phrases, Proverbs, Proper Names, and many other useful things mentioned in the Preface to the Work. By Elisha

Coles, Late of Magdalen Colledge, Oxon., now one of the Ushers in Merchant-Taylors School, London. London, Printed by John Richardson for Peter Parker at the Leg and Star over against the Royal-Exchange: And Thomas & John Gay, at the Corner Shop of Little Lumbard-Street and Cornhill, 1677.

In an interesting address to the reader, Coles clarifies some of the phrases on this title page. For example, English lexicographers from Thomas Thomas to Francis Gouldman, except Christopher Wase, had in general employed the alphabetical order in entering terms to be defined, but for the proper names they had had a separate section. Coles reverts, as he explains, to the method of Calepine in placing all, both common and proper, in one list, though unlike Calepine, Coles has a strictly alphabetical arrangement of all entries. Similarly, the separate lists of birds, beasts, and other things—a heritage from the vocabulary tradition—which were placed at the end of Rider-Holyoke dictionaries, Coles distributes alphabetically in the text proper. The alphabetical order throughout, Coles insists, makes for "quickness of dispatch" and helps to escape excessive repetition.

The phrase "Explained in the Mother Tongue," on the title page, has reference to Francis Holyoke's method of frequently throwing explanations into Latin—a habit introduced, as we have seen, in the enforced augmentation of the 1633 issue, and thereafter retained. Such explanatory phrases Coles rightly translated into English or, if they seemed unnecessary, omitted entirely.

Coles's own language in "To the Reader" is explicit about the ways he sought to "retrench" and "to rectifie" and is descriptive of his procedure. He writes:

> In the Latin part, many Words and Phrases are much more properly rendred than they were in any other; and where a single Word could conveniently be had, we chose it rather than a long and tedious Periphrasis.
> We have not heap'd up Synonyma's but yet took care that Words (especially the Primitives) should have the whole variety of their several Significations.
> Such usefull Explications, Directions and References as were wont to be in Latin, are here in plain and intelligible English. But such Latin Explications as were afterward repeated again in English, were judged a needless Vanity and therefore we have omitted them. We have also omitted the superfluous and tedious Etymologies, which (for the most part) depended merely upon Conjectures, and were of little or no Use at all to Children: but have given them where they are plain, and rationally to be deduced. . . .
> The quantities are here made compleat, by being placed over initial Vowels, as well as other Syllables.

To those familiar with Latin-English lexicography antecedent to Coles, in the seventeenth century, it is obvious that he is critical of the Rider-Holyoke and the Gouldman dictionaries. In these are the "tedious

Periphrasis," the explications in Latin often repeated in English, and the "superfluous and tedious Etymologies." To use one word, when possible, instead of a periphrasis, to avoid heaping up of synonyms, to make explanations in plain English, and to avoid etymologies based on conjectures—these were timely aims in 1677. They are nearer in spirit to Wase than to other contemporaries of Coles. And Wase is probably his most important source in the English-Latin and the Latin-English, though there is obvious indebtedness to Gouldman.

Of the English-Latin part of his text, Coles writes:

> In the English Part, the Corrections are so many and so great, as would take up too much Time and Room to relate.
>
> Thousands of Words, Particles, Idioms, Phrases and Proverbs are added. Together with the whole body of Proper Names (not in the English-Latin section of previous dictionaries), not only of Men and Women, and places here in England . . . but also the Modern names of Foreign Countries, Islands, Mountains, Cities, etc.

A comparative study of Rider-Holyoke, Gouldman, Wase, and Coles indicates Coles's predilection for Gouldman and Wase. The parallels which follow represent such a scrutiny, though only those most nearly related are set down. First are entries from Gouldman and Coles.[2]

Gouldman (1674)	Coles (1677)
Abacted. V. Driven away [Driven away. *Abactus, profligatus*].	Abacted [driven away] *abactus, a, um.*
To Abandon, put away, or forsake. *Amando, amoneo, abjicio, relinquo, derelinquo, desero, destituo.*	To Abandon [forsake] *amando, are, desero, derelinquo, destituo, ere.*
Abandoned or forsaken. *Amandatus, relictus, derelictus, desertus, destitutus.*	Abandoned, *derelictus, desertus, amandatus, a, um.*
An abandoner or forsaker. *Amandator, relictor, desertor.*	An Abandoner, desertor, *Amandator, oris, m.*
An abandoning or forsaking. *Amandatio, relictio, derelictio, desertio, destitutio.*	An Abandoning, *derelictio, amandatio, onis, f.*
To Abase, or bring low. *Humilio, dejicio, abjicio, demitto, deprimo.*	To Abase [bring low] *humilio, are, deprimo, ere, minuere, gradu dejicere.*
Abased or brought low. *Humiliatus, dejectus, demissus, depressus, p.*	Abased, *humiliatus, depressus, a, um.*
An abasement or bringing low. *Humiliatio, dejectio, demissio, depressio, f.*	Abasement, An Abasing, *humiliatio, onis, f.*
To Abate or diminish, (Act.) *Demo, minuo, detraho, imminuo, comminuo, attenuo, decoquo, subduco.*	To Abate [act.] *Subduco, detraho, minuo, ere.*
To abate, (neut.) *Decresco.*	To Abate [neut.] *Decresco, ere, minuo, ere.*
. . . . . .	. . . . .
An abecedary or alphabet, an A, b, c. *Alphabetum, abecedarium, n.*	An Abecedary, [A.B.C.] *Alphabetum, i.* An A.B.C. boy, *puer elementarius.*

In only the last entry in this group does Coles draw anything from Wase.

The parallels which follow show Coles generally preferring Wase to Gouldman.

Wase (1675)	Coles (1677)	Gouldman (1674)
A Nagge. *Asturco nis. Mannus i.*	A Nag. *Asturco, mannus.*	A nag, *Mannus, gradarius, asturco, equulus, musimon.*
The nail of a mans hand or foot. *Unguis is.*	The Nail of ones hand } foot } *Unguis.*	Nails of the fingers and toes. *Unguis, onyx.*
To scratch or mark with the nail. *Scabo, ere.*	To Mark } with the Scratch } Nails, *Scabo.*	
To pare ones nails very near. *Praecidere unguiculos advivum.*	To pare the Nails, *unguiculos praecidere.*	
Naked. *Nudus* Stark belly-naked. *Nudus velut ab utero materno.*	Naked, *Nudus* Stark Naked, *Nudus velut ab utero materno.*	Naked. *Nudus, inopertus, investitutus, intectus, adj.*
As naked as ones nail. *Nudior ovo, leberide.*	As Naked as ones Nail, *Nudior ovo, Leberide.*	
A name. *Nomen inis.*	A Name. *Nomen.* . . .	A name. *Nomen, vocabulum.*
The proper name. *Praenomen, inis.*	A proper Name, *Praenomen.*	
A sir-name. *Cognomen inis.*	A sur-name, *Cognomen.*	A surname. *Cognomen, cognomentum.*
A nick-name. *Ignominiosa, cognominatio.*	A Nick name, *Ignominiosa, cognominatio.*	A nick name. *Improperium.*
A good name. *Honesta fama.*	A good Name, *Fama honesta.*	A good name or report. *Existimatio, laus, fama, gloria.*

The two blocks of parallels are designed to show only that Coles borrowed from both Gouldman and Wase, not that these are sole sources of Coles. He has probably derived illustrations from other lexicographers and from his own reading.

Proper names which Coles includes in the English-Latin part of his text are hardly more than identifications, such as "Nab [a River in Germany] *Nabus*," "Nabel [in Africa] *Neapolis*," "Niddisdale [part of Scotland] *Nithia*," "Newcastle [in Northumberland] *Novum Castellum*," and "Newnham [in Hertfordshire] *Villa Nova*." He also inserts proper names with brief sketches in the Latin-English section. These, Coles asserts, he has added from Calepine, Ferrarius, and others. The "and others" includes Gouldman, to whom he owes much. Compare, for example, the entries below.

Gouldman (1674)

Brundunum, urbs Bavariae, vulgo Brau-naw.

Brundŭsiŭm . . . Graeci Brentesium, appel. a Brento quodam Herculis filio. A city of Calabria by the Adriatick sea, which hath a very commodius haven, long. 42. lat. 40. Clav.

Bruxella. A city of Brabant called Brussels, long. 26. lat. 52. Merc.

Bryas. A Grecian captain of the Argives against the Lacedaemonians.

Bryax, An engraver that helped to make that famous monument of Mausolus.

Bubassus, Cariae regio, Cujus mulieres Bubasides ab Ovidio voc.

Būbălus. A painter of Clazomene, who in his painting did expose Hipponactes to laughter: whereupon the Poet wrote such bitter verses against him that he hanged himself.

Būtes, gr. i. bubuculus. The son of Amycus king of Bebrycia, who being expelled for his fathers cruelty, came into Sicily, and was there in great favour with the strumpet Lycaste, called Venus for her beauty: he had a son by her called Eryx; whereupon rose the fable that Butes begat Eryx of Venus: also the son of Cecrops: also a river in Scythia near the Agathyrsi. . . .

Coles (1677)

Brundunum, the City Braunaw in Bavaria.

Brundŭsium, issum, Brendestium, or *Brentesium,* a City of Calabria by the Adriatick Sea, with a very commodius Haven.

Bruxellae, the City Brussels in Brabant.

Bryas, a General of the Argives, against the Lacedaemonians.

Bryaxis, a Worker of Marble, who helped to make the Mausoleum.

Bubasus, a Country in Caria, whose Women are called Bubasides in Ovid.

Būpălus or *Bubalus,* a Painter of Clazomene, who in his painting exposed the Poet Hipponactes to Laughter, who thereupon wrote such bitter verses against him, that he hanged himself.

Būtes, the son of Amycus, King of Bebrycia, who was expelled for his Fathers Cruelty, and settled in Sicily. Also a River in Scythia, and several other men.

There are in each text proper names and sketches not found in the other.

For the Latin-English of Coles, Wase and Gouldman are the more important sources. The parallel entries indicate that Coles drew from both the others.

Gouldman (1674)

Condŭco, is, xi, ctum, ere [Greek omitted]. To bring with: to hire or procure: to buy: to take an house or land . . . Also to gather or assemble together in one place: to convert: to take in hand: to undertake to do a thing at a price: to do a work or

Wase (1662, 1675)

Conduco, ĕre. To bring together. *In unum locum conducere. Domum conducere,* to hire or take an house. *Coquum conducere,* To hire a man cook. *Conducere opus faciendum,* To agree for, or take work by the great.

Coles (1677)

Condŭco, xi, ctum, to bring with or together, Lead, Assemble, Rent, to Hire, Agree for. *Conducere opus faciendum,* to take work by the great. *Quae ad ventris victum conducunt,* Belly-timber. *Reipublicae*

Gouldman (1674)	Wase (1662, 1675)	Coles (1677)
business for hire or wages . . . *Exercitus in unum conducere*, To gather together.	*Foricas conducere.* To undertake to cleanse a privy at such a rate. *Conducit*, It helps toward, it is gainful or profitable. *Id minime conduxit agricolae*, That was no wages available or advantageous to the husbandman. *Quae ad ventris victum conducunt*, What things make toward food. Belly timber. *Reipub. rationibus putem conducere*, I think turn to the publick advantage.	*rationibus conducere*, to turn to the publick advantage. *Conducere vulnus*, to skin or heal up a wound. *Nimium magno conducere*, to buy too dear. *Non aedepol conduci passum vita uxoris annua*, I can't believe my wife will live a year to an end.
Aliquem ad caedem faciendam conducere, To hire or procure one to. *Qui columnam illam de Cotta conduxerat*, Who undertook at Cotta's hand to make, &c. *Conducit hoc tuae laudi*, This maketh much for your praise. *Conducunt haec ad ventris victum*, Prud. Are good to fill the belly.		
In rem quod recte conducat tuam, Plaut. Maketh well for thy profit. *Conducere vulnus, idem quod Obducere cicatricem*; to skin or heal up a wound.		
Conducor, eris; pass. To be lead or brought together: Firm.		*Conducor, eri.* to be Led or Brought together.
Conductārius, a, um; Gloss. That guideth together.		*Conductarius, a, um;* Guiding together.
Conductilis, le; Firm. Easie to be hired.		*Conductilis, le,* Easily to be Hired.
Conductim, adverb. Capit. Bringing joyntly.		*Conductim,* Bringing joyntly.
Conductio, onis; f. verb. . . . An hiring, a taking to do at price; a gathering together.		*Conductio, onis, f.* a Gathering together, Hiring, Undertaking.
Confabulo, as; & Confābulor, aris; depon. Plaut. . . . To tell tales: to commune, talk or chat together.	*Confabulo, are.* (Anciently,) *Confabulor, ari.* To discourse together, to talk or prate one with another.	*Confabulo, are, Confabulor, ari,* To Discourse, Talk or Prate together, Tell tales.

Other entries in the three texts confirm the practice obvious in these above, namely, Coles's free borrowing from both his predecessors. Under *confero*, Coles takes nine of his dozen illustrations from Wase; under *conficio* his English definitions are largely from Gouldman and only one illustration from Wase. Compare also the entries, under *configo*, *conflo*, *confringo*, and *conglomero*.

It may be recalled that the title page of Coles's *Dictionary* states that here are added "Thousands of Words, Phrases, Proverbs, Proper Names." Of the proper names we have spoken above. Proverbs, hardly to be numbered by thousands, are distributed here and there in alphabetical order. Under the phrase *out of*, for example, we read: "Out of sight, out of mind, *sematus ab oculo, sematus ab animo*," and "Out of God's blessing into the warm sun, *ab equis ad asinos*." In the English-Latin, Coles, like Wase before him, gives emphasis to the different meanings of English words. He achieves this end by bracketing words or phrases to indicate the special meanings of terms to be defined, as in these entries:

> Ability [riches] *facultates.*
> Ability [of body] *robur, vires.*
> Ability [of parts] *solertia, peritia.*
> Above [not below] *super, supra.*
> Above [in greatness, place] *major, superior. . . .*
> Above [more or longer than] *plus, amplius, magis quam.*
> Above [beyond or more than] *ultra, praeter, supra.*

This valuable practice was to be followed, with modifications, by other lexicographers in Latin and English.[3]

At the end of the English-Latin part of his *Dictionary*, Coles adds three pages (of three columns each) of special words under this heading: "A Collection of some *English* Words which agree in Sound, yet differ in Sense and Orthography; with their Several Significations explained by English for the Benefit of our own Nation, and the Latin for the Good of Strangers." Here are examples of Coles's collection:

Are (be) *sunt.*
Air (Element) *aer.*
Heir (to an Estate) *Haeres.*

Belly (of man) *venter.*
Bely (to speak lies) *calumnior.*

Bile (on the body) *tuberculum.*
Boil (to seeth) *coquo.*

Carnal (fleshly) *carnalis.*
Kernel (of a nut) *nucleum.*

Debter (that owes) *Debito.*
Deterr (to frighten) *Terreo.*

Decent (seemly) *Comptus.*
Descent (of a place) *Descensus.*

Far (distant) *Procul.*
Fur (a Hairy skin) *Pellis.*

Moth (flye) *Tinea.*
Mouth (in head) *Os.*

Poor (needy) *Egenus.*
Poor (of the body) *Porus.*
Pour (to empty out) *Fundo.*
Power (strength) *Vis.*

Sheep (of the flock) *Ovis.*
Ship (of the sea) *Puppis.*

Besides reflecting pronunciation in the late seventeenth century, this collection of words reveals Coles's interest in the English vocabulary, an interest confirmed by his compilation of his *English Dictionary*, in 1676.

Although the *Dictionary, English-Latin, and Latin-English* of Elisha

Coles continued to be printed at fairly regular intervals until 1772,[4] it had no substantial augmentation. Title pages of the first edition (1677), the second (1679), the seventh (1711), the ninth (n.d.), the eleventh (1727), and the thirteenth (1736) are identical, excepting the specification of edition and the imprints. Almost without change also are the address to the reader, the printers' signatures, and the catchwords. Of these editions, only that of 1736 claims amplification. On the title page we read: "The Thirteenth Edition, with Large Additions." Also at the end of the preliminary matter the Booksellers assert that this edition has "many Thousand Additions, for the sake of the young Beginner: And with one material Part; the Parts of Speech, Declension of Nouns, Pronouns and Participles, and the Conjugation of Verbs, added to the Latin of the English Part, which are either entirely or very superficially noted in any other English-Latin Dictionary extant." The language is equivocal; the additions are for the most part abbreviations to indicate grammatical information, not new entries as seems to be implied. These abbreviations the revisers (Coles died in 1680) were able to insert in the hitherto unfilled spaces in the columns, without increasing the number of entries. The method may be illustrated by a few entries from the eleventh and the thirteenth editions:

Eleventh (1727)	Thirteenth (1736)
Just so, *haud aliter, haud secus.* . . .	. . . adv. *haud aliter, haud secus.* . . .
A just *hastiludium.*	. . . *hastiludium, i; m.*
Justs	
Justice *justitia.*	. . . *justitia, ae; f.*
Justness	
A justice *justitiarius.*	. . . *justitiarius, i; m.*
Justicer	
To justifie, *justifico, absolvo.*	. . . *justifico,* 1, *absolvo,* 3.
Justified, *justificatus.*	. . . *justificatus, a, um.*

On the basis of the inserted abbreviations the booksellers would doubtless justify their statement of "many Thousand Additions," but the phrasing, as they probably knew, would convey a different meaning to prospective purchasers of the text. This may have been an attempt to anticipate competition of Ainsworth's *Thesaurus,* published in 1736. Apparently there were no further changes in subsequent editions of Coles. The "with Large Additions" on the title page of the fifteenth edition (1749) was carried over from 1736.

The recurrent printings of Coles's *Dictionary* are evidence of great popularity. In the eleventh edition the booksellers state that "this Book hath sufficiently commended it self to the World by the Sale of 2000 every Year"; and in the thirteenth, that there has been a sale of "2000 every Year, since its first Publication." This would mean, if accepted literally, that from 1677 to 1736, approximately 120,000 copies had been sold. Granted these are extravagant claims, there is still ample evidence of very wide vogue. Broad in range, concise in expression, inexpensive in format, the Coles had for the average user the advantage over the large quartos of Gouldman and Littleton and the folio of Thomas Holyoke. Small print, its chief defect, seems not to have hindered its popularity.

CHAPTER XXI

Adam Littleton's *Latine Dictionary,*
in Four Parts (1678)

A MONG THE best-known lexicographers of the Restoration was Adam Littleton (1627–94). Littleton was educated at Westminster and Christ Church, Oxford. In 1658 he became second master at Westminster and, like many of his predecessors in lexicography, probably became interested in compiling a dictionary as a result of his teaching experience. In 1669 he was made rector of Chelsea, and in the following year chaplain to Charles II. Littleton was a classical scholar, a good mathematician, and was skilled in Oriental languages and rabbinical learning. He is said to have collected books and manuscripts from all parts of Europe, Asia, and Africa, to the great impoverishment of his estate. According to Collier (*DNB*) his erudition procured for him the title of "Great Dictator of Learning."

An interesting story has come down to us concerning Littleton's work on his dictionary.

When Dr. Adam Littleton was compiling his latin dictionary, and announced the verb *concurro* to his amanuensis, the scribe imagining that, from an affinity of sound, the six first letters would give the translation of the word, said, "*concur*, I suppose, Sir"; to which the doctor replied, peevishly, "*concur! condog!*" The Secretary, whose business it was to write what his master dictated, accordingly did his duty; and the word *condog* was inserted, and was actually printed as one interpretation of *concurro* in the first edition, 1678, (to be seen in the British Museum) though it has been expunged, and does not appear in subsequent editions! [1]

Whether this story is literally true, we do not know; the fact remains, however, that *condog* as one of the meanings of *concurro* does appear in the 1678 edition and also in what seems to be an irregular edition of Littleton published at Cambridge in 1693.

His *Latine Dictionary, in Four Parts* was first published in London (1678) in large quarto. Other issues appeared in 1684, 1693, 1703, 1715, 1723, and 1735. The sixth edition was published a few months before the first issue of Robert Ainsworth's well-known lexicon.

The title page of Littleton's dictionary is as follows:

Linguae Latinae Liber Dictionarius Quadripartitus.
A Latine Dictionary, In Four Parts.

| I. An English-Latine | III. A Latine-Proper |
| II. A Latine-Classical | IV. A Latine-Barbarous |

wherein

The Latine and English are adjusted, with what care might be, both as to Stock of Words and Proprieties of Speech Particularly,

1. In the English-Latine, more Words and Proprieties of our Language, as now spoken, are set down, by several Thousands, than in any other Dictionary yet extant.
2. In the Latin-classic, the Etymologies, Significations, and Phrases are fully and plainly, yet briefly discoursed: together with the several Kinds and Constructions of the Verbs; a thing hitherto not much regarded.
3. In the Latine-proper, the Expressions of Story, which were taken mostly out of Cooper, are much amended; and many useful things are now added, which were formerly omitted; with two Mapps, one of Italy, another of old Rome.
4. In the Latine-barbarous, those words which through Mistake of writing have been corrupted from the Latine, or by Ignorance or Boldness of later Authors have crept into the Latine are exposed and expounded.

And in all Four Parts, many things that were utterly impertinent and cumbersom to School-Institution and to the true uses of Learning, are laid aside. Of all which several performances, together with considerable Additions of new matter by way of Appendage to the main Work, a fuller account is given in the Prefaces. Operâ & Studio Adami Littleton, S.T.D. Capellani Palatini [Quotation in Greek & Latin.] London, Printed for T. Basset at the George in Fleet-street, J. Wright at the Crown on Ludgate-Hill, and R. Chiswell at the Rose and Crown in St. Paul's Churchyard, 1678.

Preliminary matter following the title page is made up of the Latin dedication to Charles II, a Latin "Erudito Lectori," and "To the English Reader." Then comes the heading "The English-Latin Dictionary," and the text, four columns to the page. At the end of this text are "The most usual Christian Names of Men and Women Rendered into Latine," including "Nick-Names" (3 pages); a list of special tracts in the book; and abbreviations of authors referred to in the text. Here follows, without title page, the Latin-English dictionary, under the heading "Linguae Latinae Dictionarium Classicum." This part comprises approximately two-thirds of the large quarto. Two maps follow, one of ancient Italy and one of Rome. Here is the proper-name section, with the heading "Dictionarium Poeticum, Historicum & Geographium, Nomina Propria exhibens." The dictionary of barbarous Latin words, which follows, has its own title page:

Dictionarium Latino-Barbarum. Cui praemittitur Praefatiuncula, docens Quo pacto Barbaries in Latinitatem Irrepsecit. [Woodcut] Londini, Typis J. C. Impensis Johannis Wright & Richardi Chiswell. MDCLXXVII.

This text has the heading "Glossarium sive Dictionarium Latino-barbarum," and consists of twenty-six pages, three columns to a page. Then follow a "Syllabus Vocabulorum" (six pages of law terms), a Roman calendar, "Tabula Chronologia" of illustrious persons' memorable deeds, from the creation to A.D. 1666 (an abridgment of Christopher Helvicus' book on chronology), and finally tables of weights, coins, and measures of the Romans.

As Littleton's "To the English Reader" states his general aims and discourses briefly on various divisions, it requires summary comment. The compiler explains that, though he has traveled all along in the "Old beaten Road of Alphabet," as the method most conducive to the study of youth, he has made amendments and supplements and the like so that in matter and manner of handling it his book is "as free from Incroaching upon any others Copyhold, as any that has been writ in English of the king since Thomasius his time." His great aim, he insists, has been "to carry the purity of the Latine Tongue throughout," not to take things or words upon trust, to avoid transcribing the mistakes of others, and wherever possible to get more certain information from the authors themselves. Littleton's laudable aim of compiling a classical dictionary, emphasized here and upon the title page, is hardly attained. He follows too closely some of his immediate predecessors; he prepares the way, however, for Ainsworth, who more nearly realizes this purpose.

After these remarks, the compiler makes pertinent comment on each of the four parts of his dictionary. In the English-Latin part he has endeavored to present English as it is now spoken, together with suitable Latin. As a result he has supplied "several Thousands of Words and Proprieties formerly wanting." On the several "notions and importances" of words, especially verbs, he has had assistance from "the Reverend Dr. Lloyd, Dean of Bangor, in his Philosophical Dictionary at the end of Bishop Wilkins his Universal Character." "Idiotisms" (idioms?) and proprieties of speech have been enlarged; old-fashioned words, such as *abarstick,* thrown out; and circumlocutions, such as "the inward top of the finger next to the Nail," have been discarded.

In the "Latine-Classick," "besides the Etymology, Signification and Use of each word," other things are supplied: parts of speech are indicated; the Hebrew is continued throughout; primitives are put in capitals; words taken from the Greek are noted with an asterisk; obsolete words and those peculiar to a particular science are marked with an obelisk; synonyms are designated by an equal sign, and antonyms (*antithetae*) by a special symbol.

In giving Etymons, wherein we have been obliged to be the larger by other Examples rather than our own Judgment . . . we have endeavoured to be close and pertinent; as resolving no great matter of learning to lie in forced and affected derivations, unless they be brought to some true measures of Analogy.

The Significations of words are adjusted, as near as might be to the present English expression, and deduced orderly along; beginning either with that which is the most natural and proper importance, or with that which is most ordinary and common.

The use, more especially of Verbs, is represented in such pertinent Instances, as to show at once their Grammatical Construction and Government, together with the Latin Propriety or Phrase.

In the dictionary of proper names, or "Latine-Proper," Littleton states that he has tried to keep history, poetic fiction, and geography within the compass of Latin classic writers unless there is special reason for going beyond. Stories continued from Elyot and Cooper he has amended and brought nearer to our present dress.

As for the glossary, or "Latine-Barbarous" words, the compiler thinks that no "right-bred Latinist" can take offense at seeing them "thrown into a Lay-stall" by themselves. It is, he thinks, possible to distinguish classical words from those that are not such, and it is necessary for youth that they should be so distinguished. Littleton concludes:

Let it suffice thee, Reader, that thou hast here the whole body of the Latine Tongue, with all its natural and genuine branches, delivered to thee; whereby thou mayst be inabled to speak and write Latine by the same authority as the Romans themselves spoke and wrote it, when Rome was at her height. For as to those words, which thou missest here, and meetest with elsewhere, thou must know that they being but corruptions and abuses of Latine, are better let alone than taken notice of.

On this note of the classical quality of his dictionary, Littleton ends his discourse. But his achievement hardly corresponds with his expressed aims. There is progress as compared, for example, with the dictionary of Thomas Holyoke, but Littleton has been too content to follow the lead of other compilers and, notwithstanding his aim to the contrary, has copied their mistakes.

What then are the immediate sources of his text? Let us consider them according to the arrangement indicated on the title page and also in "To the English Reader."

Antecedents of the English-Latin part extend back to the Rider of 1589. This, with few changes, was printed repeatedly in the Rider-

Holyoke dictionaries, and followed with supplements and changes by Gouldman. Wase's English-Latin (1662) was also used by Gouldman. In 1677 appeared Coles's dictionary, owing something to both Gouldman and Wase. By the time of Littleton, the pattern had become somewhat complicated, and all texts must be examined to determine direct sources. The tendency is, however, for a given lexicographer to borrow most from his more recent predecessors, though there are some exceptions. Littleton follows the general tendency. The parallels which follow show that he depends largely upon Gouldman and Coles.

Gouldman (1674)	Coles (1677)	Littleton (1678)
A face. *Facies, vultus, os.*	A face, *facies, vultus.* . . .	A Face. *Facies, vultus, os.*
With the face upward. *Supinus, adj.*		With the face upward. *Supinus, adj.*
With the face downward. *Pronus, adj.*		With the face downward. *Pronus, adj.*
He that hath two faces. *Bifrons, adj.*		One with two faces. *Bifrons.*
Face to face. *Adversus, adj. coram, facie tenus.*	Face to face, Before one's face. *Coram.*	Face to face. *Adversus, adj. coram, facie tenus.*
To set a good face on a bad matter. *Spem vultu simulare.*	Set a good face on it, *Bene adsimula, Spem vultu simula.*	To set a good face on it. *Spem vultu simulo, bene adsimulo.*
	Faceles (a kind of pulse), *Phaseolus.*	Faceles, a kind of pulse. *Phaseolus.*

Of the seven entries from Littleton transcribed above, five come from Gouldman and two from Coles. Littleton's *to face a garment*, omitted from the list above, may have been suggested by Wase's *to face (a Garment)*, though generally matter from Wase derives through the medium of Gouldman or Coles. A comparison of the first twenty-five entries under "*H ante A*" (*a haak*, *a haberdasher*, etc.) produces similar results. There are also some striking correspondences between Littleton's English-Latin and the *Phraseologia generalis* (Cambridge, 1681), an English-Latin phrase book compiled by William Robertson. But as Littleton has the priority of three years, the debt is by Robertson to Littleton.

What is said above concerning the complicated pattern of the English-Latin is applicable also to the Latin-English, except that the ultimate source here is Thomas Thomas, not to go further back. Entries in Thomas were carried on by Francis Holyoke in *Dictionarium etymologicum* of the Rider-Holyoke dictionaries. Gouldman used both Holyoke and Thomas. In Littleton there are close correspondences to Thomas in many of the entries, but these apparently come through Gouldman, as indicated by other elements in the same entries common to Gouldman and Littleton (e.g., Hebrew and Latin from Calepine) and not in Thomas. Study of the seventeenth-century dictionaries gives evidence of Littleton's indebtedness to Gouldman, with occasional borrowings from Coles. In the list of authors consulted in compiling the text, Littleton places also Cooper and Wase. To these he gives credit for some entries. But to Gouldman, who is also in the list, Littleton apparently owes most. Compare the following entries:

Littleton (1678)

Expeditio, onis; f. verb ἐισβολή . . . A setting forward to the war, an expedition, a voyage; a dispatch. . . .

Expeditus, a, um; part. & adj. Cic. Dispatched, freed, rid out of, provided, prepared, etc. Adj. Ready, in a readiness: quick, nimble, light, easie. *Expeditus eques,* Salust . . . A light horseman.

Expello, is, ere; puli, pulsum; act. . . . To expel: to put, thrust, drive, or chase forth, out or away: also to reject: also to thrust forth in length. *Expellere aliquem regno,* Caes. *ex urbe,* Cic. *in opus,* Plin. *animam per vulnera,* Ovid. . . .

Expensus, a, um; part . . . Weighed, pondered, considered, laid out, reckoned. *Expenso gradu,* Propert. With a slow pace, step by step. *Expensum alicui ferre,* Cic. To set down his hand in his creditors book and acknowledge so much money borrowed.

Gouldman (1664)

Expeditio, onis; f. verb ἐισβολή . . . *exercitus, apparatus belli, bellum.* A setting forward to the war, an expedition, a voyage.

Expeditus, a, um; promptus, facilis, nullis impedimentis oneratus. Expeditior comp. facilior. Ready, in a readiness: not letted or troubled: soon provided and gotten, quick, nimble, light, prompt, easie to dispatch, delivered, dispatched, rid out. *Expeditus miles,* Salust . . . A light harnessed souldier.

Expello, is, puli, pulsum, ere . . . To expel: to put, thrust, drive, or chase out or away: also to reject. *Expellere aliquem regno;* Caes. *ex urbe;* To expell or drive out of. *Expellere aliquem in opus,* Plin. To drive out to work. *Per vulnera animam expellere,* Ovid. To kill. . . .

Expensus, a, um; part. . . . Weighed, pondered, considered, laid out, reckoned. *Expenso gradu,* Propert. With a slow pace. *Mihi feras expensum,* Write or set this on my head in your book: or Write that you have lent or delivered it to me.

F. Holyoke (1649)

Expeditio, onis, f. verb ἐισβολή . . . *Exercitus, apparatus belli, bellum.* A setting forward to the war, a voyage.

Expeditus, a, um . . . *promptus, facilis, nullis impedimentis oneratus. Expediti milites dicuntur levioris armaturae & sine impedimentis. Expeditior comp. facilior:* Ready, soon provided, quick, light, dispatched, rid out: also light harnessed.

Expello, is, puli, ulsum, ere . . . To put or chase one out of the way, also to reject, to thrust forth, to expell.

Expensus, a, um. . . . Weighed, considered, laid out, reckoned.

On the title page Littleton states that the "Expressions of Story," which were taken mostly out of Cooper, are much amended. A similar statement in "To the English Reader" refers to Elyot and Cooper as sources. Numerous sketches in the "Latine-Proper," or "Dictionarium Poeticum," seem to support the assertion of direct indebtedness to Cooper's *Thesaurus*, as under *Acco, Acadinus, Adamitae, Admetus, Aegeon, Aegeus, Aegium, Agrippina, Alexander, Anabaptistae, Anacharsis, Anaxagoras,* and *Anaxarchus.* But for many entries in the proper names the debt is to Gouldman.

Gouldman (1674)	Littleton (1678)
Ababa, Maximini Senioris Romani Imperatoris mater, Capital.	*Ababa, Maximini Senioris Romani Imperatoris mater,* Capital.
Abacaena, civitas Medorum, & item Siciliae.	*Abacaena, Civitas Medorum,* Ptol.
Abacus. The chief city of Cevola in India; now called Granata.	*Abacus,* The chief City of Cevola in India: now called Granata. Nizz.
Abaddon, ἀβαδδὼν, *destruens, ex* אבר, *perdidit,* Revel. 9. 11. ἀπολλύων, *angelus abyssi.*	*Abaddon,* ἀβαδδὼν, אברון *ex* אבר *periit, in Piel, perdedit.* Gr. *redditur* Ἀπολλύων, *i. perdens,* Apoc. 9. 11. The Destroyer, the Angel of the bottomless Pit.
Abadir, lapis teste, Prisc. A stone which Saturn devoured instead of his son Jupiter: For it was prophesied, that Saturn should be driven out of his kingdom by some of his sons; that he might elude this prophesie, he devoured all the sons that he begat of his wife Ops: but when Jupiter was born, she deceived him, and in stead of her son Jupiter, put the stone Abadir into his mouth, and saved Jupiter alive.	*Abadir vel Abaddir, m. ind.* Prisc. *vox exotica.* Gr. βαίτυλος. A stone which Saturn devoured instead of his son Jupiter: For it having been prophesied that Saturn should be driven out of his Kingdom by some of his sons; that he might elude this Prophesie, he devoured all the sons that he begat of his wife Ops: but when Jupiter was born, she deceived him, and instead of a child, put the stone Abadir in his mouth, and so saved the Godling alive.

Cooper and Gouldman are thus seen to be direct sources of Littleton. Back of these, and not unknown to the compiler, are Calepine, the *Thesaurus* of Robert Stephanus, and the *Dictionarium poeticum* of Charles Stephanus.

Although the "Latine-Barbarous" is contained on thirteen leaves, the compiler, for some reason, dignified it with a special title page. Many of these terms first appeared in the Thomasius at the end of the sixteenth century. These, with some augmentations, were arranged in a special section of the earlier Rider-Holyoke dictionaries, but by Gouldman again distributed through the alphabet. In Littleton are correspondences to all these. He may have used a 1617 edition of the Rider-Holyoke as a convenience in making his word list. He seems also to have consulted both Gouldman and Thomas. Referring to the terms in this section, Littleton describes them as "many such words as our Glosses have holp us to." He may have consulted glosses, but, as most of the terms are in the dictionaries of the predecessors mentioned, Littleton's own contribution is probably slight.

After the dictionary of Latin-barbarous terms is placed a "Syllabus Vocabulorum quorundam Forensium," a glossary of terms of common law. Similar terms, drawn from Rastell and Cowell, had been included in English dictionaries from the time of Blount's *Glossographia* (1656) and Phillips' *New World of English Words* (1658) to the eighteenth century. Discussing common-law terms in "To the English Reader," Littleton refers to Spelman, Cowell, and his "worthy progenitor" Sir Thomas Littleton, without making specific acknowledgment. To all of these he may be indebted, but especially to Spelman's *Glossarium archaiologicum*. Out of Littleton's first thirty-five entries, all but six could have come from the *Glossarium*.

The Roman calendar and the tables of weights and measures and coins, inserted in most of the larger dictionaries since Thomas and Rider, were now common property. Among these special features was the "Tabula Chronologica." This appears to be Littleton's own abridgment, or that of an assistant, from Christopher Helvicus' book on chronology, entitled *The Historical and Chronological Theatre of Christopher Helvicus*, translated and enlarged (London, 1687).

As to marking of vowels, presenting grammatical information, etymology, illustrations of usage, and Greek and Hebrew equivalents, in the Latin-English section, Littleton tends to follow Gouldman. The Hebrew is more consistently inserted. For the extra terms, Littleton may have employed William Robertson's *Compendious Hebrew Lexicon* (London, 1654). Of etymologies, of "forced and affected derivations," Littleton is somewhat wary; yet, as he explains to the reader, he has been obliged to include them, following the example of others rather than his own judgment. The result is that most of the farfetched etymologies of his predecessors—Gouldman and Rider-Holyoke—reappear in Littleton's *Dictionary*.

In discussions of the letters of the alphabet, Littleton reverts to the precedent of John Baret in the late sixteenth century. At the beginning of the entries under each letter, Littleton has a long discussion, in Latin, varying from a half-page to a page or more, of the significance and history of the letter. These erudite essays are later continued by Ainsworth, who, for his *Thesaurus*, translates Littleton's essays into English, often making revisions.

In 1684 a second edition of Littleton appeared. In phrasing, arrangement of lines, and punctuation, the title page is identical with that of 1678. The only difference is in date. This edition claims no augmentation; and the printer's signatures correspond throughout the two editions.

Not until 1703 did another edition of this dictionary appear with Adam Littleton's name on the title page. Meantime, in 1693, there was published by anonymous editors at Cambridge and London, with a different title and title page (though in phrasing obviously imitative of the Littleton), a dictionary which incorporated practically all of the Littleton. This was not printed as an edition of the Littleton, but later it came to be regarded as the third edition. Since this is so, the "Cambridge Dictionary," as Ainsworth called it and as we shall refer to it, requires discussion in this chapter. It poses questions which in the present state of our knowledge cannot be satisfactorily answered. But we shall present the facts which are available. The title page of the 1693 text follows.

Linguae romanae dictionarium Luculentum Novum. A New Dictionary, in Five Alphabets: Representing

I. The English Words and Phrases before the Latin; among which latter, no Word or Expression is admitted, but what is Classic, and of an approved Authority.

II. The Latin-Classic before the English; wherein Care is taken, that the Proper and Original Signification of each Word is first set down, which is followed by those that are Derivative, Metaphorical or Remote.

III. The Latin-Proper Names of those Persons, People or Countries that frequently Occur, or are any way Remarkable in Classic Authors, with Explications from their several Languages, and a short Account of them Historical and Geographical.

IV. The Latin-Barbarous, Explaining as well such Technical Words, or Terms of Art, as are made necessary to us by the many Inventions and Discoveries not known to the Ancients, as those which crept into the Latin Tongue during the Ignorance and Darkness of the Middle Ages.

V. The Law-Latin, Comprehending those Words, which are made use of by the Common-Lawyers in their particular Profession, very necessary for the understanding of Charters, &c.

The Whole Completed and Improved from the several Works of Stephens, Cooper, Gouldman, Holyoke, Dr. Littleton, a Large Manuscript, in three Volumes, of Mr. John Milton, &c. In the Use of all which, for greater Exactness, Recourse has always been had to the Authors themselves.

. . . .

Cambridge, Printed for W. Rawlins in St. Bartholomew's Close, T. Dring at the Harrow near the Inner-Temple Gate in Fleetstreet, R. Chiswell at the Rose and Crown in S. Paul's Churchyard, C. Harper at the Flower de Luce over against S Dunstan's Church in Fleet street, W. Crook at the Green Dragon without Temple-Bar, J. Place at Furnival's Inn Gate in Holborn, and the Executors of S. Leigh. M DC XC III.

There appear to have been two other issues of this *New Dictionary* in the year 1693, one exactly as this described above, except that *London*

LINGVÆ ROMANÆ
DICTIONARIUM
Luculentum Novum.

A NEW
DICTIONARY,
In Five Alphabets:

REPRESENTING

I. The ENGLISH WORDS and PHRASES before the *Latin*; among which latter, no Word or Expression is admitted, but what is Classic, and of an approved Authority. *English proper names of persons and places, with their proper Latin: first place's the proper persons: Nic*

II. The LATIN-CLASSIC before the *English*; wherein Care is taken, that the Proper and Original Signification of each Word is first set down, which is followed by those that are Derivative, Metaphorical or Remote. *Abbreviations used in my work —*

III. The LATIN-PROPER NAMES of those Persons, People or Countries that frequently Occur, or are any way Remarkable in Classic Authors, with Explications from their several Languages, and a short Account of them Historical and Geographical.

IV. The LATIN-BARBAROUS, Explaining as well such *Technical* Words, or Terms of Art, as are made necessary to us by the many Inventions and Discoveries not known to the Ancients, as those which crept into the *Latin* Tongue during the Ignorance and Darkness of the Middle Ages.

V. The LAW-LATIN, Comprehending those Words, which are made use of by the Common-Lawyers in their particular Profession; very necessary for the understanding of Charters, &c. *The Roman Kalender; An Account of weights measures coins. A Cronology of all*

The WHOLE Completed and Improved from the several Works of *Stephens, Cooper, Gouldman, Holyoke*, Dr. LITTLETON, a Large Manuscript, in three Volumes, of Mr. John Milton, &c. In the Use of all which, for greater Exactness, Recourse has always been had to the Authors themselves.

Τῷ δὲ Θεοὶ νεμεσῶσι καὶ ἀνέρες, ὅς κεν ἀεργὸς
Ζώῃ, *Hesiod.*

CAMBRIDGE,
Printed for W. Rawlins, T. Dring, J. Place, and the Executors of S. Leigh:
And are to be Sold at the *Harrow* in *Fleet-street*, and at *Furnivals-Inn-Gate* in *Holborn.*
M DC XC III.

in the imprint is substituted for *Cambridge*. The other has this imprint:

Cambridge, Printed for W. Rawlins, T. Dring, J. Place, and the Executors of S. Leigh: And are to be Sold at the Harrow in Fleet-street, and at Furnivals-Inn-Gate in Holborn. M DC XC III.[2]

According to the title page, this is *A New Dictionary*, not designated as another edition of Littleton or any other lexicon. The unnamed compilers admittedly use Littleton's text as well as five others, including the three-volume manuscript of Mr. John Milton, we are told. Though ostensibly a new dictionary, the Cambridge volume has a title and a title page, detailing the various parts and the arrangement, strangely similar to those of Littleton. The Littleton and the Cambridge, respectively:

> *Linguae Latinae Liber Dictionarius Quadripartitus.*
> *A Latine Dictionary, in Four Parts.*
> *Linguae Romanae Dictionarium Luculentum Novum.*
> *A New Dictionary, in Five Alphabets.*

And so throughout, the Cambridge title page echoes that of Littleton. In content also the two texts are similar, not only in the larger divisions but in the smaller items of the Christian names of men and women, nicknames, the Roman calendar, and weights and measures. It is as if the Cambridge publishers were saying, in effect, "Here is something of the same kind as Littleton, but much better." Their text, in fact, follows Littleton throughout, notwithstanding the implications of the title and title page. The Cambridge editors do somewhat augment and perhaps improve Littleton, but the product is after all only a revision. The changes they wrought will be here given in some detail.

The English-Latin part of the book is based on Littleton, with some augmentation, to be specified below. In the address to the reader the Cambridge editors acknowledge indebtedness to Dr. Littleton, though they do not state that his text is the basis of their own. They say they have added whole classes of words, including terms of trade, building, physic, and heraldry. Their claims are exaggerated, but they have some basis in fact. The editors add a certain number of place names and proper names under the first three letters of the alphabet, more derivatives of the main English or Latin words, synonyms, and technical terms.[3] The amplification, not extensive, derives largely from Elisha Coles's *Dictionary, English-Latin, and Latin-English*, a source not mentioned by the editors. An illustration of the debt to Coles appears at the beginning

Title page of A New Dictionary, in Five Alphabets, *from a copy in the University of Texas Library (opposite)*

of the letter *A*. For eight entries ("*A* Before a Consonant") the Little-ton of 1678 and the Cambridge text correspond verbatim; then follow in the Cambridge six entries not in Littleton. These derive from Coles.

Cambridge (1693)	Coles (1677)
Aa, the name of several rivers. *Aa*, *Aae*, *f.*	Aa [the name of several rivers] *Aa*, *Aae*, *f.*
Aarasso, in Pisidia, *Aarassus, i. f.*	Aarasso [in Pisidia] *Arassus, i. f.*
Aare, and Are, a river in Germany. *Abrinoa, ae, f.*	Aare, & Are [a river in Germany] *Abrinoa, ae, f.*
Aaron, a man's name, *Aaron, onis, m.*	Aaron [a mans name] *Aaron, onis, m.*
Abacoa, an Island in America. *Abacoa, ae, f.*	Abacoa [an island of America] *Abacoa, ae, f.*
Abacted, or driven away. *Abactus, a, um.*	Abacted [driven away] *abactus, a, um.*

Other entries common to the Cambridge and the Coles and not in the 1678 or 1684 Littleton are these:

Cambridge	Coles
Brampton, by Huntington, *Bramptonia.*	Brampton [by Huntington] *Bramptonia.*
Brampton, in Cumberland, *Brementuracum.*	Brampton [in Cumberland] *Brementuracum.*
Brampton, in Northamptonshire, *Brementum.*	Brampton [in Northamptonshire] *Brementum.*
Brancaster, in England, *Branodunum.*	Brancaster [in England] *Branodunum.*
. . . . .	. . . . .
Branches of a deer's head. *Cervinorum, Cornuum, medii arculi, intermedii ramusculi.*	Branches [of a deer's Head] *cervinorum, cornuum, medii arculi, intermedii ramusculi.*
A branch-pease. *Pisum.*	A Branch-pease, *Pisum.*
A brancher-hawk. *Eutraphus, Accipiter junior.*	
Branchester, in Norfolk. *Brannodunum.*	Branchester [in Norfolk] *Brannodum.*

Some additions by the Cambridge editors, for example, under *half, hand*, etc., seems to derive from William Robertson's *Phraseologia generalis* (1681). But since Robertson himself compiled his work from various dictionaries, it is difficult to determine exact relationships.

The matter, including proper names of places and Christian names of men and women, placed between the English-Latin and Latin-English parts of the Cambridge text, follows Littleton closely.

For the Latin-English section the Cambridge editors assert that they gathered their materials (1) from a careful perusal of Lucretius, Terence, Caesar, Petronius, and others; (2) from Robert Stephanus' *Thesaurus*— "the second Edition of it lay open before us"; (3) from "a Manuscript Collection in three Large Folio's digested into an Alphabetical order, which the learned John Milton had made, out of Tully, Livy, Caesar, Sallust, Quintus Curtius, Justin, Plautus, Terence, Lucretius, Virgil,

Horace, Ovid, Manilius, Celsus, Columella, Varro, Cato, Palladius; in short out of all the best and purest Roman Authors." [4] Since Lucretius, Terence, and the other classical writers are cited in almost all the dictionaries, it is impossible to determine whether the editors drew firsthand from these authors; probably not. Evidence of their use of Robert Stephanus is found under *confido, confiteor, conflagro, facio, iaceo, iacio,* and *iactura.* As far as I can determine, Milton is nowhere cited in the entries; the citation of authorities used by Milton, such as Tully, Livy, and Caesar, does not help us to determine whether his manuscript, if in existence at this time, contributed anything to the Cambridge text. Since the editors tend to follow printed dictionaries, and since the augmentations are not so large as to have received much help from a three-volume manuscript, we may discount their claims.

Once again, though Littleton is basic in the Latin-English of Cambridge, there are revisions. In 129 entries between *confero* and *confluxio* in the two dictionaries, the word lists are identical, though in four of these—*confido, confirmatio, confiteor,* and *conflagro*—there are added illustrations. There are also expansions in the entries *necessitudo, negotium, pars, parvus,* and *praetereo,* to mention a few. In general there are revisions and amplification in varying degrees in many of the entries under *A, B, C, D, E, F, G, H, I, M, N, O,* and *P.* The changes consist in the reduction of speculative etymologies and of synonyms; in the increase of illustrative quotations; in rewriting and rearranging certain long entries, as *abeo, facio,* and *misceo.* There are few changes of importance under *K, L, Q, R, S, T, V, X, Y,* and *Z.*[5]

Discussions of the letters of the alphabet, extensive in Baret's *Alvearie* (1573) and revived in scanty treatments by Gouldman, are given much prominence in Littleton. The Cambridge editors continue the practice, rewriting the introductory essays on *A, B, C, D, E, F, G, M, N, O,* and *P.*

In "The Latin-Proper Names," the Cambridge has some new entries. These are from Gouldman, as in *Aetius, Aalac,* and *Aarassus,* and from Coles, as in *Dabanegoris, Dactonium,* and *Daedalian.* "The Latin-Barbarous" remains unchanged, as do the Roman calendar and various tables at the end of the texts. "The Law-Latin" is enlarged by about seven columns. The sources suggested by the anonymous editors are Spelman's *Glossarium,* Cowell's *Interpreter,* and *Terms of the Law,* ascribed variously to William Rastell and to John Rastell.

What we have in the "Cambridge Dictionary," announced as *A New Dictionary,* is a somewhat revised and amplified edition of the Littleton of 1678 and 1684. The change of title, the anonymity of the revisers, and the reduction of Littleton's name to one of a half-dozen whose works the revisers have consulted seem a strange procedure, even though the address to the reader does imply throughout that Littleton is the real basis of the new dictionary. No less odd is it that in 1703 the name of Adam Littleton, in black type is restored to the title page of the text and the lexicon is published as "The Fourth Edition," the "Cambridge Dictionary," by implication, having been the third.

It is interesting to compare the 1703 title page with that of the 1693 Cambridge text. First, the former title of the Littleton dictionaries—*Linguae Latinae* . . . —replaces the *Linguae Romanae* . . . of Cambridge; and the descriptive phrases "Luculentum Novum" and "A New Dictionary" disappear. Then, in boldface, "Dr. Adam Littleton's," and beneath, in capital letters, "Latine Dictionary." Thereafter the title page of the 1703 text follows that of 1693, excepting the imprint. The edition of 1703 reprints the "To the Reader" of the earlier Littleton, and also that of the Cambridge, and includes, as we shall see below, only part of the revisions of the 1693 text. As the publishers term the 1703 volume "The Fourth Edition," it would seem that they have now decided that the 1693 Cambridge was, after all, not "A New Dictionary," but a third edition of Littleton.

We might expect that the fourth edition would incorporate the revisions and alterations of the third, or Cambridge. It does so only in part; it is eclectic. In the English-Latin, for example, the 1703 text takes over the added phrases under *break, busie, carry,* and *dash.* But the proper names which the Cambridge had supplied in this section do not reappear in the 1703 Littleton.

Matter between the English-Latin part and the Latin-English, including names of places and the Christian names of men and women, remain unchanged; so also do the entries in the "Latin-Barbarous" glossary and the items at the end of the texts, such as the Roman calendar and the various tables.

Likewise in the "Latin-Classic," or Latin-English of 1703 there is eclecticism. Revisions and expansions of *confido, confirmatio, confiteor, conflagro, iaceo,* and *iacio,* made by the Cambridge editors, are omitted. But the 1693 revisions of *necessitudo, negotium, pars, parvus,* and *praetero* are included. Revised discussions of the letters of the alphabet in this part of the Cambridge are disregarded in 1703, the earlier discussions by Littleton being retained. Finally, revisions and enlargements of the proper names and the law terms in 1693 do not appear in 1703. In other words, for these sections the text of the earlier Littleton is used.

These are some of the facts concerning the relationship of the so-called "Cambridge Dictionary" and the Littleton. They hardly make clear the reasons for the puzzling procedure of printers and publishers. Nor are we much further enlightened about what was going on behind the scenes in the publishing world by the fact that the names of four of the persons—W. Rawlins, R. Chiswell, C. Harper, and J. Place—for whom the dictionaries were printed are common to the imprints of the Cambridge text of 1693 and the Littleton of 1703.

The issue of Littleton in 1715 appears to be a reprint of the 1703 edition. The title page is the same down to the imprint, which reads: "London, Printed for D. Brown, A. & J. Churchill, M. Lawrence, J. Rawlins, J. Walthoe, S. and B. Sprint, B. Tooke, D. Midwinter, B. Cowse, T. Varnam, and J. Osborn. 1715." In black type on the title page of the 1715 is "The Fourth Edition," that is, the edition of 1703.

In 1723 another edition of Littleton's dictionary was printed. There is no change in the phrasing of the title page from that of 1703, except that this is called "The Fifth Edition," and the imprint is somewhat changed:

Printed for D. Brown, M. Lawrence, R. Bonwicke, J. Walthoe, J. Knapton, J. Wyat, R. Wilkin, J. and B. Sprint and S. Tooke, D. Midwinter, T. Osborn, B. Cowse, R. Gosling, W. Taylor, J. Osborn, R. Robinson, T. Ward, and J. Bateman. M,DCC,XXIII.

This volume contains the dedication to Charles II, the original preface of Littleton, and the preface of the improvers and editors of the 1693 dictionary. There is no claim of enlargement. This edition contains all of the materials of the 1703 edition, in the same order of arrangement. Each part corresponds also, in printer's signatures and catchwords, to the analogous division in 1703. The 1723 edition represents no essential changes.

The sixth and last edition was published in 1735. Omitted from the title page is the former general title *Linguae latinae . . . quadripartitus.* The present one begins: *Dr. Adam Littleton's Latin Dictionary in Four Parts.* As in former editions, the four general divisions are specified, but there are definite changes in phrasing. The more important variations are "The English before the Latin containeth many thousand Words more than hitherto extant" and "The Sixth Edition with Large Amendments and Improvements." Along with the usual preliminary matter— the original dedication and prefaces—is a new preface by the unnamed editor. Again we are told that thousands of words and proprieties wanting in the older editions are supplied.[6]

Numerous tests in the English-Latin part, as in the entries *break, busy, carry, charge, dash, half, hand, loss,* and *order,* most of which have many subentries, show no amplification or change. Main topics of entries, in black letter, under "*D* ante *A*," "*E* ante *A*," and "*R* ante *O*" in the two texts are the same. Other tests give a similar result. In each text, for example, are seventy-eight phrases applicable to *day* and thirty-five applicable to *eat*. The publishers' claim of "many thousand Words more than hitherto extant" is not supported by comparison of the texts.

In the proper-name dictionary; in the barbarisms; in the law terms; and in the shorter parts, such as the proper names of places, the Christian names of men and women, the Roman calendar, and the tables of weights and measures, the 1735 edition exhibits no amplification.

The "Tabula Chronologica" is slightly revised and is brought up to date (from 1703 to 1734) by the addition of twenty-three items at the end of the list.

Only the Latin-English part shows signs of revision, and this is not extensive. Etymologies, as in *conniveo* and *exercitus*, are somewhat reduced; and here and there are added more grammatical information and illustrative phrases. But it would be hard to support the assertion that this sixth and last edition of Littleton's dictionary has "Large Amendments and Improvements."

The fact remains that Dr. Adam Littleton's dictionary was in high repute in its day, partly perhaps because of the celebrity of its author, and was in fairly constant demand for a period of more than fifty years.

CHAPTER XXII

Robert Ainsworth's *Thesaurus linguae Latinae compendiarius* (1736)

ABOUT ONE YEAR after the sixth edition of Adam Littleton's *Latine Dictionary* had come from the press, there was printed in London *A Compendious Dictionary of the Latin Tongue,* compiled by Robert Ainsworth. This was a lexicon destined to supersede the Littleton and all other English-Latin and Latin-English dictionaries hitherto published, and to continue its vogue to the nineteenth century.

Robert Ainsworth was, like many of his predecessors, a schoolmaster. Born at Woodgate, near Manchester, in 1660, he was educated at Bolton, Lincolnshire. He kept a school at Bolton and, after going to London, about 1698, was master of a school near Bethnal Green and later at Hackney. His interest in the teaching of Latin is revealed in *The Most Natural and Easie Way of Institution* (1698), outlining a plan by which children in the first years of their schooling should live together in small groups and learn Latin as they learn their mother tongue. The rod was to be spared, and children encouraged by generous rewards, to which parents would be expected to contribute.

As early as 1714 the proposal for the new dictionary was made, and Ainsworth was induced to become editor.[1] The "execution of it," writes Dr. Samuel Patrick in the "Preface to the Second Edition," "was attended with so many difficulties, that it went on very slowly for a long time, and for some years was entirely suspended." Finally, with the assistance of Dr. Patrick himself, the work was completed and published. The phrasing of the rather elaborate title page follows:

GEORGE R.

GEORGE the Second, by the Grace of God, King of *Great Britain*, *France* and *Ireland*, Defender of the Faith, &c. to all to whom these Presents shall come, Greeting : Whereas our trusty and well beloved *William Mount* and *Thomas Page*, *William Innys*, *Richard Ware*, *John* and *Paul Knapton*, *Aaron Ward*, *John Clarke* in St. *Paul*'s Church-Yard, *Thomas Cox*, *Thomas Longman*, *Charles Hitch*, *Richard Hett*, *Andrew Millar*, *Joseph Pote*, *James Hodges*, *John Oswald*, *Edward Wicksteed*, *Jacob* and *Richard Tonson* and *Somerset Draper*, *Joseph Davidson*, *John* and *James Rivington*, *Mary Cooper*, and the Executors of the late Mr. *John Darby* ; have by their Petition humbly represented unto Us, that they have been at great Expence and Labour in preparing for the Press, and printing a Second Edition, with many Improvements, of a Work entituled,

THESAURUS LINGUÆ LATINÆ COMPENDIARIUS : Or, a compendious Dictionary of the *Latin* Tongue : Designed for the Use of the *British* Nations : In three Parts. Containing, I. The *English* appellative Words and Forms of Expression before the *Latin* ; in which will be found some thousand *English* Words and Phrases, several various Senses of the same Word, and a great Number of proverbial Expressions, more than in any former Dictionary of this Kind, all carefully endeavoured to be rendered in proper and classical *Latin*. To which are subjoined, 1. The proper Names of the more remarkable Places rendered into *Latin*. 2. The Christian Names of Men and Women. II. The *Latin* Appellatives before the *English* ; in which are given the more certain Etymologies of the *Latin* Words, their various Senses in *English* ranged in their natural Order, the principal Idioms under each Sense explained and accounted for, all supported by the best Authorities of the *Roman* Writers ; with References to the particular Book, Chapter, or Verse, where the Citations may be found. III. The ancient *Latin* Names of the more remarkable Persons and Places occurring in classic Authors, with a short Account of them both historical and mythological ; and the more modern Names of the same Places, so far as they are known, collected from the most approved Writers. To which are added, 1. The *Roman* Calendar, much fuller than any yet published. 2. Their Coins, Weights, and Measures. 3. A Chronology of the *Roman* Kings, Consuls, and more remarkable Events of that State. 4. The Notes of Abbreviation used in ancient *Latin* Authors and Inscriptions. 5. A short Dictionary of the more common *Latin* Words occurring in our ancient Laws. By *Robert Ainsworth*. The Second Edition, with Additions and Improvements, by *Samuel Patrick*, LL.D. and Usher of the *Charter-House* School.

Which Work the Petitioners, with the utmost Submission, apprehend will be of great Advantage to the Publick ; and being desirous of reaping the Fruits of their Expence and Labour, and of enjoying the full Profit and Benefit that may arise from printing and vending the same, without any other Person interfering in their just Property, which they cannot prevent without Our Royal Licence and Privilege : Wherefore the Petitioners most humbly pray Us, to grant them Our Royal Licence and Privilege for the sole printing, publishing, and vending the said Work, in as ample Manner and Form as has been done in Cases of the like Nature ; We being willing to give all due Encouragement to this their Undertaking, are graciously pleased to condescend to their Request : *And We do* therefore by these Presents, so far as may be agreeable to the Statute in that Behalf made and provided, grant unto them the said *William Mount* and *Thomas Page*, *William Innys*, *Richard Ware*, *John* and *Paul Knapton*, *Aaron Ward*, *John Clarke* in St. *Paul*'s Church-Yard, *Thomas Cox*, *Thomas Longman*, *Charles Hitch*, *Richard Hett*, *Andrew Millar*, *Joseph Pote*, *James Hodges*, *John Oswald*, *Edward Wicksteed*, *Jacob* and *Richard Tonson* and *Somerset Draper*, *Joseph Davidson*, *John* and *James Rivington*, *Mary Cooper*, and the Executors of the late Mr. *John Darby*, their Executors, Administrators and Assigns, Our Licence for the sole printing and publishing of the said Work for the Term of Fourteen Years, to be computed from the Date hereof, strictly forbidding all Our Subjects within Our Kingdoms and Dominions to reprint or abridge the same, either in the like, or in any Size or Manner whatsoever, or to import, buy, vend, utter, or distribute any Copies thereof, reprinted beyond the Seas, during the aforesaid Term of Fourteen Years, without the Consent or Approbation of the said *William Mount* and *Thomas Page*, *William Innys*, *Richard Ware*, *John* and *Paul Knapton*, *Aaron Ward*, *John Clarke* in St. *Paul*'s Church-Yard, *Thomas Cox*, *Thomas Longman*, *Charles Hitch*, *Richard Hett*, *Andrew Millar*, *Joseph Pote*, *James Hodges*, *John Oswald*, *Edward Wicksteed*, *Jacob* and *Richard Tonson* and *Somerset Draper*, *Joseph Davidson*, *John* and *James Rivington*, *Mary Cooper*, and the Executors of the late Mr. *John Darby*, their Executors, Administrators and Assigns, under their Hands and Seals first had and obtained, as they will answer the contrary at their Peril : Whereof the Commissioners and other Officers of Our Customs, the Master, Wardens, and Company of *Stationers* are to take Notice, that due Obedience may be rendred to Our Pleasure herein declared.

Given at Our Court at St. *James*'s, the Thirty-first Day of *January*, 1745-6, in the Nineteenth Year of Our Reign.

By His Majesty's Command,

HARRINGTON.

Thesaurus Linguae Latinae Compendiarius: Or, a compendious Dictionary Of the Latin Tongue, Designed for the Use of the British Nations. In Three Parts. Containing,

  I. The English Appellative Words and Forms of Expression before the Latin; in which will be found some thousand English Words and Phrases, several various Senses of the same Words, and a great number of proverbial Expressions, more than in any former Dictionary of this kind, all carefully endeavoured to be rendered in proper and classical Latin. To which are subjoined

    1. The Proper names of the more remarkable Places rendered into Latin.

    2. The Christian Names of Men and Women.

 II. The Latin Appellatives before the English; in which are given the more certain Etymologies of the Latin Words, their various Senses in English ranged in their natural Order, the principal Idioms under each Sense explained and accounted for, all supported with the best Authorities of the Roman Writers; with References to the particular Book, Chapter, or Verse, where the Citations may be found.

III. The ancient Latin Names of the more remarkable Persons and Places occurring in the classic Authors, with a short Account of them both historical and mythological; and the more modern Names of the same Places, so far as they are known, collected from the most approved Writers, to which are added

    1. The Roman Calendar, much fuller than any yet published.

    2. Their Coins, Weights, and Measures.

    3. A Chronology of the Roman Kings, Consuls, and more remarkable Events of that State.

    4. The Notes of Abbreviation used in ancient Latin Authors and Inscriptions.

    5. A short Dictionary of the more common Latin words occurring in our ancient Laws.

By Robert Ainsworth [Greek quotation from Longinus.] London: Printed for J. and P. Knapton, R. Knaplock, D. Midwinter, A. Bettesworth and C. Hitch, W. Mount and T. Page, B. Sprint, W. Innys and R. Manby, J. Clarke in Duck-Lane, J. Pope, J. and R. Tonson, and the Executor of Mr. J. Darby. M DCCXXXVI.

Among the interesting features in the preliminary matter—all reproduced in the second edition of 1746—are the royal license granted to the sponsors by George II; an address to the "Very Learned" Richard Mead, physician to George II; a Latin address to all lovers of pure Latin; and a Preface of about forty pages, surveying the history of Latin-English lexicography and setting forth in explicit detail the plan and objectives of the new dictionary. In the text proper the headings of the larger divisions do not correspond in phrasing with the parts specified on the title page. We have, instead: "Thesauri Linguae Latinae Compendiarii Pars Prima" [English-Latin]; "Thesauri Linguae Compendiarii Pars Secunda" [Latin-English]; and "Thesauri Linguae Latinae Pars Extrema" [proper names].

The royal privilege of King George II for the printing of Robert Ainsworth's Thesaurus, from a copy of the 1742 edition in the University of Texas Library (opposite)

If we compare the title page of Ainsworth's text with that of Littleton, we shall note striking similarities. The principal difference is the omission in Ainsworth of the section devoted to barbarisms and obsolete Latin. Otherwise, the Littleton is, in contents and arrangement, the pattern for Ainsworth—a fact which becomes important in the course of this discussion. Like Littleton, Ainsworth emphasizes the classical quality of his Latin; but unlike his predecessor, Ainsworth has a definite plan, explained in the Preface, and adheres to it tenaciously, to realize his aim. In definition also he is far superior to the learned chaplain of Charles II. But this is to anticipate.

This title page suggests a definite order for a particularized discussion of Ainsworth's text. Before proceeding with the discussion, however, it seems appropriate here to glance at the author's stated reasons for his work. These are clearly expressed in his "Preface to the Reader." As preliminary to his statement of the need for a new dictionary, the author surveys the history of Latin-English and English-Latin lexicography from the *Promptorium parvulorum* to his own day. Unfortunately for his purpose, Ainsworth was not well acquainted with the work of his earlier predecessors in the field. He refers to a 1542 edition of Elyot's dictionary as if this were the first; he thinks Cooper's first revision of the *Bibliotheca Eliotae* was in 1552; he knows only the 1580 edition of Baret's *Alvearie;* he has seen only a 1615 edition of Thomas's *Dictionarium*, and states that the author died in 1585; he has not seen Rider's dictionary, but quotes Anthony à Wood's misleading comment on it; he knows nothing of the real relationship of Francis Holyoke to Thomas Thomas; he quotes Dr. Littleton on Wase and Gouldman, whose works he has apparently not examined; and he makes no mention of the dictionaries of Huloet and Withals. Significantly, Ainsworth seems well acquainted with the dictionaries of Coles and Littleton and with the anonymous compilation at Cambridge, based on Littleton.

Notwithstanding his meager acquaintance with the work of his predecessors, Ainsworth asserts that as a teacher of youth he recognizes the defects of all Latin dictionaries, which, he says, have made additions rather than reformed errors or rejected barbarous Latin words. He himself wishes to preserve Latin pure for the British youth. To do so, he will depart from the dubious system of other dictionaries. These are wont to cite no Latin authors in support of definitions, or to cite them in so loose a manner as to be of no value. Ainsworth proposes to make specific and exact citations by way of illustration and to take these from only classical authorities. This is a definite step toward making his dictionary an authority for classical Latin. Among English lexicographers he had no precedent for specific citation of text and page. In this procedure he followed the practice of the French lexicographer Robert Stephanus, in his Latin *Thesaurus*. What Ainsworth further writes in his Preface pertains to the specific divisions of his text. And in the account of these divisions other pertinent matter from the Preface will be introduced.

The purpose of the first part of his text, the English-Latin, says Ainsworth in his Preface, is to assist learners to translate English into proper Latin. In this respect no extant dictionary was adequate. It had been, in fact, about forty years, he remarks, since any new English-Latin dictionary had been published. The earlier lexicographers overlooked many terms in good standing, such as *acceptation, accomplice, actuate, alcove, alleviate, assemblage, atrocious, attainable,* and technical terms in philosophy, botany, and physic. And since the last dictionary was published, other changes in English had come about. Hence the need for a new dictionary.

The earlier dictionaries, Ainsworth further suggests, were defective in finding proper Latin equivalents for English phrases, such as, for example, "to pass an account," "to state an account," "to place to account," "to take an account of," and various other phrases associated with such words as *bear, bargain, battle,* and *beat.* These deficiencies our compiler expects to remedy.

Furthermore, he will give special attention to an English word used in different senses and to denote various ideas. The different meanings of a given English word must be distinguished and explained so that the learner may find the right classic equivalent. To expedite the recognition of the different senses and the search for the proper Latin equivalents, Ainsworth indicates within brackets after the lead word the sense in which it is employed. Take, for example, the word *ability.* We find *ability* [skill], *ability* [power], *ability* [strength], *ability* [riches] with the appropriate Latin word or words for each specialized meaning.

Finally, the author's aim in this part of his dictionary is: (1) To admit only classical Latin words, if such can be found; otherwise to use periphrases, and afterward to add the Greek or bad Latin word, marking the Greek thus: *, and the bad Latin thus: II. (2) Constantly to compare the two parts, English-Latin and Latin-English, to see that they are consistent. This was not the practice of earlier compilers, Ainsworth rightly asserts.

The author's statements about the inadequacy of earlier English-Latin dictionaries and the need for a new one are justified. His expressed aim to seek only classic Latin words and to make the two parts of his dictionary consistent may be regarded as an innovation at least partially realized. And in this effort is his importance from the standpoint of the classical student. The impression which he seeks to make, however, that his method is wholly new must be qualified. From Elyot through Cooper, Thomas, Holyoke, and Littleton, there was recognition of the various meanings and usages of a given Latin word, but no systematic method of making distinctions. And Coles used the system of indicating by bracketed words the special meanings of English entries. To Coles, indeed, and somewhat less to Gouldman, Littleton, and the Rider-Holyoke, was Ainsworth indebted for many of his definitions as well as his method. In using the symbols 1, 2, 3, 4, 5 to indicate declensions of nouns or conjugations of verbs in the Latin, Ainsworth went beyond earlier lexicographers. But much of the spadework was already done by his immediate predecessors. The close relation of the Ainsworth to the Coles in content and method may be illustrated by the following entries:

Coles, *A Dictionary, English-Latin, and Latin-English* (1677)

Able [adj.] *potens, valens, tis; idoneus.*
. . .
Very able [adj.] *praevalidus, praepollens, praepotens, ntis.*
An able man [strong] *validus.* He was so able a man, *ita bonis viribus fuit.*
Able [wealthy] *opulentus, a, um.*
Able [skilful] *solers, gen. entis.* . . .
Able to rule himself, *compos sui.*
To be very able, *praepossum, esse.*
To be more able, *praepolleo, ere.*
An able Scholar, *vir apprime doctus.*
To be able [neut.] *possum, valeo,* 2. *queo.* Every one provideth according as he is able, *pro sua quisque facultate parat.* He is not able to bear so great an envy, *tam magnae non est par invidiae.* As far as I am able, *quod queo, pro mea parte, pro virile parte.* None is able to come near him for skill, *artifex longe citra aemulum.* We were not able to do it for poverty, *non finit nos egestas facere.* He is hardly able to hold his eyes open, *vix sustinet palpebras.* He is not able to pay, *non est solvendo.* I am able to do or allow it, *est mihi unde haec fiant.* He was not able to speak a word more, *vox ei defecit.* I am afraid he will not be able to stand to him, *metuo ut substet.* He owes more than he is able to pay, *animam debet.* He gives more than he is

Robert Ainsworth, *Linguae Latinae compendiarii, Pars Prima* (1736)

Able [fit] *Capax, idoneus, potens, valens.*
Able [skilful] *Gnarus, peritus, solers.*
Able [strong] *fortis, robustus, validus, magnis viribus praeditus.*
Able [wealthy] *Dives, itis; opulentus, re lauta constitutus.*
Able to rule himself, *compos sui, potens sui.*
To be able. *Possum, queo,* 4. *valeo,* 2.
    Everyone provided as he was able, *pro sua quisque facultate parabat.* He was not able to bear so great envy, *tam magnae non erat par invidiae.* I bare it as well as I was able, *ut potui, tuli.* He was an able spokesman considering those times, *multum, ut temporibus illis, valuit dicendo.*
    As far as I was able, *quoad possem.* He was not able to do it through poverty, *non finit eum egestas facere.*
    You are hardly able to hold your eyes open, *vix sustines palpebras.* I am able to allow these expenses, *est mihi unde haec fiant.* He is not able to pay his debts, *non est solvendo.*
    She was not able to speak a word more, *vox eam defecit.* He is more liberal than his income is able to allow, *benignior est quam res patitur.* I assisted him all I was able, *pro mea re adjuvi.* I am afraid he will not be able to maintain his resolution, *metuo ut*

Coles (1677)

well able, *benignior est quam res patitur.* One of his age is able to be of
Nero's guard, *praestare Neronem se-
curum valet haec aetas.* He is not able
to resolve upon anything, *cui parata
est ne quidem gutta certi consilii.* He is
able to spend a king's revenue, *vel Her-
culi conterere quaestum possit.* He is
able to split a hair, *ille milvo volanti
poterat ungues resecare.*

Ainsworth (1736)

substet. They owe more than they are
able to pay, *animam debent.*

It will be remembered that Coles's *Dictionary, English-Latin and
Latin-English,* first published in 1677, had gone through twelve impressions before Ainsworth published his text. Although Ainsworth criticized
Coles's book for having some obsolete words and others interpreted in
a wrong sense, he praised the English-Latin part as containing "more English words and phrases than any dictionary published before his time." A
comparative study of the typical entries above, under *able* and *to be able*
shows how near in method and matter Ainsworth is to Coles. Study of
similar entries in the English-Latin section of the Rider-Holyoke and of
the Littleton shows that, not these, but Coles was the principal immediate
source of Ainsworth's text. Comparison of the latter two in the entries
under *above, about, bread, busy, buy,* and *egg* further support this conclusion. In the case of *above,* for example, Ainsworth has nine out of
eleven items corresponding to those in Coles; in *bread,* twenty out of
twenty-nine. The point need not be labored. Ainsworth's avowed purpose was not to find new words and definitions, but, using materials
amassed, to systematize, correct, verify, and supply for the Latin words
grammatical information. In this effort he made great progress.

Under the heading "The Latin Appellatives before the English"
on the title page the author states concisely his aim. The more detailed
exposition of his procedure appears, however, in his Preface. As this more
adequately sets forth his purpose and method, we shall here paraphrase
in brief what he writes. He there asserts that a Latin-classical dictionary
should contain

all the words found in any good edition of the several Latin authors generally allowed
to be classical, with proper marks and notes accurately distinguishing those which
rarely occur, or are only read in authors of an inferior class, or in the poets which
are undoubtedly classical, and used by good writers in prose; together with their
etymologies, so far as they can be fixed with any certainty or good probability; and an
exact and clear interpretation of all their different senses, ranged in their due order,
beginning with those nearest to their originals; as also the proper vouchers or authorities for every sense so given.

The author insists that the justness and propriety of any word or expression must be settled by pertinent examples out of classic authors, and all citations should have the exact references to author, text, and page. In this respect the lexicographers before Ainsworth are not dependable.

The author's remarks show that he was most familiar with the dictionaries of his immediate predecessors—with those of Littleton, Coles, and the anonymous Cambridge editors. Ainsworth writes, for example, that "no author is cited for any of them [the phrases] in the Cambridge dictionary or any edition of Littleton . . . which yet in such cases are generally the only books the learner hath to rely upon; for Coles hath omitted almost all citations of this nature."

As to etymologies, Ainsworth explains that he has confined himself to one or two "which seemed to me the most probable. . . . The Hebrew and Greek words, except where the Latin is derived from them, are omitted, as serving rather for a vain ostentation of learning than affording any real benefit in a work of this nature."

For clearness in recording and for the benefit of the student, the author reduces the Latin tongue to six classes of words: (1) words and phrases used in purest Roman authors and in common use; (2) those found seldom in good authors and not commonly made use of later; (3) those that were regarded as obsolete when the Latin tongue was at its most flourishing state (these are marked "T"); (4) those met with chiefly in Latin poets (denoted by the fleur-de-lis); (5) Greek words which occur in some Latin writers; and (6) words in authors of inferior rank. To most words in this last group, Ainsworth subjoins better words. In general, he seems to have carried out this laudable scheme of selection and classification.

Ainsworth's method of entering Latin words and their definitions may be best explained in his own language.

The several significations of such words as admit of various senses are ranged in a method entirely new, with regard to our Latin dictionaries . . . being all numbered by figures, 1, 2, 3, &c., and ranged together in their natural order beginning with that signification which semeth nearest to the etymology of the word, where that is known, and proceeding gradually to those that are more remote from the original sense though sometimes most usual. The primitive signification of words may generally be known by their etymology, their relation to their subject or some parallel or opposite word joined to them. One or more Latin examples are added by way of confirmation to each signification, which are likewise ranged together in the same order as the English and marked by figures; and the particular book, chapter, or verse, wherein these passages in Roman authors so cited may be found, are for the most part carefully referred to.

Ainsworth is right in his assertion that his method of defining words and illustrating usage is "entirely new," with regard to Latin dictionaries;

and yet the various elements that constitute his plan may be found, though not in combination, among his antecedents. Phrases to illustrate meaning and usage appear in Calepine, Stephanus, Elyot, Cooper, Thomas, Gouldman, and Littleton. But no one of these has a systematic method of showing the immediate pertinency of the illustrative phrases to the term being defined. In Robert Stephanus' *Thesaurus*—a book which Ainsworth used, as we shall see below—the compiler gave exact references to particular books, chapter, and verses. Finally, in Abel Boyer's *Dictionnaire royal, francois-anglois et anglois-francois* (1699) was the practice of distinguishing the several meanings of a word, proceeding from the etymological to the more remote.[2] These elements Ainsworth synthesizes: he has the divided and numbered definition, proceeding from the primitive and well-known to the metaphorical and more remote; the illustrative phrase, keyed to the word being defined; and the exact and specific reference to classical authors, citing book, chapter, etc. This is the method adopted by Benjamin Martin in his English dictionary, *Lingua Britannica reformata* (1749), and by Dr. Samuel Johnson in his monumental *Dictionary of the English Language* (1755).

Ainsworth, unlike many of his predecessors, could devote himself to a more critical treatment of his materials, to supplying classical authorities, to numbering and arranging, because the task of laborious accumulation of materials for a dictionary had already been done. In the later editions of Littleton, Ainsworth obviously found the best source for his own work. Although in his English-Latin division, our author had turned chiefly to Coles, he now rejected the Latin-English of the Coles for the more richly illustrated work of Adam Littleton. Note, for example, the definitions of the test word *confero*.

Adam Littleton's *Dictionary* (1703)

Confero, fers, tuli, collatum . . .[3] To bring, carry, put, set or lay together; to profit or avail, to do good . . . to contribute, to give or bestow, to collate, to compare or vie with . . . to confer or discourse and talk together; to lay out, bestow or employ, to dispose of; to go or come to, to betake; to lay, impute, attribute or cast upon: to defer or put off, Caes. to turn, set, bend or apply to. To change, Coop. ex Ovid. *Conferre pedem*, Cic. to set foot to foot, to stand close, to come to the point; *manum*, Vir. to fight hand to hand; *gradum*, To go in even pace one with another, as horses in a coach; to

Robert Ainsworth's *Thesaurus* (1736)

Confero, tuli, ferre, collatum a con & fero (1) To bring, carry, put set or lay together. (2) To advantage, or avail, to do good. (3) To confer, discourse, or talk together. (4) To contribute, or give, to bestow. (5) To collate, compare, or vy with. (6) To lay out, bestow, or imploy. (7) To lay, impute, attribute, or cast upon. (8) *Conferre se*, To go, to betake himself to. (9) To defer or put off. (10) To join. (11) To bend, or apply. (12) To refer to, or be judged by another. (13) To compose or digest. (1) *Horreum, quo conferatur rusticum instrumentum,* Varr. 1, 6. (2) *Comoedia ad eloquen-*

Adam Littleton's *Dictionary* (1703)
set step by step; *signa*, Liv. to engage in battle; *consilia*, Ter. to lay their heads together; *animum*, *id.* to set or bend his thoughts; *lites*, Hor. to chide and scold; *rationes*, Cic. to cast account or reckon with; *se*, Cic. to go, to betake himself. *Conferre castra castris*, Caes. To pitch their camp over against one another. *Novissima conferre primis*, Cic. To bring or lay them together. *Aliquod stipendium nostro studio contulerunt*, Col. Given us some help or assistance . . . *Culpam conferre in aliquem*, Plaut. To lay the blame on one. *Rem in pauca conferre*, Id. To make short. *Conferre beneficium in aliquem*, Cic. To do one a courtesy. *In pedes se conferre*, Plaut. To run away.

Robert Ainsworth's *Thesaurus* (1736)
tiam confert. Quint. 1, 8. (3) *Coram brevi tempore conferre, quae volumus, licebit*, Cic. Att. 2, 25. *Conferunt capita*, Liv. 2, 45. (4) = *Nos dabimus, nos conferemus nostro sumptu*, Plaut. Most. 5, 2, 39. (5) *Non illi quisquam bello se conferet heros*, Catull. (6) *Cum studia, & officia in me contulisset*, Cic. (7) *Verum ne post conferas culpam in me*, Ter. Eun. 2, 3, 96. (8) *Cum se contulisset Rhodum*, Cic. de Orat. 3, 56. *Conferre in fugam*, *Id.* pro Caec. 8. (9) *Quae omnia in Martium mensem sunt collata*, Cic. (10) *Novissima primis conferam*, Cic. (11) *Omnia mea studia in istum unum conferam.* Cic. (12) *Id omne ad tuum arbitrum conferemus*, Cic. Fam., 1, 9. (13) *De cultu hortorum in carmen conferemus*, Col. 9, 16.
Conferre pedem, To set foot to foot, to come to the point, Cic. pro. Planc. 19. *manum, ferum*, to fight, *Id. capita*, to consult, *Id. signa*, to engage in battle, Liv. *rationes*, to cast account, or reckon with one. Cic. (Att. 5, 21.) *Castra castris*, to pitch their camps over against one another. Cic. de Div. 2, 55.

It will be seen that the new matter in Ainsworth's entry is the careful numbering of the meanings and the corresponding illustrative Latin phrases, and supplying these phrases themselves with the references to authors and texts. Practically all the English definitions in the first part of Ainsworth's entry are from Littleton, as are the phrases, Latin and English, after the last numbered illustration. Incidentally, eleven of the references to authors and texts for the illustrative phrases are from Robert Stephanus' *Thesaurus*.

Compare also the parallel entries which follow:

Littleton (1703)
Degravo, as; act. Ovid. . . . To weigh down.

Ainsworth (1746)
Degravo, are. act. To weigh down, to sink down. *Vitis degravat ulmum*, Ov. Trist. 5. 3. 35. *Degravat unda caput*, Prop. 3. 7. 58. *Etiam peritos nandi lassitudo & vulnera & pavor degravant*, Liv. 4. 33.

Littleton (1703)	Ainsworth (1746)
Degravor, aris; pass. Col. To be weighed down, to be wearied.	*Degravor, ari, atus. pass.* To be weighed down, to be wearied. *Labore operis degravari*, Col. 6. 2.
Degredior, eris, ssus; ex De & Gradior . . . To go down, to descend. *Cum Abl.* Tac. *Degredi ad pedes;* Liv. To alight off his horse.	*Degredior, i, ssus (ex de & gradior)* . . . To go down, to descend. *Postquam Alpibus degressi sunt*, Tac. Hist. 2. 66. *Degredi ad pedes*, To alight off his horse, Liv. 3. 62.
Degressus, a, um; part. Liv. *Cum Abl.* Going down, or being come down.	*Degressus, a, um, part.* (1) Going down, or being come down. (2) Alighting from horseback. (1) *Degressos tumulos mantanos sensit*, Liv. 21. 32. (2) *Cum equitibus ad pedes degressis*, with his dragoons, Liv.
Degulatus, a, um; part. Plaut. Devoured, wasted, guzzled down.	*Degulatus, a, um. part.* Devoured, wasted, guzzled down, Plaut. in Frag.
Degustandus, a, um; part. Quint. To be lightly touched or spoken of.	*Degustandus, a, um. part.* To be lightly touched, or, Met. spoken of, Quint. 4. 1.
Degusto, as; act. Cic. . . . To taste or assay, to have a taste or smack of a thing: to touch slightly: to smatter or have a smattering: to speak briefly of a thing; Quint. to catch, as fire; Lucre.	*Degusto, are. act.* (1) To taste. (2) Met. To sound or try one. (3) To touch slightly, to speak briefly. (4) To catch, as fire doth. (5) To essay, to prove. (6) To conceive. (1) *Vinum degustare*, Cato 148. *fruges*, Plin. 18. 2. *cruorem*, Sil. Ital. 5. 275. (2) *Tu velim a Fabio odorere, & istum convivam tuum degustes*, Cic. Attic. 8. 8. (3) *Degustare genus aliquod exercitationum*, Cic. Parad. 5. (4) *Ignes degustant tigna*, Lucr. 2. 192. (5) *Visne ipse tandem degustare, & fortunam experiri meam?* Cic. Tusc. 5. 21. (6) *Aliquid speculae ex sermone alicujus degustare*, Cic. *pro.* Cluent. 26.

A checking of the entries above with Thomas, Gouldman, Thomas Holyoke, Coles, and Littleton shows that Ainsworth is, in the English phrasing, nearest to Littleton; and twelve of sixteen illustrations, with their specific references, derive from Stéphanus.

An unpublished study, "Robert Ainsworth and Latin-English Lexicography," by Charles E. Noyes, made when he was a graduate student working with me (1948) offers additional proof of Ainsworth's dependence upon Littleton for his Latin-English word list. Noyes studied the first twenty words defined by Littleton under each of six letters—*A, B, E, F, M,* and *N*—and checked against them similar material from Ains-

worth, observing also corresponding entries in Gouldman, Thomas Holyoke, and Coles. The results, as they pertain to each letter, are too long
to present here in full details, but here is his summarizing paragraph:

> Thus, of one hundred and twenty words placed in order in the Littleton, Ainsworth
> omits twenty. Nine of these are admittedly not classical; four are comparative or
> superlative degrees treated by Ainsworth under their positives; two are words of
> Greek origin; and one is a variant form of another word. Only four words of the one
> hundred and twenty are dropped for no immediately assignable reason. To all these,
> Ainsworth adds only five new terms. The inference to be drawn is that Ainsworth
> worked from a copy of the Littleton, eliminating many words in his quest for purity
> of language, but adding comparatively few.

We have noticed above that in the Latin-English part of his text Ainsworth often depended upon the *Thesaurus linguae Latinae* of Robert
Stephanus for illustrative phrases and specific references to their classical
sources. Although most English lexicographers from Cooper to Littleton
had supplied illustrations, they had not referred these to specific texts.
Stephanus had done so and had furnished his *Thesaurus* with examples
in great abundance. For the fulfillment of Ainsworth's plan, no other
dictionary would have been so helpful as Stephanus' *Thesaurus*. Without
it, the *Compendious Dictionary* of Ainsworth would have been an even
longer time in the making. With the Stephanus at hand, the task of
Ainsworth and Patrick and probably other assistants was one of choosing
illustrations and verifying. Other lexicographers had borrowed freely
from the riches of Stephanus, disregarding the specific citations.

The *Thesaurus* of Robert Stephanus was first published in 1531. Other
editions with augmentations followed until the posthumous edition of
1573, published in three folio volumes. While Ainsworth was compiling
his book, a new edition of the *Thesaurus* (1734–35) in four volumes,
folio, was printed in England. This edition, which corrected errors in
earlier issues and added illustrative examples in some entries, was probably printed too late for extensive use of Ainsworth. But whatever edition
Ainsworth and his assistants consulted, they found in it the necessary
illustrations with the specific references.

Various tests we have made, including those mentioned above, indicate
that Stephanus was in constant use by the compilers of Ainsworth. Similar
results appear in Charles Noyes's study (*op. cit.*, 44–45). Noyes finds
that of the twenty-two quotations given by Ainsworth to illustrate the
meanings of *canis*, seventeen may be found in the Stephanus. Of fifteen
quotations listed under the definitions of *caput*, ten match ones found in
Stephanus. Under the various significations of the words *amabiliter*,
amanuensis, *caballus*, *cacoethes*, *cacumen*, *calamarius*, and *calleo*, Ainsworth furnishes twenty-one quotations, and eighteen of them could have

been located through Stephanus' *Thesaurus*. Additional evidence would seem to be superfluous. There can be no doubt that for illustrations in Ainsworth the Stephanus was a principal source.

It is in the Latin-English part of the dictionary that Ainsworth includes disquisitions on the letters of the alphabet. These are distributed through the text, the entries under each letter being prefaced by a discussion of the particular letter. The etymology, formation, and the use of the letter in various languages is considered. These discourses are in English, as in Baret's *Alvearie*, but Baret is not the source. Ainsworth's discussions are paraphrases, with some corrections and modifications, of the Latin essays found in Littleton.

"The ancient Latin Names of the more remarkable Persons and Places occurring in the classic Authors" is the title Ainsworth gives to the proper-name section. This is the conventional "Dictionarium Poeticum et Historicum" appearing in the larger dictionaries from Cooper to Littleton. And once again Littleton is the principal source, as is evidenced by a comparison of the items under *Acteon, Actania, Actia, Achilles, Acusilaus, Acontius, Admetus, Adonis, Crates, Creon,* and *Creusa.* Ainsworth supplies, where lacking, specific citations to classic authors, makes changes and corrections, and adds new items. The matter under *Absyrtes* and *Acastus* shows how Ainsworth modified what he found in Littleton; and the explanations under *Abdera, Accius,* and *Acco* exemplify his addition of new material.[4] In accordance with his plan to compile a classical dictionary, Ainsworth rules out the Biblical proper names which had been so prominent in Littleton and his predecessors. Although Littleton is basic for the proper-name word list, Ainsworth makes some additions from other sources. In keeping with his aim also, he numbers the meanings if a proper name applies to more than one person or place, and he generally cites the specific classical source of information.

For his legal terms Ainsworth has a heading beginning "Index Vocabulorum Quorundum," imitative of the heading of an analogous list in Littleton. From Littleton a number of entries are borrowed. But Ainsworth's list is much augmented. For additional matter he seems to have drawn from Spelman's *Glossarium*, with which there are numerous correspondences, from a late seventeenth-century edition of Cowell's *Interpreter*, and from Giles Jacob's *A New Law Dictionary* (1729).[5]

Other features of Ainsworth's dictionary may be touched upon briefly. The proper names of remarkable places, or "Index Geographicus," represents a fourfold expansion of Littleton; the "Christian Names of Men and Women" follows largely Littleton's word list, inserting meanings and derivations. The "Fasti Romanii Consulares," to which there is no corresponding section in Littleton, derives, according to Ainsworth, from an account printed by Almeloveen, at Amsterdam, in 1705; the matter on abbreviations and inscriptions, from the *Breviarium* of Sertorius Ursalus; and the tables of coins, weights, and measures, from published data by Pope's friend, Dr. Arbuthnot.[6]

My account, thus far, of the purpose, the provenience, the method, and the sources of Ainsworth's *Thesaurus, or Compendious Dictionary* is based largely upon a study of the first (1736) and second (1746) editions of his work. As far as Ainsworth's individual contribution was concerned—he died in 1742—we might stop here. A word must be said, however, concerning the subsequent history of the text.

At the beginning of this chapter we quoted in full the wording on the title page of the first edition (1736) of Ainsworth's dictionary. This wording is followed closely on the title page of the 1746 edition, down to the imprint, where we read: "The Second Edition, with additions and improvements. By Samuel Patrick, LLD." [7] This edition reprints all the preliminary matter, including the lengthy Preface, of the 1736 edition and adds the "Preface to the Second Edition," by Dr. Patrick. As the introductory matter was noted above, we need only remark upon the added Preface. In this, Dr. Patrick has a brief biographical sketch of Ainsworth and an account of his work. He then states what he himself has done to improve the dictionary. Much of his time has been devoted to the correction of errors that slipped into the first edition. He also claims a modest amount of augmentation, the insertion of illustrations, references, etc., discovered just too late to get into the 1736 edition.

Most of Dr. Patrick's additions appear in the English-Latin. Many new phrases for this part he claims to have found in a manuscript compilation by Samuel Morland.[8] Among these, he tells us, are new illustrations for *to scruple, to shew, short, the sight, to signify, the soul, a stranger,* and *a year.* All of these are expanded in the second edition; also, there are a few new illustrations under *fall, to fall,* and other entries.

In the Latin-English of 1746, evidences of correction appear in the matter under *confero, conficio, confido,* and other entries. In certain groups of a hundred entries or more, we find some additions. Between the first and the last entry in "*E ante O,*" there are no new entries; but in "*E ante P,*" there are seven; and in "*H ante I,*" seven. Many other groups of entries show no sign of amplification.

Various tests applied to the proper-name section and to the discussion of letters of the alphabet reveal corrections of mistakes and insertions of some additional references, but no essential augmentation.

In 1751 there was printed another edition, in quarto, "The Third Edition, with Additions and Improvements. By Samuel Patrick, L.L.D.

and Usher of the Charter-House School." Excepting the imprint, the title page is unchanged; the claim of enlargement is simply a repetition of that found in the 1746 edition. This issue contains the introductory and textual matter of the earlier edition. The 1751 edition appears to be virtually a reprint of the 1746, provided to fill a gap before the new and revised volume of 1752.

The fourth edition of Ainsworth's dictionary was published in 1752, in two volumes, folio, edited by William Young. This contains the preliminary matter of former editions, and a "Preface to the Fourth Edition," by the editor. The first volume contains the English-Latin, the proper names of persons and places, and "several appendages relating to Roman antiquities"; the second has the Latin-English. In his Preface, Young recalls the work of Ainsworth and Dr. Patrick and lists the improvements which he himself endeavored to make. These are the insertion of the derivations of many words which Latin writers had borrowed from the Greek language, the addition of several classical words not hitherto found in classical dictionaries, the correction of imperfectly cited sentences, and the exercise of utmost care in eliminating typographical errors. Examination of the larger sections, the English-Latin and Latin-English, reveals some corrections and a few additions, but the slightest augmentation. The great merit of this edition is in the printing. Earlier editions in thick quarto and fine print are trying for the student. The larger print of the folio volumes of 1752 is in pleasing contrast. Of the earlier editions, this is the most desirable to possess.

There is no gainsaying the popularity of Ainsworth's dictionary in its own day and the continued demand for it in the eighteenth and early nineteenth century. To give a full account of subsequent printings is beyond the scope of this study. It is, however, instructive to read the list by Kennedy (No. 2863), and also those in the *British Museum Catalogue*. In the latter are these recordings: 1758, an abridgment by "Mr. Thomas"; 1761, a reissue of the fourth edition (in two volumes, quarto); 1773, a "new edition," by T. Morell, reissued in 1796; 1812, a "second American edition," published in Boston; 1823, a "second" edition of Morell's version; 1827, the same version corrected by A. Jamieson; 1828, an edition called the "thirteenth"; 1829, an edition printed from the folio of 1752 with improvements by B. W. Beatson, revised by William Ellis; and yet later editions.[9]

Such is the story of Ainsworth's dictionary. To evaluate his achievement, we need to view his work in the right perspective. There is perhaps no feature of his lexicon that in itself is entirely novel or original. The idea of compiling a classical dictionary had obtained, in England, from the first half of the sixteenth century. This was in the mind of Elyot, of

Cooper, and of Thomas; and they made progress. But apparently the time was not ripe for such a lexicon. Many words in old books, charters, and documents, regarded by the classicist as barbarous, still had to be defined. Renaissance lexicographers hardly deserve criticism for the inclusion of nonclassical Latin words. They were serving their day and time. After the Restoration, Wase and, later, Littleton re-emphasized the notion of classical Latin. So too in the matter of defining terms, Cooper and, after him, Thomas and their imitators listed various meanings, though apparently without any definite order of arrangement in mind. Illustrations of meaning and usage were supplied, but without any attempt to correlate them with the definitions or give exact and specific references to the classic authors whence they derived. In the English-Latin of Elisha Coles was a crude system of dividing definitions and indicating distinctions in meaning; in Abel Boyer's English-French was the system of numbering the different meanings of a given term; and, finally, in the Latin *Thesaurus* of Robert Stephanus was copious illustration with specific citations to book, chapter, and verse in the classic sources.

What then was the problem of Ainsworth when, in 1714, he was requested to compile a new dictionary? In a word, it was that of formulating a definite plan, motivated by a central and impelling idea; then of judiciously selecting and rejecting and combining materials from the riches of his predecessors, devising methods to fit the predesigned pattern. Now Ainsworth is his own best expositor, and in his Preface he has told his story well. This I have freely drawn upon in this discussion to make explicit his procedure. It is hardly necessary to recount in detail his aim and methods. It is perhaps sufficient to say that his achievement was the exercise of sound critical judgment in devising his plan for a classical dictionary and in selecting and synthesizing techniques of his antecedents. The results are the divided and numbered definition and the illustration of meaning and usage keyed to the definition and supported by exact reference to classical authorities. This was the system endorsed and adopted by Dr. Samuel Johnson.

CHAPTER XXIII

Conclusion

IT REMAINS to draw together the main threads of this fabric and to suggest briefly the significance. Beginning with the *Promptorium* about the middle of the fifteenth century, English-Latin lexicography continues its history as an independent genre in the *Catholicon Anglicum* (*ca.* 1483), in Huloet's *Abcedarium* (1552), in Withals' *Dictionarie* (1553), in Baret's *Alvearie* (1573), and in Rider's *Bibliotheca scholastica* (1589). The *Ortus vocabulorum* (1500) was the earliest printed Latin-English dictionary. This species persists in the *Dictionary* (1538) of Sir Thomas Elyot, in the various augmentations of Elyot (1548–59) by Thomas Cooper, in Cooper's *Thesaurus* (1565), and in Thomas Thomas's *Dictionarium* (1587).

Proper-name dictionaries as an independent type were not compiled in England during the Renaissance; yet proper names of men and places were not neglected. In the Elyot-Cooper dictionaries these names were distributed throughout the alphabet in the general word list. For the first time in the history of Latin-English lexicography proper names were placed together in a separate part of the text in Cooper's *Thesaurus*. In 1606 Francis Holyoke revised Rider's *Bibliotheca,* adding to it a Latin-English and a proper-name section. He was thus the first in England to bring together under one cover an English-Latin, a Latin-English, and a proper-name dictionary. For the larger dictionaries, with one or two exceptions, this method of assembling the various parts in one text became the established practice for the next one hundred and fifty years.

Lexicographers of the fifteenth century, probably because citation of well-known authorities would lend prestige, were more likely to give

341

specific acknowledgment of major sources than were the compilers of the Tudor and Stuart periods. The *Promptorium*, for example, lists in the *Preambulum* twelve compilatious from which the author drew materials, and which he cites, severally, in various entries of the text. In the *Catholicon Anglicum* eight earlier works are referred to as authorities and sources of illustration; and in the *Ortus*, five. Of the host of bilingual vocabularies, class names, and glossaries which must have been known and useful to our compilers, no mention is made. The authors and books cited as authorities are better known: Hugo of Pisa's *Magnae derivationes*, Joannes Balbus' *Catholicon*, John of Garland's *Dictionarius*, Alexander Neckam's *De nominibus utensilium*, and others. Most influential of all probably was the *Catholicon* of Balbus.

From Sir Thomas Elyot on, in the sixteenth century, there was a shift away from the medieval lexicographers as authorities and sources to authors and compilers regarded as more nearly classical in content. There was also a tendency to refrain from acknowledgment of specific sources, or to bury the names in long lists of authors allegedly consulted in the compilation of the dictionary. This procedure is exemplified in the lists cited in the preliminary matter of the *Bibliotheca Eliotae* (1542) and of the *Abcedarium* (1552). Within such blanket acknowledgments, however, are usually found the names of authors whose works have been most frequently employed by the compilers. Among these are Calepine, Perottus, Grapaldus, Suidas (especially for proper names), Robert Stephanus (titles of whose works are not mentioned, though English lexicographers drew freely from the Latin *Thesaurus* and the Latin-French and the French-Latin dictionaries), Erasmus, Plutarch, and others. In the course of the sixteenth century the problem of sources becomes increasingly complex as the lexicographers borrow not only from common sources but also from each other.

By the end of the century the dictionary-makers in England had accumulated a considerable body of lexical lore in such texts as the Elyot-Cooper dictionaries, the Huloet-Higgins, the Rider, the Baret, and the Thomas Thomas. These, especially the lexicons of Cooper and Thomas, constitute the basic sources for the compilers of the seventeenth century. The Rider-Holyoke dictionaries, extending through the first half of the century, depend largely on Thomas and Rider, with borrowings from Calepine and others for etymologies. Gouldman admittedly compiled his dictionary from those of his English predecessors, deriving most from Thomas and the Rider-Holyoke. Thomas Holyoke built upon Gouldman and the Rider-Holyoke of his father, Francis, supplementing these texts with generous borrowings from Spelman's *Glossarium*. Littleton owes much to his immediate antecedents as well as to the earlier Elyot-Cooper dictionaries. To his countrymen Coles and Gouldman, Ainsworth is a heavy debtor in content and method, but for classical illustrations and references he reverted to the Latin *Thesaurus* of Robert Stephanus and to actual texts of classical authors. Thus the influence of Stephanus first exerted in England on Elyot's *Bibliotheca* of 1542, becomes even more potent in Ainsworth's dictionary of 1736.

In the sixteenth century three methods of arranging words in the dictionary were in vogue: the topical, in which words are collected under general headings according to association and use; the etymological, in which the primitive or root word is placed first and the derivatives after; and the alphabetical, or ABC, order of arrangement. Until near the end of the century, no one of these methods was followed meticulously.

Of the first, or topical, method, Withals' very popular *Dictionarie* is the chief example. Withals was in the tradition of the medieval bilingual vocabularies and perhaps under the immediate influence of a Latin edition of Julius Pollux' *Onomasticon* and Franciscus Grapaldus' *Lexicon de partibus aedium*. Although the topical system was not destined to prevail in the larger dictionaries, it lingers in wordbooks for schoolboys, such as John Ray's *Nomenclator classicus* (1675) and James Greenwood's *London Vocabulary* (*ca.* 1700), through the eighteenth century.

Using Calepine as his model, Elyot at first observed the etymological order of word entry. In revisions and augmentations of his dictionary by himself and by Thomas Cooper, an approximate alphabetical order was employed. In his *Thesaurus* Cooper, following the arrangement of the *Dictionarium Latino-Gallicum* of Robert Stephanus, uses a modified etymological plan, with alphabetical cross references. Influential as the *Thesaurus* was in the last thirty years of the century, its system of word arrangement did not prevail.

The reasons are obvious. Many doubtless felt it impracticable, even with the cross references, to turn from one part to another of the thick folio of Cooper to find the meaning of a given word. A strictly alphabetical arrangement would have expedited the use of the text. There were also other factors making for an alphabetical order. Such an order, or the approximation of it, had persisted in the English-Latin dictionaries from the *Promptorium* (which, however, tends to group words alphabetically according to the parts of speech) through Huloet, Higgins, Baret, and others. So, too, proper names, whether distributed through the text, as in Elyot's *Bibliotheca,* or grouped together in a special section, as in Cooper's *Thesaurus,* were in the order of the alphabet. Finally, Thomas Thomas, following the word order of G. Morelius, observed a strictly alphabetical arrangement. The high repute and the immense vogue of the Thomasius through a period of twenty-five years seem finally to have fixed the alphabetical system.

With few exceptions, lexicographers from the compiler of the *Promptorium* to Ainsworth included a certain amount of grammatical information on terms entered and defined. The *Promptorium* designates adverbs, the nominative forms of adjectives, the gender and declension of nouns, and the principal parts and the conjugation of verbs. The manuscript of the *Catholicon Anglicum,* edited by Herrtage, gives no grammatical information, but the *Ortus* designates the gender and declension of nouns and the conjugation of verbs.

The editions of Elyot issued before 1548 present the nominative forms of the adjective and the genitives of nouns (not consistently) and designate the conjugation of verbs. Cooper's revision of the *Bibliotheca Eliotae* (1548) gives full grammatical information, though no instruction concerning accent and pronunciation or derivation. This aspect of lexicographic technique appears fully developed in the *Thesaurus* (1565). In this we see indicated for each word the part of speech, the accent and pronunciation, the gender and declension of nouns and substantives, the conjugation of verbs, and the arrangement of derivatives under their primitives.

Thomas Thomas gives the same grammatical information, except that he arranges the derivatives alphabetically and uses diacritical marks, instead of the abbreviations *pen. corr.* and *pen. prod.,* employed by Cooper, to indicate the long and the short vowels, and therefore accent and pronunciation. The grammatical system thus established by Thomas prevails in Holyoke, Littleton, and Ainsworth.

Despite the precedent from early times—from Varro and Festus, from Isidore of Seville, from Hugo of Pisa, and from Joannes Balbus—most lexicographers in the Latin-English or English-Latin tradition refrained from etymologizing, beyond the statement that a Latin word was derived from the Greek or was composed of two other Latin words, or indication, by arrangement, that a family of Latin words derived from a common stem. There are, however, two notable exceptions in our period. These are John Baret and Francis Holyoke.

In the *Alvearie* (1573, 1580) of Baret, Professor James Sledd has noted, without exhausting the list, seventy-odd examples of etymology, true and false. Baret is concerned with English words. Though some of his etymologies appear to be original, he borrows many from the Latin dictionary of Friar Calepine and the French-Latin text of Robert Stephanus.

Francis Holyoke devoted his attention to the etymology of Latin

words. In 1606 he published as a Latin-English supplement to Rider's
Bibliotheca his *Dictionarium etymologicum,* "deriuing euery word from
his natiue fountaine, with reasons of his deriuations." Although his Latin
word list and English definitions are borrowed mainly from Thomas
Thomas's dictionary, Holyoke is indebted to various others for his etymologies. He cites Festus, Varro, Isidore, and Perottus, but rarely Calepine, whose dictionary is frequently the source of Holyoke's references
to the earlier etymologists.

Many of the etymologies of Francis Holyoke, fantastic and otherwise,
persisted, after the Restoration, in the lexicons of Gouldman, Thomas
Holyoke, and Littleton, but were rejected by the more critical Elisha
Coles, who stated: "We have . . . omitted the superfluous and tedious etymologies, which (for the most part) depended merely upon conjectures."
Ainsworth retained, he tells us, only those etymologies that "can be fixed
with any certainty or good probability."

The ultimate test of a dictionary is in the accuracy and completeness of
definition. In the Renaissance this subject is to some extent bound up with
those of translation, synonymy, copiousness, and the employment of quotations from standard classical authors to illustrate meaning and usage.
Definition is thus a complex subject. For the present, we can do no more
than clear the ground and indicate the beginning and persistence of general trends in definition, or explication of meaning.

In the sixteenth century, progress in defining words is best represented
in the Elyot-Cooper dictionaries, including the dictionary of Thomas
Thomas. These constitute a unified group of texts in which it is possible
to trace the lexical fortunes of individual terms. Definitions in these lexicons are by no means uniform in quality or fullness. Some are literal translations of the Latin from foreign sources, such as Calepine or Stephanus.
Some are expanded by the use of English synonyms. Some are elaborate
but vague and inexact; others are concise and adequate. In his *Thesaurus*
Cooper includes most of the definitions, often rephrased and improved,
which he and Elyot had developed in the *Bibliotheca.* To these he adds
scores of new entries from other sources, and hundreds of classical phrases
and quotations to illustrate meaning. In the definitions both Elyot and
Cooper give careful attention to English idiom, and both group immediately after the Latin term to be defined a series of English words or
phrases, almost synonymous, designed to suggest shades of meaning which
the Latin term contains. The meaning or meanings thus expressed are
reinforced by quotations from classical Latin. This procedure assists the
student to the attainment of copiousness and variety of expression in both
Latin and English. Thomas Thomas, selecting and condensing from his
antecedents, frequently shows improvement of definition.

Progress in the framing of definitions in the Elyot-Cooper-Thomas texts could be amply demonstrated by tracing through them a considerable number of terms, such as *daemon, definitio, fanaticus,* and *harmonia* —a procedure not practical here. A few abbreviated interpretations of words less representative must suffice. *Adulator,* for example, means "a flatterer," in the Elyot-Cooper dictionaries, and in Thomas "a flatterer, a clawbacke, a picke-thanke." Elyot renders *idiota* as "a man or woman unlearned"; Cooper retains these words and adds "one that is not very fine witted, an ideot. Also one out of office"; and Cooper's definition is borrowed by Thomas. Elyot renders *indignor* "to disdeygne, to fume, to fret, to chafe, to thinke scorne, to be made angry, to be stampyng and staryng wood." Cooper uses the same words with slight change of spelling; Thomas adds "repine, grudge, to be displeased, out of patience, and discontented." *Noverca,* in the Elyot-Cooper dictionaries, is translated as "a stepmother," whereas Thomas renders the same word as "a stepmother or mother in law; also hurtfull." Thomas defines *meretrix* as "a harlot, a light housewife." But here he is not following closely his predecessors. Elyot, after Calepine, renders the phrase *diobolares meretrices* "women who be hyred for little money"; Cooper, more concise and idiomatic, writes "three halfe pennie harlots." And this is more elegant than Adam Littleton's "common sluts."

Definitions developed in the Elyot-Cooper texts persist in the Latin-English dictionaries of the seventeenth century, though in the Rider-Holyoke texts they are often cluttered up with fantastic etymologies in Latin and with insertions of long Latin expositions between the terms to be defined and the English definitions. In Wase and Coles and Littleton, after 1660, excessive Latin verbiage is excluded, more prominence given to English definitions, and more emphasis placed on classical Latin terms and illustrations. In Ainsworth's *Thesaurus,* the wording of his predecessors, even back to Thomas and Cooper, is still in evidence; but there is great gain in the elimination of extraneous verbiage, in the reduction of etymologizing, in orderly arrangement, and in supplying classical examples of usage keyed to the definitions.

The illustration of meaning and usage, a topic adumbrated in the foregoing paragraphs, requires little further elaboration. Quotation from classical authors to illustrate the meaning of Latin words was in vogue, at the end of the fifteenth and in the early sixteenth century, in the works of Perottus, Calepine, and Robert Stephanus. For Sir Thomas Elyot these were precedents in his efforts to compile a Latin-English dictionary more nearly in keeping with classical usage. Elyot at first uses illustrative phrases sparingly, occasionally citing the authors' names. In the 1542 and

1545 editions of the *Bibliotheca,* he much increases the number of classical illustrations, borrowing generously from the Latin-French dictionary of Robert Stephanus. Expansion of the illustrative matter, largely from the same sources, continues in Cooper's revision of the *Bibliotheca,* though Cooper fails to cite the names of his authorities. The great expansion appears, however, in his *Thesaurus.* Here Cooper, depending on the augmented *Dictionarium Latino-Gallicum* of Stephanus, adds literally thousands of illustrative phrases, together with the authors' names, but with too little regard to practical usefulness. Here, however, is "copie," in the Elizabethan meaning, and a treasure-trove for subsequent lexicographers.

From the abundance of the *Thesaurus,* Thomas selects illustrative phrases, making it possible to reduce the size of his text while increasing the number of entries (I refer especially to the Thomasius of 1596 and after). In the seventeenth century, lexicographers—excepting Francis Holyoke, who reduced illustrations to a minimum—tended to follow Thomas, with occasional borrowings from Cooper. Only in Ainsworth is there a more critical selection and orderly arrangement, and also the addition of new illustrations, with specific citations of author and text for all examples.

The search for illustrations of usage in reputable Latin authors of antiquity is evidence of the desire for a classical dictionary. Elyot's general purpose was to compile a dictionary which would concern itself with standard classical Latin words, and his illustrations and authorities were generally classical. He was, however, under the necessity of retaining many Latin words which, though current in his day, were medieval or, as Erasmus might term them, "barbarous." Under the stimulus of Budaeus, Robert Stephanus, and other Humanists of the early sixteenth century, Cooper ruled out many of the terms of doubtful classical Latinity and, from Stephanus, supplied a host of classical illustrations. He thus made progress and perhaps approached, in his *Thesaurus,* nearer to the ideal than any other English lexicographer in the sixteenth century. Though much under the influence of Cooper, Thomas and his later editors and redactors introduced much matter from medieval glossaries and documents and thus moved a step away from a classical dictionary. While making the Thomasius more useful in reading all sorts of Latin, the editors and revisers did not improve its classical quality. And the Rider-Holyoke dictionaries apparently moved a step farther away from classicism.

In the Restoration, first Wase and then Coles, Littleton, and the Cambridge editors re-emphasized the idea of classical Latin, but made little progress in realizing the proclaimed ideal. It remained for Ainsworth, at the beginning of the eighteenth century, to analyze the work of his predecessors, which he was to use advantageously; to formulate a definite plan for a classical Latin dictionary; and meticulously to carry out the plan.

Establishing the authority of the dictionary is a subject on which little direct information is available. Puttenham's statement in 1589 does, however, seem significant. Discussing pure English and warning the poet against linguistic affectation, Puttenham writes, "Herein we are already ruled by th' English Dictionaries and other bookes written by learned men" ("The Arte of English Poesie," in G. G. Smith's *Elizabethan Critical Essays* [Oxford, 1904], II, 150–51). As there were no purely English dictionaries in his day, Puttenham probably had in mind the well-known bilingual dictionaries—Elyot's *Dictionary* and *Bibliotheca* and Cooper's *Thesaurus*. We know that a copy of the *Thesaurus* was presented to the Stratford school by Brechtgirdle and retained for reference. Withals' *Dictionarie* (1553) was prepared especially for schoolboys and, judging from its popularity, was long in use. At least three editions of Thomas (1600, 1610, 1619) were prepared for use in schools. Evidence that dictionaries were kept as reference works in school libraries as well as in private collections in the sixteenth and seventeenth centuries is plentiful. In *A Consolation for Our Grammar Schooles* (1622) John Brinsley recommends, "for both English and Latin," Rider's "dictionarie of the last" (1617) edition, Thomas's dictionary, and the *Ianua linguarum*. In 1650, Charles Hoole, giving instructions on developing a theme, writes:

Now to furnish themselues also with copy of good words and phrases, besides what they haue collected weekly, and what hath been already said of varying them; they should haue these and the like Books reserued in the Schoole-Library: viz., *Sylva Synonymorum* . . . Barrets *Dictionary*, Huloet or rather Higgins *Dictionary*; Drax' *Bibliotheca*, A little English Dictionary, 16° . . . and if at any time they can wittily and pithily inuent any thing of their own brain; you may help them to express it in good Latine, by making use of Cooper's Dictionary, either as he himself directed in his preface, or Phalerius will more fully show you in his *Supplementa ad Grammaticam*.[1]

In the schools, dictionaries seem to have been regarded as authoritative in Latin and English discourse, oral and written. How far applicable outside the classroom is Puttenham's remark that "we are ruled by th' English Dictionaries" it is not possible with certainty to say.

In content and in technique the English dictionary owes much to the bilingual English-Latin and Latin-English dictionaries. In the hard-word English dictionaries, beginning with Cawdrey's *A Table Alphabeticall* (1604) and including Bullokar's *English Expositor* (1616), Cockeram's *English Dictionarie* (1623), and Blount's *Glossographia* (1656), there is fairly constant borrowing of definitions from the Latin-English dictionaries of Thomas and Holyoke.[2] And the debt for definitions continues to some extent in subsequent English dictionaries of the seventeenth and eighteenth centuries.

Probably of more importance is the developed technique of the Latin-English dictionary, which was adapted by the English lexicographers. Two aspects of this technique are exhibited in Ainsworth. First are the divided and numbered definitions which take account of the various meanings of a term and arrange them in logical and intelligible order. This practice was adopted by Benjamin Martin in *Lingua Britannica reformata* (1749). The second aspect is illustrating meanings by use of quotations from standard classics, specifying author and text. It is not a far cry to Johnson's quoting English authors to confirm the usage of English words; and Johnson, following Martin, employed the divided definition, first used by Ainsworth.

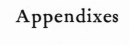

Appendixes

Appendix I

Related Dictionaries

1. PETER LEVINS' *Manipulus vocabulorum* (1570)

The *Manipulus vocabulorum* is an English-Latin dictionary of some nine thousand entries, arranged in the alphabetical order of the last syllables and designed especially for "such as vse to write in English meetre." As this is the single example of a rhyming dictionary in the sixteenth century and is not therefore in the genre of English-Latin dictionaries proper, it seems fitting to give the *Manipulus* brief notice apart from the foregoing general history. Since the text has been re-edited, with a preface and an alphabetical index of the English words by Henry B. Wheatley (for the Camden Society [No. XCV], 1867), and since the editor has given the essential information concerning the author and the text, no lengthy additional account seems required.

The wording of the title page in the original edition follows:

Manipulus Vocabulorum. A Dictionarie of English and Latine wordes, set forthe in suche order, as none heretofore hath ben, the Englishe going before the Latine, necessary not onely for Scholers that wāt varietie of wordes but also for such as vse to write in English Meetre. Gathered and set forth by P. Leuins, Anno 1570. For the better vnderstanding of the order of this present Dictionarie, read ouer the Preface to the Reader, and the Epistle Dedicatorie, and thou shalt finde it easie and plaine, and further thereof thou shalt gather great profite. Imprinted at London by Henrie Bynneman, for John Waley.

In the dedicatory epistle to Lord Stanley, Levins refers to those writers who "by their friends counsell" set forth to the public what "first they thought should be but a priuat exercise." As for himself, "when I first began to collect this booke . . . I thought and did always entend, with so much speed as I could, to publishe and set abroade the same."

On the arrangement of entries, Levins writes that "this Booke is deuided into ix. partes, according to the ix. vowels, which come before the consonant in the last syllable; of the which vowels, these fyue be simple, *a, e, i, o,* and *u,* & these four, *ay, ea, oy,* & *ou,* be Diphthonges." He explains that the diphthongs are always long, and the vowels short with some exceptions, which he notes. Typical entries are these:

A ante *T*	*Ea* ante *L*
A Date, *dactilus, i.*	An Eale, *anguilla, ae.*
A State, *status, us.* . . .	A Beale, den, *spelunca, ae.*
A Gate, *porta, ae, ianua, ae.*	A Deale, *portio, onis.*
A Grate, *crages, is, haec.*	Meale, *farina, nae.*
A Mate, *socius, sodalis, is.*	A Peale of gunnes, &c., *classicum, i.*
A Pate, *caput, itis, hoc.*	A Queale, *pupula, lae.*
	A Seale, fish, *phoca, ae.* . . .

The concise entries make difficult determination of sources. Wheatley does not discuss this topic, but his annotations of many words in his English index point to the English-Latin dictionaries—*Promptorium parvulorum* and Huloet's *Abcedarium* (1552)—as the texts which Levins most frequently consulted. Correspondences between Huloet and Levins may be seen in the entries which follow.

Huloet (1552)	Levins (1570)
Almerye, *Almariolum . . . Scrinium, ij.*	An Almerie, *scrinium, almariolum.* [col. 103, 26]
Almesse, *Agapu . . . Elemosina.*	Almose, *eleemosyna.* [col. 222, 3]
Ancker, *Anchora.*	An Anker, *anchora, rae.* [col. 70, 45]
Artochokes herbe. *Cynara.*	A Artochocke, *cynara, ae.* [col. 159, 5]
Bable, *pegma, tis.*	A Bable, *pegma, atis, hoc.* [col. 1, 34]
Ballocke of man or beast . . . *genitale, testiculus.*	A Ballocke, *testiculus, scortum.* [col. 158, 35]
Bansticle. *Trachida.* . . .	A Banstickle, *trachyda, ae.* [col. 122, 8]
Barnacle byrdes, *chelonalopices.*	A Barnacle, bird, *chelonalops, idis.* [col. 6, 1]
Barnacles or burnacles to putte on a horse nose to make hym to stande. *Pastomis.*	Barnacles, bonds, *pastomis, idis.* [col. 6, 2]

The parallel entries above, not noted by Wheatley, indicate a possible dependence of Levins on the *Abcedarium.* Further confirmation of this relationship is found in Wheatley's annotations of the following English words in Levins: *apostume, aule, balesse, blache, bodge, bottes, bounce, brache, brake, brocke, buffe, bum, bush, butte,* and *byrlet,* not to mention all.

Levins seems also to have been familiar with the Elyot-Cooper *Bib-*

liotheca Eliotae. Because this lexicon was a principal source of Huloet, the debt of Levins is not easy to assess. Here are, however, a few of the correspondences.

Elyot-Cooper	Levins
Hinnio, iui, ire, to neie lyke an horse.	To Nie as an horse, *hinnire.* [col. 102, 2]
Eupatorium . . . an herbe called Agrimonie, looke *Agrimonia.*	
Agrimonia . . . an herbe commonly called in englyshe Egrimoyn.	Egrymonye, *eupatorium.* [col. 102, 10]
Gastrimargia, gluttony, ingurgitacion.	Gluttony, *gastrimergia.* [col. 102, 13]
Baeticus, blacke or brown . . . tauny.	Taunye, *baeticus.* [col. 102, 41]
Dehonesto, aui, are, to dishonest.	To Dishonest, *dehonestare.* [col. 92, 24]
Astur . . . *Astur equus,* a Spanyshe horse, called a genet.	A Genet of Spayne, *astur equus.* [col. 86, 42]
Minutal . . . a meate made with herbes . . . a iussell.	Iussell, meate, *minutal.* [col. 57, 22]

In his search for rhyming words, Levins not infrequently consulted some edition of the *Promptorium parvulorum.* Among the words noted by Wheatley in his Index (pp. 245 ff.) are these: *basnet* ("light helmet"), *batte* ("to beat"), *bazelharde* ("a dagger"), *beald* ("build"), *big* ("build"), *blabbe, boose* ("cattle stall"), *booste* ("a box"), *brosten* ("burst"), *bruste* ("a bristle"), and *burgen* ("to burgeon").

Wheatley observes (Preface, *iv*) that the *"Manipulus* has a double interest, as at once an early collection of English words, and the first Rhyming Dictionary." Some of the unusual English words are noted above. Rhyming dictionaries after Levins—T. Willis's *Vestibulum linguae Latinae* (1651), J. Poole's *English Parnassus* (1657), E. Bysshe's *Art of English Poetry* (1702), and J. Walker's *Rhyming Dictionary* (1775)—are treated concisely by Wheatley in the Preface (pp. *viii–xv*) to his edition of the *Manipulus.*

2. SIMON PELEGROMIUS' *Synonymorum sylva* (1580)

The *Sylva,* a book of Latin synonyms, was originally published on the Continent, in Latin and Flemish. In 1580 the Flemish headings or topics were converted into English by a certain "H. F." (not identified), and thereafter the *Sylva* was of wide vogue and influence in England. As an adjunct to the dictionaries proper, this book requires notice.

Simon Pelegrom, or Pelegromius, was born at Bois-le-Duc about 1507 and lived until 1572. He was a Humanist who rose to be prior of the convent of Baeseldonck, in 1542, and provincial of the order in 1557. In 1537 he published, under the title *Synonymorum sylva,* a list of Latin synonyms with Flemish translations, a work which appeared in a new edition, *une refonte complete,* in 1546. The book went through many editions (*Biographie nationale . . . de Belgique* [Brussels, 1899], XV, 875).

By the patent of June 19, 1574, Thomas Vautrollier was given a ten-year privilege of printing the *Sylva* (*STC;* also Baldwin, *op. cit.,* I, 510; see also various other references to the *Sylva* by Baldwin). Wording of the title page of the English-Latin edition of the *Sylva* is as follows:

Synonymorum Sylva Olim a Simone Pelegromio collecta, & Alphabetico Flandrico ab eodem Authore illustrata: nunc autem e Belgarum sermone in Anglicanum transfusa, & in alphabeticum ordinem redacta per H. F. & ab eodem denuo multis locis emendata, & aucta . . . [1609].

The book is dedicated by "H. F." to Sir Francis Walsingham. A lengthy Ad Lectorem is supplied by Ioannis Serranus (1540–98). On the subject of synonyms as a means of varying expression, Serranus writes ten pages in Latin, reflecting in substance the discourse of Erasmus in *De copia.* The emphasis on copiousness may have enhanced the vogue of the *Sylva.*

Typical entries in the *Sylva* are these:

to Breake or Burst. *Frangere. Confringere. Infringere. Rumpere. Dirumpere. Crepare. Frigidus in Prato contundo rumpitur anguis. Limina perrumpit, posteque a cardine vellit.*

to Cut, to Rid, to Strike off. *Amputare. Abscindere . . . Truncare. Detruncare, Defalcare. Auellere caput humeris. Deturbare, scindere, auferre ense caput. Iugulum mucrone resoluere . . . Desecare. Praecidere. Resecare. Decurtare . . . Descerpere. Destringere.*

Entries vary greatly in length, some, such as *to deceiue, to beguile,* filling more than a column with Latin synonyms and synonymous phrases.

Numerous editions of the *Sylva* in England attest its popularity. The *STC* lists editions in 1580, 1585, 1603, 1609, 1612, 1615, 1619, 1622, and 1639. Kennedy (No. 2758) notes editions also of 1598, 1632, and 1650. Of the lexicographers, John Rider borrowed from the *Sylva* to supplement his *Bibliotheca scholastica,* and through Rider the impact of the *Sylva* continued in the Rider-Holyoke dictionaries in the seventeenth century.

3. HADRIAN JUNIUS' *Nomenclator or Remembrancer* (1585)

The *Nomenclator,* like the *Sylva,* was first published on the Continent, where it was in great esteem. After a period of twenty years, English equivalents were supplied by Higgins, and the Higgins-Junius text extended the influence of the *Nomenclator* in England.

Hadrian Junius (1511–75), whose original Dutch name was Adriaen de Jongh, was a Humanist physician and classical scholar. Born at Hoorn, he studied at the Latin school at Haarlem, and later at the University of Louvain. At Louvain he studied philosophy and medicine. At Bologna, Italy, in 1540, he got the degree of doctor of philosophy and doctor of medicine. From about 1543 to 1550, Junius was in England, first as family physician to the Duke of Norfolk, and afterward to a noble lady. In 1548 he dedicated his *Lexicon Graeco-Latinum* to Edward VI.

In 1555, Junius published at Augsburg his *Nomenclator omnium rerum propria nomina variis linguis explicata indicans*. This was a text in the tradition of Julius Pollux' *Onomasticon* and also of the less pretentious bilingual vocabularies from the Middle Ages. The *Nomenclator* went through many editions, being printed at Antwerp in 1557, 1567, 1576, and 1583; at Frankfurt in 1591, 1596, and 1611; at Paris in 1602; at Geneva in 1619; and at London (in English) in 1585. This list is not exhaustive (see T. DeVries' *Holland's Influence on English Literature* [Chicago, 1916], Chapter 22, "Hadrianus Junius"; also "Adrien Junius" in *Nouvelle Biographie*, ed. Michaud; *Catalogue Général . . . de la Bibliothèque* [Paris, 1924], V, 79; *British Museum Catalogue*). Of most interest to our study is the edition of the *Nomenclator* published in London, 1585.

The title page of the 1585 edition is phrased thus:

The Nomenclator, or Remembrancer of Adrianus Iunius Physician, diuided into two Tomes, conteining proper names and apt termes for all thinges vnder their conuenient Titles, which within a few leaues doe follow: Written by the said Ad. Iu. in Latine, Greeke, French and other fc.iein tongues: and now in English, by Iohn Higins: With a full supplie of all such words as the last inlarged edition affoorded; and a dictional Index, conteining aboue fourteene hundred principall words with their numbers directly leading to their interpretations: Of special vse for all scholars and learners of the same languages. . . . Imprinted at London for Ralph Newberie, and Henrie Denham. 1585.

This edition consists of two volumes in one, with consecutive pagination (I, 1–359; II, 360–539). The matter is printed in double columns. At the end is a helpful Latin Index by Abraham Fleming, referring to the page and column in which any Latin word may be found. The entries are in Latin, Greek, French, and English in the order named, though the French is often omitted. In the first volume are sixty-three different headings under which entries are grouped: "Of bookes, of writings . . ."; "Of Man and woman"; "Of the lims and members"; "Of liuing creatures fourefooted"; etc. The second volume, containing twenty-six topics, begins: "Of the elementes & their appurtenances"; "Of yeres, daies, times, seasons and festiuals"; "The names of earthes or grounds, waters, and places . . ."; "Of mettals and minerals."

A suggestive entry appears under *"Cerites tabulae . . . Tables of waxe, or the Censors tables, wherein their names were set downe, who had an ill name and report, and were thought unworthie of a voice."* Compare *Hamlet:* "My tables, my tables,—meet it is I set it down! That one may smile, and smile, and be a villain! (I, v, 107–108).

In supplying English equivalents in the *Nomenclator*, Higgins in many cases made his own translation of the Latin or French of Junius. In other instances, his English phrasing is determined by *Huloets Dictionarie* (which Higgins himself had revised in 1572), by Cooper's *Thesaurus*, and probably by others.

Of the impact of the *Nomenclator* on contemporary lexicographers, we have spoken. It may be recalled, however, that the influence of Junius on *Huloets Dictionarie* as revised by Higgins (1572) has been noted, and through the Huloet-Higgins this finds reflection in Baret's *Alvearie*. Both Thomas and Rider borrowed freely from the 1585 *Nomenclator*, and through these compilers the influence of Junius continues to the end of the seventeenth century.

4. *A Dictionarie English and Latine*

A Dictionarie English and Latine: Wherein the knots and difficulties of the Latine tongue are vntied and resolued, and the elegancies and proprieties thereof fully declared and confirmed by examples. A Worke new, and treading the steps of no former example: and yet very profitable for such as translate English into Latine, and generally for those that learn to write or speake properly and purely, according to the naturall idiome of the Latine tongue. London, Printed by Iohn Haviland, for Samuel Man, and are to be sold at his shop in Pauls Church-yard at the signe of the Swan. 1623.

So reads the title page of this anonymous seventeenth-century dictionary. On the following page is the heading "A Table Alphabeticall." Then follows an alphabetical list of contents, that is, of English phrases, such as *aboue, about, abroad,* and *according to,* which appear as headings in the text, though the Latin phrases on the page actually precede the English. Compare, for example, the following:

Alone

Solae sumus, Ter. Wee be lone women without husbands or defenders.
Solitarius homo, Cic. A lone or solitarie man.
Missa facio, Ter. I let all alone.
Aliquem missum facere, To let one alone.
Mitte me, Cord. Let me alone.
Omitte me posthoc, Cor. Let me alone.

In *A Dictionarie, before* has the general heading, followed by related topics: *before, little before, long before, ever and never before, streight before, before that,* and *before a ivdge.* Here is transcribed part of the matter under the heading:

Before

Ante, Coram, Palam, doe differ each from other: *Ante* is most generall, signifying not only Neere before, but also Farre off. *Coram* is limited to proximity, signifying Before in presence. Lastly, *Coram* respecteth certaine persons: *Palam* all univer- sally, though sometimes it happeneth otherwise, as *Palam me,* Before me: *Coram* is used also aduerbially; and *Ante,* which then may elegantly be interserted or interposed in the sentence, as *Paucis ante annis,* Cic. A few yeeres before.

Ante lucem, Cic. Before day. *Ex ante-lucano tempore,* Cic. Before day-breaking.

Ante oculos coram, Ter. In presence before my face.

A fronte & a tergo, Cic. Before and behind.

Incertior, multo quam dudum, Ter. I am more in doubt than I was before.

Si in ora parentum filios jugulat, Sen. Before the parents faces.

Subjicere aliquid oculis, Cu. To put before ones eies.

Ob oculum habebat, Plaut. He wore before his eye.

Ob, quandoque significat Ante, Desp. *vt.*

Foeda mors ob oculos erat, Liu. Death was before his eyes.

Ob oculos mihi saepe mors versata est, Cic. I had oftentimes death before my face. . . .

Palam populo, Liu. Before all the people. . . .

I prae, sequar, Ter. Goe before, I will follow.

Praeter suorum ora, Tac. Before the face of his men.

The examples above will give an idea of this anonymous *Dictionarie.* It is not, in fact, a dictionary proper but a sort of adjunct to dictionaries, a phrase book, doubtless prepared for schoolboys and based on the larger dictionaries, such as Thomas Thomas and Rider-Holyoke.

Appendix II

Excerpts from Plutarch's *Lives*
in the Elyot-Cooper Dictionaries

Pericles, a noble and valyaunte Capytayne of the Atheniensis, excellent in wytte and naturall eloquence, and was instructed in philosophy by Anaxagoras, so that therby he atteined to meruaylouse great knowlage, and noble courage and patience, in so much as whā a lewde person folowed hym to his house reuylynge hym by all the waie, whan he was come to his dore, than beinge nyghte, Pericles commaunded one of his seruauntes to take a torche and bring hym which had rebuked hym home to his house: Also he being in great estimation and auctoritee amonge the people of Athenes, wolde neuer be at any feastes or bankettynges, nor receyue of any man any presentes or gyftes, nor dyd go to euerye assembly or counsayle, or beinge there dydde speke or reason in euery matter, but reserued him self to thinges of very great importance, & yet than semed he to be very tymerouse, but yet was his eloquence so excellent, his voyce and pronounciation soo plesaunt, his sentences so ponderouse and vehement, that he neuer spake, but that therto all men consented, and therefore it is wrytten of him that he did fulminate his wordes, that is to saye, that they proceded from him as thūder and lightnynge. He was of suche temperaunce, that althoughe he semed to haue al the Athenyensis at his commaundement, yet he neuer increased his owne reuenewes the worthe of oone ferthynge, but augmented the commune tresure excedyngelye, and suche spoyle as came to his parte in the warres, he dydde employe vpon grayne and vittayle diuiding it among the people, in the tyme of necessitie, onely he was infortunate in his owne children, his eldest sonne Xantippus, persecuting hym with sundry displesures and openly mockyng him. Not withstandynge as it was reason, he dyed miserably before his father. Fynally Pericles beinge sycke vnto death, the noble men commen vnto him to comforte hym, spekynge softly, they communed of his prowesse, where he had victorie in nyne great battayles, he herynge what they spake, sayde vnto theym, that he muche maruayled that they extolled so muche that thynge, wherof the more part perteyned to fortune, and had hapned to dyuers other capitayns, as well as to hym, and that whyche was moste to be praysed, they spake

NOTE: Elyot's translation was made from a Latin edition of Plutarch.

360

nothyng of it, for neuer man (saied he) by mine occasion had cause to put mournyng garmentes vpon hym. Plutarchus in vitis. He was afore thincarnatiō of Christ 441. yeres.—*Bibliotheca Eliotae* (1545).

Photion, a noble Atheniense, which had ben disciple to Plato & Xenocrates, afterward one of the chief gouernors of the citie of Athenes was a man of suche wonderfulle grauitie and constāce, that he was not lyghtly sene to change his countenance, eyther to laugh or to mourne, nor to haue his handes out of his habyte, excepte in warre, and whan he was in the countrey, he went alwaie bare foted, except it were in the colde wynter, wherof there was no better token than to see Photion goo shodde. His speche was short, graue, vehement, and full of quycke sentences, and therefore the moste eloquente oratoure Demosthenes, callyd hym the hatchette that dyd cut of his wordes. He was of suche a constaunce, that where Apollo at Delphos made aunswere, that one man in Athenes was of a contrary opynion to all the citie. Whan that was reported, Photion rose vp and sayde, Leaue (sayde he) countrey men, to searche whome youre god meaneth, for I am that one manne, whome nothynge lyketh, whyche is nowe doone in the commune weale of this citie, whan he hadde made an oration vnto the people, and they praysynge hym consented vnto hym, he tourned hym to theim that were nexte hym, and sayde, Alas what haue I doone, I feare lest some foolysshe woorde hath escaped unwetynge me, sygnyfyenge that the people seldomme allowed any thynge that was good, or not foolysshe. On a tyme when he raisonned contrary to the mynde of the people, Wherfore they murmured and wolde haue let hym, It is at youre pleasure country menne, saied he, to compell me to do that that I would not, but to speake otherwyse than I thynke, that no man liuing can cause me: he was so reuerende a personage, that the great kinge Alexander in the begynninge of his letters after that he hadde vanquisshed Darius, he saluted no man but hym and Antipater. He refused infinite treasure sent vnto hym by Alexander, and although he hadde bene the generall capitayne of the Athenienses in sundrye warres, and honourably achieued his enterprises, yet was he best content to lyue poorely. Fynally he was of his vnkynde countrey menne condempned to deathe, whereto he went with the same countenaunce, that he hadde in authoritie, whan one whyche was condempned with hym, lamented and feared to dye, Phocion tournynge vnto hym sayde: Why arte thou not gladde, that thou shalt dye with Phocyon? And whan one of his frendes asked hym, yf he wolde any thynge to his sonne, I woulde saied he, that suche wronge as the Atheniensis dooe to me, he shall not remembre. What a wounderfulle woorde of a paynyme was this, who folowed Christis doctrine, ere Christe was borne .333. yeeres.—*Bibliotheca Eliotae* (1545).

Priamus, the sonne of Laomedon, and kyng of Troye, a notable paterne and example of fortunes frowarde vnconstancie and mutabilitie. Neuer lyued Prince more adourned with prosperitie: Neuer was there man more wounded with aduersitie. For, what benefite faire fleeing fortune in wealth could shew one, in his royall estate he enioyed it: what griefe and sorrowe hir frowning lookes could turn man to, in his wofull fall hee felte it. Before the siege of Troye he flourished a long tyme in great power, glory and riches, with many nations subiect to him, and hauing a great number of sonnes and daughters, in his life tyme risen to greate fame of prowesse, chiualrye, personage and beautie, himselfe a prince of great worthinesse, and indued with sundry noble qualities. In body strong, and (while youth flourished) of much actiuitie, when age grew on, reuerende and full of maiestie. In counsayle, wyse, in maners, sober and graue, as best might become his princely person. When fortune began to chaunge her copy, and the Grecians had beset his royall citie, hee lyued to see his power debated, his honour and glory decayed, his riches and treasure wasted, his realmes spoyled, his subiectes pitifully killed, all his children slayne and put to vilany before his face, his citie and palaice burned to ye ground and himselfe finally in his last dayes and reuerend olde age dispiteously drawen by the heare of the heade, and slayne by Pyrrhus, on the body of his young sonne Polytes, by the aulter whither he had fledde for succoure, and so ended his tragicall lyfe and wofull dayes.—Cooper, *Thesaurus* (1565).

Notes

Notes

CHAPTER I

1 The first modern edition of the *Promptorium* was edited by Albert Way and printed by the Camden Society: Part I (*A–L*), 1843; Part II (*M–R*), 1853; Part III (*S–Z*), 1865. Part III has a Preface (pp. *xiii–xlix*) treating the author of the *Promptorium*, the sources from which his Latinity was derived, and the manuscripts of the work; an Appendix (pp. *l–lxxxv*) containing notices of glossaries, vocabularies, and other works illustrative of the English language and of medieval Latinity; an Orthographic Index (pp. 541–50); and an index to the notes (pp. 551–59).

Another modern edition of the *Promptorium* is that by A. L. Mayhew (EETS, Extra Series 102, London, 1908), "edited from the manuscript in the Chapter Library at Winchester, with introduction, notes, and glossaries." Mayhew's Introduction is largely a summary of Way's Preface in the Camden Society edition. The notes by Mayhew (pp. 552–744) are extremely valuable to all students of the English language.

To these editions, with their introductions and commentaries, my account of the *Promptorium* is heavily indebted, as these notes will indicate.

2 Early printed editions of the *Promptorium* in the British Museum are those printed by Richard Pynson, 1499; Julian Notary, 1508; and Wynkyn de Worde, 1510, 1516, and 1528. A comparative study of these together with the later editions by Way and Mayhew, printed from manuscript, forms the basis for conclusions here drawn.

3 The Notary edition is described also by Way, *op. cit.*, Part III, *xlvi–xlvii*.

4 *Op. cit.*, Part III, *xliv*. Way describes a copy of only the 1516 edition, though he had examined others.

5 C. 40. d. 59, G. 7497, and G. 7496 in the British Museum.

6 *Promptuarium*, employed by Wynkyn de Worde in the title, seems to have been synonymous with *promptorium*, both meaning "storeroom" or "repository." See Mayhew's edition, p. *xiii*.

7 Part III, Preface, *xxxvi–xli*.

8 Mayhew, *op. cit.*, *viii–ix*. See Way, *op. cit.*, Part III, *xxxix–lx*, for a description of the Winchester manuscript.

9 Mayhew, *op. cit.*, *xvi–xvii*, cols. 1, 3; Way, *op. cit.*, Part I, 1–4.

10 Way places on the title page of his edition "Circa A.D. M.CCCC.XL," and avers that we "ascertain with certainty" from the author's own statement in the Preambulum that the date was 1440. Mayhew (p. *xiii*) repeats the statement without demur.

11 Quoted from the Preambulum of Mayhew's edition (cols. 1–3), based on the Winchester manuscript. For similar information see Way's edition (Part I, 2–3), based on Harleian MS 221.

12 Peter Langtoft's *Chronicle*, ed. Thomas Hearne, II, 624. Quoted from Way's Preface, *op. cit.*, Part III, *xvi.*

13 *Op. cit.*, Part III, *xvi–xix*. Mayhew (*op. cit.*, *xiii–xvii*) summarizes Way's account, omitting, however, the reference to Richard Frauncis.

14 Summarized by Way, *ibid.*

15 *Ibid.*, *xix*; Mayhew, *op. cit.*, *xvi.*

16 H. B. Wheatley, in his Preface to Sidney J. H. Herrtage's edition of *Catholicon Anglicum*, EETS, Original Series 75 (London, 1881), *ix.* My own estimate is approximately the same.

17 Wright's *Vocabularies* was privately printed (London, 1857); Wülcker's revision appeared in two volumes (London, 1884). For a discussion of some of these vocabularies, see DeWitt T. Starnes and Gertrude E. Noyes, *The English Dictionary from Cawdrey to Johnson, 1604–1755* (Chapel Hill, University of North Carolina Press, 1946), 197–211.

18 Way, *op. cit.*, Part III, *xxiii–xxxvi*; Mayhew, *op. cit.*, *xvii–xxvi.*

19 Way, *op. cit.*, Part III, *xxiii*; Mayhew, *op. cit.*, *xvii*; Charles du Fresne, Sieur du Cange, *Glossarium mediae et infimae Latinitatis* (10 vols., Niort, 1883–87), Praefatio, *xxxiv* ff.; E. E. Brandon, *Robert Estienne et le dictionnaire français aux XVIᵉ siècle* (Baltimore, 1904), 27–28; Robert Stephanus, *Thesaurus linguae Latinae* (4 vols., London, 1734–35), Praefatio.

20 Glossarium, *xxxiv.*

21 J. C. Brunet, *Manuel du libraire* (5 vols., Brussels, 1838–45), II, 527–28; *Nouvelle biographie*, ed. Michaud (Paris, n.d.), *s.v. Balbe*. The full title of the Mayence edition, published in 1460 by Ioannem Faustum, is *Summa grammaticalis valde notabilis, quae Catholicon nominatur*. Other editions were printed at Augsburg (1469); at Nuremberg (1483, 1486), by Koburger; and at Strasbourg (1483). The *Catholicon* was often printed at Venice, Lyons, Rouen, Paris, and Vienna. There were many printings, also of *Vocabularius breviloquus* (1476), an abridgment.

22 In Rare Books Collection, University of Texas.

23 Brandon, *op. cit.*, 27–28.

24 Way, *op. cit.*, Part III, *xxiii–xxiv*; Mayhew, *op. cit.*, *xviii–xix*; Du Cange, *op. cit.*, I, *xxxiv*; Stephanus, *op. cit.*, Praefatio.

25 Du Cange, *op. cit.*, I, *xxxiv*; quoted by Way, *op. cit.*, Part III, *xxiii–xxiv.*

26 Way lists some of the manuscripts (*op. cit.*, Part III, *xxiv*, n. *a*).

27 Mayhew, *op. cit.*, *xix*; Paget Toynbee, "Dante's Latin Dictionary," in *Dante Studies and Researches* (London, 1902), 97–114.

28 "John Garland" in *DNB*; Wright, *op. cit.*, 120; Du Cange, *op. cit.*, I, *xxxiv.*

29 See the discussion of Stanbridge, in Chapter 5. Similar lists are in Holyband's *The French Littleton* (1566) and *The French Schoolmaster* (1575) and Florio's *First Fruites* (1578).

30 Printed by Wright, *op. cit.*, 120 ff.

31 *Ibid.*, 123.

32 The *STC* lists editions of *Equivoca* as follows: 1496, 1503, 1508, 1514 by Pynson; 1499, 1502, 1505, 1514, 1517 by Wynkyn de Worde. Editions of the *Synonyma*: 1496, 1500, 1502, 1509 by Pynson; 1500, 1502, 1505, 1514, 1517, 1518 by Wynkyn de Worde.

33 Brief accounts of these three and other authorities listed in the Preambulum or cited in the text proper are found in the preliminary matter to Way's edition of the *Promptorium* and to Mayhew's.

34 Way, *op. cit.*, Part III, *xxxiv.*

CHAPTER II

1 *Ibid.*, Part I, *x.*

2 For an account of the Monson manuscript and Addit. MS 15562, see *ibid.*, Part III, *lxiv–lxv*, and Herrtage's edition of the *Catholicon Anglicum*, xiv ff.

3 Herrtage, *op. cit.*, *xiii.*

4 *Ibid.*, *xv.*

5 *Ibid.*, *xvii.*

6 *Ibid.*, *xvi*; Way, *op. cit.*, Part III, *lxiv.* "Hugutio," "Uguitio," and "Ugucio" are variant spellings in these texts for Hugo of Pisa.

7 See n. 32, Chapter 1.

8 Examples from Pynson's 1509 edition of the *Synonyma* and Herrtage's edition of the *Catholicon.*

9 Compare the following pairs of words in the respective texts: *a dike, fossa; to dowte, dubito; a felde, campus; a felay* [*fellow*], *comes; swerde, gladius; water, aqua; wrath, ira.*

10 See the discussions of Higgins's revision of *Huloet's Dictionarie* and Rider's *Bibliotheca scholastica* in Chapters 12 and 15.

CHAPTER III

1 Written also as *Medulla grammaticae* and *Medulla grammatices*, "The Marrow of Grammar," obviously including a knowledge of Latin words as well as grammatical information.

2 See Way's edition of the *Promptorium*, Part I, *ix–x.* Both Way and Mayhew drew words from the *Medulla* to illustrate terms in the *Promptorium*, as did Herrtage in annotating his edition of the *Catholicon Anglicum.*

3 "The Sources of the Stonyhurst Medulla" (doctoral dissertation, University of Michigan, 1943).

CHAPTER IV

1 Modern editors generally write [*H*]*ortus*, supplying the *H* and thus modernizing the Latin. In nearly all printed editions of the *Promptorium* and in the *Catholicon Anglicum* edited by Herrtage, *ortus* is the word used to mean "garden." Hence my use of *Ortus vocabulorum* as the title. For Way's account of the *Ortus*, together with his list of printed editions, see his edition of the *Promptorium*, Part III, *liv–lxiv.* See also *STC*, *s.v.* [*H*]*ortus vocabulorum.*

2 Mayhew (*op. cit.*, *xv–xvi*) quotes Bale.

3 Way, *op. cit.*, Part III, *lxiii.*

4 *Op. cit.*, 13–14.

5 For the quotation, see page 5 above.
6 Way, *op. cit.*, Part III, *liv–lxix.* Cf. also No. 2733 in A. G. Kennedy, *A Bibliography of Writings on the English Language from the Beginning of Printing to the End of 1922.* The *STC* lists editions by Wynkyn de Worde as follows: 1500 (folio), 1511, 1514, 1516, 1518, 1528, 1532; by Pynson: 1509; by Olivier: (Rouen) 1520.
7 Quoted by Way, *op. cit.*, Part III, *lxiii.*
8 *Ibid., lvii.*
9 I have written out the abbreviations in this as in other quoted passages from the texts.
10 I have not examined Pynson's 1509 edition of the *Ortus.* The paraphrase is based on Way's transcript (*op. cit.*, Part III, *lvii*) of the title page.
11 *Ibid., liv–lv.*
12 Entries from the *Medulla* are transcribed from Harl. MS 2257, in the British Museum. All abbreviations are written out.
13 Copies of the *Breviloquus* in the British Museum are dated 1478, 1482, 1487, 1488, 1489, and 1495.
14 Copies of the *Gemma* in the British Museum are dated 1504, 1505, 1507, 1508, 1512, 1514, and 1518. A copy of a 1514 edition is in the Rare Books Collection of the University of Texas. See also Du Cange, *op. cit.*, I, 851; Way, *op. cit.*, Part III, *lxii.*
15 Copies of *Vocabularius Latino-Teutonicus* in the British Museum are dated: Spire, 1479; Eichstadt, 1480? ; Nuremberg, 1480 (2 editions) ; Ulm, 1480.
16 This book, often referred to with the abbreviated title *Equivoca,* has these words on the title page of a 1494 edition: "Multorum Vocabulorum equivocorum interpretatio grammatico et volente latine loqui maxime necessaria."
17 See n. 32, Chapter I.

CHAPTER V

1 See *The Vulgaria of John Stanbridge and the Vulgaria of Robert Whittinton,* edited by Beatrice White for EETS, Original Series 187 (1932). I am indebted to the informative Introduction of this volume for the biographical details concerning Stanbridge.
2 All printed in Wright's *Volume of Vocabularies.*
3 See *ibid.,* 206 ff., for a fifteenth-century *nominale.*

CHAPTER VI

1 See E. Greswell's *A View of the Early Parisian Greek Press* (2 vols., Oxford, 1833) for an account of the Stephanus (Estienne) family. See also *Nouvelle biographie générale,* ed. Didot (Paris, 1856).
2 For a full account of Elyot's life and work, see H. H. S. Croft's edition of *The Gouernour* (London, 1883), I, Introduction.
3 *Ibid.,* II, Glossary; E. E. Hale, "Ideas on Rhetoric in the Sixteenth Century," *PMLA,* XVIII (1903), 424 ff.; Samuel Jesse McCoy, *The Language and Linguistic Interests of Sir Thomas Elyot* (doctoral dissertation, University of North Carolina, 1933); J. L. Moore, *Tudor-Stuart Views on the Growth, Status, and*

Destiny of the English Language, "Studien zur Englischen Philologie," XLI (Halle, S. M. Niemeyer, 1910).

4 See the Preface to his *Dictionary* (1538) for his discussion of the then available lexicons.

5 Croft (*op. cit.,* I, *cxxxiii*) quotes Vives' *De tradendis disciplina* as follows: "Ex quibus universis confletur dictionarium T.... ..ae linguae, quod nullum est plenum satis et justum. . . . Expediet in quaque etiam vulgari lingua geminum pueris tradi unum quo Latina verba reddantur vulgaribus, alterum quo vice versa vulgaria Latinis: quod in nostro sermone Antonius Nebrissensis fecit, opus non satis exactum, tyronibus magis cum provectioribus utile."—*Opera,* I (1555), 475.

6 The volume in the British Museum is a presentation copy to Thomas Cromwell with an autographed Latin letter addressed to him, on the flyleaf. Croft (*op. cit.*) prints this letter in full.

7 In the editions of 1542 and 1545 all the quoted definitions are retained, but slightly rearranged to make an alphabetical order; and three new entries are inserted: *idipsum, idomeneus,* and *idume.* In the 1548 and subsequent editions, four additional entries appear: *idonie, idonea, idotaea,* and *idyia. Idem* is expanded by supplying ten illustrative Latin phrases with their English equivalents; and *idoneus,* with two illustrations.

8 Cf. the Preface of Calepine's *Dictionarium* (1510): "Hoc unum affirmare ausim, nostrum hoc opus et vocabulorum multitudine, et propositionum interpretamento, et auctorum citatione ordineque, Dictionaria cuncta superare."

Cf. also Du Cange, *op. cit.,* I, 37 ff., where the same statement is quoted from the 1502 edition of Calepine. The curious claim of superiority on the basis of the number of terms defined in their dictionaries has persisted among lexicographers (or publishers) to the present day.

9 *The Governour,* "Everyman's Library," 42 ff.

10 Sextus Pompeius Festus (date uncertain) was the author of *De verborum significatione,* only a portion of which has come down to modern times. His work was printed at Milan in 1471, at Cologne in 1473, and in other editions.

M. Terentius Varro (116–27 B.C.). His treatise *De lingua Latina* was printed at Rome by Pomponius Laetus in 1471.

Nonius Marcellus. The first edition of his *De proprietate sermonisi* was printed at Rome in 1476.

Dionysius Nestor, of Novara, in Italy, compiled *Onomasticon,* a Latin dictionary, which was published at Milan in 1483.

Joannes Tortellius Aretinus, author of *Commentariorum grammaticorum libri duo* (Rome, 1471).

Laurentius Valla (1406–57). His *De elegantia Latinae linguae* was published simultaneously at Rome, Venice, and Paris in 1471.

Nicolas Perottus, or Perotti, bishop of Siponto (d. 1480). His *Cornucopiae sive linguae Latinae commentarii* was first published in 1489.

Ambrosius Calepinus was born at Bergamo in 1435 and died in 1511. His *Dictionarium* was first published at Reggio, in 1502.

Elio Antonio de Lebrixa, who turned his name into Aelius Antonius Nebrissensis in Latin, was born in 1444 at Lebrixa, Spain. He was a lecturer at the Universities of Seville and Salamanca. He published in 1506 his *Vocabularius* (*Dictionarium ex sermone Latino in hispaniensem, et dictionarium ex hispaniense in Lat. sermonem*), the work to which Elyot refers.

11 DeWitt T. Starnes, "Sir Thomas Elyot and the Sayings of the Philosophers," University of Texas *Studies in English*, Vol. XIII (1933), 11–12. Many of the biographical sketches and proverbs persist in the revisions of the dictionary and are taken over by Thomas Cooper in his *Thesaurus*.

12 *Op. cit.*, I, 410–11. Cf. also Didot's *Nouvelle biographie générale*.

13 See n. 10 above, on Festus, Varro, Perottus, Valla, and Tortellius.

Aelius Donatus was a celebrated grammarian of the fourth century, and the preceptor of St. Jerome. His most popular work was the *De octo partibus orationis*, a Latin grammar in great vogue during the Renaissance.

Servius Honoratus was the author of *Libellus de ultimis syllabis, et centrimentum* (Bergamo, 1476) and *Commentarii in bucolica, georgica et Aeneidem Virgilii* (Venice, 1471).

14 Pronunciation is indicated, at the author's discretion, by the abbreviation *pen. cor.* (*penultima correpta*), meaning that the penult is short and that the accent is therefore on the antepenult; or by *pen. prod.* (*penultima prodita*), showing that the penult is long and so receives the accent.

15 For convenience of comparison, the order of the entries in the Calepine has been slightly changed to correspond to the order in Elyot. Abbreviations in the Calepine have been written out.

16 It can hardly be said that Elyot ever followed scrupulously any order of arrangement. In 1538 he did approximate the etymological order of Calepine. In subsequent editions of his *Dictionary*, he approximated the alphabetical order.

17 Elyot gives for the Latin verbs the first person of the present indicative, active; the first person of the perfect indicative; and the present infinitive.

18 A copy of the edition I have used for this part of my study is in the British Museum. It is undated (the title page is missing), but given in the British Museum *Catalogue* is the conjectural date of 1542. Comparison with the dated volumes, 1538 and 1545, shows that the undated volume falls between these two. This is probably a copy of the 1542 edition referred to by Ames.

In their *Catalogue* for December, 1948, John Grant, Booksellers, Ltd., 31 George IV Street Bridge, Edinburgh, offered for sale a copy of *"Bibliotheca Eliotae: Eliotis Librarie*. Londini anno verbi incarnati. 1542." As this date is on the title page, this appears to be an authentic copy of the rare 1542 edition.

19 In the list of authors are 119 names, representing almost every branch of knowledge—history, geography, philosophy, theology, poetry, law, medicine, architecture, and lexicography. Although the majority of writers are of ancient Greece and Rome, there are included names of the Church Fathers and of contemporary scholars of Italy and France.

20 Suidas (fl. late tenth century). Suidas' *Lexicon*, Greek, was printed at Milan (1498), Venice (Aldine, 1514), and Basel (Froben, 1544). It is not only a dictionary of words but also a geographical and biographical work. A modern reprint is the folio by Ludolph Kuster (3 vols., Cambridge, 1705).

21 Elyot is mistaken here. The *Vocabula* of John Stanbridge, in Latin and English, still current in the thirties, contained classified lists of maladies, of beasts and birds and fishes, and of herbs, trees, and fruits. See Chapter 5. Elyot's statement ignores also similar lists in the vocabularies and glosses of the fifteenth century, in the *Dictionarius* of John of Garland and the *De nominibus* of Alexander Neckam. Cf. Wright, *op. cit.*

22 See n. 20 above and Elyot's use of Suidas, *s.v. abyrtace, Agapius, Amelius, Amilcar, Amphictiones, amphitetum, anagyris, analphabeti, Babylus, Bacelus,*

Basilius, Burdegala or *Burdigala, Didymus, Dionysius, Dithyrambus,* and *dipsas.*

23 See n. 11 above. Laertius and Erasmus are among the authorities listed in the Proheme of the 1542 and 1545 editions of the *Bibliotheca.*

24 For a thorough general study of Budaeus, see Louis Delaruelle's *Études sur l'humanisme français: Guillaume Budé, les origines, les débuts, les idées maîtresses* (Paris, 1907). Chapter 3 is devoted to the *Annotationes.*

   See also Jean Plattard's *Guillaume Budé (1468–1540) et les origines de l'humanisme français* (Paris, 1923).

   For Budaeus' influence on Greek-Latin lexicography, see F. L. Schoell's *Études sur l'humanisme continental, en Angleterre à la fin de la Renaissance,* in "Bibliothèque de la Revue de Littérature Comparée," XXIX (Paris, 1926), 143 ff.

25 *Op. cit.,* 18.

26 *Op. cit.,* 113.

27 See Richard Copley Christie's *Estienne Dolet, the Martyr of the Renaissance, 1508–1546: A Biography* (London and New York, 1899).

28 *Ibid.,* 204.

29 Published in two volumes, 1536–38. See *ibid.,* 242 ff.; Brunet, *op. cit.,* II, 88–89.

30 Quoted from Christie, *op. cit.,* 245.

31 For Doletus' own explanation of his system, read these lines from the Introduction to his *Commentaries:*

   "That the method of these my *Commentaries* may be more clearly seen and more easily understood, I wish to explain the arrangement I make use of. In the first place I give the meaning of each word, both its primary and its secondary or tralatitious meaning. Then I distinguish the different uses of the words. Lastly I adduce examples, but of each kind separately, so that instances are given of the words used in their original signification, and again in their secondary. But in setting forth the different uses of a word, I have so separated the examples, that immediately after showing as accurately as possible the primary signification of a word and the tralatitious one (if it has a tralatitious meaning), I adduce simple examples of the different uses. I call them simple because they are set forth with no special grace or elegance of construction of the word. When I have shown both in my own language and by examples drawn from Cicero, the primary and secondary meanings of the word in question, I then subjoin other words of a cognate meaning, and so continue in a connected series. When I have exhausted a series of congruent words I naturally proceed to their contraries, and with them I use as far as possible the same plan. . . . For example, after the words *conciliare, conjungere,* on the next page are opposed the words *alienare, abalienare.* So to *consentire, convenire, congruere, concordare, coire, conspirare, conjurare,* succeed *dissentire, dissidere, discordare, discrepare,* like opposing standards brought together for hostile encounter. But I must pursue my course in my own stupid way. I directly join opposites to opposites, so only that the series of words is not interrupted, and thus when the forms of similar and dissimilar words are extended somewhat more at length, my system becomes plain."—Christie, *op. cit.,* 245–46.

32 We use in this study the Latinized "Stephanus" instead of "Estienne," since the Latin form was employed on the title pages of the lexicons we refer to. The vogue and influence of Robert Stephanus' lexicographical works, and to a less extent that of his brother Charles, will appear in the course of this study. See also E. Greswell, *op. cit.*

For the influence of Henri Stephanus' Greek-Latin *Thesaurus* in England, see Schoell, *op. cit.*, 147 ff. The Greek-Latin *Lexicon* of John Scapula, an unauthorized abridgment of Henri's *Thesaurus*, went through nineteen editions between 1580 and 1687. See also Brunet, *op. cit.*, IV, 258 ff.

33 In the Preface to the *Thesaurus* (1531), Stephanus writes: "Ex ipso autem Budaeo, quem nostra aetate praecipuum omnis eruditionis lumen optimus quisque indicat, tam multa ad verbum transcripsimus, ut paene omnia et rara et exquisita illi in hoc opere debeantur." In the text proper, also, Stephanus frequently refers to Budaeus as authority. Cf. Delaruelle, *op. cit.*, 113, n. 2.

For examples of Stephanus' debt to Calepine, compare the various entries under *confero* and *conficio* in the *Thesaurus* and the *Dictionarium Latino-Gallicum* with the corresponding entries in Calepine.

34 The title page runs thus: "Dictionarium Latino-Gallicum, Thesauro Nostro Ita ex Adverso Respondens, vt extra pauca quaedam aut obsoleta, aut minus in vsa necessaria vocabula, & quas consulto praetermisimus, authorum appellationes, in hoc eadem sint omnia, eodem ordine, sermone patrio explicata . . . Parisiis. Ex Officina Roberti Stephani. M.D.XXXVIII."

35 Compare the entries below.

Calepine's *Dictionarium* (1520)	Stephanus' *Dictionarium Latino-Gallicum* (1538)
Conferre in pauca est concludere. . . .	*In pauca conferre, Conclure,* Faire fin.
Quandoque pro disputo seu in comparationem deduco. . . . Et dicimus confero te illi & cum illo.	*Conferre, Comparare. Dicimus autem, Confero te isti & cum isto,* comparer.
Conficio . . . finio: perficio.	*Conficio . . . idem significat,* Acheuer & parfaire.
Item colligere. Permagnam . . . dices ex illa re pecuniam confici posse.	*Pecuniam ex re aliqua conficere,* Faire argent & amasser.

36 I follow the order of entries in the *Bibliotheca*, making some rearrangement of the order in Stephanus. Elyot selects his illustrations, not attempting to use all from Stephanus or to follow the order of entry. Elyot does, however, adopt Stephanus' plan of giving each example a new line. Elyot may be utilizing also a suggestion from Doletus in beginning each illustration with the infinitive form of the verb.

37 Diogenes Laertius relates that Anaxarchus bit out his tongue and spit it in the face of Nicocreon, the tyrant. This story is repeated by Calepine (1502) and by Adam Littleton in his *Dictionary* (1678). Cf. Elyot's *Governour* (ed. Croft, II, 315–16) for the story of the young Christian gentleman who bites off his tongue rather than yield to the seductions of the woman with whom Valerian tempts him. Bolingbroke's speech in *Richard II* runs thus:

> ". . . Ere my tongue
> Shall wound my honour with such feeble wrong,
> Or sound so base a parle, my teeth shall tear
> The slavish motive of recanting fear,
> And spit it bleeding in his high disgrace
> . . . even in Mowbray's face." (I, i, 190–95)

38 The edition of 1538 has "———— Goodman." In a 1545 copy someone has inserted in longhand "Rowland."

39 This is hardly the place for a complete list of the proverbs in the *Bibliotheca*, but a few others may be indicated: *s.v. aedilitas; s.v. Aegeum, Aegeum nauigat; s.v. aequalis, aequalis calculi; s.v. Aethiopia, Aethiopem lauas; s.v. Anticyra, nauiga ad Anticyras; s.v. aurus, aurum Tolosanum habere; s.v. Cadmus, Cadmaea victoria; s.v. caesus, inter caesa & porrecta; s.v. calcar, calcar addere, calculo mordere, calculum album addere; s.v. camarina, camarinam mouere; s.v. canis, canina facundia, canis festinans caecas aedit catulos, canis reuersus ad uomitum;* and *s.v. carceres, a carceribus ad calcem.* In the *Bibliotheca* of 1559, I have counted 275 proverbs.

40 Two minor sources of Elyot's *Dictionary*, not discussed in the foregoing pages, are F. M. Grapaldus' *Lexicon de partibus aedium* (editions 1494 to 1535) and Robert Stephanus' *Hebraea, Chaldaea, Graeca et Latina nomina* (Paris, 1537). Although Elyot derived through Calepine much matter from the *Lexicon*, he also consulted Grapaldus directly, as these entries show: *anguilla, cribrum, mullus,* and *rana.* Echoes of the *Hebraea* appear under *Abdias, Abel, Abraham, Adam, Adrumetum, Amos, Ascalon, Astaroth, Baal, Babel, Caesarea, Carmelus, Cedar,* and *Edom.*

CHAPTER VII

1 See *DNB* and Anthony à Wood, *Athenae Oxonienses,* ed. Philip Bliss (3rd ed., London, 1813), I, 610 ff.

2 The heading is "Tho. Cooperus Candido Lectori Salutem." This address first appeared in the preliminary matter of the 1548 edition and was reprinted, without alteration, in the issues of 1552 and 1559. The gist of it is given near the end of this chapter.

3 The colophon reads: "Thus Endeth This Dictionarie, printed at London in the house of Thomas Berthelet, Anno Domini. M.D.XLVIII. The viii daie of August. Cum priuilegio."

4 *Shakespeare's Books* (Berlin, 1904), 15–16, 16 n.

5 The Latin sentence in the *Bibliotheca* (1548) is as follows: "Udallo viro doctissimo, cuius eruditissimo annotationibus multis locis leuati sumus, dignas laudes gratiasque tribue."

6 Cooper's *Thesaurus* (1565, 1573, 1584) gives this interpretation of the phrase: "Raunsome or delyuer thyselfe being taken in loue snares as good cheape as thou canst." This is nearer to the context in *The Taming of the Shrew.* Tranio says to Lucio, who has fallen desperately in love with Bianca,

> If love has touch'd you, nought remains but so
> "Redime te captum quam queas minimo."

7 In the address to the reader Cooper's words are these: "Praeterea, propria nomina deorum, virorum, regionum, fluminum, oppidorum, que prius magna ex parte neglecta erant, . . . ad poetarum lectionem maxima necessaria, tum ex Stephano, tum ex aliis, qui de eis scripserunt, in hanc editionem transtulimus."

8 DeWitt T. Starnes, "The Poetic Dictionary and the Poet," *The Library Chronicle of the University of Texas,* Vol. II, No. 2 (Summer, 1946), 75–85.

9 See *DNB.*

10 Although Turner's book on birds was published at Cologne in 1544, Cooper apparently did not make use of it in the revision of the *Bibliotheca* in 1548. He simply continued the entries on birds which he found in the 1545 edition by

Elyot. In 1552, however, many of Elyot's entries are revised and new entries are added.

11 I have used the text entitled *Turner on Birds*, edited, with Introduction, translation, Notes, and Appendix by A. H. Evans (Cambridge, 1903). The text gives the Latin with English translation on the opposite page. All page references are to this text.

12 Marius Nizolius, *Observationes in M. Tullium Ciceronem* (Pratalboino, 1535). Also *Thesaurus Ciceronianus* (Basel, 1548; Venice, Aldus Manutius, 1570, folio). Other editions, with augmentations by Aldus Manutius, 1576 and 1591. Cf. Brunet, *op. cit.*, III, 347–48.

13 This idea Cooper continues to emphasize in his *Thesaurus* (1565 and later editions). In doing so he has, perhaps unconsciously, pointed out to posterity the real value of his lexicographic work: it is a great monument of the English language in the Tudor period.

14 It is difficult to determine to what extent Cooper actually consulted craftsmen, farmers, etc. Some of his definitions seem to support his claim. See, for example, *ager, architectus, arena, coquo, culter, fabrica, faber, ferrarius, olitor, texo,* and *textor*.

The method suggested is extremely interesting, anticipating as it does Edward Phillips with his array of specialists from whom he allegedly got aid in compiling his *New World of Words* (1658), and later lexicographers.

Cooper's language, in the address, runs thus:

"His ergo qui lexicon ex omni parte perfectum, et in quo nihil desyderetur, sibi conficiendum proponunt: omnes simul artifices in consilium adhibere oportet, ut ab illis rerum nomina discant, quibus singuli artificia sua tuentur. Quemadmodum et nos frequenter ad materiaros fabros, ad olitores, ad textores, ad agricolas, ad rusticam turbam de nomenclaturis retulimus, et ab illis sumpsimus etiam, quae propositae rei congruerent. . . ."

15 In his *Thesaurus* (1565) Cooper uses the modified etymological order, presumably following Robert Stephanus.

16 Cooper does not cite his authorities in the text of the *Bibliotheca*, though he mentions Cicero, Terence, and others in his address to the reader.

CHAPTER VIII

1 See Cooper's address to the reader, opposite the first page of the brief proper-name section, in the *Bibliotheca* (1559).

2 Anthony à Wood (*op. cit.*, I, 610) quotes one of the scurrilous poems of twelve quatrains on the reputed intrigues of Mrs. Cooper and Thomas Day.

3 *The Martin Marprelate Tracts* (*1588, 1589*), ed. William Pierce (London, 1911); see especially "Hay Any More Worke for the Cooper," p. 234, and Pierce's n. 3, pp. 234–35.

4 The story of the burning of the manuscript is told by Aubrey, as follows: "Dr. Edw. Davenant told me that the learned man had a shrew to his wife, who was irreconcileably angrie with him for sitting-up late at night compileing his Dictionarie. When he had halfe-donne it, she had the opportunitie to gett into his studie, tooke all his paines out in her lap, and threw it into the fire, and burnt it. Well, for all that, the good man had so great a zeale for the advancement of learning, that he began it again, and went through with it to that Perfection that he

hath left it to us a most useful Worke."—*Aubrey's Brief Lives,* ed. Oliver Lawson Dick (London, 1949), 71.

5 Wood (*op. cit.*, I, 609) writes: "[Cooper] was indeed a reverend man, very well learned, and exceeding industrious, as it appears by that great Dictionary, which yet [*ca.* 1690] bears his name, and was the cause of his preferment."

6 Pierce, *op. cit.*, 90.

7 Quoted by J. E. B. Mayor in his "Latin-English and English-Latin Lexicography," *Journal of Classical and Sacred Philology,* Vol. IV (March, 1857), 16–17. Mayor has some interesting observations on Cooper's *Thesaurus,* and I am indebted to him, as I shall point out from time to time, for suggestions in this part of my study. In treating the Elyot-Cooper dictionaries, Mayor was, however, at a disadvantage in not having seen several of the texts. He had seen no copies of Elyot's *Dictionary* of 1538, 1542, or 1545; and had perused a copy of the 1548 edition only after his article was finished.

8 See the Preface to the Rider-Holyoke dictionary, published in 1633.

9 Quoted by Mayor, "Latin-English and English-Latin Lexicography," *Journal of Classical and Sacred Philology,* Vol. IV (March, 1857), 40–41. Cf. also Kennett's "Life of Somner," prefacing Somner's *Treatise of the Roman Ports and Forts in Kent* (Oxford, 1693), 75, 76, 79, 90.

The *Dictionarium* here ascribed to Charles Stephanus was, in fact, the Latin-French dictionary of his brother Robert Stephanus, published for the third time in 1552, not 1553.

10 This generous tribute to Elyot did not appear in the earlier editions (1565, 1573, 1584) of the *Thesaurus.* Cooper may have used this statement as a means of counteracting rumors already current of his appropriating Elyot's *Bibliotheca.*

11 For the bibliography of these dictionaries, see E. E. Brandon's "Bibliographie de l'oeuvre lexicographique de Robert Estienne," in *Robert Estienne et le dictionnaire français* (Baltimore, 1904), 116–23.

12 *Dictionarium Latino-Germanicum,* the title page of which reads in part, "Joanne Frisio Tigurino interprete . . . 1556," is the text used in this study. In his address to youth, Frisius pays tribute to the labors of Robert Stephanus in the *Thesaurus* and the *Dictionarium Latino-Gallicum,* adding that he could have done little without these works of Stephanus, Frisius' chief work being to put the definitions into German. "Omnino nihil, nisi solum . . . Germanicam versionem, veram tamen illam, & adscribimus, atque attribuimus."

13 Note that, of the Latin phrases in Stephanus' *Thesaurus,* the Latin-French dictionary omits that beginning *vulgatos taceo,* the *aes conferre,* the first *amorem conferre,* part of the *ne id quod,* and the *haec ubi;* it omits, also, the specific references to books cited in the *Thesaurus.* The *Dictionarium,* but not the *Thesaurus,* gives definitions and translates illustrations into the vernacular. The Frisius and the Cooper have in common with Stephanus' *Dictionarium* the identical omissions of phrases, the abbreviated citations of authorities, and definitions and illustrations in the vernacular.

14 Compare, for example, the vernacular interpretations, in the French and the English, respectively, of *conficere hominem, ignes conficiunt, diem extremum, exercitum, famam, flagitium,* and *funera iusta (s.v. conficio).*

15 Cf. *Bibliotheca Eliotae* (1545): "*Conferre in pauca.* To conclude shortely."

Did Cooper, in the *Thesaurus,* alter his definition to conform to what he found in Frisius?

16 Elyot's *Dictionary* (1538): "To breake a nutte with his teeth."

17 Although the Latin phrases are the same in the three texts, Frisius and Cooper write "Ovid," Stephanus, "Ovidius." Did Frisius abbreviate Stephanus' citation, and Cooper follow Frisius, or are the abbreviations independent?

18 The French phrase in Stephanus' *Dictionarium* is the same (as above) in all editions of the Latin-French text; the *Bibliotheca* (1548) translates the French as "to walke." The *Thesaurus* here seems to follow Frisius.

19 Both Frisius and Cooper omit "Bud." (Budaeus).

20 Cf. *Bibliotheca* (1545): *"Animum alio conferre,* to sette hys mynde els where."

21 See n. 12 above.

22 It is to be remembered here that in augmenting the *Bibliotheca,* Cooper, following Elyot, borrowed freely from Stephanus' *Dictionarium Latino-Gallicum* of 1538. By 1552 the *Dictionarium* had been considerably augmented. In compiling the *Thesaurus,* Cooper employed the Stephanus of 1552, or a reissue of this text in 1561.

23 Several entries near the beginning of the proper-name section of Cooper's *Thesaurus,* though they constitute but little of the comparative study, illustrate Cooper's method of borrowing from the Stephanus dictionaries. From Robert Stephanus' *Thesaurus,* generally through the revised *Bibliotheca,* comes the matter under the following entries: *Aba, Abae, Abaris, Abas, Abantes, Abaster* or *Abastrus, Abaton, Abatos, Abderita* or *Abderites, Abderitanus,* and *Abella* or *Avella.* From Charles Stephanus' *Dictionarium* come these: *Abacaena, Abala, Abalites, Abaortae,* and *Aborigines.* Longer items also, such as *Lucretia* and *Lycaon,* are from the *Dictionarium.* The sources of certain entries it is impossible to determine. The following, for example, might have come from either Charles or Robert Stephanus: *Abalus, Abantes, Abarimon,* and *Abaucas;* and the longer entries, *Aegeus, Ancaeus,* and *Lucullus.*

24 The practice of arranging the derivatives under their primitives, even when they belong, alphabetically, elsewhere in the text, is known in lexicography as the etymological system as distinguished from the alphabetical. Cooper uses the etymological arrangement in the *Thesaurus* with alphabetic cross references to the derivatives.

25 In his revisions of the *Bibliotheca,* Cooper had used illustrative quotations, but omitted the names of his authorities. In the *Thesaurus,* he increases the number of examples and cites names of approved writers but not specific works.

In a Latin note, Cooper explains that if no authority for a word is cited in the *Thesaurus,* one may know the word is of Greek origin or not used by approved Latin writers.

26 Mayor ("Latin-English and English-Latin Lexicography," *Journal of Classical and Sacred Philology,* Vol. IV [March, 1857], 25 ff.) notices this tendency and gives the list of words which I here set down. Mayor does not observe, however, that these terms were in the Latin-French source which Cooper was following.

27 Listed by Mayor, *ibid.*

28 See the address to the reader, reprinted in the editions of 1552 and 1559.

29 "Latin-English and English-Latin Lexicography," *Journal of Classical and Sacred Philology,* Vol. IV (March, 1857), 31–32.

30 "A Footnote on the Inkhorn Controversy," University of Texas *Studies in English,* Vol. XXVIII (1949), 49–56.

31 Cooper's Latin is as follows: "Vnicuique dictioni uernacula uocabula accommodata et conuenientia, quasi uno aceruo congesta, tanta uarietate subtexuimus. ut hic

noster labor non tam ad expeditam Romani sermonis notitiam, quam ad nostrae linguae ornatum, et elegantiam plurimum conferat."

32 *Scholars' Facsimile and Reprints*, d. Sanford V. Larkey and Philip M. Wagner (New York, 1941), sig. *D4*^v.

33 "A Footnote on the Inkhorn Controversy," University of Texas *Studies in English*, Vol. XXVIII (1949), 55.

34 See J. N. Madvig's commentary on Cicero's *De finibus bonorum et malorum*, Book I, Chapter 10, sec. 34.

35 Mayor, "Latin-English and English-Latin Lexicography," *Journal of Classical and Sacred Philology*, Vol. IV (March, 1857), 32.

36 For Shakespeare's familiarity with Cooper's *Thesaurus*, a copy of which was in the Stratford Grammar School which Shakespeare attended, see T. W. Baldwin's *Shakspere's Small Latine and Lesse Greeke* (2 vols., Urbana, Illinois, 1944), II, Index and *passim*.

CHAPTER X

1 *Athenae Cantabrigienses*, ed. C. H. Cooper, II, 29–30.

2 The *STC* gives the date of publication as 1588[?].

3 My translation. Holyoke's Latin runs thus:
"Suum [*Dictionarium*] autem Thomasius, ex Calepino & Coopero primum compilavit, quod vestigia adhuc recentia ostendunt. Postea ex Iunij nomenclature & quibusdam glossarijs & herbarijs auxit & ampliavit: tandem reverendus vir D. Philemon Hollandus doctissimus medicus iuxta ac philologus, ipsum Thomasium ex bonis auctoribus, adeo mirifice ditavit, ut nullum eo genere Dictionarium adhuc exstet, quod pro vocabulorum numero, perfecta vocum interpretatione & phrasibus selectis huic Thomasiano adaequari merito possit. . . . "

4 "Sententiam Georgij Agricolae, potissimum sequar." The reference is to Agricola's *De mensuris et ponderibus Romanorum atque Graecorum* (Basel, 1550).

5 Budaeus, *Libri V de asse et partibus ejus* (1514).

6 Scapula's text is an abridgment of the *Thesaurus Graecae linguae* (4 vols., 1572), by Henri Estienne. The abridgment was extremely popular.

7 The table is based upon groups of 100 consecutive words in the 1592 edition. Beginning with *confero*, for example, I find that the one hundredth entry is *confugella*. Using the same terminal words in the 1596 copy, I count the number of entries within the group, which is 207.

8 Edward Arber, *A List of London Publishers*, 19. The dedicatory letter in the edition of 1619 (*q.v.*) is written by the younger Legate, and is addressed to Lord Bacon, Baron Verulam, chancellor of England. In this letter Legate complains that the dictionary, his adopted child, has been taken without permission into a strange family (*alienam familiam*) and is being sold under another name. This charge of plagiarism is reserved for discussion later (see the discussion of Francis Holyoke's work, Chapter 16). The point of interest here is Legate's implication of printing rights for himself because he is a member of the Thomas family.

Legate's meaning becomes clearer in a similar dedicatory letter addressed to Thomas, Baron Coventry, of Aylesborough, and prefixed to the edition of 1631. Legate writes: "Huiusce Author Dictionarij primarius, Thomasius erat, Avus meus maternus: cuius famae, me nepotem eius pijssime parentatum indicabunt omnes, ubi Posthumo suo Thomae, Sponsorem Te (nobilissime Domine) accersere conatus fuⴹrim." The dedication to Baron Coventry is reprinted in the Thomasius of 1644, and the statement above is repeated verbatim. We have here in explicit language thⴰ signed statement of John Legate the Younger that Thomas Thomas, the first author of the dictionary, was his maternal grandfather. Perhaps it is a wise man that knows his own grandfather. But here is the best evidence so far presented of family relationship of the Thomases and the Legates. Young Legate's statement above obviously means that, sometime between July 28, 1588, and June 8, 1600, John Legate the Elder was married to Joan Thomas, the only daughter of the printer and lexicographer. (In his will, of date July 28, 1588, Thomas bequeaths £50 to Mary Barnes, his sister's daughter, and the rest of his property to his daughter Joan Thomas and his wife Anne [cf. *Athen. Cantab.*, II, 29–30]. June 8, 1600, is the date of the younger Legate's baptism in the parish of St. Mary the Great, Cambridge. Cf. *DNB*.) Such a union would seem natural enough.

But what of the records of these families? With a single exception, none of the accounts of printers which we have found even intimates the kinship of Legate to Thomas. According to Herbert-Ames (*Typographical Antiquities* [1785–90], III, 1414 ff.) and C. H. Timperley (*A Dictionary of Printers and Printing* [1839], 479), John Legate was married to Agatha, the daughter of Christopher Barker; according to Nichols, he was married to Agatha, the daughter of Robert Barker. Robert Bowes and Dr. R. B. McKerrow (cf. *DNB* and McKerrow, *A Dictionary of Printers and Booksellers in England, 1557–1640*) say Legate was married to Alice Sheirs, February 4, 1588–9, at St. Mary the Great, Cambridge, and within twenty years (1589–1609) nine daughters and three sons were born to the union. The first part of this statement has support in the parish register of St. Mary the Great. The register records the marriage of John Leggat [*sic*] and Alice Sheirs as of February 6, 1588 (cf. "Marriages," in *Cambridge Parish Registers*, ed. Evelyn Young [1927], VII, 6).

The exception referred to above is by one of the editors of the *Athen. Cantab.*, ed. C. H. Cooper and Thompson Cooper (II, 29–30). The editor, writing of Thomas's dictionary, states that "John Leyalt [*sic*], Thomas's grandson, wrote a dedication to one of the editions." But, as far as we can discover, this clue has never been followed up.

Meanwhile, of the statements we have recorded concerning the Legates, only two are of consequence; and they are apparently contradictory. John Legate the Younger's public assertion that Thomas Thomas was his maternal grandfather we must accept. As to the recorded marriage of John Leggat and Alice Sheirs, one might query whether this was the John Legate who succeeded Thomas as University printer and as editor of the Latin-English dictionary. If this is the same Legate, then we must assume that, sometime before 1600, Legate's wife (the former Alice Sheirs) died, or was divorced, and John Legate married Joan Thomas. It is a reasonable inference, I think, that somewhere in Cambridge, or possibly in London, there is a record of this marriage. Until such a record is found, we have to rely on John Legate the Younger's assertion that Thomas Thomas was his maternal grandfather. And this surely is sound evidence.

The significance of this relationship is that the right of printing the Thomasius was kept within the Thomas family; and John Legate the Younger, as an heir, could have brought action against those who were transcribing the Thomasius and, under another title, printing it as their own.

9 Nonius Marcellus, *De proprietate sermonis* (1471); M. Terentius Varro, *De lingua Latina* (Rome, 1471); Ammianus Marcellinus, *Historiarum libri XIII* (Rome, 1474); Petronius Arbiter, *Fragmenta* (Venice, 1499); and *Satyricon*.

10 Dioscorides: see *alypon, alysson, amiantus, ammoniacus sal, amorgine, anactorion, antimelon, anytos,* and *apocynum*. Celsus: see *alphos, anasarca, anastomosis, ancteres, ancycloblepharon,* and *andronyum*. Paracelsus: see *almizadir, altey, plumbi, alusar, anathron, anatrum, anthos, aquaster,* and *aquila*.

11 Way, in his edition of the *Promptorium* (Part III) for the Camden Society, lists a number of manuscripts of the *Medulla*, one of which was in the Library of St. John's College, Cambridge, and another in the Pepysian collection at Cambridge. Holland, a Cambridge man, may have used one or both of these manuscripts.

12 For the influence of Thomas on English dictionaries (Cawdrey, Bullokar, Cockeram) of the seventeenth century, see Starnes and Noyes, *The English Dictionary from Cawdrey to Johnson, 1604–1755,* Chapters 2–4.

CHAPTER XI

1 *DNB.*

2 Brandon, *Robert Estienne et le dictionnaire français aux XVIe siècle,* 116–23.

3 Comparison of about two hundred entries, from *condemno* to *conniuentia,* in Stephanus' *Dictionariolum* (1544) and Veron's edition of 1552 shows that Veron followed his original closely, simply adding his English translation of the French.

4 John Baret published his *Alvearie, or Triple Dictionarie, English, Latin, and French,* in 1573. For a discussion of Baret, see Chapter 14.

5 Additional examples of this procedure may be found by examination of the following entries in the four texts specified: *incontinens, incontinenter, incontinentia, inconueniens, incoquo, incorporeus, incorruptus, incorrupte,* and *increbresco*.

6 Abraham Fleming (1552–1607) seems to have had a hand in several dictionaries in the 1580's. He revised and augmented Baret's *Alvearie* (second edition, 1580) and edited and augmented the 1584 edition of Withals' *Dictionarie* and the 1584 edition of Veron. The *DNB* makes no mention of Fleming's work with the dictionaries of Baret and Veron.

7 The reference is apparently to John Higgins's translation of Junius' *Nomenclator,* in 1585.

CHAPTER XII

1 Among these are the elementary texts of Robert Stephanus: *Dictionnaire francois-latin* (Paris, 1539, 1549); *Dictionariolum puerorum* (1544, 1547, 1550). The *Dictionariolum,* with English equivalents for the French, supplied by John Veron, was published in London, in 1552. In Ghent, in 1549, Joannes Paludanus printed his *Dictionariolum,* in Latin, French, and Flemish; and in London, in 1553, John Withals first published his *Dictionarie for Yonge Begynners*.

2 See Brandon, *op. cit.,* 64 ff., and Bibliographie, where Brandon lists the various editions of the French-Latin dictionary. The three which follow are pertinent to this study: *Dictionnaire francois-latin, contenant les mots et manieres de parler francois tournez en latin* (Paris, De l'imprimerie de Robert Estienne, 1539, folio); *Dictionnaire francois-latin, autrement dict, Les mots francois* (Paris, 1549, folio); *Dictionnaire francois-latin . . . corrigé & augmenté par Maistra Jehan Thierry* (Paris, Chez Jehan Mace, 1564, folio).

3 John of Garland's *Synonyma* and *Equivoca,* products of the thirteenth century, had wide vogue after the advent of printing. See *STC* for editions printed in England.

4 See Henry B. Wheatley's Preface to the *Manipulus vocabulorum, iv.* Wheatley probably reckons not only main entries but what may be regarded as subsidiary entries.

5 For convenience in illustration, I have placed under *continuo* several entries in abbreviated form.

6 For further evidence, see the entries in the *Abcedarium* under *borage, bote, cycory herbe, cynque foyle, cypres, cocke, wede, condempned,* and *delay,* and compare the Latin equivalents of these terms with corresponding entries in the *Bibliotheca.*

7 Huloet's entry "Brittayne . . . *Britannia*" also paraphrases Calepine.

8 In my copy of the *Etymologiae,* printed by Iehan Petit, Paris, 1520, the *arbor consanguinitatis* is on folio *L*^r.

9 At least six editions of the *Promptorium* were printed between 1499 and 1528 (cf. *STC*). The *Catholicon Anglicum* was not printed until 1881, but Huloet might have had access to a manuscript of this book.

10 See Anthony à Wood, *Athenae Oxonienses,* I, 374–75; and also *DNB.*

11 Compare with the two entries from Huloet-Higgins the following from R. Stephanus' *Dictionarium Latino-Gallicum* (1561): *s.v. mitto:* "*Mitte Vnam hanc noxiam.* Pardonne moy ceste faulte"; *s.v. accedo:* "*Ad hominem accedam.* Terent. l'iray yers luy."

12 Brandon, *op. cit.,* 117–19.

13 *Ibid.,* 68.

14 In many instances Higgins does not supply the symbol *S,* as he claims to have done, after phrases borrowed from Stephanus.

15 *H* seems to signify Hadrianus, that is, Hadrianus Junius (1511–75). Junius first published the *Nomenclator* in 1567 with the title *Nomenclator omnium rerum propria nomina variis linguis explicata, indicans.* Higgins supplied English equivalents in 1585. For a sketch of Junius and his work, compare T. DeVries' *Holland's Influence on the English Language and Literature,* 182–86.

16 The essays on the letter *G* in both texts derive from Calepine.

17 *S.v. gods,* Huloet writes (and Higgins retains this in the 1572 edition): "Here you shall haue as it were a Pantheon or temple full of Goddes & Goddesses, the whyche I proteste to be but *Figmenta poetica,* and be put here to the only purpose that yong gramarians whiche do reade Poetrye, maye the soner fynde them for their purpose, in this place, as in Penario, or conuenient place for them, and so take it."

18 Sources of the verses distributed through the Huloet-Higgins text are indicated in the following table:
   Catullus: in the discussion of the letter *H.*
   Horace: *s.v. playe.*
   Juvenal: *s.v. Nestor.*
   Lucretius: *s.v. antipodes, care.*
   Magnus Cato: *s.v. Athenodorus.*
   Mantuan: *s.v. chewe, cockatrice.*
   Martial: *s.v. Attalus, babion, doue, figge, ladies, lettuce, peache, playe, purblynde.*
   Ovid: *s.v. Aeacus, detract, drinke, garde, peace.*

Persius: in the discussion of the letter *A*.

Priscian: *s.v. diamonde.*

Statius: *s.v. care.*

Suetonius: *s.v. Cato.*

Terence: *s.v. ah.*

Virgil: *s.v. ah, alder, amomum, aracynthus, bewitche, brode, Brutus* (two Latin quotations), *cease, coole, cuntrey, deformed, despised, dogge, drawe, dronkard, enuy, faire, fiere, gaggle, grasshopper, heate, inuersion, lizarde, lopper, pype, rust.*

"Pil." (unidentified): *s.v. if, kalendes* (mnemonic verses on the calendar, including "Thirty dayes hath November").

For a discussion of some of Higgins's verses, especially those under the entry *Brutus*, see James Sledd's "The English Verses in the Huloet-Higgins *Dictionarie* of 1572," *MLN*, Vol. LXIII (April, 1948), 251–54.

19 For an informative discussion of synonymy, see Roy Hugh Schram's "Synonymy in the English-Latin and Latin-English Dictionaries, 1440–1589" (master's thesis, University of Texas, 1950).

Chapter XIII

1 There seems to be no basis for the suggestion (Herbert-Ames, *Typographical Antiquities* [1785], I, 203) that Withals' *Dictionarie* was first printed *ca.* 1510 by Wynkyn de Worde. *STC* records a copy of a 1553 edition, owned by W. A. White. Cf. also Bibliography.

2 Professor A. G. Kennedy, in *A Bibliography of the Writings on the English Language* (Cambridge and New Haven, 1927), No. 2786, etc., lists twenty editions of the *Dictionarie*. For some of these, especially those dated 1554 and 1623, I do not find adequate evidence, though they may have existed. *STC* lists fourteen editions. In this study I have consulted editions dated as follows: 1556, 1568, 1574, 1579, 1581, 1584, 1586, 1594, 1599, 1602, 1608, 1616, and 1634.

3 The later editions have only the English headings.

4 The English words and phrases are printed in Tudor black type; the Latin, in roman.

5 See Thomas Wright's *Volume of Vocabularies* and Richard Paul Wülcker's revision of Wright's work under the title *Anglo-Saxon and Old English Vocabularies*. Volume I reprints the vocabularies, with some omissions and some additions. See also Starnes and Noyes, *op. cit.*, 197 ff.

6 Cf. *Biographie universelle ancienne et moderne*, 367–68. The *Biographie* lists editions of the *Lexicon* in quarto in 1494, 1501, 1506, and 1516; and later ones which are reprints of the 1516 issue. I have used a copy of the edition printed at Lyons, in 1535. All references are to this edition. Grapaldus drew freely from Pliny and Columella; Withals' indebtedness to these authors is probably by way of Grapaldus.

7 For information on Julius Pollux and his *Onomasticon*, see *The Universal Cyclopedia*, ed. C. K. Adams, IX, 338; also *A Dictionary of Greek and Roman Biography and Mythology*, ed. William Smith, III, 440; and Brunet's *Manuel du libraire*, III, 562. Editions of the *Onomasticon*, in Greek, were printed in 1502, 1520, 1536, and later. The authorities consulted make no mention of the Latin edition by Rudolphus Gualtherus (Basel, 1542). All references are to this

edition, a copy of which I have consulted in the Rare Books Collection, University of Texas.

8   Brunet (*op. cit.*, I, 410) states that there were sixteen editions printed by Aldus, in Venice, between 1542 and 1583. Du Cange (*Glossarium mediae et infimae Latinitatis*, I, *xxxviii–xxxix*) discusses Calepine and reprints the Preface of the 1502 edition. I have used in this study the Aldus edition of 1542.

9   Editions of the *Vocabula* published by Wynkyn de Worde appeared in 1510, 1525, and 1531; by Richard Pynson, in 1496, 1513, 1516, and 1519.

10 See pp. 61, 68, above for an account of the editions of Elyot's *Dictionary* and *Bibliotheca*. Cooper claims to have augmented the 1548 *Bibliotheca* by 33,000 words.

11 See the accounts of Turner in Agnes Arber's *Herbals* (Cambridge, 1938) and Charles E. Raven's *English Naturalists from Neckham to Ray: A Study of the Making of the Modern World* (Cambridge, 1947).

12 The original edition of the *Historia* was printed at Cologne, in 1544, with the title *Avium praecipuarum apud Plinium et Aristotelem mentio est, breuis & succincta historia*. I have used the edition entitled *Turner on Birds: A Short and Succinct History of the Principal Birds Noticed by Pliny and Aristotle*, ed. A. H. Evans (Cambridge, 1903). This is a reprint of the original Latin together with a translation in English. Page references are to this edition.

13 References are to *The Names of Herbes* (1548), edited with an Introduction by James Britten for the English Dialect Society (London, N. Trubner & Co., 1881).

14 Withals is probably indebted also to Joannes Paludanus' *Dictionariolum . . . puerorum* (Ghent, 1549). This dictionary for children is in Latin, Flemish, and Gallic, and in aim and organization has much in common with Withals.

15 The quoted matter beginning *s.v. sea* is based on the *Adagia*. The Latin quotation *Vita haec est fabula quaedam . . .* (p. 176) derives directly from the *Zodiacus vitae* of Palingenius, as Professor T. W. Baldwin (*Shakspere's Small Latine and Lesse Greeke*, I, 652 ff.) and others have noted. Professor Baldwin thinks that the lines in the *Zodiacus* are based upon a passage in Vives' *Satellitium*. Detailed discussion of the point is here impracticable. In my opinion, however, the following lines from Erasmus' *Encomium moriae* are a more likely source: "Porro mortalium vita omnis quid aliud est, quam fabula quaepiam, in qua alii aliis obtecti personis procedunt, aguntque suas quisque partes, donec choragus educat e proscenio?"—*Opera*, IV (1703), 428 C.

For Shakespeare's probable use of Withals in various other passages in the plays, compare Baldwin, *ibid.*, 710–14.

16 Much of the matter added by Clerk appears on pages 324–450 of the 1602 edition (and also on the same pages in 1608, which is unchanged), and on pages 386–524 in the editions of 1616 and 1634. The *DNB* mistakenly asserts that Clerk's augmentation was first made in the issue of 1608.

17 Clerk does not indicate the edition of Martial which he uses, but he generally gives the number of the epigram and the title. For extensive use of Martial by the Renaissance lexicographers, see Nicholas Perottus' *Cornucopiae* (1489 and later editions) and John Higgins's edition of *Huloets Dictionary* (1572).

18 The edition of 1616 contains, all told, 125 pages more than that of 1608; the pagination and the catchwords of the 1634 issue are the same as those of the 1616.

19 The *Dictionarius* includes many of the topics and much of the word list in the

conventional medieval vocabularies, but the method of presentation is similar to that of an interlinear gloss.

20 The selections from Locher and Barclay appear in the text (1602) on pages 391–445. These are concerned with the fools who collect fine books, which they never read; with physicians, lawyers, the devotees of Venus, benefices, fools of contention, tame fools, and usurers.

21 For a discussion of these characteristics in Withals and other lexicographers, see DeWitt T. Starnes, "Literary Features of Renaissance Dictionaries," *SP*, Vol. XXXVII (1940), 26–50.

22 See Starnes, "*The London Vocabulary* and Its Antecedents," University of Texas *Studies in English*, 1939, pp. 114–38.

Chapter XIV

1 This chapter owes much to Professor James Hinton Sledd, of the University of Chicago. His unpublished doctoral dissertation on "The *Alvearie* of John Baret" and his article "Baret's *Alvearie*, an Elizabethan Reference Book" (*SP*, Vol. XLIII, No. 2 [April, 1946], 147–63) are rich sources of information. Thanks to the generosity of the author, I have drawn freely from these sources.

2 See the sketch of Baret by Sidney Lee in *DNB*; and John Venn and J. A. Venn, *Alumni Cantabrigienses* (Cambridge, at the University Press, 1922), I, i, 96.

3 Cited by Sledd, "The *Alvearie* of John Baret," 13.

4 "Maister Powle" and "Maister Garth" have not been positively identified. Professor Sledd ("The *Alvearie* of John Baret," 8) suggests that "Maister Powle" might possibly refer to David Powell, a fellow of Trinity College, Cambridge, and University preacher in 1566; or to the printer Thomas Powell, Berthelet's assistant. "Maister Garth" may have been Gregory Garth of Cambridge, Lady Margaret preacher in 1562, and rector of Chalfont St. Giles from 1562 to 1585 (Venn, *Alumni Cantabrigienses*, I, ii, 198).

5 For the discussion of "M. Claudius" and "M. Chaloner" see pp. 196–98 below.

6 In his "Address to the Reader" Baret explains that "*pen. corr.* standeth for *penultima correpta*, when the last syllable save one is short, or without anie rising and lifting of the voice at the same, but rather at some other syllable before it, as *Dominus*; and *pen. prod.* for *penultima producta*, when it is long, as *Urtica*, with such a little strike, or accent commonlie over that vocall, where the voice riseth in pronouncing of it." This is the method used in Baret's sources, Robert Stephanus and Cooper.

7 These entries show the order of languages: (1) the English, in black letter; (2) the Latin, in roman; (3) the Greek, when given; (4) the French, in italic. Analysis of this block of entries shows the Greek terms to be from Calepine, the English mostly from Cooper's *Thesaurus*, and the French from Robert Stephanus' *Dictionarium Latino-Gallicum*.

8 It is possible, of course, to assume that the *Thesaurus* was used from the beginning and no revision was necessary. Such an assumption would place the beginning of Baret's work definitely after 1565 and contradict his whole discourse to the reader.

9 Since only the English phrasing is under consideration here, the French and occasional Greek phrases in the *Alvearie* are omitted.

10 Cited by Sledd ("The *Alvearie* of John Baret," 62–65), who writes out the

definitions. I have verified them and compared entries from the 1559 *Bibliotheca*, which was not available to him.

11 These and the parallels above were noted by Sledd, *ibid.*, 66 f.

12 Compare also the following entries in Levins and Baret: *caponet, to faffle, fourdye, to frubbish, muckye, newish,* and *to pickle flesh.*

13 Sledd, "The *Alvearie* of John Baret," 69–70.

14 Quoted by Sledd (*ibid.*, 78–80), who cites fifteen other passages for comparison.

15 *Ibid.*, 9; *DNB*; and Cooper's *Athenae Cantabrigienses*, I, 235–37.

16 Lucy E. Farrer, *La vie et les oeuvres de Claude de Sain Liens alias Claudius Holyband* (Paris, 1908), 70.

17 *Ibid.*, 21–23; Sledd, "The *Alvearie* of John Baret," 90.

18 Farrer, *op. cit.*, 70.

19 *Ibid.*, 70–71.

20 *The Teaching and Cultivation of the French Language in England During Tudor and Stuart Times* (Manchester, at the University Press, 1920), 188.

21 *Notes and Queries*, Vol. CLXXVII (September 30, 1939), 239.

22 *Ibid.* Cf. also Sledd's "A Note on the Use of Renaissance Dictionaries," *MP*, Vol. XLIX (August, 1951), 10–15.

23 Sledd, "The *Alvearie* of John Baret," 94.

24 Brandon, *Robert Estienne et le dictionnaire français aux XVIe siècle*, 116–23.

25 *DNB*; Venn, *Alumni Cantabrigienses*, I, i, 384, *passim.*

26 *Athenae Cantabrigienses*, II, 459–64. Cf. also *DNB*. Neither of these mentions Fleming's revision of the *Alvearie* or of the Veron-Waddington dictionary. Cf. also Kennedy, Nos. 2715, 2716, 2797, 2802.

27 For information on Henry Lyte (1529?–1607) see *DNB*; for Rembert Dodoens, or Dodonaeus (1517–85), see *Biographie nationale*, VI, 85 ff.; and Sledd, "The *Alvearie* of John Baret," 56.

28 The six proverbs listed appear also, with the same English translations, in the "Dictionarium Poeticum" of Cooper's *Thesaurus*. Fleming could have drawn from this source.

29 Quotations from the *Adagia* are taken from Erasmus' *Opera* (1703), II.

30 Compare the following entries:

1573	1580		1573	1580
A, 626	A, 731		C, 924	C, 955
B, 20	B, 22		D, 406	D, 472
C, 880	C, 910		D, 546	D, 632

31 Sledd, "The *Alvearie* of John Baret," 23–24.

32 *Ibid.*, 120 ff.

33 *Ibid.*, 152.

34 "Baret's *Alvearie*, an Elizabethan Reference Book," *SP*, Vol. XLIII, No. 2 (April, 1946), 147 ff. Cf. especially 162, 163. This is a very small part of the more detailed study in Sledd's doctoral dissertation.

Chapter XV

1 *DNB*; *Athenae Oxonienses*.

2 See the discussion of Francis Holyoke, in Chapter 16.

3 Sir Henry Radcliffe, fourth earl of Sussex (1530?–93), succeeded his brother as earl, 1583; K.G., 1589. Sir William Waad (1546–1623), ambassador to Portu-

gal, 1580; clerk of the Privy Council, 1583–1613; seized Mary Stuart's papers, 1586; tracked out Roderigo Lopez' plot, 1594; knighted, 1603.

4 Sir Francis Walsingham (1530?–90), M.P., Banbury, 1559; Surrey, 1574–90; secretary of state, 1573–90; knighted, 1577.

5 John Case (d. 1600), Aristotelian commentator; chorister at Oxford; M.A., St. John's College, Oxford, 1572; M.D., 1589; practiced medicine in Oxford; published *Sphaera civitatis*, 1589; *Apologia musices*, 1588.

6 The English entries in the Rider text are in italic; the Latin equivalents, in roman of somewhat larger size.

7 Grammatical information and citation of classical authorities for Latin terms appear in the text proper of the *Alvearie*.

8 See Chapter 12.

9 The title page reads: "Synonymorum Sylva Olim a Simone Pelegromio collecta, & Alphabetico Flandrico ab eodem Authore illustrata: nunc autem e Belgarum sermone in Anglicanum transfusa, & in alphabeticum ordinem reducta per H.F. . . . London, 1609." The Ad Lectorem, by "Jo Serranus" is a ten-page Latin discourse on the subject of synonymy and the principle of varying. The essay follows that of Erasmus in *De copia verborum et rerum*.

10 See Schram, "Synonymy in the Latin-English and English-Latin Dictionaries of the Sixteenth Century." Schram cites (pp. 169–71) most of the examples mentioned in this list.

11 The inflectional endings in the Huloet-Higgins are omitted for economy in these illustrations.

12 Abraham Fleming, who in 1580 had revised Baret's *Alvearie*, added to Junius' *Nomenclator* in 1585 an index patterned after that in the *Alvearie*. Rider was of course familiar with both indexes.

13 Many entries in Rider, especially those involving groups of Latin synonyms, derive ultimately from the French-Latin dictionaries of Robert Stephanus. Such entries come, however, by way of the Huloet-Higgins or Baret.

14 On the title page: "The Nomenclator or Remembrancer of Adrianus Iunius Physician, divided into two tomes, conteining proper names and apt termes for all things under their convenient titles . . . Written by the said Ad. Iu. in Latine, Greeke, French and other forrein tongues: and now in English, by Iohn Higins . . . Imprinted at London for Ralph Newberie, and Henrie Denham, 1585." I have used a copy of this edition.

15 As recorded by Rider, the list is as follows: "Black-foot . . . *Melampus*"; "Blanch, or white-coat . . . *Leucon*"; "Chaunter, or ring-wood . . . *Hylactor*"; "Kill-buck, or fierce-looke . . . *Theron*"; "Make-swift, or make-speed . . . *Anyte*"; "Rauener, or eat-all . . . *Pamphagus*"; "Rug, ruffin, or shag-haire . . . *Lachne*"; "Scalecliffe, or rangehill . . . *Oribasus*"; "Swift-foot . . . *Podargus*"; "White-tail, or fox . . . *Lampurus*"; "Whirlewind, or tempest . . . *Laelaps*"; "Wolfe, or churle . . . *Lycisca*." Thomas's list is the same, except that *s.v. hylactor & hylax*, he gives "Ring, chaunter, or barker"; and he ascribes each one to Ovid. Rider could have followed either Thomas or Junius. He is less likely to have followed Ovid.

16 For the entries on birds and herbs Thomas drew from the Elyot-Cooper dictionaries and also directly from Turner and Junius.

CHAPTER XVI

1 *DNB.*

2 *Stationers' Register*, III, 207, 223, 225, 276. See also Holyoke's Ad Lectorem in the 1606 edition of Rider-Holyoke.

3 *DNB.*

4 *The History of the Worthies of England* (3 vols., London, 1840), III, 287. This book was first published in 1662.

5 See n. 2 above.

6 Falconer Madan seems to suggest that publication of the Rider was hindered by the Stationers' Company. See his *Oxford Books: A Bibliography of Printed Works Relating to the University and City of Oxford or Printed or Published There* (3 vols., Oxford, 1912). Madan writes (II, 28–29):

"The Oxford press was bold in issuing this dictionary, for the Cambridge one by T. Thomas, issued in 1587, was the subject of complaints in the following year, the Stationers' Company threatening to reprint it, as holding the privilege of printing all dictionaries. So too the book was only transferred to John Barnes on June 7, 1602, 'Salvo jure cujuscunque,' and on Dec. 6 on condition that it should be printed in London: Barnes re-transferred it on Jan. 27, 1602/3, to Cuthbert Burby, and he to a syndicate on Nov. 26, 1604."

7 Holyoke's statement is somewhat misleading: the objection was to what Holyoke himself had put into his *Dictionarium etymologicum*, the Latin-English section he had added to Rider's English-Latin.

8 See the bibliographical discussion in the latter part of this chapter.

9 In the transcribed entries Greek terms of the Thomas and grammatical information from all three are, for the most part, omitted.

10 For the phrasing of the title pages and further details of the 1612 text, see pp. 264–65 below.

11 See p. 265.

12 See p. 265.

13 See p. 266.

14 See p. 267.

15 Although Holyoke's defence is similar to that he had made in 1606, namely, that he was following the practice of other lexicographers, he has changed his accusation of Cooper. Earlier he had asserted that Cooper had compiled his *Thesaurus* from Stephanus and Elyot; now he holds that Cooper had translated his book from Frisius' Latin-German dictionary.

16 See p. 268.

17 For clearness in the illustrations Greek terms, grammatical information, etc., are omitted.

18 See p. 269.

19 But see pp. 267–70.

20 See p. 270.

CHAPTER XVIII

1 For this information, I am indebted to Professor James Sledd, who kindly collated for me the 1664 and 1678 editions of Gouldman. I have since compared with these the 1674 edition.

2 The statement of the *DNB*, under *Thomas Thomas*, that "Francis Gouldman of Christ's College brought out a new edition of Thomas's Dictionary" is erro-

neous. Although Gouldman admittedly owes much to Thomas, he draws freely from Rider and the augmented Holyoke.

3 The compilers of the *New Dictionary in Five Alphabets* (Cambridge, 1693) claim to have used a manuscript in three folio volumes, by John Milton. Assistants in preparation of Ainsworth's *Thesaurus* also claim use of manuscript collections.

4 For simplification, I have omitted Greek equivalents of the Latin and, in Rider-Holyoke and Gouldman, Hebrew.

CHAPTER XIX

1 It is curious to note that through his use of Rider-Holyoke and Gouldman, Thomas Holyoke is, like his father before him, ultimately most heavily indebted to Thomas, whose dictionary was first published ninety years before.

2 A number of long sketches, largely in Latin, have no basis in Rider-Holyoke, Gouldman, or Wase. Such are the items under *asinus* and *canis*, with the various proverbs associated with each; also *abanec*, *buttu*, *aedes*, and *lex*. These are from a seventeenth-century edition of Calepine. I have noted the correspondence in my edition of 1609. From Sir Henry Spelman's *Archaeologus in modum glossarii* (*Glossarium*, 1626, 1664), Thomas Holyoke takes over long passages, such as those under the following entries: *abba*, *abbas*, *abbatia*, *abbatis*, *abbatissa*, *abbay*, *abbettator*, *abeyantia*, *abhaeredes*, *abiectire* (*abiectum*, *abiectiuum*, *iactiuum*, *iectiuum*), *abiaticus*, *abishersing*, *absida*, *absque hoc*, *abutto* (*abuttare*), *acceptor*, *accesorius*, *accionarius* (*actionarius*), *accola* (*accolana*, *accolanus*, *acolabium*), *aclea*, *acoluthi*, *acquietancia*, *acra*, *actor* (*Actor Dominicus*), *adaero* (*adaerare*), *adelingus*, *adalingus*, *adelscale*, *adelscalche*, *adelscalcus*, *adfatomia* (*affatomia*), *adiurnare* (*adiurnatus*), *adiurnamentum*, *admallo*, *admezatores*, *admineculator*, and *admiralias* (*amirallas*, *admiralis*, *admirans*). These are successive entries, each of which Holyoke condenses and uses.

CHAPTER XX

1 For an account of Coles's *English Dictionary*, see Starnes and Noyes, *op. cit.*, 58 ff.

2 A few entries, where there are no correspondences, are omitted from each column. Coles did not, of course, take all of his matter from Gouldman.

3 Compare Littleton, Ainsworth, and Dr. Samuel Johnson.

4 See Kennedy, *op. cit.*, No. 2827: 1st ed., 1677; 2nd, 1679, 1703; 7th, 1711; 8th, 1716; 10th, 1722; [12th, 1730]; 13th, 1736, 1742; 15th, 1749; 17th, 1764; 18th, 1772.

CHAPTER XXI

1 These words are from a clipping from the *Hull Advertiser*, November 22, 1806. I found the clipping pasted in my copy of the 1678 Littleton, opposite the entry *concurro*. This story, substantially as it appears in the *Advertiser*, is repeated by Allibone (*Critical Dictionary of English Literature* [1882], I, 1108). In a book entitled *Extracts from Curiosities of Natural History* (Second Series [1879], 349), by Frank Buckland, is a much embellished version of the story, in which the writer states that *condog* for *concurro* appears in a copy of Ainsworth in his possession, and he attributes the incident to Ainsworth and his scribes. But the

first edition of Ainsworth did not appear until 1736, and this does not contain the *condog*. Moreover, the *OED* points out that the concur-condog pun was used by John Lyly as early as 1592, in *Galathea* (3. 3. 247). Regrettably we must abandon the pretty fiction concerning Littleton.

2 From a copy in the Rare Books Collection, University of Texas.

3 For this information and other used in this chapter, I am glad to acknowledge, once again, indebtedness to Professor Sledd, who collated for me the Cambridge text and Littleton. Since his collation, I have been able to verify the results for myself.

4 Both Milton's nephews, John and Edward Phillips, have testified that Milton was compiling a Latin *thesaurus* after the manner of Robert Stephanus; and, according to Edward Phillips, he continued his collection almost to his dying day. See *The Early Lives of Milton*, ed. H. Darbishire (London, 1932), 29, 44–45, 71–72.

5 See Sledd, n. 3.

6 This language is almost identical with that employed by Littleton in the first edition of the dictionary, and the claim of enlargement requires verification.

CHAPTER XXII

1 See the Preface to Ainsworth's dictionary.

2 See Starnes and Noyes, *op. cit.*, 154–56.

3 Greek and Hebrew words and phrases in Littleton are omitted as not pertinent to the illustrations, as there are no correspondences in Ainsworth.

4 Charles Noyes, *op. cit.*, 31.

5 The third edition of Jacob's *New Law-Dictionary* appeared in 1736, the year that the first edition of Ainsworth was printed. Ainsworth may have consulted the first or the second edition of Jacob's. As Jacob's law lexicon draws upon all its antecedents, it is difficult to determine often whether Ainsworth is borrowing from Jacob or one of his sources. Compare, however, the first thirty entries in Ainsworth and Jacob, noting especially *abgatoria, acra* (*acre*), *affidari ad arma*, and *affretamentum*.

6 See Ainsworth's Preface.

7 The imprint of the 1746 Ainsworth: "London: Printed for W. Mount and T. Page, W. Innys, R. Ware, J. and P. Knapton, A. Ward, J. Clarke in St. Paul's Church-Yard, T. Cox, T. Longman, C. Hitch, R. Hett, A. Millar, J. Pote, J. Hodges, J. Oswald, E. Wicksteed, J. and R. Tonson and S. Draper, J. Davidson, J. and J. Rivington, M. Cooper, and the Executors of Mr. J. Darby. MDCCXLVI."

The same list, with given names substituted for initials, appears in the royal license for printing this edition.

8 In his "Preface to the Second Edition" (p. *xxvii*) Dr. Patrick writes: "Having consulted a very valuable manuscript of the late learned Mr. *Samuel Morland*, in five volumes in *folio*, which furnished me with a large number of *English* and *Latin* phrases not to be found in any dictionary, I have inserted as many of them, as was consistent with the brevity and expedition required in this edition."

Compare with this the claim of the Cambridge editors and, from 1703, the editors of Littleton to having used a Milton manuscript collection, in three volumes, folio.

Dr. Patrick's reference seems to be to Sir Samuel Morland, first baronet (1625–

95), of Winchester School and Magdalene College, Cambridge. He was, according to *DNB*, diplomatist, mathematician, and inventor. If he compiled such a manuscript as Dr. Patrick describes, it has, regrettably, disappeared.

9 Information on listings in the *British Museum Catalogue* was gathered by Charles Noyes, *op. cit.*, 14–15.

Chapter XXIII

1 *A New Discovery of the Old Art of Teaching School*, ed. T. Mark (Syracuse, New York, 1912), 209–10. Hoole's book was first published in 1659.
2 Starnes and Noyes, *op. cit.*, Chapters 1–5.

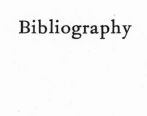

Bibliography

Bibliography

References pertaining to the history of Latin-English lexicography

Ainsworth, Robert. *Thesaurus linguae Latinae compendiarius: Or, a Compendious Dictionary of the Latin Tongue*. 1736. The Preface has an inadequate survey of Latin-English lexicography from the fifteenth to the end of the seventeenth century.

Gouldman, Francis. *A Copious Dictionary in Three Parts*. 1664. The Preface, outlining the history of Latin lexicography to about 1660, is reprinted at the end of the chapter on Gouldman.

Kennedy, Arthur G. *A Bibliography of Writings on the English Language from the Beginning of Printing to the End of 1922*. Cambridge and New Haven, 1927. See, especially, "Interlingual Dictionaries," pp. 99–108. An indispensable guide in this study.

Mayor, J. E. B. "Latin-English Lexicography," *Journal of Classical and Sacred Philology*, Vol. II (November, 1855), 271–90.

———. "Latin-English and English-Latin Lexicography," *Journal of Classical and Sacred Philology*, Vol. IV (March, 1857), 1–44.

Sledd, James Hinton. "The *Alvearie* of John Baret." Unpublished doctoral dissertation, University of Texas, 1947.

———. "Baret's *Alvearie*, an Elizabethan Reference Book," *SP*, Vol. XLIII, No. 2 (April, 1946), 147–63.

———. "A Footnote on the Inkhorn Controversy," University of Texas *Studies in English*, Vol. XXVIII (1949), 49–56.

———. "The English Verses in the Huloet-Higgins *Dictionarie* of 1572," *MLN*, Vol. LXIII (April, 1948), 251–54.

Starnes, DeWitt T. "Thomas Cooper's *Thesaurus:* A Chapter in Renaissance Lexicography," University of Texas *Studies in English*, Vol. XXVIII (1949), 15–48.

———. "An Elizabethan *Dictionarie for Yonge Beginners*" [Withals], University of Texas *Studies in English*, Vol. XXIX (1950), 51–76.

———. "Thomas Cooper and the *Bibliotheca Eliotae*," University of Texas *Studies in English*, Vol. XXX (1951), 40–60.

———. "Richard Huloet's *Abcedarium:* A Study in English-Latin Lexicography," *SP*, Vol. XLVIII (1951), 717–37.

Stephanus, or Estienne, Robert. *Thesaurus linguae Latinae. Ed. nova prioribus multo*

393

auctior et emendatior. 4 vols. London, 1735. The Praefatio (Vol. I, fols. 1–24) surveys Latin lexicography from the Middle Ages to 1735.

Way, Albert, ed. *Promptorium parvulorum sive clericorum.* Camden Society, 1843–65. Way's Pref·ce (pp. *xiii–xlix*) on the author, sources, and manuscripts and editions, and the Appendix (pp. *l–lxxxv*) on Medieval glossaries, vocabularies, and other works are of immense value in the history of English-Latin lexicography.

Wheatley, Henry B. "Chronological Notices of the Dictionaries of the English Language," *Transactions* of the Philological Society, 1865, pp. 218–93. The author notices briefly bilingual and trilingual dictionaries published before 1616, "in which the English precedes the other language."

Wing, Donald, comp. *Short-Title Catalogue of Books Printed in England, Scotland, Ireland, Wales . . . 1641–1700.* New York, Index Society, 1945——. Only Volumes I and II had appeared when this study was in progress.

Worcester, Joseph E. *A Dictionary of the English Language.* Boston, 1860. The Introduction (pp. *liii–lviii*) has notices of early lexicographers other than English, including Suidas, Joannes Balbus, Calepinus, *Ortus vocabulorum*, Huloet, and Rider.

Short-title list of Latin-English and English-Latin dictionaries (1500– ca. 1800) in American libraries

NOTE: This list of dictionaries is compiled from a survey of forty American libraries, public and private. It refers only to printed texts, microfilms being excluded. Though widely representative, the list cannot be regarded as exhaustive.

Ainsworth, Robert. *Thesaurus linguae Latinae compendiarius.*
1736   Quarto. Harvard, University of Illinois.
1746   Quarto. Boston Public Library, University of Texas.
1751   Quarto. University of California (Berkeley), Columbia, University of Illinois, Newberry Library, New York Public Library, Rutgers, Yale.
1752   Folio, 2 vols. Brown, Library of Congress, Harvard, Johns Hopkins, University of Michigan, University of Virginia, Watkinson Library.
1761   Quarto, 2 vols. University of California (Berkeley), University of California (Los Angeles), University of Chicago, University of Illinois, University of Minnesota, University of Texas, University of Virginia, Yale.
1773   Quarto, 2 vols. Boston Public Library, Cornell, Folger Library, Yale.
1783   Quarto. Folger Library, Harvard, University of Minnesota, Princeton.
1796   Quarto, 2 vols. Boston Public Library, University of California (Berkeley), Huntington Library, University of North Carolina.
1798   Quarto. Boston Public Library, University of Minnesota.
Cf. Kennedy: Nos. 2863, 2866, 2868, 2884.

Baret, John. *An Alvearie or Triple Dictionarie.* Folio.
1573   Boston Public Library, Library of Congress, Folger Library, Harvard, Huntington Library, University of Minnesota, Newberry Library, New York Public Library, University of Texas, Yale.
——. *An Alvearie or Quadruple Dictionarie.*
1580   University of California (Berkeley), University of California (Los Angeles), University of Chicago, Columbia, Library of Congress, Duke, Folger Library, Harvard, Huntington Library, University of Illinois,

University of Iowa, University of Michigan, Newberry Library, New
York Public Library, Princeton, University of Texas, Watkinson Library,
University of Wisconsin, Yale.

Cf. Kennedy: Nos. 2712, 2714.

Coles, Elisha. *A Dictionary, English-Latin, and Latin-English.*
1677   Quarto. Library of Congress, University of Illinois, University of Iowa,
      Stanford.
1679   Quarto. University of Minnesota, New York Public Library, Yale.
1711   University of Illinois, University of Michigan.
1717   Octavo. New York Public Library.
1722   Harvard, University of Illinois.
1727   Cornell, University of Texas.
1730   University of Illinois, Yale.
1736   Octavo. Harvard, University of Texas.
1742   Dartmouth, University of Michigan.
1749   Harvard.
1755   Rutgers, Yale.
1764   Octavo. Boston Public Library, University of Michigan.
1772   Octavo. Library of Congress, Harvard, Yale.
Cf. Kennedy: Nos. 2827, 2854, 2867, 2883; Wing, I: Nos. 5068, 5069.

Cooper, Thomas. *Thesaurus linguae Romanae et Britannicae.* Folio.
1565   University of Chicago, Folger Library, Huntington Library, University
      of Illinois, University of Iowa, New York Public Library, New York
      University, Ohio State University, Princeton, Stanford, University of
      Texas, University of Virginia, Watkinson Library, Yale.
1573   Boston Public Library, University of California (Los Angeles), University
      of Chicago, Columbia, Folger Library, Huntington Library, University of
      Illinois, New York Public Library, Wellesley, Yale.
1578   Boston Public Library, University of California (Berkeley), University
      of Chicago, Library of Congress, Duke, Folger Library, Harvard, Hunt-
      ington Library, University of Illinois, University of Iowa, University of
      Minnesota, University of Missouri, Newberry Library, New York Public
      Library, University of North Carolina, Princeton, University of Virginia,
      Yale.
1584   Boston Public Library, Brown, University of California (Berkeley), Uni-
      versity of Chicago, University of Cincinnati, Columbia, Cornell, Duke,
      Folger Library, Harvard, Huntington Library, University of Illinois,
      University of Michigan, Northwestern, Princeton, University of Texas,
      Watkinson Library, University of Wisconsin, Yale.
1587   University of Texas (private collection of Rudolph Willard).
Cf. Kennedy: Nos. 2754, 2757.

Elyot, Thomas. *The Dictionary of Syr Thomas Eliot, knyght.* Folio.
1538   Folger Library, Harvard, University of Illinois, University of Michigan,
      University of Virginia, Watkinson Library, Yale.
————. *Ibid.* In subsequent editions entitled *Bibliotheca Eliotae: Eliotis Librarie.*
1542   Harvard.
1545   Columbia, Harvard, University of Michigan, Yale.
1548   Revised by Thomas Cooper. Library of Congress, Folger Library, Harvard,
      Huntington Library, University of Michigan, Newberry Library, Yale.

1552   Folger Library, New York Public Library, Watkinson Library, Yale.
1559   Columbia, Folger Library, University of Illinois, University of Michigan, New York Public Library, Stanford, University of Texas, Yale.
Cf. Kennedy: Nos. 2748, 2749, 2750, 2751, 2752.

Gouldman, Francis. *A Copious Dictionary in Three Parts*. Quarto.
1664   Boston Public Library, University of Michigan, Newberry Library.
1669   University of Illinois, University of Texas, Yale.
1674   Library of Congress, University of Illinois, University of Texas, Watkinson Library, Yale.
1678   University of California (Los Angeles), Columbia, Library of Congress, Harvard, Newberry Library.
Cf. Kennedy: Nos. 2818, 2819, 2822a, 2829; Wing, II: Nos. 1443, 1444, 1445, 1446, 1447.

Holyoke, Thomas. *A Large Dictionary in Three Parts*. Folio.
1676–77   Boston Public Library, University of California (Berkeley), University of Chicago, Library of Congress, Cornell, Harvard, University of Illinois, University of Minnesota, Princeton, University of Texas, University of Wisconsin, Yale.
Cf. Wing, II: No. 2535.

[*H*]*ortus vocabulorum*.
1500   Folio. Huntington Library.
1508   Not located.
1509   Not located.
1511   Octavo. Library of Congress, Yale.
1514   Quarto. Huntington Library.
1516   Not located.
1517   Not located.
1518   Quarto. Harvard, University of Illinois.
1520   Not located.
1528   Not located.
1532   Not located.
1533   Not located.
Cf. Kennedy: Nos. 2737, 2739, 2741, 2744.

Huloet, Richard. *Abcedarium Anglico Latinum, pro tyrunculis*. Folio.
1552   Folger Library, Harvard, University of Michigan, Newberry Library, Yale.
————. *Huloets Dictionarie, Newly Corrected by J. Higgins*.
1572   Boston Public Library, Columbia, Folger Library, Harvard, Huntington Library, University of Virginia, Yale.
Cf. Kennedy: Nos. 2785, 2792.

Junius, Hadrian. *The Nomenclator, or Remembrancer . . . in English by Iohn Higgins*. Octavo.
1585   University of Chicago, Columbia, Duke, Folger Library, Huntington Library, University of Illinois, University of Texas, Yale.
Cf. Kennedy: No. 2716.

Linguae Romanae dictionarium luculentum novum. A New Dictionary, in Five Alphabets. Quarto.

1693 Boston Public Library, Brown, University of Chicago, Harvard, University of Illinois, Princeton, University of Texas, Yale.

Littleton, Adam, *A Latine Dictionary, in Four Parts.* Quarto.

1678 Brown, University of California (Los Angeles), Dartmouth, Folger Library, Harvard, Huntington Library, University of Illinois, Johns Hopkins, University of Michigan, New York Public Library, Northwestern, Princeton, University of Texas, Yale.

1684 University of California (Berkeley), Newberry Library, Watkinson Library.

1703 Brown, Library of Congress, Harvard, University of Illinois, Ohio State University, University of Texas.

1715 Boston Public Library, University of Chicago, Columbia, University of Michigan.

1723 Harvard, University of Illinois, Newberry Library, New York Public Library, Rutgers, University of Texas, Watkinson Library.

1735 Boston Public Library, Brown, Harvard, University of Minnesota, University of Texas.

Cf. Kennedy: Nos. 2830, 2848, 2862; Wing, II: Nos. 2563, 2564, 2565.

Pelegromius, Simon. *Synonymorum sylva.* Octavo.

1585 Huntington Library, University of Illinois.
1603 Not located.
1606 University of Chicago.
1609 Not located.
1612 Folger Library.
1615 Folger Library, University of Texas.
1619 Not located.
1632 Folger Library.
1639 University of Chicago, Folger Library, Harvard, University of Illinois, Yale.
1650 Boston Public Library, Brown, University of Illinois, University of Texas.
1663 University of Illinois.
Cf. Kennedy: Nos. 2758, 2769, 2773.

Promptorium parvulorum. Quarto.

1499 Not located.
1508 Not located.
1510 University of Illinois.
1512 Folger Library, Huntington Library.
1516 Huntington Library.
1528 Not located.
Cf. Kennedy: No. 2442.

Rider, John. *Bibliotheca scholastica. A Double Dictionarie.* Quarto.

1589 Folger Library, University of Illinois.
————. *Riders Dictionarie.* Revised by Francis Holyoke.
1606 Folger Library.

1612   University of Illinois.
1617   Library of Congress, Harvard, University of Illinois (2 issues), North-
       western.
1626   Revised by N. Gray. University of Illinois, Watkinson Library, Yale.
1627   Columbia, New York Public Library, Yale.
1633   Boston Public Library, Huntington Library, New York University, Yale.
1639   University of Texas (copy contains only the *Etymologicall Dictionarie*,
       by F. Holyoke).
1640   Boston Public Library, Folger Library (2 issues), Huntington Library,
       University of Illinois, University of Michigan, Newberry Library.
1648–49   Boston Public Library, University of Chicago, Library of Congress,
       University of Michigan, New York University, University of Texas, Wat-
       kinson Library.
1659   Harvard, University of Illinois.
Cf. Kennedy: Nos. 2761, 2798; also *s.v. Holyoke, Francis:* Nos. 2768, 2772,
       2777, 2803, 2806, 2808, 2826.

Stanbridge, John. *Vocabula.*
  n.d.   (Wynkyn de Worde) Folger Library.
1496   Not located.
1510   Not located.
1513   Not located.
1516   Not located.
1519   Not located.
1525   Not located.
1531   Not located.
1562   Not located.
1577   Not located.
1600   Huntington Library.
1635   Folger Library.
Cf. Kennedy: Nos. 2734, 2735, 2738, 2740, 2742.

Thomas, Thomas. *Dictionarium linguae Latinae et Anglicanae.*
1587   Not located.
1589   Quarto. University of Illinois, University of Texas.
1594   Octavo. Folger Library, Harvard, Yale.
1596   Quarto. Folger Library, Huntington Library, University of Illinois,
       University of Texas.
1606   Quarto. Folger Library, University of Michigan, University of Texas.
1610   Octavo. Folger Library.
1615   Quarto. University of Chicago.
1619   Octavo. Johns Hopkins.
1620   Quarto. University of Illinois.
1631   Quarto. University of Texas.
1644   Quarto. Library of Congress.
Cf. Kennedy: Nos. 2760, 2763.

Veron, John. *Dictionariolum puerorum, tribus linguis.* Quarto.
1552   Not located.
————. *A Dictionary in Latine and English Corrected by R. Waddington.* Quarto.
1575   Huntington Library.

1584   Columbia, Folger Library, Harvard.
Cf. Kennedy: Nos. 2711, 2756, 2759.

Wase, Christopher. *Dictionarium minus: A Compendious Dictionary.* Quarto.
1662   Not located.
1675   Boston Public Library, Harvard, New York Public Library, University
        of Texas (private collection of De Witt T. Starnes).
Cf. Kennedy: No. 2825.

Withals, John. *A Shorte Dictionarie English and Latin for Yonge Begynners.*
1553   Quarto. Columbia.
1556   Quarto. Huntington Library, University of Michigan.
1568   Quarto. Library of Congress, Folger Library, Huntington Library.
1579   Quarto. Folger Library.
1584   Quarto. Folger Library.
1586   Quarto. Folger Library.
1594   Quarto. Huntington Library.
1599   Quarto. Folger Library.
1602   Octavo. Folger Library, Harvard, Yale.
1608   Octavo. Folger Library, University of Illinois.
1616   Octavo. Folger Library, Harvard, Newberry Library.
1634   Octavo. University of Chicago, Columbia, Folger Library, Huntington
        Library, Johns Hopkins, University of Illinois, Newberry Library.
    Cf. Kennedy: Nos. 2786, 2787, 2788, 2789, 2793, 2795, 2796, 2797, 2799,
2801, 2802, 2807.

Index

Index

DeWITT T. STARNES, coauthor or coeditor of four other books, has published many articles in the field of Renaissance language and literature. Out of his study of the writings of Sir Thomas Elyot grew his interest in the bilingual dictionaries of the period. Several of these old lexicons, beautiful examples of Renaissance typography, are in his private collection, and others have been bought on his recommendation for the Rare Books Collection of the University of Texas Library.

The study of Renaissance dictionaries has taken the author to some of the world's most famous libraries: the Huntington, the Folger, the Bodleian at Oxford, the University of Cambridge Library, and the British Museum.

Mr. Starnes holds an A.B. degree from the University of Chattanooga and A.M. and Ph.D. degrees from the University of Chicago. A native of Tennessee, he came to Texas in 1921 to teach at Rice Institute. Since 1926 he has been on the faculty of the University of Texas, where he is professor of English.

A UNIVERSITY OF TEXAS PRESS BOOK

The type is linotype Caslon Old Face, monotype Caslon Old Style No. 337, and Goudy Text. The illustrations are line plates from photographs by the Walter Barnes Studio, Austin. Printed on 60 lb. white Warren's Olde Style antique paper.